Criminal Behavior

Theories, Typologies, and Criminal Justice

For those who have been harmed by criminal behavior

Criminal Behavior

Theories, Typologies, and Criminal Justice

Jacqueline B. Helfgott

Seattle University

Los Angeles • London • New Delhi • Singapore

For information:

 Sage Publications, Inc.
2455 Teller Road
Thousand Oaks, California 91320
E-mail: order@sagepub.com

Sage Publications Ltd.
1 Oliver's Yard
55 City Road
London EC1Y 1SP
United Kingdom

Sage Publications India Pvt. Ltd.
B 1/I 1 Mohan Cooperative Industrial Area
Mathura Road, New Delhi 110 044
India

Sage Publications Asia-Pacific Pte. Ltd.
33 Pekin Street #02-01
Far East Square
Singapore 048763

Printed in the United States of America.

Library of Congress Cataloging-in-Publication Data

Helfgott, Jacqueline B.
Criminal behavior: theories, typologies, and criminal justice/Jacqueline B. Helfgott.
    p. cm.
Includes bibliographical references and index.
ISBN 978-1-4129-0487-2 (cloth)
    1. Criminal behavior—Textbooks. 2. Criminal justice, Administration of—Textbooks. I. Title.

HV6080.H42 2008
364.3—dc22   2007052837

This book is printed on acid-free paper.

08   09   10   11   12   10 9 8 7 6 5 4 3 2 1

Acquisitions Editor:	Jerry Westby
Editorial Assistant:	Eve Oettinger
Production Editor:	Karen Wiley
Copy Editor:	Dorothy Hoffman
Typesetter:	C&M Digitals (P) Ltd.
Proofreader:	Theresa Kay
Indexer:	Kathy Paparchontis
Cover Designer:	Gail Buschman
Marketing Manager:	Jennifer Reed Banando

Brief Contents

Detailed Contents

Preface

This text offers a comprehensive exploration of criminal behavior for upper-level undergraduate and graduate students in criminology, criminal justice, sociology, and psychology and for criminal justice and mental health practitioners and others who want to better understand the nature of criminal behavior and types of crime. The goals of the text are to

1. Link theory and practice in a way that facilitates understanding of the importance of theory and typology development in making sense of and responding to criminal behavior

2. Highlight gaps in the literature with respect to the evolving nature of crime in the 21st century, with attention to the role of media and pop culture in the development of criminal behavior and its response

3. Provide concrete examples of the ways in which theories and typologies impact each stage of the criminal justice process

The text includes an interdisciplinary overview of theories of crime, explanation of how and why criminal typologies are constructed, a literature review for each major crime category, and discussion of how theories and typologies of crime are used at different stages of the criminal justice process. Unique features of the book include an emphasis on the role of mass media and computer technology and popular culture in understanding crime and its response (including sections on cyber and copycat crime); attention to the gendered nature of crime and the influence of sex-role stereotypes in the development, perceptions, and understanding of criminal behavior; and a dynamic approach that notes the cultural and subcultural nature of crime and changes in the manifestation of criminal behavior across time, situations, and culture.

The text can be seen as a comprehensive typology of crime, offering an integrative theoretical framework for understanding criminal behavior grounded in real-world examples of crime and criminal justice practice. The approach is "broad brush" with respect to criminological theory and the overview of criminal types, but detailed with respect to the nuts and bolts of typology development and criminal justice applications. It combines theory, literature review, and discussion of the nexus between theory and practice, focusing on understanding criminal behavior through an interdisciplinary framework, concrete examples of criminal justice applications, and the role of media and pop culture in shaping crime and its response. Central themes addressed throughout the text include gender and crime, computer and mass media technology and crime, theory integration, and criminal justice applications. Topics such as age and crime, career criminality, juvenile delinquency, gender and crime, and feminist criminology are integrated throughout the text.

The book is organized into three parts: Theories and Typologies; Criminal Typologies; and Applying Theories and Typologies to Criminal Justice Policy and Practice. Part I includes chapters on the nature, extent, and measurement of crime (Chapter 1), theories of criminal behavior (Chapter 2), typologies of crime and mental disorders (Chapter 3), and psychopathy and criminal behavior (Chapter 4). Part II includes comprehensive chapters on crime types including violent crime (Chapter 5), sex crime (Chapter 6), economic crime (Chapter 7), public order crime (Chapter 8), political crime (Chapter 9), and technology, media, and criminal behavior (Chapter 10). Part III covers applied criminology (Chapter 11) and challenges for the future (Chapter 12).

To promote an integrative understanding of crime through material of practical relevance and high interest to students, major theories of crime are reviewed in Chapter 2, followed by a chapter (Chapter 3) that explains how these theories are used to develop typologies that can be applied to the criminal justice system in law enforcement (investigation, interviews and interrogation, profiling), courts (drug and mental health courts, sexual predator laws, insanity defense), and corrections (classification, management, treatment, community supervision). Because the text focuses on an integrative understanding of theory and its practical application, more time is spent on the nexus of theory and practice than on the nuances of the individual schools of criminological thought. A technology and crime chapter covering "cybercrime" and "copycat crime" highlights the role of technology and media in shaping criminal behavior (Chapter 10). This chapter emphasizes important work that has been done in the area of "cultural criminology" to understand the changing nature of crime and the links between criminal behavior and contemporary culture (e.g., Ferrell, *Cultural Criminology* [1995], Baily & Hale, *Popular Culture, Crime, & Justice* [1998], Surette, *Media, Crime, & Criminal Justice* [1992], Jenkin, *Using Murder: The Social Construction of Serial Homicide* [1994], Black, *Aesthetics of Murder* [1991]), which deserves attention in criminal behavior texts.

My hope is that students, scholars, mental health and criminal justice practitioners, and others who read this book will come away reminded of several important things that can take us further toward preventing, controlling, and responding to crime. First, crime is a common everyday occurrence with very real and often tragic consequences we are all forced to deal with at some level in our everyday lives, whether we are offenders, victims, witnesses, citizens, jurors, or professionals in criminal justice, mental health, or social service. Second, feasible and effective solutions to the prevention and control of crime can come only from the conjoining of scientific and practical perspectives of different disciplines, keeping in mind that nothing about real crime will ever fall as neatly into place as the theories suggest and no empirical study can be so perfectly designed as to provide definitive answers. Third, crime types included in this text that are rarely covered in traditional criminology texts, such as political and copycat crimes, will hopefully inspire researchers to pursue otherwise untouched avenues of research. Finally, criminal behavior is not a static phenomenon. Crime is a subcultural and cultural product—a human behavior that changes in form and meaning across time, place, culture, subculture, gender, and so on. The hope is that this book will inspire students, researchers, criminal justice professionals, and citizens to think creatively about crime, to work together across disciplines and arenas to make use of the best theories and practices, and to never forget that for every crime that is prevented, every offender who is (even slightly) reformed, every victim who is better supported, every citizen who is less afraid of crime, and every criminal justice professional who is given better tools with which to do his or her job, many lives and communities will be affected and improved.

Acknowledgments

I would like, first, to acknowledge Jerry Westby, Sage Publications executive editor—with whom I consider it an honor and great fortune to have had the opportunity to work—for his encouragement, patience, and suggestions throughout the long course of this project. I would like to thank Denise Simon for her assistance with chapter reviews and revisions and other components of the project throughout the process. I am grateful to many others at Sage for their help at different stages of the project—Deya Saoud for assistance with photo permissions and chapter revisions, Dorothy Hoffman for the copy editing, Gail Buschman and the art department for the cover design, and Karen Wiley, production editor. The Sage editors and production staff have made the process of writing and completing this text a positive experience on many levels.

Many students, colleagues, and others have offered support throughout this project. My teaching, research, and service endeavors have offered me the opportunity to get to know and learn from a wide range of people who have been influential in my professional and academic life. Students, criminal justice professionals, academic colleagues, prisoners, and ex-offenders have shaped and guided my research and thinking and have enabled me to approach the study of criminal behavior with attention to the critical role of research, the realities of practice, and with deep understanding that crime is a social, interpersonal, and personal harm that, more often than not, has tragic and enduring consequences. Special thanks go to student research assistants who assisted with library research for different parts of the book, including Kevin Trujillo, Brandy Olson, Sonja Wilbanks, John Misko, Elizbeth Neidhart, and Ha Fong Ieong; prisoners at the Washington State Reformatory and Washington Corrections Center for Women and ex-offenders at Interaction Transition halfway house who have shared their insights with me and my students over the years including Patrick Bolt for assistance with prison programs I have coordinated (and for taking on more responsibilities during the time it took me for this project) and Jon Fleming for allowing me to include his essay "A Day in the Life of a Burglar" as Box 7.2 in Chapter 7; Seattle University staff including Rebecca Watson, who designed Figures 2.2, 3.1, and 5.1, Kate Reynolds, who assisted in typing several box features, and John Harrison, who assisted with library research; Seattle University Criminal Justice Department faculty—Elaine Gunnison, A. Daktari Alexander, Matthew Hickman, and Michael Kelliher, adjunct faculty, and other Seattle University colleagues who have provided a positive and supportive work environment; my mentors and colleagues from the University of Washington and Penn State, especially William Parsonage, Penn State Administration of Justice professor emeritus, who has been an important influence in my academic career and always cheers me on, and long-time colleagues and friends Faith Lutze from Washington State University and Frances Bernat from Arizona State University–West for their enduring encouragement and support.

I am grateful to the reviewers who offered critical feedback in the review and revision stages of the process. The book is the product of much time and care on the part of many reviewers who provided an enormous amount of constructive feedback throughout the text. These reviewers included

Bart Abplanalp
McNeil Island Corrections
  Center

William Archambeault
Louisiana State University

Michael Bailey
Columbus State University

Patricia Brennan
Emory University

Jay Strike Carlin
Canyon College

Trina Cyterski
University of Georgia

Lloyd V. Dempster
Texas A&M
  University–Kingsville

Robyn L. Diehl
Virginia Commonwealth
  University

Jason Doll
Marymount University

Joseph Dwyer
Webster University

Michael M. Eagen
Webster University

Peter English
California State
  University–Fresno

Cynthia Gallagher
New England College

Kelly Goodness
University of Texas at Dallas

Nancy Horton
University of Maryland
  Eastern Shore

Steven Hundersmarck
Ohio Northern University

Travis Langley
Henderson State University

Suzanne Lenhart
Tri-State University

Don Mohr
Purdue University

Catherine Orban
Marygrove College

Corinne Ortega
John Jay College of
  Criminal Justice

Robert Schug
University of Southern
  California

Amy Thistlethwaite
Northern Kentucky
  University

Finally and most important, I would like to thank my family and friends who have provided much support throughout the process of writing this book—my mom Esther, who as a feminist, writer, and historian has been my role model in so many areas of my life; my dad Oscar, who constantly tells me how proud he is (and promised to read this entire book); my grandmother Anna, who is no longer alive but always with me; my daughter Zalia and husband Zach, who have been especially patient with the schedule I have had to keep in writing this book; my brothers Ian and Scott and their families; stepparents Abe and Bea; friends Sharon, Jill, Rowena, Rina and their families; and many other family members and friends—too many to list—who have offered all kinds of support and words of encouragement throughout this project.

PART I

Theories and Typologies

Criminal Behavior

Nature, Extent, and Measurement

We can count in advance how many individuals will soil their hands with the blood of their fellows, how many will be swindlers, how many poisoners, almost as we can the number of births and deaths that will take place . . . .

—19th-century French mathematician-astronomer
Adolphe-Jacques Quetelet (Radzinowicz, 1966, p. 29)

. . . once we view the study of crime as a process of invention rather than the simple discovery of what is already in place, then the division between fact and fiction begins to break down, and perhaps in a highly productive fashion.

—Ngaire Naffine (1996, p. 123)

Human beings commit all sorts of crimes from the bizarre to the mundane. Consider the following:

- A man in Germany places an Internet advertisement for a young man interested in being "slaughtered and consumed." When the ad is answered, the two meet and the man cuts off the other man's penis, fries it up in a pan, and both the man and the victim try to eat it with a bottle of wine. When the victim finally bleeds to death, the man chops him into pieces and eats him over a six-month period.

- A 15-year-old runaway hitches a ride from her home in Las Vegas to her grandfather's home in California. She is picked up by a 51-year-old man in a truck. The man drives to an isolated area where he bludgeons and repeatedly rapes the girl and then hacks off her forearms with a hatchet leaving her to die in a culvert on the side of the interstate.

Twenty years later after serving less than 10 years in prison for the rape/mutilation of the teen, the man stabs to death a 31-year-old prostitute in his apartment.

- A woman meets a pregnant woman with a dog breeding business on the Internet. She claims to want a dog and arranges to meet but instead kills the woman, slices open her abdomen, and steals the baby to try to pass as her own.

- Two male teenagers known to be involved in the "Goth" lifestyle and role-playing games stomp, kick, and strangle to death a female teenage friend in a park. They then go to her house where they beat and stab her parents and sister to death with a baseball bat and combat knife. When they leave they take a telephone, CD player, and VCR.

- A man abducts a 4-year-old boy from a park. He takes him to his home where he sexually assaults him for several days, takes nude Polaroid pictures of him, and then hangs the boy in the closet. The man takes more pictures of the boy after he is dead hanging from a rope in the closet.

- A young couple in the United States and two couples in France become fascinated with the film *Natural Born Killers* and go on their own murder sprees, closely reenacting events in the film.

- During a one-week period in the United States, a man walks into a Colorado high school, sends the boys and teachers out, and lines up a row of teenage girls in front of the classroom. He holds them hostage and sexually assaults them over a period of several hours, finally releasing all but one who he shoots in the head before killing himself when police attempt to overtake him. Days later, a man in Pennsylvania walks into a small Amish schoolhouse, sends the boys and teachers out, lines ten little girls up at the chalkboard and shoots each one in the head before shooting himself.

- A teenager plays a violent video game, *Grand Theft Auto Vice City*, for 17 hours, steals a car, and gets arrested. During booking at the police station he grabs an officer's gun and shoots two officers and a 911 dispatcher.

- Two college-educated women in their early 30s set fire to a university research center and claim the Earth Liberation and Animal Liberation Fronts are responsible.

- A young man has sex with his dog while the dog squeals in pain. His wife catches the act on her cell phone video and the man is charged with animal cruelty.

- A group of Islamic terrorists hijacked four commercial passenger airliners, crashing two into the World Trade Center, one into the U.S. Pentagon, and the final jet crashing in Pennsylvania after passengers and crew attempted to overtake the hijackers. The act resulted in the deaths of 2,973 people and the 19 hijackers and 24 missing persons.

- Two young men in Wyoming lure a young man from a bar, targeting him because he is gay. They take him to a field, pistol whip him 18 times, and leave him to die tied to a rail post in near-freezing temperatures.

- Over 400 protesters at a World Trade Organization conference in Seattle violate city ordinances by protesting in police-designated no-protest zones, some engaging in peaceful protests, others throwing objects at officers and setting fires to businesses. They are arrested and charged with a range of offenses.

- A woman waits until her abusive husband falls asleep and then sets his bed on fire.

- Two teenage boys storm their high school armed with automatic weapons shooting classmates and teachers and killing 12 students and 1 teacher, and wounding 24 students before killing themselves.

- Nigerian fraudsters make hundreds of millions of dollars annually by sending out polite letters and e-mails inviting people to participate in bogus real estate deals and financial schemes in return for "advance fees."

- A girl is abducted from her home, kidnapped, and forced to travel with a couple who sexually assault her for a year.

- A 60-year-old man sexually assaults his two granddaughters over a 5-year period before he is caught when the children are aged 6 and 9.

- A 20-year-old woman gives her niece a bath and inserts her finger into the child's vagina.

- A woman is found drunk and passed out on a city street and charged with public drunkenness.

- A movie star has sex with a prostitute in a car and is arrested for lewd conduct.

- A Pennsylvania man drags a woman off a city street into an abandoned warehouse, rapes her, ties her to a chair, douses her with gasoline, and sets her on fire, burning her alive.

- A woman injects her infant daughter's feeding tube with an unknown substance while her daughter is under hospital care for unknown illness and is charged with child abuse.

- A Web site devoted to men who solicit prostitutes provides tips for connecting with prostitutes and an avenue to exchange contact information.

- A teenager skilled in computer technology hacks into the computer system of a large-scale company.

- Two East Coast real estate moguls operate a $20 million illicit business involving the theft, stripping, and reassembly of high-end cars ranging from BMWs to Land Cruisers and resell to innocent dealers and the public through the cover of a legitimate car sales business.

- A man shoplifts $315 of Aleve from a grocery store.

- A juvenile girl runs away from home, lives on the street, and has sex for money to support herself.

- A young girl who recently graduated from high school leaves a friend's house after having a few beers. On her way home she hits and kills a woman on a motorcycle.

- A 29-year-old Oregon woman steals five cars parked in front of homes in a month and sells them to buy drugs.

- A young man and woman go out on a date for the first time and return to the man's apartment. The man asks the woman for sex. When she says she's not ready, he pins her down, forces her to undress, and rapes her.

- A man breaks into dorm rooms at a university and steals panties from female students.

- A man sends e-mails out with links to phony bank Web sites, getting people to give their personal Social Security, address, and bank information. The man uses the private information to steal the identity of multiple victims and acquires credit in their names, resulting in losses of thousands of dollars.

- A drunk man in Boston goes to a gas station snack shop, grabs a bag of Cheetos, and offers the attendant 50 cents for the $2.49 bag while yelling obscenities. He is arrested for public drunkenness and disorderly conduct.

This list of crimes, some of which are highly publicized cases and others lesser known offenses, offers nothing more than a brief flash of the amount and range of criminal behaviors in which human beings have been known to engage. If it were possible to produce a complete catalog of human criminal behavior over time and around the world, such a document would likely be one of the most fascinating reads of all time.

The popularity of TV crime shows like *Law and Order, CSI,* and the long-running *NYPD Blue*; films such as *Taxi Driver, Silence of the Lambs, Natural Born Killers,* and *Ocean's Eleven, Ocean's Twelve,* and *Ocean's Thirteen*; and classic literature such as *In Cold Blood* and *Crime and Punishment* suggests that most people are fascinated with the deviant and criminal side of human behavior. However, fictional accounts of crime (many of which are loosely or not-so-loosely based on real-life events) rarely compare to the reality of crime. Any law enforcement officer, medical examiner/death investigator, crime scene technician, criminal attorney, judge, juror, criminologist/researcher, or citizen who has been exposed to some or all aspects of real-life criminal events knows that real-life crime is just as fascinating as if not more so (and in some cases much more horrific) than what our imaginations can come up with.

On the other hand, media focus on the most extreme variants of criminal behavior often makes people forget that most crime does not involve stranger abductions, sadistic torture, chopping off body parts, elaborate Internet schemes, or using commercial airliners as bombs. Although the real-life catalog of bizarre and extreme crimes is filled with horror, tragedy, and untold human harm and loss, it includes an even larger list of more benign offenses that most TV producers would have no interest in devoting a 1-hour prime time show to; and even if they did, most of us would probably rather do our laundry than watch. This list would include a kid putting a candy bar in his pocket at a grocery store, a man shoving his wife into a wall during an argument, a homeless person camped out on a city street and drinking, a woman growing a few marijuana plants in her basement, a teenage babysitter becoming frustrated and hitting a child under her care, college students illegally copying software or music CDs, an argument at a bar that ends in a fist fight between two patrons, a pharmacist pocketing prescription medication to give to a friend, a man going to a bar after work for a few too many beers and getting in his car to drive home, someone driving a U-Haul without properly securing the load in the back of the truck, a couple of youths hailing a cab and jumping out without paying the driver after they reach their destination, vandalism or theft at a local school, and so on.

In some ways, crimes that fall on the more "normal" side of the continuum of criminal behavior are even more interesting because they involve regular people in usual settings making decisions (some spontaneous, some not) about violating the law. The nature and dynamics of these sorts of everyday crimes provide a great deal of information about the root of criminal behavior—in fact, probably more than the extreme forms of criminal behavior, which can often be explained in terms of severe psychopathology or social or political conflict (see the Criminal Behavior Continuum in Figure 1.1).

At one end of the continuum are regular people who sometimes use poor judgment and make bad choices that, mixed with particular situational factors and circumstances, may result in behavior that violates the law such as driving too fast, taking something that doesn't belong to them, cheating on their taxes, buying or selling illegal drugs, painting graffiti on fences, crashing computer systems for fun, or illegal gambling. Some people have problems such as drug and alcohol addiction and steal to

❖ **Figure 1.1** Criminal Behavior Continuum

Normal →	Everyday Problems in Living →	Pathological
Behavior resulting from Poor judgment Bad decisions Situational factors Environmental context	Behavior resulting from Minor medical or mental health condition Drug or alcohol addiction Severe poverty and deprivation	Behavior resulting from Severe medical or mental health condition Long-term development of deviant identity and behavioral conditioning processes involving interaction of some combination of biological predisposition, childhood trauma, and environmental- cultural facilitators

support their habit, fall asleep on the street, drive under the influence, lose their temper and hit someone, or crash their car into a building and drive away. At the more extreme end of the continuum are people who are severely disturbed; they may inject their own children with poison to make them sick, walk into public restaurants and start shooting complete strangers, rape children and hang them in closets, or experience contemptuous delight or sexual arousal through torture and murder. The study of criminal behavior provides a fascinating look at the continuum of behavior, from the mundane to the bizarre, that falls outside the bounds of the social contract.

Crime exists only to the extent to which behavior is legally defined as criminal by the larger society and culture. In some contexts (e.g., war, executions in correctional contexts) it is not a crime to kill another human being. In some states (e.g., Nevada) it is not a crime to engage in prostitution. Until 2003 engaging in a homosexual act was a crime in many states in the United States, and it is currently illegal in some places around the world.[1] "Crime is not an entity in fact but an entity in law" (Radzinowicz, 1966, p. 22) and "technically speaking, there is no 'crime' without 'criminal law'" (Shelden, 2001, p. 23). *Criminal behavior is a special category of behavior that has been defined through socio-cultural-legal-political-economic processes as outside of the bounds of the law.* This is important in reviewing criminal behavior research because theoretical concepts central to understanding the mechanisms of criminal behavior such as *antisocial behavior, aggression, psychopathy*, or *deviance* are sometimes confounded with criminality in the research literature and popular discourse. For example, studies on aggression are often conducted in laboratory settings with animals or humans who are engaged in some laboratory task. *Can research on aggression in rats be applied to human crime and violence? Are the processes that produce antisocial behavior, such as lying or cheating on a spouse, the same processes as are involved in violating the law? Can theories explaining how people develop deviant identities also explain how people develop criminal identities?* Much of the current knowledge base on crime and criminal behavior draws from research focusing on these other concepts.

The term *social and behavioral sciences* is often used to encompass the many disciplines and subdisciplines involved in the study of criminal behavior, with scholars from a wide range of fields in sociology, psychology, criminology, and criminal justice engaged in the study of crime. The scientific study of crime evolved from the classical and positivist schools of thought and the disciplines of sociology and psychology. Eighteenth-century discourse on criminal behavior came from the work of classical theorists Cesare Beccaria and Jeremy Bentham, who saw crime as a product of free will, committed by people who made cost-benefit analyses regarding the pleasure crime would bring. The positivist school of thought emerged in the early 1800s with the writings of Cesare Lombroso (*The Criminal Man*) and with French mathematician-astronomer Adolphe-Jacques Quetelet's "social physics" and French lawyer Andre-Michel Guerry's "moral statistical analysis," supporting the notion that crime could be measured and predicted. Criminology emerged as a sub-field of sociology in the 1930s, and Criminology and Criminal Justice as a distinct academic discipline originated in the 1960s and 1970s. Psychologists have been interested in criminal behavior since the advent of psychology as a discipline (Blackburn, 1993).

The study of criminal behavior is much more interdisciplinary today than in the past. However, scholars continue to be divided into the same two camps that have historically defined the study of crime. More than 40 years ago, criminologist Sir Leon Radzinowicz wrote:

> We are here at the sources of the two fundamental approaches to the study of crime; crime as a product or expression of society and crime as a product or expression of individual constitution. From them developed two schools of thought. To one the central task of criminology was to explain the existence and distribution of crime in society: its natural tendency was to see the social factors as of overwhelming importance. To the other, the purpose of criminology was to discover why certain individuals became criminal. The tendency here was to stress the significance of constitutional factors. (Radzinowicz, 1966, pp. 29–30)

The long history of these two general schools of thought—criminal behavior as a product of social forces versus criminal behavior as a product of individual constitution—has been somewhat resistant to change, and even the titles of texts about crime have historically reflected one or the other perspective. Texts titled *Criminology* tend to approach the study of crime from a macrosociological framework whereas texts titled *Criminal Behavior* often focus more on the micro-level dynamics of individual criminality.

This text uses the term *criminal behavior* because the focus is less on crime in the aggregate and the ways in which crime is situated within society than on the nature and dynamics of criminal behavior in general and individual types of crime in particular. *Criminal behavior* is an individual-level behavioral product of an infinite array of factors and forces that converge at a given point in time. The term *crime* can be understood more broadly as the collective amount of criminal behavior in a society. The focus here is on how and why individuals commit crime more than on why crime increases or decreases in society over time. Unlike texts on criminology that broadly review theories of crime or offer a general theory of crime, this text offers a brief overview of theories of crime, and a look at how typologies of crime are constructed and how they are practically applied in the criminal justice system, with particular attention to the nature and dynamics of specific types of criminal behavior.

Over the past 200 years, a large body of literature has accumulated on crime and criminal behavior. Advances in the academic fields of criminology, criminal justice, and forensic psychology have led to recognition that theory and empirical research is critical to effective and efficient use of social resources to respond to crime. Old "tough on crime" approaches that called for harsh response to crime without attention to the nature of different types of offense behavior, rehabilitative potential, and levels of risk have been replaced by a trend favoring "smart on crime reforms" such as elimination of mandatory minimum sentences, more effective response to technical violations of probation and parole, and prison closures (Greene, 2003). These reforms rely heavily on theory and empirical research on the nature and extent of criminal behavior and the accurate measurement of crime. "Prevention and corrections have moved from 'nothing works' through 'what works' to 'making what works work'" (Andrews & Bonta, 2006, p. iii). More than at any other time in history, the science of criminal behavior today is making its way into policy and practice at every stage of the criminal justice system.

Why Do People Commit Crime?

When a crime occurs, the first question that tends to comes to people's minds is *"Why?"* This is especially true when the crime in question is heinous or extraordinary. Many prominent scholars have attempted to answer the question, *"What makes people commit crime?"* In 1988, Jack Katz, author of *Seductions of Crime,* wrote:

> The social science literature contains only scattered evidence of what it means, feels, sounds, tastes, or looks like to commit a particular crime. Readers of research on homicide and assault do not hear the slaps and curses, see the pushes and shoves, or feel the humiliation and rage that may build toward the attack, sometimes persisting after the victim's death. How adolescents manage to make the shoplifting or vandalism of cheap and commonplace things a thrilling experience has not been intriguing to many students of delinquency. Researchers of adolescent gangs have never grasped why their subjects so often stubbornly refuse to accept the outsider's insistence that they wear the "gang" label. The description of "cold blooded, senseless murders" has been left to writers outside the social sciences. Neither academic methods nor academic theories seem to be able to grasp why such killers may have been courteous to their victims just moments before the killing, why they often wait until they have dominated victims in sealed-off environments before coldly executing them, or how it makes sense to kill when only petty cash is at stake. (Katz, 1988, p. 3)

Twenty years later, many integrative theories have been developed to explain how biological, developmental, personality, social, and situational factors and forces converge to produce criminal behavior (e.g., Agnew, 2005; Barak, 1998; Elliott, Ageton, & Canter, 1979; Gottfredsen & Hirschi, 1990; Moffit, 1993; Robinson, 2004; Thornberry, 1987; Tittle, 1995), yet none sufficiently answers all of the questions about all types of crime nor do they bring us much closer to understanding, as Katz suggests, "what it means, feels, sounds, tastes, or looks like to commit a particular crime."

In his book *Why Do Criminals Offend?* criminologist Robert Agnew says that after 25 years studying crime, "I have never been able to provide an answer that is clear and concise on the one hand, but reasonably complete on the other" (Agnew, 2005, p. 1). Agnew offers his integrated general theory of crime as a "reasonably complete," clear and concise explanation of individual criminal behavior that explains crime in terms of personality, social environment, and situational factors and the variables and intervening mechanisms associated with most crime theories. Tunnell (1992), author of *Choosing Crime: The Criminal Calculus of Property Offenders,* writes, "Crime is not an isolated phenomenon but is meticulously and historically woven into the fabric of this society" (p. 173) emphasizing that it is impossible to make sense of, or effectively respond to, criminal behavior while focusing solely on the offense or the offender without attention to the cultural-historical-political-economic infrastructure within which crime is rooted. In his book *Why Crime?* Robinson (2004) offers an integrated systems theory that illustrates "how risk factors at different levels of analysis from different academic disciplines interact to increase the probability that a person will commit antisocial behavior" (p. 271). In *The Psychology of Criminal Conduct,* Blackburn (1993) extensively reviews the social, individual, biological theories and the research on classifying crime. In their text also called *The Psychology of Criminal Conduct,* Andrews and Bonta (2006) offer a psychology of criminal conduct that describes and accounts for "the fact that not all human beings are equally into criminal activity," explaining differences in terms of when and under what circumstances they commit criminal acts and the number, type, and variety of antisocial acts they engage in. There is no shortage of theories or texts attempting to answer the question of why people commit crime.

However, as Agnew's comments suggest, the most experienced and respected criminologists have a difficult time answering the question of why criminals offend. Issues that have historically complicated the study of criminal behavior include the following:

- General theories are often so general they offer few answers to questions about specific subtypes of criminal behavior or the individual, situational, contextual dynamics within which a particular criminal act occurs.

- Empirical research on criminal behavior is largely based on data collected many years ago, and findings may have little relevance to crime committed in contemporary times.

- Most theories and research on criminal behavior focus on male offenders and male criminality with little, if any, direct attention to female criminality or acknowledgment of the ways in which gender stereotypes, sex-role socialization, institutionalized sexism, and biological sex differences influence criminal behavior or how it is defined and responded to.

- The study of criminal behavior is fragmented by disciplinary insulation and the tendency of researchers to keep within their own disciplinary frameworks. As a result, research conducted in the fields of sociology, psychology, criminal justice/criminology, social work, political science, anthropology, and other disciplines has stayed (for the most part) within these fields. Interdisciplinary theories have therefore not developed to the point where key theories and empirical findings from the different fields are consistently connected, synthesized, and discussed within the different schools of thought.

In thinking about and responding to criminal behavior, we should add some important questions to the "why" question:

- Is there a single theory that can explain all criminal behavior?
- What's the difference between explaining criminal behavior and predicting it?
- How is criminal behavior different from other human behavior?
- Can one form of criminal behavior be the product of different types of motivation?
- Can the same motivation produce different types of criminal behavior?
- Do certain types of crimes share particular features?
- Does gender, culture, or time period influence the types of crimes people commit?
- How much crime is there and how can we best measure it?

The study of crime and criminal behavior involves asking these and other complex questions about the nature, extent, and measurement of crime.

Clearly, there is no simple answer to the question, "Why do people commit crime?" The history of criminal justice is filled with responses to crime based on flawed ideas about offenders and the causes of criminal behavior. If we could only identify a single answer—bad parenting, drugs and alcohol, hormones, or a crime gene—then maybe we could make some gains at reducing crime and protecting the public. From the eugenics movement in the early 1900s (fueled by the notion that crime is genetically based and sexual sterilization of offenders would prevent the birth of criminal offspring), to the social welfare programs of the 1960s-70s (based on recognition of environmental and social influences on crime and promoting social services as a means of crime prevention), to the risk assessment mentality of the late 20th and early 21st centuries (founded on the idea that dangerousness can be scientifically assessed, crime can be controlled by assessing potential for offender-environment risk, and the "us" can be kept away from the "them"), all crime prevention strategies are based on some idea about the causes of crime. Rather than searching for a single answer, however, researchers and criminal justice practitioners recognize that no single factor can completely explain criminal behavior.

It may be useful to think about the answer to "Why do people commit crime?" with an analogy that has nothing to do with crime. On August 17, 2006, two Coast Guard divers died of asphyxia in a cold-water dive 500 miles north of Alaska. The divers, Lieutenant Jessica Hill and Petty Officer Steve Duque, were part of a group including 35 scientists in the Arctic to collect data to map the ocean floor. The dive was conducted at the same time as an "ice liberty," an on-board version of shore leave in which the crew were allowed to drink alcohol, play football, and take dips in the cold (29°F) water. During the party, Hill got permission to do a training dive with Duque to get some experience. Both Hill and Duque died during the dive. The investigation into the accident revealed failures in oversight at every level on the icebreaker *Healy*, including the divers' lack of experience and departure from Coast Guard policy. Among the many factors the investigation concluded played a role in the deaths of Duque and Hill were commingling the ice liberty festivities and the dive, inexperienced dive tenders who were drinking during the dive, equipment malfunction and damaged gear, and diver carelessness and misjudgment. The investigation found that the diver deaths were preventable and attributable to failures in leadership, training, judgment, experience, and program management to properly plan for and execute a standard cold-water dive. According to Vice Admiral Charles Wurster, head of the Coast Guard's Pacific fleet, "The investigation uncovered a chain of events and decisions which, had any link been broken, this tragedy would not have occurred" (Barber, January 13, 2007).

The botched Arctic training dive from the icebreaker has nothing to do with criminal behavior, except that the conclusion of the *Healy* investigation is a useful analogy in thinking about the causes of crime. Like the botched dive resulting in the accidental deaths of the *Healy* divers, *criminal behavior occurs as a result of a series of interlocking events and would not occur if any link in a chain of events and decisions were broken.* This notion of a series of intertwined factors that converge to produce a particular outcome, whether accidental death or medical disease or criminal behavior, is far from novel and not especially exciting. Furthermore, such a complex explanation does not lend itself to a single concrete answer to the problem of crime. However, it is important to note that the outcome of the *Healy* investigation led to concrete changes in the Coast Guard in memory of Officer Duque and Lieutenant Hill, with the goal of preventing future diver deaths by breaking links in the events and decisions that led to the botched dive. If every crime were analyzed to the extent that this Coast Guard tragedy was investigated and data collected to determine the successive events linked to produce the criminal act, then the science of criminal behavior would be much more advanced and steps could be taken to prevent future crimes. The final action memorandum from the U.S. Coast Guard said, "We will honor our lost shipmates and keep faith with our Core Values of Honor, Respect, and Devotion to Duty by diligently directing our energies toward improving our performance through the elimination of the shortfalls that led to this tragedy" (Final Action, 2007, p. 27). Like the *Healy* diving incident, many criminal acts result in tragic consequences for victims and communities who would be similarly honored by "directing energies toward improving performance through the elimination of shortfalls" that led to the criminal event. *In thinking about and researching what makes people commit crime, it is important to think in terms of a chain of events that can be closely examined and deliberately interrupted.* Like the *Healy* incident, if we were to retrospectively analyze every criminal event, we would likely find that most crime is preventable—that if one link in the chain had been missing, the crime would not have occurred. Identifying how to prevent and respond to crime requires this sort of detailed analysis of criminal events.

It is unlikely that each and every criminal behavior committed will ever be retrospectively scrutinized in the same manner as accidental deaths (whether in the line of duty, in the medical field, or from accidents resulting from product malfunction or negligence in other arenas). However, understanding why crime occurs requires focus on both aggregate-level factors (e.g., factors statistically associated with criminal behavior across large groups of offenders) and individual-level factors (the unique influences and chain of events in an individual's life contributing to the criminal behavior). Theory and research directed toward identifying correlates of crime at the aggregate level as well as detailed analysis of individual-level offenses are necessary to explain why crime occurs. For example, research shows that gender, age, and social class are highly correlated with criminal behavior, with young males of lower socioeconomic status being more likely to commit crime. However, knowing that a person is young, male, and poor tells us very little about why a particular person decides to engage in an individual criminal behavior or a lifestyle of crime, nor can these factors be used to predict or clearly explain the dynamics of individual-level criminal acts.

Extent and Measurement of Crime

The second most frequently asked question about crime is, *"How much crime is there?"* Criminal justice policies and practices are generally tied to both the nature and the extent of crime. Attention and resources are allocated based on where the greatest need arises, which can depend on the amount of social harm or public fear crime causes. For example, even though some types of crime are particularly shocking or horrific, such as cannibalism and fetus theft, these crimes are extremely rare. It is unlikely that a great deal of resources will be directed to preventing or responding to crimes that almost never occur. On the other hand, some types of crime are so common people almost forget that they are crimes at all, such as drunk driving and domestic violence. With these types of crimes, all it takes is a few atrocity tales and a moral panic to generate a wave of concern that sometimes leads to increased resources and attention.

How much crime exists is a question of great interest to the news media, who often report when crime in general or certain types of crime are on the rise or falling, crime sprees in a certain location, or particular areas experiencing disproportionate amounts of certain types of crimes. This information is also important to the public, politicians, and policymakers who use official crime rates to make decisions about allocation of resources to law enforcement agencies. Newspaper headlines typically provide a snapshot of information from governmental reports or studies informing the public about the rise, fall, or pattern of crime, such as the following recent examples:

- "Most types of crime declined last year" (Rondeaux, January 7, 2007).
- "Homicides up, but violent crime down: City recorded 466 murders last year" (Rozek, January 2, 2007).
- "City sees 13.5% rise in slayings for 2006" (O'Hare, January 1, 2007).
- "No pattern to rise in murders, police say" (Reid, December 31, 2006).
- "Domestic violence found to fall by half over decade; the statistics mirror a national crime drop, but some are skeptical" (Fiore, December 29, 2006).
- "Violent crime rates on the rise nationwide" (NBC News, July 14, 2006).

However, criminologists have proven to be notoriously bad predictors of crime rates. This is because there are so many factors that converge to produce increases or decreases in aggregate levels of crime.

For example, the most powerful correlates of crime are age, gender, and socioeconomic status. Males between the ages of 14 and 24 from impoverished backgrounds are disproportionately represented in both offender and victimization statistics. This means that a criminologist could safely predict that when demographic shifts occur in society, such as decreasing number of male youth age 14 to 24 in the population, crime will decrease. However, crime rates in aggregate and individual-level criminal behavior are much more complicated than the theories would lead us to believe, and some might say virtually impossible to accurately predict given the varieties of human behavior and the endless parade of variables that affect criminal behavior.

The Dark Figure of Crime

Similar to that old philosophical conundrum, "If a tree falls in the forest and no one hears it, does it make a sound?" criminologists ask "if you're not caught, is it really a crime?" The term *dark figure of crime* refers to all of the unknown crimes that do not make it into official crime data, victimization surveys, or research studies or the discrepancy between crime known to police and the true extent of crime. The amount of crime that actually occurs far exceeds the amount of crime reported to police. The majority of crime becomes known to police through citizen complaints. However, in many cases citizens do not report crime to the police. Mosher, Miethe, and Phillips (2002) offer some of the many reasons crimes are not reported to police:

> Some victims lack trust in the police or have severe reservations about the ability of law enforcement officials to solve crimes. Some fear retaliation and reprisals from offenders for reporting crimes; others think it is not worth their while to report offenses because, for example, the property is uninsured and probably will not be recovered. The victims in some crime situations may also be involved in criminal activities themselves (e.g., drug sellers or prostitutes who are victims of robbery) which decreases their likelihood of reporting. Others believe the incident was a "private matter," "nothing could be done," or "was not important enough." Public apathy and the desire to "not get involved" may underlie some witnesses' reluctance to report offenses they observe. (p. 84)

Other reasons include the belief that someone else will report the crime (e.g., in the case of nuisance offenses such as disorderly conduct or vandalism against public property) or a belief that calling the police may cause more harm than good to a family (e.g., in the case of domestic violence). Whether or not a crime makes its way into official statistics also depends on police discretion in recording an incident as a crime. There are many offenses that never make it past 911 dispatchers and many that officers choose not to report either because the evidence is weak, the crime has no clear victim, the crime is not serious, or the complainant prefers not to press charges. In many such situations, criminal behavior has occurred, however the behavior does not make it into official statistics. Even in cases in which the offense is reported to and by police, many details about the criminal behavior never make it into the police report and are forever lost.

In thinking about the dark figure of crime and the gap between the true extent of crime and crime known to police, it is important to realize that, for any behavior to be defined as criminal, it has to be prohibited by law. *Crime is a social construction* that depends on cultural, social, political, economic, and legal decisions about what is and what is not outside the bounds of the law. If there is no law against a particular behavior, then that behavior is not criminal behavior. Or, if certain people are not perceived as offenders, they may not show up in official statistics. For example, until relatively recently law enforcement did not recognize female gang members because females were excluded from official definitions of gang membership (Sikes, 1996). Thus, even though criminal behavior is studied by psychologists and other behavioral scientists who research anger, aggression, impulsivity, and other characteristics associated with behavior that violates the law, criminal behavior cannot be understood without recognizing that *criminal behavior is a special category of human behavior that is defined by a broad range of cultural forces.*

Crime also requires that certain elements be present—most important, *mens rea* (criminal intent) and *actus reus* (act violating the law). Furthermore, if a person intentionally engages in behavior that violates the law, to be considered a criminal (and recorded in official statistics), the person would have to be convicted of the offense in a court of law. Thus, to be defined as a crime, a behavior must be an intentional violation of the law. An interesting question to consider is, *if a person commits a crime— steals something or kills someone—and isn't caught, has that person committed a crime?* One of the most notorious examples of a crime that wasn't is the case of O.J. Simpson and the 1994 murder of his wife Nicole Brown Simpson and her friend Ronald Goldman. O.J. Simpson was charged and tried for the crime and, after a year-long highly publicized (and televised) trial, received a verdict of "not guilty." In 1997, Simpson lost a civil suit filed against him by the Goldman family, who received a $33.5 million judgment. In 2006, ReganBooks, an imprint of HarperCollins, almost published a book by Simpson (that was yanked at the last minute), called *If I Did It, Here's How It Happened,* describing how Simpson would have committed the murder had he done it. Publisher Judith Regan said about the book, "This is an historic case, and I consider this his confession" ("Publisher considers O.J. Simpson book 'his confession,'" November 15, 2006). The book was later published in 2007 by the Goldman family with Beaufort Books, with the added subtitle *Confessions of a Killer.* Almost 15 years after the murders, many people still believe O.J. Simpson committed the murders of Nicole Brown Simpson and Ronald Goldman. However, he was not convicted for the offense, so even if he now decided to confess to the crime in a book or any other forum, he did not commit the crime. The homicides of Nicole Brown Simpson and Ronald Goldman were obviously reported to police, someone was arrested, and the crime was reflected in the Uniform Crime Reports for 1994. However, O.J. Simpson himself did not make it into the official data as a convicted or incarcerated offender.

What if Simpson did commit these murders? What if, even though he was acquitted for the offense, he "confessed" years later? Can Simpson's behavior be considered criminal? How can we understand the universe of criminal behavior, when there are so many offenses for which we don't have all the information because the offender is not caught or convicted, or because the offense never comes to the attention of the police in the first place? While most homicides do come to the attention of police, only *half of all crimes are reported to police* (Hart & Rennison, 2003). This means that official data collected by police tell only half of the story. And, as the O.J. Simpson case illustrates, even crimes that do make it into official statistics sometimes go unsanctioned with the offender unknown. *The 50% of all crime that is never reported to police is the dark figure of crime.* Beyond this, there are many details of criminal acts for which offenders aren't caught or aren't talking. Thus, even when offenses are known to police, many unknown features of criminal behavior are never uncovered.

Measuring Crime

Crime in the United States is generally measured through three sources: *The Uniform Crime Reports, National Crime Victimization Survey,* and *Self-Report Surveys.* The Uniform Crime Reports (UCR) represents all crimes that come to the attention of the police. The National Crime Victimization Survey and Self-Report Surveys represent attempts to capture information about crimes that do not come to the attention of the police. The amount of crime that can be measured through the combination of these three data sources reflects the crime we know about (and can study). Used together, these sources allow us to know something about more than the 50% of crime reflected in the UCR data, but still do not give the whole picture. These sources are a starting point for understanding crime in general and specific types of crime in particular. The amount of crime that is not captured through these sources is the true dark figure of crime.

The Uniform Crime Reports

The Uniform Crime Reporting Program was developed by the International Association for Chiefs of Police (IACP) in 1927 in response to the need for a reliable national crime reporting system. The system was developed out of a Rockefeller Foundation working group that included the IACP, the FBI, and leading criminologists of the time. Under the leadership of Herbert Hoover, all law enforcement agencies were required to submit arrest data to the FBI. Hoover added other features including the "Crime Clock" and the "Ten Most Wanted List" that brought publicity to the FBI (Walker, 1998). The UCR was criticized early on because it reported only crimes known to police and local police records were not independently audited. However, it remained the leading source for crime data in the United States until the 1970s. Today, the UCR publishes three publications annually based on data collected from 17,000 law enforcement agencies: *Crime in the United States, Hate Crime Statistics,* and *Law Enforcement Officers Killed and Assaulted.* Over 97% of the U.S. population is reflected in the UCR data.

The UCR is a starting point for understanding the extent of different types of crime in the United States. The UCR collects data on two groups of offenses—Part I offenses and Part II offenses. *Part I offenses* are serious crimes including criminal homicide, aggravated assault, robbery, forcible rape, burglary, larceny-theft, motor vehicle theft, and arson. *Part II offenses* include less serious offenses such as simple assault, forgery, fraud, embezzlement, prostitution, and gambling (Table 1.1). The

❖ Table 1.1   UCR Part I and Part II Offenses

Part I Offenses	Part II Offenses
Criminal homicide	Other assaults (simple)
Forcible rape	Forgery and counterfeiting
Robbery	Fraud
Aggravated assault	Embezzlement
Burglary	Stolen property
Larceny-theft	Vandalism
Motor vehicle theft	Weapons
Arson	Prostitution and commercialized vice
	Sex offenses
	Drug abuse violations
	Gambling
	Offenses against family and children
	Driving under the influence
	Liquor laws
	Drunkenness
	Disorderly conduct
	Vagrancy
	Suspicion
	Curfew and loitering laws
	Runaways
	All other offenses

Adapted from *Crime in the United States* 2005 http://www.fbi.gov/ucr/05cius/about/offense_definitions.html

UCR includes data collected monthly from law enforcement agencies on known Part I offenses cleared by arrest as well as the sex, age, and race of persons arrested for the offenses. Data provided on Part II offenses are arrest data only.

A number of issues should be kept in mind when using UCR data. First, all crimes are not legally defined in exactly the same way across states and jurisdictions, which results in ambiguity in classifying offenses. Data collected for the UCR program are collected monthly from law enforcement agencies that voluntarily submit the information. Law enforcement agencies are provided with training services and data collection manuals by the FBI, so that procedures for classifying and recording offenses are standardized. However, classifying offenses in UCR categories requires translating offense titles in the different jurisdiction to the UCR crime categories. Second, the hierarchy rule is used in collecting data, collapsing lesser offenses into the more serious offense, which is the one recorded in the UCR, with the exception of arson, which is always recorded in UCR data (in other words, a crime involving a homicide, rape, and robbery would be classified as a homicide). Finally, the UCR data do not give detailed information about offenses such as situational and contextual factors and victim-offender relationship.

In 1987, the *National Incidence Based Reporting System* (NIBRS) was piloted and added to the Uniform Crime Reporting Program. Designed to be a more comprehensive and in-depth source of information about criminal events, the NIBRS views crimes as incidents and collects detailed information about crime and all of its components. Whereas the traditional UCR collects data in aggregate, the NIBRS categorizes each incident and arrest into one of 22 categories that span 46 offenses and 53 data elements about the victim, property, and offender are collected. The NIBRS was developed to collect data on important features of offenses not available in the UCR data. However, the time it takes law enforcement agencies to record and report the detailed data is problematic. Many critics see the NIBRS as less important for law enforcement than for researchers and there is little incentive for agencies to participate. As of 1999, 6% of the U.S. population was reflected in NIBRS data.

An article entitled "Crime Reporting in the Age of Technology" in the *FBI Criminal Justice Information Services Newsletter, NIBRS Edition,* offers an example to illustrate the detailed information collected in the NIBRS and the difference in reporting between the NIBRS and the UCR summary data:

> At approximately 8 p.m. on December 23, 1999, two young males approached a 28-year-old Asian female in a parking garage. The first man, who was black, held the woman at knifepoint, reached for her purse, and demanded her jewelry. The female, unwilling to cooperate with the robber, tried to hold on to her purse. A brief struggle ensued during which the second male, a white man, began laughing and pulled a gun. The white male then grabbed the woman, threw the purse at the black male, and said, "I'll have her!" After the second man raped the woman, both men fled the scene, leaving her in the parking garage. (US Department of Justice, FBI, 2000, p. 2)

This criminal event would be reported in the UCR as one occurrence of rape. In the NIRS, the robbery and rape would be counted and information about critical elements of the offense including sex, age, race of victim and offender, nature of the victim-offender relationship, date and time of the incident, and the type and value of the lost property included.

How do NIBRS data compare with UCR data? NIBRS and UCR crime rates differ slightly. On average the NIBRS Index crime rate was 2% higher and the property crime rate was over 2% higher. Murder rates are the same, but robbery, aggravated assault, and rape are, on average, 1% higher, burglary rates are 0.5% lower,[2] larceny rates are 3.4% higher, and motor vehicle theft rates are 4.5% higher in NIBRS data than in the UCR (Rantala, 2000). Following are other differences between the two:

– NIBRS collects data on male victims of female rapists.

– NIBRS records justifiable homicide separately, not including it with murder and manslaughter.

– NIBRS restructures assault into three categories: aggravated, simple, and intimidation.

– The UCR *hotel rule* (if a number of dwelling units under a single manager are burglarized and the offenses are most likely to be reported to the police by the manager rather than the individual tenants, the burglary should be scored as one offense) is expanded in the NIBRS to include burglaries in temporary rental storage facilities, and if three units are burglarized, this counts as only one burglary in the NIBRS.

The NIBRS is an important step in collecting more detailed and meaningful crime data to capture the dark figure of crime and the nature of individual offenses. However, critics argue that it is more helpful to researchers than to law enforcement and law enforcement has few incentives to participate, the coding scheme is too complex (documented in four volumes published by the FBI), and these problems leave too much missing data to be useful on a widespread scale to accurately reflect crime in the United States (Mosher, Miethe, & Phillips, 2002).

National Crime Victimization Survey

The *National Crime Victimization Survey* (NCVS), previously called the National Crime Survey, was developed in 1972 and is the most comprehensive victimization survey in the United States. Conducted by the National Institute of Justice, Bureau of Justice Statistics, the NCVS obtains annual data from a nationally representative sample of 77,200 households, including approximately 134,000 individuals, on the frequency, consequences, and characteristics of criminal victimization in the United States. The survey, intended to complement UCR data, records incidents not reported to police, providing detailed information about crime incidents from the victim's perspective. The data allow for estimation of likelihood of victimization for the population by assault, robbery, rape, sexual assault, theft, motor vehicle theft, and burglary.

The NCVS was redesigned in 1989 to accommodate increased interest in certain types of victimization such as different types of sexual offenses. The revised survey includes more explicit questions regarding sexual victimization, with the goal of improving reporting for these types of crime. The first data from the redesigned version were published in 1993. This has resulted in an increase in reports of rapes and sexual assaults. With the increase in victims reporting victimization experiences, the redesigned survey is able to produce a more comprehensive picture of crime in the United States.

Other victimization surveys include smaller-scale surveys such as the victimization components of the General Social Survey, college campus surveys, sexual assault surveys, neighborhood quality of life surveys, the City-level Survey of Crime Victimization and Citizen Attitudes, Emergency Room Statistics on Intentional Violence, the National Computer Security Survey, and surveys outside of the United States such as the British Crime Survey that collects data on victimization in England and Wales and the International Crime Victimization Survey that collects data from different countries, with the most recent wave of data collected in 2000 from 47 countries (Table 1.2).

❖ Table 1.2   Vicitimization Surveys

National Crime Victimization Survey (NCVS) http://www.ojp.usdoj.gov/bjs/cvict.htm#ncvs	The NCVS is the most comprehensive victimization survey in the United States. Conducted by the National Institute of Justice, Bureau of Justice Statistics, the NCVS obtains annual data from a nationally representative sample of 77,200 households including approximately 134,000 individuals on the frequency, consequences, and characteristics of criminal victimization in the United States.
General Social Survey (GSS)—United States http://webapp.icpsr.umich.edu/cocoon/ ICPSR-SERIES/00028.xml *General Social Survey* (GSS)—Canada http://www.statcan.ca/english/Dli/Data/Ftp/gss.htm	The GSS is a general social survey that has been conducted in the United States since 1972 and has been administered 26 times to over 45,000 respondents (total). The GSS includes over 4,200 variables including questions regarding victimization. Similar GSSs are conducted in Ireland, Britain, Australia, Canada, Germany, Taiwan, Korea, Japan, and other countries. The GSS Canada Module 18 was designed in 1988 to collect victimization data from Canadians aged 15 years and older about their experiences of being a victim of crime and their fear, perceptions of crime and the criminal justice system. Four GSS victimization surveys have been conducted by Statistics Canada in 1988, 1993, 1999, and 2004.
Violence Against Women Survey (VAWS) http://www.statcan.ca/cgi-bin/imdb/p2SV.pl? Function=getSurvey&SDDS=3896&lang= en&db=IMDB&dbg=f&adm=8&dis=2[DH1]	Designed in 1993 to collect data on women's experiences of physical and sexual violence and sexual harassment committed by men, and perceptions of personal safety. VAWS was adapted for use as a module in the GSS Canada to provide periodic estimates of violence against both women and men.
National College Women National Victimization Study (NCWSV) http://www.ncjrs.gov/pdffiles1/nij/182369.pdf	NCWSV study, funded by the National Institute of Justice, collected data from a telephone survey of a randomly selected, national sample of 4,446 women who were attending a 2- or 4-year college or university during fall 1996. The questions were asked in 1997. The results are reported in the NIJ research report *The Sexual Victimization of College Women* (Fisher et al., 2000).

(Continued)

❖ Table 1.2 (Continued)

Comprehensive Sexual Assault Assessment Tool (CSAAT) *Comprehensive Sexual Assault Assessment Tool for Elders* (CSAAT-E) http://www.ncjrs.gov/pdffiles1/nij/grants/216550.pdf	The CSAAT is widely used to collect clinical and forensic data when investigating sexual assault crimes and to train sexual assault nurse examiners and other health and investigator professionals. The CSAAT was adapted to measure elderly sexual assault with the creation of the CSAAT-E, which includes questions pertinent to elderly sexual abuse.
Neighborhood Quality of Life Surveys http://www.sustainableseattle.org/Programs/SUNI/researchingconditions/communitysurveys/surveys/index_html	Neighborhood quality of life surveys are conducted in local communities to measure the perception of community members regarding quality of life in local neighborhoods such as social, physical, and economic environment, community involvement, crime and pollution, and other issues. Questions about victimization and public safety are generally included and respondents have an opportunity to provide open-ended responses to questions such as "what would you say are the three most pressing neighborhood concerns?"
City-Level Survey of Crime Victimization and Citizen Attitudes http://www.ojp.usdoj.gov/bjs/pub/pdf/cscvca.pdf	Joint effort of Bureau of Justice Statistics (BJS) and the Office of Community Oriented Policing Services (COPS) conducted in 12 selected cities. The survey combines standard National Crime Victimization Survey instrument with questions about citizen perceptions of community policing and neighborhood issues. All sampled household residents age 12 or older were included in the survey.
Emergency Room Statistics on Intentional Violence http://www.ojp.usdoj.gov/bjs/pub/ascii/vrithed.txt	The instrument provides data on intentional injuries, such as domestic violence, rape, and child abuse, from a national sample of hospital emergency rooms. Through the Consumer Product Safety Commission's National Electronic Injury Surveillance System, information is obtained on characteristics of the victim and perpetrator, victim-perpetrator relationship, alcohol/drug involvement in the incident, and description of circumstances of injury.

National Computer Security Survey (NCSS) http://www.ncss.rand.org/	The NCSS is a national survey, the first of its kind, sent to thousands of businesses across 37 industry sectors, including critical infrastructure. The NCSS, launched in 2006, is sponsored by the U.S. Department of Justice, Bureau of Justice Statistics, and the U.S. Department of Homeland Security, National Cyber Security Division. The NCSS collects data on the nature and extent of computer security incidents, monetary costs and other consequences of these incidents, incident details such as types of offenders and reporting to authorities, and computer security measures used by companies.
National White-Collar Crime Center Survey http://www.nw3c.org/research/visitor_form_val.cfm	National survey completed in 1999 examined public's perceptions of and experiences with white-collar crime. The survey was administered to 1,169 U.S. citizens. The results of this survey (published in 2000 with a follow-up report in 2005) provide information on public attitudes regarding crimes such as fraud and embezzlement. They also tell us how often American households are victimized by these crimes.
British Crime Survey (BCS) http://www.homeoffice.gov.uk/rds/bcs1.html	The BCS has been conducted annually since 1982, collecting data on victimization in England and Wales. Over 50,000 interviews are conducted annually with respondents aged 16 and over. Results are published in the report *Crime in England and Wales.*
International Crime Victimization Survey http://webapp.icpsr.umich.edu/cocoon/NACJD-STUDY/02973.xml	International crime victimization survey collects data from different countries with the most recent wave of data collected in 2000 from 47 countries. The survey is funded by the Ministry of Justice of the Netherlands. Four waves of the survey have been administered to date.
Idaho Crime Victimization Survey http://www.isp.state.id.us/pgr/PDF/cvs2000.pdf	Initiated in 2000 to enhance knowledge and understanding of crime victimization phenomena in Idaho, the survey instrument is modeled after the National Crime Victimization Survey, including additional questions regarding domestic violence, child abuse, sexual harassment in the workplace, hate crime, perceptions of crime, and police services. It was administered to household residents age 18 and older in 2000 to a random sample of 2,489 Idaho households.

Victimization data supplement UCR data by providing information about crimes not reported to police, but they are still not able to capture the entire dark figure of crime. Victimization surveys are, of course, not able to capture offenses where there is no identifiable victim, such as public order offenses like drug offenses, gambling, disorderly conduct, trespassing, public drunkenness, and prostitution. Other excluded crimes include murder, bank robbery, and nonresidential economic crimes such as tax evasion, nonresidential burglary, possession of stolen property, and employee theft. Thus, since a large majority of offenses involve public order and nonresidential economic crime, victimization surveys are able to provide information about only a small subset of crimes, primarily violent and sex crimes, personal theft, motor vehicle theft, and residential burglary.

Mosher, Miethe, and Phillips (2002) caution that using victimization data has four inherent problems:

1. Victimization surveys cover only a small range of crimes.

2. Victimization surveys are based on sample data rather than population counts, subjecting them to distortion from sampling error and sampling bias.

3. Victimization surveys are based on victims' perceptions without independent confirmation.

4. Question wording and technical elements of the survey, including the use of different procedures over time, make it difficult to compare victimization rates over time.

These problems do not diminish the value of victimization data, given that official UCR data have their own flaws. Victimization data are important in minimizing the dark figure of crime and necessary to understanding criminal behavior. A first step in studying any form of criminal behavior should involve consulting both UCR and victimization data (and any other available data) for crime categories in which data are available.

Self-Report Surveys

Beyond official statistics collected by the FBI in the UCR and victimization surveys, there are many self-report surveys that attempt to gather information from the offenders' perspective. Self-report surveys provide information about criminal incidents from the offenders' perspective and are able to capture information about crimes that do not come to the attention of the police, that victims are not willing to report, as well as public order and other offenses that may not have a clearly identifiable victim.

Self-report surveys were developed beginning in the 1940s and 1950s out of concern among criminologists that official statistics were reflecting a distorted picture of crime. Self-report measures have developed substantially over the past 50 years and are now considered a fundamental reliable and valid method of scientifically measuring criminality and the bedrock of etiological studies (Thornberry & Krohn, 2000).

Self-report surveys provide information about criminal events that is not translated into legalistic definitions and the victim perspective and are one of the few means through which information about offender motivation can be obtained. Information about offender motivation generally comes from two sources: self-report of involvement in crime or inferences made by researchers from behavioral evidence. Obtaining accurate data on offender motivation is problematic because it involves either trusting the offender's account or making inferences from behaviors.

There are two general types of self-report surveys: (1) surveys of unknown offenders and (2) surveys of known offenders. Surveys of unknown offenders provide information that has not made it into official police data. Surveys of known offenders may provide insight into the details of a criminal event including offender motivation, situational factors, and thoughts and feelings of the offender before, during, and after the event. Surveys of unknown offenders can be problematic in that respondents may not want to share information that they fear may be reported to police. Surveys of known offenders may not provide a completely accurate picture if offenders are fearful that the information could be used against them in some way. With both types of self-report surveys, results may not be valid and reliable because they depend on the offender's memory of a criminal event, recall ability, and the extent to which the offender is willing to share information about the event. Furthermore, offenders may experience memory lapses or want to present themselves in a more positive light. In some cases, this may not even be a conscious decision because oftentimes people remember what they want to remember about an event, especially in recalling a criminal event in which the offender's behavior may cause shame or embarrassment.[3]

Examples of large-scale self-report surveys of unknown offenders are the *National Youth Survey* (NYS), *National Survey on Drug Use and Health* (formerly called the National Household Survey on Drug Abuse, NHSDA), and *Monitoring the Future Survey* (MTF). These surveys provide information about offenses committed that have not come to the attention of the police (Table 1.3). The NYS, now called *National Youth Survey Family Study (NYSFS),* is a longitudinal survey that began in 1976 that uses a national sample of youth who were age 11 to 17 at the time of the first interview. The study has followed the individuals (currently age 39 to 45) over time, measuring their changing attitudes, beliefs, and behaviors about topics such as community and family involvement, career goals, and attitudes about social values, violence, and drugs. The NYS includes 47 activities that parallel UCR offenses, excluding homicide. More than 90% of the originally 1,725 survey respondents have remained in the survey over time. The *National Survey on Drug Use and Health (NSDUH)* is an annual survey sponsored by the Substance Abuse and Mental Health Services Administration (SAMHSA). The survey, conducted by the federal government since 1971, is the primary source of information on the use of alcohol, tobacco, and illicit drugs in the civilian, noninstitutionalized population of the United States. *Monitoring the Future (MTF)* is an ongoing study of the behaviors, attitudes, and values of American secondary school students, college students, and young adults.

❖ Table 1.3   Self-Report Surveys

National Youth Survey (NYS) http://webapp.icpsr.umich.edu/ cocoon/ICPSR-SERIES/ 00088.xml *National Youth Survey Family Study* (NYSFS) http://www.colorado.edu/ibs/ NYSFS/index.html	The NYS is a longitudinal survey begun in 1976 that uses a national sample of youth who were age 11–17 at the time of the first interview. The NYS was designed to gain a better understanding of both conventional and deviant types of behavior by youths, and involved collecting information from a representative sample of young people in the United States. The survey is now called National Youth Survey Family Study (NYSFS), and the original respondents are age 39–45. The study has followed the individuals over time measuring their changing attitudes, beliefs, and behaviors regarding topics such as community and family involvement, career goals, social values, violence, sexual activity, and drugs. The NYS includes 47 activities that parallel UCR offenses, excluding homicide. More than 90% of the originally 1,725 survey respondents have remained in the survey over time.
National Survey on Drug Use and Health (NSDUH) (formerly called the Household Survey on Drug Abuse [NHSDA]) http://www.oas.samhsa.gov/ nsduh.htm	NSDUH is an annual survey sponsored by the Substance Abuse and Mental Health Services Administration (SAMHSA). The survey, conducted by the federal government since 1971, is the primary source of information on the use of alcohol, tobacco, and illicit drugs in the civilian, noninstitutionalized population of the United States. The survey involves face-to-face interviews at the respondent's residence with approximately 67,500 persons aged 12 years or older each year.
Monitoring the Future Survey (MTF)	Monitoring the Future (MTF) is an ongoing study of the behaviors, attitudes, and values of American secondary school students, college students, and young adults. Approximately 50,000 8th-, 10th-, and 12th-grade students participate in the survey annually (12th graders since 1975, and 8th and 10th graders since 1991). Annual follow-up questionnaires are also mailed to a sample of each graduating class for a number of years after their initial participation. The MTF has been funded by investigator-initiated research grants from the National Institute on Drug Abuse, a part of the National Institutes of Health, and is conducted at the University of Michigan Survey Research Center in the Institute for Social Research.
The Offending, Crime, and Justice Survey http://www.homeoffice.gov.uk/ rds/offending_survey.html	The Offending, Crime, and Justice Survey (OCJS) is the national longitudinal, self-report offending survey for England and Wales that measures the extent of offending, antisocial behavior and drug use among the household population, aged 10 to 25. The survey was first conducted in 2003 and was repeated annually until 2006.

Approximately 50,000 8th-, 10th-, and 12th-grade students participate in the survey annually (12th graders since 1975, and 8th and 10th graders since 1991).

In addition to these large-scale national self-report surveys, the National Institute of Justice, Bureau of Justice Statistics, regularly collects data from adult offenders under jurisdiction of probation authorities, jails, prisons, or parole agencies (Greenfeld, 1998), and there are literally thousands of studies that utilize self-report measures of criminal behavior. Self-report studies that collect data from the offender's perspective offer a rare glimpse into motivational elements of criminal behavior in addition to providing information about offenses that do not make their way into official police statistics or victimization data.

All three of these methods of obtaining information about crime are important in understanding criminal behavior. Measuring the extent of crime through official statistics, victimization surveys, and self-report measures is a necessary starting point for any study of criminal behavior or a particular crime category.

Crime in the United States

How much crime is there? Does the United States have more crime than other countries? Are some types of crimes more or less of a problem than others? Is crime, or certain types of crime, on the rise or falling? Determining how much crime exists is important for resource allocation in communities in terms of directing focus of criminal justice resources, prevention programs, and law enforcement response, and evaluating whether or not implementing certain programs and practices has any impact on crime. Measuring crime through the UCR, NCVS, and self-report measures allows researchers to get as close as possible to the true extent of crime. Unfortunately, "the absolute volume of crime in a given jurisdiction is anyone's guess" (Mosher, Miethe, & Phillips, 2002, p. 172). Thus, it is important to critically evaluate available crime statistics with an understanding that there is always some (possibly large) amount of unknown crime and hidden and complex reasons that influence the extent to which the true amount of crime can be accurately measured in any given time and place.

For example, in the mid-1990s the crime rate in the United States dramatically decreased to a rate lower than it had been for 40 years. Criminologists had predicted just the opposite—that the mid-1990s would bring a large increase in crime consistent with the increase in the population of youth ages 14 to 24. However, according to Levitt (2004), different factors influence crime rates in different time periods and prominent criminologists completely missed the mark. The usual factors such as strong economy, changing demographics, better policing strategies, gun control laws, concealed weapons laws, increased use of the death penalty did not explain the mid-1990s drop in crime. Rather, Levitt (2004) argues that the increased number of police, rise in prison population, receding crack epidemic, and the post–*Roe v. Wade* (1973) legalization of abortion were the real reasons for the decrease in crime.

The association of legalization of abortion and crime rates is a novel and controversial suggestion based on the notion that unwanted children are at greater risk for crime and abortion reduces the number of unwanted children. In other words, unwanted children born after 1973 would have become the criminals who elevated the crime rate in the mid-1990s.[4] Others have argued that the dramatic drop in crime in the mid-1990s was the result of changing sensibilities. According to Tonry (2004), "Crime rates change slowly, in response to long-term social and normative changes" (p. 112) and when people's attitude toward a particular criminal behavior changes and becomes less tolerant, citizens are more likely to report crime to the police. Thus, at times when people are less tolerant of drug crime, more drug crimes will be noticed and reported to police, which in turn will inflate the statistical incidence of this type of criminal behavior. Still others have argued that the peak in crime rates in 1980 was the result of the expansion of the crack cocaine market coupled with the spread of youth gangs and increased access to firearms. When the crack cocaine market matured and turf battles ended, crime began to decrease. The 1990s crime decrease in all offense categories suggests that "something fundamental was changing in the United States and it affected each of these major crimes in the same ways" (Tonry, 2004, p. 116). For example, historians have found that homicide rates since the 12th century (the earliest time for which quantitative data are available) declined steadily in England, Holland, Belgium, Germany, Scandinavia, and Switzerland from between 30 and 100 per 100,000 in the population to 10 per 100,000 in the 18th century, to 1 to 2 per 100,000 in the 20th century. Considering more recent periods in Western countries in the mid-1990s, historians have described the violent crime rate as a "U" or "reversed J-Shaped" curve (Tonry, 2004).

To make sense of criminal behavior at any given time and in a particular society or community, it is important to know whether or not a particular criminal behavior is a statistical anomaly or so common a behavior it can be said to be barely a crime at all, and to pay attention to the differences in the extent of crime types across geographical areas, communities, cultures, and time periods. It is also important to recognize that it is no easy task to compare/contrast and synthesize data across sources, and an even more difficult challenge to compare crime rates across time periods and cultures. For example, UCR crime categories are not the same as NCVS categories and self-report studies such as the NYS and NSDUH measure crimes and crime categories at a level not possible with official police data and victimization surveys (e.g., NSDUH provides data on drug use that are not available through other sources). Official statistics present only a limited picture of the extent of crime in the United States, and making sense of the nature and extent of crime in general or of a particular type of crime requires synthesizing multiple sources of data. Figure 1.2, Table 1.4, and Table 1.5 present UCR data on crime types from 1986 to 2006, the NCVS data for 2005, and a rough look at the difference in the amounts of violent and property crime reported by the UCR and NCVS.

❖ Table 1.4a   Crime in the United States by Volume and Rate per 100,000 Inhabitants, 1986–2005

Year	Population[1]	Violent crime	Violent crime rate	Murder and non-negligent man-slaughter	Murder and non-negligent man-slaughter rate	Forcible rape	Forcible rape rate	Robbery	Robbery rate	Aggravated assault	Aggravated assault rate	Property crime	Property crime rate	Burglary	Burglary rate	Larceny-theft	Larceny-theft rate	Motor vehicle theft	Motor vehicle theft rate
1986	240,132,887	1,489,169	620.1	20,613	8.6	91,459	38.1	542,775	226.0	834,322	347.4	11,722,700	4,881.8	3,241,410	1,349.8	7,257,153	3,022.1	1,224,137	509.8
1987	242,288,918	1,483,999	612.5	20,096	8.3	91,111	37.6	517,704	213.7	855,088	352.9	12,024,709	4,963.0	3,236,184	1,335.7	7,499,851	3,095.4	1,288,674	531.9
1988	244,498,982	1,566,221	640.6	20,675	8.5	92,486	37.8	542,968	222.1	910,092	372.2	12,356,865	5,054.0	3,218,077	1,316.2	7,705,872	3,151.7	1,432,916	586.1
1989	246,819,230	1,646,037	666.9	21,500	8.7	94,504	38.3	578,326	234.3	951,707	385.6	12,605,412	5,107.1	3,168,170	1,283.6	7,872,442	3,189.6	1,564,800	634.0
1990	249,464,396	1,820,127	729.6	23,438	9.4	102,555	41.1	639,271	256.3	1,054,863	422.9	12,655,486	5,073.1	3,073,909	1,232.2	7,945,670	3,185.1	1,635,907	655.8
1991	252,153,092	1,911,767	758.2	24,703	9.8	106,593	42.3	687,732	272.7	1,092,739	433.4	12,961,116	5,140.2	3,157,150	1,252.1	8,142,228	3,229.1	1,661,738	659.0
1992	255,029,699	1,932,274	757.7	23,760	9.3	109,062	42.8	672,478	263.7	1,126,974	441.9	12,505,917	4,903.7	2,979,884	1,168.4	7,915,199	3,103.6	1,610,834	631.6
1993	257,782,608	1,926,017	747.1	24,526	9.5	106,014	41.1	659,870	256.0	1,135,607	440.5	12,218,777	4,740.0	2,834,808	1,099.7	7,820,909	3,033.9	1,563,060	606.3
1994	260,327,021	1,857,670	713.6	23,326	9.0	102,216	39.3	618,949	237.8	1,113,179	427.6	12,131,873	4,660.2	2,712,774	1,042.1	7,879,812	3,026.9	1,539,287	591.3
1995	262,803,276	1,798,792	684.5	21,606	8.2	97,470	37.1	580,509	220.9	1,099,207	418.3	12,063,935	4,590.5	2,593,784	987.0	7,997,710	3,043.2	1,472,441	560.3
1996	265,228,572	1,688,540	636.6	19,645	7.4	96,252	36.3	535,594	201.9	1,037,049	391.0	11,805,323	4,451.0	2,506,400	945.0	7,904,685	2,980.3	1,394,238	525.7
1997	267,783,607	1,636,096	611.0	18,208	6.8	96,153	35.9	498,534	186.2	1,023,201	382.1	11,558,475	4,316.3	2,460,526	918.8	7,743,760	2,891.8	1,354,189	505.7
1998	270,248,003	1,533,887	567.6	16,974	6.3	93,144	34.5	447,186	165.5	976,583	361.4	10,951,827	4,052.5	2,332,735	863.2	7,376,311	2,729.5	1,242,781	459.9
1999	272,690,813	1,426,044	523.0	15,522	5.7	89,411	32.8	409,371	150.1	911,740	334.3	10,208,334	3,743.6	2,100,739	770.4	6,955,520	2,550.7	1,152,075	422.5
2000	281,421,906	1,425,486	506.5	15,586	5.5	90,178	32.0	408,016	145.0	911,706	324.0	10,182,584	3,618.3	2,050,992	728.8	6,971,590	2,477.3	1,160,002	412.2
2001[2]	285,317,559	1,439,480	504.5	16,037	5.6	90,863	31.8	423,557	148.5	909,023	318.6	10,437,189	3,658.1	2,116,531	741.8	7,092,267	2,485.7	1,228,391	430.5
2002	287,973,924	1,423,677	494.4	16,229	5.6	95,235	33.1	420,806	146.1	891,407	309.5	10,455,277	3,630.6	2,151,252	747.0	7,057,379	2,450.7	1,246,646	432.9
2003	290,788,976	1,383,676	475.8	16,528	5.7	93,883	32.3	414,235	142.5	859,030	295.4	10,442,862	3,591.2	2,154,834	741.0	7,026,802	2,416.5	1,261,226	433.7
2004[3]	293,656,842	1,360,088	463.2	16,148	5.5	95,089	32.4	401,470	136.7	847,381	288.6	10,319,386	3,514.1	2,144,446	730.3	6,937,089	2,362.3	1,237,851	421.5
2005	296,410,404	1,390,695	469.2	16,692	5.6	93,934	31.7	417,122	140.7	862,947	291.1	10,166,159	3,429.8	2,154,126	726.7	6,776,807	2,286.3	1,235,226	416.7

[1] Populations are U.S. Census Bureau provisional estimates as of July 1 for each year except 1990 and 2000, which are decennial census counts.
[2] The murder and nonnegligent homicides that occurred as a result of the events of September 11, 2001, are not included in this table.
[3] The 2004 crime figures have been adjusted.
Note: Although arson data are included in the trend and clearance tables, sufficient data are not available to estimate totals for this offense.

❖ Table 1.4b   Crime in the United States Percent Change in Volume and Rate per 100,000 Inhabitants for 2 years, 5 years, and 10 years

Years	Violent crime	Violent crime rate	Murder and nonnegligent manslaughter	Murder and nonnegligent manslaughter rate	Forcible rape	Forcible rape rate	Robbery	Robbery rate	Aggravated assault	Aggravated assault rate	Property crime	Property crime rate	Burglary	Burglary rate	Larceny-theft	Larceny-theft rate	Motor vehicle theft	Motor vehicle theft rate
2005/2004	+2.3	+1.3	+3.4	+2.4	-1.2	-2.1	+3.9	+2.9	+1.8	+0.9	-1.5	-2.4	+0.5	-0.5	-2.3	-3.2	-0.2	-1.1
2005/2001	-3.4	-7.0	+4.1	+0.2	+3.4	-0.5	-1.5	-5.2	-5.1	-8.6	-2.6	-6.2	+1.8	-2.0	-4.4	-8.0	+0.6	-3.2
2005/1996	-17.6	-26.3	-15.0	-24.0	-2.4	-12.7	-22.1	-30.3	-16.8	-25.5	-13.9	-22.9	-14.1	-23.1	-14.3	-23.3	-11.4	-20.7

❖ Table 1.5   Personal and Property Crimes, 2005: Number, Percent Distribution, and Rate of
Victimizations, by Type of Crime

Type of Crime	Number of Victimizations	Percent of All Victimizations	Rate per 1,000 Persons or Households
All crimes	**23,440,720**	**100.0%**	. . .
Personal crimes	**5,400,790**	**23.0%**	**22.1**
Crimes of violence	5,173,720	22.1	21.2
Completed violence	1,658,660	7.1	6.8
Attempted/threatened violence	3,515,060	15.0	14.4
Rape/Sexual assault	191,670	0.8	0.8
Rape/Attempted rape	130,140	0.6	0.5
Rape	69,370	0.3	0.3
Attempted rape[a]	60,770	0.3	0.2
Sexual assault[b]	61,530	0.3	0.3
Robbery	624,850	2.7	2.6
Completed/property taken	415,320	1.8	1.7
With injury	142,830	0.6	0.6
Without injury	272,490	1.2	1.1
Attempted to take property	209,530	0.9	0.9
With injury	64,450	0.3	0.3
Without injury	145,090	0.6	0.6
Assault	4,357,190	18.6	17.8
Aggravated	1,052,260	4.5	4.3
With injury	330,730	1.4	1.4
Threatened with weapon	721,530	3.1	3.0
Simple	3,304,930	14.1	13.5
With minor injury	795,240	3.4	3.3
Without injury	2,509,690	10.7	10.3
Purse snatching/Pocket picking	227,070	1.0	0.9
Completed purse snatching	43,550	0.2	0.2
Attempted purse snatching	3,260*	0.0*	0.0*
Pocket picking	180,260	0.8	0.7
Total population age 12 and over	244,493,430	. . .	. . .
Property crimes	**18,039,930**	**77.0%**	**154.0**
Household burglary	3,456,220	14.7	29.5
Completed	2,900,460	12.4	24.8
Forcible entry	1,068,430	4.6	9.1
Unlawful entry without force	1,832,030	7.8	15.6
Attempted forcible entry	555,760	2.4	4.7
Motor vehicle theft	978,120	4.2	8.4
Completed	774,650	3.3	6.6
Attempted	203,470	0.9	1.7
Theft	13,605,590	58.0	116.2
Completed	13,116,270	56.0	112.0
Less than $50	4,079,120	17.4	34.8
$50–$249	4,656,120	19.9	39.8

(Continued)

❖ Table 1.5 (Continued)

Type of Crime	Number of Victimizations	Percent of All Victimizations	Rate per 1,000 Persons or Households
$250 or more	3,231,440	13.8	27.6
Amount not available	1,149,590	4.9	9.8
Attempted	489,320	2.1	4.2
Total number of households	117,110,800	. . .	. . .

Note: Detail may not add to total shown because of rounding.
*Estimate is based on about 10 or fewer sample cases.
Percent distribution is based on unrounded figures.
. . . Not applicable.
ªIncludes verbal threats of rape.
ᵇIncludes threats.

❖ **Figure 1.2** Extent of Violent, Property, and All Crime by Millions, UCR and NCVS Data

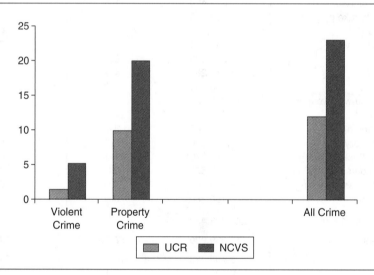

In addition to the Uniform Crime Reports, National Crime Victimization Survey, and self-report surveys, a number of sources serve as a central clearinghouse and starting point for research on crime and characteristics of different types of criminal behavior. The *Bureau of Justice Statistics* compiles data from the UCR, the NCVS, and self-report measures to give an estimate of crime trends based on multiple data sources. The *National Criminal Justice Reference Service* is a central clearinghouse offering justice and substance abuse information with links to resources, reports, and data sources to support research, policy, and program development. The *Sourcebook of Criminal Justice Statistics* brings together data from more than 100 sources about many aspects of crime and criminal justice in the United States. For example, the *Sourcebook* presents statistics from UCR, NCVS, and self-report surveys and a combination of multiple sources. Tables 1.6, 1.7, 1.8, and 1.9 present examples of the different types of statistical tables available in the *Sourcebook* from sources including the UCR, NCVS, and self-report surveys. The study of criminal behavior requires bringing together data from all of these sources. Important information about the nature and extent of a particular type of criminal behavior at a particular time period or location is often not available from these public sources, but these data sources are an important starting point to situate crime or a type of crime within the larger context.

The Changing Nature of Crime in the 21st Century

Crime is often approached as if it were an unchanging phenomenon—as if the reasons why a person would commit crime in one time period or context carry over to very different or distant times, cultures, and situations. Perhaps this is because scientific paradigms do not shift fast enough to keep up with the many social and cultural forces at the heart of definitions of crime and individual-level criminal behavior. Politics influence what behaviors are legally defined as criminal. Economics shape individual choices, who has power to make and enforce the law, who will be targeted, and what items in society are valuable targets for crime. Technological advances, which have far surpassed any gains the social sciences have been able to make in the study of criminal behavior, have had an enormous impact on methods of committing and detecting certain types of crime and mass communication, through which people learn about and are influenced by crime in society.

A number of themes emphasized throughout this text are of critical importance for the study of criminal behavior in the 21st century. First, the typology approach to understanding similarities and differences of various types of crime lets us refine theories of how types and subtypes of crime are similar and different, allowing for concrete application of theory to practice. Second, the disciplines of sociology, psychology, and more recently criminology and criminal justice have historically operated in their own disciplinary vacuums. The time has come to connect and synthesize the longstanding theoretical and empirical dots to make a more sophisticated understanding of criminal behavior possible. Third, as the number-one correlate of crime, the role of gender needs to be more central in developing theory and empirical research on crime. Finally, how and why technology shapes criminal behavior is only beginning to be explored. Theories of the future must be able to explain how crime and criminal behavior is influenced by rapid changes in technology over short periods of time. Dynamic theories and creative research methodology is needed to tap into the ways in which technological and cultural changes quickly alter the face of crime.

All criminal behavior is not alike in terms of motivation, offender-victim dynamics, situational factors, social harm, legal sanctions, and so on. While it is important to develop general theories of crime that attempt to explain most, if not all, criminal behavior, it is also important to identify the similarities and differences between types

❖ Table 1.6   Reported Drug Use, Alcohol Use, and Cigarette Use in Last 12 Months Among College Students. (Selected Table From the *Sourcebook of Criminal Justice Statistics*: http://www.albany.edu/sourcebook/pdf/t374.pdf)

By type of drug, United States, 1988–2003

Question: "On how many occasions, if any, have you used . . . during the last 12 months?"

Percent Who Used in Last 12 Months

Type of Drug	1988	1989	1990	1991	1992	1993	1994	1995	1996	1997	1998	1999	2000	2001	2002	2003
Marijuana	34.6%	33.6%	29.4%	26.5%	27.7%	27.9%	29.3%	31.2%	33.1%	31.6%	35.9%	35.2%	34.0%	35.6%	34.7%	33.7%
Inhalants[a]	4.1	3.7	3.9	3.5	3.1	3.8	3.0	3.9	3.6	4.1	3.0	3.2	2.9	2.8	2.0	1.8
Hallucinogens[b]	5.3	5.1	5.4	6.3	6.8	6.0	6.2	8.2	6.9	7.7	7.2	7.8	6.7	7.5	6.3	7.4
LSD	3.6	3.4	4.3	5.1	5.7	5.1	5.2	6.9	5.2	5.0	4.4	5.4	4.3	4.0	2.1	1.4
MDMA (ecstasy)[c]	NA	2.3	2.3	0.9	2.0	0.8	0.5	2.4	2.8	2.4	3.9	5.5	9.1	9.2	6.8	4.4
Cocaine	10.0	8.2	5.6	3.6	3.0	2.7	2.0	3.6	2.9	3.4	4.6	4.6	4.8	4.7	4.8	5.4
Crack[d]	1.4	1.5	0.6	0.5	0.4	0.6	0.5	1.1	0.6	0.4	1.0	0.9	0.9	0.9	0.4	1.3
Heroin	0.2	0.1	0.1	0.1	0.1	0.1	0.1	0.3	0.4	0.3	0.6	0.2	0.5	0.4	0.1	0.2
Other narcotics[e,f]	3.1	3.2	2.9	2.7	2.7	2.5	2.4	3.8	3.1	4.2	4.2	4.3	4.5	5.7	5.9	8.7
Amphetamines[e]	6.2	4.6	4.5	3.9	3.6	4.2	4.2	5.4	4.2	5.7	5.1	5.8	6.6	7.2	7.0	7.1
Crystal methamphetamine[g]	NA	NA	0.1	0.1	0.2	0.7	0.8	1.1	0.4	0.8	1.0	0.5	0.5	0.6	0.8	0.9
Barbiturates[e]	1.1	1.0	1.4	1.2	1.4	1.5	1.2	2.0	2.3	3.0	2.5	3.2	3.7	3.8	3.7	4.1
Tranquilizers[b,e]	3.1	2.6	3.0	2.4	2.9	2.4	1.8	2.9	2.8	3.8	3.9	3.8	4.2	5.1	6.7	6.9
Alcohol[h]	89.6	89.6	89.0	88.3	86.9	85.1	82.7	83.2	83.0	82.4	84.6	83.6	83.2	83.0	82.9	81.7
Cigarettes	36.6	34.2	35.5	35.6	37.3	38.8	37.6	39.3	41.4	43.6	44.3	44.5	41.3	39.0	38.3	35.2

Note: These data are from a followup survey of respondents 1 to 4 years past high school who are presently enrolled in college. Included are those registered as full-time students in March of the year in question and who report that they are enrolled in a 2- or 4-year college. Those individuals previously in college and those who have already completed college are excluded. The approximate N for each year is as follows: 1988, 1,310; 1989, 1,300; 1990, 1,400; 1991, 1,410; 1992, 1,490; 1993, 1,490; 1994, 1,410; 1995, 1,450; 1996, 1,450; 1997, 1,480; 1998, 1,440; 1999, 1,440; 2000, 1,350; 2001, 1,340; 2002, 1,260; 2003, 1,270. Readers interested in responses to this question for 1980 through 1987 should consult previous editions of SOURCEBOOK. Some data have been revised by the Source and may differ from previous editions of SOURCEBOOK.

Since 1982, new questions were introduced on the use of controlled and noncontrolled stimulants in order to exclude over-the-counter amphetamines, which were believed to have been inflating the statistic for earlier years. Figures presented for "stimulants" are based on the data obtained from these new questions. For survey methodology and definitions of terms, see Appendix 6.

[a]This drug was asked about in four of the five questionnaire forms in 1988 and 1989, in five of the six questionnaire forms in 1990–98, and in three of the six questionnaire forms beginning in 1999.

[b]In 2001, the question text was changed on half of the questionnaire forms. The 2001 data are based on the changed forms only. Beginning in 2002, all forms include the revised wording.

[c]This drug was asked about in two of the five questionnaire forms in 1989, in two of the six questionnaire forms in 1990–2001, and in three of the six questionnaire forms beginning in 2002.

[d]This drug was asked about in two of the five questionnaire forms in 1988 and 1989, in all six questionnaire forms in 1990–2001, and in five of the six questionnaire forms beginning in 2002.

[e]Only drug use that was not under a doctor's orders is included here.

[f]In 2002, the question text was changed on half of the questionnaire forms. The list of examples of narcotics other than heroin was updated by replacing "Talwin," "laudanum," and "paregoric" with "Vicodin," "OxyContin," and "Percocet." The 2002 data are based on the changed forms only; N is one-half of N indicated. Beginning in 2003, all forms include the revised wording and data are based on all six forms.

[g]This drug was asked about in two of the six questionnaire forms.

[h]In 1993 and 1994, the question was changed slightly in half of the questionnaire forms to indicate that a "drink" meant "more than a few sips." Data for 1993 and 1994 are from the revised and unrevised forms combined. Beginning in 1995, all forms include the revised wording.

Source: Lloyd D. Johnston et al., *Monitoring the Future National Survey Results on Drug Use, 1975–2003*, Vol. 2, College Students and Adults Ages 19–45 (Bethesda, MD: U.S. Department of Health and Human Services, 2004), p. 237. Table adapted by SOURCEBOOK staff.

❖ Table 1.7 Students Reporting Involvement in Delinquent Activities at School. (Selected Table From the *Sourcebook of Criminal Justice Statistics:* http://www.albany.edu/sourcebook/pdf/t358.pdf)

By grade level of respondent, 2002–2003[a]				
Question: "While at school have you . . . ?"				
	Never	One time	2 to 5 times	6 or more times
Carried a gun	96.3%	1.2%	0.6%	1.8%
Grades 6 to 8	96.9	1.2	0.5	1.5
Grades 9 to 12	95.7	1.3	0.8	2.2
12th grade	94.8	1.4	0.8	3.0
Carried a knife, club or other weapon	85.0	6.7	3.5	4.8
Grades 6 to 8	87.7	6.7	2.6	3.0
Grades 9 to 12	82.4	6.6	4.3	6.6
12th grade	82.1	5.5	4.2	8.1
Threatened a student with a gun, knife or club	94.6	2.2	1.2	1.9
Grades 6 to 8	95.6	2.0	1.0	1.4
Grades 9 to 12	93.7	2.5	1.5	2.4
12th grade	93.6	2.3	1.2	2.9
Threatened to hurt a student by hitting, slapping or kicking	62.6	11.1	12.8	13.6
Grades 6 to 8	62.6	12.0	12.0	13.3
Grades 9 to 12	62.5	10.1	13.6	13.8
12th grade	67.1	8.9	12.1	11.9
Hurt a student by using a gun, knife or club	96.5	1.2	0.8	1.5
Grades 6 to 8	97.2	1.0	0.6	1.2
Grades 9 to 12	95.8	1.5	0.9	1.8
12th grade	95.1	1.5	1.0	2.4
Hurt a student by hitting, slapping or kicking	68.3	11.6	10.8	9.3
Grades 6 to 8	66.6	12.9	10.9	9.6
Grades 9 to 12	69.9	10.4	10.8	9.0
12th grade	75.2	8.3	8.9	7.5

[a]Percents may not add to 100 because of rounding.

Source: PRIDE Surveys, "2002–2003 PRIDE Surveys National Summary, Grades 6 through 12," Bowling Green, KY: PRIDE Surveys, 2003. (Mimeographed.) Pp. 212, 213. Table adapted by SOURCEBOOK staff. Reprinted by permission.

❖ Table 1.8   Workplace Homicides. (Selected Table From the *Sourcebook of Criminal Justice Statistics:* http://www.albany.edu/sourcebook/pdf/t3135.pdf)

By victim characteristics, type of event, and selected occupation and industry, United States, 1992–2002[a]	1992	1993	1994	1995	1996	1997	1998	1999	2000	2001[b]	2002[c]
Total	1,044	1,074	1,080	1,036	927	860	714	651	677	639	609
Victim characteristics											
<u>Employee status</u>											
Wage and salary workers[d]	793	786	818	823	675	632	526	485	488	470	449
Self-employed[e]	251	288	262	213	252	228	188	166	189	169	160
<u>Sex</u>											
Male	862	884	895	790	751	715	550	525	543	513	473
Female	182	190	185	246	176	145	164	126	134	126	136
<u>Age</u>											
Under 16 years	(f)	6	(f)	(f)	(f)	(f)	(f)	(f)	(f)	(f)	(f)
16 to 17 years	11	11	10	6	8	9	(f)	8	(f)	(f)	(f)
18 to 19 years	19	16	27	26	21	16	12	11	14	14	10
20 to 24 years	105	89	102	70	74	60	44	49	41	45	34
25 to 34 years	271	294	280	264	220	215	178	145	142	136	147
35 to 44 years	275	295	290	258	228	216	199	166	177	174	167
45 to 54 years	186	194	205	215	189	171	139	155	165	151	147
55 to 64 years	116	108	104	127	120	120	82	74	100	81	76
65 years and older	56	61	61	65	65	51	52	38	31	34	24
<u>Race, ethnicity</u>											
White	597	583	592	578	504	500	399	346	344	331	309
Black	192	164	210	206	171	146	128	116	118	113	111
Asian or Pacific Islander	105	128	129	100	105	104	74	85	84	72	54
American Indian, Eskimo, or Aleut	(f)	6	7	5	6	(f)	(f)	(f)	(f)	(f)	(f)
Other or unspecified	14	8	(f)	17	11	5	10	5	20	13	26
Hispanic[g]	132	185	139	130	130	101	99	95	108	106	107
<u>Type of event</u>											
Shooting	852	884	934	762	761	708	574	509	533	505	469
Stabbing	90	95	60	67	80	73	61	62	66	58	58
Hitting, kicking, beating	52	35	47	46	50	48	48	48	37	36	34
Other	30	48	31	153	29	26	24	26	38	38	38
<u>Major occupation</u>											
Managerial and professional specialty occupations	185	162	149	200	184	156	132	117	141	120	104
Technical, sales, and administrative support jobs	353	404	426	381	332	305	239	197	235	203	210
Service occupations	228	212	251	216	188	181	146	156	130	171	156
Police and detectives	62	68	70	81	55	66	53	47	49	62	57
Guards	56	55	76	61	52	43	39	36	33	38	37
Farming, forestry, and fishing	15	11	17	20	18	10	19	19	14	11	13
Precision production, craft, and repair jobs	43	67	39	40	37	36	41	35	38	34	28
Operators, fabricators, and laborers	211	204	178	160	154	162	130	118	113	96	96

By victim characteristics, type of event, and selected occupation and industry, United States, 1992–2002[a]	1992	1993	1994	1995	1996	1997	1998	1999	2000	2001[b]	2002[c]
Major industry											
Agriculture, forestry, fishing	15	13	18	19	18	9	19	19	12	9	(f)
Construction	20	20	16	15	12	14	20	6	21	26	18
Manufacturing	32	46	33	44	40	43	38	26	25	32	24
Transportation and public utilities	117	126	118	98	76	110	69	70	65	52	49
Taxicabs	86	96	87	68	50	74	48	51	42	33	27
Wholesale trade	25	25	20	25	24	21	21	26	16	6	18
Retail trade	503	525	530	422	437	395	287	264	310	280	263
Grocery stores	166	176	196	152	146	141	95	78	111	92	77
Eating and drinking places	145	145	135	121	135	109	69	95	91	93	86
Gasoline service stations	41	53	41	36	23	34	25	17	14	16	17
Finance, insurance, real estate	37	35	31	53	41	28	22	34	21	20	28
Services	175	155	193	141	169	146	139	136	127	125	110
Detective and armored car services	23	32	49	27	29	21	18	17	16	21	19
Government[h]	104	124	104	212	100	88	94	66	78	88	83
Federal	11	18	12	109	11	7	16	7	6	9	5
State	11	20	12	17	20	19	22	11	11	10	16
Local	80	86	80	84	69	60	56	48	61	68	61

Note: These data were collected through the Census of Fatal Occupational Injuries conducted annually by the Bureau of Labor Statistics in cooperation with numerous federal, state, and local agencies. Data were compiled from various federal, state, and local administrative sources including death certificates, workers' compensation reports and claims, medical examiner reports, police reports, news reports, and reports to various regulatory agencies.

The Census of Fatal Occupational Injuries, therefore, includes data for all fatal work injuries, whether they are covered by the Occupational Safety and Health Administration (OSHA), another federal or state agency, or are outside the scope of regulatory coverage. Federal agencies participating in the census include OSHA, the Employment Standards Administration, the Mine Safety and Health Administration, the Federal Aviation Administration, the Federal Railroad Administration, the Department of Energy, and the U.S. Coast Guard. State and local agencies participating in the census include state and local police departments; state vital statistics registrars; state departments of health, labor, and industries; state farm bureaus; and local coroners and medical examiners. Multiple sources were used because studies have shown that no single source captures all job-related fatalities. Source documents were matched so that each fatality is counted only once. To ensure that a fatality was work related, information was verified from two or more independent source documents or from a source document and a followup questionnaire.

[a]Detail may not add to total because of the omission of miscellaneous categories.
[b]The workplace homicides that occurred as a result of the events of Sept. 11, 2001, are not included in this table.
[c]Data for 2002 are preliminary.
[d]May include volunteers and other workers receiving compensation.
[e]Includes paid and unpaid family workers, and may include owners of incorporated businesses or members of partnerships.
[f]No data reported or data did not meet publication criteria specified by the Source.
[g]Persons identified as Hispanic may be of any race; therefore, detail will not add to total.
[h]Includes fatalities to workers employed by government agencies regardless of industry.

Source: Table adapted by SOURCEBOOK staff from data provided by U.S. Department of Labor, Bureau of Labor Statistics.

❖ **Table 1.9** Terrorist Incidents and Preventions, United States, 1980–2001. (Selected Table From the *Sourcebook of Criminal Justice Statistics:* http://www.albany.edu/sourcebook/pdf/t3173.pdf)

	Terrorist Incidents	Suspected Terrorist Incidents	Terrorism Preventions
Total	294	55	133
1980	29	0	1
1981	42	4	0
1982	51	1	3
1983	31	2	6
1984	13	3	9
1985	7	6	23
1986	25	2	9
1987	9	8	5
1988	9	5	3
1989	4	16	7
1990	7	1	5
1991	5	1	5
1992	4	0	0
1993	12	2	7
1994	1	1	0
1995	1	1	2
1996	3	0	5
1997	4	0	21
1998	5	0	12
1999	10	2	7
2000	8	0	1
2001	14	0	2

Note: A terrorist incident is a violent act, or an act dangerous to human life, in violation of the criminal laws of the United States or of any state, to intimidate or coerce a government, the civilian population, or any segment thereof, in furtherance of political or social objectives. A terrorism prevention is a documented instance in which a violent act by a known or suspected terrorist group or individual with the means and a proven propensity for violence is successfully interdicted through investigative activity. (Source, p. iv.) A suspected terrorist incident is a potential act of terrorism in which responsibility for the act cannot be attributed at the time to a known or suspected terrorist group or individual. Some data have been revised by the Source and may differ from previous editions of SOURCE BOOK.

Source: U.S. Department of Justice, Federal Bureau of Investigation, *Terrorism 2000/2001* [Online]. Available: http://www.fbi.gov/publications/terror/terror2000_2001.pdf [Sept. 14, 2004], p. 10. Table adapted by SOURCEBOOK staff.

and subtypes of crime. Focus on typologies of criminal behavior and the distinct and overlapping features of crime categories offers a more nuanced understanding of the nature of different types and subtypes of crime. *Can a single theory explain why a woman kills her abusive husband, why a teenager steals a car, and why a group of people engage in drug smuggling? Are there features of the many different types of criminal behavior that are so distinct that they call for minitheories to explain subtypes of offense behaviors? What details do general theories of crime overlook regarding the nature and dynamics of distinct types of offense behaviors? How can understanding these details enhance opportunities for meaningful criminal justice policy and practice at different stages of the criminal justice process?*

Dynamic theories and creative research methods designs are needed to tap into the ways in which changes in technology and culture quickly alter the nature and dynamics of criminal behavior. Much of the empirical research is based on data collected many years ago and even recently published results often utilize aging data sets or involve secondary data analysis based on surveys from sources such as the National Youth Survey that, though it has been changed over time, is not designed to answer questions relevant to particular time periods, places, subcultures, communities, gender, ethnic groups, and so on. Findings based on data collected 10, 20, or 50 years ago assume that there is little relationship between cultural changes and individual-level criminal behavior. *Does it make sense to explain criminal behavior using the same theories over time? Is crime committed in 2008 the same as it was in 1908, 1948, or 1988? Has popular culture and technology played a role in shaping criminal behavior in terms of offender motivation? Do the ways in which offenders commit their crimes change over time in relation to changes in technology and culture? Have advances in computer and media technology shaped criminal behavior in ways that call for new theories and empirical research that utilizes timely samples?* Surprisingly, researchers have only begun to ask these questions, and there is little empirical research to shed light on how or if crimes of today and in the future may be different from or similar to crimes of the near or distant past.

Insulation and disconnection across disciplines is a major hindrance to advances in criminal behavior research. Even though the study of crime has become much more interdisciplinary over time, with a greater number of scholars coming from PhD programs in criminology/criminal justice (that emphasize multiple disciplinary perspectives on the study of crime and its societal response), important work being done in many fields remains disconnected. Even scholars whose academic background is heavily interdisciplinary often have a particular allegiance to one or another disciplinary camp. The more students and researchers of criminal behavior are willing to cross disciplinary boundaries to make critical theoretical linkages, the more advanced our understanding of crime will be. Contributions from the fields of psychology, sociology, anthropology, social work, political science, communications, cultural studies, women studies, ethnic studies, theology, philosophy, biology, neurochemistry, neuropsychology, computer science, and other disciplines must be linked and synthesized to advance the knowledge base. Many pockets of important work are being done in multiple disciplines. Critical research necessary to further knowledge on criminal behavior is being conducted in areas such as offender motivation and cognitive distortions, career criminality and anti-social persistent behavior across the life course, psychopathy and its role in criminal behavior, sexual deviancy and family violence, and media effects. *What the study of criminal behavior needs for the 21st century is a true and meaningful synthesis of disciplines and respect among scholars whose work converges,* perhaps not with respect to disciplinary terminology and nomenclature, but in theoretical linkages that allow for a more nuanced understanding of the nature of crime. Such synthesis could have powerful implications for understanding and responding to crime. This does not mean that criminology/criminal justice is not a discipline in and of itself, but rather distinguishes the field as truly and uniquely interdisciplinary.[5] In his 2001 presidential address to the Academy of Criminal Justice Sciences, Todd Clear said the field of criminology/criminal justice is "multidisciplinary always, interdisciplinary at our best" (Clear, 2001, p. 711).

Finally, and perhaps most important, *the study of crime and criminal behavior must finally and at once address the gender issue.* Criminologists have done a poor job explaining why the vast majority of all crimes are committed by men (Messerschmidt, 1993). Across all time periods and cultures, the vast majority of crime is committed by men. The bulk of what has been written about criminal behavior has been by men and about men. Gender is the strongest predictor of criminality. However, the discipline of criminology has been gender-blind for most of its history. Criminologists have been bizarrely silent about the reasons why masculinity is so strongly associated with criminal behavior. If, across all time periods and cultures, almost all crime is committed by men, why have criminologists devoted such a small amount of attention to the issue of gender? Why is it that the variable that has so consistently been empirically established as the single most important predictor of criminal behavior has been so blatantly ignored? The answers to these questions need to be examined without delay. Anything less reflects negligence of criminal behavior scholars to address the most fundamental feature of crime.

In the 1970s, discourse on female involvement in crime and the gendered nature of criminal behavior emerged, spawning a subfield called *feminist criminology.* Influential early works include Freda Adler's (1975) *Sisters in Crime,* Rita Simon's (1975) *Women in Crime,* Carol Smart's (1977) *Women, Crime, and Criminology: A Feminist Critique,* and Chapman's (1980) *Economic Realities and the Female Offender.* Adler and Simon suggested that, as women gain more economic power in society, they will engage in more criminal behavior. This notion that increased participation in crime by women is a byproduct of the feminist movement came to be known as the controversial *liberation hypothesis.* Smart, Chapman, and other feminist scholars such as Susan Brownmiller (1975), Andrea Dworkin (1987), and Katherine MacKinnon (1983) challenged this hypothesis, suggesting that female criminality and victimization could be explained by patriarchal oppression, economic depravation, and sexual subjugation.

In 1988, Kathleen Daly and Meda Chesney-Lind wrote a now classic article entitled "Feminism and Criminology," highlighting the *generalizability problem* (the misapplication of male theories of crime to female offending) and calling for theory development on gender and crime and gender equality in the criminal justice system.

Since then, increasing attention has been paid to the applicability of male theories of crime to women and girls, the male as predator/female as victim dichotomy maintained by patriarchy, and gender discrimination and disparity in the criminal justice system. Meda Chesney-Lind, author of *The Female Offender: Girls, Women, and Crime* (1997) and numerous other books and articles, has been referred to as the "Mother of feminist criminology" (Belknap, 2004) and is one of the most prolific writers and outspoken voices on feminist criminology. Her work highlights the contextual features of the lives of girls and women that influence their involvement in crime as offenders and victims and the disparate and discriminatory practices in the criminal justice system.

Feminist criminology raised issues regarding not only the applicability of male theories of crime to female offenders, but also the gendered nature of crime. In his important work, *Masculinities and Crime,* Messerschmidt (1993) called for attention to the masculinity-crime connection, arguing that criminology has ignored the most central predictor of crime. According to Messerschmidt, "Crime by men is a form of social practice invoked as a resource, when other resources are unavailable, for accomplishing masculinity" (p. 85). In *Feminism and Criminology,* Naffine (1996) offered a critical analysis of the impact of masculinity and femininity on criminal behavior and the discipline of criminology, arguing that the gendered nature of crime is perpetuated by "a desperate desire to preserve men from associations with the feminine and its supposed weakness and subordination" (p. 148). Gerbner (1994) and Jhally (1999) have highlighted the role of mass media technology in shaping and solidifying the masculinity-crime/femininity-victim ideology, giving attention to the ways in which media images pit the male aggressor against the female victim and make it virtually impossible for males or females to break out of these culturally designated roles.

This research suggests that there is still a lot of work to be done to unravel the gendered nature of criminal behavior. Katz (2006) argues that violence against women is a men's issue and men need to take action and personal responsibility for the problem of crime. Others such as Naffine (1996) emphasize the need to address the gendered nature of criminology as a discipline more centrally:

> The most pressing intellectual and ethical obligation of those of us who wish to persist with the study of crime, its meaning and reasons, is to bring women (and other exiles) in from the cold. In order to know more about who we are as criminologists, about the very nature of our enterprise and whether it is worth pursuing at all, we need to open up the conventional borders of the discipline. (Naffine, 1996, p. 153)

This important work in the area of feminist criminology and gender and crime has set the theoretical foundation for future research that may begin to explain the masculinity-crime link and gender differences and similarities in offending patterns.

In the last 30 to 40 years, male and female crime rates have converged and the gender gap in offending has narrowed considerably (Heimer, 2000). Some argue that there has been a rise in female crime and violence (Kirsta, 1994), whereas others caution that increases in official rates of female offending reflect changes in law and criminal justice policy and practice that have disproportionately targeted girls and women (Chesney-Lind, 1997; Daly & Chesney-Lind, 1988). It is unclear, however, whether this convergence is the result of actual differences in male and female offending patterns or an artifact of increased police attention to female offenders and society's acceptance of the notion that girls and women are just as capable as boys and men of committing crime. Important gains have been made in recent years in research on female aggression and the application of historically male constructs such as psychopathy to female offender populations. This research suggests that females are just as aggressive as males but that behavior manifestations of aggression in females (and males) depend on cultural, situational, and individual-specific factors (Bjorkqvist & Niemela, 1992; Campbell, 1994).

One of the most promising areas of research explaining gender differences in manifestations of aggression is cognitive modeling. Identification with aggressive models is an important factor in explaining the effect of television violence (Bjorkqvist & Niemela, 1992). People are more likely to imitate the thinking and behavior of role models they closely identify with, and the sorts of role models that exist in any given culture are limited to its norms, values, and social structure. Girls and women are presented with the widespread cultural view in American and most other cultures that *males are predators and females are prey*. The maintenance of this masculinity-predator/femininity-prey dichotomy is central to patriarchal societies, ensuring that men stay in power and women are kept out. Entire literatures and disciplines (e.g., women studies, feminist jurisprudence) have been devoted to the social, economic, political, and legal oppression of women; however, links between sex-role stereotypes, patriarchal ideology, and gender differences in the manifestation of aggression and criminal behavior have not been clearly (or empirically) drawn. Boys and men commit more crime than girls and women because they are exposed to and inundated by aggressive role models in everyday life, the media, and popular culture. In contrast, girls and women are exposed to and inundated by the image of the victim. With little exposure to aggressive and powerful female role models, girls and women cognitively model what they see. However, aggression has a biological basis. Most aggression is instigated by real-life frustration, but the manifestation of frustration-induced aggression is highly dependent on social learning.

Some would argue that images of aggressive and powerful women in American and other cultures are increasing, providing girls and women with a new set of role models that may alter cognitive scripts and increase the amount of crime among women. However, the relationship between gender, aggression, patriarchal ideology, social learning, cognitive modeling, and criminal behavior is complex. What is clear is that criminal behavior is a product of the interactions of biological predisposition; psychological factors such as social learning and cognition and information processing; sociocultural influences such as values, ideology, and media images; and phenomenological influences such as the meanings people attribute to their and others' behaviors. What is not clear, given the state of the literature on gender and crime, is how all of these influences simultaneously bind masculinity and crime or how variations across time, place, situations, and individuals influence gender manifestations of aggression and criminal behavior.

Unraveling the association between masculinity and criminal behavior and understanding the nature of female offending is a critical challenge for 21st-century criminologists. There is no shortage of questions for researchers of the future: *How do images of the first female speaker of the house, or a woman running for president, or media images of violent females influence gender differences in crime? What mediating factors intercept the power-crime association? When aggressive female characters are presented in the media, and what patriarchal features of the presentation co-occur to ensure that female viewers still see themselves as victims rather than predators? What is the interaction between biological sex differences, sex-role conditioning, patriarchal ideology, economic factors, race/ethnicity, and media effects in shaping criminal behavior and differential gender manifestations of aggression? Can existing theories of crime be applied to female offenders and, if so, with what modifications?*

Summary

Two questions are usually asked about crime and criminal behavior: *Why do people commit crime?* and *How much crime is there?* Criminologists have had a difficult time answering the first question and recognize that no single factor can completely explain criminal behavior. In some respects, criminal behavior is analogous to a tragic accident— *criminal behavior occurs as a result of a series of interlocking events and would not occur if any link in a chain of events and decisions were broken.* A first step in studying criminal behavior involves determining its nature and extent. Measurement of crime involves synthesizing data from multiple sources including official police data, victimization surveys, and self-report measures to get as close as possible to the true amount of crime while minimizing the dark figure of crime—the amount that remains unknown. Primary sources for crime data in the United States include the Uniform Crime Reports (UCR), the National Crime Victimization Survey (NCVS), and the National Youth Survey (NYS). Challenges for the study of criminal behavior for the 21st century include understanding similarities and differences of various types of crime, meaningful synthesis of theory and research on criminal behavior across multiple disciplines, the gendered nature of crime, the role of technology in shaping criminal behavior, and the development of dynamic theories and creative research methods to tap into the relationships between crime, technology, and culture.

This text examines major theories of crime and typologies of criminal behavior within an interdisciplinary framework, focusing on the link between theory and practice and the changing nature of crime in the 21st century. Real-life stories of criminal behavior are discussed throughout the text within an interdisciplinary theoretical framework and with emphasis on the critical relevance of theory to criminal justice practice. Chapter 2 presents the major theories of crime from an interdisciplinary perspective. Chapter 3 illustrates how theories are transformed into typologies that have practical applications for criminal justice practice. Chapter 4 introduces the concept of psychopathy, examining its central relevance to the study of criminal behavior and implications for risk assessment and prediction of dangerousness. Chapters 5 through 9 provide detailed overviews of the major categories of crime—violent, sex, economic, public order, and political crime. Chapter 10 discusses the role of mass media and computer technology in shaping criminal behavior, focusing on copycat crime and cybercrime.

Chapter 11 illustrates how theories and typologies of crime and criminal behavior directly influence criminal justice policy and practice. Chapter 12 discusses the future of the study of criminal behavior, highlighting knowledge gaps and suggestions for future research that attend to the evolving nature of crime in the 21st century.

DISCUSSION QUESTIONS

1. Discuss the difficulties criminologists have in answering the two primary questions that are usually asked about criminal behavior: Why do people commit crime? How much crime is there?

2. Explain the different sources of available data on crime. Compare/contrast these different data sources and discuss their strengths and weaknesses.

3. What are some of the most pressing challenges for scholars of criminal behavior in understanding crime in the 21st century?

4. In the last 30 to 40 years, male and female crime rates have converged, considerably narrowing the gender gap in offending, and scholars differ in their interpretations of this convergence. Discuss the different explanations for the lessening gender gap in criminal behavior. What are your thoughts on why this has occurred?

5. One suggestion made in this chapter is that criminal behavior in the 21st century may be different from criminal behavior of the past. Discuss your thoughts on this—how is criminal behavior this year similar to and different from criminal behavior in time periods of the past?

On Your Own: Log on to the Web-based student study site at http://www.sagepub .com/helfgottstudy/ for the URL links in the Web Exercises, study aids such as review quizzes, and research recommendations including links to journal articles specifically selected for this book.

WEB EXERCISES

1. Go to the U.S. Coast Guard's electronic library and read the report on the deaths of Lt. Hill and Officer Duque in the botched diving incident of the icebreaker *Healy*: http://www.uscg.mil/foia/reading_room.asp. Read about the linked events and decisions that were attributed to the accident and the measures recommended to prevent future incidents from occurring. Using this case as a framework for an analogy to understand criminal behavior, discuss how a similar report might be generated in the aftermath of a crime, what factors are likely to be identified, and what concrete changes could be made to prevent future similar crimes.

2. Explore the major sources for U.S. crime statistics:

    Uniform Crime Reports: http://www.fbi.gov/ucr/ucr.htm

    National Crime Victimization Survey: http://www.ojp.usdoj.gov/bjs/cvict.htm#Programs

    Bureau of Justice Statistics: http://www.ojp.usdoj.gov/bjs/welcome.html

    Sourcebook of Criminal Justice Statistics: http://www.albany.edu/sourcebook/

    National Criminal Justice Reference Service: http://www.ncjrs.gov/index.html

    What can these sources tell you about the nature and extent of crime in the United States? Examine a particular crime category that interests you: Describe the nature and extent of the crime category using these sources. What information are these sources not able to provide regarding your topic?

3. In 2000, the National Institute of Justice, Bureau of Justice Statistics, published data on the sexual victimization of college women in the report, "The Sexual Victimization of College Women" (Fisher, Cullen, & Turner, 2000). The report is available from NIJ: http://www.ncjrs.gov/pdffiles1/nij/182369.pdf. Read the report and discuss how the data add to the official police data available through the UCR and what sort of information about sex crimes against college students might be obtained from self-report surveys. Would combining UCR, NCVS, and self-report data tell us all we need to know about sexual victimization of college students? What is likely to remain part of the dark figure of crime regarding this type of offense?

4. An example of the use of UCR, NCVS, and self-report survey data is available at http://www.ojp.usdoj.gov/bjs/pub/ascii/ac.txt in the BJS report, *An Analysis of National Data on the Prevalence of Alcohol Involvement in Crime*. Read the report and discuss how these data collection methods are used in this study to explain alcohol-related criminal behavior. What information is still needed to fully understand this form of criminal behavior?

5. Read Jeff Ferrell's (1995) article "Culture, Crime, and Cultural Criminology" in the *Journal of Criminal Justice and Popular Culture*: http://www.albany.edu/scj/jcjpc/vol3is2/culture.html and Jackson Katz's "10 Things Men Can Do to Prevent Gender Violence": http://www.jacksonkatz.com/topten.html and respond to the following three questions raised in this chapter: (1) How is the notion of males as predators/females as prey culturally perpetuated? (2) How do you think this notion may or may not influence criminal behavior and victimization on societal and individual levels? (3) Pose a research question for 21st-century criminologists that you would like to see explored to address issues raised by Ferrell, Katz, media-crime scholars, and feminist criminologists.

6. Violence scholar Jackson Katz argues that the normalization of violent masculinity in American culture has to be acknowledged and challenged. Visit Katz's Web site: http://www.jacksonkatz.com/ and watch the YouTube video of Katz speaking about Virginia Tech, Columbine, and other school shootings. Discuss your thoughts on the issue of masculinity, crime, and violence.

Theories
of Criminal
Behavior

It's, I don't know, maybe a messed up gene somewhere.

—Alex Baranyi, quadruple murderer (Johnson, 1998)

At midnight on January 3, 1997, 20-year-old Kimberly Wilson was strangled and kicked to death in a Bellevue, Washington, park. Her body was found a day later lying in a heap with a cord wrapped around her neck. When the police went to her nearby home to inform her family of her murder, they found blood spatter on the walls and ceilings. Kimberly's parents, Rose and Bill Wilson, and 17-year-old sister, Julia Wilson, were dead in their beds. Rose Wilson's head had been crushed by blows of a blunt object and there were through-and-through stab wounds in her throat. Bill Wilson's skull had been crushed and he had stab wounds to the neck, face, and head. Julia Wilson had defensive injuries including slash wounds on her hands and a broken arm with blunt force injuries and stab wounds in her head, face, and throat.

Investigators discovered that Kimberly Wilson had been involved with a group of friends who were into the "Gothic" lifestyle. They called themselves "Goths," dressed in dark clothing, wore dark make-up, played role-playing games pretending to be witches and vampires, and possessed a worldview of gloom and death. The group hung out at a Denny's restaurant and were part of the "Saturday Night Denny's Club." Most of the group considered the Gothic lifestyle fun and did not take it too seriously. However, investigators discovered that two of the group's members, David Anderson, a friend of Kimberly's since elementary school, and Alex Baranyi were known to take the lifestyle to extremes and had often talked about committing murder.

Less than a week after the murders, police arrested 17-year-old Alex Baranyi, who confessed to the murders. He told detectives that he had strangled Kimberly in the park and, on realizing she may have told her parents she was meeting him, he went to her home to kill them with a baseball bat and combat knife. Baranyi acknowledged that he had an accomplice who beat Kimberly as he strangled her and helped kill her family. Later police arrested David Anderson, also 17, after compiling evidence including bloodstained items found at Baranyi's and Anderson's homes that DNA tests matched to the blood of the victims. Baranyi and Anderson were convicted on four counts of aggravated murder in 1998 and 2000, respectively, and received sentences of life without parole.[1]

Photo 2.1   Alex Baranyi.

Photo Credit: *Seattle Times*

Photo 2.2   David Anderson.

Photo Credit: *Seattle Times*

Why did two teenagers in an upper-middle-class Seattle suburb commit this horrific quadruple murder? What factors converged to produce their criminal behavior? As we go about our daily lives—on the Web, watching TV, listening to the radio in our cars, reading news headlines while waiting in line at Starbucks for the morning coffee— we read and hear about all sorts of horrendous stories of crime. What happened to the Wilson family becomes part of the ongoing chatter of incomprehensible criminal events in the background of our lives. Headlines and images of crime bombard us:

- "Mother and 2 daughters killed in Connecticut home invasion" (Lueck, Stowe, & Hussey, 2007)
- "Prison gang linked to 16 Dallas murders" (Lopez, 2007)
- "Girl fatally stabbed before decapitated" (Associated Press, 2007)
- "Gunman kills girls 'execution style' at Amish school" (Reid & Baldwin, 2006)
- "Woman rips off husbands testicles with bare hands" (6 ABC Action News, May 17, 2006)
- "Woman charged with scalping Mohawk-wearing teen" (Associated Press, 2005)
- "Gary Ridgway said: 'I killed so many women I have a hard time keeping them straight'" (Ho, Johnson, & Castro, 2003)

- "Woman kills pregnant woman and cuts out fetus" (Shortnews.com, 2003)
- "Abducted 5-year-old girl is found dead in what investigators say is a 'calling card' from killer" (Carter, 2001)
- "Man kills wife with telephone cord during sex" (Shortnews.com, 2004)
- "Family's horror at mother and daughter's stabbing" (Laddin, 2004)
- "Teen charged with 4 murders—Police say he planned to kill for a year" (Wilson & Byrnes, 1997)
- "The Matrix made me do it" (Stern, 2003)
- "Expert links sniper, violent video games" (Pierce, 2002)

Fortunately, the statistical likelihood of being the victim of a heinous crime is slim to none. Most of us are more likely to die or become incapacitated by our own bad habits than by violent crime. However, crime touches all of our lives. Most of us will be, or will come into personal contact with, victims or perpetrators of some type of crime during our lifetimes. Even for the rare person who manages to avoid personally experiencing crime, daily consumption of crime in the media ensures that fear of crime and public safety have a permanent place as one of the top priorities for communities, politicians, local and federal government, and citizens.

Much public and media attention is directed to the business of how to catch, convict, and punish criminals. It is impossible to respond to crime without asking, "*What causes a person to engage in criminal behavior?*" Beyond natural human curiosity, we need to know something about why crime occurs and who we're dealing with in order to control and respond to crime. Knowing something about the factors associated with criminal behavior, the characteristics of offender types, and the "causes" of crime provides information with which to pursue and investigate suspects, adjudicate defendants, make sentencing determinations, manage offenders in correctional institutions, make parole and reentry decisions, and design crime prevention and crime control strategies. All kinds of theories about why individuals commit crime are bandied about in public discourse. Crime is the product of rational choice and free will. Crime is caused by parental neglect and sexual and physical abuse. Crime is caused by poverty and social disorganization. Crime is caused by too much TV, mental illness, peer influences, the quest for power, violent films and video games, bad genes, head trauma, lack of attachment, too much attachment, pornography, social isolation, being bullied in school, Twinkies, PMS, *Beevis and Butthead*, *The Catcher in the Rye*, and so on . . . .

In recent years criminologists have recognized that comprehensive and accurate understanding and prediction of criminal behavior require theoretical and disciplinary integration. Many disciplines and knowledge bases are necessary to fully understand criminal behavior. Crime has been explored within the disciplines of criminology and criminal justice, sociology, psychology, psychiatry, neuroscience, biology, philosophy, social work, law, anthropology, political science, economics, cultural and media studies, women's studies, and others. Though no unified theory or model yet exists that can be considered truly integrative (Fishbein, 2001;

Schmalleger, 2004), promising integrative models that have emerged (Barak, 1998; Hickey, 2002; Robinson, 2004) offer insight into the developmental pathways and manifestations of criminal behavior. Criminologists are challenged to develop a comprehensive and coherent explanation of criminal behavior that takes into account the diverse and sometimes conflicting theories, frameworks, and perspectives across the range of disciplines from which criminal behavior has been historically approached.

The lack of complex integrated theory construction (largely rooted in historical competition between macro-level sociological theories and micro-level psychological theories) and inability to come up with a general theory to explain all types of criminal behavior call into question how much criminologists really know about crime. Criminologists' analyses are rarely heard in mass media, which are dominated by the perspectives of criminal justice professionals and news journalists (Tunnell, 1998). However, "the mass media pundits, the public cultural critics, and the professional politicians who are all engaged in the business of talking about crime know far less than criminologists do" (Barak, 1998, p. 5). This "talking about crime" that inundates us on a daily basis through news media, pop culture, the Internet, and politics makes it especially important to be able to sort fact from fiction, theory from anecdote, and scientific methodology from everyday observation and the many fallacies that exist about crime (Felson, 2002).

Interdisciplinary Criminology

Criminology is an interdisciplinary field of study focusing on crime, criminal behavior, and its social response. *Criminologists* are researchers, academics, and policy analysts with advanced degrees (usually in criminology, criminal justice, or sociology) who study crime, crime trends, and social reactions to crime (Schmalleger, 2004). Contemporary criminology is historically rooted in two schools of thought—positivist criminology and classical criminology. *Positivist criminology* locates the root of criminal behavior in identifiable factors such as biological, psychological, and environmental forces. *Classical criminology* identifies free will as the root of criminal behavior, based on the notion that all human beings make choices about the behaviors they engage in, and offenders engage in a cost-benefit analysis before choosing to commit a crime.

Contemporary criminologists recognize that criminal behavior involves both free will and deterministic forces. A clear line cannot be drawn between classical and positivist thought (Barak, 1998), and an individual's decision to engage in criminal behavior cannot be viewed as an either-or phenomenon. According to Katz (1988):

> The statistical and correlational findings of positivist criminology provide the following irritations to inquiry: (1) whatever the validity of the hereditary, psychological, and social-ecological conditions of crime, many of those in the supposedly causal categories do not commit the crime at issue, (2) many who do commit the crime do not fit the causal categories and (3) what is most provocative, many who do fit the background categories and later commit the predicted crime go for long stretches without committing the crimes to which the theory directs them. (pp. 3–4)

On the other hand, explanations of crime that hinge solely on the classical free will argument do not take into account genetic and biological influences (Fishbein, 2001), unconscious dynamics (Gacono & Meloy, 1988), conditioning mechanisms (Laws & Marshall, 1990), facilitators (Hickey, 2002), temptations versus controls (Felson, 2002), background factors and "foreground dynamics" (Colvin, 2000), the interaction between the offender, victim, and context (Miethe & Meier, 1994), and influence of cultural values, style, aesthetics (Black, 1991; Ferrell & Sanders, 1995; Presdee, 2000) that shape conscious choice and create the push and pull compelling an individual to commit a particular criminal act.

Crime scholars have called for integration of the many theories and perspectives on the continuum from classical to positivist criminology. According to Barak (1998), criminology has spun out of control with too many perspectives, disciplines, frameworks, and criminologies—each operating as if no others existed. Many criminologists now argue for an interdisciplinary approach to the study of crime that integrates the natural sciences, social sciences, and humanities with the view that no single discipline can explain crime alone (Barak, 1998; Colvin, 2000; Ferrell & Sanders, 1995; Robinson, 2004; Walsh & Ellis, 2007). Criminologists have adopted three general positions: (1) sociological traditionalists; (2) multidisciplinary specialists; and (3) interdisciplinary generalists (Barak, 1998, p. 8). *Sociological traditionalists* approach crime from the sociological perspective, with the view that criminology is a subfield of sociology and other fields play a subordinate role in the study of crime. *Multidisciplinary specialists* are criminologists from social and behavioral science disciplines outside of sociology (e.g., psychology, biology, political science, economics) who do not see criminology as a subfield of sociology. *Multidisciplinary generalists* acknowledge the necessity of studying crime from multiple disciplines, but elevate their own particular discipline's importance in the study of crime while minimizing or neglecting the importance of others. *Interdisciplinary generalists* include an emerging group of criminologists who believe that the study of crime and its response must involve equal integration of knowledge from many fields including, but not limited to, psychology, sociology, biology, cultural studies, law, philosophy, political science, history, and economics.

Interdisciplinary criminology rejects the notion that scientific evolution is achieved through the falsification of theories, with the view that criminal behavior is so complex that most theories have something to offer, explain part of the picture, for at least some types of crimes. As a result, criminal behavior scholars have moved toward focus on risk and protective factors that increase or decrease the likelihood of crime rather than on theory falsification. The important question is "What variables are related to crime, and in what ways?" with the focus on "variables and relationships among variables, rather than on theories themselves" (Vold, Bernard, & Snipes, 2002, pp. 313–314). This approach to the study of crime is known as a risk factor approach. The risk factor approach integrates multiple theories (many of which have been historically viewed as contradictory) with the view that many factors contribute to crime—some playing more of a role than others—and that some theories may explain more or less of the variation in crime than others.

The *interdisciplinary risk factor approach* challenges the either-or view that criminal behavior is the product of free will (classical criminology) or determinism (positivist criminology). Viewing criminal behavior in terms of free will or determinism is problematic because human beings are not born with equal abilities nor can they be neatly divided into criminal and noncriminal groups. Furthermore, it is impossible to empirically verify or falsify free will/rational choice or to demonstrate deterministic causality. The interdisciplinary approach addresses these problems by explaining criminal behavior in terms of probability rather than choice or causality. The interaction between risk (e.g., genetic predisposition for antisocial behavior) and protective factors (e.g., family support) increases or decreases the likelihood of criminal behavior (Robinson, 2004). In other words, a person is able to "freely choose" within deterministic constraints that involve a continuous push and pull of risk versus protective factors that increase the probability that some of us will engage in criminal behavior more than others. We can all choose to be law abiding, but self-control and inclinations toward such behavior depend on a multitude of factors and forces that dictate our choices.

Felson (2002) uses the *potato chip principle* to explain this complex interaction between free will and determinism:

> We could all make a decision that nearly enslaves us for some time afterward. Then a flash of freedom arises, a crucial junction for the next decision. Moving through life, a person never has complete freedom or complete constraint, but the degree of constraint shifts by time, place, and setting. (Felson, 2002, p. 42)

A bag of potato chips has the potential to constrain choice for certain people some of the time. Eating the entire bag of chips is not unlike a burglary committed by a group of youths whose night out drinking escalates into an exhilarated frenzy with some choosing to go home and others deciding to burglarize someone else's (Felson, 2002). Explanation of the factors and forces that explain who will eat the chips and who will stop after just one requires integration of the research findings and perspectives of a range of disciplines.

Interdisciplinary criminology is the most comprehensive, theoretically rich, and practically applicable approach to make sense of the reality of crime. This text approaches the study of criminal behavior from the "interdisciplinary generalist" position, with focus on risk factors that increase the probability of criminal behavior and the view that theories and knowledge bases from different disciplines can be used as integrative tools to explain, predict, and respond to criminal behavior. Although detailed summary of the many approaches and theories of different disciplines is beyond the scope of this text, the following section provides a brief overview of important research findings from multiple knowledge bases with attention to the ways in which each contributes to the study of crime and to the analysis of criminal behavior.

Integrating Theories of Criminal Behavior

Crime is an illegal behavior committed by an individual or group of individuals that occurs at a particular moment within a specific social context. Like any human behavior, crime is the end-product of a complex interplay between individual and environmental forces. Most crimes are adaptive, normal, and easy to understand, and (in legalistic terms) all crime can be explained by the existence of a criminal law prohibiting such behavior (Robinson, 2004). Some crimes are much more difficult to understand and explain. It is not hard to comprehend why someone would steal because they're hungry or to support a drug addiction. But understanding and explaining why a woman would shoot a pregnant acquaintance in the head and then cut out her fetus or why a young man would abduct, rape, torture, and murder a child is much more difficult and requires attention to research and theory from multiple disciplines.

Multiple theories can be used to explain criminal behavior, with recognition that no single discipline is capable of offering "the answer." The study of criminal behavior has historically been approached from a range of disciplines and perspectives with minimal theoretical integration. Many theories of crime, antisocial behavior, and deviance overlap and cannot be neatly separated by discipline.[2] For purpose of clarity, disciplinary perspectives and criminology knowledge bases are broken down into six general areas and related research questions:

1. **Biological:** What are the biological roots of criminal behavior?

2. **Psychological:** What psychological factors contributed to this behavior?

3. **Sociological:** What sociological forces contributed to this behavior?

4. **Routine Activity/Opportunity/Ecological:** What situational, contextual, environmental factors provided the setting and opportunity for this crime to occur?

5. **Cultural:** What cultural forces provided the context in which this crime could occur?

6. **Phenomenological:** What personal meaning does the crime hold for the offender?

Although there is much disciplinary and theoretical overlap,[3] the six bodies of knowledge represent unique ways of looking at crime and offer specific tools with which to analyze criminal behavior. Each area represents particular factors that contribute to criminal behavior and is briefly summarized to provide a general overview of the knowledge bases from which interdisciplinary criminology draws.[4]

Biological Theories—What Are the Biological Roots of Criminal Behavior?

Biological theories explain crime in terms of the interaction between biological predisposition and environmental conditions on behavioral outcomes (Fishbein, 2001). Studies show that behaviors, characteristics, and traits associated with crime such as aggression, impulsivity, antisocial personality, and psychopathy are influenced by a range of biological factors including evolution and genetics, brain biochemistry and function, brain injury, hormonal influences, physiology, physical anomalies and body build, diet and blood sugar levels, and cognitive deficits (Raine, 1993). Proponents of the biological perspective argue that biological theories of criminal behavior offer more sophisticated theories, models, concepts, instruments, and methodology that can serve traditional criminology as quality control devices (Walsh, 2002).

Much of the research on biology and crime is based on the assumption of a relationship between aggression, antisocial behavior, impulsivity, psychopathy, and criminal behavior. Different studies use different concepts and variables, which makes determining the biology-crime relationship problematic. Because criminality is a socially constructed concept, findings on the biological factors associated with crime are based on research on the biological roots of behaviors and traits empirically linked to criminality such as aggression, impulsivity, violence, and other crime-related variables. Given the vast amount of research on biology and crime, selective coverage is provided here, with attention to some of the more interesting theories, findings, and hypotheses that are being actively explored in criminological research.[5]

Evolution and Genetics

In April 2003, The International Human Genome Sequencing Consortium, led in the United States by the National Human Genome Research Institute (NHGRI) and the Department of Energy (DOE), announced the successful completion of the *Human Genome Project,* which finished the reference sequence of the human genome. The finished sequence covers 99% of the human genome's gene-containing regions, and it has been sequenced to an accuracy of 99.99% (National Human Genome Research Institute, 2003). This means that 99% of the human blueprint has now been discovered, with widespread implications for the discovery, treatment, and prevention of human diseases and conditions, including criminal behavior. Many contend that mapping the human genome may bring new cures for human afflictions and diseases including drug addiction, mental illness (Recer, 2001), aggression, violence, and crime (Montgomery, 1995).

Human behavior is the product of an evolutionary process involving chance, natural selection, and cultural influences (Ehrlich & Feldman, 2003). *Genes do not cause human (or criminal) behavior. They predispose individuals to particular conditions.* Whether or not a person will develop a disease or condition depends on chance and environment, referred to as *genotype-phenotype interaction.* A *genotype* is the genetic constitution of an individual encoded in the DNA contained within chromosomes and other structures inside cells. A *phenotype* is the observable product of the interaction between the genotype and the environment, such as physiological response and behavior. At the most basic level, genes determine what we are (e.g., type of animal, human) but do not solely determine who we are (Robinson, 2004). Phenotypic expression—intelligence, personality, physical behaviors, mental disorders, medical and behavioral conditions—is determined through interaction between genetics and environment. Criminal behavior is a phenotypic expression produced through genetic-environment interaction.

Evolutionary theories of crime contend that criminal behavior evolves through natural selection. *Evolutionary psychology* is a branch of psychology that uses a Darwinian framework to explain human behavior in terms of processes of natural selection and adaptation. *Evolutionary criminology* applies theory from evolutionary psychology to criminal behavior. Evolutionary criminologists explain criminal behavior in terms of evolutionary history, arguing that behaviors seen as criminal today were adaptive in ancestral environments. Evolutionary theories of crime are based on the notion that natural selection is the inevitable result of three fundamental features of life:

1. *Heredity*—physical and behavioral traits are genetically passed from parent to offspring.

2. *Variation*—individuals differ in their physical traits and behaviors.

3. *Differential reproduction*—the inherited traits of some individuals will result in the reproduction of more offspring.

Hereditable traits are reproductively *adaptive* (advantageous), *maladaptive* (disadvantageous), or *neutral* (Jones, 1999). The accumulated effects of natural selection impact the brain's neural structure and information processing predisposing certain behaviors that facilitate reproductive success (Jones, 1999). Rooted in neo-Darwinian theories of evolution, these theories state that genes dictate that reproduction is the most vital function of an organism, and that DNA codes for priority reproduction must take in order for a species to survive (Fishbein, 2001). Reproduction is a genetically driven evolutionary process that codes for anatomical and physiological traits. Criminal behavior, like all behaviors, revolves around reproductive drives. Proposed evolutionary theories relevant to antisocial and criminal behavior include the r/K theory, the cheater theory, the adaptation hypothesis, and evolutionary theories of rape.[6] All attempt to explain criminal behavior in terms of its long-term reproductive consequences.

Heritability studies (involving twin and adoption studies) suggest that personality factors and traits linked to aggressive and violent behavior may be heritable. Findings suggest that childhood aggression, disruptive behavior, and aggressive behavior across the life course may be mediated by genetic factors (Mik et al., 2007). Some research suggests that aggressiveness is transmitted across generations within families (Huesmann, Enron, & Lefkowitz, 1984) and that alcoholism, susceptibility to aggressive and impulsive behaviors, and personality disorders including conduct disorder, borderline personality disorder, attention deficit disorder, and antisocial personality disorder are genetically influenced (Fishbein, 2001). Studies have found that children who have mothers with histrionic personality disorder (HPD)[7] and fathers with antisocial personality disorder (APD) are more likely to have the disorders themselves (histrionic personality disorder if female and antisocial personality disorder if male) and that HPD and APD are sex-typed manifestations of psychopathy (Spalt, 1980; Warner, 1978). However, heredity studies do not identify the genetically influenced biological mechanisms that may contribute to these traits (Fishbein, 2001), which may be identified in the future through the discovery of the human genome sequence.

One of the more interesting of the biological theories is the *cheater theory*. This theory holds that, in some species, alternative reproductive strategies have evolved in some males. In these species, at least two types of males have evolved—"dads" and "cads." Because males do not need to grow offspring to reproduce as females do, they have greater latitude in their reproductive behavior. Dads reproduce by accommodating female preferences for males who are prone to provide parental care for their offspring. Cads reproduce by using force or deception to mate without providing adequate care for their offspring. According to this theory, chronic offenders are "human cads," and cheater males are more likely to evolve in large, impersonal societies where their adaptive strategy is likely to go undetected. This tendency to use deception in the mating process extends to other situations, resulting in the use of cheating, theft, risk-taking, and other antisocial behaviors and crimes (Fishbein, 2001, pp. 22–23).

In recent years, there has been considerable interest in *evolutionary theories of rape*. These theories hold that rape is a "normal" male natural selection strategy. Evolutionary theorists argue that forced copulation occurs in many species, and the key to understanding rape in humans is the wide disparity in parental investment between the sexes. The female reproductive strategy is to resist casual sexual relations with men, whereas the male reproductive strategy is to inseminate as many females as possible. From this perspective, all males are potential rapists, but whether or not they become rapists depends on environmental factors that affect their ability to obtain resources that will put them in a position to attract mates (Walsh & Ellis, 2007). Consistent with the cheater theory, males who are not successful in the mating process by way of noncoercive methods or deception must resort to forced copulation. In *The Natural History of Rape*, Thornhill and Palmer (2000) suggest that rape would not occur if human females had been selected to be willing to mate with any male under any circumstances, and if human males had been selected to be sexually attracted to only certain females under limited circumstances, rape would be far less frequent. Of the biological theories of crime, this theory is one of the more controversial in terms of its implications. Box 2.1 offers an example of how evolutionary theory of rape can be applied to a contemporary rape case and the criminal justice implications of this theoretical perspective.

Other evolutionary theories, such as the *r/K theory*, have been offered as an explanation for sex differences in offending behavior. The concept of r/K selection is based on a continuum along which organisms function. Organisms that are r-selected produce large numbers of offspring with little or no parental care. K-selected organisms produce few offspring and devote inordinate energy and time to their care and nurturing, maximizing each offspring's potential for reproduction. As applied to criminal behavior, this theory assumes that altruistic and criminal behavior are at opposite ends of a continuum and that criminality should be found among individuals who exhibit all or most r-selected traits, including shorter periods of gestation (premature births), early sexual experiences, sexual promiscuity, child abandonment, neglect, abuse, and short life expectancy (Ellis, 1989, Ellis, 2001; Fishbein, 2001). Studies have shown that offenders possess more r-selected traits than do nonoffenders, and the reason males engage in more criminal behavior than females is that they are more r-selected (Ellis, 2001).

Brain Chemistry and Function

Neurotransmitters

Neurotransmitters are chemical messengers in the brain that convey "information" in the form of an electrically charged signal across neurons and from brain structure to brain structure. The balance, metabolism, and activity level of neurotransmitters (in part, a function of genetics) regulate emotion, impulse control, mood,

BOX 2.1

BIOLOGY AND CRIME: THE CASE OF THE "Mall Rapist"

Case Example

James Perry, a 34-year-old married father of two, committed over two dozen rapes and attempted sexual assaults in southern Wisconsin and northern Illinois shopping malls from 1999 until his arrest in 2004. Known as the "Mall Rapist," Perry attacked female clothing store employees in stores and mall parking lots. In addition to the mall rapes, he made pornographic videos of himself raping two girls under the age of 10 and was charged with a 2001 sexual assault where he allegedly approached a woman at a laundromat, threatened her with a screwdriver, and forced her into a bathroom, where he raped her. Sometime around 2003, authorities believe he changed his behavior from raping adult women to raping young girls. Also during this time he was arrested for domestic violence, charged with disorderly conduct and sentenced to 20 months probation, which he later violated and was reincarcerated for 5 days (Blume, 2004). After eluding police for five years, Perry was captured in early 2004 when he was caught on surveillance tape at a Comfort Inn in Madison. When spotted on the tape, he put a gun to the head of a 13-year-old girl. The girl escaped unharmed from what police believe was an attempted kidnapping. Perry was sentenced in July 2004 to 180 years in prison for the federal sexual exploitation convictions.

Madison Detective Lieutenant Jay Lengfeld described the case as "probably the worst sexual predator case that I have seen in 23 years" ("Police Say Madison's 'Mall Rapist' Behind Bars," 2004). Perry's employer, National Tower Service of Madison, issued a statement saying they were "shocked." Perry's wife of eight years and mother of his two daughters said after his arrest:

> I guess that's how good they are . . . . They know how to keep secrets and live separate lives. They do these things yet they are able to come home to their family and make us feel safe. . . . I don't know this man. I was married to him for eight years, but I don't know him. This is all a

huge shock. He's done a lot of bad things. I don't know what else there is for me to say. (Blume, 2004)

Maggie Thurs, a member of the Wisconsin Coalition Against Sexual Assault, commented that for sex offenders who live double lives

. . . home is somewhere where they have the opportunity to become that kind, loving, warm person that they know they are suppose to be . . . . Sex offenders spend a lot of time working on this. They know that if they are going to get away with a crime, they need to do this. They need to go home and be the perfect husband, and then they'll go out and be a rapist or be violent. (Blume, 2004)

Analysis of Case From the Biological Perspective

Biological theories of rape are highly controversial. The dominant view since the 1970s has been that rape is a crime of violence, not sex. This view and the sociopolitical implications of associating rape behavior with biological forces have ensured that biological theories of rape have met with a great deal of criticism. One of the best-known (and controversial) biological theories of rape is the theory of *evolutionary adaptation* (Thornhill & Palmer, 2000). From this perspective, rape is an adaptation designed by sexual selection to facilitate reproductive success. The accumulated effects of natural selection impact the brain's neural architecture and information processing pathways predisposing certain behaviors that facilitate reproductive success. In other words, evolutionary processes create species-typical, sex-typical, and age-typical "evolved psychologies" that have probabilistic effects on behavior (Jones, 1999, p. 846).

Evolutionary theories of rape rest on the biological principle of sexual selection. Sexual selection (human mating rituals) is dictated by evolutionary pressures to sexually reproduce. Biological sex differences determine how many offspring males and females can reproduce and the amount of time, energy, and general investment it takes. Females are much more invested in reproduction because of the limits of their own bodies. The theoretical maximum number of children a female could mother would be approximately 100, whereas a man could father into the thousands. Male reproductive success is limited by access to fertile females; female reproductive success is limited by the time and energy it takes for each reproductive episode. Because of these differences, male-male competition for mates is greater and female choice is greater than male choice regarding who one's mate will be. Different male and female psychologies concerning willingness to copulate indiscriminately have evolved as a result of these differences in sexual selection (Jones, 1999). According to leading biology and rape researchers Thornhill and Palmer (2000), "If human females had been selected to be willing to mate with any male under any circumstances, rape would not occur. On the other hand, if human males had been selected to be sexually attracted to only certain females under certain limited circumstances, rape would be far less frequent" (p. 84).

(Continued)

(Continued)

How does all of this help us understand and explain the rapes and sexual assaults committed by James Perry? From the perspective of adaptation theory, Perry's behavior was the result of the evolved behavioral predisposition to rape that exists in all males. However, all males do not rape, and all rapists are not sexual predators. As is the case with any human behavior, the heritable predisposition to rape is influenced by individual, environmental, and contextual factors. Studies comparing human rape to "rape" among insects and primates have found that contextual factors such as male-male competition, the extent to which a male possesses resources necessary to attract a mate, and so on influence whether or not a male will rape. Causes of behavior can be proximate and ultimate. Proximate causes are short term whereas ultimate causes are long term (in the evolutionary sense). Proximate explanations of behaviors have to do with *how* certain mechanisms caused something to happen, and ultimate explanations deal with *why* particular mechanisms exist in a species (Thornhill & Palmer, 2000). Thus, the *ultimate cause* of Perry's rape behavior was that he was biologically propelled to rape as an evolutionarily adaptive means of mating and reproducing. Even though rape may not produce increased likelihood of offspring in today's world, the behavior can be seen as an evolutionary byproduct of the intense sexual desires of human males and the sexual choosiness of human females that in earlier times increased the chances of reproductive success. Proximate causes such as childhood experiences, behavioral conditioning, stress, cultural images and rape myths, use of pornography, contextual factors, and other factors played a role in the manifestation of his rape behavior, but the ultimate cause of his behavior was natural selection and adaptation.

Perry was married with two children, so why rape to reproduce? Perry's rape behavior increased his base of mating partners and his chances of producing a greater number of offspring. From the evolutionary perspective, human males are in a better position to reproduce the more sex partners they have. In other words, rape is an *additional* mating tactic, not a substitute for consensual intercourse. In addition, whether or not his rapes actually produced offspring or made him less likely to attract consensual mating partners in the future (i.e., by going to prison) is irrelevant because the evolutionary forces that drove his behavior are based on "evolutionary time"—how such behaviors worked in the past, not necessarily the present.

How does the adaptation theory explain Perry's move from young women to children? Biological theorists argue that rape victims in their teens and early 20s are overrepresented around the world (Thornhill & Palmer, 2000). However, victim selection depends, in part, on accessibility and vulnerability. In Perry's case, his move to children occurred after having eluded police for several years. His change in behavior to child rape can be explained as a move to more vulnerable/accessible victims in an attempt to continue his behavior and to evade police. James Perry's behavior may have been influenced by multiple adaptations to rape. His ability to elude police and go undetected by his wife, employer, and family for so many years suggests that he may be psychopathic. According to Thornhill and Palmer, psychopathic and normal men possess distinct psychological adaptations. Psychopathy is associated with criminal behavior, exploitation of others, and rape, and human rape behavior may be the product of one or multiple rape adaptations. In other words, individuals with a high level of psychopathy are more inclined to harm others and to engage in predatory violence. Perry's biological predisposition to psychopathy *and* rape were the ultimate or distal causes of his predatory rape behavior.

Criminal Justice Application

The most direct application of biological theories to rape behavior is chemical castration. Chemical castration involves administering a drug (Decapeptyl) that decreases sexual impulses. The practice has been used in the United States, Israel, and Europe. The practice has been controversial on legal and moral grounds for many years. The first known offender in the United States to receive chemically castrating injections as a condition of probation was Joseph Frank Smith in 1983 in San Antonio, Texas (Jones,1999). Chemical castration is now mandatory for some types of sex offenders in some jurisdictions (e.g., for pedophiles in California). The success of chemical castration as a rape-reducing tool depends on the extent to which rape is sexually motivated. From an evolutionary perspective, sexual desire plays a significant role in rape. Studies suggest that chemical castration significantly reduces paraphilic behavior (e.g., exhibitionism, voyeurism, pedophilia), but less is known about its effects on rapists.

The evolutionary theory of rape causation provides strong (or perhaps the only) support for chemical castration. If rape is not influenced by the evolutionary adaptation of sexual desire, then chemical castration is difficult to defend. However, in contrast to surgical castration, the chemical version is reversible and would have no more impact on a person's future reproduction than would a period of incarceration (provided the incarceration did not involve conjugal visits).

In Perry's case, he was sentenced to 180 years in prison, so chemical castration would serve only to reduce his sexual desires in the prison setting (which may be advantageous from a correctional management perspective). Certainly, Perry's movement to child rape suggests that he has engaged in behaviors that are evolutionary byproducts of the rape adaptation. Perry's predisposition to rape may thus extend to male rape or rape of female correctional staff, or it may act as impetus to escape or to disruptive or violent acts. In his case, chemical castration would decrease sexual desire and reduce the likelihood of behaviors that can be seen as evolutionary byproducts of the rape adaptation (male rape) and frustrations associated with the inability to reproduce (escape attempts, disorderly conduct, violence).

Of course, had James Perry's sexual deviance and sex-offending patterns been identified earlier, perhaps at the time when he was arrested for domestic violence and convicted of disorderly conduct, chemical castration might have been a particularly useful sanction to reduce his inclination to rape or have decreased the number of victims and incidents over time.

hunger, thirst, arousal of the nervous system, and other psychological and behavioral processes. Certain neurotransmitters have been strongly and consistently associated with aggressive and antisocial behavior (Fishbein, 2001) and appear to play a primary role in the behavioral display of different types of aggression (Meloy, 1988). Most of the research on neurochemistry and aggression has been conducted on animals. However, results of the few human studies that have been conducted validate the animal research findings.

Aggression can be classified as instrumental/predatory (planned, purposeful, emotionless) or expressive/affective (spontaneous, reactive, emotional). The two types of aggression are controlled by different sets of neurotransmitters with distinct neuroanatomical pathways, and studies have shown that four neurotransmitters (serotonin, norepinephrine, dopamine, and acetylcholine) correlate in a distinctive manner with behavioral displays of predatory and affective aggression. The following example illustrates the differences in the display of predatory and affective aggression:

> When a household cat is cornered and threatened, the neurochemical set produces a display of affective aggression: hissing, hair standing on end, dilated pupils, active clawing, arching back. When the same cat is stalking a bird in the backyard, predatory aggression dominates: quiet stalking of prey, the absence of ritualistic display, and focused attention on the target (Meloy, 1988, p. 25).

Studies show that affective aggression is associated with low levels of serotonin and high levels of norepinephrine, dopamine, and acetylcholine whereas predatory aggression is associated with low levels of serotonin, norepinephrine, dopamine, and high levels of acetylcholine (Meloy, 1988).

These findings do not support a link between specific neurotransmitters and crime because crime is a heterogeneous category consisting of subtypes of differentially motivated criminal behaviors. For example, most homicides are committed in the context of interpersonal disputes and are motivated by affective aggression whereas serial murder is generally motivated by predatory aggression (Miethe & McCorkle, 2001). However, the findings offer insight into the biochemical mechanisms associated with different behavioral outcomes. In addition to aggression, specific neurotransmitters (e.g., serotonin and norepinephrine) are correlated with low heart rate and skin conductance, which are both associated with antisocial behavior. Thus, neurochemical levels and activity have important implications for understanding and responding to criminal behavior.

Brain Function

Biological predisposition to crime may be the result of a disruption of normal neural mechanisms that control and mediate behavior. Neuropsychological theories of crime suggest that dysfunction or damage to areas of the brain contribute to aggression, violence, and antisocial behavior. This research assumes that individual differences in the functioning and quality of parts of the brain can be measured by neuropsychological tests, and that such differences predispose an individual to commit criminal behavior (Raine, 1993).

The brain can be divided into two parts—the cortex and subcortex. The cerebral cortex is made up of four regions or lobes: frontal, temporal, parietal, and occipital. Most neuropsychological research has focused on the left hemisphere of the brain, specifically on the anterior region made up of the frontal and temporal lobes. Some inconsistent evidence links frontal lobe and left hemisphere dysfunction to aggression violence, and antisocial behavior. Other research suggests that dysfunction in the limbic regions of the brain, particularly the amygdala and hippocampus (which regulate emotion), and reduced lateralization for language are associated with violence and aggression (Raine, 1993).

The story of Phineas Gage illustrates how damage to the brain can impact behavior. In 1848, Phineas Gage was the foreman of a Burlington Railroad work crew. In the process of trying to blast rock with gunpowder an accident occurred. A 3½ foot iron rod (a tamping rod used to prepare the rock for blasting) blasted out of the rock like a cannon, striking Gage just below the left eye. The rod blew through Gage's skull and frontal lobe with great speed, exiting through the midline of his skull (just above where the hair meets the forehead). The rod flew 50 feet in the air before landing covered with brains and blood. After the accident, Gage's crew was shocked to find that he was still able to speak and walk. Over a period of several weeks he made an almost complete physical recovery. However, his personality was severely altered. Previously said to be a well-balanced, energetic, and smart businessman, he became obstinate, impatient, and antisocial, engaging in unpredictable and unrestrained behavior. Research inspired by Gage's experience has found that the area damaged in his case—the orbitofrontal cortex within the prefrontal cortex—is responsible for social skills, impulse control, forethought, and assessment of consequences. More recent research has found that damage to this area appears associated with a number of behavioral problems, such as alcoholism, drug abuse, conduct disorder, and antisocial behaviors (Fishbein, 2001).

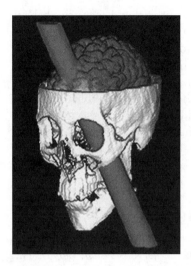

Photo 2.3 Phineas Gage's Brain Injury

Hormones

Studies on the relationship between hormones and crime have focused on testosterone and other male hormones called androgens. Data from animal and human studies suggest that male hormones are associated with aggression in some individuals under some circumstances (Fishbein, 2001). The surge of testosterone in postpubertal males (10 times greater than in postpubertal females) partially accounts for the onset of antisocial behavior in most adolescent males and the differences in offending rates between males and females of any age (Walsh, 2002). Male sex hormones operating on the human brain appear to increase the probability of "competitive/victimizing behavior"—behavior directed at others that exists along a continuum from altruistic acts that make no profit to acts that intentionally and directly harm or dispossess others of their property (Ellis, 2005). There is some evidence to suggest that testosterone is associated with juvenile delinquency, but the association between testosterone and antisocial behavior diminishes in adulthood (Vold, Bernard, & Snipes, 2002). Other findings suggest that the link between testosterone and adult aggressive and violent behavior is well established but this relationship may be absent, or reversed with respect to aggression in children (Raine, 2002). Regarding sex offenders, testosterone provides the basis for general sexual drive, but research linking abnormality of androgen metabolism with aberrant sexual behavior is not strongly supported and is characterized by conflicting results (Hucker & Baine, 1989). The testosterone-aggression relationship appears to be dependent on contextual, social circumstance, and personality factors (Fishbein, 2001). A critical question is whether or not the relationship between testosterone and aggression and violence is causal (Raine, 1993). It is unclear whether increased testosterone causes increased aggression or increased aggression and other behaviors, such as exposure to erotica and success in competition, results in increased testosterone levels (Fishbein, 2001; Raine, 1993; Vold, Bernard, & Snipes, 2002).

Female hormones have also been associated with antisocial and aggressive behavior. A number of studies support the hypothesis that a higher percentage of crimes of convicted women are committed four days before and four days after menstruation. Some women may be particularly susceptible to hormonal changes in the menstrual cycle that contribute to proneness to hostility during the menstrual phase (Raine, 1993). This research has led to the use of the "PMS defense," though public interest in the PMS-crime link far exceeds the level of scientific support for the hypothesis. Evidence also suggests the influence of male hormones on muscular physique, masculine self-identity, and aggressiveness in adult females (Fishbein, 2001). However, research on the links between hormones and criminal behavior in women is scarce and no causal relationship has been established.

Psychophysiology and Other Biological Factors

The human nervous system is made up of the *central nervous system (CNS)* and peripheral nervous system, which includes the *autonomic nervous system (ANS)*. The ANS resides outside of the brain and is responsible for functions necessary for survival, including regulation of heart rate, digestion, blood pressure, circulation, and body temperature. The ANS is activated under stress situations. Individuals who respond to stress by becoming anxious have higher levels of ANS activity than those who do not. CNS and ANS activity are genetically determined, but behavioral manifestations are highly influenced by environmental factors such as learning experiences and stressors. *Research shows that individuals prone to antisocial, sensation-seeking, and risk-taking behavior have unusually low physiological levels of CNS and ANS activity.* A great deal of research has accumulated over the past 60 years on the link between underarousal and early disinhibited temperament, a childhood forerunner to antisocial behavior. Researchers have explored this link with a range of measurement techniques including analysis of heart rate, skin conductance activity, electroencephalograms (EEGs), and event-related potentials (ERPs) (Raine, 1993). These autonomic responses are also measured through the polygraph because they are considered to be indicators of anxiety and arousal.

Individuals with underactive CNS and ANS activity do not experience physiological and emotional discomfort to the same degree as individuals with average or above average ANS and CNS activity levels. Individuals who do not feel discomfort do not respond appropriately to punishment or threats of punishment and, as a result, are not effectively deterred from engaging in antisocial behavior. Researchers have measured low CNS and ANS activity in antisocial individuals through EEG differences and ERPs (the signals received by the EEG recorder), skin conductance (electrical activity in the skin), heart rate, and startle reflex. *Study after study has found that antisocial, psychopathic, and violent offenders are more likely to be underaroused*—to have low skin conductivity, low pulse rate, slow-wave activity in their EEG, and delays in their evoked potentials (Fishbein, 2001; Hare, 2001; Raine, 1998), as well as a deviant pattern of startle reactivity (Patrick, 2001). These deficits in emotional processing may be the physiological result of neurotransmitter imbalance (Fishbein, 2001; Raine, 1993).

Recent research addressing the interaction between biological and environmental factors shows that biological and social factors interact to produce antisocial and criminal behavior. The best-replicated biosocial effect appears to be the interaction of birth complications with negative home environments in predisposing adult violence (Raine, 2002). Sophisticated theories, particularly in the area of evolutionary psychology, are now being developed to explain the complex relationship between biology and environment in producing criminal behavior. Ellis (2005) proposes the evolutionary neuroandrogenic (ENA) theory, which envisions criminality as the result of a complex interaction between biological factors resulting from evolutionary history, social learning, and social environmental factors.

Psychological Theories—What Psychological Factors Contributed to This Behavior?

Psychological theories attribute criminal behavior to individual differences resulting from early psychodynamic development, information processing and cognition, and conditioning processes. Psychological theories of crime are micro-level theories that locate the source of criminality within the individual, with the idea that crime is a symptom of an individual's internal psychological condition. Much of the psychological research on criminal behavior has focused on the relationships between personality, mental disorder, and crime. Research at the intersection of psychology and criminology has emphasized integration of cognitive, behavioral, and psychodynamic perspectives in the development of functional concepts of psychopathy and criminality (Meloy, 1988; Walters, 1990). Because crime is a social construct, psychological research on criminal behavior involves study of internal psychological conditions that produce behaviors associated with crime such as antisocial behavior, psychopathy, aggression, and impulsivity. From this perspective, *crime is a behavioral symptom that is a manifestation of an internal psychological condition.* Recent research has focused to a large extent on the role of psychopathy in criminal behavior and the predictive utility of the construct in assessing dangerousness and future violence.

Psychodynamic and Personality Theories

Psychodynamic theories of criminal behavior focus on development of the psyche in infancy. From this perspective, motivation for criminal behavior is rooted in an individual's psychodynamic structure and development. Contemporary psychodynamic theories of criminal behavior are rooted in Freud's theory of the id, ego, and superego. Freud postulated that behavior is the product of the interaction of the id, ego, superego with the environment. The id represents the human drive for pleasure, the ego regulates the id in accordance with the demands of the external environment, and the superego reflects the conscience and ego ideal or the parental voice inside one's head that says "Do the right thing."

Offender Types in Psychodynamic Theory

Many theories and typologies developed from the psychoanalytic perspective suggest that there are different developmental routes to criminal behavior. Andrews and Bonta (2003) review four offender types that have emerged from psychodynamic theory: (1) weak superego type, (2) weak ego type, (3) the "normal" antisocial offender, and (4) the neurotic offender. The *weak superego type* needs immediate gratification and does not hear or respond to that "voice inside the head." The *weak ego type* is immature and has poorly developed social skills, gullibility, and dependence resulting in criminal behavior through misreading of the external environment and stumbling into crime (e.g., following the leader). The *"normal" antisocial offender type* passes through normal stages of development as a fully functioning adult but possesses a procriminal superego as a result of identification with a criminal parent and ego-mastery of criminal skills. The *neurotic offender type* has an overactive superego that results in criminal behavior to fulfill the wish to be punished for "past sins."

The *weak superego theory* is the most popular of the theories in the psychodynamic literature and was the topic of much discourse and discussion in the 1940s, 1950s, and 1960s. Behavioral indicators of a weak superego include reckless disregard for conventional rules, lack of conscience and antisocial cognitions, weak ambition, absence of guilt, early conduct problems, expressions of bravado, authority conflicts, and isolation (Andrews & Bonta, 2003). These features have been consistently associated with antisocial personality disorder, psychopathy, and criminal behavior. An example of a the weak superego theory is Hervey Cleckley's (1941) classic work, *The Mask of Sanity*, which, though not solely focused on criminal behavior, offers case study illustrations of criminal and noncriminal psychopaths. According to Cleckley, psychopaths have a "defect in affect" that enables them to harm and manipulate others without remorse. Psychopaths delight in shocking others and have no interest in engaging in conformist behaviors. Cleckley identified 16 characteristics of the psychopath (discussed in Chapter 4), such as unreliability, lack or remorse or shame, and failure to learn from experience, that reflect defect in interpersonal relations and unwillingness or inability to adhere to social (and superego) norms, rules, and values.

Kernberg's Theory of Borderline Personality Organization

Another prominent superego pathology theory is Kernberg's theory of *borderline personality organization (BPO)*. BPO theory is particularly helpful in terms of understanding how internal conditions across the continuum of personality produce a tendency toward criminal behavior. According to Kernberg (1966, 1967, 1984, 1985a, 1985b, 1992), personality is organized along a continuum from "psychotic" to "borderline" to "neurotic" and defined by capacity for reality testing and unconscious defensive process. Psychotic personality organization is characterized by absence of reality testing and the use of primitive defenses, borderline personality organization by capacity for reality testing and use of primitive defenses, and neurotic personality organization by capacity for reality testing and use of higher-level defenses (Figure 2.1).

Kernberg's *primitive defenses* center around the lower level mechanism of *splitting*, and the related mechanisms of *primitive idealization, projective identification,*

❖ Figure 2.1   Kernberg's Theory of Borderline Personality Organization

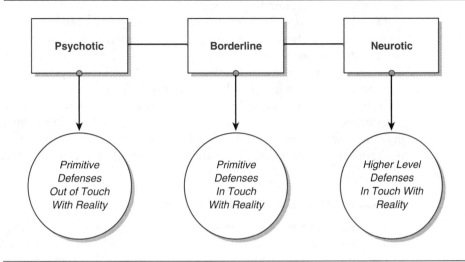

denial, omnipotence, and devaluation. Splitting is a genotypic defensive operation that is expressed through the phenotypic defensive process of dissociation. This defensive operation is pathognomonic of general borderline ego functioning, particularly in the psychopath (Meloy, 1988). Kernberg (1976) views splitting as alternating ego states, each consisting of completely separate complex psychic manifestations, a fundamental feature of the borderline ego functioning experienced by the narcissistic, histrionic, borderline, and psychopathic personalities. Splitting is a defensive process exemplified by lack of personality integration, and the coexistence of distinct cohesive personality attitudes with conflicting aims, goals, and moral and aesthetic values (Kohut, 1971). Put simply, splitting is the view of oneself and others as all good or all bad with an inability to reconcile the two identities.

The subsidiary defenses of primitive idealization, projective identification, omnipotence, devaluation, and denial protect the ego from conflict by dissociating or actively separating contradictory experiences of the self and of others. As a result, the contradictory ego states (e.g., good/bad) are alternatively activated, and as long as they are kept apart, anxiety related to these conflicts is controlled or prevented. Although these defenses protect the individual from intrapsychic conflict, they do so at a cost of weakening the person's ego functioning and reducing adaptive effectiveness and flexibility (Kernberg, 1985b). This "lower level" of the borderline personality organization differs from "higher-level" functioning that centers on repression and other higher-level operations such as reaction formation, intellectualization, rationalization, and isolation, all of which protect the ego from intrapsychic conflict. The lower-level defenses are shared by the psychotic and the borderline personality, wheras the neurotic uses higher-level operations. Individuals with borderline disorders are set apart from the psychotic by their capacity for reality testing, which is not present in psychotic organization (Kernberg, 1985b).

Kernberg (1985a) views borderline personality organization as an intermediary stage between psychosis and neurosis. Primitive defenses facilitate criminal behavior because they enable an individual to objectify and harm other human beings while maintaining an image of themselves as all-good. By definition, crime requires *mens rea* (a guilty mind); thus, individuals who are psychotic may commit criminal behavior, but if they are determined to be out of touch with reality they are not legally responsible for their behavior. On the continuum from psychotic to borderline to neurotic, individuals with personalities organized at the borderline level of functioning are most susceptible to criminal behavior by the very nature of their defensive structure.

Antisocial Personality Disorder and Psychopathy

According to the *Diagnostic and Statistical Manual of Mental Disorders,* Fourth Edition, Text Revision (*DSM-IV-TR*) (American Psychiatric Association, 2000), a personality disorder is "An enduring pattern of inner experience and behavior that deviates markedly from the expectations of the individual's culture" (p. 686). To be diagnosed with a personality disorder, an individual must manifest the disorder in two or more of the following areas: cognitions (ways of perceiving the world), affectivity (emotional response), interpersonal functioning, and impulse control. The enduring pattern must also be inflexible and pervasive across a range of circumstances and situations, lead to clinically significant impairment or distress, and be stable, having originated in adolescence or early adulthood. The pattern also cannot be the product of another mental disorder, substance abuse, or a medical condition.

Of the personality disorders defined in the *DSM-IV-TR*, the *Axis II, Cluster B* disorders are most relevant to the study of criminal behavior. These disorders include *Antisocial Personality Disorder, Borderline Personality Disorder, Histrionic Personality Disorder,* and *Narcissistic Personality Disorder.* These four disorders share behavioral features such as impulsive acting out, unpredictable behavior, and dramatic presentation, as well as a common intrapsychic structure centered on a lower-level defensive organization that uses primitive defenses. Wulach (1988) suggests that features of each of these disorders comprise the *criminal personality* and there is evidence to suggest that each may represent distinct behavioral expressions of psychopathy. Much of the psychological research on criminal behavior has focused on *antisocial personality disorder* and *psychopathy*. In fact, the concepts of criminality, insanity, antisocial personality, and psychopathy have been so intertwined over the past two centuries that much of the research, particularly in the discipline of psychology, has failed to clearly differentiate between mental disorder (an internal condition) and crime (a behavioral symptom and social construct). Researchers have spent the last 20 years trying to sort out the conceptual differences and in recent years there have seen rapid advancement in our understanding of the relationship between antisocial personality disorder, psychopathy, and crime.

According to the *DSM-IV-TR*, the essential feature of APD is "a pervasive pattern of disregard for, and violation of, the rights of others that begins in childhood or early adolescence and continues into adulthood" (p. 701). The *DSM-IV-TR* definition goes on to say that "Antisocial Personality Disorder must be distinguished from criminal behavior undertaken for gain that is not accompanied by the personality features characteristic of this disorder" (p. 705). Although the *DSM-IV-TR* states that "this pattern has also been referred to as psychopathy, sociopathy, and dyssocial personality disorder" (p. 702), researchers have criticized the APD classification because it is not able to differentiate between criminal behavior (again, a social construction and symptom) and personality features of the disorder. In other words, 50 to 75% of offenders in forensic populations can be diagnosed with APD because the criteria on which the classification is based are predominantly antisocial and criminal behaviors. Psychopathy, in contrast, is characterized by specific personality characteristics with only 15 to 25% in forensic populations meeting the criteria. According to Robert Hare, foremost researcher on psychopathy, "Although my colleagues and I have taken great pains to differentiate between psychopathy and APD, some clinicians and investigators use the labels as if the constructs they measure were interchangeable. They are not, and the failure to recognize this results in confusion and misleading conclusions" (Hare, 1998, p. 193).

Psychopathy and antisocial personality disorder are overlapping but distinct clinical constructs. Diagnosis of APD is based primarily on behavioral features such as failure to conform to social norms, deceitfulness and lying, impulsivity, irresponsibility, harm to others, and other traits, whereas psychopathy is defined by a "constellation of affective, interpersonal, and behavioral characteristics including egocentricity; impulsivity; irresponsibility; shallow emotions; lack of empathy, guilt, or remorse; pathological lying; manipulativeness; and the persistent violation of social norms and expectations" (Hare, 1998, p. 188). Understanding psychopathy as a clinical entity distinct from APD is particularly important in differentiating between criminal behavior rooted in psychopathology from criminal behavior committed by individuals who do not possess a personality disorder or other type of mental illness.

Psychopathy is now considered to be one of the most important, if not *the* most important, clinical constructs in the criminal justice system (Hare, 1998). A large body of research has accumulated linking psychopathy and criminal recidivism, violence, and dangerousness. The Psychopathy Checklist–Revised (PCL-R; see Hare, 1991, 2003), a 20-item checklist that measures the affective, interpersonal, and behavioral features of the disorder, has become a popular tool in research, clinical assessment, and criminal justice practice. The PCL-R is a valid and reliable measure of psychopathy that is a strong predictor of violent recidivism and dangerousness (Gacono, 2000; Hare, 2001, 2003; Harris, Rice, & Cormier, 1991; Hart, 1998; Hemphill, Templeman, Wong, & Hare, 1998; Hodgins, 1997; Litwack & Schlesinger, 1998; Salekin, Rogers, & Sewell, 1996; Serin & Amos, 1995), and a determinant of high criminogenic offender risk/needs (Simourd & Hodge, 2000). The PCL-R has gained widespread attention and is now used at various stages of the criminal justice system in Canada and the United States (Hare, 1998).[8]

Cognitive Theories

Cognitive theories focus on the thinking errors and information processing anomalies that lead to and are associated with criminal behavior. From this perspective, criminal behavior is the product of cognitive defects and cognitive schemas that facilitate and support criminal behavior. Cognitive theories of criminal behavior include *rational choice theories* that suggest crime is a conscious, freely chosen activity produced by thinking errors and particular cognitive style, and information processing theories that identify specific cognitive deficits that contribute to a tendency to commit criminal behavior.

The Criminal Personality

According to the *criminal personality theory* (Yochelson & Samenow, 1976), a subset of chronic offenders possess a "criminal personality." These offenders engage in chronic criminal behavior across their lifespan as a result of a unique pattern of thinking and specific thinking errors. From this perspective, offenders consciously choose to commit crime and maintain a criminal lifestyle through the use of a cognitive style that enables them to "cut off" deterrents and feelings of remorse and guilt that would otherwise stop them from committing crime. Offenders with "criminal personalities" use thinking errors such as *uniqueness, ownership, concrete thinking, lying, victim stance, fragmentation,* and *power thrust,* which they have practiced from childhood, forming a unique cognitive style. These offenders engage in the conscious mechanisms of *corrosion* and *cut-off*—slowly eliminating external deterrents (corrosion) until feelings of guilt are quickly cut off in the moment before they commit a criminal act.

Information Processing

Cognitive/information processing studies have focused on information processing deficits in antisocial personality disordered offenders and, more recently, psychopaths. Researchers have attempted to empirically explore Cleckley's (1941) *semantic dementia*— the psychopath's attempt to mimic emotion and manipulate meaning through language. Reiber and Vetter (1995) suggest that the language of the psychopath reflects underlying personality dynamics, in particular the ability to dissociate feelings of guilt. Other researchers have found that psychopaths use fewer cohesive ties when telling stories (Brinkley, Newman, Harpur, & Johnson, 1999) and extract less information from affective words than nonpsychopaths (Williamson, Harpur, & Hare, 1991). Research by Blair et al. (1995) suggests that psychopathy is the result of early dysfunction within the *violence inhibition mechanism* (VIM), a cognitive mechanism that reduces the likelihood of aggressive attack when the aggressor is faced with the display of distress cues. Blair and his colleagues found that, when psychopaths are asked to identify with protagonists in stories where someone is harmed, their dominant attribution to story protagonists is indifference and happiness in striking contrast to the guilt and regret attributed by the controls.

Other studies suggest that crime is the product of culturally supported cognitive schemas and *techniques of neutralization* (Sykes & Matza, 1957).[9] People use a range of neutralization techniques to rationalize their behavior and maintain a positive self-image, including condemnation of the condemners, appeal to higher loyalties, denial of injury, denial of victim, and denial of responsibility (Sykes & Matza, 1957). Acceptance of neutralizations has a positive effect on violence (Agnew, 1994). For example, Stermac, Segal, and Gillis (1989) found that rape is the product of traditional male sex-role stereotypes, and rapists (seen as having an excess of stereotypical maleness) express more positive attitudes toward women and less endorsement of rape myths than controls. Rapists excuse or deny their behavior by employing distinct excuses and justifications that reflect cognitive schemas that allow them to rationalize their behaviors. Rape "excusers" maintain a positive image of themselves by attributing their behavior to alcohol and drug use, emotional problems, or compartmentalizing their rape behavior by presenting themselves as "good guys" in other areas of their lives. Rape "deniers" use cognitive schema such as "nice girls don't get raped," "women mean yes when they say no," and "women are seductresses" (Scully & Marolla, 1984). These cognitive distortions allow rapists to neutralize (and continue) their behavior.

Wallace, Schmitt, Vitale, and Neman (2000) suggest that individuals who score above 30 on the PCL-R likely have a *cognitive deficit* characterized by failure in the response modulation process. These individuals are unable to attend to nonsalient stimuli and alter their behavioral sequence accordingly. They are inclined to engage in criminal behavior because they are unable to "pause" once they begin a behavioral course, as a result of this deficit in response modulation. Individuals who score below 30 on the PCL-R do not have this deficit, but may employ *cognitive distortions* to provide justification and excuses that will enable criminal behavior—the higher the PCL-R score up to 30, the more likely the individual will experience cognitive distortions conducive to antisocial and criminal behavior. This research makes room for the notion of a categorically distinct group of individuals whose behavior is the product of a cognitive deficit (primary psychopaths), while at the same time acknowledging that most people (nonpsychopaths) use cognitive distortions that may increase their likelihood of antisocial and criminal behavior along a continuum of severity.

Behavioral Theories

Operant and Classical Conditioning

Conditioning theories explain crime in terms of the ways in which behaviors are shaped through stimulus pairing (classical conditioning) and reinforcement and punishment (operant conditioning). *Operant conditioning* involves the increase of behaviors through reinforcements and decrease of behaviors through punishments. *Classical (Pavlovian) conditioning* involves the increase or decrease of behaviors through pairing and removal of stimuli. Conditioning theories are based on the work of early behavioral theorists B.F. Skinner (operant conditioning) and Ivan Pavlov (classical conditioning). Skinner believed that behavior could be changed by altering environmental stimuli (i.e., reinforcers, punishments), whereas Pavlov found that behavior could be conditioned by pairing primary and secondary stimuli based on his famous salivating dog experiment. Pavlov found that after feeding his dogs following the ringing of a bell, the dogs began to salivate when they heard the bell even if food was not presented. The dog's primary or unconditioned stimulus was the food, which caused a primary physiological response. The secondary or conditioned stimulus was the ringing of the bell, which by itself would not cause salivation. The dogs learned to salivate at the sound of the bell with or without the presentation of food. This is classical conditioning.

Applying operant and classical conditioning theory to criminal behavior, crime (a behavior) can be increased or decreased through exposure to various stimuli. For example, operant conditioning can increase criminal behavior when such behaviors are immediately followed by positive or negative reinforcement. Positive reinforcement involves delivering a reward, whereas negative reinforcement involves withholding something. Criminal behavior can also be classically conditioned when such behavior is associated with a secondary or conditioned stimulus. A simple example: A teen runaway who's been living on the streets for some time finds a gun and decides to commit an armed robbery to acquire money to live. Immediately following the robbery, the offender is rewarded with a wallet full of cash. The anxiety the offender had been experiencing over having no financial resources is immediately alleviated. In this case, the offender's robbery behavior is positively reinforced by acquiring the cash and negatively reinforced by the alleviation of anxiety. However, what if immediately following the robbery a bystander intervenes, tackling and severely beating the offender? Rather than receiving reinforcements (money, decreased anxiety), the offender receives punishment (attack, beating) and the likelihood of repeating the behavior is reduced. This is an example of *operant conditioning*.

Classical conditioning is somewhat different in that behavior is increased through pairing of stimuli. When the offender commits the robbery, the act of robbing someone at gunpoint generates feelings of exhilaration. After committing a number of subsequent robberies and experiencing this physiological arousal each time, the offender begins to associate armed robbery with feeling good. This pairing of an unconditioned or secondary stimulus (the act of robbing someone) with unconditioned or primary stimuli (physiological arousal produced by fear and uncertainty) increases the likelihood of future robbery behavior.

Learning Theory

Skinner's and Pavlov's early behavioral theories were based on experiments with animals. Though strict behaviorists support the application of conditioning theories to human behavior, many contend that these theories do not take into account human agency. Learning theories deal with this problem by considering how individual human beings interpret, perceive, and make decisions in response to environmental cues. Learning theorists contend that behavior is learned through a combination of environmental influences and individual interpretation and response to those influences. For the learning theorist, crime is a product of social learning whereby an individual's decision to commit crime results from observation and association.

Returning to the armed robber example, when the teenager found the gun, where did he get the idea to rob someone with it instead of turning it into the police? Learning theory offers the missing piece not answered by operant and classical conditioning theories. Perhaps the teen was an avid *NYPD Blue, Law and Order,* or *CSI* fan and had seen countless television accounts of armed robbery. Or maybe he'd been hanging out with other homeless teens who he regularly watched commit these sorts of acts. Or maybe he came from a family or community in which the act of armed robbery was seen as a common means to obtain resources.

There are a number of variations on learning theory including expectancy theory, imitation or modeling, and differential association (a sociological theory discussed in the following section). Expectancy theory suggests that people act on the basis of what they expect will happen as a result of a particular act. In other words, people act based on what they perceive the consequences and benefits will be. Imitation or modeling theories suggest that people imitate or model what they see. Imitation theories are based on the work of Albert Bandura, whose famous 1960s study showed that preschool-aged children who viewed a film of an adult assaulting a rubber "Bobo" doll behaved more aggressively after viewing the film than did a control group of children who viewed a film depicting more passive behavior. Differential association theory suggests that individuals act on the basis of who they associate with. People learn criminal behavior through interaction with friends and family members who engage in such behavior. Burgess and Akers's (1966) differential association–reinforcement theory combines differential association with conditioning theories to suggest that people learn to engage in crime through differential association but criminal behavior is then maintained through operant and classical conditioning.

A great deal of research has accumulated applying social learning theory to analyzing the impact of crime and violence in media and pop culture.[10] Early studies (called the Payne Fund Studies) conducted in the 1930s found that many in a sample of 2,000 respondents were conscious of having directly imitated acts of violence they saw in films. This research spawned decades of controversy and research on the subject of media violence (Sparks & Sparks, 2002). A more recent study found that 25% of juvenile offenders got ideas about how to commit their crimes from popular culture (Surette, 2002). From the perspective of social learning theory, expectations and ideas are conveyed through television, film, music, computer games, and other forms of popular culture and are mimicked by youth in particular. Although there is some disagreement in the literature about whether or not media violence is criminogenic (crime producing) or cathartic (crime reducing) or both, a large and growing body of research suggests media violence triggers the occurrence of criminal behavior and shapes its form (Surette, 1998). Most of the studies on the effects of TV and computer game violence, however, have been conducted in laboratory settings and measured levels of aggression in response to violent stimuli (rather than actual criminal behavior), which is problematic for drawing conclusions.

Beyond anecdotal accounts of media-mediated violence, little empirical research supports a direct criminalizing effect of violent media. Findings suggest that media depictions of violence are more likely to shape criminal behavior than trigger it (Surette, 1998). People already inclined to commit a crime get ideas about how to commit the crime from media images, but few otherwise law-abiding citizens will be influenced by media to commit a crime. On the other hand, compelling case study evidence suggests that the behavior of a small group of "media junkies" may be unduly influenced by media violence though the potential for violent media to trigger criminal behavior is very small.[11]

Sociological Theories—What Sociological Forces Contributed to This Behavior?

Sociological theories explain criminal behavior in terms of social influences such as community disorganization, stigmatization and labeling, peer influences, delinquent subcultures, and social bonds. Sociological theories of crime are macro-level theories that locate the source of criminality outside the individual, with the idea that "nurture" rather than "nature" shapes criminal behavior. There is considerable overlap between sociological theories of crime and theories of (noncriminal) deviance. Sociological theories that explain criminal behavior also explain deviant behavior such as college student cheating, eating disorders, bad habits, and unusual sexual behaviors.

Sociological theories can be broken down into three general types: *structural, cultural,* and *interactionist*. Structural theories see criminal behavior as a product of social structure, cultural theories contend that criminal behavior is rooted in and shaped by delinquent subcultures, and interactionist theories look at the interactional forces that explain why some people commit crime while others from the same background and social circumstances do not.

Structural

Structural theories view crime as a product of the structure of society, asking the question, *"Why do some societies have more crime than others?"* From this perspective, crime is rooted in two primary factors—differential opportunity and discrimination toward certain (powerless) groups within society. In a society where the rich and poor live in relatively close proximity, the poor turn to crime as an alternative pathway to success. Crime is defined by the powerful, and laws are created to ensure that the group or groups in power retain the resources. Examples of structural theories are structural functionalism, strain theory, and conflict theory.

The dominant sociological theory of crime for the first half of the 20th century was *structural functionalism*. According to Durkheim, founding father of sociology and structural functionalist, crime and deviance is the product of social distancing and *anomie*—a state of normlessness. Durkheim also believed that deviance and crime, despite their negative effects, serve a social function by promoting social solidarity among the law abiding. When a criminal or deviant act is committed and made public, law-abiding members of society are united in pointing their fingers at the perpetrators. Law-abiding citizens can also look to deviant behavior to help them define the boundaries of acceptable behavior (Durkheim, 2003). Structural functionalism is illustrated by Kai Erickson's (1966) case study analysis of Puritan response to revolutionaries in 17th-century Bay Colony, showing how societal response to these "offenders" served to solidify the rest of the community and strengthen their moral convictions.

Strain theory is another example of a structural theory of crime. According to strain theorists, crime is the product of differential opportunity. Robert Merton extended Durkheim's ideas, suggesting that anomie results when access to prescribed goals and availability of legitimate means to obtain those goals are lacking. Crime occurs when individuals do not have access to legitimate noncriminal means to obtain the success everyone strives for. Cloward and Ohlin (1960) took this idea further, suggesting that crime is more likely to occur when particular illegitimate opportunities are present, and some people have greater access to particular types of illegitimate opportunity.

Conflict theories locate the cause of crime in the incompatible interests of multiple groups in society. Conflict theories became prominent in the 1960s and 1970s with the work of Quinney (1970, 1977). Whereas structural functionalists view society from a consensus perspective in which norms are created through a shared understanding of the majority, conflict theorists contend that society is heterogeneous and conflictual. Crime is defined by the dominant class to include behavior patterns of those who do not have power in society and used as a tool to serve the interests of the powerful. A reflexive relationship exists between the definers of crime (the powerful) and those defined as criminal (the powerless) whereby those defined as criminal begin to see themselves as such and learn to play the role with increasing probability of being defined as criminal in the future. Those in power construct an ideology of crime to make sure they stay in power. A social reality of crime is created by defining crime, creating and applying laws, and constructing behavior patterns in such a way that the probability of criminality (and sanctions for criminality) is high for powerless members of society. Conflict theory offers an explanation of both criminal behavior and criminal justice.

Marxist and critical theories are historically related to conflict theories, and many of the conflict theorists are also considered Marxist theorists. The terms *critical criminology* and *radical criminology* are often used synonymously with Marxist criminology, though critical criminology has branched out considerably from Marxism. Some suggest that critical criminology does not reflect a coherent body of theories and should be viewed under the umbrella term *constitutive criminology*[12] along with other critical approaches such as postmodernism, chaos theory, semiotics, edgework, catastrophe theory, critical race theory, and peacemaking criminology (Akers & Sellers, 2004).[13] Like conflict theory, Marxist theory locates the cause and legal definitions of criminality in power relations, but rejects the idea that the conflict is between multiple groups. From the Marxist perspective, there are two groups—the power elite and the masses or working class. Laws are constructed by the power elite—the small group of ruling class who has all the social, economic, and political power. The power elite manipulate social institutions such as the academic community, mass media, and other sources of public opinion to make it appear that the law protects everyone's interests so that the masses will continue to believe the system is legitimate.

Marxist theory contends that the criminal justice system is a tool to repress the working class, but the theory has little to say about crime. Karl Marx himself did not write about criminal behavior. Marxist (and conflict) theorists explain criminal behavior as an inevitable response to the capitalistic system. People engage in crime because either they are brutalized by and trying to accommodate the capitalistic system or their crimes are conscious or unconscious acts of revolution and resistance. Marxist theories can be particularly useful in explaining certain types of crime (e.g., political crime), but fall short in offering etiological explanation for most types of criminal behavior.

Feminist theories of crime focus on gender issues as central to understanding criminal behavior. Feminist criminology asks the questions, *"Do theories of men's criminality apply to women?"* (generalizability problem) and *"Why do girls and women commit so much less crime than boys and men?"* (gender ratio problem; see Daly & Chesney-Lind, 1988). Feminism is a "set of theories about women's oppression and a set of strategies for social change" (Daly & Chesney-Lind, 1988, p. 502). Feminist criminology and feminist thought consist of a range of perspectives including Marxist, socialist, radical, liberal, power, postmodern, Black feminist, and critical race feminisms.[14] Feminist criminology raises issues regarding the applicability of male theories of crime to female offenders and the gendered nature of crime. Scholars such as Klein (1973), Adler (1975), Simon (1975), Daly and Chesney-Lind (1988), Simpson (1989), Naffine (1996), and Messerschmidt (1993) have contributed to the body of work now known as feminist criminology. Feminist criminologists argue that feminist inquiry should be applied to all facets of crime, deviance, and social control (Daly & Chesney-Lind, 1988) and that the striking gender difference in crime suggests that gender should be the central focus of criminology and anything less is disciplinary negligence (Naffine, 1996).

The *power-control theory* of gender and delinquency integrates conflict, Marxist, and control theories. Power-control theory asks, "What differences do the relative class positions of husbands *and* wives in the workplace make for gender variations in parental control and in delinquent behavior of adolescents?" (Hagan, Simpson, & Gillis, 1987, p. 789). According to power-control theory, the predominantly male pattern of crime and delinquency is the result of the class structure of patriarchal families. The parent-daughter relationship is an "instrument-object relationship" in which fathers and especially mothers are expected to control their daughters more than they control their sons. This instrument-object relationship between parents and daughters exists in the extreme in the patriarchal family. As a result, daughters are prepared for a "cult of domesticity" that significantly reduces their involvement in delinquency. In contrast, reduced parental controls on boys encourages risk-taking behaviors associated with criminality.

Cultural

Cultural theories recognize that society is made up of conflicting subcultures with different norms, values, beliefs, and characteristics. Cultural conflict exists between different subcultures and those whose values conflict with the dominant culture. When a subculture conflicts with dominant culture, the norms, values, and behaviors of that subculture are deemed deviant or criminal. When members of a subculture are defined as deviant by the larger society, they adopt and solidify values and norms that contrast with those of the dominant culture. Subcultures that conflict with the dominant culture ensure their survival through cultural transmission, passing their norms and values from one generation to the next, ensuring the continuation of cultural conflict and placement outside the dominant culture (Adler & Adler, 2003).

The *subculture of violence theory* is an example of a cultural theory. This theory (originally developed by Wolfgang and Ferracuti in their text *The Subculture of Violence*) states that more violence occurs in lower-class subcultures as a result of particular norms, values, expectations, and behaviors. Values such as honor, masculinity, defense of status, and the use of physical violence to settle disputes define subcultures of violence. Some researchers suggest that a subculture of violence exists in the American South, and among African Americans, and delinquent gangs (Vold, Bernard, & Snipes, 2002). In general, cultural theories suggest that crime is the product of criminal subcultures within a society whose values conflict with the dominant culture. Features of criminal subcultures include an exaggerated sense of masculinity, toughness, thrill-seeking, fatalistic philosophy, getting into trouble, and an antiauthority stance.

Interactionist

Interactionist theories explain crime in terms of the interactional dynamics between people. These theories come from a social-psychological perspective focusing, at a more micro-level, on the ways in which individuals are defined and come to define themselves as criminal. Interactionist theories help explain why some individuals within subcultures of violence or those who belong to powerless groups in society do not engage in criminal behavior. Interactionist theories also explain why some members of the dominant culture engage in criminal behavior. From this perspective, peer groups, family dynamics, and attribution of meaning are important determinants of criminal behavior. Interactionist theorists are concerned not only with why crime occurs, but also with how it occurs (Adler & Adler, 2003). Examples of interactionist theories include Sutherland and Cressey's differential association theory, Becker's labeling theory, and Hirschi's social bond theory.

According to differential association theory, crime is a product of association between friends and family members. The crux of this theory is social learning—people who associate with friends and family members who engage in criminal behavior are more likely to learn how to commit crime and how to rationalize their behavior. Values, norms, and traditions that promote crime are transmitted interpersonally between people who are close to each other. From the perspective of differential association theory, "hanging out with the wrong crowd" is the primary explanation for why and how crime occurs.

Labeling theory suggests that many people engage in deviant and criminal behavior at some point in their lifetimes. However, only some people are caught and labeled as deviants or criminals. According to Becker (2003), "Social groups create deviance by making the rules whose infraction constitutes deviance" (p. 70). Individuals who are caught and defined as criminals develop an identity consistent with this view. A self-fulfilling prophecy ensues when the person who is defined as criminal self-identifies as such and continues to commit criminal behavior. Individuals labeled and stigmatized as criminals develop a criminal identity, style of behaving, and associated auxiliary traits consistent with the "stigma-theory" (Goffman, 1963) imposed by rule creators (the dominant and powerful groups who decide what's normal and do the labeling).

Hirschi's *social bond theory*, also referred to as *control theory*, is the most frequently tested and discussed of all theories in criminology (Akers & Sellers, 2004). Social bond theory asks, "Why do people conform/why don't we all violate the rules?" The main proposition in social control theory is that crime occurs when an individual's bond to society is weak or broken. Social bonds consist of four elements: *attachment* to others, *commitment* to conventional goals, *involvement* in conventional community activities, and *belief* in conventional norms and values. According to social bond theory, people who are attached, committed, involved, and believe in conventional values are less likely to engage in criminal behavior because they have a stake in the community and have too much to lose. Most social bond research has supported the theory (Akers & Sellers, 2004).

Routine Activity/Opportunity Theories[15]—What Situational, Contextual, Environmental Factors Provided the Setting and Opportunity for This Crime to Occur?

The routine activity theory states that crime occurs as a result of increased temptations and reduced controls. From this perspective, *setting* and *opportunity* are the most important factors contributing to criminal behavior. According to this theory, crime is a normal everyday activity that occurs when opportunities in the environment support or encourage criminal behavior. Crime can be controlled through strategies that harden targets and alter settings in ways that make crime less opportune and desirable for offenders (Felson, 2002). For example, an individual inclined to commit burglary will be less tempted to carry out the behavior if natural social controls exist such as observers or place managers and targets are hardened (e.g., adequate lighting, locked doors and windows, territorial markers, alarms, visibility, etc.). According to Felson (2002), people, including offenders, have varying degrees of self-control; some have more self-control than others and most people have more at some times than at others, depending on circumstance, mood, and other factors. Most people cannot abstain from criminal behavior when the opportunity to commit crime is too tempting and controls too few.

The routine activity theory rests, in part, on the *"broken window theory."* This theory uses the analogy of the "broken window" to describe how social disorganization leads to crime:

> A stable neighborhood of families who care for their homes, mind each other's children, and confidently frown on unwanted intruders can change, in a few years or even a few months, to an inhospitable and frightening jungle. A piece of property is abandoned, weeds up, a window is smashed. Adults stop scolding rowdy children; emboldened, the children become more rowdy. Families move out, unattached adults move in. Teenagers gather in front of the corner store. The merchant asks them to move; they refuse. Fights occur. Litter accumulates. People start drinking in front of the grocers; in time, an inebriate slumps to the sidewalk and is allowed to sleep it off. Pedestrians are approached by panhandlers.

> . . . serious street crime flourishes in areas in which disorderly behavior goes unchecked. The unchecked panhandler is, in effect, the first broken window. Muggers and robbers, whether opportunistic or professional, believe they reduce their chances of being caught or even identified if they operate on streets where potential victims are already intimidated by prevailing conditions. If the neighborhood cannot keep a bothersome panhandler from annoying passersby, the thief may reason, it is even less likely to call the police to identify a potential mugger or to interfere if the mugging actually takes place. (Wilson & Kelling, 1982, quoted in Kelling & Coles, 1996, pp. 19–20)

Thus, in the mind of the potential offender, the presence of disorder is a temptation because it sends the message that no one cares. When communities or neighborhoods are abandoned or people look the other way, the social controls are removed and there is no reason *not* to commit crime.

The routine activity theory is a type of *rational choice theory*. Rational choice theories suggest that individuals freely choose to engage in criminal behavior when the benefits outweigh the costs. The routine activity theory is unique in that the theory recognizes that the degree to which a person can freely choose is constrained by a multitude of factors and forces. For example, if an individual who is biologically predisposed to commit crime (i.e., a person with low autonomic arousal, low self-control, and traits such as impulsivity, irresponsibility, etc.) finds him- or herself in a situation in which there are high temptations and low controls (e.g., brand new Range Rover with keys in the ignition left in a dark parking lot with no one around), he or she would be more inclined to "choose" to steal the car than someone who is not biologically predisposed to commit crime.

From the perspective of the routine activity theory, crime is the product of the interaction between individual, situational/contextual, and environmental factors that converge in a way that increases the likelihood that crime will occur. Certain types of crime are more likely to occur in certain contexts where there are particular presences and absences. For example, violent crime is more likely to occur in a setting such as a bar where there are a high number of young males drinking alcohol. In such a setting, there are presences (young males, alcohol) and absences (a prosocial audience—elderly individuals, children). A particular *chemistry for crime* exists in this setting, with elements such as a likely offender, a suitable target, and the absence of capable guardians converging to produce a crime-generating context that produces a crime-attracting sequence of events (Felson, 2002). Routine activity theory is one of the more applicable theories in terms of providing concrete recommendations to policymakers charged with increasing public safety. Box 2.2 provides an example of how routine activity theory has been applied to community gang problems.

Cultural—What Cultural Forces Provided the Context in Which This Crime Could Occur?

In their book *Cultural Criminology*, Ferrell and Sanders (1995) argue that to make sense of crime, it is necessary to make sense of culture. The authors propose the development of a *cultural criminology* that recognizes criminality and criminalization as cultural enterprises that must be studied through a synthesis of divergent perspectives including social, feminist, and cultural theories. From this perspective, criminal behavior (and its control) is constructed, in part, through media, popular culture, and the "aesthetics" of authority that dictates what is "beautiful," "decent," "clean," and "appropriate" (p. 15). Criminal identities are born and shaped within culture and within criminal subcultures—collective criminal aesthetic and style, symbolism, and meaning are important factors in understanding the criminality.

Ferrell and Hamm (1998) suggest that "jailhouse criminology," which has attempted to study crime through official sources, social science surveys, and traditional quantitative measures, has prohibited true understanding of crime or *criminological verstehen*. Criminologists have neglected findings produced through ethnographic studies that offer the insider perspective on crime and deviance. To truly

BOX 2.2

COMBATTING STREET GANG VIOLENCE

Although violent crime has been at 20-year lows across the country, many cities have experienced a dramatic rise in gang violence. In Los Angeles, there was a 14% increase in gang-related violent crime despite a citywide decrease in crime. Other cities across the country have seen similar increases in gang behavior. Juvenile street gangs are distinguished by their ability to intimidate through group threat and their reliance on illusion to perpetuate threat of violence (Felson, 2006). Most gang experts agree that juvenile street gangs are smaller and much less organized than media images suggest, with many disconnected smaller gangs subsumed under a larger umbrella term such as "crips," "bloods," or "Latin Kings" that is more image than reality. The notion of juvenile gangs as highly organized has been referred to as the *juvenile gang fallacy* (Felson, 2002). Leading gang researcher Malcolm Klein (1971, 1995) found that gangs consist of a small core of active members, with the majority of members serving only peripheral functions and leaving the gang after a very short time. Data on known gang activity supports this finding (Moore, 2006). In Los Angeles there are an estimated 720 street gangs with 40,000 members. Of the 720 gangs, 11 gangs and their 800 members are being targeted by LAPD and are said to be responsible for 1,700 violent crimes in 2006. Felson argues that most gangs are like turtles. "Most turtle eggs fail to become turtles, and very few turtles reach old age. So it is with gangs . . . most gangs disappear in a couple years or less" (Felson, 2006, p. 308).

Routine activity theory says that crime occurs when temptations are high and controls are low. All crimes contain three elements: a likely offender, a suitable target, and the absence of a capable guardian against the offense. The juvenile street gang is "an imperfect adaptation to its surroundings" (Felson, 2006, p. 320). Juveniles join gangs because membership in the group meets their individual needs for peer involvement, support, activity, excitement, and a sense of power and control. According to Felson, a gang policy should have four main features:

1. Reduce general local crime rates in gang areas to reduce incentives to form and join gangs.

2. Suppress places, not people. Remove the places where gang members hang out and gangs will fizzle.

3. Stop publicizing gang behavior and enhancing the image of gangs as more powerful than they actually are.

4. Regularly (every 6 months or less) remove the gang label from police files and the minds of police officers unless there is real evidence the gang still exists and a particular individual is still a "gang member." Refrain from exaggerating the gang's impact.

Routine activity theory can be applied to the juvenile gang problem by attending to the settings that provide incentive for the formation of gangs. For example, the Crowe-Zahm mixing principle (Felson, 2002)—placing safe activities in unsafe locations and unsafe activities in safe locations—can be applied to reduce the likelihood of gang violence in a community. Gang members need suitable targets and victims. If all three elements of crime are not present, crime is less likely to occur. In some settings community response to gang violence has been citizens taking back their streets by engaging in activities such as round-the-clock dog walkers and senior citizens playing pinochle on high-crime street corners. Other communities have introduced youth programs in communities with high numbers of gang activity.

The U.S. Department of Justice, Bureau of Justice Assistance monograph (1997, 1999) *Addressing Community Gang Problems: A Model for Problem Solving* offers the *Comprehensive Gang Initiative model,* which involves the SARA approach to responding to gang problems in communities. The SARA model, largely based on principles of routine activity theory and situational crime prevention, involves four components:

1. *Scanning:* Looking for/identifying problems (consisting of specific victims who are harmed by behaviors of offenders at certain times and in specific places).

2. *Analysis:* Developing a thorough understanding of a problem. Analysis consists of straightforward and creative investigation of concrete problems.

3. *Response:* Developing response options consistent with the information analyzed, selecting responses, and implementing the responses.

4. *Assessment:* Providing useful feedback on effectiveness of response. Information can be used to change the response, improve the analysis, or even redefine the nature of the problem.

According to the report:

A high-rise retirement complex probably houses few gang members but may attract gang members from the surrounding area who are would-be robbers, if they think the resident retirees carry cash and would not resist an attack. Property crime rates are often high in college communities because students are more likely to leave cars and bicycles unlocked and often leave wallets and purses where they can easily be taken. However, a neighborhood with many potential offenders or victims can have a low crime rate if the victims and offenders do not come into contact with each other. For example, apartment complexes for the elderly separate this group of potential victims from people who might prey upon them. Thus, neighborhood gang problems differ in predictable ways for comprehensible reasons. The implications for gang problem prevention are obvious: to reduce the rate of gang problems in an area, it is important to determine the problems in the neighborhood and the actions needed to reduce the number of available offenders or victims or to separate potential offenders and victims. Addressing the entire social problem of gangs is not necessary to realize a substantial impact; selecting a smaller gang problem can yield disproportionately large benefits. Because neighborhoods differ, the best prevention strategies will vary from one neighborhood to the next. Community problem solvers must

(Continued)

(Continued)

study an area's social and physical conditions before developing and implementing strategies (U.S. Department of Justice, BJS, 1999, p. 7).

The SARA model illustrates the application of the routine activity theory to community crime problems such as gang violence. Law enforcement and community efforts rely on this and other models to focus on the unique aspects of gangs in local communities.

understand criminal behavior, researchers must study crime with quantitative (surveys, available data) and qualitative (ethnographic) methods that together are able to tell the complete story of crime. For example, official statistics tell us things like what percentage of armed robbers are male, what percentage of known serial killers have been physically and sexually abused, the correlation between age and violence, and so on. However, this sort of information tells us little about the personal style and aesthetics of bank robbers, the nature of the communities and subcultures within which they spend their time, the specific ways in which girls and women learn that aggression is not a tool with which they are able to obtain resources, the process by which a serial killer comes to attach meaning to particular types of victims or crime scene trophies, or the complex nature of the collusion between youth culture, media and pop culture, alternative style and meaning, and crime.

Culture plays a contributing role in the development and expression of criminal behavior. In her book *Zero Tolerance: Punishment, Prevention, and School Violence,* Casella (2001) states, "Whether people in the United States are willing to accept it or not, violence is a defining characteristic of U.S. Culture" (p. 2). According to Levin and Fox (2001),

> We used to put our heroes on pedestals where they could be admired, revered, and emulated, but those days are long gone. Today's children grow up collecting trading cards which bear the images of mass murderers rather than baseball players. On their bedroom walls youngsters hang calendars featuring Ted Bundy and the Hillside Strangler. Instead of chronicling the good deeds of superheroes, cartoons and comics today depict the seedier side of life. Batman and Robin have been supplanted by Beevis and Butthead as well as South Park. The conquests of Superman have been replaced by a comic book version of Jeffrey Dahmer. Children can also locate killer websites, wear killer t-shirts, and join killer fan clubs. They listen to the lyrics of Marilyn Manson who inspires them to try Satanism, vampirism, Gothic fashion, and mass murder. (p. 83)

Criminal behavior is a cultural and subcultural product. Media and popular culture and the escalating number of "media junkies" and media-mediated crimes (Black, 1991) call attention to the need to make sense of how media and popular culture shape criminal behavior. People who engage in criminal behavior do so within the context of subcultural and cultural contexts that inform cognitive scripts and schema—what kinds of music, clothing, weapons, language, mannerisms, accessories, and so on are associated with what types of people, places, and behaviors. Any given type of criminal behavior brings with it some cultural or subcultural understanding of the style, symbols, and accessories associated with that type of behavior. The behavior (modus operandi, criminal acts, selection of victims) of serial killers and sex offenders is shaped by the sorts of behaviors known in culture to be humiliating, and the types of people who are targeted has some relationship to cultural notions and stories about who is in power and powerful and who is not. Insulated Internet chat rooms for sex predators have the potential to normalize, reinforce, and exacerbate the fantasies of sex offenders. The aggressive hypermasculinity that characterizes many youth subcultures (and some would argue American culture as a whole) plays a key role in violent criminal behavior of all kinds. Political criminals are able to neutralize their behaviors through common values, beliefs, aesthetics, and style that provide a rationale for their behavior. Even computer criminals and economic offenders are influenced by the norms, values, symbols, and aesthetics of the group with which they identify.

Certain cultural artifacts are criminalized by popular culture in ways that feed back and further influence criminal subcultures (Ferrell, 1995). The process by which certain pop cultural artifacts become criminalized is socioeconomic and political—usually the music or aesthetic of marginalized individuals in society becomes criminalized, and then these violent or dangerous music, art, or clothing styles feed back into pop culture and the artifact appeals to groups in society that want to defy mainstream culture and aesthetic values. For example, heavy metal and rap music have been targeted by media watchdog groups and linked with violent behavior. However, the more criminalized a cultural artifact becomes (e.g., through public outcry over the link to violence and aggression, X or Violence rating), the more likely it will be appealing to individuals and groups who do not identify with prosocial values, messages, and behaviors.[16]

A related issue is the impact of penal culture on chronic offenders and their behavior across the life course. Punishment is a cultural artifact reflecting the symbols and signs of the larger culture. Cultural sensibilities (emotions) and mentalities (ways of thinking) have implications for the ways in which offenders are punished (Garland, 1990). At the same time, punishment feeds back into culture projecting "definite notions of what it is to be a person, what kinds of persons there are, and how such persons and their subjectivities are to be understood" (p. 268). While punishment practices help shape the emotional experience, ways of thinking, and decisions of the general public and penal professionals, the most immediate recipients of the messages conveyed through punishment are offenders. It is through punishment (as an extension of other social institutions) that offenders learn the moral order of things, and the signs and symbols that secure a particular place for particular sorts of people. Furthermore, offenders who are imprisoned for extended lengths of time become "developmentally frozen" (Zamble & Porporino, 1990), "prisonized" (Abbott, 1981; Clemmer, 1958), and/or "institutionally dependent" (Helfgott, Lutze, Chang, & Goodstein, 1990), experiencing difficulties on release that contribute to their likelihood to reoffend. Such offenders are also impacted by aspects of the prison culture including the ultramasculinity (in male prisons) (Sabo, Kupers, & London, 2001), infantilism (in female prisons), racial divisions, the convict code, and the deprivations of imprisonment, all of which are important factors that may contribute to and shape postrelease offending behavior.

Phenomenological—What Personal Meaning Does the Crime Hold for the Offender?

Phenomenology is the science of being. German philosopher Edmund Husserl, the founder of phenomenology, used archeology as a metaphor to describe phenomenology because it gets to what's simple, genuine, and uncontaminated. "To study being is not to turn to another reality . . . it is to penetrate deeper and deeper into the same—the one and only—reality" (Jones, 1969, p. 410). In the criminological literature, the work of Jack Katz (1988), the concept of *criminological verstehen* (Ferrell & Hamm, 1998; Ferrell & Sanders, 1995), and research and writing by criminological ethnographers (Cromwell, 1996; Ferrell & Sanders, 1995) and "convict criminologists" (Ross & Richards, 2003) reflect a phenomenological approach to the study of criminal behavior. A number of theoretical approaches discussed in this chapter (e.g., cultural criminology, symbolic interactionism, social learning, criminal personality theory) address aspects of the offender's perception, decision-making processes, and the personal meaning of crime. However, the *phenomenology of offending—the unique meaning of the offense in the moment it is committed—* deserves separate attention and is presented here as a distinct theoretical perspective.

Crime holds different meaning for different offenders. Katz's phenomenological theory of crime is grounded in symbolic interactionism and existentialism. Symbolic interactionism argues that human behavior is best understood through the meanings attributed to the behavior. Existentialism is a body of philosophical thought that emphasizes uniqueness and individual experience.[17] The phenomenology of crime is an important component of criminal behavior that has been underresearched and only vaguely articulated in the criminological literature:

> The social science literature contains only scattered evidence of what it means, feels, sounds, tastes, or looks like to commit a particular crime. Readers of research on homicide and assault do not hear the slaps and curses, see the pushes and shoves, or feel the humiliation and rage that may build toward the attack, sometimes persisting after the victim's death. How adolescents manage to make the shoplifting or vandalism of cheap and commonplace things a thrilling experience has not been intriguing to many students of delinquency. Researchers of adolescent gangs have never grasped why their subjects so often stubbornly refuse to accept the outsider's insistence that they wear the "gang" label. The description of "cold-blooded, senseless murders" has been left to writers outside the social sciences. Neither academic methods nor academic theories seem to be able to grasp why such killers may have been courteous to their victims just moments before the killing, why they often wait until they have dominated victims in sealed-off environments before coldly executing them, or how it makes sense to them to kill when only petty cash is at stake (Katz, 1988, p. 1).

The dominance of quantitative criminology and devaluation of the qualitative research and the ethnographic method (Ferrell & Hamm, 1998) has left a void in the study of criminal behavior. The motivations, meanings, and experience of criminal behavior and the distinctive contextual, interpersonal, private factors that shape offenders' decisions before, during, and after the moment a crime occurs are not well or widely understood.

Jack Katz's classic work, *Seductions in Crime,* embodies the phenomenological perspective. According to Katz (1988), the central problem in understanding crime is to understand the sensual dynamics at the *foreground* rather than the background of the criminal event. Katz attempts to fill a void left by positivist quantitative criminology that leaves unanswered questions (raised at the beginning of this chapter). *Why do some people who possess the background factors statistically correlated with crime turn out to be law-abiding citizens? Why do people who possess none of the background factors associated with crime go on to become hard-core criminals? Why do people who possess background factors correlated with crime commit the predicted crime and then desist for long periods of time? Why do some people who are statistically crime-prone stop for 5 or 10 or 20 years and then commit another crime?* According to Katz (1988):

> If as social researchers, we are to be able to explain more variation in criminality than background correlations allow, it appears that we must respect these sensual dynamics and honor them as authentic. But now we seem caught in a new dilemma. How can we simultaneously discredit the determinism of psychological and social background factors while crediting the determinism of sensually dynamic attractions and compulsions? Put another way, how can we find, through studying how people construct their experience as an artifact, the emergence of new forces that shape the actors themselves? Can we really see any novel causal forces in the black box between background factors and subsequent acts? After we have refined correlations between problematic acts and explanatory background factors, is there anything more to say other than that those whose actions do and those whose actions do not line up with predictions just "choose" to act that way? (p. 5)

The concept of *criminological verstehen* (criminological understanding; see Ferrell & Hamm, 1998; Ferrell & Sanders, 1995) offers a methodology for exploring criminal behavior from the phenomenological perspective with focus on understanding offense behavior from the inside out—from the unique perspective of the individual or individuals engaged in the offense behavior. A number of studies have emerged that focus on the study of crime from the offender's viewpoint (Cromwell, 1996) and Ross and Richards (2003) propose a "convict criminology" that approaches the study of crime and imprisonment from the ethnographic "insider" perspective. According to John Irwin, "Even horrendous acts make some sense if you fully appreciate the perpetrator's viewpoints or the full contexts of their crimes" (in Ross & Richards, 2003, p. xx).

An example of a phenomenological account of criminal behavior (murder) is offered by Mersault, the lead character in Camus's (1942, 1988) *The Stranger:*

> . . . my forehead was especially hurting me, all the veins in it throbbing under the skin. It was this burning, which I couldn't stand anymore, that made me move forward. I knew that it was stupid, that I wouldn't get the sun off me by stepping forward. But I took a step, one step, forward. At this time, without getting up, the Arab drew his knife and held it up to me in the sun. The light shot off the steel and it was like a long flashing blade cutting at my forehead. At the same instant the sweat in my eyebrows dripped down over my eyelids all at once and covered them with a warm, thick film. My eyes were blinded behind the curtain of tears and salt. All I could feel were the cymbals of sunlight crashing on my forehead and, indistinctly, the dazzling spear flying up from the knife in front of me. The scorching

blade slashed at my eyelashes and stabbed at my stinging eyes. That's when everything began to reel. The sea carried up a thick, fiery breath. It seemed to me as if the sky split open from one end to the other to rain down fire. My whole being tensed and I squeezed my hand around the revolver. The trigger gave; I felt the smooth underside of the butt; and there, in that noise, sharp and deafening at the same time. I shook off the sweat and sun. I knew that I had shattered the harmony of the day, the exceptional silence of a beach where I'd been happy. Then I fired four more times at the motionless body where the bullets lodged without leaving a trace. And it was like knocking four quick times on the door of unhappiness. (pp. 56–57)

Though fictional, this account illustrates the phenomenology of crime and the importance of understanding what meaning a particular criminal act holds for the offender.

A similar account of murder is offered by Abbott (1981) in his book *In the Belly of the Beast,* in which Abbott describes the experience of stabbing another prisoner to death. Abbott claimed this account was fictional, but many did not believe him, and the passage was subsequently used against him in a murder trial in which he was convicted (Abbott & Zack, 1987):[18]

Here is how it is. You are both alone in his cell. You've slipped out a knife (eight- to ten-inch blade, double edged). You're holding it beside your leg so he can't see it. The enemy is smiling and chattering away about something. You see his eyes: green-blue, liquid. He thinks you're his fool, he trusts you. You see the spot. It's a target between the second and third button on his shirt. As you calmly talk and smile, you move your left foot to the side to step across his right-side body length. A light pivot toward him with your right shoulder and the world turns upside down; you have sunk the knife to its hilt into the middle of his chest. Slowly he begins to struggle for his life. As he sinks, you have to kill him fast or get caught. He will say "Why?" Or "No!" Nothing else. You can feel his life trembling through the knife in your hand. It almost overcomes you, the gentleness of the feeling at the center of a coarse act of murder. You've pumped the knife in several times without even being aware of it. You go to the floor with him to finish him. It is like cutting hot butter, no resistance at all. They always whisper one thing at the end: "Please." You get the odd impression he is not imploring you not to harm him, but to do it right. If he says your name, it softens your resolve. You go into a mechanical stupor of sorts. Things register in slow motion because all of your senses are drawn to a new height. You leave him in the blood, staring with dead eyes. (Abbott, 1981, p. 76)

The phenomenological approach to the study of criminal behavior can explain the convergence of background and foreground factors in the moment crime occurs. This is a missing component of many analyses of criminal behavior that has the potential to uncover answers not attainable through other theoretical perspectives. While Katz's phenomenological theory of crime focused specifically on the emotive and sensual attractions to crime, other researchers have extended his work to address the role of other (foreground) factors (cognition, opportunity, instrumental goals, etc.) that are part of the offender's experience of crime (McCarthy, 1995). Consideration of the unique experience, motivations, and decision-making processes of the offender at the moment crime is committed provides important information not available through traditional analyses and theoretical approaches. This information is necessary in making sense of violent crimes that are often the product of fantasy and unique motivational factors (Hickey, 2002; Keppel

& Birnes, 1997; Keppel & Walter, 1999; Meloy, 2000), in addition to providing insight into the individual, contextual, gender, and other variations across all crime categories.

Applying Interdisciplinary Criminology: Analysis of the Baranyi/Anderson Case

Integrated Theories of Crime

A number of theories have emerged that attempt to incorporate multiple theories and perspectives in explaining crime. Some are more integrated than others in that they incorporate a wider range of theories. Examples of (partially) integrated theories include general theory of crime (Gottfredson & Hirschi, 1990), developmental (Moffit, 1993) and life-course criminology (Farrington, 2003),[19] integrated systems theory (Robinson, 2004), control balance theory (Tittle, 1995), integrated theory of delinquency (Elliot, Ageton, & Canter, 1979), and interdisciplinary criminology (Barak, 1998).[20] The following descriptions of some leading partially integrated theories of crime illustrate criminologists' attempts to address complexities of criminal behavior that cannot be explained by single perspectives.

Gottfredson and Hirschi's General Theory of Crime

Gottfredson and Hirschi (1990) developed the *general theory of crime*, which explains criminal behavior as a failure in self-control. The authors contend that their theory can explain all crimes in all places at all times. The general theory of crime is commonly viewed as a sociological theory. However, it can be considered a partially integrative theory in that it uses both sociological and psychological concepts. For example, the authors state that self-control is an "enduring tendency well within the meaning of 'personality trait'" (Gottfredson & Hirschi, 1990, p. 109) but is largely the product of child-rearing practices and influenced by a range of social forces. Self-control is conceptualized along a continuum from low/immediate gratification on one end to high/deferred gratification on the other, and the theory attempts to explain both the stability and versatility of crime over time. Social bonds are subsumed under the umbrella of self-control (i.e., individuals with low self-control are less likely to be attached, committed, involved, or to share community beliefs). Research suggests that learning processes may link social bonds, self-control, and deviant and criminal behavior. This theory has generated a great deal of interest, and some argue may supplant social bond theory as the major control theory of crime (Akers & Sellers, 2004).

Developmental and Life-Course Theories

Developmental theories of crime focus on how individual offenders' lives unfold to influence crime patterns across the life course. Crime is seen as a dynamic developmental process that begins in childhood and occurs across the life course. Developmental theories are now "center stage in criminology" (Cullen & Agnew, 2006, p. 492). Like Gottfredson and Hirschi's general theory of crime, developmental and life-course theories synthesize psychological and sociological concepts and can be considered partially integrative. Life-course criminology emerged from recent developments in sociology and psychology focusing on critical life events and the interaction between the individual and their social environments in connection with life events, transitions, and turning points. The life-course perspective addresses criminological controversies such as the age-crime curve (the unimodal distribution of crime peaking in adolescence and declining dramatically in adulthood), career criminality, juvenile delinquency and adult criminality, as well as the pushes and pulls toward and from criminality and the persistence and desistance in crime for different populations at different times and situations across the life course (Cullen & Agnew, 2006; Piquero & Mazerolle, 2001).

The most exciting thing about developmental and life-course theories is that they represent a historically rare attempt to connect the dots between sociological, psychological, and biological theories of crime. Life-course criminologists (Laub & Sampson, 2003; Moffit, 1993; Sampson & Laub, 1993; and others) recognize research in psychology that has consistently shown childhood antisocial behavior is empirically linked to juvenile delinquency and persistent adult criminality. At the same time, life-course criminology addresses social and situational contexts and changes over time that influence individual criminal behavior, focusing on differences across individuals and subsets of offenders in continuity and change.

Sampson and Laub's (1993) *Crime in the Making* is considered one of the early classics in life-course criminology. The authors offered a theory of criminal behavior that explained crime across the life course in terms of changing social controls. Their theory combined Hirschi's social bond theory with developmental theories. Sampson and Laub hypothesized that people can be caught in life trajectories that involve crime and that can extend to childhood, but people experience turning points and changes in their attachment, commitment, involvement, and beliefs that may influence their propensity to continue crime over the course of their lives. The authors revised their theory in 2003 (Laub & Sampson, 2003), retaining their core thesis that structural turning points such as marriage, employment, and military service serve as sources of social control, but broadening their theory to better explain the multiple processes that characterize informal social controls across the life course.

Moffit's *Adolescent-Limited and Life-Course Persistent Theory of Antisocial Behavior* is one of the best known of the developmental theories of crime. Moffit's theory has been described as "one of the best attempts to integrate biological, psychological, and sociological variables in the recent literature" (Cullen & Agnew, 2006, p. 502). The theory identifies two qualitatively distinct groups of offenders who differ in their developmental pathways into crime. *Life-course–persistent* offenders represent a small group of offenders who engage in a high rate of antisocial behavior throughout their lives. *Adolescent-limited* offenders are a larger group who limit their antisocial behavior to adolescent years (Moffit, 1993). The antisocial and criminal behavior of these two groups can be explained by fundamentally different causal influences. A theory of antisocial behavior in life-course–persistent offenders must locate causal factors in early childhood and explain the continuity of crime over time. The antisocial behavior of adolescent-limited offenders may be specific to situations and events in adolescence and must account for the discontinuity of crime in their lives. Moffit's theory is compatible with much of the literature on antisocial behavior and has empirical support.

Barak's (1998) vision of interdisciplinary criminology provides a framework for attempting the dauntingly complex task of integrating theories to explain and predict criminal behavior. The task of interdisciplinary criminology is to discuss and articulate the ways in which constitutive elements interact to generally coproduce criminal behavior and its control. Integrative theories emerging over the past 15 years have made considerable gains in linking critical and complementary findings from different perspectives. However, criminologists are still faced with the task of integrating a much wider range of theoretical perspectives. Few if any theories, integrative or not, can explain all forms of criminal behavior, criminal events, or all individuals or groups who engage in crime. Some scholars are skeptical that a true integrative theory of crime is possible at all. However, it is unlikely that any criminal behavior can be explained by a single theory.

According to Bartol (2002), "Criminology needs all the interdisciplinary help it can get to explain and control criminal behavior. An integration of the data, theories, and general viewpoints of each discipline is crucial"(p. 2). Figure 2.2 shows the factors contributing to crime that can be explained by different theoretical perspectives and knowledge bases.

❖ **Figure 2.2**   Factors That Contribute to Criminal Behavior

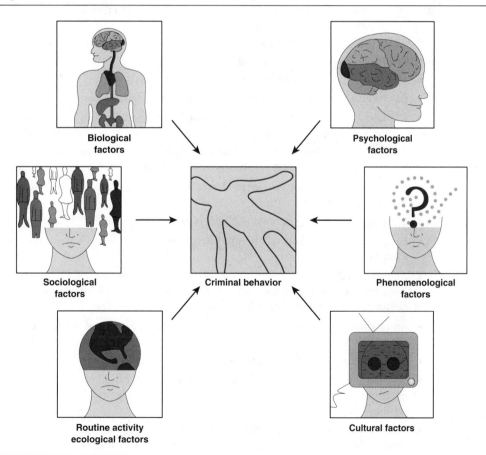

Biological factors

Psychological factors

Sociological factors

Criminal behavior

Phenomenological factors

Routine activity ecological factors

Cultural factors

Each of these perspectives can explain aspects of criminal behavior. Some crimes may be better explained by biological theories, others by psychological theories, and so on. Given the complexity of crime, all theoretical perspectives have something to offer that helps us understand and explains a piece of each and every criminal event.

Applying Interdisciplinary Criminology to a Specific Case: Alex Baranyi and David Anderson

The Baranyi/Anderson case presented at the beginning of this chapter illustrates the application of interdisciplinary criminology. To make sense of criminal behavior, it is important to identify the many factors and forces that provide the impetus and ingredients for a particular crime to occur. Interdisciplinary criminology can be thought of as a criminological toolbox. The different theories and knowledge bases are distinct tools that can explain converging parts of the whole story. Just as a hammer cannot be used to hammer a nail *and* turn a bolt, putty a wall, and dig a hole, a single theoretical framework is not sufficient or appropriate to explain all aspects of criminal behavior.

To make sense of crime—in this case, the quadruple murder of the Wilson family—it is important to identify key elements of the crime. The following is a list of elements from the case taken from news coverage and court reports:[21]

- Murders were committed by two individuals.
- Victims were acquaintances.
- Murder weapons were baseball bats, knives, and swords.
- Baseball bats, knives, and swords were seized from Anderson's home.
- Offenders and one of the victims (Kimberly Wilson) were part of a group considered "Goths," who hung out together at a local Denny's, dressed in black, and glorified death.
- One of the offenders (Anderson) had previously dated one of the victims (Kimberly Wilson) and owed her $350, which she tried to collect shortly before the murders.
- Forensic evidence (DNA analysis of blood on Baranyi's shoelaces and Anderson's shoes) supported convictions.
- Witnesses testified that Baranyi and Anderson were inseparable.
- Baranyi had been arrested 10 months prior to the murders for a domestic dispute with a female friend.
- Anderson had no prior record but had previously been investigated for property damage, a hit-and-run accident, attempted arson, and grand theft in the disappearance of a cash-machine card from his parent's house.
- Anderson was reported as a runaway in 1995 and wasn't accepted back home by his parents.
- Baranyi refused to "rat" on his friend as part of his confession.
- Witnesses testified that Baranyi and Anderson had spoken about plans to commit a range of crimes, including specific statements about murdering the Wilson family and stealing items in their home.
- Baranyi was a devoted fan of the TV show *Highlander*. He wore his hair long and in a ponytail like the show's main character and collected swords and knives. A witness

testified that in the context of role-playing games, Baranyi believed he was a demigod named "Slice" or "Thunderclap" and that he had concocted a make-believe love interest for his character named Rose.

- Baranyi and Anderson were both involved in role-playing games such as *Dungeons and Dragons*.

- Baranyi and Anderson played computer games including *Streetfighter* and *Supernintendo*.

- Items from the Wilsons' home were found in Baranyi's apartment.

- Baranyi's attorneys argued that he was bipolar.

- The prosecutors in both Baranyi's and Anderson's cases argued that they had antisocial personality disorder and felt no remorse for the murders.

- Baranyi confessed that he committed the murders because he was bored, "in a rut," and in danger of becoming "decadent." He said he had wanted to kill someone for years to "experience something truly phenomenal."

- Baranyi's writings included a to-do list of crimes with an entry about reading obituaries and robbing the families' homes while they were at the funeral.

- Witnesses indicated that Baranyi got too involved in role-playing games and was generally calm except while playing computer games.

- Baranyi's parents divorced when he was 8 years old, at which time he was shuffled back and forth between his parents who lived in Washington and Pennsylvania.

- Baranyi and Anderson were both living away from home at the time of the offense.

- Baranyi and Anderson had both attended an alternative high school and had dropped out before the murders.

- Anderson was described by witnesses as a charming "ladies man" with a "mean streak," whereas Baranyi was described as a sullen, aloof follower who "fumbled" with women and shrunk around large groups of teenagers.

- Baranyi indicated that he had no motivation for committing the murders except that he thought Kimberly Wilson was selfish because she didn't share her cigarettes.

- Witnesses testified that Anderson had expressed anger at Kimberly Wilson because she asked him to pay her back money he owed her and he felt insulted by this.

- After being convicted and sent to the Washington State Penitentiary, Anderson paid $80 to set up a Web site in which he proclaimed his innocence and solicited female companionship.

What theories best explain Baranyi and Anderson's criminal behavior? What factors converged to produce the behavior in this case? The following are (hypothetical) theoretical explanations that can be offered from within each knowledge base.

Biological. Baranyi had a biological predisposition to bipolar disorder and experienced symptoms of both bipolar disorder and antisocial personality disorder. Anderson had a biological predisposition to antisocial personality disorder. Both are physiologically hyporeactive and underaroused.

Psychological. Witnesses testified that both Baranyi and Anderson had antisocial traits and expressed no remorse for the crimes. There was disagreement between expert witnesses for defense and state attorneys as to whether Baranyi was manic-depressive (bipolar) or had antisocial personality disorder. Both Baranyi and Anderson were referred to in court and by the news media as "sociopaths" who showed no remorse, though some accounts suggest Baranyi showed some evidence of remorse and regret at different points throughout his trial. In the absence of results from forensic assessment measures, the evidence lends itself to the hypothesis that Anderson may have been the leader and Baranyi the follower, that Baranyi had co-occurring bipolar disorder and antisocial personality disorder, and that Anderson had antisocial personality disorder. Both used cognitive thinking errors, distorted schema, and neutralization techniques to carry out and provide accounts of the murders.

Sociological. The theories that best explain Baranyi and Anderson's behavior are differential association theory, social bond, and delinquent subcultures. Anderson and Baranyi committed the crime at a time in their lives in which family and community bonds had been severed (e.g., leaving home, dropping out of school). The fantasy building up to the crime was a joint endeavor produced through the interaction between the two friends, who had similarly deviant and distorted views, and values. Both Baranyi and Anderson were part of a gothic youth subculture with unique norms, values, and beliefs.

Routine Activity. Opportunity and setting facilitated Baranyi and Anderson's behavior. The initial victim was known to both, and they were able to get her to go with them to an isolated situation with no place managers or social controls. After killing Kimberly Wilson, they were able to go to her home and commit the subsequent murders without anyone noticing. This was possible because they were part of the community and known to the victims. Temptation was high, controls were low, and the setting and opportunity facilitated the behavior. Had someone passed by or intervened in the park (a jogger, park employee, etc.), the setting would not have been conducive to the crime.

Cultural. The most striking explanation for the behavior in this case is that Baranyi and Anderson appeared to have been influenced by cultural factors and artifacts that shaped their cognitive distortions. Their affinity for the gothic lifestyle, black clothing, and malevolent worldview primed and shaped the fantasy to commit murder. Baranyi's fascination with *Highlander*, violent computer games, and role playing, coupled with his own confession about his motivation for murder, suggest that his behavior was media-mediated and largely influenced by cultural factors that led him to the notion that he needed to kill to avoid becoming decadent and to experience something "phenomenal." His media-saturated lifestyle, level of physiological arousal, mood and personality disorder, involvement in a deviant subculture, and association with Anderson converged to make him highly susceptible to (pop) cultural forces that blurred the boundaries between fantasy and reality and served to maintain his cognitive schema and facilitate his behavior.

Phenomenological. Baranyi's confession yields information suggesting that the motivation for the Wilson murders was sheer boredom and the desire for experience of killing. Baranyi told detectives that he wanted to kill someone for years to "experience something truly phenomenal." In an audiotaped confession presented to jurors in court, Baranyi described the sounds and smells he experienced during the murders. He compared beating William and Rose Wilson to "jackhammering out a chunk of concrete," and he remembered apologizing to Julia Wilson as he stabbed her in the hallway. He told police he really didn't have a motive except to say that he was "getting into a lifestyle that was too stagnant and needed change." He said the concept of death fascinated him for years and that he had nothing against Kimberly Wilson except that he considered her selfish. He told police that the smell of the bloody crime scene lingered in his mind in the way his mother remembered the scent of baking chocolate chip cookies from her childhood and said, "Every now and then I'll, I will just, I'll, it'll, it will just come back to me and I'll remember what it smelled like. Then I remember what I did and really regret it."

Developmental and life-course theories can also offer insight into the behavior of Anderson and Baranyi. Available evidence suggests that Anderson was likely a life-course–persistent offender who, had he not been imprisoned, would have gone on to commit crimes throughout his life. Baranyi, on the other hand, may have been influenced at the particular time in his life by his relationship with Anderson, his adolescent propensity to engage in antisocial behavior, and his history of psychiatric illness. Although neither is likely to ever be released from prison, their propensity for violent crime will likely decrease (though perhaps at different rates) as they age.

Summary

To respond to crime, we have to know what it is, who commits it, and why. It is impossible to respond to crime without asking, *"What causes a person to engage in criminal behavior?"* In recent years criminologists have recognized that comprehensive and accurate understanding and prediction of criminal behavior requires theoretical and disciplinary integration. Disciplinary perspectives and criminology knowledge bases can be broken down into six general areas and related research questions:

1. *Biological:* What are the biological roots of criminal behavior?

2. *Psychological:* What psychological factors contributed to this behavior?

3. *Sociological:* What sociological forces contributed to this behavior?

4. *Routine Activity/Opportunity/Ecological:* What situational, contextual, environmental factors provided the setting and opportunity for this crime to occur?

5. *Cultural:* What cultural forces provided the context in which this crime could occur?

6. *Phenomenological:* What personal meaning does the crime hold for the offender?

Each perspective has something to offer in terms of understanding criminal behavior. Some crimes may be better explained by one or another of the perspectives, but integration of all of the perspectives is necessary to fully understand and unravel complexities of criminal behavior.

DISCUSSION QUESTIONS

1. How do contemporary criminologists reconcile the conflicting perspectives of classical and positivist schools of criminology? Explain.

2. What is *interdisciplinary criminology*? Define and discuss the ways in which criminologists have attempted to integrate theoretical perspectives.

3. This chapter divides the different theories of crime into six distinct theoretical perspectives. Explain each and discuss the strengths and weaknesses of this framework for making sense of the different theories of crime.

4. Discuss the contributions of developmental and life-course criminology to the study of criminal behavior.

5. The Baranyi and Anderson case was used in this chapter to illustrate the application of different theoretical perspectives to explain a criminal event that involved criminal behavior committed by two individuals. Select a more recent case example and apply the theories to the offense behavior. Does one or another theoretical perspective do better or worse in contributing to our understanding of the offense? Does any one theory explain all aspects of the behavior? Does more than one theory explain any one aspect of the criminal behavior?

On Your Own: Log on to the Web-based student study site at http://www.sagepub .com/helfgottstudy/ for the URL links in the Web Exercises, study aids such as review quizzes, and research recommendations including links to journal articles specifically selected for this book.

WEB EXERCISES

1. Take the CrimeTheory.com survey: http://www.crimetheory.com/Stuff/timepage.htm. Which theories of crime do your views most correspond with?

2. Read Greg Barak's "Integrative Theories, Integrating Criminologies" on CritCrim.org: http://critcrim.org/critpapers/barak_integrative.htm. What are your thoughts on interdisciplinary criminology. Is a true integrative theory of criminal behavior possible?

3. Sampson and Laub's (2005) "A Life-Course View of the Development of Crime" is available at http://www.aapss.org/uploads/Annals_Nov_2005_Sampson_Laub.pdf. Read the article and discuss what life-course criminology can and cannot say about crime. What, if anything, is missing from this theory to be a truly integrative approach to understanding criminal behavior?

4. Read "Gothic Murders" by Gary Boynton in *Crime Magazine:* http://crimemagazine .com/gothic.htm. After reading more of the details from the Baranyi and Anderson case, what can you add to the interdisciplinary analysis of this case?

Typologies of Crime and Mental Disorders

There are two types of people in this world, good and bad. The good sleep better, but the bad seem to enjoy the waking hours much more.

—Woody Allen

Have you ever heard someone say, "There are two types of people in this world . . ."? If you have, then you have some understanding of what a typology is. To make the world manageable, human beings mentally organize the world into categories. In order to comprehend the world we

> . . . reduce the infinite variety of life to categories. We construct images or concepts in our attempt to "know" the world around us. These constructs are a reduction of our experiences, a reduction that treats occurrences as if they were similar, recurrent and general. Phenomena thus become comparable, and comparison is the beginning of scientific and philosophical reflection (Clinard, Quinney, & Wildeman, 1994, p. 1).

Whether you are fully conscious of it or not, from the moment you wake up in the morning to the moment you go to sleep at night, you are observing, categorizing, and classifying the world around you: good/bad, rich/poor, optimist/pessimist, strong/weak, and so on.

What Is a Typology?

Typology construction is a fundamental component of human cognition and scientific investigation. *A typology is an abstract category or class (or set of categories or classes) consisting of characteristics organized around a common principle relevant to a particular analysis.* Actually, most people (and scientists) classify the world into more than two categories. Cognitive psychologists tell us that human beings naturally process information in manageable chunks (Bourne, Dominowski, Loftus, & Healy, 1986). To make information meaningful, we need to organize the stimuli around us into categories or units of information:

> The identification, organization, and integration of elements that share common characteristics has been shown to be an essential component of perception and cognition. The critical function of classification in scientific investigation mirrors its central role in general cognition. (Knight & Prentky, 1990, p. 23)

Thus, scientists do the same thing that the rest of us do on a more systematic and complex level. Biologists classify plants, zoologists classify animals, astronomers classify planets, chemists classify chemicals, pathologists classify diseases, anthropologists classify cultures, psychologists classify mental disorders, and criminologists classify crimes and criminals.

One way to think of a typology is that it is theory made manageable. On a practical level, typologies provide information with which to make decisions, policies, practices, and laws. Let's say you theorize that the world is made up of good and evil. As a result, you find yourself grouping people into categories of "safe" versus "dangerous" as you go about your day. Your general theory and applied typology provides you with information that guides your decision making and actions. When you walk down a city street you look around—you see "safe" and "dangerous" types of people, based on whatever personal criteria you've developed to (unscientifically) make this determination. When a "safe" person walks your way, you may smile and say hello. When a "dangerous" person crosses your path, you will probably take action to avoid this person by looking away or crossing the street. You constantly ask yourself the question, "What type of person is this?" in order to place people into their respective boxes so you can guide your actions accordingly.

At the institutional level, a similar activity takes place, though the classification process is guided, to a greater extent, by the scientific method and a theoretical knowledge base. Scientists must simplify complex theories so that they can be applied in everyday policy and practice. In hospitals, doctors diagnose and classify diseases in order to treat patients. In schools, students are tested and grouped as "average" or "accelerated" in order to place them into appropriate educational programs. In mental health settings, individuals are diagnosed with particular mental disorders such as "bipolar disorder" or "anxiety disorder" or "antisocial personality disorder" in order to determine appropriate treatment. In the criminal justice system, offenders are classified into types such as "violent" and "nonviolent" to make determinations regarding a range of criminal justice responses.

Most citizens and policymakers recognize that quick and easy solutions are rarely possible and real people don't fit neatly into theoretical boxes. Typologies are often based on complex theories and statistical analyses. In the criminal justice system, where critical public safety decisions have to be made every day, however, social science research has to be accessible to nonscientists. "Impelled by a public desire for simple descriptions and explanations on the one hand, and the academic pursuit of accuracy on the other, social scientists often straddle the proverbial fence between parsimony and complexity" (Miethe & McCorkle, 2001, p. 1). *Typologies are theoretical frameworks that can be practically applied to organize, classify, and make sense of the wide range of behaviors that violate the law.*

Typologies not only reduce phenomena to more systematic observation, they also help in formulating hypotheses and guiding research. "While types may emerge from theory, they are also instrumental in the reformation and expansion of theory"(Clinard et al., 1994, p. 2). Understanding the characteristics of a particular type is the "keystone of theory building and the cornerstone of intervention. It provides a pivotal underpinning for research on a population and is an essential prerequisite for determining the optimum response of a society to deviance" (Knight & Prentky, 1990, p. 23). Typologies guide research by formulating hypotheses based on the characteristics of specific types, giving characteristics an empirical interpretation, and incorporating a special case into a more comprehensive theory (Clinard et al., 1994).

In the criminal justice system, decisions have to be made efficiently and effectively regardless of the current state of the research. Social scientists are charged with explaining and describing the complex world of crime in simple terms for practical purposes. Criminal justice policymakers, practitioners, attorneys, jurors, and citizens have to know something about how offenders whose behavior falls into one or another category of crime are alike and different in order to meaningfully respond to crime. Police need to know how to deal with different types of suspects to guide investigations, attorneys need this information to argue guilt or innocence, judges and juries need it to evaluate mitigating and aggravating factors in sentencing, correctional officials need to know about the nature of the offender groups under their care for purposes of treatment and management and determining which offenders pose more or less risk to public safety in making release decisions, and communities need this information to implement crime prevention strategies and to better meet the needs of victims.

Typologies inform real-world criminal justice policy and practice and influence popular understanding of complex concepts. For theory to be applied it has to be meaningful and understandable to a wide range of people, including citizens, policymakers, attorneys, judges, law enforcement officers, and correctional staff and administrators. And when the criminal justice system applies theory in policy and practice, official classification systems, terminology, and concepts often make their way into everyday discourse informing the public about how offenders should be viewed, treated, and dealt with:

> When the penal system adopts a particular conception of criminals and criminality, or a specific way of classifying prisoners, or a particular psychology of motivation or reform; or when it begins to use a particular vocabulary to describe offenders and to characterize their conduct, such conceptions and vocabularies are never confined to the in-house activities of expert practitioners. Instead they feed back into the wider society, and frequently enter into

conventional wisdom and general circulation. Terms such as "degenerate," "feeble-minded," "imbecile," "delinquent," "kleptomaniac," "psychopath," and "career criminal" quickly become common currency after only a few years of official use, as did the associated vocabularies of "treatment" and "rehabilitation." (Garland, 1990, p. 257)

The following are some examples of how information about (or references to) criminal typologies make their way into public discourse:

- *"The judge described him at the time as a 'professional criminal' who showed no remorse for his actions and had little chance of being rehabilitated"* (news article from *Las Vegas Review Journal* on Dennis Nikrasch who masterminded one of the biggest slot machine cheating scams in Nevada history; Greer, 1998).

- *"Police have rated Vasquez as a **Level III Sex Offender** based on his history. Because of the number of offenses he committed against his children and his failing to participate in treatment, he is rated as a high risk to reoffend"* (Bellingham, Washington, Police Department Sex Offender Notification flyer posted on department Web site; Bellingham Police Department, 2002).

- *"Experts at top-security Rampton hospital have diagnosed Ian Huntley as a **psychopath** who 'feels nothing' after the murders of Holly Wells and Jessica Chapman. Psychiatrists believe the double child killer, who showed no emotion as he was jailed for life yesterday, has no mercy and no guilt."* (news article on UK double murderer Ian Huntley; Yates, Shaw, & McGurran, 2003).

- *" . . . these two young people were not 'natural' born killers, but manipulated '**copycat**' killers. . . . Yes, such 'copycats' are responsible for their crimes"* (in reference to Sarah Edmonson and Benjamin Darrus, who went on a murder spree after repeatedly watching the film *Natural Born Killers*; Reisman, 1999).

- *"The prosecution wrapped up its case on Monday before the court in Kassel after a psychiatrist testified on Friday that Meiwes, while **criminally perverted**, is **legally sane**— bolstering the defence's hopes that he will one day be a free man again"* (news article about Armin Meiwes, a self-professed cannibal who murdered a Berlin computer engineer who consented to be mutilated, slaughtered, and eaten; News 24.com, 2004).

- *"You do not want to challenge or enrage **this type of rapist [Anger Retaliatory]**. . . . You could try to escape. If you cannot get away or incapacitate the assailant, it's best to submit and try to limit the level of violence of the assault to the extent that you can"* (forensic psychologist Robert Geffner, founder and president of the Family Violence and Sexual Assault Institute of San Diego, California, on what to do if confronted by an Anger Retaliatory rapist on the *Women's Firearm Network Website*; Women's Firearm Network, 2000).

These are just a fraction of the ways in which information about offender types enter public discourse. Many (if not most) news articles about crime and information provided to the public by criminal justice agencies (e.g., sex offender notifications) refer to particular criminal types in statements about how such information should be used. Though many references to offender types are not scientifically based or originated from pop culture (e.g., "copycat crime"), popular images of crime often make their way into scholarly research and play a central role in shaping crime control policy (Baily & Hale, 1998; Ferrell & Sanders, 1995).

Mental Disorders and Criminal Behavior

Many high-profile (and everyday) cases that don't make it into the news have involved the intersection of mental disorder and criminal behavior. Mental illness is just one factor that may play a role in some incidents and types of criminal behavior. However, the overlap between mental disorder and criminal behavior and the fact that both conditions reflect human behavior or mental condition that crosses the line of statistical, psychological, or social deviance warrant attention to the relationship between the two concepts and review of typologies of mental disorders as they relate to typologies of crime. Virginia Tech gunman Seung-Hui Cho, who killed 32 students and faculty members in April 2007 before killing himself, had a history of mental illness and had expressed suicidal thoughts. Andrea Yates, who murdered her five young children in Texas in 2001, had suffered from depression and psychosis and been treated for psychiatric problems prior to the murders. John Hinkley, who attempted to assassinate Ronald Reagan in 1981, had a history of depression and was determined "not guilty by reason of insanity" after his defense attorneys successfully argued that his fixation with the film *Taxi Driver* and inability to distinguish between reality and fantasy indicated psychosis. This list could go on and on, and beyond these extreme cases are an enormous number of public order offenses such as loitering, vagrancy, illegal drug use, and public drunkenness that are largely rooted in mental illness.

Mental disorder and criminal behavior are distinct concepts that sometimes overlap. The concept of "mental disorder" is problematic for a number of reasons. The term implies a distinction between mental and physical disorder that ignores the connection between the mental and physical, and the term is defined in different ways by different people—some limit the term to the major clinical disorders such as schizophrenia and mood disorders, others include the personality disorders, and others use the term as a wastebasket category for all forms of mental abnormality whether or not the condition is clinically diagnosable. "No definition adequately specifies precise boundaries for the concept of 'mental disorder'" (APA, 2000, p. xxx). Thus when people speak of "mental disorder," this term encompasses an enormous range of human behavioral symptoms and conditions, from everyday problems in living to severe psychopathological disturbances.

Compounding the problem of understanding the relationship between mental illness and crime are the conflicting goals of the mental health and criminal justice systems. According to Blackburn (1993, p. 246), concerns about the "'psychiatrisation' of crime . . . have been paralleled by concerns over the 'criminalisation' of mental disorder." Further difficulties have arisen in arriving at consensus on the definitions of *mental disorder* and *mental illness* as clinical or scientific concepts. Though mental disorder and crime are conceptually distinct, psychiatric illness and mental disorders are often implicated as influences in criminal behavior. In the case of personality disorders, specifically antisocial personality disorder and psychopathy, a strong empirical relationship has been established between these disorders and violent criminal behavior.[1] Although most people who are mentally ill do not commit crimes and many serious mental illnesses render a person unable to form *mens rea* (criminal intent), which prohibits legal sanctions in the criminal justice system, some research suggests that certain risk factors, some of which may be associated with specific mental disorders, are linked to criminal behavior and that, on an individual level, mental disorder in conjunction with other influences may be a contributing factor in criminal behavior (Andrews & Bonta, 2006; Blackburn, 1993; Hodgins, 1993; Monahan et al., 2001).

To understand the role of mental disorder and crime, it is important to recognize the overlaps between the concepts of mental illness and criminal behavior and to have an understanding of both typologies of mental disorders and criminal behaviors. *What are mental disorders? How are they classified? What are the traits and symptoms associated with the different types of mental disorders across the spectrum of human psychopathology? Are symptoms of particular mental disorders risk factors for some but not other types of crime? How do risk factors associated with specific types of mental disorders interact with other types of risk factors (e.g., biological, sociological, phenomenological, situational/opportunity, cultural)?* A strong foundation in psychopathology and the classification of mental disorders is important for understanding (and constructing) typologies of criminal behavior.

The *Diagnostic and Statistical Manual of Mental Disorders*

The typology approach to understanding human behavior is best typified by the *Diagnostic and Statistical Manual of Mental Disorders,* commonly referred to as the *DSM.* The current edition of the *DSM* is the *DSM, 4th Edition–Text Revision (DSM-IV-TR).* The *DSM,* published by the American Psychiatric Association, is a categorical classification system of mental disorders for the purpose of communication, diagnoses, education, research, and treatment. The *DSM* divides mental disorders into types based on sets of criteria with defining features. The categorical approach used in the *DSM* is based on the "traditional method of organizing and transmitting information in everyday life" and the fundamental approach used in medical diagnosis (APA, 2000, p. xxxi). Disorders in the *DSM* are viewed as a "clinically significant behavioral or psychological syndrome or pattern that occurs in an individual and is associated with present distress . . . or disability . . . or with a significantly increased risk of suffering death, pain, disability, or an important loss of freedom" (APA, 2000, p. xxxi). The authors of the *DSM* acknowledge the limitations of the categorical model (heterogeneity of diagnostic classes, lack of clear boundaries between types), and state that there is no assumption of complete homogeneity with the view that the categorical model is superior to the dimensional perspective in clinical practice or stimulating research.

Historically, the initial impetus for developing a classification of mental disorders was the need to collect statistical information. The first attempt to collect data about mental illness in the United States began with one category in 1840 ("idiocy/insanity") and was expanded by 1880 to seven categories (dementia, dipsomania, epilepsy, mania, melancholia, monomania, and paresis). In 1952 the first edition of the *DSM* was published based on the *International Classification of Diseases, Sixth Edition (ICD-6),* published by the World Health Organization (WHO). To date, six editions of the DSM have been published (*DSM-I, DSM-II, DSM-III, DSM-III-R, DSM-IV,* and *DSM-IV-TR*). The *DSM* classifications are empirically based and developed through a three-stage empirical process that included comprehensive literature reviews, reanalysis of already-collected data sets, and issue-focused clinical field trials.

The *DSM* is organized around a multiaxial system that involves assessment on several axes. Each axis represents a different domain of information that may help a clinician create a treatment plan and predict treatment outcome. The *DSM-IV-TR* consists of five axes:

Axis I—Clinical Disorders
Other conditions that may be a focus of clinical attention

Axis II—Personality Disorders
Mental retardation

Axis III—General Medical Conditions

Axis IV—Psychosocial and Environmental Problems

Axis V—Global Assessment of Functioning (APA, 2000, p. 27)

The distinction between Axis I and Axis II in the *DSM* reflects the recognition that there is a distinction between mental illness and personality and that the two are not mutually exclusive and frequently coexist (Blackburn, 1993). Clinical disorders include schizophrenia, substance-related disorders, mood disorders, anxiety disorders, dissociative disorders, sexual and gender identity disorders, eating disorders, sleep disorders, adjustment disorders, and disorders first diagnosed in infancy, childhood, or adolescence such as learning disorders, conduct disorder, and attention deficit/hyperactivity disorder. Personality disorders are divided into subcategories—Cluster A, Cluster B, and Cluster C. Individuals with Cluster A disorders (paranoid, schizoid, and schizotypal) appear odd or eccentric. Individuals diagnosed with Cluster B disorders (antisocial, borderline, histrionic, narcissistic) appear dramatic, emotional, or erratic. Individuals with Cluster C disorders (avoidant, dependant, obsessive-compulsive) appear fearful or anxious (one way to think of the clusters is that Cluster A individuals act odd, Cluster B individuals act out, and Cluster C individuals act afraid).

A number of Axis I disorders have been associated with criminal behavior including substance use disorders, sexual disorders, childhood disorders such as conduct disorder, attention deficit/hyperactivity disorder, and oppositional defiant disorder. Impulse control disorders such as intermittent explosive disorder, kleptomania, pyromania, and pathological gambling are disorders that clearly overlap with criminal behavior; however, Blackburn (1993) argues that

> the validity of impulse control disorders as a distinct class is questionable on conceptual grounds. An "impulse" is a circular inference of cause from the behaviour it supposedly impels, and "failure to resist and impulse" is similarly inferred from the observation that an act has been performed. (p. 74)

This (and antisocial personality disorder) is an example of what Blackburn calls the psychiatrization of crime, whereby the domain of social deviance (behavior) is confounded with personal deviance (underlying traits). Axis II disorders, in particular the

Axis II, Cluster B disorders—antisocial personality disorder, borderline personality disorder, histrionic personality disorder, and narcissistic personality disorder—have also been linked to criminal behavior. A number of researchers have noted that psychopathy may be more appropriately constructed as a higher-order category comprising criteria from all four Axis II, Cluster B disorders (Blackburn, 1993; Wulach, 1988).

The Relationship Between Mental Disorder and Crime

The relationship between mental disorder and crime has long been examined with conflicting findings. Research in the early 1900s found that the criminality rate of the mentally ill was the same as or lower than that of the general population. Later studies in the 1970s found a higher rate of criminal behavior among the mentally ill compared to the general population. The deinstitutionalization of the mentally ill in the 1960s led to an increased percentage of offenders in correctional settings diagnosed as mentally ill. More recent research has found a relationship between certain mental illnesses such as substance abuse disorders, but major mental illnesses such as schizophrenia and affective disorders show a marginal relationship to criminal behavior (Modestin & Ammann, 1995). However, Belfrage (1998) found an overrepresentation of criminality in a sample of mental patients diagnosed with schizophrenia, affective psychosis, or paranoia who were discharged from mental hospitals in Stockholm, Sweden, in the 1980s and followed up 10 years later.

Other research has examined the relationship between specific Axis I (e.g., schizophrenia, substance use disorders) and Axis II or other personality disorders (e.g., antisocial personality disorder, borderline disorder, psychopathy), and some studies have looked at the relationship between Axis I and Axis II disorders and different crime types. For example, Tengström et al. (2004) found that psychopathic traits, not substance abuse, are associated with criminal offending and that there was no difference in nonschizophrenics and schizophrenics who scored high on psychopathy between those with and those without substance use disorders. An interesting study by Stuart et al. (2006) reported results on the prevalence of psychopathology among 103 women arrested for domestic violence in Rhode Island. The study found that the women arrested for domestic violence had high rates of posttraumatic stress disorder depression, generalized anxiety disorder, panic disorder, substance use disorders (Axis I disorders) and borderline personality disorder, and antisocial personality disorder (Axis II, Cluster B disorders).

The Macarthur Study of Mental Disorder and Violence has been described as the best designed study ever done on violence risk assessment, involving over 1,000 psychiatric patients. The study examined the relationship between 134 potential risk factors (identified from theory and research on violence and mental disorder and clinical experience) and subsequent violence in a large sample of people diagnosed with mental disorders. Monahan et al. (2001) concluded:

> A historical view of the study of violence by persons with mental illness reveals a determined quest for the single variable (or sometimes a small set of variables) that will determine whether a person will act aggressively toward others. Once in hand, knowledge of this

variable would lead inexorably to strategies for prediction or control. . . . Among the causative factors postulated at one point or another have been electrical discharges in the temporal lobe; physical abuse in childhood; a vulnerability to shame; overcontrol of violent impulses or its opposite; the failure to inhibit their expression; and most recently, for the people with mental illness in particular, the presence of one or another set of psychotic symptoms. . . .

Of the scores of variables whose relationship with violence we studied in this project, many (indeed most) had some significant association with future violence. None of these relationships was sufficiently strong, however, for it to be fairly said that a given variable constituted the cause of violence, even for a subgroup of patients. Nor . . . does any single concatenation of variables account for violence as a unitary phenomenon. Our data are most consistent with the view that the propensity for violence is the result of the accumulation of risk factors, no one of which is either necessary or sufficient for a person to behave aggressively toward others. People will be violent by virtue of the presence or absence of different sets of risk factors. There is no single path in a person's life that leads to an act of violence. (p. 142)

While the Macarthur study focused specifically on actuarial prediction of violence in a psychiatric population, it is clear from this and other research (e.g., Andrews & Bonta, 2006) that it is not the mental disorder itself that is linked to crime, but the behavioral symptoms and traits that make up the disorder that are, in conjunction with other factors, risk factors for criminal behavior. It is also important to keep in mind that certain risk factors associated with certain disorders may converge with other factors in such a way as to produce certain types of criminal behaviors but not others.

Criminal Typologies: Theory and Purpose

Criminal typologies are necessary to understand, identify, and respond to crime. In the criminal justice system, knowing how a rapist differs from a pedophile, whether an individual with a history of residential burglary is likely to escalate to armed robbery, or whether a violent offender is too dangerous to release requires knowledge of the distinct nature, extent, features, and dynamics of types and subtypes of crimes as well as how offenses and offenders differ across crime categories. The criminal justice system cannot respond to crime with a "one size fits all" approach. Sanctions, management strategies, treatment approaches, and public safety policies and practices are highly dependent on differentiation of types of crimes and criminals.

Typologies differ with respect to *theoretical foundation* and *purpose*. Typologies of crime and criminals have emerged from legalistic, sociological, psychological, biological, or multiple (interdisciplinary) perspectives. They can be offender-based, victim-based, situation-context–based, or organized around multiple traits. Levels of theoretical sophistication and complexity and the purpose for which the typologies are constructed and applied also differ. Three main purposes of crime and criminals typologies exist:

1. *Management.* Classification in correctional settings, prediction of dangerousness, and implementation of measures to enhance public safety

2. *Treatment.* Determining the appropriate treatment and rehabilitative programming to target particular needs of types and subtypes of offenders

3. *Understanding.* Knowledge of nature and dynamics of specific types and subtypes of offenders at a level of specificity not possible with general theories of crime (Blackburn, 1993)

Typologies are also used for other purposes such as law enforcement investigations (referred to as "criminal profiling" or "offender profiling"), in conjunction with victim typologies to determine the best way to assist victims, and for crime prevention.

The question, *"What type of person are we dealing with?"* is of central importance at every stage in the criminal justice process. In law enforcement, decisions have to be made regarding investigative strategy, interviewing and interrogation of suspects, hostage negotiations, and officer safety. These decisions depend on the type of suspect officers are dealing with. *At the law enforcement stage of the process, "who, what, and why" are crucial to criminal profiling and the investigative process* (Douglas, Burgess, Burgess, & Ressler, 1997). At pretrial, adjudication, and sentencing, decisions have to be made about charges, mitigating and aggravating circumstances, type of defense (e.g., insanity), and sentence severity. *At the courts/sentencing stage, the "what and why" continue to be important. In corrections and reentry, the focus is on "what now?"* with treatment, management, release decisions, community supervision, and public safety decisions dependent on the type of offender under consideration. Knowledge of the differences and similarities within and between different types of offenders can also yield information that can be used to develop crime prevention strategies (Miethe & McCorkle, 2001) and appropriate treatment and outreach programs for victims (Silverman, Kalick, Bowie, & Edbril, 1988; see Figure 3.1).

❖ Figure 3.1   The Use of Typologies in the Criminal Justice System

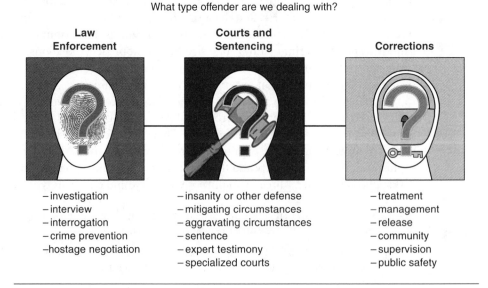

What type offender are we dealing with?

Law Enforcement	Courts and Sentencing	Corrections
– investigation	– insanity or other defense	– treatment
– interview	– mitigating circumstances	– management
– interrogation	– aggravating circumstances	– release
– crime prevention	– sentence	– community
– hostage negotiation	– expert testimony	– supervision
	– specialized courts	– public safety

Examples of Different "Types" of Typologies

Biological

Biological typologies are rooted in biological theories and organized around features such as genetics, evolutionary development, and body type. One of the earliest typologies was developed by Cesare Lombroso, often referred to as the "father of positivist criminology." Lombroso, an Italian physician is best known for his work *L'Uomo delinquente (The Criminal Man),* published in 1876, in which he offered a typology of criminals based on evolutionary development and physical traits. Lombroso contended that different types of criminals differ (by type and degree) in terms of genetic evolution, physical traits, and criminal propensities along a graduated scale from "born criminal" to "normal individual." According to Lombroso, there are "born criminals," "criminaloids," "occasional" and "habitual" offenders, and so on (Lombroso, 2003).

William Sheldon's body type theory is another example of a biological typology. Sheldon constructed a physical and mental typology based on embryology and the physiology of development composed of three body types—the *endomorph, mesomorph,* and *ectomorph.* According to Sheldon, the endomorph is characterized by roundness, short limbs, velvety skin, and tendency to put on fat. In terms of temperament, the endomorph is *viscerotonic*—a comfortable, generally relaxed, extroverted "softie." The mesomorph is characterized by predominance of muscles and bone, large trunk, heavy chest, and large hands and wrists. The mesomorph is *somotonic*—active, dynamic, assertive, and aggressive. The ectomorph is characterized by predominance of skin and limbs, and is lean, fragile, and delicate with a small face, fine hair, sharp nose. The ectomorph is *cerebrotonic*—introverted, sensitive to noise and distractions, socially anxious, and expresses physical complaints and troubled by allergies and skin problems. Sheldon's studies and later research by the Gluecks (1956) revealed that mesomorphs were more likely to possess traits associated with aggression, delinquency, and crime (Vold, Bernard, & Snipes, 2002).

The r/K selection theory is an example of a biological typology. This is an evolutionary theory that explains different evolutionary survival strategies. Based on this theory, r-selected types produce a large number of crime-prone offspring each of whom is unlikely to survive to adulthood. K-selected types produce fewer offspring, investing heavily in each one, each of whom are likely to survive to adulthood and not likely to be crime-prone (Ellis, 2005).

Legalistic

Legalistic typologies are organized around violations of the criminal law. Legalistic typologies are the oldest and most frequently used classifications of crimes and criminals (Clinnard, Quinney, & Wildeman, 1994). An example of a simple legalistic typology is the distinction in the criminal law between "misdemeanors" and "felonies." The primary organizing feature for the misdemeanor-felony typology is seriousness of offense, with felonies involving imprisonment of more than one year. A more complex example of a legalistic typology is the FBI's Uniform Crime Reports (UCR), which classifies offenses based on Part I or Part II offenses in terms of severity of offense, but is more complex because it breaks down each type into multiple subtypes. Another common legalistic typology groups crime in terms of "crimes against the person," "crimes against property," and "crimes against public order." The organizing principle behind this typology is type of victimization (Miethe & McCorkle, 2001).

The FBI's UCR is the most widely accepted legalistic typology. The UCR classifies crimes in terms of *Part I* and *Part II* Offenses. Part I offenses include the following crime categories:

- Murder and Nonnegligent Manslaughter
- Forcible Rape
- Robbery
- Aggravated Assault
- Burglary
- Larceny/Theft
- Motor-Vehicle Theft
- Arson

Part II of the UCR includes less serious crimes such as drug offenses, sex crimes and assaults (that do not involve Part I offenses), fraud, embezzlement, vandalism, disorderly conduct, possession of stolen property, commercialized vice, weapons violations, forgery and counterfeiting, gambling, driving under the influence, liquor law violations, vagrancy, and traffic violations. The UCR Part I make up what is referred to as the *Crime Index*. The Crime Index is the average of all Part I offenses. It provides a measure of crime often reported in the form of the crime rate (x number of offenses per 100,000 people), which can be compared over time and across geographical location.

Sociological

Sociological typologies are based on sociological theory and organized around social and cultural interactions and social context. Sociological typologies classify offenders and offenses based on features such as place of crime, relationship to victim, and the activities involved in the crime. Early sociological typologies developed in the 19th century distinguished between "professional criminals" (who made a living through crime), "accidental criminals" (who stumbled into crime), and "habitual criminals" (who engaged in crime for diverse, more inherent reasons). Other sociological typologies include those based on organizational sophistication of the offender and a combination of background (e.g., social class, family background, peer associations) and definitional factors (e.g., nature of offense, offender self-concept, and attitude toward social control agencies). An example of a sociological typology is Gibbon's role-career model in which he identified 20 offender types based on background and definitional factors including *amateur shoplifters, violent sex offenders, psychopathic assaultists, white-collar criminals, automobile thieves—joyriders, semiprofessional property criminals, professional thieves, white-collar criminals, naïve check forgers, incest offenders,* and others (Clinnard, Quinney, & Wildeman, 1994).

Sociological typologies of offenders have been used to describe prisoner adaptation. For example, Irwin (1980) described three types of inmates and prison adaptive modes: *doing time* (avoiding trouble and getting out as soon as possible), *jailing* (immersion in the prison world), and *gleaners* (inmates attached to the formal institutional rules who tried to improve themselves by using available prison resources). Other sociological typologies applied to prisoners are organized around the prison hierarchy. For example, *right guys* are at the top of the hierarchy because they adhere to the convict code, *politicians, characters,* and *prison toughs* are considered upper middle class, *square johns* the middle class, and *prison queens, rapos,* and *punks* the lower class (Silverman, 2001). These sociological typologies are organized around status, behaviors, and interactions between inmates.

Sociological typologies can also be based on situation and context. Hickey (2002) offers a *mobility typology* of serial murderers. This typology classifies serial murderers in terms of their mobility in the commission of crime. *Traveling* serial killers are those who travel from place to place such as Ted Bundy and Henry Lee Lucas and Otis Toole. *Local* killers commit their crimes in their own neighborhoods and communities such as the Seattle area Green River Killer Gary Ridgway. *Place-specific* killers murder in their own homes or places of employment such as Jeffrey Dahmer, who murdered in his own home, or Christine Falling, who murdered children she babysat. Other typologies are organized around the offender-victim relationship. For example, researchers have studied the differences between stranger, acquaintance, date, and partner rape (Cowan, 2000) and offenders' method of "confidence" versus "blitz" attack (Silverman et al., 1988).

The purposes of sociological typologies are theoretical understanding and social policy development. Knowing the social and situational-contextual factors that distinguish particular categories of crimes and criminals is crucial to theoretical understanding and policy and practice. For example, studies involving rapist typologies have found that victims of confidence attacks need different services than victims of blitz attacks because they engage in a greater degree of self-blame, which needs to be addressed through aftercare services. Knowledge about the different types of serial killers provides insight that may aid law enforcement investigations. And understanding the types of prisoners that emerge through interactions in the prison subculture is important for informal and formal correctional management strategies.

Psychological

Psychological typologies are based on psychological theories and organized around personality or some other individual psychological feature (e.g., mental illness, intelligence, cognition, psychodynamic development, motivation). Examples of psychological typologies include the *Diagnostic and Statistical Manual of Mental Disorders,* the *Crime Classification Manual* developed by the FBI's National Center for the Analysis of Violent Crime, the distinction between psychopathy and other types of personality disorders and conditions, and the Massachusetts Treatment Center rapist and child molester typologies.

The purposes of psychological typologies are theoretical understanding and correctional management and treatment. Sometimes psychological theories are also used by law enforcement to better understand the nature and dynamics of offenders for investigative, hostage negotiation, or public safety purposes. Crime is a behavioral symptom that can be the product of a broad range of underlying conditions. For treatment programs to be successful in correctional populations, they must target the risks, needs, and responsivity of particular types of offenders (Andrews & Bonta, 2003; Dowden & Andrews, 2004). Furthermore, correctional management often depends on and can be enhanced by identification of offender types theoretically rooted in psychological theories.

A classic example of a psychological typology can be found in Hervey Cleckley's (1941) *The Mask of Sanity.*[2] *The Mask of Sanity* brought attention to the phenomenon of psychopathy, in particular to the notion of noncriminal psychopaths. Cleckley's work describes what is known in the literature as the classic conception of psychopathy. Cleckley proposed the notion of psychopathy as a taxon characterized by 16 distinct characteristics:

1. Superficial charm and good intelligence
2. Absence of delusions
3. Absence of nervousness
4. Unreliability
5. Untruthfulness and insincerity
6. Lack of remorse and shame
7. Inadequately motivated antisocial behavior
8. Failure to learn from experience and poor judgment
9. Pathologic egocentricity and incapacity for love
10. Lack of affect
11. Loss of insight
12. Unresponsiveness to interpersonal relations
13. Fantastic and uninviting behavior (with and without alcohol)
14. Suicide rarely carried out
15. Impersonal, trivial, poorly integrated sex life
16. Failure to follow any life plan (Cleckley, 1941, p. 204)

Cleckley contended that the primary or true psychopath can be distinguished from all other psychological conditions by the *defect in affect*, or the inability to feel, and contrasted psychopaths with other types and conditions including psychotics, psychoneurotics, mental defectives, sexual deviants, ordinary criminals, geniuses, and hedonists. Cleckley's work has been the foundation for much of the contemporary research on psychopathy (discussed in detail in Chapter 4), distinguishing the condition as a unique clinical entity (or type) with implications for correctional classification, management, treatment, and risk assessment.

Lykken (1995) offers a classification of criminal types rooted in psychological theory. He proposes three types of offenders: *normal offenders, psychotic offenders*, and *antisocial personalities*. Lykken's criminal types are organized with respect to the level of pathological disturbance present. Normal offenders are not psychopathologically disordered. Their crimes include normal people reacting atypically to provocative situations (e.g., passion murder), innocent people who have been wrongly convicted, and "career" or white-collar criminals who commit crime because of life circumstance and opportunity. Psychotic offenders are out of touch with reality and, although most are not violent, may commit crime when they fail to take their medication. Antisocial personalities are the largest and most complex type, characterized by a "persisting disposition toward antisocial behavior" (p. 21). Within the antisocial personalities category, Lykken distinguishes three subtypes (sociopathic, psychopathic, character neurosis), each broken down into further designations.

Another example of a psychological/motivational typology is the *power assertive, power reassurance, anger retaliatory, anger excitation* rape/sexual homicide typology originally developed by Groth (1979), expanded by Knight and Prentky (1987, 1990), and applied to sexual homicide by Keppel and Walter (1999). This typology is based on offender motivation and behavioral features and is used in law enforcement investigation for investigation, interview/interrogation, and case linkage (Turvey, 1999, 2002). The following are the types of rape/sexual homicide included in this typology:

- *Power Assertive (PA)* (rape planned–murder unplanned, power driven, increasing aggression to control victim)
- *Power Reassurance (PR)* (rape planned–murder unplanned, power driven, fantasy acted out while seeking reassurance from victim)
- *Anger Retaliatory (AR)* (rape and murder planned, anger/revenge driven, may select symbolic victim)
- *Anger Excitation (AE)* (rape and murder planned, anger driven, prolonged torture, exploitation, mutilation that energizes killer's fantasy)

The FBI's *Crime Classification Manual* (CCM) was modeled after the *Diagnostic Manual of Mental Disorders* as a catalog of violent crime (Douglas et al., 1992). The CCM can be considered a psychological typology in the sense that it, like the PA, PR, AR, AE typology, is based on motivational features. The CCM classifies violent crime into three categories—homicide, arson, and rape/sexual assault—based on motivational features of offenses. Offenses are classified based on victimology, crime scene characteristics, staging/nature of offense, and forensic findings. Information is presented for each offense category including distinguishing features of each offense. The FBI is also responsible for the well-known *organized/disorganized typology,* which distinguishes between offenders who leave organized, mixed, or disorganized crime scenes, each type of which possess certain features; that is, whether a crime scene is left organized or disorganized tells something about the offender's criminal sophistication and personality. The organized offender has psychopathic characteristics, needs power and control, and exhibits controlled and organized behaviors during the commission of a crime such as planning and staging, bringing weapons to the scene, and hiding evidence. In contrast, the disorganized offender is said to display characteristics of psychosis; commits crime out of passion, compulsion, frustration, or anxiety; and engages in reactive violence, using whatever objects are found at the scene as weapons. The organized/disorganized typology was developed by FBI profilers from the *National Center for the Analysis of Violent Crime* and based on interviews conducted by FBI agents with incarcerated sexual murderers from 1979 through 1983 (Ressler, Burgess, & Douglas, 1992). The typology has been heavily criticized by a number of authors (Alison, Bennell, Mokros, & Ormerod, 2002; Canter, Alison, Alison, & Wentink, 2004; Godwin, 1998) for being too simplistic, encouraging law enforcement officers to engage in pseudopsychological diagnosis for which they are untrained (Turvey, 1999, 2002); however, the typology has been commonly cited in the history of profiling (Woodworth & Porter, 2001) and is a good example of a typology that attempts to make theory manageable for practical application in the criminal justice system.

Multitrait

Multitrait typologies attempt to combine dimensions of crime into a single typology. Rather than just using a single trait or dimension (e.g., biological, legal, social, psychological), around which types are organized, multitrait typologies incorporate multiple theoretical perspectives and crime dimensions. Clinnard, Quinney, and Wildeman's (1994) *Criminal Behavior Systems* and Miethe and McCorkle's (2001; Miethe, McCorkle, & Listwan, 2006)[3] *Crime Profiles* are examples of multitrait typologies. The purposes of multitrait typologies include theoretical understanding and social policy development, crime prevention, and criminal investigation. Multitrait typologies include multiple dimensions and are theoretically interdisciplinary. Although some biological, psychological, and sociological typologies include other factors (e.g., Meloy's sexual homicide typology is grounded in biological and psychological theories), multitrait typologies attempt to incorporate legalistic, sociological, psychological, and biological dimensions to create a general typology of crime.

Clinard, Quinney, and Wildeman's (1994) multitrait typology is organized around five theoretical dimensions:

1. Legal aspects of selected offenses
2. Criminal career of offender
3. Group support of criminal behavior
4. Correspondence between criminal and legitimate behavior
5. Social reaction and legal processing

The authors construct the following nine theoretical types of criminal behavior in relation to these five dimensions, which are used to explain each type of criminal behavior:

1. Violent personal (including homicide, rape, assault)
2. Occasional property (including forgery, shoplifting, theft)
3. Public order (including prostitution, public drunkenness, vagrancy)
4. Conventional (including larceny, burglary, robbery)
5. Political (including conspiracy, political demonstrations)
6. Occupational (including workplace theft, embezzlement)
7. Corporate (including insider trading, false advertising, environmental pollution)
8. Organized (including racketeering, organized criminal activity in legitimate business)
9. Professional (including counterfeiting, forgery, confidence games)

Although the purpose of Clinnard, Quinney, and Wildeman's typology is primarily theoretical, Miethe and McCorkle (2001) incorporate the routine activity theory into their multitrait typology with direct application for crime prevention. Relying on information from the UCR, the National Crime Victimization Survey (NCVS), local police data, and interviews with offenders, they offer a typology of crime organized around five dimensions:

1. Offenders' criminal careers
2. Offender versatility
3. Level of crime planning
4. Offender motivation
5. Target selection factors

The authors apply these dimensions to each of seven crime categories:

1. Murder and aggravated assault
2. Sexual assault
3. Personal and institutional robbery
4. Residential and nonresidential burglary
5. Motor vehicle theft
6. Occupational and organizational crime
7. Public order crime

Miethe and McCorkle's (2001) typology is unique in that it offers an "anatomy of dangerous persons, places, and situations" (p. 236) with direct implications for crime prevention and public safety strategies.

Meloy (2000) offers an integrative psychobiological sexual homicide typology with biological and psychological features including *DSM* classification, level of psychopathy, physiological arousal, type of aggression, early childhood trauma, among others. This typology can be seen as a multitrait typology because it integrates biological and psychological findings to support a theoretically and empirically based psychobiological typology. The typology distinguishes between two types of sexual homicide offenders—*compulsive* and *catathymic*.[4]

These two types of sexual homicide offenders are distinguished by underlying psychopathology (*DSM* Axis I and II diagnoses, level of psychopathy, attachment pathology), nature of sexual homicide (organized/disorganized), and biological factors (autonomic nervous system) as well as traumatic reinforcers (childhood trauma). Meloy's typology is one of the more sophisticated typologies because it integrates motivational/psychological and biological features and draws from research in biology, psychology, and law enforcement/criminal profiling (see Table 3.1).

How Are Criminal Typologies Constructed?

Scientific advancement depends on "descriptive analytic schemes which identify similarities and differences between the entities comprising the universe of interest"

❖ Table 3.1   Meloy's Sexual Homicide Typology

	Compulsive	Catathymic
Nature of sexual homicide	Organized	Disorganized
Axis I diagnosis	Sexual sadism	Mood disorder
Axis II diagnosis	APD/NPD	Various traits & PDs
Psychopathy	Severe (primary)	Mild-moderate
Attachment pathology	Chronically detached	Attachment hunger
ANS	Hyporeactive	Hyperreactive
Early Trauma	Often absent	Often present

Adapted from J. R. Meloy. (2000). The nature and dynamics of sexual homicide: An integrative review. *Aggression and Violent Behavior, 5,* 1–22.

(Blackburn, 1993, p. 60). *Classifying events or people into types is a necessary function of science, theory development, and professional practice.* The classification of crime and criminals has direct implications for the way offenders are identified and dealt with in the criminal justice system. Scientific typology construction is a systematic activity that differs from everyday classifications that tend to be based on stereotypes and observational errors. Informal and unscientific classification of individuals into groups is problematic because there is potential for stigmatization, stereotyping, and denial of individual uniqueness.

An example of typologies rooted in stereotypes is racial profiling in law enforcement, which involves making predictions about how people behave based on the category to which they are classified using race as the organizing characteristic. *Racial profiling is based on stereotype and stigma, not science.* There is little in the way of theory or empirical research that links particular racial groups to specific types of offenses. Without an empirically established link between race/ethnicity and criminal behavior, the practice of racial profiling by law enforcement threatens the civil rights of citizens who are targeted by police for nothing more than the color of their skin. However, scientifically based typologies that attempt to avoid stereotypes and everyday errors in reasoning are necessary for communication, program development, policy, prediction, and decision making.

Scientific typologies are based on the traditional Linnaean classification of plants:

Attributes, events, or individuals are divided into classes on the basis of a common principle, such as a variation in form or function. Classes are defined by necessary and sufficient criteria of class membership, and assumed to be homogeneous and mutually exclusive. (Blackburn, 1993, p. 61)

Classifications are rarely truly *homogeneous* (the same); most are based on relative homogeneity and the identification of a set of defining criteria that all members of the group share. In the real world there is no such thing as a homogeneous category or type in which all members are the same and possess no features of any other group. For example, all blue-eyed people are not the same nor are they completely different from green- or brown-eyed people. A typology based on eye color would yield groups of people who are similar with respect to the color of their eyes, but the group would be *heterogeneous* (different) with respect to hair color, body type, personality style, economic status, education, and other factors. A typology based on eye color would be useful only to the extent that the categories "blue eyed," "brown eyed," "green eyed," and "hazel eyed" are meaningfully homogeneous. If eye color were predictive of a particular behavior or associated with amenability to a particular approach or treatment, then the typology would be useful—perhaps for suitability for particular contact lenses or a type of eye surgery.

In the social sciences, criminology and psychology in particular, "the systematic study of behavior is based on an ordering of the diversified world of discrete phenomena" (Clinnard, Quinney, & Wildeman, 1994, p. 1). To make sense of the range of human behaviors and conditions, individuals are grouped into types based on shared characteristics (e.g., personality type). Human types may be more appropriately viewed along a continuum or dimension rather than as discrete categories or *taxa*. In other words, most people are a little of this and a little of that, for example, a little narcissistic or a little obsessive compulsive. This is a dimensional view of personality. A taxon is an either/or classification. Pregnancy is an example of a taxon—a person is either pregnant or not. A categorical classification or taxonomy of personality would hold that a person is either narcissistic or not, obsessive-compulsive or not.

Categories or types that are not inherently taxonomic (where there are no clear boundaries) are often formed by empirically grouping those who share features on several dimensions by means of statistical methods such as cluster analysis (Blackburn, 1993). "This preserves naturally occurring interactions between attributes, and yields polythetic categories defined by continuous rather than dichotomous criteria . . . categorical classification in psychiatry frequently imposes artificial boundaries between normality and abnormality" (Blackburn, 1993, p. 61). For example, though you cannot be a little bit pregnant, you can be a little bit psychopathic. Thus, dividing people up into pregnant or not pregnant is a relatively easy task requiring a pregnancy test, but dividing people up into psychopathic or nonpsychopathic types is not so simple and requires assessing particular clusters of traits and behaviors. For example, psychopathic personality disorder is generally assessed with the *Psychopathy Checklist-Revised (PCL-R)*, a 20-item assessment tool that measures level of psychopathy on a 0- to- 40-point scale. A score of 30 or greater is indicative of primary psychopathy, a condition that many researchers suggest is categorically distinct and should be considered a taxon. Does this mean that someone who receives a score of 30 is a psychopath and someone who receives a score of 29 is not? This is a difficult (theoretical, philosophical, and empirical) question that illustrates the artificiality of boundaries separating most psychological (and criminological) "types."

Typologies are constructed in two general ways. First, *ideal types* are inductively constructed based on a subjective clinical impression, for example, if a psychologist were to form the impression that particular personality types exist based on observations in clinical practice or a theorist were to construct a type based on attributes of central concern to a particular theory or to pragmatically combine variables of immediate interest (Blackburn, 1993). This is sometimes referred to as "armchair" theorizing. The ideal type can never be found in reality and "may be conceived as a distortion of the concrete" (Clinnard, Quinney, & Wildeman, 1994, p. 11). Second, *empirical* types are deductively constructed through multivariate statistical methods to describe patterns that exist in the real world (Blackburn, 1993; Clinnard, Quinney, & Wildeman, 1994). For example, hierarchical cluster analysis is used to specify clusters of cases based on their similarity across a number of variables. This allows examination of each cluster to reveal salient features (Silverman, Kalick, Bowie, & Edbril, 1988), yielding a distinct empirical type. However, the distinction between ideal and empirical typologies is somewhat arbitrary. Ideal types are not the result of induction alone, nor are empirical types formed solely through deduction. "To conceive of types as developing from either source is to ignore the metaphysical problem of the nature of reality and our grasp of it. We construct that which gives meaning to our lives and to the problems of living that are posed by our need to survive" (Clinnard, Quinney, & Wildeman, 1994, p. 11).

Knight and Prentky Typology of Sexual Offenders: An Example

Knight and Prentky's (1990) typology for classifying sex offenders illustrates the simultaneous use of both inductive and deductive approaches to typology construction. The authors identified ideal typologies of sex offenders, empirically testing them with statistical methods. Most sex offender typologies are speculative models of ideal types that have been constructed from the "armchair," with little evidence of reliability or validity. Their model is one of the most sophisticated and complex typologies of sex offenders developed to date in criminal justice decision making for treatment and management of sex offenders (Fisher & Mair, 1998). The construction of the model is reviewed here to illustrate how complex typologies are constructed.

Knight and Prentky (1990) sought to determine the validity and reliability of tests of existing (speculative) sex offender typologies:

> Identification of a preliminary target for such a critical assessment required a thorough evaluation of the current status of the theory and research on sexual offenders. In a relatively undeveloped area like the study of sexual aggression, where data on the validation of typological systems were virtually nonexistent, we had to use other factors to guide our choice of a preliminary model. We compared the available typologies of sex offenders to determine whether specific types of offenders were described across a number of systems (see Knight et al., 1985). We reasoned that if such types could be identified, they would represent a consensus among clinicians of the most salient subtypes of sexual offenders and thus would provide the best available guesses about taxonomic structure. (1990, p. 25)

The development of the typology involved four stages: theory formulation, implementation, validation, and integration. What follows is a summary of the stages of the construction process of the first version of the Massachusetts Treatment Center Rapist and Child Molester typologies adapted from Knight and Prentky (1990):

Stage 1—Theory Formulation

The authors compared available typologies to determine whether consensus exists regarding specific types of sex offenders. They developed two typologies representative of the types most frequently described in the literature—the Massachusetts Treatment Center: Child Molester Typology 1 [MTC: CM1] and the Massachusetts Treatment Center: Rapist Typology 1 [MTC:R1]. They then identified the type-defining dimensions (e.g., amount and nature of aggression, lifestyle impulsivity, etc.) and tested them using cluster analysis to come up with the variables that most differentiate the types.

Stage 2—Implementation

At the next stage, Knight and Prentky clearly defined the types and dimensions and assessed interrater reliability (the degree to which multiple raters agree that specific offenders should be classified as specific types within the typology of interest). They then determined the coverage and degree to which the typology was exhaustive (applicable across the spectrum of offenders) and homogeneous (how cohesive the types are). On finding inadequate reliability and coverage for one of the typologies (child molester typology), they had to circle back and make revisions (e.g., omitting variables, adding dimensions) to the typology before moving to the next stage. Finally, less relevant variables were excluded in an effort to include only the most reliable and relevant variables. In other words, variables that multiple raters did not clearly identify and/or that were not found to be mutually exclusive across types were discarded. For example if "victim selection" were a variable hypothesized to distinguish between types of child molesters and cluster analysis revealed that different types of child molesters select similar types of victims and raters did not consistently classify offenders into the same types based on this variable, then this would not be a distinguishing variable and would be discarded.

Stage 3—Validation

In the validation stage, the authors looked to the research literature and theory on the developmental roots of sex offending to determine whether the constructed types could be shown to have "distinctive, theoretically coherent developmental roots" (Knight & Prentky, 1990, p. 28). The purpose of linking the typology with theories of the etiology and development of sex offending is to establish *construct validity*. Construct validity, which involves examining converging lines of evidence to support a particular theory of types, is an important step in the empirical construction of typologies.

Stage 4—Integration

The integration stage involved responding to the analyses of construct validity to determine which dimensions of the typologies needed modification. Cluster analyses and other statistical methods were used to determine which dimensions carried more or less weight as discriminating factors. For example, in their analysis and validation of the child molester typology, the authors found that two constructs—*fixation* and *regression*—which originally represented separate types, were problematic. The fixation type was said to be characterized by "high intensity" (high level of pedophilic interest) and "low social competence," whereas the regression type was associated with "low intensity" and "high social competence." The fixation-regression types were crossed with an instrumental-expressive aggression distinction to yield eight separate types of child molesters. However, when attempting to classify a group of 68 child molesters using this eight-group typology, the authors found that interrater reliabilities were unacceptably low, certain types were extremely heterogeneous, and some offenders fell between the types (e.g., offenders who were highly fixated and had high social competence). As a result, the typology had to be revised to improve and ensure reliability, homogeneity, and validity.

The MTC typologies have continued to be improved and are now in the third version (MTC:R3 and MTC:CM3; Prentky & Burgess, 2000). Figures 3.2 and 3.3 provide visual illustration of the MTC:R3 and MTC:CM3 typologies.[5]

Evaluating Typologies

A criminal typology is useful only to the extent that it describes *homogeneous* categories of offending, is *comprehensive/exhaustive* with respect to the stated purpose (i.e., Is it a general typology of crime? psychopaths? serial killers? organized criminals? etc.), contains categories that are *mutually exclusive* (do not overlap), and is *complex* enough to have explanatory value and simple enough to be *applied* in criminal justice policy and practice. In evaluating offender typologies, it is important to ask the following questions:

- *Are the typology and the categories it includes homogeneous?*
- *Are the typology and the categories it includes heterogeneous?*
- *Are the typology and the categories it includes exhaustive?*
- *Are the categories included in the typology mutually exclusive?*
- *Is the typology too simple?*
- *Is the typology too complex?*

Homogeneity/Heterogeneity

A typology is homogeneous if it can be said to describe a category of offending consisting of offenders or behaviors that are the same with respect to principle unifying dimension and purpose. For example, we can ask this question about the legalistic *misdemeanor/felony* typology. Are all crimes that fall under the heading of "misdemeanors" the same along the principle unifying dimension? In this case, the organizing principle is severity of offense and sentence. Classification as a felony is based on the seriousness of the offense and punishment of more than one year in prison. But are all felonies the same? Yes and no. The "felony type" is homogeneous with respect to offense severity and punishment. If the purpose of the typology is simply to differentiate for the purpose of legal sanction, then the typology is sufficiently homogeneous with respect to the central organizing principle. However, for other dimensions the felony category is actually quite heterogeneous. Felony offenses include murder, rape, robbery, assault, drug offenses, arson, sex offenses, embezzlement, fraud, and many other offenses. For any purpose beyond legal sanctions, this typology is much too heterogeneous to be of use. For example, can we say anything about felony offenders that would be helpful in

❖ **Figure 3.2** Massachusetts Treatment Center Classification System for Rapists: Version 3 (MTC:R3).

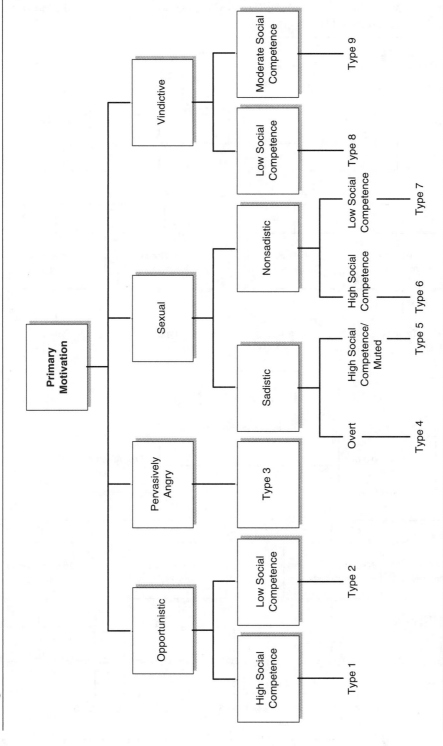

Adapted from Prentky & Burgess (2000). *Forensic management of sexual offenders.* New York: Kluwer/Plenum, p. 62.

❖ **Figure 3.3**   Massachusetts Treatment Center Classification System for Child Molesters: Version 3 (MTC:CM3).

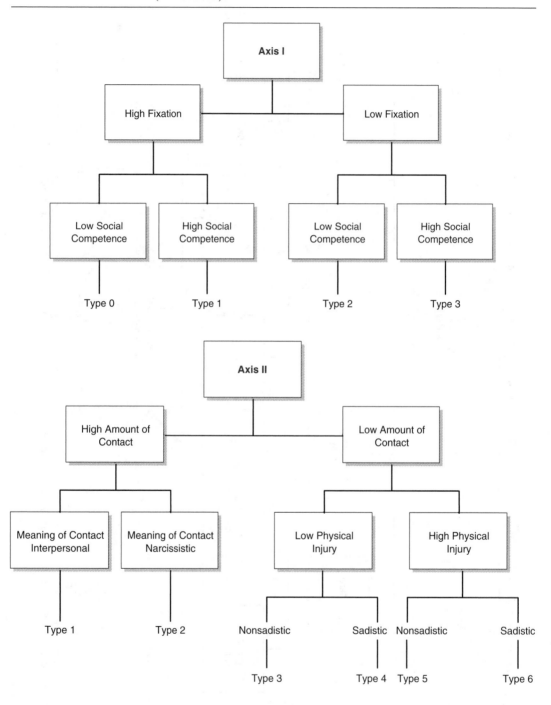

Adapted from Prentky & Burgess (2000). *Forensic management of sexual offenders.* New York: Kluwer/Plenum, p. 62.

determining correctional management and treatment strategies? Perhaps to some extent; we could say that felony offenders have committed more serious crimes, pose a greater risk, and should be placed in more secure correctional facilities. Or could we? Could we devise an appropriate "treatment" approach for felony versus misdemeanor offenders? Would a treatment program devised for all felony offenders be beneficial for sex offenders, drug offenders, and murderers? Given that these two categories (felony and misdemeanor) incorporate a diverse array of offender types, this legalistic typology is not of much use for treatment programs.

Exhaustiveness/Exclusiveness

A typology is useful only to the extent that it is exhaustive with respect to the concept it is describing and exclusive in the sense that categories do not overlap. Miethe and McCorkle (2001) state that "a definitive typology of crimes or criminals is not possible" (p. 14). Criminologists disagree on which dimensions are most important, definitions of crimes and criminals are socially constructed, and typologies serve different purposes. Thus, there is no such thing as a "perfect" typology of criminal behavior. Typologies should be assessed with respect to their ability to explain a central concept and the degree to which real-world crimes and criminals exclusively fall into the designated types.

It is probably not possible to come up with a completely exhaustive criminal typology. Such a typology would have to include all possible types of crime. Because definitions of crime change across time and place, typologies of crime are, to some extent, time and culture bound. For example, most typologies of crime constructed before the last decade or so do not include the categories "cybercrime" and "copycat crime." These crime categories have been identified and have gained attention only in recent years and thus were historically not recognized as specific crime types. Within a typology of crime, however, it is crucial that each category be exhaustive, including all possible instances of the offense type. For example, until recently, typologies of serial killers did not include women or instrumentally motivated offenders (Hickey, 2002). The FBI definition of serial murder, "three or more separate events in three or more separate locations with an emotional cooling-off period between homicides" (Douglas et al., 1992, p. 21), did not capture many female and instrumental offenders. Thus, a crime category must be evaluated in terms of the degree to which it is exhaustive and able to explain all possible expressions of the crime/criminal it proposes to describe.

More important, typologies must be assessed in terms of the mutual exclusivity of the categories within it. In other words, a theoretical "type" is meaningful only to the degree that it tells us something about those who are classified within it. For example, one of the major problems with the UCR is that people who commit more than one crime are classified in the most severe offender category. What this means is that a person who commits a rape/murder is classified as a "murderer" in the UCR. This alleviates the problem of mutual exclusivity but distorts the reality of crime in official statistics. In reality, many offenders commit (to use the typology of Clinard, Quinney, & Wildeman, 1994) public order *and* violent personal *and* occasional property criminal behavior. Theoretically, this is not much of a problem as long as each category is conceptually distinct. However, many existing typologies lack conceptual distinction (and mutual exclusivity) between categories.

Simplicity/Complexity

If a typology is too simple, it will be criticized as being unsophisticated. If a typology is too complex it will not have real-world application. A balance must be achieved between simplicity and complexity. This is one of the most crucial considerations in typology construction.

For example, one of the more heavily criticized typologies in the criminal justice literature is the FBI's *organized/disorganized* typology; however, this typology is probably the best-known and most often applied typologies in research and law enforcement practice.[6] According to Ressler, Burgess, and Douglas (1992), whether the crime scene is left *organized* or *disorganized* tells something about the offender's criminal sophistication and personality. Organized crime scenes are said to reflect an offender who commits crime out of a need for power and are associated with psychopathy. Disorganized crime scenes are said to reflect an offender who commits crime out of passion, compulsion, frustration, or anxiety and are associated with psychosis. Organized offenders tend to engage in specific behaviors such as premeditation, transporting the victim's body to another location, bringing weapons to the scene, and not leaving evidence behind. Disorganized offenders tend to use weapons found at the scene, leave the victim's body and other evidence in full view, and seek victims known to them. The organized/disorganized typology has been used in case linkage, to provide investigative direction, and to inform interrogation and interview strategies with suspects.

Turvey (1999, 2002) argues that the organized/disorganized typology is a "false dichotomy" developed for "unsophisticated law enforcement agencies requesting profiles" (p. 145). He criticizes the typology for being too simple and suggests it can be used "without thinking," making it "seductive to those without any education in, or knowledge of, human psychology," which he says is the "majority of law enforcement" (p. 146). From Turvey's perspective, the organized/disorganized classification is an "invitation to be misled" by what is a "badly thought out set of offender generalizations," a "beautiful theory that cannot withstand the scrutiny of critical analysis" designed for training those without a basic knowledge of human psychology (p. 149).

At root of these criticisms, Turvey (1999, 2002) finds the following problems:

- Most crime scenes will not be one or the other, but present on a continuum.
- Only a competent forensic analysis can give insight on how and why a crime scene presents as it does.
- Crime scenes that appear disorganized can be created by nonpsychotic, nonmentally ill offenders.
- Crime scenes that appear organized are not necessarily committed by "psychopaths."
- The dichotomy does not take into account an offender's development over time.
- The dichotomy ignores distinctions between MO and signature, focusing only on the physical scene and not on "why" the crime occurred as it did.
- It can be misused in court if framed as a clinical assessment.

Thus, this behavioral typology is problematic with respect to a number of factors we have reviewed so far. The types are not homogeneous constructs (more than one "type" of offender can be "organized" or "disorganized"). The types are not mutually exclusive (a person can be classified as both organized and disorganized). And most important, the typology as a whole is too simple, particularly regarding the association with psychopathy and psychosis, which are highly complex constructs.

On the other hand, theorists who construct typologies might take a few notes from the FBI profilers who developed the organized/disorganized typology. Criminologists often complain that their research and theories are not practically applied in the criminal justice system. The task at hand is to develop sophisticated typologies that can be simply presented for use in criminal justice policy and practice. A number of empirically derived typologies that have made their way into criminal justice policy and practice have influenced correctional classification and management, treatment programs, and sex offender classification levels (discussed in Chapter 11).

Summary

To make the world manageable, human beings mentally organize the world into categories. Typology construction is a fundamental component of human cognition and scientific investigation. Typologies inform and are informed by theory. One way to think of a typology is that it is theory made manageable. *A typology is an abstract category or class (or set of categories or classes) consisting of characteristics organized around a common principle relevant to a particular analysis.* Typologies of crime and criminals provide information with which to make decisions, policies, practices, and laws.

Typologies are used at all stages of the criminal justice process—from profiling in law enforcement, to expert testimony on categories of criminal behavior in adjudication and sentencing, to offender classification in corrections, to dangerousness predictions at the parole reentry stage, typologies of crime and criminals make their way into the criminal justice system. In the criminal justice system, decisions have to be made efficiently and effectively regardless of the current state of the research. Social scientists are charged with explaining and describing the complex world of crime in simple terms for practical purposes. Criminal justice policymakers, practitioners, attorneys, jurors, and citizens have to know something about how offenders whose behavior falls into one or another category of crime are alike and different in order to respond meaningfully to crime.

Typologies are constructed in two general ways. *Ideal types* are inductively constructed based on a subjective clinical impression, and *empirical* types are deductively constructed based on research and statistical analysis that determines the degree to which characteristics cluster together. Typologies differ with respect to *theoretical foundation* and *purpose*. Typologies of crime and criminals have emerged from legalistic, sociological, psychological, biological, or multiple (interdisciplinary) perspectives. A criminal typology is useful only to the extent that it describes homogeneous categories of offending, it is comprehensive/exhaustive with respect to the stated purpose, its categories are mutually exclusive, it is complex enough to have explanatory value, and it is simple enough to be applied in criminal justice policy and practice.

DISCUSSION QUESTIONS

1. What is a typology? Explain.

2. How are typologies used in the mental health and criminal justice systems? Provide examples of specific typologies used in both systems.

3. The Crime Classification Manual (CCM) developed by the FBI (Douglas et al., 1992) is an interesting example of an attempt to model a crime typology after the American Psychiatric Association's *Diagnostic and Statistical Manual of Mental Disorders* (which many consider the clinicians "bible" in mental health settings). However, unlike the *DSM-IV-TR*, which is the standard tool of psychologists, psychiatrists, social workers, and clinicians, the CCM did not become a popular widely used tool in the criminal justice system. Discuss your thoughts on why the CCM has not taken off in criminal justice system as the "bible" of criminal justice professionals.

4. Explain the difference between legalistic, sociological, psychological, and multitrait typologies. Provide examples of each.

5. What is the difference between an ideal and an empirical type? How are empirical typologies constructed? Explain.

6. What are the features of a good typology? Choose a typology discussed in this chapter or another typology and evaluate it. Discuss its strengths and weaknesses with attention to the features of a good typology discussed in this chapter.

 On Your Own: Log on to the Web-based student study site at http://www.sagepub .com/helfgottstudy/ for the URL links in the Web Exercises, study aids such as review quizzes, and research recommendations including links to journal articles specifically selected for this book.

WEB EXERCISES

1. In *The Mask of Sanity*, Cleckley says:

   Is it an exaggeration if we say that the difficulties confronting the psychiatrist who has had to approach the psychopath through such a tangle of concepts (and it has been our traditional method) are comparable with those that would be faced by a general practitioner discussing leukemia if this term meant also a broken leg, hemorrhoids, pregnancy, brain tumor, and the common cold? (p. 233)

   He then goes on to compare the psychopath with other "types." Read Section III, Part II (pp. 244–316) of Cleckley's *The Mask of Sanity:* http://www.cassiopaea.org/cass/sanity_1.PdF. How does this comparison/contrast help in better understanding the nature of the psychopath?

2. Review the *DSM-IV-TR* classification of mental disorders on the BehaveNet Web site: http://www.behavenet.com/. Evaluate the *DSM-IV-TR* classification system asking the questions discussed in this chapter.

3. Read the article "Fighting Back Against Rapists" on the Woman's Firearm Network Web site: http://www.womenandguns.com/wfn/fight.html. Discuss your thoughts on this example of the use of a criminal typology as a tool to enhance personal safety.

4

Psychopathy and Criminal Behavior

Psychopathy is one of the best-validated clinical constructs in the realm of psychopathology, and arguably the single most important clinical construct in the criminal justice system.

—Robert Hare (1998, p. 189)

In 1993, Richard Allen Davis kidnapped 12-year-old Polly Klaas from a slumber party at her home in California. Polly had been playing a game with friends while her mother and sister were sleeping in a room down the hall when Davis abducted her at knifepoint. Her body was found two months later 25 miles from her home after Davis, arrested for drunk driving, confessed to her murder when his fingerprints were identified as those of the kidnapper. At the time of Polly Klaas's murder, Davis was on parole after serving 8 years on a 16-year sentence for a prior kidnapping. On August 5, 1996, a jury decided that Richard Allen Davis should be executed. Following the verdict, Davis turned to the courtroom audience and TV cameras, and with a glaring smirk, gestured with his middle fingers without a flicker of remorse. Later, Polly's father, Marc Klaas, said in a television interview that he hoped the verdict would send a message to "all of the other psychopaths out there" (King 5 News, August 5, 1996). Davis now sits on San Quentin's death row seeking pen pals through his personal Web site.[1]

I t did not seem difficult for Marc Klaas to determine that a psychopath was to blame for the death of his daughter, but psychologists and criminologists have long struggled to understand psychopathy, to identify psychopathic individuals, and to use scientific knowledge about the condition to explain, predict, and control criminal behavior. The term *psychopath* is common in everyday language, media, and pop culture. Images of psychopaths are projected through news media, television, film, music, literature, art, myth, fairy tale, and the Bible. We all know who Marc Klaas was talking about. We may not know the scientific terms or how to diagnose personality disorders, but we know what it feels like when someone makes the hair rise on the backs of our necks. When it comes to making decisions about crime, it is this feeling that drives us.

Psychopathy is historically, theoretically, and practically important to the study of criminal behavior. Research on the links between psychopathy, criminal behavior, and violence has grown at an enormous pace over the past 30 years and made its way into the criminal justice process at a number of critical junctures. A large and growing body of literature indicates that psychopathy is highly predictive of recidivism, treatability, and violence. "Indices of psychopathy are rapidly becoming a routine part of assessment batteries used to make decisions about competency, sentencing, diversion, placement, suitability for treatment, and risk for recidivism and violence" (Hare, 1998, p. 205). In law enforcement, determining whether or not a suspect is psychopathic is useful in criminal profiling (Hare & O'Toole, 2006; O'Toole, 2007; Turvey, 1999, 2002) and hostage negotiations (Greenstone, Kosson, & Gacono, 2000). Identifying psychopathy in incarcerated offenders is important in correctional classification, management, and treatment (Wong & Hare, 2005; Young, Justice, Erdberg, & Gacono, 2000), and expert testimony on psychopathy has been introduced in a broad range of court cases including sexually violent predator determinations, capital sentencing, determinations of competency and insanity, juvenile transfers to adult court, and making predictions of dangerousness for sentencing and release decisions (DeMatteo & Edens, 2006; Lyon & Ogloff, 2000).

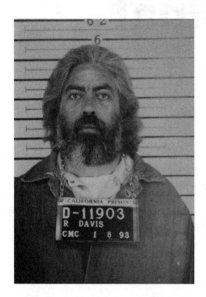

Photo 4.1   Richard Allen Davis's Mugshot.

Photo credit: © Forden Patrick J./Corbis Sygma.

Throughout history, the concepts of criminality, delinquency, antisocial personality, sociopathy, and psychopathy have been intertwined and misunderstood. Much of the research conducted on criminal and antisocial behavior overlaps with the literature on psychopathy. Research on criminal behavior conducted before the last 15 years uses heterogeneous offender samples (with no clear distinction between "criminals" and "psychopaths"). In 1991, the first edition of the *Psychopathy Checklist–Revised (PCL-R),* developed by Robert Hare, was published by Multi-Health Systems. The second edition of the PCL-R was published in 2003. As the first standardized, valid, and reliable tool for assessing psychopathy, the PCL-R offered researchers a means to measure psychopathy to ensure all studies were measuring the same clinical entity. Since publication of the PCL-R, there has been a surge in research on psychopathy and attempts to practically apply the concept in North America and internationally in critical criminal justice decision making.

Research conducted since the publication of the PCL-R has shown that psychopathy is a robust predictor of violent recidivism and dangerousness (Douglas, Vincent, & Edens, 2006; Hare, 1998, 2003), leading to the contention that psychopathy is the "*single most important clinical construct in the criminal justice system*" (Hare, 1998, p. 189). California's "Three Strikes You're Out" law requiring mandatory life sentences for repeat felony offenders was, in part, motivated by the murder of Polly Klaas and the notion of the *six percent solution,* which hypothesizes that incarcerating a small number of dangerous offenders will significantly reduce the crime rate and protect public safety. This theory, derived from criminologist Marvin Wolfgang's cohort studies of career criminals in the 1940s and 1950s, showed that 6% of the cohort was responsible for over 50% of total crime (Beres & Griffith, 1998). Based on this, three strikes would enhance public safety by identifying and incarcerating those inclined to reoffend. Along these lines, psychopathy can be viewed as a scientific reconceptualization of evil that has been used to contain and control threatening and unexplainable behavior. "Get tough" laws are enacted through the image of the psychopathic predator— Three (and Two) Strikes You're Out legislation, sexual psychopath/predator laws, capital punishment, the federal Violent Crime Control and Law Enforcement Act of 1994—have all been championed as weapons with which to aggressively attack the incorrigible criminal. In the public mind, the incorrigible criminal is the psychopath.

Defining Psychopathy

Psychopathy is a personality disorder characterized by an inability to form human attachment, aggressive narcissism, and antisocial behavior (Meloy, 1992). Robert Hare, foremost researcher on the subject, creator of the PCL-R, and author of *Without Conscience: The Disturbing World of the Psychopaths Among Us*, describes psychopathy as a personality disorder defined by a constellation of affective, interpersonal, and behavioral characteristics most of which society views as pejorative (Hare, 1993, 1998). According to Hare:

> Psychopaths are social predators who charm, manipulate, and ruthlessly plow their way through life leaving a broad trail of broken hearts, shattered expectations, and empty wallets. Completely lacking in conscience and feelings for others, they selfishly take what they want and do as they please, violating social norms and expectations without the slightest sense of guilt or regret. (Hare, 1993, p. xi)

Psychopaths are hardwired to commit antisocial and criminal behavior because they have an emotional dysfunction that interferes with their ability to feel.

If you went to a library just 20 years ago to answer the question, "What is a psychopath?" you would have had a difficult time finding a simple answer. The terms *sociopath, psychopath*, and *antisocial personality* (and sometimes *psychotic*) have been confused and used interchangeably over the years by researchers, clinicians, criminal justice professionals, and the general public. For many years, the term psychopathy was considered by many to be a "wastebasket" category with no clear definition. Hervey Cleckley, in his classic work *The Mask of Sanity,* called the psychopath "the forgotten man of psychiatry" (Cleckley, 1941, p. 16) because the term had, for so many years, represented a "loose and variously understood" heterogeneous group. Research conducted over the past several decades, however, suggests that psychopathy is a unique clinical condition characterized by the "juxtaposition of affective interpersonal traits with antisocial behavior" (Hare & Neumann, 2006, p. 84) that is empirically associated with criminal behavior and violent recidivism.

The sudden clarity and consensus regarding the meaning of *psychopath* can be largely attributed to the development and standardization of the PCL-R (Hare, 1991, 2003), which has become the standard measure of psychopathy in research, clinical assessment, and criminal justice practice. The PCL-R is a 20-item scale that assesses psychopathy using a semistructured interview, file, and collateral information that measures personality traits and behaviors associated with a widely understood, historical, and traditional conception of psychopathy (Hare, 1991, 2003). Researchers consider the PCL-R's ability to predict violence to be unprecedented and unparalleled (Salekin, Rogers, & Sewell, 1996). The PCL-R is a valid and reliable measure of psychopathy that is a strong predictor of violent recidivism and dangerousness (Douglas et al., 2006; Hare,1998; Porter & Porter, 2007),[2] and a determinant of high criminogenic offender risk/needs (Simourd & Hodge, 2000). The PCL-R has gained widespread attention and is now used at various stages of the criminal justice system in Canada and the United States (Hare, 1998).

The advent and standardization of the PCL-R has made it possible for researchers to distinguish between offenders who are antisocial (the majority of offenders in prison populations) and those whose criminal behavior is rooted in psychopathology. The PCL-R is composed of two categories of the distinguishing personality (Factor 1) and behavioral features (Factor 2) of the disorder. Table 4.1 shows the PCL-R items and factors. Factor 1 items are associated with affective and interpersonal personality characteristics derived from Cleckley (1941). Factor 2 items reflect the social deviance component of the disorder, including antisocial behaviors similar to those included in the Antisocial Personality Disorder classification in the *Diagnostic and Statistical Manual of Mental Disorders* (APA, *DSM-IV-TR*, 2000). Recent research using *Item Response Theory (IRT)* has provided support for a four-factor model of psychopathy with specific PCL-R items associated with interpersonal, affective, lifestyle, and antisocial factors (Hare & Neumann, 2006; Neumann, Kosson, & Salekin, 2007; see Figure 4.1).[3]

Psychopathy as a Categorical or Dimensional Construct

Psychopathy can be considered *categorically* as a discrete clinical disorder of personality (or taxon) or *dimensionally* along a continuum as a personality dynamic all individuals use to a greater or lesser degree as a tool for committing immoral acts without remorse or shame. The categorical model of psychopathy holds that a person either is or is not a psychopath. Researchers have generally used a PCL-R cutoff score of 30 and above as the criterion for classification as a primary or "true" psychopath. However, some researchers suggest that a lower score may differentiate psychopaths from nonpsychopaths (Harris, Rice, & Cormier, 1991; Harris, Rice, & Quinsey, 1994). The dimensional model holds that all human beings possess characteristics of

❖ Table 4.1   PCL-R Factors 1 and 2

• FACTOR 1	• FACTOR 2
— Item 1: Glibness/Superficial charm	— Item 3: Need for stimulation/Proneness to boredom
— Item 2: Grandiose sense of self-worth	— Item 9: Parasitic lifestyle
— Item 4: Pathological lying	— Item 10: Poor behavioral controls
— Item 5: Conning/Manipulative	— Item 12: Early behavior problems
— Item 6: Lack of remorse or guilt	— Item 13: Lack of realistic, long-term goals
— Item 7: Shallow affect	— Item 14: Impulsivity
— Item 8: Callous/Lack of empathy	— Item 15: Irresponsibility
— Item 16: Failure to accept responsibility for own actions	— Item 18: Juvenile delinquency
	— Item 19: Revocation of conditional release
	— Item 20: Criminal versatility

• *PCL-R items not included in factors:*

— Item 17: Many short-term marital relationships
— Item 11: Promiscuous sexual behavior

psychopathy to greater or lesser degrees (Figure 4.2). In other words, a person can be more or less psychopathic with psychopathy level reflecting greater inclination toward criminal behavior and violence.

Research and strong arguments support both models. Gacono and Meloy (2002) stress the importance of understanding psychopathy as a taxon (PCL-R > 30) for research purposes and as a dimensional construct along a continuum of severity in clinical/forensic settings, and they recommend that other tests (including assessment of defensive process) be used in conjunction with the PCL-R to further delineate the dimensional aspects (behavioral and intrapsychic characteristics) of antisocial and psychopathic subjects.[4] Wallace et al. (2000) suggest that PCL-R scores above 30 reflect the categorical phenomenon (e.g., the true or primary psychopath), whereas PCL-R scores below 30 reflect the dimensional construct (e.g., the secondary psychopath or antisocial personality disorder).

❖ **Figure 4.1**   PCL-R Four-Factor Model of Psychopathy

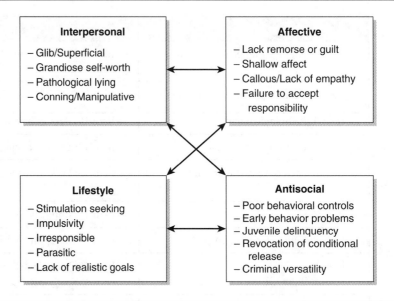

Adapted from Hare & Neuman (2006). The PCL-R assessment of psychopathy. In C.J. Patrick (Ed). *Handbook of psychopathy.* New York: The Guilford Press, 58–90.

❖ **Figure 4.2**   Categorical and Dimensional Models of Psychopathy

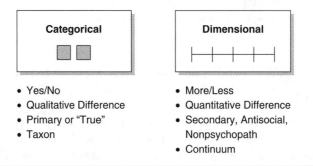

Psychopathy and Antisocial Personality Disorder

Much has been written on the subject of psychopathy over the past 200 years. Within this discourse has been debate over what to call the condition, how it should be classified in relation to other disorders, and whether it exists at all. Since the inception of the *Diagnostic and Statistical Manual of Mental Disorders* (*DSM*; APA, 1952), the American Psychological Association (APA) has not used the historical term *psychopath* as an official diagnostic category, but instead (depending on the edition) the terms *sociopathic personality, dyssocial personality, antisocial personality,* and presently, *antisocial personality disorder* (APD). Despite the APA's abandonment of the term, researchers agree that the psychopath is a distinct clinical entity that has not been adequately conveyed through the diagnostic categories in the various editions of the *DSM* (Reid, 1985). Researchers continue to use the term *psychopathy* in discussion and empirical study, referring to a distinct phenomenon that is not necessarily synonymous with associated terms used over time in the *DSM, DSM-II, DSM-III, DSM-III-R, DSM-IV,* and *DSM-IV-TR*.

The *DSM-III* (1980) and *DSM-III-R* (1987) versions of APD were extensively criticized because they were long and cumbersome, overfocused on behaviors, underfocused on personality, and incongruent with international criteria[5] (Hare, Hart, & Harpur, 1991). The criteria were considered "too descriptive, inclusive, criminally biased, and socioeconomically skewed to be of much clinical or research use" (Meloy, 1988). APD classifications of the *DSM-IV* and *DSM-IV-TR* are shorter than their predecessors but the criteria remain behaviorally focused, including personality features such as lack of empathy, superficial charm, and inflated and arrogant self-appraisal under the subheading "Associated Features and Disorders."

However, the APD classification remains the diagnostic category closest to the historical concept of psychopathy. Its diagnostic criteria are as follows:

- A pattern of disregard for the rights of others as indicated by at least three subcriteria (e.g., failure to conform with respect to lawful behavior, deceitfulness, impulsivity, irritability and aggressiveness, consistent irresponsibility, lack of remorse)

- Individual at least 18 years of age

- Diagnosis of conduct disorder with onset before age 15

- Occurrence of antisocial behavior not exclusively during the course of schizophrenia or manic episode (*DSM-IV-TR*, APA, 2000, p. 706)

Although APD is the official classification most resembling the traditional concept of psychopathy, its strict behavioral criteria have led researchers to conclude that the classification is not a useful measurement for empirical study of psychopathy as traditionally defined.

The PCL-R scale differs from the *DSM* classification of APD in that its criteria capture both the personality (Factor 1) and behavioral (Factor 2) features of the traditional psychopathy concept, based on the work of Cleckley (1941). The PCL-R measures a unitary syndrome composed of two distinct underlying mechanisms—*aggressive narcissism* (Factor 1) and *antisocial behavior* (Factor 2) (Meloy, 1992). The distinctiveness of these mechanisms and the relationship between them play an important role in differentiating psychopathy from criminality, in understanding the relationship between personality and crime, and in identifying psychopathy independent of cultural influences that shape its manifestation. The two PCL-R factors are correlated (.56 in prison inmates and .53 in forensic patients; Hare, Hart, & Harpur, 1991). Factor 1 reflects core personality features of the condition and is considered to infer interpersonal style. Factor 1 is positively correlated with clinical ratings of psychopathy, prototypicality ratings of narcissistic and histrionic personality disorder, and self-report measures of

Machiavellianism and narcissism, and negatively correlated with measures of empathy and anxiety (Hare, 1991; Harpur, Hare, & Hakstian, 1989; Hart & Hare, 1989). Factor 2 reflects a chronically unstable and antisocial lifestyle and is considered to be a measure of social deviance. It is positively correlated with criminal behaviors, socioeconomic background, self-report measures of socialization and antisocial behavior, and diagnosis of APD (Hare, 1991; Harpur et al., 1989).

The Psychopath's Inability to Feel

Many authors consider the fundamental feature of psychopathy to be a lack of attachment to other human beings. This feature has been referred to as a "defect in affect" (Cleckley, 1941), "lack of empathy" (Hare, 1991, 2003), absence of conscience (Hare, 1993), "failure to put oneself in another's position" (Yochelson & Samenow, 1977), and "fundamental disidentification with humanity" (Meloy, 1988). This inability to experience human emotion is what makes psychopaths more prone to criminal behavior than individuals who do not have the disorder. Attachment is a fundamental human need. A person who is not attached to others is not constrained by guilt or remorse and consequently can harm others with no emotion.

The emotional experience of the psychopath has been the focus of much research attention. Many scholars, forensic practitioners, and laypersons share the view that psychopaths are emotionless. However, broad generalizations about the emotional experiences of psychopaths are contradicted by the disorder's complexity and inconsistent with research suggesting that psychopaths are capable of experiencing some emotional states (Steuerwald & Kosson, 2000) including momentary anxiety, sadness (Reid, 1978), anger, exhilaration, and contemptuous delight (Meloy, 1988). Although there is no direct test of whether a person feels a particular emotion, researchers have measured emotion in psychopaths indirectly by examining the attribution of emotion to others (Blair et al., 1995), emotional reactivity to positive or negative mood induction (Habel et al., 2002), startle reactivity (Patrick, 2001), physiological arousal to aversive stimuli (Steuerwald & Kosson, 2000), and amygdala[6] dysfunction (Blair et al., 2005).

This growing body of research on the emotional experience of the psychopath suggests that the core emotional detachment factor of psychopathy is related to a weak defensive activation system (low avoidance) and to traits of high dominance and low anxiousness (Patrick, 2001). Psychopaths are able to extrude painful elements from conscious self-experience (Lafarge, 1989), have a reduced sensitivity to emotion (particularly fear and anxiety) mediated by attentional differences and coping mechanisms, and emotional impairment may be specific to situations in which the psychopath is not experiencing strong emotion (Steuerwald & Kosson, 2000). Recent research by Patrick (2007) suggests that emotional processing in the psychopath can be viewed as a dual process whereby different affective processing deviations are associated with the different facets of psychopathy. High Factor 1 scores are associated with "diminished defensive reactivity to aversive cues and a temperament profile involving agency and stress resistance" and high Factor 2 scores are associated with "a range of externalizing syndromes that are marked by traits of low constraint and heightened NEM [negative emotionality]" (pp. 240–242).

As a result of this incapacity for human emotion and attachment to others, the psychopath learns early on how to read other people and manipulate them to meet personal needs. The psychopath is able to mimic, or unconsciously simulate and consciously imitate, human emotion (Meloy, 1988). Yochelson and Samenow (1977) refer to the psychopath's imitation of emotional expression as "sentimentality," a cognitive thinking error unique to the "criminal personality" (a term they use synonymously with psychopathy). This view is supported by Cleckley (1941), who contended that, absent true affect, the psychopath is a "subtly constructed reflex machine that can mimic the human personality perfectly" (Cleckley, 1941, p. 228). Blair et al. (2005) suggest that dysfunction of the amygdala in the psychopath contributes to impaired aversive conditioning, processing of fear and sad expressions, and instrumental learning.

Psychopaths are often referred to as "snakes" or "reptiles" in popular culture. Meloy (1988) proposes the reptilian-state theory suggesting that the emotional state of the psychopath is more similar to that of reptiles than humans. The reptilian cerebrotype (brain structure) is the first evolutionary step in the development of the human brain. The common denominator among mammals is the structure of the limbic system in the brain that is responsible for the experience and expression of emotion supporting behaviors such as parental response to offspring, hoarding, and sociability. The brain structure of the reptile supports certain behaviors such as establishment and defense of territories, hunting, feeding, mating, dominance, competition, aggression, and imitation. Like reptiles, psychopaths are missing behaviors that are products of the limbic system, including hoarding (to protect the future) and social behavior. Unlike most mammals, the primary psychopath does not become attached to others, express emotion, or engage in hoarding behavior (i.e., saving for a rainy day). Like the reptile, the primary psychopath is defensive, predatory, aggressive, competitive, and imitative (superficial). Clinical observations support the idea psychopaths engage in acts of visual predation or a "reptilian stare." According to Meloy (1988), the psychopath's reptilian state is a psychobiological state that can be momentary or long-lasting and the conceptual parallels between psychopathic behavior and the "functional prevalence of the reptilian cerebrotype" are striking (p. 69). No neurophysiological or neuroanatomical research supports the association between the brain structures and behaviors of psychopaths and reptiles; however, the psychopath-reptile analogy, discussed in the research literature and more widely in popular culture, may provide additional insight into the distinctive emotional life of the psychopath.

What *Causes* Psychopathy?

In *The Psychopathic Mind*, Meloy (1988) explains the underlying dynamics involved in the development of psychopathy, offering what he considers to be the most fundamental feature of the condition. He defines psychopathy as a

> . . . deviant developmental disturbance characterized by an inordinate amount of instinctual aggression and the absence of the object relational capacity to bond. Psychopathy is a process: a continuous interplay of factors and operations that are implicitly progressing or regressing toward a particular end point . . . a fundamental disidentification with humanity. (Meloy, 1988, p. 5)

Meloy's definition reflects a synthesis of theories from a variety of disciplines (e.g., biology, psychology, sociology) and perspectives (psychodynamic, behavioral, cognitive), emphasizing the developmental context in which the disorder emerges. This attention to developmental issues illustrates the particular dynamics involved in the disorder's etiology. From this perspective, psychopathy is not necessarily inherent, but it is deeply rooted in complex psychodynamic processes. Psychopathy is the product of neither an unchangeable inborn defect or purely environmental factors.

Biological Predisposition

A body of research has accumulated on the biological factors that predispose an individual to psychopathy. Though biological factors do not "cause" the disorder, research supports a link between psychopathy and a number of biological deficits and anomalies, including genetic predisposition, neurotransmitter imbalance, low autonomic arousal, brain damage (Raine, 1993; Raine & Sanmartin, 2001), and dysfunction in the amygdala, part of the limbic system associated with fear and other emotions (Blair, 2006). Much of the research on the biological factors associated with psychopathy also applies to criminality and antisocial behavior and violence. Anatomical research focusing specifically on psychopathy is "nearly non-existent" (Raine & Yang, 2006, p. 290). Research has focused more generally on antisocial conditions based on heterogeneous samples (including psychopathic and nonpsychopathic offenders), so it is difficult to sort out whether the findings apply to psychopaths or to offenders more generally.

For example, Raine (Raine & Sanmartin, 2001) found that violent offenders are more likely to have preshrunken prefrontal cortexes, though this anomaly is found in offenders who engage in affectively motivated violence more than those who engage in predatory violence (usually committed by psychopaths). Similarly, research on the neurochemical basis of psychopathy has targeted the antisocial behavior component of the condition (Factor 2), but has little to say about the affective-interpersonal component (Factor 1). There appears to be a relationship between impaired central serotonergic activity and impulsive and aggressive behavior, but as with other findings, this says little about the neurotransmitter role in instrumental predatory aggression and the affective component of psychopathy (Minzenberg & Siever, 2006). With respect to the relationship between genetics and criminal behavior more generally, there is unlikely to be a genetic contribution to specific antisocial or criminal behaviors. Rather, genetics likely play a role in determining the probability that a person will learn an antisocial rather than a prosocial strategy to get his or her needs met. Thus, the emotional dysfunction in the psychopath that makes it so easy to harm and take advantage of others may have a genetic contribution (Blair et al., 2005). Some research suggests that environmental stressors such as birth complications in pregnancy are associated with conduct disorder, delinquency, and violence in adulthood. However, these stressors appear to be associated with reactive aggression rather than instrumental aggression (Blair et al., 2005).

One of the most consistent findings is that psychopaths experience low anxiety and low fear reactions to aversive stimuli. Both the *low-fear hypothesis* (Lykken, 1957) and the *behavioral inhibition system (BIS) deficit* in psychopaths have been consistently supported in a range of studies that measured the psychopath's avoidance to punishment and aversive conditions and autonomic arousal and startle reflex. Fowles and Dindo (2006) propose a dual-deficit model of psychopathy, suggesting that the deficit in psychopathy is a combined deficit of low fear and low anxiety and hypothesizing that low fear makes anxiety less likely in the psychopath. However, both low fear and low anxiety, though rooted in temperament, are highly dependent on environmental influences, producing a developmental failure associated with deficits in anxiety and fear reactions shaped by parent-child interactions and other environmental contributors.

Environmental and Cultural Influences

Biological influences alone do not "cause" psychopathy. Environmental forces such as attachment in infancy, family factors, and culture play a critical role in the development and manifestation of psychopathy and may actually be responsible for many of the differences found in neuroanatomy and neurochemistry research. Like the biological research, much of what is known about psychopathy and environmental factors comes from the more general research on environmental causes of antisocial and criminal behavior.

From a psychodynamic and developmental perspective, psychopathy is the product of genotypic-phenotypic interaction—a biologically predisposed condition exacerbated by environmental forces that develops in infancy prior to 36 months of age. Infants who are biologically predisposed develop psychopathy as a result of an interactive process between the individual and environment. According to Meloy (1988), all infants experience "hard" and "soft" sensations. Hard sensations can be anything that the infant experiences as harshness (e.g., parental abuse, neglect, loud noises, cold expressions). Soft sensations are perceived by the infant as comforting, soothing, and facilitating human bonding. Psychopaths experience a preponderance of hard sensations and as a result turn inward, attach to the narcissistic core of their personality, and build an impenetrable wall of primitive defenses that impede human bonding. Beyond infancy and into adulthood, environmental forces can shape the manifestation of psychopathy. Hare (1996a) suggests that differential environmental circumstances can lead a psychopath raised in a privileged environment to engage in phony stock trading or manipulative power politics while those reared in disadvantaged situations may engage in violent crime.

Research on the influence of family factors on psychopathy is sparse to nonexistent. Early work in the 1950s, 1960s, and 1970s suggested that maternal deprivation, parental rejection, erratic discipline, an antisocial parent, and poor parental supervision could have negative effects resulting in delinquent and antisocial behavior; however, few studies have examined the influence of these factors on psychopathy. Virtually all of the findings on family contributors to psychopathy are extrapolated from longitudinal studies of criminal behavior that have focused on career criminality, with the idea that the group that life-course researchers consider *chronic offenders* is equivalent to the group personality researchers have called *primary psychopaths*.[7] This is highly problematic for making sense of the role of family influences in psychopathy, because the constructs overlap but are not identical.

The only longitudinal study including childhood risk factors that has measured psychopathy is the *Cambridge Study in Delinquent Development,* a 40-year longitudinal survey of offending and antisocial behavior development that followed 411 London boys from age 8 to age 48. The PCL-SV was administered and a subset of "most psychopathic" males who scored 10 or more were identified. While none of these men could be considered to be clinical psychopaths suffering from a severe personality disorder (a high score in a community sample is considered 16 or above) and cannot be considered in the same category as individuals who would score about 30 on the PCL-R (primary psychopaths), the study found that the best predictors of the "most psychopathic" males were having a convicted father or mother, physical neglect, low family income, low involvement of the father with the boy, and coming from a disrupted family (Farrington, 2006).

What about the influence of cultural factors? Can cultural influences cause psychopathy? Researchers have only just begun to explore this question, recognizing that the more we know about the differences and similarities across culture, the better we may understand the etiology of psychopathy. Most researchers acknowledge that the manifestation of psychopathy may be shaped by environmental and cultural influences such as gender-role socialization, ethnic background, and culture. However, the PCL-R was developed and normed almost exclusively on European-American males in the United States and Canada, so results from studies employing the PCL-R with other samples have to be interpreted with caution (Hare, 2003). Results to date suggest that international prison populations have lower mean scores on the PCL-R and lower base rates of psychopathy compared with North American prison populations, that sociocultural variables may contribute to behavioral differences in psychopathy across ethnicity (Sullivan & Kosson, 2006), and that lower rates of psychopathy are found in female samples (Jackson & Richards, 2007b; Verona & Vitale, 2006).

Cognition and Behavior

The historical link between psychopathy and criminality rests on the psychopath's absence of cognitive defect. Unlike psychotics, who are out of touch with reality and can be considered legally insane, psychopaths know the difference between right and wrong and cannot be considered under the insanity defense. However, despite the recognition of the psychopath as cognitively intact for legal purposes and culpable for criminal behavior, research suggests that the psychopath's information processing abilities and mechanisms are intact, but dysfunctional. Recent research suggests that the assumption that psychopaths are not cognitively impaired may stem from oversimplified models of cognitive functions, and psychopaths may be impaired in more subtle aspects of cognition not captured by standard measures of intelligence or executive ability (Hiatt & Newman, 2006).

Yochelson and Samenow's (1977) theory of the *criminal personality* (a term the authors use in reference to psychopaths rather than criminals) offers a glimpse at what the cognitive thinking patterns of the psychopath may look like and provides a foundation on which to construct a method for measuring these patterns (from which unconscious process may be inferred). In their three-volume work, *The Criminal Personality,* the authors offer detailed description of the thinking errors and patterns of the psychopath. At the core of the psychopaths' cognitive style are mechanisms that Yochelson and Samenow term *corrosion* and *cut-off.* These mechanisms enable the psychopath to gradually eliminate any thoughts that would deter the commission of a particular act, and ultimately to abruptly cut off such thoughts in order to complete the act with no remorse or feelings of guilt. These mechanisms are supported by a cognitive style that shapes the psychopath's every attitude, value, and belief. The psychopath's behavior is dictated by cognitive thinking errors that facilitate chronic criminal and manipulative behavior. These thinking errors include a sense of uniqueness, thrust for power, fragmented thinking, lying, victim stance, failure to put oneself in another's position, lack of trust, pretentiousness, ownership, lack of interesting responsible performance, and superoptimism, among others.

Psychopaths engage in a particular style and pattern of thinking and expression that involves communication of deceit and deception. Cleckley (1941) suggested that the psychopath suffers from *semantic dementia*—discordance between an emotion and the attempt to mimic emotion and manipulate meaning through language. The psychopath's language is seen as a tangible and analyzable trait through which to identify the processes by which psychopaths "cut off" feelings of guilt about their antisocial behavior (Helfgott, 2004; Reiber & Vetter, 1995). A number of studies support Cleckley's concept of semantic dementia. Psychopaths use fewer cohesive ties while telling stories (Brinkley, Newman, Harpur, & Johnson, 1999), and extract less information from affective words (Williamson et al., 1991). Furthermore, Blair et al. (1995) suggest that psychopathy may be the result of early dysfunction in the violence inhibition mechanism (VIM), a cognitive mechanism that reduces the likelihood of aggressive attack when the aggressor is faced with distress cues.

More recent findings support the notion that psychopaths experience cognitive deficiencies and use distorted cognitive schema that support antisocial behavior. Wallace et al. (2000) found that psychopaths have cognitive deficiencies rather than distortions, and the core feature of psychopathy is a deficit in attention resulting from impairment of the response modulation process and self-regulation. Psychopaths are unable to shift attention from carrying out a behavior to evaluating behavior and, once fixated on a goal, are unable to stop or change their behavior in response to nonsalient stimuli (e.g., recognition of long-term consequences). Antisocial personality disordered offenders (who are not necessarily psychopaths) use maladaptive cognitive schemas (e.g., "weak people get what they deserve"), but such schemas are cognitive distortions, not deficits, and not themselves indicative of psychopathy. Deficit in response modulation paired with cognitive distortions and antisocial personality style, however, is a compelling explanation for psychopathic behavior. Wallace et al. (2000) suggest that the PCL-R can be viewed along a continuum where scores less than 30 reflect the degree of cognitive distortion used whereas a score of greater than 30 reflects evidence of cognitive deficit seen only in psychopaths (and not antisocial personality disordered offenders).

The literature on cognitive and language processing of psychopaths shows a broad array of deficits. Psychopaths appear to perform well on explicit tasks performed in isolation but not as well on complex dual-task paradigms and show poor performance in response modulation. In processing language, psychopaths use fewer cohesive ties and elaborate associations. Hiatt and Newman (2006) identify two emergent themes from the cognition and information processing research—difficulty in accommodating unintended secondary cues and cerebral processing abnormalities—and hypothesize that these two components of cognitive deficits may stem from a common mechanism.

Primary and Secondary Psychopathy

At what point on the continuum can an individual be deemed psychopathic? What factors enable the condition to progress from a few traits and behaviors to the full-blown clinical condition? Central to these questions is the long-standing idea that psychopathy exists in primary and secondary forms. Throughout history, primary psychopathy has been thought of as inherent and untreatable (a discrete clinical condition) whereas secondary psychopathy has been described as a more superficial condition caused by environmental factors (a dimensional perspective). The inclusion of secondary psychopathy in the general definition of the concept has been the crux of the historical struggle to identify the condition as a homogeneous entity. The criteria for primary psychopathy have been based on characterological defect and criteria for secondary psychopathy on behavioral symptoms. Many writers have suggested that primary and secondary psychopaths share the common bond of antisocial, manipulating, or immoral behavior, but they are divided by the etiology of this behavior.

The following definition is a synthesis of the many ways in which primary and secondary psychopathy has been presented in the literature:

> The primary psychopath engages in antisocial behavior as a result of a genetic or biological predisposition directed by particular psychodynamic forces that occur in infancy. The secondary psychopath's antisocial behavior, on the other hand, is the result of strictly environmental forces (such as membership in a deviant group) that occur at developmental stages beyond infancy. The fundamental distinction between the two types is the ability to attach emotionally to others and to experience the natural anxiety associated with human attachment. The primary psychopath forms no attachments as a result of early developmental obstruction, and thus is capable of harming others with little or no anxiety. The secondary psychopath forms human attachments, possibly to deviant subgroups, or possibly not. However, whether or not the secondary psychopath appears to be attached to others, emotional connection to other human beings is present. (Helfgott, 1992)

Psychologically, the distinction between the types depends on particular developmental phenomena. The primary psychopath, consistent with Meloy's (1988) definition, does not successfully pass through the developmental stages necessary for an individual to form human attachment, to develop one's own identity, and to experience other human beings as separate from oneself. With this psychic awareness comes the ability to empathize, to know that others are not unfeeling objects but, like oneself, human beings who feel pleasure and pain. The secondary psychopath successfully passes through the developmental stages considered necessary to form human attachment, and thus is not deeply void of anxiety associated with harming others. The secondary psychopath may separate from already formed attachments later in life (e.g., a teenager who joins a gang, a young adult who becomes a member of a cult) but is likely to separate and attach to other individuals for emotional reasons. The secondary psychopath's antisocial behavior may be the result of a variety of forces—high anxiety or some other uncomfortable mental condition, attachment to a deviant subculture, or basic need. Secondary psychopaths are a heterogeneous group in the sense that the etiology of their antisocial behavior cannot be explained by one single psychological phenomenon, whereas primary psychopaths are a homogeneous group in the sense that they are deficient in the ability to emotionally attach to other human beings.

Secondary psychopathy is not a categorical psychopathological condition (though both the scientific and popular definitions of psychopathy are often expanded to include this group). The separation of psychopathy into the two types clouds the relationship between personality deviance (primary) and social deviance (secondary). Blackburn (1998) emphasizes this problem of conceptualizing psychopathy based on heterogeneous elements, and considers psychopathy a mythical disorder based on cultural norms and a "moral judgement masquerading as a clinical diagnosis." According to Blackburn, the concept of psychopathy has historically contained the domains of personal deviance and social deviance. These two distinct concepts have been used to explain the disorder in different terms dependent on place and time. North American concepts of psychopathy emphasize social deviance, whereas personal deviance is associated with European conceptualizations. There has been minimal commonality psychometrically across the two concepts, which may be etiologically as well as conceptually distinct (Barbour-McMullen, Coid, & Howard, 1988). These issues have made the psychopathic disturbance difficult to distinguish independent of sociocultural influence.

Sociocultural Influences on Manifestations of Psychopathy

How do sociocultural influences affect the manifestation of psychopathy? Are certain cultures breeding grounds for psychopaths? What is the relationship between masculinity or masculine stereotypes and psychopathy? How do race/ethnicity and social class influence both the presentation and assessment of psychopathy? These and other questions regarding sociocultural influences on the development and manifestation of psychopathy are only beginning to be understood. Research on the relationship between psychopathy and culture has taken a back seat to the surge of research published in recent years in the areas of violence risk assessment and psychopathy and neurobiological studies. The increasing acceptance of psychopathy in Western culture and use of the PCL-R internationally have created renewed interest in the cross-cultural validity of psychopathy as well as interest in cultural and ethnic differences in its manifestation (Sullivan & Kosson, 2006).

Psychopathy and Culture

An interesting body of literature exists that has examined psychopathy as a disturbance of culture (Harrington, 1972; Mailer, 1959; Reiber & Green, 1989; Smith, 1978).[8]

Several authors portray the psychopath as an existentialist antihero who is "the man of the future" (Harrington, 1972), at once admired and condemned for his rational rebellion (Mailer, 1958) and "extrasocial" ways (Smith, 1978). From this perspective, psychopathy is a way to get ahead in America (and other individualist cultures)—a societal value that embodies a toleration for lawlessness, conning, and cheating that is "as American as apple pie" (Reiber & Green, 1989, p. 85). According to Reiber and Green (1989), the conflict between rugged individualism and community values in the larger urban landscape has resulted in a tendency "to wink at successful evasions of the moral code" (p. 85), creating what the authors call the "psychopathy of everyday life." Meloy (1988) cites the rise in stranger homicides and serial murder as evidence that psychopathy is a growing clinical and sociocultural phenomenon in the United States and other cultures, and Reiber and Green (1989) suggest that the public tolerance of the actions of political and governmental figures reflects a type of "bystander intervention" whereby the psychopathy of everyday life is tolerated and admired.

This notion of the psychopathic culture raises a fundamental issue relevant to the distinction between primary and secondary psychopathy. Cultural values may inhibit, disinhibit, and generally shape psychopathic expression and the ways in which psychopathy is defined in the larger social context. This does not necessarily mean that particular cultures will produce a greater number of primary psychopaths. However, a culture that glorifies, condones, or accepts the characteristics of the psychopath (e.g., superficial charm, a grandiose sense of self-worth, conning, lying, need for stimulation, impulsivity, many marital relationships, sexual promiscuity, and failure to take responsibility for actions) may inadvertently support the existence of the secondary psychopath, whose behavior may be deemed psychopathic, but is not likely to produce a significantly greater number of primary psychopaths, who have not developed a sense of attachment in the early years of psychodynamic development.

This raises the question, *How many psychopaths are roaming about in free society, the workplace, the college classroom, or the school playground who have escaped the attention of the criminal justice system?* Cleckley (1941) was the first to popularize the notion of the successful, noncriminal psychopath with case study examples of psychopaths (a "businessman," "gentleman," "man about the world," "scientist," "physician," and "psychiatrist") able to maintain a facade of normality—a "mask of sanity." Reiber and Green (1989) use the term *adaptive psychopaths* to refer to individuals whose day-to-day functioning is not characterized by the impulsivity, hostility, and chaos associated with the clinical condition as it is generally understood, but who exhibit certain hallmarks of psychopathy such as thrill seeking through dangerous behavior, omnipotence expressed in the feeling that they will never get caught, and an innate dissociative capacity that enables them to demarcate periods of antisocial behavior from their "normal" periods, one of the most troublesome aspects of the condition. According to Hare (1993), *white-collar psychopaths* are lawyers, doctors, politicians, teachers, or counselors who hold any high status or respected position. These upper-level psychopaths "are aided by the common expectation that certain classes of people are presumably trustworthy because of their social or professional credentials" (p. 107). Given this selective trust afforded to certain groups (and the selective enforcement of laws that goes along with it), the enigma of the socially adaptive psychopath remains unsolved (Reiber & Green, 1989).[9]

The notion of successful, industrial, or "corporate" psychopaths has been fully described in Babiak and Hare's (2006) *Snakes in Suits: When Psychopaths Go to Work.* According to the authors:

> . . . psychopaths do work in modern organizations; they often are successful by most standard measures of career success; and their destructive personality characteristics are invisible to most people with whom they interact. They are able to circumvent and sometimes hijack succession planning and performance management systems in order to give legitimacy to their behaviors. They take advantage of communication weaknesses, organizational systems and processes, interpersonal conflicts, and general stressors that plague all companies. They abuse coworkers and, by lowering morale and stirring up conflict, the company itself. Some may even steal and defraud. (Babiak & Hare, 2006, p. xiv)

Understanding the nature of noncriminal psychopathy is important in sorting out the relationship between psychopathy and criminal behavior. Recent research suggests that similar etiological processes underlie criminal and noncriminal psychopathy. However, criminal and noncriminal psychopaths are differentiated by the latter's ability to evade the law, higher socioeconomic status, higher levels of executive function, elevated physiological reactivity, and a greater push toward psychopathic behavior by environmental circumstances. Studies to date suggest that high levels of fearless dominance, but not impulsive antisociality may characterize the noncriminal psychopath (Hall & Benning, 2006).

The phenomenon of the noncriminal psychopath raises a number of important questions. Are noncriminal psychopaths less extreme versions of criminal psychopaths or do they represent a more adaptive variant of the personality that perhaps should not be considered disordered? How does noncriminal psychopathy overlap with its criminal expression? If the psychopathic behavior of noncriminal psychopaths appears to be more influenced by environmental forces, then are certain cultures, subcultures, career paths/workplaces, and so on more or less likely to breed psychopathy?

Psychopathy and Gender

Psychopathy, antisocial personality disorder, and crime are overwhelmingly male phenomena. Part of this sex difference can be attributed to sex-role socialization in general and the socialization of aggression in particular. Sex-role socialization shapes the ways aggression manifests across gender. Boys are encouraged to play rough, to contain emotion, and to fight for what they believe in. The most remarkable thing about the socialization of aggression in girls is its absence (Campbell, 1994). As a case in point, a young girl who possesses aggressive narcissism (the personality component of psychopathy) is taught, throughout her childhood, that she will receive attention when she cries but not when she hits. She learns that little girls do not misbehave. Little girls are pretty, patient, and quiet. They should not expect too much. And when they grow up, they will be valued more highly if they find a man. But she is filled with aggression, coupled with the narcissistic need for attention and admiration. What does she do? As she grows up, she masks her aggression with tears, passivity, and physical attractiveness, finding that she gets what she wants this way. Because her aggressive narcissism renders her more forceful and in need of attention than those without this interpersonal style, she is excessively emotional, overly attentive to her physical appearance, and adept at getting whatever she wants. Her behavior does not appear to be antisocial at all. Rather, as a woman she emerges as a dramatically flamboyant social butterfly.

This hypothetical example illustrates the complexity of the relationship between traits and symptoms in the manifestation of psychopathy (and other conditions). The woman possesses the internal personality trait of aggressive narcissism. However, as a result of the ways in which she has been socialized, she does not display the antisocial behaviors commonly associated with the psychopathic disorder. In fact, her behavior appears quite the opposite—as pathologically prosocial. Research shows that women tend to experience internalizing symptomatology such as depression and anxiety, whereas men tend to experience externalizing psychopathology such as antisocial behavior, aggression, and substance abuse (Verona & Vitale, 2006). When women do "act out," anger and aggression are often (re)directed inward and manifest in the form of eating disorders, self-mutilation, or psychiatric or physical illness. Even when women engage in extreme forms of criminal behavior, this behavior is often directed toward their own children or family members, who they are more likely to see as extensions of themselves than strangers or nonfamily members.[10]

Many authors suggest that the female manifestation of psychopathy is not APD, but histrionic personality disorder (HPD; see Ford & Widiger, 1989; Helfgott, 1992; Horowitz, 1977; Lillienfeld, Van Valkenburg, Larntz, & Akiskal, 1986; Spalt, 1980; Warner, 1978). Studies show that APD and HPD represent sex-typed categories of a single disorder (Warner, 1978), that HPD is most often diagnosed in women whereas APD is most often diagnosed in men (Spalt, 1980), and that clinicians are influenced by the labels given to the disorders (Ford & Widiger, 1989). HPD is characterized by excessive emotionality, attention-seeking, self-centeredness, superficial charm, flirtatiousness, dramaticization, sexual provocativeness, seductiveness, use of physical appearance to attract attention, inappropriate and excessive reactions, theatricality, suggestibility, and flights into romantic fantasy (*DSM-IV-TR*, APA, 2000). Studies have shown that the APD criteria reflect stereotypically masculine behaviors and HPD criteria reflect stereotypically feminine behaviors (Horowitz, 1977); that manifestations of the hysterical personality are learned, have symbolic meanings, and are culturally defined (Horowitz, 1991); and that sex bias in clinician expectations account for the sex differentiation between APD and HPD (Ford & Widiger, 1989).

The *DSM* in general, and personality disorder classifications in particular, have been criticized for embodying sexist concepts and values with an androcentric bias that pathologizes stereotypically feminine behaviors (Brown & Ballou, 1992). In their review of the literature on psychopathy in women, Verona and Vitale (2006) conclude that although evidence suggests there is sex bias in diagnosis of psychopathy, data from a range of studies suggest that men and women manifest antisociality and psychopathy differently. PCL-R scores are lower in female prison populations than they are in male prison populations, with lower Factor 2 scores in women. Women are less likely than men to show aggressive symptoms and early behavioral problems and more likely to exhibit higher rates of HPD, BPD, and somatization, prostitution, and sexual misbehavior. Furthermore, the PCL-R does not do a good job predicting violence in women, and some researchers have suggested that the PCL-R items need to be modified to adequately discriminate between psychopathic and nonpsychopathic women. In this new and important area of research on psychopathy, gender, and criminal behavior, "a call for 'more research' is insufficient; what is needed is more theory development, testing, and refinement that accommodate what is known about gender differences in developmental processes, temperament, biology, and socialization" (Verona & Vitale, 2006, p. 432). Jackson and Richards (2007b) suggest generation of new models with female psychopaths in mind, with attention to possible gender differences in the role of childhood physical and sexual abuse in promoting the development of psychopathy, modification of laboratory techniques used in measuring cognitive affective correlates that are more oriented toward women,[11] and examination of noncriminal female psychopaths.

Social Class and Race/Ethnicity

Research on psychopathy that is cognizant of feminist, multicultural, and socioeconomic perspectives calls for a new definition of antisocial behavior that better applies to individuals whose aggressive narcissism has been shaped, through cultural forces, into behavior that *appears* to be prosocial when it is nothing of the kind. The two-factor structure of the PCL-R better integrates traits with symptoms than does the behaviorally weighted classification of APD, and may be able to identify psychopathy independently of cultural influences. It is likely that a female psychopath or a noncriminal psychopath would score high on Factor 1 of the PCL-R, and perhaps on items 11 (promiscuous sexual behavior) and 17 (many marital relationships). However, such a score may not be high enough to warrant a diagnosis of psychopathy. The PCL-R was developed through study of male criminals. Though some evidence suggests that use of the PCL-R may be warranted in minority populations (Kosson, Newman, & Smith, 1990) and noncriminal groups (Hare, 1993), these applications are only beginning to be explored. Use of the PCL-R to assess psychopathy in females may be more problematic, given the gender differences that have been found in the manifestation of psychopathy (Hare, 1991; Peaslee, 1993; Raine & Dunkin, 1990; Warner, 1978) and the ways in which gender stereotypes have influenced psychological classifications (Hamilton, Rothbart, & Dawes, 1986), criminal law (Faith, 1993; Naffine, 1996), criminal justice and mental health policy (Allen, 1987; Brown & Ballou, 1992, Daly, 1995), and definitions of antisocial behavior and aggression (Campbell, 1994; Kirsta, 1994).

Social class and racial/ethnic background may also affect how antisocial behavior is manifest and defined. Cleckley (1941) has said that many psychopaths "mask" their condition and exist quite successfully without coming into contact with the criminal justice system or ever receiving a diagnosis of psychopathy. Furthermore, because nonWhites are more likely to come into contact with the justice system, through the practice of selective enforcement of laws, the label of psychopathy may be overapplied to this group in the criminal justice context.

Returning to the PCL-R, Factor 2 items (which are closely associated with APD criteria) such as early behavioral problems, juvenile delinquency, lack of realistic long-term goals, irresponsibility, and revocation of conditional release are likely to be rated higher in individuals who, as a result of socioeconomic conditions, are forced into situations in which they must behave in these ways to survive. These criteria are designed with the image of the common criminal in mind—prototypically a young, economically disadvantaged male who is a member of a minority group. The criteria may be completely inapplicable to women, whose aggressive narcissism is tempered or rerouted in response to social pressures to prosocial rather than antisocial behavior, except in the case of girls and women who are forced to shed stereotypically female behavior in order to survive.[12]

The "Levels Hypothesis"

Gacono and Meloy (1988, 1994) propose the levels hypothesis to explain the relationship between defensive process, cognitive style, and psychopathic behavior. According to the levels hypothesis, the psychopath's defensive process can be inferred from cognitive style (Figure 4.3). The psychopath's defensive process consists of primitive defenses that make up borderline personality organization (Kernberg, 1966, 1967, 1984, 1985a, 1985b, 1992; described in Chapter 2) and the conscious cognitive style of the psychopath involves the use of cognitive thinking errors that Yochelson and Samenow (1977) suggest are distinctive to the "criminal personality."

To illustrate the unconscious defensive process (UDP)/conscious cognitive style (CCS) relationship, Gacono and Meloy (1988) offer a hypothetical scenario of the

❖ **Figure 4.3** The Levels Hypothesis

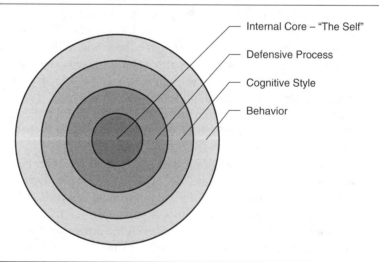

Internal Core – "The Self"

Defensive Process

Cognitive Style

Behavior

mental mechanisms of a psychopath before, during, and after the commission of a violent rape, consisting of pairings of particular unconscious defenses and conscious cognitive thinking errors. The hypothetical rape scenario shows how particular thinking errors and defenses are associated with each other during the commission of a violent act. Pairings of defense mechanisms and thinking errors represent different stages of the mental mechanisms of a psychopath prior to, during, and after the commission of a violent crime. Examples of associations within the stages are splitting/cut-off, shut-off; primitive idealization/grandiosity; projective identification/anger; omnipotent control/power thrust; devaluation/sexuality; and denial/entitlement. Each of the pairs consists of a primitive defense and a "criminal personality thinking error" (Yochelson & Samenow, 1977) representing successions of the mental process involved in the psychopath's ability to commit a violent act. For example, in the first stage, idealization/grandiosity, the psychopath idealizes the object (victim) based on a "goodness of fit" stereotype derived from previous experience with persons symbolized by the victim (e.g., viewing the victim as a person in the psychopath's life such as his mother or father). The conscious component of this stage takes the form of a grandiose identification of the object in which the psychopath convinces himself that the object is attracted to him in some way. The subsequent stages continue the mental process through various defensive techniques and cognitive distortions that enable the psychopath to commit a violent act while maintaining a grandiose self-image and preventing the "zero state" described by Yochelson and Samenow as a state of nothingness that the psychopath continually flees from.

Psychopathy, Crime, and Criminal Justice Policy and Practice

Study of psychopathy is crucial to the understanding of criminal behavior and criminal justice policy and practice. Psychopathy explains human predatory violence. The emotional dysfunction in the psychopath and associated traits are empirically associated with aggressive behavior, particularly instrumental, cold-blooded, predatory behavior. However, the condition calls to question fundamental premises on which the criminal justice system is based. To understand psychopathy is to doubt the basic notions of free will, determinism, insanity, criminality, personality, and person. Psychopaths choose to commit immoral and criminal acts freely (Yochelson & Samenow, 1977), although their choices may be determined in early infancy (Meloy, 1988). Psychopaths are not legally insane, yet they are personality disordered and more dangerous and difficult to explain than those who are (Cleckley, 1941). Most psychopaths are criminals, but most criminals are not psychopaths (Hare, 1993). Psychopaths are not attached to others (Meloy, 1988), but attachment is universal to humans and mammals (Ainsworth, 1989). Psychopaths lack moral sense, though morality distinguishes person from animal (Murphy, 1972). Psychopathy can be considered categorically or dimensionally, but where the line is drawn is often arbitrary or based on psychometric tests that do not measure a homogeneous condition.

What this means for the study of criminal behavior is that psychopathy presents a condition that explains criminality in terms of psychopathology. This presents a number of dilemmas because the criminal law is based on the notion that individuals rationally choose to commit crime. These dilemmas are dealt with in social policy through the dichotomizing of the concepts of criminality and insanity and the separation of criminal justice and mental health into two distinct systems with conflicting objectives. The goals of the criminal justice system are due process, punishment, and public protection. The goals of the mental health system are individual functioning and psychological change. Individuals who do not function properly (with respect to their cognitive capacities) are not held responsible and are dealt with in the mental health system.

By definition, psychopaths are not psychotic. They know right from wrong, are responsible for their actions, and with their lack of conscience are inclined to commit criminal behavior. Simply put, "Given the characteristics of psychopathy . . . it comes as no surprise that the disorder is implicated in a disproportionate amount of serious repetitive crime and violence" (Hare & Hart, 1993, p. 106). Although some psychopaths do not come into contact with the criminal justice system, managing to restrict their antisocial behaviors to noncriminal manipulation and deceit or to avoid detection, psychopathy is clearly compatible with the propensity to commit crime (Hare, 1998).

Psychopaths are criminally versatile. Those who break the law "run the gamut from petty theft and fraud to cold-blooded violence" (Hare, 1998, p. 195). Cleckley (1941) distinguishes the psychopath from the typical criminal who has passion, purpose, and loyalty to a particular group or code of conduct. The criminal works consistently for a goal that can be understood by the average person, sparing him- or herself as much shame and discomfort as possible at the expense of another. The typical murderer kills in the heat of passion, for a particular purpose such as obtaining money or fame, or as the result of psychosis, neurotic compulsion, or some other psychopathological condition. Unlike the typical criminal, the psychopath is not purposive at all, engaging in acts that make no sense to the average observer without the slightest attention to consequences and with absolutely no sense of loyalty to anything or anyone. And unlike the psychotic criminal, who is exempt from legal responsibility, the psychopath does not "have the common decency to go crazy" (Reiber & Green, 1989, p. 48).

Sociologists and criminologists have addressed the relationship between emotional attachment, cognition, and behavior with different terminology and a more general application than psychologists use. In sociological terms, crime is associated with weak or broken social bonds (Hirschi, 1969), defensive techniques (Sykes & Matza, 1957), and linguistic accounts that justify and excuse behavior (Gabor, 1994; Scully & Marolla, 1984). Direct parallels can be drawn between Hirschi's (1969) social bond theory and Meloy's (1992) theory of violent attachments, between Sykes and Matza's (1957) techniques of neutralization and Kernberg's (1985) primitive borderline defenses, and between Scully and Marolla's (1984) findings on the vocabulary of rapists, Gabor's (1994) study of crime by the public, and Reiber and Vetter's (1995) research on the deceptive aberration of language in the psychopath. The similarities across disciplines in the explanations of antisocial behavior reflect an important theoretical link that is necessary to examine the congruence between the psychopathy as a categorical and a dimensional concept.

Because nonpsychopaths have formed attachment in infancy, it makes sense to analyze the ways in which they detach from a sociological, rather than psychological, perspective. The techniques used in ordinary life to detach from others in order to engage in an antisocial act are superficial in the sense that they are not deeply rooted in the psyche, and are primarily learned through culture. According to Blackburn (1993):

> Deviant acts may or may not be a consequence of personality characteristics, but they are not in themselves traits, and belong in a different conceptual domain of *social deviance*. . . . Socially deviant behaviors, then are neither necessary nor sufficient criteria of a disorder of personality, and there is no *a priori* reason for expecting those who are homogeneous in terms of social deviance to belong to a single category of personality deviation. (p. 84–85)

It is important to remember that crime is a *behavioral manifestation,* whereas psychopathy is an *internal psychological condition* that produces a particular set of traits and behaviors. In some cases, psychopathy may produce crime. However, not all criminals are psychopaths. Clinically and categorically, psychopathy is a personality disorder an individual has that is shaped by environmental, situational, and biological factors. Culturally and dimensionally, psychopathy can be conceptualized as a continuum of traits and behaviors that all human beings possess to a lesser or greater degree. Criminal behavior may be produced by a clinically and categorically psychopathic individual or by nonpsychopaths (with any one of a number of internal conditions) who have psychopathic traits that relieve the guilt associated with committing a particular act.

Summary

Psychopathy is historically, theoretically, and practically important to the study of criminal behavior. The *Psychopathy Checklist–Revised (PCL-R)* (Hare, 1991, 2003) has become the standard measure of psychopathy in research, clinical assessment, and criminal justice practice. Research conducted since the publication of the PCL-R has shown that psychopathy is a robust predictor of violent recidivism and dangerousness, with some referring to psychopathy as the "*single most important clinical construct in the criminal justice system.*" This construct is now being used in making decisions at all stages in the criminal justice system.

Psychopathy is a personality disorder characterized by an inability to form human attachment, aggressive narcissism, and antisocial behavior defined by a constellation of affective, interpersonal, and behavioral characteristics, most of which society views as pejorative. Psychopathy can be considered *categorically,* as a discrete clinical disorder of personality, or *dimensionally* along a continuum, as a personality dynamic used to a greater or lesser degree. The PCL-R differs from the Antisocial Personality Disorder classification in that its criteria capture both the personality and behavioral features of traditional concept of psychopathy based on the work of Cleckley. Psychopathy is the product of biological, environmental, and cultural influences. It explains human predatory violence and has important implications for criminal justice policy and practice in law enforcement, adjudication and sentencing, and correctional classification, management, and treatment.

DISCUSSION QUESTIONS

1. What is psychopathy and why is it important in the study of criminal behavior?

2. The *Psychopathy Checklist–Revised* is considered one of the single most important contributions to the scientific study of psychopathy. Explain what the PCL-R is and why it has become so important in research on psychopathy.

3. What are the characteristics of the psychopath? How does psychopathy relate to the Axis II Cluster B personality disorders discussed in Chapter 3? Why isn't psychopathy included as one of the personality disorders in the *DSM-IV-TR*? If the disorder is not listed in the *DSM*, then why do so many researchers continue to use the term?

4. What role do you think environment and culture plays in the development and manifestation of psychopathy? Discuss how gender, ethnicity, subcultural, and cultural factors might shape both the development and behavioral symptoms of psychopathy.

5. The empirical link between psychopathy and general and violent recidivism has made an enormous impact in terms of the applicability of the construct in the criminal (and civil) justice systems. Discuss your thoughts on whether or not and how psychopathy (and PCL-R scores) should be used in the criminal justice system. Should scores on the PCL-R be used at different stages of the criminal and civil justice systems (e.g., bail decisions, sentencing decisions, correctional classification and management, death penalty decisions, juvenile waiver hearings, child custody determinations, etc.)?

On Your Own: Log on to the Web-based student study site at http://www.sagepub .com/helfgottstudy/ for the URL links in the Web Exercises, study aids such as review quizzes, and research recommendations including links to journal articles specifically selected for this book.

WEB EXERCISES

1. Familiarize yourself with the different versions of the PCL-R now available: http://www.hare.org/scales/pclr.html. Explain each and discuss examples of the sort of research that might use these measures.

2. Visit the Web site for the *Society for the Scientific Study of Psychopathy* (SSSP): http://www .psychopathysociety.org/index.php.

3. Read Dr Robert Hare's profile on the Crime Library Web site: http://www.crimelibrary .com/criminal_mind/psychology/robert_hare/index.html.Discuss Dr. Hare's contributions to the study of psychopathy.

4. Read the WebMD article on the BTK Killer and watch the video footage of his courtroom testimony: http://www.foxnews.com/story/0,2933,161145,00.html. Is Rader a successful or unsuccessful psychopath? How does this case illustrate definitional issues with the concept of "successful" or "noncriminal" psychopathy?

5. Review news coverage of the sexually violent predator civil commitment trial of Kevin Coe (subject of Jack Olsen's book *Son: A Psychopath and His Victims*): http://www.spokesmanreview .com/sections/coe/. Discuss the role of psychopathy in Coe's rape behavior and the state's decision to attempt to civilly commit him.

6. Read the story of Elizabeth "Diane" Downs: http://www.crimelibrary.com/notorious_ murders/famous/downs/index_1.html (subject of Ann Rule's book *Small Sacrifices*). Discuss gender differences in the manifestation of psychopathy.

Part II

Criminal Typologies

5

Violent Crime

Well, they started complaining about being tied up, and I re-reloosened the bonds a couple of times, tried to make Mr. Otero as comfortable as I could. Apparently he had a cracked rib from a car accident, so I had him put a pillow down on his—for his—for his head, had him put a—I think a parka or a coat underneath him. They—You know, they talked to me about, you know, giving the car whatever money. I guess they didn't have very much money, and the—from there I realized that, you know, I was already—I didn't have a mask on or anything. They already could ID me, and made—made a decision to go ahead and—and put 'em down, I guess or strangle them.

—Dennis Rader, the "BTK Killer" confessing
to the murders of the Otero family

In February 2005, Dennis Rader was arrested for 10 murders committed in Wichita, Kansas, from 1974 to 1991. The murders went mysteriously unsolved for many years. Dennis Rader, a 60-year-old, churchgoing, married father of two and Cub Scout leader who held a bachelor's degree in Administration of Justice from Wichita State University and worked as the supervisor of the compliance department in Park City, Kansas, gave himself away after he sent an envelope to KSAS TV in Wichita containing a computer disk and letter. The disk was traced to Rader and he was arrested. He confessed and pled guilty, offering a detailed account of the murders, which he referred to as "projects" in court, was convicted of 10 counts of first-degree murder, and sentenced to 10 consecutive life terms.

Media images of rare and extreme forms of violent predatory crime like the BTK murders saturate evening news and popular culture. Violence is primed in the public mind in such a way that many people grossly overestimate the likelihood that they will be victims of violence at the hands of strangers. Armed robberies, homicide-suicides, serial murders, mass murders, family annihilation murders, spree murders, terrorism, child abductions, and school shootings are at the forefront of public consciousness. As a result, *most people are disproportionately fearful of statistically rare violent stranger crimes that make news headlines while they grossly underestimate the chances of violent victimization at the hands of people they know.* For example, though carjacking occurs less frequently than other types of violent offenses, public fear of carjacking exceeds that of robbery and murder as a result of heightened media attention to carjacking compared to other, more usual types of violent offenses (Haghighi & Sorensen, 1996). Similarly, serial murder is a statistically extremely rare phenomenon. Most people have a much higher likelihood of dying from their own bad habits than they do at the hands of a serial killer. Yet, with every Hannibal Lecter sequel on the big screen, a new serial killer to replace every Dennis Rader, Gary Ridgway, Jeffrey Dahmer, or Ted Bundy in the news, it is all too easy to overestimate how many extreme violent offenders are roaming the streets.

Despite the understandable tendency to selectively attend to the more unusual, shocking, or frightening violent crimes, most violent crime does not involve predatory serial murder committed by grandpa-looking strangers who troll the streets in search of helpless families to murder. Of the 14, 860 total murder victims reported in the UCR data for 2005, only 2,070 (14%) were committed by strangers (UCR, 2005).[1] Many violent offenses, some just as gruesome as the higher-profile stranger murders, are committed by family members. For example, on Friday evening January 12, 2007, a North Carolina mother, Amber Violette, returned home from work to find her 4-year-old daughter in the hallway of their home, decapitated. A butcher knife and a serrated kitchen knife were found at the scene. Hours later, the U.S. Marshals Service arrested her husband, John Patrick Violette, at a hotel in Washington, DC, where he had flown and was tracked through his credit card transactions. Violette was sent to a mental hospital for evaluation, and it was uncovered that 10 years earlier he had suffered from paranoid schizophrenia. Neighbors knew the family as loving and stable churchgoers.

This and other cases illustrate that violence is a varied behavioral outcome of a complex web of motivational, situational, and contextual factors. Most violent crime involves offenders and victims who know each other. Most violence is an emotional reaction, not diabolical, methodical, or predatory. A large percentage of violent crime is mundane and ordinary. Spousal abuse, elder abuse, child abuse, barroom brawls, gang fights and shootings, robberies, assaults in the heat of an argument, and so on constitute the bulk of violent crime. For every high-profile serial murder case, there are hundreds of thousands of violent crimes that occur between family members or acquaintances, on city streets, in school hallways, and in workplaces that never make the headlines.

Serious violent crime (murder and non-negligent manslaughter, forcible rape, robbery, and aggravated assault) accounted for only 4.3% of all 14,094,186 arrests in the United States in 2005. In 2005, there were 1,390,695 violent crimes reported to police, resulting in 603,503 arrests.[2] From 2004 to 2005, the estimated volume of violent crime increased 2.3%, with the 5-year trend showing a 3.4% decrease and the 10-year trend (1996 compared with 2005) showing a 17.6% decline in violent crime. Aggravated assault accounted for 62.1%, robbery for 30%, forcible rape for 6.8%, and murder for 1.2% of the violent crimes in 2005. Of the 603,503 arrests for violent crime, approximately 74% were for aggravated assault, 19% were for robbery, 4.2% for forcible rape, and 2.3% for murder. For every 100,000 people, about 469.2 violent crimes occurred in the United States in 2005, down from a rate of 620.1 in 1986 (UCR, 2005).

National Crime Victimization Survey (NCVS) data shows that *47% of all violent crime is reported to police.* According to NCVS data for 2005, the violent crime rate dropped 58% from 1993 to 2005, from 50 to 21 victimizations per 1,000 persons age 12 or older, a reported 5.2 million violent crimes. Of the violent victimizations in 2005, 24% involved a weapon, including 9% in which the weapon used was a firearm. The rate of firearm violence increased slightly in 2005 over 2004 from 1.4 to 2.0 victimizations per 1,000 persons 12 or older. In 2005, there were 191,670 rapes/sexual assaults, 624,850 robberies, 1,052,260 aggravated assaults, and 3,304,930 simple assaults. Males, Blacks, and persons under age 24 are victimized at higher rates than females, Whites, and persons age 25 or older. Males are more likely to be the victims of violent crime overall (homicide, robbery, assault), wheras females are more likely to be sexually assaulted. Males are more likely to be victimized by strangers, and females are more likely to be victimized by someone they know (Catalano, September 2006).

Violent victimization rates (and property crime rates) are the lowest recorded in 20 years (U.S. Department of Justice, 2003). Most criminologists attribute changes in crime rates over time to multiple factors, most important, demographic shifts in the proportion of the population who are of the crime-prone age of 14 to 24. Put in the context of such concerns as public health and mortality rates, homicide did not make it into the top 15 causes of death in 2004 (the latest data available). In 2005, the rate of death by assault/homicide was 5.6 per 100,000, and the death rates by heart disease, accidents, influenza/pneumonia, and suicide were 222.7, 37.0, 20.9, and 10.8, respectively (Minoño, Heron, & Smith, 2004). However, statistics and changes in the overall crime rates over time are no consolation to those personally affected by violent crime. Despite representing only a small portion of all crime, the personal and physical harm caused by violence, its extensive media coverage ("if it bleeds it leads"), and the fear violent crime generates in most people guarantees its status as a social problem of primary concern.

To understand the interplay of biological, sociological, psychological opportunity, cultural, and phenomenological factors from which violent criminal behavior emerges, the offense itself must be the central focus of analysis. Motivation, factors, and forces contributing to violent crime can be uncovered only with careful analysis of offense characteristics. West (2000) suggests that forensic assessment of offenders should include "offense analysis" that uses thematic research-based schema to uncover the phenomenology of offending. This is a theoretically rich method with which to uncover the dynamics of violent offending behavior. Offense analysis is based on the idea that the crime scene and the criminal event hold information necessary to understanding the offender and the offense. The schema, based on a body of specialized knowledge called *forensic psychological assessment,* focuses on the phenomenology of the offense using "theoretical and other research-derived organizing principles as a route map" (West, 2000, p. 227).

One of the problems with many crime typologies is that offenders often do not fall neatly into types (whether theoretically are statistically constructed). The rigid classification schemes often used to define a particular type can be problematic in understanding and classifying offenders in the real world. Dixon and Browne (2003) suggest a "scientific profiling" approach (similar to offense analysis) that bases classification on dominant themes of behavior: "The central hypothesis of scientific profiling is that assailants will carry out crimes using different actions and that these actions will reflect features of the offender" (Dixon & Browne, 2003, p. 123). Typologies are devised based on behavioral actions that can be associated with maladaptive characteristics of the offender (e.g., personality pathology, attitudes, attachment style, social skills deficit). Thus, to identify differences between offenses and offenders, themes of behavior need to be established.

The dynamics of violent offending (and other types of offending) can be understood at an interdisciplinary level by asking, *Why was the offense committed at this time and place and with this victim? What was going on with the offender both internally and externally—what factors, forces, and precipitating events led to the offense?* Additional questions of central importance in uncovering the dynamics of violent offending include

- *What is the victim-offender relationship and situational context of the offense?*
- *What is the degree of predatory versus affective aggression within the offense?*
- *What themes (fantasy, motivation, psychopathology, opportunity, modus operandi) are demonstrated in the commission of the offense?*

Answers to these questions enhance our understanding of the similarities and differences between violent and nonviolent criminal behavior and the ways in which different types of violent crime are distinct.

Aggression and Violence

Although often used interchangeably, violence and aggression are not synonymous terms. There is no generally accepted definition of aggression, but there is agreement in the research literature that *violence is a behavioral manifestation of aggression* (Suris et al., 2004). Violence is a behavior that involves overt threat or application of force likely to result in injury. Aggression is a component of normal behavior that has similar neural bases in animals and humans (Weinshenker & Siegel, 2002). Violence is an expression of a need mediated by environmental, social, and cultural forces that may or may not manifest in violence. The distinction between violence and aggression is illustrated by cases in which aggression (hostility, threat) actually reduces the probability of violence (injury, abuse) (Lederhendler, 2003), for example, when an assault is diffused by a victim's verbal or physically aggressive stance. "Modes of aggression may include acts of violence, but not necessarily. On the other hand, aggression is a necessary component of all acts of violence" (Meloy, 1988, p. 192).

Animal research on aggression suggests that a neural mechanism underlying the different types of aggression produces particular physical responses. In humans, aggression produces much more complex responses. Biological, psychological, socio-logical, cultural, and contextual factors shape the ways in which aggression is behav-iorally displayed in humans. For example, because boys are generally socialized to behave aggressively while girls are not (Campbell, 1994), aggression manifests differ-ently across gender; girls and women are more likely to engage in nonphysical forms of aggression that is more relational than physical (Crick & Nelson, 2002). Whether or not a woman engages in physical violence appears to depend to some extent on the degree to which she is connected to middle-class values and cultural contexts in which female physical aggression and violence are tolerated and reinforced. In some working-class and street cultures, female aggression and violence are survival tools that are rewarded and reinforced (Campbell, 1994; Day, Gough, & McFadden, 2003). Social class, cultural context, media images and role models, the personal meanings attributed to stimulus events, and a cluster of related risk factors shape individual manifestations of aggression.

Cultural context and ethnic differences mediate child and adolescent externalizing outcomes such as aggression, delinquency, and criminality. Ecological niches (unique environments in which children are raised composed of cultural context, parenting style, ethnic background, family characteristics, parents' socialization goals, etc.) affect the manner in which parents use physical discipline, the meanings children attach to that discipline, and its effects on adjustment and behavior. The experience of physical discipline in the first five years of life and during adolescence is associated with more externalizing behavior problems for European American adolescents but lower rates for African American adolescents. For example, African American children may regard spanking as legitimate parenting practice carried out in their best interest whereas European American children view it as a frightening experience in which their parents are out of control (Lansford et al., 2004). These findings illustrate the importance of understanding human aggression within the context of complex interactions and forces, and how critical phenomenological factors—the meanings attached to events throughout the life course—are influencing behaviors, including the manifestation of aggression, violence, and crime.

Two Types of Aggression and Violence: Predatory and Affective

Researchers have identified many forms of aggression—maternal, territorial, irrita-ble, intermale, fear-induced, sex-related, among others (Moyer, 1968). Different authors distinguish between the types[3] and compare conceptual classifications;[4] however, the literature suggests that aggression is not a unitary phenomenon and the many forms of aggression can be divided into two distinct types—*predatory* and *affective*. Predatory aggression is instrumental and proactive, whereas affective aggression is expressive and reactive. Human violence can be motivated by either or both types of aggression.[5]

The bimodal predatory/affective classification is an important theoretical tool in distinguishing violent crime from other types of crime and understanding the moti-vations of different types of violent offenders. *The motivation for violence lies in the mode of aggression underlying a violent act.* However, a critical problem in classifying offenders as predatory or affective aggressors is that many offenders have a history of both instrumental and reactive violent offenses and some acts of violence are motivated by both modes of aggression. Cornell et al. (1996) suggest classifying violent offenders into those with a history of at least one instrumental (predatory) offense and those with a history of reactive (affective) offenses but no instrumental offenses.[6] An individual offender who engages in violent criminal behavior may be simultaneously motivated by predatory and affective aggression or by one or the other at different times, but could be classified based on the quantity of predatory and affectively motivated violent acts in their offense history.

A number of authors (Meloy, 1988; Moyer, 1968) have used the example of the physiological features of a cat in a stalking or fear reaction stance to explain the differences between predatory and affective aggression. When a cat stalks prey, it behaves quite differently from when it is defending itself from attack. The cat that stalks a bird or a mouse slinks silently, close to the ground, and makes its deadly attack. The cat that is threatened by a raccoon or dog hisses and growls, and arches its back with its tail fluffed out and ears back. The cat may then attack with a frenzy of biting and scratching. These two types of behavioral responses differ in terms of the stimulus inducing the response and the sympathetic arousal associated with the response (Figure 5.1).

Affective Aggression

The vast majority of human violence is motivated by affective aggression—barroom brawls, domestic violence, child abuse, and most murders are the unplanned result of a physiological and emotional reaction to a real or imagined threat. These types of violent acts could also be committed by people engaging in predatory aggression (e.g., spousal violence involving a batterer with psychopathic characteristics who engages in violence

❖ **Figure 5.1**   Features of Predatory and Affective Aggression

Predatory	Affective
No perceived threat	Perceived threat
Goal oriented	Goal threat reduction
No conscious experience of emotion	Conscious experience of emotion
Planned purposeful violence	Reactive unplanned violence
Increased self-esteem	Decreased self-esteem
Unimpaired reality testing	Possible loss of reality testing

including methodically planned stalking behaviors), but the bulk of them involve people who react violently to threat, frustration, anger, anxiety, confusion, or other uncomfortable emotional state (e.g., disturbances of perception such as hallucinations or delusions suffered by schizophrenics). Affective aggression is characterized by

> an intense and patterned sympathetic activation of the autonomic nervous system due to external or internal threatening stimuli. It is accompanied by threatening and defensive postures and increased vocalization. Often it is an end in itself and seldom correlates with feeding or predation in animals. It may, however, subsequently precede or follow predatory aggression in humans. (Meloy, 1988, p. 192)

Affective aggression is a defensive behavioral response accompanied by physiological changes and a particular behavioral posture similar to that found in cats and other animals. Unlike in animals, however, affective aggression in humans, in some cases, is part of a range of behavioral responses that may include predatory aggression.

Meloy (1988, pp. 193–211) identifies 13 discrete characteristics of affective aggression:

1. Intense sympathetic arousal of the autonomic nervous system

2. Subjective experience of conscious emotion

3. Reactive and immediate violence, if present

4. Internally or externally perceived threat

5. Goal of threat reduction

6. Rapid displacement of the target of aggression

7. Time-limited behavioral sequence

8. Prefaced by public ritual

9. Primary affective dimension

10. Heightened and diffuse sensory awareness

11. Self- and object percept dedifferentiation

12. Possible loss of reality testing

13. Lowered self-esteem

Affective aggression is the reaction to a stimulus perceived as a biological or psychological threat that can be external (e.g., another person) or internal (e.g., auditory hallucination or cognitive distortion). Affective aggression is precipitated by sympathetic motivation of the nervous system that prepares the person for increased muscular activity necessary for attack. *A person experiencing affective aggression is in a physiological alarm state* associated with heightened sensory awareness, momentary loss of sensory-perceptual distinction (between past/present, self/other, reality/fantasy, human/nonhuman), and behavioral cues such as dilated pupils, increased perspiration, increased and shallow breathing, flushed skin, defensive posturing, and increased loudness and frequency of vocalizations. Individuals who have engaged in affective violence retrospectively report intense feelings of fear or anger at the time of the violent incident.

The immediate goal of affective aggression is threat reduction, which involves a "fight-or-flight" behavioral response. Violence motivated by affective aggression lasts seconds or minutes. It is the end product of a behavioral sequence that enables the individual to return to a state of biological efficiency and psychological homeostasis as quickly as possible. *One of the most salient characteristics of affective violence is that it is associated with lowered self-esteem,* which takes the form of fear, anger, and anxiety prior to or during the violence or profound feelings of guilt, remorse, and shame following the event. The following is an offender's retrospective account of the affectively motivated murder of his wife (taken from a prison encounter program in which offenders shared their stories with victims of crime and community members; see Helfgott, Lovell, & Lawrence, 2002; Helfgott, Lovell, Lawrence, & Parsonage, 2000; Lovell, Helfgott, & Lawrence, 2002):

> Graduated. . . . Bought a house. . . . Had a daughter. Marriage was going pretty well . . . but I was irresponsible with money . . . too many credit cards . . . marriage suffered, was young. I was a good father, not a good husband, didn't know what to do. Went to a church person who suggested a therapist. Therapy brought up childhood stuff, but didn't know what to do with the stuff. Became very suicidal . . . therapist didn't take me seriously. . . . [I was] depressed. Bought a shotgun and drove around with it in the car. Wanted to just jump on a plane to Sweden . . . then nothing would have happened. Went home . . . Left the shotgun in the car. My wife was there. We got in an argument. . . . My first impulse was to throw the TV through the window. Wish I'd have done that. Anger built up inside me, nowhere to go. It had been building for two weeks. . . . Ended up in the kitchen . . . had to make an effort to get the knife. . . . I stabbed her. She was an innocent mother. I'd never been to jail, never abused her. She died. I panicked, didn't have intention to do it. . . . I left . . . drove to Canada . . . turned around . . . went to a hotel . . . called 911 and told them I killed my wife and my daughter was still in the house. I was going to kill myself. I didn't. Had the shotgun, not pleasant having it in your mouth. I'd trade places with my wife. She deserves to be alive.

This offender narrative illustrates the emotional nature of affective aggression and violence—the flight-or-fight response to a perceived threat (in this case the stress and pressure of an overwhelming family situation), the building frustration and anger, and decreased self-esteem present before, during, and after the event (anger, lack of control, guilt/regret). This was the first and only criminal offense committed by this individual, he confessed to the crime upon arrest, was convicted of first-degree murder, and sentenced to life in prison.

Predatory Aggression

Some human violence is motivated, at least in part, by predatory aggression—serial murder, murder-for-hire, and incidents in which violence is used as a means to an end are examples of predatory or instrumentally violence. In animals, predatory aggression occurs between species resulting in the destruction of prey to secure food.

In humans, predatory aggression occurs within species. Some psychopathological conditions such as psychopathy are particularly suited to predatory aggression. Features of predatory aggression contrast with those of affective aggression, yet often the behavioral result (violence) produced by these contrasting modes of aggression can appear very similar. Meloy (1988, pp. 212–234) identifies 13 discrete characteristics of predatory aggression:

1. Minimal or absent autonomic arousal

2. No conscious experience of emotion

3. Planned and purposeful violence, if present

4. No or minimal perceived threat

5. Multidetermined and variable goals

6. Minimal or absent displacement of the target of aggression

7. Time-unlimited behavioral sequence

8. Preceded or followed by private ritual

9. Primary cognitive-conative dimension

10. Heightened and focused sensory awareness

11. Self- and object concept dedifferentiation

12. Unimpaired reality testing

13. Heightened self-esteem

One of the most striking examples of human predatory aggression is the case of Dennis Rader, the BTK Killer. Dennis Rader recounts the murder of his fifth victim, Shirley Vian:

> I told Mrs.—Miss Vian that I had a problem with sexual fantasies, that I was going to tie her up, and that—and I might have to tie the kids up, and that she would cooperate with this—cooperate with me at that time. We went back. She was extremely nervous. Think she even smoked a cigarette. And we went back to the—one of the back—back areas of the porch, explained to her that I had done this before, and, you know, I think she—at that point in time I think she was sick 'cause she had a night robe on, and I think, if I remember right, she was—she had been sick. I think—I think she came out of the bedroom when I went in the house. So anyway, we went back to the—her bedroom, and I proceeded to tie the kids up, and they started crying and got real upset. So I said oh, this is not gonna work, so we moved 'em to the bathroom. She helped me. And then I tied the door shut. We put some toys and blankets and odds and ends in there for the kids, make them as comfortable as we could. Tied the—We tied one of the bathroom doors shut so they couldn't open it, and we shoved—she went back and helped me shove the bed up against the other bathroom door, and then I proceeded to tie her up. She got sick, threw up. Got her a glass of water, comforted her a little bit, and then went ahead and tied her up and then put a blag (sic)—a bag over her head and strangled her. (Court Transcript of BTK's Confession)

Rader's description of his behaviors in the course of the murders are chilling examples of human predatory violence.

In some individuals, the distinction between predatory and affective violence may not be so clear and affective aggression may appear predatory.[7] Individuals with borderline personality organization (e.g., psychopaths, narcissists) are able to dissociate or "split off" affect so they to not experience emotion during an episode of affective violence. For example, affective aggression in psychopaths tends to be masked by predatory aggression and violence occurring before and after brief periods of affective violence. Violence committed by psychopaths often appears instrumental, cold, calculated, and devoid of affect. Psychopaths are biologically predisposed to lower levels of autonomic reactivity and employ a particular set of (primitive) defenses resulting in *affect block* (Meloy, 1988, p. 204). They may experience momentary bouts of affective aggression amid periods of predatory aggression and violence, but in such cases aggression would be followed by narcissistic rage rather than remorse or guilt, and lack of overt expression of emotion requires that affect be inferred from particular behaviors. Some individuals may shift between modes of affective and predatory violence—to inflict additional injury on a victim to satisfy sadistic impulses or to conceal their true motives for the violence to deceive forensic investigators. Predatory violence may also occur along with affective violence:

> Skin-boundary contact with the victim during an act of predation may correlate with a shift to affective violence. This is a common occurrence among sexual psychopaths who are predatorily violent until they come into actual physical contact with the victim and psychobiologically shift to a state of affective aggression and violence as a result of sensory-perceptual triggers of the victim; "in a sense, the victim may be perceived as invading the psychopath's visual, auditory, olfactory, gustatory, and somesthetic fields despite *his* [the psychopath's] aggression, leading to high levels of sympathetic arousal" (Meloy, 1988, p. 214).

Thus, psychopaths, though more inclined to engage in predatory aggression and violence, given their nature, may affectively react in situations in which they are angered or insulted or a victim does not follow the predetermined script the offender imagines and plans for.

Predatory aggression is characterized by a "striking absence of autonomic arousal" (Meloy, 1988, p. 213) and the absence of emotion. The only emotions that may be experienced during episodes of predatory aggression are exhilaration and contemptuous delight.[8] *Predatory violence is planned, purposeful, and intentional.* An individual engaging in predatory violence makes a conscious choice to do so, though this choice may be fueled by unconscious motivation or compulsion. For example, a number of serial killers such as Arthur Shawcross, Edmund Kemper, and Gary Ridgway (see Box 5.1) have been explained in terms of displaced matricide—their anger and wish to destroy their mothers was displaced and fulfilled by murdering hitchhikers or prostitutes. Such cases illustrate the sequential shifts between predatory and affective violence.

The individual engaging in predatory aggression actively, intentionally, and attentionally fixates on and stalks a particular victim who is not a threat. The victim is selected based on a particular stereotype and simultaneously idealized and devalued. The predation can be momentary or may last for years. The violent event is preceded or followed

BOX 5.1

GARY RIDGWAY

THE GREEN RIVER KILLER

Gary Ridgway at sentencing.

Photo Credit: © AFP/Getty Images.

In November 2003 Gary Leon Ridgway, aka the Green River Killer, pled guilty to 48 murders in a plea agreement that spared him the death penalty in Washington State. Ridgway was convicted of more murders than any other serial killer in U.S. history. For two decades, the Green River case went unsolved until advances in DNA technology made it possible to test biological evidence collected from victims' remains found in the 1980s.

Ridgway began murdering teenage girls and women in 1982, leaving their bodies in the Green River south of Seattle and in other locations near freeways, ravines, and the SeaTac airport. Most of the victims were teenagers who were prostitutes, runaways, or hitchhikers. During the years he murdered, spanning from 1982 to the late 1990s, he was employed as a truck painter for the Kenworth Truck Company in Renton, Washington, was married several times, and had a son (whom he had wait for him in the car during a number of the murders). He was arrested, questioned, and released in the late 1980s after being seen with one of the victims. Small amounts of DNA evidence found on victims' remains were preserved for 20 years until new DNA technology linked Ridgway to several of the victims.

By Ridgway's own account (in court documents and the publicly released DVDs of the five-month investigation preceding the plea agreement), he indicated that his intent was to murder prostitutes, and that he targeted prostitutes because he hated them and thought he could kill as many as he wanted without getting caught. He referred to his victims as "ladies," whom he distinguished from "women." To Ridgway, prostitutes were "ladies" and "workers" (working-class women) were "women." Although some of his victims were not prostitutes, he insisted that they had all taken money for sex and the few who did not, "pissed him off" in some other way. His modus operandi was to pick up a woman for a "date," offer her money for sex, have her take her clothes off, have sex with her, manually strangle her from behind, and then dump her body in a remote location. He experimented with postmortem sex with at least one of his victims and with two victims inserted rocks in their vaginas. He referred to his victims as "garbage," covered them with shrubs and other debris, and left them in "clusters" near trees and other markers so he knew where they were and could return to the sites. He indicated in interviews with detectives that he did not enjoy the sex as much with the victims when they were dead, but engaged in the postmortem sex because he didn't have to pay for it, the bodies belonged to him, and it was more convenient than searching for another victim and having to go through the trouble of dumping the body (which he indicated was a big hassle for him and somewhat of a deterrent).

Ridgway was born on February 18, 1949. At age 11, he moved to South King County, Washington, where he lived for most of his life. In 1969 he joined the Navy, got married in 1970, and then was stationed for a period in the Philippines. While stationed in the Philippines, his wife became involved with another man and they divorced in 1972. Ridgway later claimed that his ex-wife became a "whore" while he was overseas. In 1971, Ridgway was employed as a painter for Kenworth Truck Company, located on East Marginal South a few miles from Pacific Highway South, where many of the victims were last seen. He worked at Kenworth for over 30 years until his arrest in 2001.

In 1973, Ridgway married his second wife, whom he had known for approximately a year. During his second marriage he lived in Renton, West Seattle, and Federal Way. He and his wife had a son on September 5, 1975. Ridgway's second wife reported that during their marriage Ridgway liked to have sex outdoors, was interested in bondage, would leave home at night for long periods and return wet and dirty, liked to hide from her and sneak up on her when she walked in the woods, and that he tried to choke her on at least one occasion. Their relationship ended in 1980, and they were divorced on May 27, 1981. After the divorce, Ridgway's wife gained custody of their son and he was awarded custody on alternate weekends.

In 1981, Ridgway bought a house in South King County, where he later admitted he had killed dozens of women, mostly during an 18-month period after his second divorce. After dating several women whom he met through Parents without Partners, he met and married his third wife in 1988. After his marriage he moved several times to different locations in South King County. He was arrested at his residence in Auburn, Washington, in 2001. Two weeks before his arrest for the Green River Murders, he was arrested for soliciting an undercover King County Sheriff detective for prostitution. During his booking, he asked the officers to not contact his wife, but to contact the Green River Task Force, saying "they know me real well" (King County Prosecutor's Summary of Evidence, p. 8).

(Continued)

(Continued)

Ridgway "had what appeared to be an innate understanding of forensic evidence" (p. 33). If a victim scratched him, he would cut her fingernails. At one crime scene he left tire tracks so he purchased new tires and threw the old ones in the river in two different locations. After one victim left deep scratches in his arms, he burned himself with battery acid to hide the scratch marks. He left phony evidence at scenes to throw off police (cigarette butts, gum, a hair pick). He wrote a letter to a local newspaper entitled "What you need to know about the Green River Man," designed to throw off the police. He avoided detection because he did not fit the profile of the typical serial killer. He did not have a history of juvenile or adult criminal behavior, maintained long-term employment, was not a loner, had a family, and did not display the grandiosity and superficial charm seen in other serial killers or keep trophies of his kills. Ridgway gained his victims' trust by being an "ordinary person," nonthreatening, meek, and average. A forensic psychologist who interviewed Ridgway reported that "his admissions reveal a deeply rooted psychopathy" that enabled him to deflect suspicion and pass a polygraph taken in the late 1980s, when he was originally suspected for the murders. When asked by the forensic psychologist if there was something missing in him that was present in other people, he replied "caring" (p. 126).

Ridgway's method of approaching, abducting, and murdering his victims was clearly an act of predatory aggression. His goal was to murder prostitutes who were not an (external) threat. He carefully planned his crimes and confessed to systematically and methodically murdering more than 70 women. His matter-of-fact account of his murders suggests that he did not consciously experience emotion during his crimes and that his self-esteem was inflated through the commission of the violent acts, which he said gave him a sense of power and control. Forensic psychological evaluations determined that Ridgway was legally sane. At the time of the murders he was in touch with reality, rationally chose to murder his victims, and took elaborate steps to avoid detection. However, his predatory acts were preceded and, in some cases, followed by affective aggression. In interviews with detectives and forensic psychologists, he expressed anger toward and sexual attraction for his mother. He referred to his first ex-wife as a "whore" and committed the bulk of his murders during an 18-month period following his second divorce. This suggests that his inclination to kill was, at its onset, an affectively motivated behavioral response to an internally perceived threat (e.g., mother, wife). Through conditioning processes and as a result of external factors, personality traits, cognitive schema, and defensive mechanisms, his aggression became predatory and instrumental on a conscious level and his affective aggression was displaced onto prostitutes who became the targets of predatory aggression.

However, at different points throughout his 20-year career as a serial killer Ridgway engaged in episodes of affective violence. He killed several of his victims with their clothes on before having sex with them. This was unusual because he killed the majority of his victims after they had removed their clothes and after having sex. In interviews with detectives, he indicated that the few victims he killed with their clothes on, with whom he did not have sex, made him angry in some way. He did not plan to kill them, but did so because they made him angry. For example, he told police that he killed one victim because she gave him a "blow job" and this "pissed him off." This is an example of an affectively motivated act of violence. In fact, Ridgway's account of this incident indicates that he did, in fact, experience emotion (anger) at the time of the murder and that his self-esteem decreased as a result because it was not his plan to kill these particular women, or at least in this way. Thus, while the majority of his murders were predatory acts, it could be argued that the underlying drive and original inclination to kill was rooted in affective aggression, and that even though this transformed into a predominately predatory mode, he engaged in affective violence with several victims at different periods throughout his life.

On December 18, 2003, King County Superior Court Judge Richard Jones imposed 48 consecutive life sentences and ordered Ridgway to pay $480,000 in fines, $10,000 for each victim. Ridgway is incarcerated at the Washington State Penitentiary in Walla Walla, Washington.

by private ritual that has symbolic meaning. For example, Gary Ridgway dumped his victims in "clusters" for the purpose of revisiting the scenes to relive the experience and enhance his feelings of grandiosity. Wesley Dodd, executed in 1993 for murdering and sexually assaulting three boys in Washington State, kept meticulous journals detailing his fantasies and plans. Unlike affective aggression, the goal of predatory violence is not to reduce a perceived threat, but to acquire resources, gratify sadistic desires, satisfy a perversion, relieve compulsion, fulfill fantasies of vengeance, or exercise omnipotent control and power over a victim. Goals of predatory aggression may also be inspired or dictated by situational or environmental forces such as media and pop culture, youth gang or organized crime subcultures, acute socioeconomic stressors, ideological or religious beliefs, or family systems or cultural contexts that disinhibit aggression.

Predatory aggression and violence is associated with heightened self-esteem. Predatory violence is a means through which confidence is increased and grandiosity and omnipotence are bolstered. The following account by an offender (scoring above 36 on the PCL-R who participated in a study on unconscious defensive process/conscious cognitive style in psychopaths) who tortured and murdered a 55-year-old man and a 20-year-old woman illustrates the self-esteem–enhancing nature of predatory violence:

> They owed money, didn't want to pay, needed a lesson. Beat 'em up, tied 'em up, stabbed 'em up, beat 'em up some more, stabbed 'em some more, threw 'em down the stairs. . . . Asked if they understand, then choked 'em to death. Was thinking it was a lot of fun—the look in their eyes—unknown terror—gives a good warm glow all over—to look . . . and say, "it's not happening to me." Power. . . . It's a small margin between pain and pleasure—people get hurt and it's like ecstasy, but if it goes further, it's not fun anymore. Like they didn't know they had really stepped in it this time and thought they were just going to get roughed up a bit. It looked like they were enjoying it at first—glazed look, nonchalant . . . then . . . terror, at the point when they realized it wasn't like other times—halfway through when hitting them in the head with a hammer. . . . (Helfgott, 1997b, 2004)

This offenders' retrospective description of a predatory violent event reveals the contemptuous delight, exhilaration, and omnipotence the offender experienced during and following the event. The feelings of power and "ecstasy" contrast markedly with the remorse and anxiety that individuals who engage in affective aggression and violence generally experience in the aftermath of the event.

Gender, Aggression, and Violence

According to 2005 UCR arrest data for which gender of offender was recorded, of the 372,962 adult arrests for violent crime in 2005, approximately 82.1% was committed by males and 17.9% by females. Of the 56,889 juvenile arrests for violent crime, 81.6% was committed by males and 18.4% by females. Table 5.2 shows UCR data on the breakdown by sex for 10-year arrest trends for violent crime from 1996 to 2005. Most violent offenders and victims of violence are male. National Crime Victimization data show that most violent crime is characterized by male-on-male violence and both male and female offenders are more likely to target male victims than female victims. For example, data on the victim-offender relationship in homicides show that most homicides involve male offenders and male victims. When females engage in violence, however, they are more likely to attack males than females, while the smallest category of violent crimes involves female-on-female violence (Table 5.2).

Given the striking sex bias in crime, the "man question" (*What is it about men that makes them commit crime and what is it about women that makes them law abiding?*) should be the central preoccupation of criminologists (Naffine, 1996):

> Sexual difference runs right through the crime statistics—from large-scale corporate fraud to petty property crime; from major to minor crimes against the person. Crime is also something that men are expected to do, because they are men, and women are expected not to do, because they are women. Crime, men, and masculinity have an intimate relationship, so intimate that we often fail to see it, and so intimate that it can seem natural. Though the vast majority of men do not enter the official criminal statistics, those individuals who do become known as criminals are usually men. Each year we know this will be true and rarely is anything made of it, even though for many it is a major concern. It would be astonishing were the crime statistics, official or informal, to reveal otherwise. Criminology would tilt on its axis. (Naffine, 1996, p. 6)

The "man question" becomes even more central with respect to violent crime, in particular armed robbery and forcible rape, which have historically been male-only offenses. In Gilligan's (1996) compelling book *Violence,* he concludes,

> If humanity is to evolve beyond the propensity toward violence that now threatens our very survival as a species, then it can only do so by recognizing the extent to which the patriarchal code of honor and shame generates and obligates male violence. If we wish to bring this violence under control, we need to begin by reconstituting what we mean by both masculinity and femininity. (p. 267)

It is impossible (and some may argue irresponsible) to speak of crime, particularly crimes of violence, without speaking specifically of gender (see Messerschmidt, 1993, *Masculinities and Crime,* and Naffine, 1996, *Feminism and Criminology,* for compelling and comprehensive discussion of the historical gender-blindness of criminology).

News headlines such as "Girls Getting Increasingly Violent" (Hall, 2004), "Violence Among Girls Growing Nationwide" (Miller, 2004), and "Teen Love, Teen Hate: Girl Gang Takes Savage Revenge" (Thompson, 2004) seem to suggest that female aggression and violence is on the rise. This is only partially true. Since 1996, violent

❖ **Table 5.1** UCR Data for Violent Crime

10-Year Arrest Trends
by Sex, 1996–2005
[8,009 agencies; 2005 estimated population 178,017,991; 1996 estimated population 159,290,470]

Offense charged	Male						Female					
	Total			Under 18			Total			Under 18		
	1996	2005	Percent change	1996	2005	Percent change	1996	2005	Percent change	1996	2005	Percent change
Murder and nonnegligent manslaughter	8,572	7,114	−17.0	1,290	664	−48.5	992	875	−11.8	98	75	−23.5
Forcible rape	18,512	14,924	−19.4	3,153	2,332	−26.0	233	205	−12.0	49	60	+22.4
Robbery	73,192	60,096	−17.9	22,962	15,118	−34.2	7,788	7,745	0.6	2,356	1,673	−29.0
Aggravated assault	260,469	224,080	−14.0	36,972	8,312	−23.4	54,936	57,923	+5.4	9,152	8,655	−5.4
Arson	9,972	8,114	−18.6	5,794	4,230	−27.0	1,626	1,602	−1.5	712	685	−3.8
Total Violent Crime (not including "other assaults")	360,745	306,214	−15.1	64,377	46,426	27.9	63,949	66,748	+4.4	11,655	10,463	−10.2
Other assaults	597,763	554,044	−7.3	99,610	95,555	−4.1	158,366	183,431	+15.8	38.240	47,402	+24.0

❖ **Table 5.2** The Victim/Offender Relationship in Homicides

Offender/Victim Relationship	Percentage of Homicides
Male offender/Male victim	65.2
Male offender/Female victim	22.6
Female offender/Male victim	9.7
Female offender/Female victim	2.4

Source: Adapted from National Crime Victimization Survey data for 2004 reported by the Bureau of Justice Statistics: http://www.ojp.usdoj.gov/bjs/homicide/gender.htm

crime arrests of adult and juvenile males decreased in all violent crime categories. Arrests of adult females decreased in all violent crime categories (murder, rape, robbery) *except* aggravated and "other" assaults, which saw a 5.4% and 4.4% increase, respectively. For females under age 18, arrests for violent crime decreased in all categories *except* forcible rape, which increased 22.4%. Murder and non-negligent manslaughter arrests for males showed a 17% decrease for adult males and 48.5% decrease for juvenile males. For females there was a smaller decrease in homicide arrests of 11.8% for adults and 23.5% for juveniles (UCR, 2005). *In general, violent crime has decreased across the board regardless of gender. However, the gap in arrest and incarceration rates between males and females is becoming increasingly smaller.*

Much of the increase in arrest and incarceration rates for female violent crime can be attributed to changes in public perception and law enforcement response to girls and women who commit crime (this is especially likely to be the case with traditionally male crimes such as forcible rape). Historically, sex differences in female aggression and violence have been systematically exaggerated, similarities between male and female aggression have been minimized, and much of the aggression and violence committed by females has historically been overlooked (Day, Gough, & McFadden, 2003). When it comes to crimes that are premeditated, intentional, and predatory, there has been much cultural resistance to recognizing the capacity of females (especially White upper-middle-class females) to commit this sort of behavior. Resistance has been particularly strong to recognizing instrumental/predatory aggression in girls and women. In fact, "Instrumental aggression in women, both of legitimate and illegitimate nature, lacks a place in our culture" (Naffine, 1996, p. 147), despite evidence suggesting that girls and women do experience and engage in instrumental aggression and violence.

In the 1990s, a great deal of media attention was given to the subject of female violence, suggesting there was a "new breed" of violent women (Kirsta, 1994). This has contributed to changing public views on the types of violence girls and women are capable of and changes in law enforcement policy and practice with respect to defining, identifying, arresting, convicting, and sentencing girls and women who commit violent crime. Films such as *Thelma and Louise, Blue Steel, True Romance, The Last Seduction, Natural Born Killers,* and *Set It Off* (and more recently *Kill Bill Volumes 1, 2,* and forthcoming 3 and 4) depicted girls and women committing traditionally male crimes. For example, prior to the 1990s, law enforcement definitions of gang members excluded females despite the fact that female gang members have existed since the early 19th century (Campbell, 1994; Sikes, 1998). Similarly, even though there are at least 64 documented cases of female serial killers since 1826, many of whom were instrumentally motivated (Hickey, 2002, 2006), Aileen Wuornos is often referred to as the "first female serial killer." Other crimes of violence such as infanticide and spousal homicide and assault have long been committed by women in the domestic sphere (Gauthier & Bankston, 2004; Messing & Heeren, 2004).

The apparent increases in some categories of violent crime may have more to do with changing perceptions of gender differences in violent crime (and the willingness to arrest, convict, and sentence female offenders), the identification of women committing traditionally male and instrumental forms of violence (e.g., armed robbery and use of firearms), and the willingness to publicly acknowledge female violence than to an actual increase in female violence. Women who act aggressively and violently have historically been dealt with through the mental health system rather than the criminal justice system, so they are less likely to show up in the official crime statistics. They are also more likely to have their crimes explained away—as the end product of sexual abuse, emotional trauma, or hysteria (Allen, 1987). Although available data from the United States and around the world across all time periods suggest that violent crime is a predominantly male phenomenon, it is highly probable that female aggression and violence is, and has always been, much more prevalent than official statistics suggest (Day, Gough, & McFadden, 2003).

The evidence suggesting that female aggression and violence has always existed does not change the fact that, throughout history and across cultures, violent crime has been disproportionately committed by males. It does suggest, however, that violent crime must be understood as if gender matters. According to Messerschmidt (1993):

> In order to comprehend what it is about men as men and boys as boys that impels them to commit more crime and more serious types of crime than women and girls—as well as different types and amounts among themselves—we need first a theoretical grasp of social structure and gendered power. (p. 29)

As discussed in Chapter 1, cultural images of males as predators and females as prey shape individual-level criminal behavior. Within each category of violent crime, questions must be asked: *What role does gender play in the motivations, factors, and forces that produce violent criminal behavior and violent victimization? What factors come into play when girls and women engage in criminal behavior, especially traditionally male forms of criminality, despite the socialization pressures for girls and women to be peacemakers? How much do ultramasculine subcultural environments increase the likelihood of criminality? How much does the cultural notion of the male predator and female victim work its way into self-images of boys and girls? How does female gender-role socialization alter behavioral manifestations of affective and predatory aggression?* Criminal behavior, particularly violent and sex crimes and violent victimization, must be understood within the context of patriarchal society, the male-predator/female-prey dichotomy, and cultural shifts in sex-role socialization practices and ideas about the sorts of behaviors males and females engage in.

Types of Violent Crime

The degree to which criminal typologies are meaningful depends on how homogeneous crime categories are. Of central importance in understanding violent crime is the question of specialization. If all criminals engaged in all types of crime, it would make little sense to break crimes into categories or types. On the other hand, if some criminals specialize in a particular type of crime, then something can be said about one category of crime and criminals that may not be said about another:

> Instead of attempting to predict "violence" as if it were a unitary, homogeneous mode of behavior, efforts should be directed at differentiating meaningful subtypes or syndromes of violent individuals and then determining the diagnostic signs in the clinical data that will enable us to identify individuals of each type. (Megargee, 1970, p. 146, in Cornell et al., 1996, p. 783)

The central task in developing a meaningful typology of criminal behavior is to identify features that are unique to each type of crime.

Is there something about violent crime that differentiates it from other types of criminal behavior? Do some offenders specialize in violent crime, and when they do commit crime, is it more likely to be violent? Research suggests that "violent and nonviolent offending may be different phenomena," and that individuals who commit violent criminal behavior differ from those who do not (Lynam, Piquero, & Moffitt, 2004, p. 226). Using self-report data, Lynman, Piquero, and Moffit (2004) found that two important factors distinguish offenders who specialize in violent crime—childhood conduct problems and negative emotionality, traits similar to those associated with psychopathy. This and other research (Cornell et al., 1996) support the strong empirical link between level of psychopathy and violent crime discussed in the previous chapter. From a continuum/dimensional perspective, one can say that violent crime is a function of psychopathy level—the greater the number of psychopathic and antisocial traits and characteristics, the greater the probability of committing, and specializing in, violent crime.

This does not mean that all violent offenders are psychopaths. Most individuals who commit violent crime would not score above 30 on the PCL-R, and some individuals may engage in violence as a result of a very different psychopathological condition (e.g., paranoid schizophrenia, mood disorder). However, *to engage in violence against another human (or living) being requires suspension, however momentary, of emotion and attachment.* To understand this, it is helpful to conceptualize the relationship between psychopathy and violence along a continuum. The more psychopathic traits an individual possesses, the more able the person is to detach or "dissociate" or "cut off" feelings of guilt, remorse, and human attachment that would otherwise be an internal deterrent to committing a violent act. But *what compels an individual to commit a violent crime?* The empirical association between psychopathy and violent crime does not provide a complete answer to this question. Most individuals with high levels of psychopathy are criminally versatile—they will engage in any type of criminal behavior if it benefits them in some way. Certainly an individual who has not developed human attachment will have an easier time committing acts of violence and other antisocial behaviors than someone who has the capacity to experience remorse and guilt. But this is only part of the story. An important challenge for criminologists is to unravel how and why some people have a stronger will to violence than others.

Do people engage in violent crime because there's something inherently appealing about the act of violence? Schinkle (2004) raises the notion of *autotelic violence,* violence committed for its own sake, and suggests that any instance of violence contains autotelic aspects. From this perspective, when people engage in violent crime they consciously or unconsciously *will* to do so because there is something intrinsically compelling about the violence itself. Schinkle (2004, p. 15) suggests, "Perhaps it is time to end the exclusivity of the 'why-question' altogether. For in the case of violence we may ask not only what its 'meanings' are, but also what its intrinsic attractiveness might be. This would mean to ask for the aesthetics of violence." As in Katz's work on the phenomenology of crime, this focus on the personal meaning of violence offers a piece of the picture that is often lost in the pursuit of an endless haze of precipitating factors and forces.

Schinkle (2004) proposes abandoning the division of violence into "types" and speaking instead of "aspects" of violence—with a particular violent act reflecting multiple aspects. For example, let's say an individual commits an armed robbery for financial gain but does not intend to use the weapon to harm or kill the victim. During the course of the act, the offender encounters unexpected resistance and shoots the victim in the heat of the moment. This offender, though not having intended to use violent force, is surprised to find the experience exhilarating. The adrenaline rush the offender experienced may then lead to subsequent acts of violence. If someone were to interview this offender after the crime, he might say he committed the offense for money and did not plan to hurt or kill the victim. He might not acknowledge, or not even be able to verbally articulate, the momentary exhilaration—the enjoyment of the violence for its own sake. But the exhilaration is only a small piece of the picture. If he were to be classified as a "type" of offender who instrumentally engages in violence for profit, would this be correct if he did, in fact, enjoy the violence even for a moment? This criticism of typologies—that strict adherence to ideal types "does violence to the reality of violence" (p. 20)—is important to keep in mind. In thinking about and utilizing typologies, we must strike a balance. On one hand, we want to theoretically explain violence and other types of crime by identifying their distinctive features. On the other hand, it is important to understand violence in the real world.

This section reviews the major violent crime categories, with attention to the distinctive features that characterize different types of violent behavior with acknowledgment that there is considerable overlap between violent crime and other types of crime. Sex crimes (rape, sexual homicide) are crimes of violence. Hate crime and terrorism involving violent acts can be classified as political crime, but are also crimes of violence. Many copycat crimes involve mimicking images of violent crimes in the media and popular culture. Given the range of behaviors that can be classified as "violent crime" and the importance of addressing these subtypes of violent behavior in detail, sex crime, political crime (including terrorism and hate crimes), and copycat crime are discussed in a subsequent chapters. This text continues to focus on the typology framework, but in keeping with Schinkle's call for attention to aspects of violence rather than ideal types, it is important to acknowledge that classification of criminal types is a theoretical undertaking. Typologies should not be viewed as either-or real-world dichotomies, but rather as a strategy for organizing and conceptualizing. They also serve, as will be discussed in depth in later chapters, as a framework for intervention, investigation, policy formulation, and criminal justice sanctions.

Assault

The majority of arrests for violent crime are for assaults. From a legal perspective, assaults are usually defined as "aggravated" or "simple." Aggravated assaults generally involve premeditated, intentional acts that result in serious injury or use of weapons. Simple assaults typically do not involve a weapon and result in minimal or no injury.[9] In 2005, there were a total of 449,297 arrests for aggravated assault and 1,301,392 arrests for "other assaults" (UCR, 2005). National Crime Victimization Survey findings reveal larger numbers—a total of 4,357,190 assault victimizations in 2005 (1,052,260 aggravated and 3,304,930 simple; Catalano, 2006). Assaults are clearly the most prevalent form of violent criminal behavior. The following are examples of offenses legally defined as aggravated assault:

- Vanessa and Raymond Jackson of Camden County, New Jersey, were charged with aggravated assault and child endangerment for starving and neglecting their four adopted sons. They were charged with aggravated assault for "failing to provide proper and sufficient nutrition, resulting in severe growth retardation and malnutrition" (Gohlke, 2004).
- Twenty-year-old Darrell Booker of Cheyenne, Wyoming, was convicted of aggravated assault for pointing a gun at his wife's head after an argument that began in the couple's car, carried into a restaurant, and then to a motel where Booker held the gun to his wife's head (Rule, 2003).
- Dieu Quang Ha of Ottowa was convicted of aggravated assault and attempted murder for hiring three teenagers to beat up his business partner in what ended up being a near-fatal attack. The teens pummeled the victim with metal weightlifting bars until he was near death (Casey, 2003).
- Danielle Rae Bird, a 20-year-old woman with connections to the Indian Posse street gang, was convicted of aggravated assault for slashing another young woman in the cheek, leaving a wound so deep it cut her gums and required 18 stitches (Adam, 2004).
- Two teenage boys were indicted for aggravated assault in Memphis for shooting a 20-month-old boy in the head as they fired at two other young men. The 20-month-old was seriously wounded while trick-or-treating with his mother (Chattanooga Times Free Press, 2004).
- Michelle Lee Murphy was convicted of aggravated assault and reckless endangerment after helping a man attack his mother and abduct his three children. Murphy assisted in cutting and slashing the victim and leaving her bound and gagged in her basement while the children were abducted (McMillan, 2004).

Miethe, McCorkle, and Listwan (2006) identify five major syndromes of homicide and aggravated assault:[10]

1. Interpersonal disputes (violence occurring out of a disagreement or conflict between parties)

2. Instrumental felony offenses (violence occurring within the context of the commission of another felony)

3. Youth group offending (violence carried out within group contexts)

4. Chronic violent offending (violence committed by individuals with a developmental history characterized by a pattern of violent offending over an extended period of time)

5. Politically motivated violence (violence used to improve the position of one group over another, to maintain prevailing conditions, or to illustrate the inadequacies of a prevailing regime)

Each of these syndromes represents a unique conglomeration of factors and forces that shape violent offending. Within each category, offenders may use predatory or affective violence, and particular victim-offender, contextual, and motivational factors shape the offense behavior.

What differentiates violent acts? How do assaults differ from homicides and other types of violent criminal behavior (e.g., robbery)? The legal difference between an aggravated assault and a homicide can depend on the culpability of the offender and whether or not the victim dies of injuries resulting from an assault and use of weapon. The method or weapon used in the assault is also a factor. An assault with a fist or a knife is much less likely to result in death than an assault with a firearm. Thus, in terms of motivation and individual factors, there may not be much difference between aggravated assault and homicide.

For example, an elderly woman was attacked by her adult son who suffered for years from schizophrenia. The son had stopped taking his medication and experienced auditory hallucinations that ordered him to attack his mother. He assaulted her for hours in her home with kitchen knives and lawn shears, fled the scene, and left her critically wounded on her doorstep with her throat cut and multiple stab wounds. The woman miraculously recovered. Her son was found and arrested nearby, but was determined to be not guilty by reason of insanity as a result of his long and documented history of schizophrenia. What differentiates this violent act from "aggravated assault" or "homicide"? If the man had been determined to be legally sane, he would have likely been convicted of aggravated assault or attempted murder. If the woman had died, the crime would have been homicide. Thus, it is important to keep in mind that the distinction between violent acts and a violent crime is a social-legal construction and the difference between an assault and homicide often depends on the type of weapon used and whether or not the victim manages to survive.

Victim-Offender Relationship and Situational Context

The preceding case received only a two-inch section of the B section of a local newspaper. However, this is a common example of the sort of situation in which violent crime is most likely to occur—in the victim's own home at the hands of a family member who is affectively motivated. Most assaults occur in the context of a domestic dispute, between acquaintances or coworkers, or in contexts in which both victim and offender are intoxicated or engaged in similar activities (e.g., drinking in a bar, using or selling drugs on the street). National Crime Victimization data for 2005 show that females are more likely to be victimized by someone they know, whereas males are more likely to be victimized by a stranger (Catalano, 2006). Assaults also occur during the commission of a crime such as street or bank robbery or a burglary where the offender is caught off guard, unexpectedly finding an occupant in the residence or business.

Predatory Versus Affective Aggression and Assault

Most assaults are the product of affective aggression in contexts where two or more people are engaged in conflict—a barroom brawl, a domestic argument, a workplace or hostile business interaction. "Affective violence is the common, garden-variety aggression we observe between people who are violent, and is preceded by heightened autonomic arousal, accompanied by anger or fear, and is a reaction to an immediate perceived threat" (Meloy, 1998, p. 16). Assaults tend to be a product of an escalating altercation between two people who know each other. In such situations, both (or in the case of groups, all) parties play a role in the escalation to the offense. According to Felson (2002), the escalation sequence plays out as follows:

- One person perceives an insult from another.
- The person responds to the insult and escalates the confrontation.
- That response induces a similar escalation.
- Someone takes the first jab, throws the first punch, and so on.

From Felson's (2002) perspective, "True, one guy might have thrown the first punch; but if the other guy insulted or taunted him, it is hard to call that a predatory crime" (p. 24).

Group fight situations (particularly in masculine contexts) further facilitate the escalation of violence because the audience becomes a catalyst for violent response. Comments such as, "Are you going to let him talk to you like that?" compel a violent response to avoid embarrassment. On the other hand, violence could be averted if someone in the audience acted as a peacemaker, offering comments such as, "Walk it off, it's not worth it." This is where gender, culture, and subcultural values come into play. In masculine environments—gangs, prisons, and certain working-class cultural contexts[11]—violence escalates within and is exacerbated by group values and norms that place aggressive prowess, the ability to physically defend oneself, personal honor, and toughness high on the list of desirable characteristics.

Many group contexts involve relatively routine activities and everyday people to set the stage for affectively motivated violence. For example, the band Guns N' Roses, popular in the 1980s and early 1990s, has been associated with a number of violent incidents, assaults, and riots. In 2002, the band, including only one of the original members, attempted to make a comeback. However, during that year concertgoers turned riotous in Philadelphia and Vancouver, B.C., leading to a cancellation of the group's tour. These riots were the end of a string of violent incidents occurring throughout the band's history. The sole original member of the band in the 2002 revival was Axl Rose, who himself had a history of assaultive behavior. Although many subcultural contexts can be used to illustrate this point, the violent history of this

BOX 5.2

GUNS N' ROSES, GROUP VIOLENCE, HYPERMASCULINITY, AND SUBCULTURAL CONTEXT FOR ASSAULT

Axl Rose, lead singer of Guns N' Roses.

Photo credit: © S.I.N. / Corbis.

In 2002 Guns N' Roses, a popular band in the 1980s and early 1990s, launched a comeback tour. However, when lead singer (and the only remaining member of the original band) Axl Rose failed to appear for the first show of the North American leg of the tour in Vancouver, British Columbia, an hour-long riot erupted. On hearing about the band's cancellation, fans (many of whom had been drinking and smoking marijuana) hoisted metal security barriers outside and rammed them through the glass entry doors. They threw bottles and rocks, yelling "Fuck Axl." The riot involved thousands of concertgoers and police had to use pepper spray and riot batons to disperse rioters. When the band failed to appear at another show in Philadelphia, the crowd of 20,000 became unruly, throwing drinks and other objects. It took 100 police officers to restore order and several people were injured.

The riots in 2002 were not the first in the band's history. In 1991, Axl Rose precipitated a riot in Maryland Heights, Missouri, when he jumped off the stage and attacked a fan who was videotaping the concert. Sixty people were hurt and a great deal of damage was caused to the Riverport Amphitheatre. In 1992, a show the band played with, Metallica, was cut short after Metallica's frontman James Hatfield caught fire in a pyrotechnic mishap during a set. When the Guns N' Roses set was cut short, angry fans became violent and unruly. In an outdoor concert in Hershey, Pennsylvania, in the early 1990s, Guns N' Roses played a show with Skid Row, another popular

(Continued)

(Continued)

1980s band. Lead singers of both bands (Sebastian Bach of Skid Row and Axl Rose of Guns N'Roses) shouted obscenities between sets. When Rose took the stage he playfully shouted out, "Rape her, man," in reference to a female fan who had taken her shirt off. During the concert, male audience members, many of whom were clad in motorcycle leather displaying biker insignia, urinated on other audience members while standing on bleacher seats. Audience members openly drank alcohol and smoked marijuana. The subcultural context—women flinging their shirts off while screaming for Bach, Rose, and other band members, the language used throughout the concert, men publicly urinating, the dominant presence of ultramasculine biker subculture, the rampant drinking and drug use, and the jovial validation of sexual assault (and implication that the women wanted it and were asking for it)—created a group contagion that was ultramasculine and aggressive.

particular band (and its lead singer), the ultramasculine values and behaviors the band invoked in audiences, and the drinking and drug use of concertgoers created the critical ingredients for assaultive behavior (Box 5.2).

This sort of environment contains the necessary ingredients for affectively motivated assaultive behavior, but emotionally reactive assault can occur between any two (or more) people in relatively benign situations. At least half of the assaults that occur in domestic violence contexts are committed by normal (nonpathological) people in their own homes. In a review of literature on typologies of spouse abusers, Dixon and Browne (2003) found that 50% of spousal assaults are committed by "family-only" abusers. Family-only abusers can be male or female and are distinguished from other types of abusers in that they have no psychopathological disturbance. Husbands and wives engage in aggressive acts at congruent rates, though wives usually initiate aggression in self-defense and are more likely to experience negative outcomes when they are victims of male aggression and violence (Dixon & Browne, 2003). These are "psychologically normal" people who engage in violence as an emotionally reactive conflict-resolution strategy often aggravated by the use of alcohol or drugs.

It is relatively easy to understand affectively motivated assault. Most people have been angry enough at someone in their lives, or in a situation where they were sufficiently antagonized to the point of behaving (or wanting to behave) aggressively or violently. But, *what about assaults rooted in predatory aggression?* If 50% of spousal assaults are committed by family-only offenders, what about the other 50%? According to Dixon and Browne (2003), 30% of spousal violence is committed by generally violent/antisocial offenders and the remaining 20% by individuals who are psychologically distressed with evidence of dysphoric/borderline personality characteristics. These individuals, particularly those in the violent/antisocial category, are much more likely to engage in predatory, instrumental, proactive, assaultive behavior.

In the case of violent/antisocial offenders, assault is often used as a way to intimidate and threaten for the purpose of obtaining power and control. Some chronic batterers and a small minority of stalkers engage in predatory assault. For example, although most stalking violence is affective, some violent stalkers engage in stalking and violence to control, devaluate, and intimidate the victim (Meloy, 1998). Individuals in the dysphoric/borderline category may engage in assaultive behavior to gain attention, and for retaliation. This latter group of offenders is at risk for homicide-suicide and more likely to use both affective and predatory aggression simultaneously.

Offense Themes

Assault is a heterogeneous category of violent behavior. People commit assault and other types of violent crime for different reasons, under different circumstances, as a result of a cumulative network of internal and external forces. Canter (2000) suggests that interpersonal aspects of criminal behavior reflect the ways in which offenders deal with people in their everyday life. Offenders interact with victims in the same way they interact with family members, coworkers, and others. Canter offers the following thematic distinctions for understanding violent crime:

- Victim as an object: Victim is something to be used and controlled.
- Victim as a vehicle: Victim is a vehicle of the offender's emotional state.
- Victim as a person: Victim is seen as a person; the offender has or perceives a relationship with the victim.

The manner in which an offender commits a crime mirrors aspects of his or her behavior in everyday life.

Assaults and other types of violent crime can be classified in terms of the theme or essence of the crime. To understand any violent offense it is important to understand the purpose of the offense in the mind of the offender. Offense behavior and behavioral evidence left at a crime scene reflect the person who committed the offense, how the offender viewed the victim, and the mode of aggression underlying the violence (Salfati, 2000). In the case of serious violent crime, a "signature" can often be identified that reflects the psychopathology of the offender (Keppel & Birne, 1997). The offender's signature—aspects of the crime that were not necessary to carry out the offense—tells something about who the offender is, why he or she committed the offense, and the theme of the offense.

A chronic batterer whose goal is power and control will engage in violence to maintain a position of omnipotence. The drunken concertgoer caught up in group contagion and drug and alcohol use who assaults a police officer is reacting to an emotional state. The spouse who engages in a one-time incident of domestic violence, lashing out in frustration, does so as a result of a close relationship with the other person. The key here is how the offender views him- or herself in relation to others and the particular meaning a violent act holds for the offender. For example, in the case of batterers, "internal thoughts and beliefs of the batterer provide important clues for the preoccupation with the estranged partner, whether it is an appropriate concern, or a stalking fantasy" (Burgess et al., 2001). Violent crime is an interpersonal act and cannot be understood apart from the psychological state of the offender, interpersonal relationships, and the contextual/situational factors that shape each and every violent act.

Homicide

Homicide is the smallest category of violent crime; however, it receives the most attention in the news media and popular culture. Legally, homicide is defined in most jurisdictions as murder or non-negligent manslaughter, with a charge of aggravated, first-degree, second-degree, or manslaughter depending on the degree of premeditation, level of intent, and circumstances. Homicide is the behavioral outcome of a wide range of motivations and circumstances. For example,

- On February 12, 2007, at 6:45 in the evening, 18-year-old Sulejman Talovic calmly started shooting randomly with a shotgun and a handgun in a Salt Lake City, Utah, shopping mall. By the time the rampage ended, many people including parents shopping with their children were injured or dead. In all, six people were dead, ranging in age from 15 to 53, including the gunman who was cornered and shot by police.

- In 2007, 33-year-old Cynthia Sommer was convicted of poisoning her 23-year-old husband, a U.S. Marine, with arsenic to cash in his $250,000 insurance policy.

- In 2005, 18-year-old Angolan refugee Roberto Malasi and three other teenage gang members stormed a christening party wearing masks to rob guests in south London. During the robbery, Malasi shot 33-year-old Zainab Kalokoh while she cradled a baby in her arms. He stabbed 18-year-old Ruth Okechukwu in the same area 15 days later.

- In April 2003, Tacoma, Washington, Police Chief David Brame shot and killed his wife Crystal Brame and then turned the gun on himself. The homicide-suicide occurred shortly after Crystal Brame filed for divorce, making public a long history of threats and domestic abuse.

- In March of 2003, members of the Texas Syndicate gunned down three men at a home in Dallas, Texas. Authorities said gang members were committing crimes to increase their positions and ranks in the group.

- In 1997, 37-year-old Rebecca Cleland had her cousins kill her 43-year-old husband for a $1 million insurance policy.

In 2005, there were 15,495 known offenses recorded in the UCR as murder and non-negligent manslaughter and a murder rate of 5.9 per 100,000. An estimated 16,692 people were murdered in these offenses. In 1.2% of the offenses, the offender was a stranger. Murder represented 1.2% of all violent crime. From 1986 to 2006, the murder rate dropped to a 20-year low from 8.6 to 5.6 per 100,000. Of the 10,335 murder and non-negligent manslaughter offenders arrested in 2005 for which the offender's sex was identified, 89% were male and 11% were female with 97 under age 15 years, 929 age 15 to 18 years, and 9,406 over age 18 (UCR, 2005).

As with assault, homicide is a heterogeneous offense category that occurs in many contexts. Murders can be classified based on organizing features such as level of intent (first-degree, second-degree, manslaughter), victim-offender relationship (stranger, acquaintance, family), nature of offense (serial, mass, spree, sexual). Within these general categories, they can be divided into subtypes consisting of more homogeneous categories. *Acquaintance homicide* includes subtypes of spousal murder, parricide, infanticide, matricide, patricide, and family annihilation murder. *Stranger homicide* includes

Photo 5.1 A Salt Lake City police officer squats with his gun drawn next to a body inside the mall after a gunman opened fire in the Trolley Square shopping mall on February 12, 2007, in Salt Lake City, Utah.

Photo Credit: Getty Images.

felony-murder (homicide committed during the course of another felony crime), serial murder, mass murder, and spree murder. Although the acquaintance versus stranger typology is not mutually exclusive for all crime types (e.g., mass murderers and some serial killers have targeted acquaintances and strangers), it is a general classification scheme that has some theoretical support. Offenders who murder strangers tend to be more predatory and have a higher level of psychopathy than those who target people they know. Copes, Kerley, and Carroll (2002) suggest that another category, "crime-precipitated homicide," can more meaningfully disaggregate homicide by focusing on the situation-context in which the offense occurs. This category is defined as "homicides in which the victim was killed in the process of participating in illegal behaviors including predatory crimes, vice crimes, and narcotics offenses" (p. 242).

A number of typologies have been developed to explain and understand the varieties of homicidal behavior beyond the more general classification of acquaintance and stranger homicides. Fox and Levin (2001) divide murder into seven categories: *intimate and family murder, young superpredators, school murders, serial killers, rampage* or *mass murderers, hate homicides,* and *cult killings.* Douglas et al. (1997) divide homicide into four general types: *Criminal enterprise homicide, personal cause homicide, sexual homicide,* and *group cause homicide.* Meyer and Oberman (2001) offer a typology of mothers who kill their children (filicide) consisting of five types: *filicide related to an ignored pregnancy, abuse-related filicide, filicide due to neglect, assisted/coerced filicide, purposeful filicide,* and *mother acted alone.* Douglas and Olshaker (1999) distinguish three types of multicide (multiple murder):

- *Serial murder:* when the offender murders on at least three occasions with an emotional cooling-off period between each incident

- *Mass murder:* when an offender kills four or more victims in one location in one incident

- *Spree murder:* when an offender murders at two or more separate locations without an emotional cooling-off period between each

Fox and Levin (2003) define mass murder as "the slaughter of four or more victims by one or a few assailants within a single event, lasting but a few minutes or as long as several hours" (p. 47). Mass murder can be further divided into five motivational types: *revenge, power, loyalty, profit,* and *terror* (Fox & Levin, 2003).

Egger (2002, p. 5) offers a comprehensive definition of serial murder, including seven components:

1. One or more individuals commit a second murder and/or subsequent murders.

2. There is generally no prior relationship between the victim and the attacker.

3. Subsequent murders occur at different times and have no apparent connection to the initial murder.

4. Subsequent murders are usually committed in a different geographical location.

5. The motive is not for material gain; it is for the murderer's desire for power and dominance.

6. Victims may have a symbolic value for the murderer and/or may be perceived to lack prestige, or to be powerless and defenseless.

7. Victims typically include vagrants, homeless, prostitutes, homosexuals, migrant workers, missing children, and single women (out by themselves), elderly women, college students, and hospital patients.

Hickey (2002, 2006) defines serial murderers broadly as "any offenders, male or female, who kill over time" (p. 19) and offers a mobility classification including "local," "place specific," and "traveling" types. Holmes and Deburger (2004) divide serial murderers into four types: *visionary* (psychotic), *mission* (retaliatory), *hedonistic* (sadistic), *power/control* (psychopathic). Clearly there is no shortage of definitions of homicide and homicide typologies, each offering important organizational and theoretical dimensions to better understand the range of homicidal behavior.

Victim-Offender Relationship and Situational Context

Murder tends to be an urban crime, with over half of all homicides occurring in cities with populations of 100,000 or more. Homicides tend to occur between people who know each other or are from similar socioeconomic, cultural, and ethnic backgrounds. Murder offenders and victims tend to be males. Males are three times more likely to be killed and eight times more likely to commit homicide than females. Blacks are disproportionately represented as homicide victims and offenders. Blacks are six times more likely to be victimized and eight times more likely to be offenders than Whites. Approximately one-third of murder victims and almost half of offenders are under age 25 (Fox & Zawitz, 2002). Thus, the victim/offender/situational context is a Black male offender under the age of 25 who murders a Black victim in a large urban area.

Cultural context also plays a role in homicide. Even though the homicide rate has declined in the United States, homicide rates in America are still much higher than rates in other Western nations. On an individual level, it can be generally (and simplistically) stated that "the greater a person's frustration and the more one has been socialized to violence, the more likely one is to commit murder" (Beeghley, 2003). However, cultural forces work together to increase the likelihood that the overall murder rate will be higher in one culture than the next. Beeghley (2003) offers a structural analysis of homicide using the analogy of a house:

In sociology, a structural analysis, whether of homicide or any other topic, is a little like examining how a house sets the context for action rather than worrying about the motives of individuals who enter and leave it. Thus, every house displays a specific arrangement of rooms, doors, and windows. These characteristics mean, for example, that most people will go in and out through the doors. In fact, most will use the front door, fewer the back. Note, however, that the combination of the footprint of the house and the shape of the lot sometimes means that most people will go in and out the back door. But doors need not always be used; it is simply easier to do so. Thus, although it is harder, some people (a teenager seeking to evade parents, a burglar) will use a window as a means of entry and exit. And, although harder still, it is possible to imagine using a sledgehammer to force an opening through a wall. Thus, the characteristic of a house (the social context) determines rates of behavior, making some acts relatively easy and others more difficult. Without knowing which individuals go through doors and which go through windows, or their motives, it remains useful to study the way the house influences how people enter and exit, as well as other behavior. Moreover, houses vary from one neighborhood to another—in size, for example—and this difference influences rates of behavior as well. (p. 28)

Beeghley argues that the high base rate of homicide in the United States reflects the impact of five forces: (1) greater availability of guns, (2) the expansion of illegal drug markets, (3) greater racial discrimination, (4) greater exposure to violence, and (5) greater economic inequality.

To take this one step further, we can examine the social context of school shootings. From 1982 to 2001 there were 28 school shootings in the United States. In a study of random school shootings in the United States, Kimmel and Mahler (2003) found that of the 28 shootings, 20 of them took place in states that are predominantly Republican (that voted for George Bush in the 2000 presidential elections). The eight that took place in Democratic states (that voted for Al Gore in the 2000 election) took place in rural Republican pockets within those states. The authors argue that school shootings are unevenly distributed and rooted, in part, in local gun culture, gender culture, and school cultures. Reviewing the cases of the 28 school shootings Kimmel and Mahler found that all of the shootings were committed by culturally marginalized boys who had stories of being constantly bullied, threatened, beaten up, and "gay-baited" (accused of being gay when they were not). According to the authors, no industrial society other than the United States has developed such a violent "boy culture" (p. 1450), and this culture has a profound effect particularly on White boys. African American boys have not been the perpetrators of mass school shootings. The authors argue that even though African Americans face a multitude of challenges in schools (that impact their behavior in different ways), when they do not succeed in school they can tap into a "narrative repertoire of resistance" (p. 1453) so that their anguish is collectivized and subsumed into readily available political rhetoric.

The role of environment and culture in the development of homicide behavior is summed up best by Nancy Gabbert, the mother of 17-year-old Gary Ridgway/Green River Killer victim Sandra:

Fifty years ago, Gary Ridgway was a little baby. . . . He's not some monster who was dropped down from another planet. He was created right here in our society. . . . How did we do this? (Talvi, 2003)

Predatory Versus Affective Aggression and Homicide

Most homicides are affectively motivated. It could, in fact, be argued that no crime is purely predatory. Even the most extreme psychopathic serial killer is internally driven by a chronic emotional starvation and a subconscious quest for attachment and reduction of anxiety (Whitman & Akutagawa, 2004). *Is it useful to classify homicide in terms of whether it is fundamentally predatory or affective in nature? Are offenders who commit predatory homicides qualitatively different from those who commit affective homicides?* Cornell et al. (1996) suggest that reactive/affective violence is a more homogeneous entity than instrumental/predatory violence. Offenders who can be classified as instrumental/predatory (having committed at least one violent instrumental act) are a distinct subgroup that is more psychopathic. Along these lines, predatory violence is indicative of a pathological development in the ability to use aggression for goal-directed purposes. Furthermore, Copes et al. (2002) found that predatory crime-precipitated homicides are distinct in that the offenders were more likely to have a history of violence and nearly half of the offenders and victims were between the ages of 15 and 24, four-fifths of the offenders and victims were Black, and they were overwhelmingly male.

The determination of the mode of aggression displayed in homicide (and other offenses) can play an important role in forensic assessment of the offender and in competency determinations and the adjudication process. For example, Meloy (1997) offers a case study analysis of a mass murder committed by a 35-year-old male. Following a week's separation from his wife and temporary loss of custody of his son, the offender went to his wife's workplace and murdered her, her store manager, and a police officer. While many mass murders are affective violence, this crime was determined to be predatory in nature. This determination has important implications for understanding the offender and enhancing the accuracy of expert testimony.

This issue arose in the case of Andrea Yates. On June 20, 2001, Yates systematically drowned each of her five children ranging in age from 6 months to 7 years old. In a taped confession to police, she explained how several months prior to the murders she had filled the tub with the intent to drown the children, but didn't go through with it. On the day of the murders, she filled the tub with water 3 inches from the top and drowned each child, one by one, by holding them under the water while they struggled. During the trial, prosecutors argued that Yates knew the difference between right and wrong while the defense argued the insanity defense based on Yates's history of mental illness and postpartum depression and psychosis. However, Park Dietz, forensic psychiatrist for the state, argued that Yates ignored every opportunity to protect her children from her own murderous intentions by not following the advice of her doctors and not responding to her delusions by getting her children to safety. Dietz said she kept thoughts about killing her children secret because she feared she would be stopped, indicating she knew what she was doing was wrong (Box 5.3).

BOX 5.3

ANDREA YATES

Andrea Yates escorted to court June 22, 2001.

Photo Credit: Steve Ueckert/Getty Images.

On June 20, 2001, the police received a telephone call from 36-year-old Andrea Yates asking them to come to her Cedar Lake, Texas, home. Shortly thereafter, Yates telephoned her husband asking him to come home and telling him, "It's time; I finally did it." What the police and Rusty Yates discovered when they arrived at the Yates residence were the dead bodies of all five Yates children.

In a taped confession, Yates explained that earlier that day, she had filled the family bathtub with cold water 3 inches from the top and drowned each of her children. She drowned each child separately. First was Paul, her three-year-old son. After Paul died, Yates carried his body into her bedroom, tucked him under the covers, and laid his head on a pillow. Next was two-year-old Luke, followed by five-year-old John. Next was six-month-old Mary, who had been on the bathroom floor crying during the first three murders. While drowning Mary, seven-year-old Noah walked in and asked what was wrong with his sister. Noah, noticing his sister's clenched fists and coloring, ran out of the bathroom. Yates had to chase after her son and drag him back into the bathroom. After drowning Noah, Yates placed Mary in the bed with her brothers, wrapping their arms around the baby, and left Noah floating in the tub. She then proceeded to give each child a baptism and call the police and her husband.

Yates claimed that she was plagued by the devil telling her to harm her children. She believed she had failed her children and that it was her duty to punish herself for being a lousy mother, as evidenced by her children's poor development. To date, Yates's crimes have been blamed on

(Continued)

(Continued)

mental illness, a poor marriage, her fundamentalist religious beliefs, her doctors, her extended family, and her suburban neighbors. Yates was described by her friends and neighbors as a quiet, thoughtful, and attentive mother. She and her husband were devout Christians who home-schooled their five children. Yates also took care of her father with Alzheimer's disease. Neighbors found her compassionate and self-sacrificing. With a deeper investigation, it became apparent that Yates's life was not as picture perfect as her neighbors and small group of friends imagined. She was diagnosed with postpartum depression with psychotic features and was said to have exhibited signs of depression as early as high school. Her first suicide attempt was in June 1999, when she overdosed on some of her father's Alzheimer's medication—four months after the birth of her fourth child. She was hospitalized and received intensive drug treatments. Yates exhibited both catatonic schizophrenia and paranoid schizophrenia. After her father died, she again attempted suicide, this time with a knife. Again she was hospitalized. When she was released, her mother—in-law came to her home to help care for the children. Yates murdered her children after she saw her husband off to work and an hour before her mother-in-law was set to arrive to help her care for the five children.

To onlookers, the marriage between Andrea and Rusty Yates appeared to be a good relationship. Rusty was a Christian traditionalist—he did not want Andrea working outside the home, did not want other people to care for his children, and wanted his children home schooled. Andrea lived an isolated life. Her family truly did not know the extent of her circumstances and her neighbors were uninformed as well.

Yates Family Photo

Photo Credit: Getty Images

Andrea Yates pleaded not guilty by reason of insanity to the capital murder charges against her. With the insanity defense, her motives and will were called into question. The Texas Penal Code uses the M'Naughten test, which states that a person is legally insane when, as a result of a severe mental disease or defect, the person did not know that his or her conduct was wrong. Both the prosecution and defense agreed that Yates was mentally ill, but the prosecution argued Yates did in fact know the wrongfulness of her actions. This, the prosecution argued, was evidenced in her premeditation; calling the police after she murdered her children, which indicated knowledge that killing was wrong; and her arrangement of the dead bodies of her children. Andrea Yates was found guilty and sentenced by Judge Belinda Hill to life in prison without the possibility of parole.

In January 2005, a Texas appeals court reversed the guilty verdict on grounds that prosecution witness Park Dietz had testified that Yates had watched an episode of *Law and Order* that depicted a woman who drowned her children. Defense attorneys discovered that no such episode had ever aired and argued that the jury was influenced by Deitz's false testimony. Yates was determined to be not guilty by reason of insanity and was granted release to a Texas mental hospital.

Were the murders of the Yates's children an act of predatory or affective violence? Can someone who is mentally ill be capable of predatory violence? Clearly, the act of planning and systematically drowning one's own children is predatory. In Yates's case, evidence and her own confession indicate that she experienced minimal autonomic arousal and no conscious experience of emotion as she murdered her children. She planned an act of purposeful violence with heightened and focused awareness. She specifically targeted her children, who were not a threat. On the other hand, she was responding to delusions—Satan ordering her to kill her children. A valid and reliable determination of the mode of violence depends on the observed behavior in the hours or days before the crime. Psychological testing in the weeks or months following a crime is generally not relevant to the mode of violence at the time of the crime (Meloy, 1997). Thus, determination of whether Yates's offense was predatory or affective hinges on the number of facts supporting the criterion for predatory violence. The case ended up going to trial twice as a result of the uncovering of faulty expert testimony. The guilty verdict in the first trial suggests that the jurors saw Yates's behavior as predatory, though their unwillingness to impose the death penalty reflects an understanding of the role mental illness played in the commission of the offense. The not guilty by reason of insanity ruling in the second trial indicates that jurors were persuaded to reconsider as a result of Yates's long history of mental illness.

With mass murders, especially family annihilation murders, it can be difficult to determine the mode of aggression underlying the violence. However, other types of murder more clearly reflect the predominance of predatory versus affective modes. Examples of murders that generally involve affective violence include spousal murder in the heat of an argument, spree murder or mass murder immediately following a traumatic event, or a murder within the context of a fight between two people under the influence of alcohol or drugs. Murders that tend to be predatory in nature include murder for hire, (some) revenge-retaliation murders committed by gangs or organized criminal groups, and serial murder.

Offense Themes

Regardless of the mode of aggression, victim-offender relationship, or situational context, the act of murder requires the ability (whether conscious or unconscious) to objectify another human being. Even in domestic violence situations in which the offender views the victim as a person and the violence is affective, the offender must, if only for a moment, suspend feelings of empathy for the murder to occur. In order to do so, the offender engages in a process called *dissociation*. Dissociation is "a phenotypic defensive process that expresses the genotypic defensive operation of splitting; it is ubiquitous in the psychopath" (Meloy, 1988, p. 151). Dissociation as a defensive process can be distinguished from a *dissociative state*. Dissociative states are noted to occur in 30 to 70% of the normal population and involve *depersonalization* (a temporary alter-ation of the perception or experience of the self in which the usual experience of the self is changed or lost) and *derealization* (a temporary alteration in the perception of one's surroundings where a sense of reality of the external world is lost; Meloy, 1988). Dissociation in psychopaths is long term and chronic. Dissociative states in normal populations can range from daydreams to pathological states such as psychogenic amnesia or experiences of depersonalization and derealization (Moskowitz, 2004).

Increased dissociation has been associated with increased violence in a wide range of populations (Moskowitz, 2004) and is crucial to understanding the act and themes of homicide. Studies have found that the majority of offenders with no psychiatric problems are in a dissociative trance or fugue state at the time of their crimes, involv-ing a shift to an altered state of consciousness immediately prior to the crime and impaired recall after the crime. Dissociative states appear to create a psychological environment in which violent and impulsive acts are more likely to occur. Dissociative symptoms are linked to violent behavior in persons with dissociative disorders (e.g., dissociative identity disorder/multiple personality disorder), other psychiatric diag-noses (posttraumatic stress disorder, personality disorders including psychopath), and normal populations. According to Moskowitz,

> the intense fantasy lives described by many violent and sadistic killers may be dissociative in nature and could lead to a form of dissociated identity, and the meek, quiet individual who explodes in a paroxysm of blind violence, the "overcontrolled" offender, could be explained from a dissociative perspective. (Moskowitz, 2004, p. 39)

Dissociation (and dissociative states) enables the offender to reconcile ambivalence and rid the mind of internal deterrents in the commission of a homicide. Through dis-sociation, a violent act can be committed without the intrusion of an internal struggle over right/wrong or the feelings of the victim.

The nature of the dissociation experienced by an offender in the commission of a homicide is a central aspect of the theme of the offense. In some homicides, the theme is readily identifiable—for example, an affectively motivated murder that is the outcome of a drunken barroom brawl or a spousal homicide committed in the context of a heated argument or assault. However, many homicides, particularly rare forms such as serial murder and sexual homicide, are complex crimes that are the behavioral outcome of predispositional factors, early trauma, years of fantasy development, conditioning processes, dissociation, and facilitators. Understanding the theme of these offenses, based on theory and research, is crucial to treatment, risk assessment, public safety, and prevention.

Hickey's (2002) *trauma control model* explains the development of a serial murderer (Figure 5.2). Based on this model, no single factor predicts or explains homicidal behavior. Homicide (and other crime) is the behavioral outcome of biological, sociological, cultural, routine activity/opportunity, and phenomenological factors. Homicidal behavior is made possible through a series of compounding factors and forces. Biological predisposition (e.g., low autonomic arousal, amygdala dysfunction), early trauma (abuse, neglect, parental rejection), and dissociation (employed to deal with the trauma) set the stage for low self-esteem and the development of fantasies that become increasingly violent. "Violent abusive behavior often leads to the development of dissociative tendencies, which in turn increase the likelihood of perpetrating violence" (Moskowitz, 2004, p. 41). Childhood trauma may act as a triggering mechanism, resulting in an inability to deal with the stress of future life events. The combined effects of traumatizations over the life course should be viewed exponentially rather than arithmetically (Hickey, 2002). Once trauma has occurred and the dissociative tendencies are

❖ Figure 5.2   The Trauma Control Model

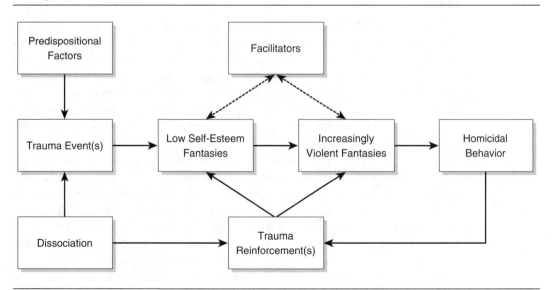

Source: From Hickey's (2006) *Serial Murderers and Their Victims.*

set in motion, future traumatizations (ostracism in school, failure, divorce, or other negative life events), in conjunction with other factors, "create a synergistic response, or enhanced reaction" (Hickey, 2002, p. 108). Facilitators such as pornography, alcohol, and drugs fuel violent fantasy, enhancing the possibility of homicidal behavior.

Using this model and theory and the research presented in this and previous chapters, we can begin to identify homicide themes. In any given case, the following questions (by no means an exhaustive list) should be asked to uncover the theme of the offense:

- What was the context (victim-offender relationship, situation) in which the offense occurred?
- How did the offender view/treat the victim?
- To what extent was the offense affective/predatory?
- What was the offender's modus operandi and signature?
- To what extent are features of the offense consistent with homicide typologies such as Keppel and Walter's (2000) PA, PR, AR, AE; Meloy's (2000) compulsive/catathymic; and the FBI's organized/disorganized typologies?
- What offense indicators suggest use of facilitators?
- What role did fantasy play in the commission of the offense?
- What cognitive schema and distortions did the offender employ?

Answers to these questions offer important information regarding the nature of homicidal behavior and the factors contributing to a particular offender's development and behavioral outcome.

Robbery

There were 417,122 robberies and 114,616 robbery arrests in the United States in 2005 with a rate of 140.7 per 100,000, down from 226 per 100,000 in 1986. From 1996 to 2005 the robbery rate decreased 30.3%, the largest decrease in any of the violent crime categories. Of the robberies committed in 2005, most (44%) were committed on streets or highways. Firearms were used in 42% of the robbery offenses, with an average dollar amount stolen of $1,230 (the highest average amount per offense taken in bank robberies). Of the 85,309 robbery arrests for which data on offender sex are available, 75,819 (89%) were committed by males and 9,490 (11%) were committed by females, with a greater percent change from 1996 to 2005 seen in male arrests (34.2%) compared to female arrests (29%). Most (84.7%) robberies were committed by adults, with 15.3% committed by juveniles age 15 to 18 and 4.6% by juveniles under age 15 (UCR, 2005). National Crime Victimization data show that there were 624, 850 robbery victimizations in 2005, with a significant decrease (-57.4%) in the average annual rate of victimization per 1,000 persons age 12 or older from 1993 to 2005 (Catalano, 2006).

One of the distinguishing features of robbery is that it is both a violent and a property crime. The Uniform Crime Reports define robbery as the "taking or attempting to take anything of value from the care, custody, or control of a person or persons by force or threat of force or violence and/or by putting the victim in fear" (UCR, 2002, p. 303).

Robberies are often classified in terms of where they occur. There are street robberies, bank robberies, home invasion robberies, gas station and convenience store robberies, and highway robberies. Robbery is legally distinguished from burglary or theft in that it involves taking something from another person with the use of some type of force. Robbery can involve different levels of force and different types of weapons, and it can be directed toward commercial or individual targets (Matthews, 2002).

Robbers are not a homogeneous group. People commit robbery for all sorts of reasons and target different types of victims. Robbery typologies are generally organized in terms of offender motivation or skill level or where the offense was committed. Miethe, McCorkle, and Listwan (2006) identify six types of (or ways of classifying) robbers:

1. Offender-based classifications (chronic, professional, intensive, occasional, career)

2. Bank robberies

3. Convenience store robberies

4. Street muggings

5. Home invasion robberies

6. Carjackings

Matthews (2002) proposes a typology that differentiates offenders in terms of criminal careers, planning, choice of target, amount of money stolen, and weapons used. He identifies three groups of robbers: *amateurs and novices, intermediate/mixed,* and *professionals.* Other typologies classify based on offender motivation such as *professional robbers, opportunistic robbers, addict robbers,* and *alcoholic robbers* (Conklin, 1972, in Siegal, 2004).

One of the most distinguishing features of robbery, compared to other crimes, is that it remains an offense overwhelmingly committed by males. The gender dimension of robbery is significant and tells something about the nature and dynamics of the behavior (Matthews, 2002). Robbery is a bold crime that requires the use of physical force. Robberies are committed by females (Box 5.4), but to a much lesser degree than any other crime category.

Victim-Offender Relationship and Situational Context

As reflected in the preceding list, robbery has historically been classified in terms of victim selection and the level of expertise or "type" of individual offender. Unlike other types of violent crime, robbery is often an interracial crime (Wright & Decker, 1997). In most cases, robbery victims are targeted strangers. Because robbery is predominantly a stranger crime that often results in injury or death (one in three robbery victims sustain at least minor injuries and 10% of homicides occur in the context of robbery; see Wright & Decker, 1997), it generates a great deal of public fear.

How do robbery offenders select their targets? Some researchers suggest that robbery is a rational crime involving cost-benefit analysis, though others question how a crime

BOX 5.4

THE QUEENS OF ARMED ROBBERY

Between May 30 and July 10, 1999, four teenage girls went on an armed robbery spree in the upper-middle-class Kingwood suburb of Houston, Texas. The girls, 16-year-old Krystal Maddox, 17-year-old Katie Dunn and Lisa Warzeka, and 18-year-old Michelle Morneau, committed five convenience store robberies after coming up with the idea while sitting in a restaurant discussing ways to get money to buy drugs and body piercings. Morneau and Maddox were from wealthy families. Dunn was a member of the Kingwood High drill team; Warzeka, a varsity volleyball player.

Calling themselves the "Queens of Armed Robbery," the girls wore gloves, masks, hoods, and sunglasses to disguise themselves as boys and brandished a semiautomatic pistol, a shotgun, and a .22-caliber rifle. The girls, who did the robberies in pairs with the others as lookouts, said they got their MO from TV, terrorized their victims, shouting "This is a hold-up" and "You have two seconds bitch, or I'm going to shoot you." They stole cash and cigarettes; $800 was their largest take. One of the girls, Katie Dunn, did not participate in one of the five robberies because she had been grounded by her mother. The four robbed Stop N Drive, Ryan's Bakery, Jack's food store in Houston, and the Porter food store and one other store in Montgomery County. Krystal Maddox, the youngest of the group, was said to be the ringleader and drove her 1999 Firebird her father had bought her as the getaway car.

The crime was big news in the Houston area and nationwide because the offenders were girls with money from an upper-middle-class suburb. The girls were known to be heavy users of cocaine, but theirs and others' accounts of the crimes suggest they did the crimes for "kicks" as a result of boredom. Local newspapers referred to the spree as, "Quentin Tarantino comes to Pleasantville," in reference to the sleepy suburb that offered little to do for teens beyond school activities and weekend keg parties. However, news stories following the event uncovered an underside of the image-oriented community, including widespread drug involvement among teens who had money to obtain them and parents who would take care of any problems their kids ran into. A Kingwood cheerleader was quoted as saying, "you have your parents around your little finger. The more you get away with, the higher your status."

The girls were arrested when an informant contacted *Crime Stoppers* after hearing the girls brag about their crimes at parties. Maddox, Dunn, and Warzeka received seven-year sentences (within a sentence range of 5-99 years). Morneau was sentenced to four months of boot camp and probation because she stayed in the car during the robberies. When sentencing Dunn and Warzeka, Judge Mark Kent Ellis said, "You made a choice. Despite all the advantages that you had, in your homes, in your school, in your neighborhood, you made a choice. And that choice was to be thugs. Spare me your tears. You have sown the wind, and you have now reaped the whirlwind."

that involves face-to-face confrontation and danger can be wholly rational. In his study of commercial armed robbers in Britain, Matthews (2002) found that violence committed in the course of a robbery is selective and instrumental. Using techniques of neutralization, robbers viewed themselves as violent, but only in specific spheres with certain types of victims (e.g., convenience store cashiers but not their own children), which allowed them to maintain a positive self-view. Miller (1998) found that female robbers tend to choose female targets, and when they choose males, they "set them up" or feign sexual interest to catch them off guard. In their study of African American street robbers in St. Louis, Missouri, Wright and Decker (1997) found that robbers consciously choose victims who themselves are involved in illegal behavior such as using drugs or soliciting prostitutes. Robbers who select noncriminal victims tend to have a concrete rationale for choosing a particular victim. Siegal (2004) suggests that some offenders engage in "acquaintance robbery," selecting a known victim who possesses a large amount of money or someone they rob as a means of retaliation or "street justice" to settle a dispute. Acquaintance robbery is attractive to some because in such cases there is an expectation that victims will not report the crime out of fear of retaliation or because they don't want to be involved with the police.

Matthews (2002) questions the notion of the rational robber, suggesting that many people who engage in robbery are drunk or on drugs prior to and during the commission of the offense and are desperate, driven by the need to find money to finance a drug habit or to feed their families. Furthermore, it is difficult to make sense of actively pursuing the risk and danger in armed face-to-face confrontation with a victim. From this perspective,

> The pursuit of risk, which becomes the trademark of the experienced professional robber, does not fit well into the notion of the armed robber as a rational actor. In fact, the rational/irrational dichotomy makes little sense in this context. There can be no doubt that robbers employ contingent rationalities and make decisions based on certain knowledge, experience and hunches. However, the contingent rationalities need to be understood in a complex and contradictory framework of motivations and values, which in turn are conditioned by a culturally generated set of attitudes and social relations and which themselves embody contradictory and inconsistent elements. (Matthews, 2002, p. 38)

In what situations or contexts does robbery occur? Offenders who commit robbery do so because they perceive themselves as having little choice. They have a strong emotional attachment to street culture. Their offending is motivated by a "desperate desire to participate in and sustain various illicit activities promoted by that culture" (Wright & Decker, 1997, p. 131). Beyond the situational and environmental factors that set the stage for robbery are immediate contextual factors that increase the likelihood of the offense. The following findings illustrate the contexts in which robbery is most likely to occur:

- Most people who are targeted by robbers are themselves engaged in some sort of illicit activity.
- When robbers do select noncriminal targets, they are attracted to victims with outward signs of wealth.
- Robbers tend to operate in socially disorganized areas and do not stray far from their own communities.

- Physical settings shielded from public view with good escape routes are most conducive to robbery.

- Locations in and around businesses that involve cash-intensive activities are highly desirable targets.

- Robbers seek cash and operate in situations in which cash (not credit cards or checks) is available.

- Automatic teller machines are a hot target for robbers.

- Lower-class communities where people are presumed to carry cash are desirable locations for some offenders.

- Victims who do not cooperate have a greater chance of serious injury or death. Most offenders respond to resistance with extreme violence.

- Most offenders do not want their victims to make eye contact for fear of being identified and are more likely to resort to violence in such situations. (Wright & Decker, 1997)

Predatory Versus Affective Aggression and Robbery

Robbery is predominantly a predatory crime. It is also a crime that illustrates how predatory and affective aggression can occur in a series of consecutive acts. No other offense so clearly distinguishes predatory from affective violence. The decision to engage in a robbery can be affectively motivated in the sense that robbery is a crime of desperation—a visceral and emotional reaction to economic and social pressures to overcome constraints. The decision to commit the act can be understood as a reaction of sorts to a perceived threat (financial hardship, social pressure). However, the actual commission of robbery is predatory. It is a goal-oriented act that involves planning, target selection, absence of emotion, and elevated self-esteem (feelings of power and control). Once the crime is underway, an offender may engage in unplanned affective violence in response to victim resistance. The following is an account of a robbery by a 17-year-old offender who was convicted of robbery and aggravated assault for hitting a 52-year-old woman over the head with a lead pipe for $60:

> Put a mask on. . . . Went to the store and waited for someone to come out. Picked up a little tire changing thing on the side of a house. Waited for someone who wouldn't give much trouble. . . . Didn't think it would take that much aggression to obtain a wallet. Lady came out. . . . The thing was light . . . if had a soft head it might crush . . . thought would only have to hit once. She started yelling, screaming. . . . I panicked and started hitting repeatedly until she stopped screaming . . . took her purse and left. I thought it would take just one hard strike . . . bang, boom that'd be it. . . . There wasn't any feeling. Not even any realistic thought. It was like I wasn't doing it—like I was watching someone else. . . . Dawned on me, was brutal, unnecessary, two or three days later. (Helfgott, 1997b, 2004)

This offender (a participant in a study on unconscious defensive process/conscious cognitive style in psychopaths who did not score above 30 on the PCL-R) clearly engaged in predatory aggression in committing this offense, but his attack of the victim was an unplanned reaction to the victim's screams, an act of affective violence.

Although the goal of robbery is primarily to obtain money or property, many robbers express satisfaction in dominating their victims. This illustrates the predatory nature of the offense. The following account illustrates the feeling of control that lies at the heart of armed robbery:

> [On one of my armed robberies] me and a friend of mine . . . was standing up over [the victims] with these big old guns and these people were saying, "Take the money! Take the money! Just don't shoot us!" I didn't have any intentions of shooting anybody anyway. But I'm just saying that when a person is telling me that, you [are] in control. You can either take their life like that or you can just let them live. That's what it is, a control thing . . . you succeeded in having the authority to control people. (Wright & Decker, 1997, p. 56)

While offenders who commit robbery can be classified and understood as predatory or instrumental offenders, identifying the affective/expressive violence within robbery incidents offers insight into important situational aspects of the offense and characteristics of the offender. Cornell et al. (1996) theorize that

> the capacity to inflict serious injury on a person for goal-directed criminal purposes is made possible by the relative lack of well-internalized social standards and associated feelings of concern and respect for others that otherwise would inhibit the offender. In those offenders with what might appear to be marginally adequate inhibitory standards and concern for others, the presence of extreme impulsivity or anger might override these inhibitions and drive them to act aggressively to achieve their instrumental objectives. (p. 789)

Thus, affective violence within the context of a predatory act of robbery offers information regarding the individual who committed the offense and the theme of the offense.

Offense Themes

In a heterogeneous crime category such as robbery, identifying the theme of the offense is all the more crucial. It could be hypothesized that the serial armed robber who robs gas stations and shoots station attendants execution style is a different sort of person from the offender who robs a convenience store with a toy gun and shakes while asking for the money. (Research supporting the categorical model of psychopathy in conjunction with the empirical link between psychopathy, violent recidivism, and predatory crime supports this hypothesis.) Though all robberies share certain elements (planning, target selection) and instrumental motivations (money, power/control), aspects of individual offenses offer information about the nature of the offense and the offender.

The following are some examples of very different types of armed robbery that occurred in different locations in 2004:

- Reubin Lamont Lacefield robbed a gas station in Boston by lifting his sweatshirt to show the butt of a Daisy BB handgun. He fled with cash and four cartons of Newport cigarettes.
- Michael Brody and Allen Wichgers of Milwaukee were charged with burglary and armed robbery. Wichgers was the getaway driver and Brody was the tipster who told two

others about a house where there was a significant sum of cash. Brody and two others entered the house and hit the resident with a baseball bat, leaving with $1,400.

- In Baltimore, a 17-year-old was arrested for holding up a pizza deliveryman and robbing him of a cell phone, money, and three pizzas.

- In Britain, a gang of seven professional armed robbers was foiled in an attempt to steal gold bullion worth a large amount of money from a warehouse in Heathrow Airport. The gang rammed a white van through the doors of a Swissport cargo warehouse on the outskirts of the airport and leapt out to threaten staff with a gun and knives. Had they pulled it off, the crime would have been one of the biggest robberies in UK history.

- In Aberdeen, Washington, 33-year-old Virginia Marie Kay, three teenage girls (one her own daughter), and 20-year-old Amber Wood robbed an Anchor Savings Bank armed with handguns. The heist, modeled after the film *Set It Off,* lasted 53 seconds with one of the three shouting out time in five-second intervals.

- Two New Orleans men were arrested for a four-hour robbery spree that involved stealing two vehicles, two wallets, jewelry, a DVD player, a computer, a TV, and cash from three victims. They carjacked a man as he was getting out of his pickup truck, then followed a man home and ordered him into his house where they took a watch and electronic equipment. An hour later they carjacked another man as he was about to enter his vehicle. They then set the stolen pickup truck on fire.

- Larry Butler, who worked at Gerald's restaurant in New Orleans, was charged with armed robbery after he went to the restaurant to pick up his paycheck wearing a T-shirt with the business' name on it and without his face covered. He went to a female employee who was counting cash, told her he had a gun and threatened to kill her, then pushed her away and took the cash.

In all of these crimes the offenders were arrested for armed robbery; however, each involves a different modus operandi and signature and involves different themes. Some of the offenders engaged in purely predatory acts in which the victims may have been viewed as objects and power and control were dominant factors (the carjackers). Others engaged in offenses that involved more of a mix of predatory and affective aggression in which victims were more likely to have been vehicles of the offender's emotional state (the employee/acquaintance robber), whereas others involved an affective/retaliatory component in which the victim was known and personalized (the Milwaukee burglary/robbery). Of course, more information is necessary to definitively identify the themes of the individual crimes, but these very different robberies illustrate the importance of attending to offense themes in understanding the nature of robbery and the forms it may take.

Summary

Violence is primed in the public mind in such a way that many people grossly overestimate the likelihood that they will be the victims of predatory violence at the hands of strangers. However, most violent crime is not predatory, nor is it committed by strangers. Violence is a varied behavioral outcome of a complex web of motivational, situational, and contextual factors. Serious violent crime accounts for only a small percentage of the total amount of crime. Violent crime has decreased considerably in the last two decades in the United States, with violent victimization rates the lowest recorded in 20 years. Violent crime is predominantly a male phenomenon; however, the gender gap in arrests for violent crime has lessened considerably in recent years.

Motivation, factors, and forces contributing to violent crime can be uncovered only with careful analysis of offense characteristics, giving attention to the link between aggression and violence. Violence is a behavioral act that is an expression of predatory or affective aggression mediated by environmental, social, and cultural forces that may or may not manifest in violence. Research suggests that violent and nonviolent offending may be distinct and different phenomena and that individuals who commit violent criminal behavior differ from those who do not. Major categories or types of violent crime include homicide, assault, and robbery. Each type of violent crime has distinct characteristics and features in terms of nature of aggression and offense themes.

DISCUSSION QUESTIONS

1. Discuss how "offense analysis" proposed by West (2000) can help in better understanding violent criminal behavior. What does this approach offer in terms of identifying homogeneous features of violent criminal behavior?

2. What are the features of predatory and affective aggression? Explain the two types of aggression and their roles in violent crime. How are violent crimes motivated by affective aggression different from those motivated by predatory aggression? Do offenders who engage in violent crime motivated by predatory aggression also engage in violent crime motivated by affective aggression and vice versa? Discuss.

3. It is a stereotyped belief that girls and women are more likely to engage in affectively motivated rather than predatory aggression. However, research on female serial killers suggests that female serial killers may be just as likely as men if not more so to engage in instrumental and predatory aggression. What are your thoughts on this—is the view that men are more predatory than women when it comes to violent crime more myth based on sex-role stereotypes than reality?

4. Describe the *trauma control model* proposed by Hickey (2002, 2006) to explain the development of serial murder. Does this model have the potential to explain other types of violent crime? Why or why not?

5. What subtypes of crime fall under the heading of "violent crime" in this chapter? Is violent crime a homogeneous crime category that is distinct from other types of crime? Are people who engage in violent crime categorically different from people who engage in nonviolent crime?

On Your Own: Log on to the Web-based student study site at http://www.sagepub .com/helfgottstudy/ for the URL links in the Web Exercises, study aids such as review quizzes, and research recommendations including links to journal articles specifically selected for this book.

1. Review the most recent violent crime statistics in the *Uniform Crime Reports* at http://www.fbi.gov/ucr/05cius/offenses/violent_crime/index.html and the *National Crime Victimization Survey* at http://www.ojp.usdoj.gov/bjs/abstract/cv05.htm. In reviewing these data, what can be said about violent crime and the types of violent crime in the United States? What cannot be said? Where would you go and how would you attempt to find answers to additional questions about violent crime that available data do not address?

2. Read about the BTK case and trial transcripts at http://crime.about.com/od/murder/p/raderbtk.htm and watch the video clip of his detailed confession at http://www.foxnews.com/story/0,2933,165957,00.html. Discuss elements of Rader's offenses that are associated with predatory violence. Could any of Rader's acts be considered affectively motivated?

3. Study the graph on the Bureau of Justice Statistics Web site, http://www.ojp.usdoj.gov/bjs/glance/vsx2.htm, "Violent Crime Rates by Gender of Victim." Why do you think the gender gap in violent victimization is decreasing? Looking further—http://www.ojp.usdoj.gov/bjs/homicide/gender.htm—at the victim/offender relationship in homicides, discuss why you think male-male homicide represents the largest percentage of homicides whereas female-female homicides represents the smallest percentage. What do these data offer in answering the "man question" in criminology?

4. Read/listen to a recent report entitled, "U.S. Violent Crime Rises at Pace Unseen in 10 Years": http://www.npr.org/templates/story/story.php?storyId=5480227. Given the overall statistics discussed in this chapter and your own review of UCR and NCVS data over the past 20 years, can we confidently say violent crime is on the rise?

5. Read through cases of "Women Who Kill" on the Crime Library Web site: http://www.crimelibrary.com/notorious_murders/women/index.html. Based on this available anecdotal case information on female killers, would you conclude that most female homicide is instrumentally or affectively motivated? Offer suggestions for ways in which this question can be empirically investigated.

6. Read about the homicide-suicide case of David and Crystal Brame: http://www.thenewstribune.com/news/projects/david_brame/. Research other news examples of homicide-suicide. What are the distinctive features of this subtype of violent crime? Is the Brame case a usual or anomalous example of homicide-suicide?

Sex Crime

Surely if humans, far and wide, wound the genitals, we hate them;
we hate where they take us, what we do with them.

—Andrea Dworkin (1987, p. 194)

In March 2001, Armin Meiwes, a 42-year-old computer expert, murdered 43-year-old Bernd Juergen Brandes, a microchip engineer, in his home in Rotenburg, Germany. The two met after Brandes answered an Internet advertisement placed by Meiwes for a young man interested in "slaughter and consumption." Meiwes testified in court that the killing began after the two engaged in sadomasochistic sex acts when, at Brandes's request, he tried unsuccessfully to bite off Brandes's penis, and then cut it off with a knife. The two then tried to eat the penis raw, then fried it in a pan trying unsuccessfully to eat it. Brandes eventually went unconscious from loss of blood after lying for hours in the bathtub while Meiwes read magazines and drank wine. Meiwes then hung Brandes from a butcher's hook and slaughtered him. The slaughter included severing his head, disembowelment, laying him out on a butcher block, and chopping his body into pieces. After the killing, Meiwes froze portions of the body, kept the skull in the freezer, buried other body parts in the garden, and ate 44 pounds of the body over the months to follow. Meiwes videotaped the entire event, watched it later to become sexually aroused, and spoke in court about how watching horror films as a child fueled his fantasies and long-time desires to commit such acts ("German Cannibal Tells of Fantasy," December 3, 2003).

Meiwes was caught in 2002 after an Internet surfer came across another one of his ads and turned him in to police. He was charged with sexually motivated murder and "disturbing the peace of the dead" for cutting up body parts. Meiwes told the court, "I wanted someone to be part of me." A psychiatrist determined that Meiwes was aware of what he was doing, legally sane, and fit to stand trial. Meiwes was diagnosed

Photo 6.1   Armin Meiwes.

Photo credit: Copyright © Alexander Heimann/Getty Images.

with *schizoid personality*, a personality disorder characterized by inability to form close relationships.[1] Psychiatrist and sexual behaviorist Dr. Klaus Beier told the court that, for Meiwes, sexual excitement was irrevocably linked to the idea of cutting up men ("Cannibal Could Kill Again," January 20, 2004). In January 2004, Meiwes was convicted of manslaughter and sentenced to 8½ years in prison. Judge Volker Muetze explained the verdict saying that Meiwes's intention was not evil but "the fulfillment of his fantasy" and that Meiwes's primary motive was "the wish to make another man part of himself," which he fulfilled through the consumption of his victim's flesh ("Smiling Cannibal Cleared of Murder," January 30, 2004). The case was later appealed and overturned by the prosecution, who ordered a retrial on the grounds that the lower court did not give sufficient consideration to the sexual motivation behind the killing ("Cannibal Case to Go to Germany's Highest Court," March 19, 2007). In May 2006, Meiwes was sentenced to life in prison ("German Court Sentences Cannibal to Life in Jail," May 9, 2006).

What is interesting about this case is that the crime (manslaughter) was a sexually motivated act involving two consenting adults. The case illustrates the distinction, and sometimes blurred boundaries, between sexual deviance and sexual crime. The term *sexual deviance* refers to sexual behavior outside the norm. This includes socially deviant as well as criminal sexual behavior. Behaviors such as sadomasochistic sexual activity (S&M) engaged in by consenting adults (such as the initial acts engaged in by Meiwes and Brandes) are sexually deviant, but not criminal. The Meiwes case was legally problematic because the offender and victim were engaging in sexually deviant acts involving consenting adults. In Germany, cannibalism is not a crime and a person cannot be convicted of murder if the victim gives consent to be killed. In this case, one could argue, as Meiwes defense attorney did in the original trial, that Meiwes committed a mercy killing, which should be construed as an assisted suicide. In other words, technically speaking, some may argue that Meiwes did not commit a sex crime (at least not sexual homicide) though few could argue that he did not engage in sexually deviant acts.

Normal Sexuality, Sexual Deviance, Sexual Disorder, and Sex Crime

To understand sex crime, it is important to understand the varieties of human sexual behavior, the processes by which certain types of sexual behaviors are deemed deviant and criminal, and the multiple perspectives from which the behavior is defined and controlled. Sexual behavior has been defined and explored in terms of *normal sexuality, sexual deviance, sexual disorder,* and *sexual crime*. Sex offenses are crimes of violence. However, the sexual nature of such acts requires understanding of the overlapping concepts of sexual deviance, sexual disorder, and sexual crime. It is important to keep in mind three key points in thinking about sexual deviance, sexual disorders, and sexual crimes:

- Overlap occurs between informal, formal, and medical definitions and control of sexual deviance.

- The designation of a variety of sexual practices as a disease or an objectively abnormal condition is inconsistent with cross-cultural evidence suggesting that sexuality norms are relative across time and place.

- There is disparity between the reality of sexual practices in American society and the formal and informal social control of sexual deviations (Heitzig, 1996).

In other words, there are a wide range of sexually deviant behaviors. What is defined as deviant or not is rooted in religion, culture, law, and science. Sexual behavior is controlled informally through stigmatization, formally through the criminal law, and medically through clinical diagnosis. Sexual disorders identified as criminal (by the legal system) or pathological (by psychology and psychiatry) are socially constructed as such despite differences in sexual norms across time and place. As a result of informal, formal, and medical definitions and control of sexual deviance, most sexual behavior is conducted behind closed doors and sexual behavior is rarely discussed openly despite major commercial and Internet markets for deviant, pathological, and criminal sexual services.

The designation of the parameters of "normal sexuality" are subjective, time and culture bound, and dependent on an array of sociopolitical forces. In fact, understanding sex crime may require more of an understanding of normal sexuality than of abnormal psychology. The finding that 65% of college-age men have engaged in some form of sexual misconduct, including sexual contact with children, coercive sex with women, frottage, and obscene phone calls (Templeman & Stinnett, 1994), suggests that the divide between people most consider "normal" and those viewed as sexually deviant or criminal may be smaller than we think.

Normal Sexuality

Definitions of sexual deviance and the social control of sexual behavior through law are based on cultural views of acceptable "normal" sexual behavior. *Normal sexuality* is rooted in Judeo-Christian doctrine and the criminal law. Normal sex is monogamous, procreative, heterosexual intercourse between married persons. Much more research attention has been given to sexual deviance than to the subject of normal sexuality. The dearth of research on normal sexuality may be, at least in part, the result of the difficulties in obtaining a sample of individuals willing to openly discuss their sexual behavior and sexual fantasies (Laumann, Gagnon, Michael, & Michaels, 2003). What is "normal" in the statistical sense (the behavior that most people actually engage in behind closed doors) does not necessarily coincide with social proscriptions for normal sexual behavior, and what's normal in one culture, time, or place may be deviant or criminal in another.

Human sexuality is a complex concept that has to be understood through multiple lenses and disciplinary perspectives. Sex researchers Masters and Johnson (1974) noted that human sexual behavior is both learned and instinctive and impacted by a range of biological, psychological, and sociocultural influences. Alfred Kinsey, a zoologist who conducted one of the first systematic studies of human sexuality, states:

> To each individual, the significance of any particular type of sexual activity depends very largely upon his previous experience. Ultimately, certain activities may seem to him to be the only things that have value, that are right, that are socially acceptable; and all departures from his own particular pattern may seem to him to be enormous abnormalities. But the scientific data which are accumulating make it appear that, if circumstances had been propitious, most individuals might have become conditioned in any direction, even into activities which they now consider quite unacceptable. There is little evidence of the existence of such a thing as innate perversity, even among those individuals whose sexual activities society has been least inclined to accept. There is an abundance of evidence that most human sexual activities would become comprehensible to most individuals, if they could know the background of each other individual's behavior. (Kinsey, Pomeroy, & Martin, 1948, p. 678)

To understand human sexuality and all of its forms requires suspension of judgment and attention to the conditioning processes, social forces, and environmental events that shape the biological (and more innate) aspects of human sexual behavior.

Research on and theories of sexuality come from a range of intersecting perspectives. Human sexuality is studied within the disciplines of psychology, sociology, sociobiology, criminology, cultural anthropology, biology, medicine, theology, history, and law (Turner & Rubinson, 1993). The *psychological perspective* focuses on the ways in which sexuality and sexual arousal are shaped by emotions, personality dynamics, motivations, attitudes, beliefs, and interpersonal behaviors. The *sociological perspective* looks at the ways in which sexuality and its definition and social control are shaped by the society in which a person lives. The *sociobiological perspective* views sexuality as a genetic adaptation to the environment with the belief that sex differences in males and females are functional and adaptive in an evolutionary sense. The *criminological perspective* focuses on sexual offenses, the causes and consequences of such behavior, and its control. The *cultural anthropology* perspective looks at cross-cultural variations in sexual behavior and the meaning that behavior holds for individuals in particular cultures and communities. The *biological perspective* focuses on the physical aspects of sexuality—anatomy, physiology, development, and maturity of the body's sexual systems. The *medical perspective* emphasizes sexual health—the maintenance of sexual well-being and the conditions associated with disease and individual and social distress. From *historical* and *theological perspectives,* sexuality is shaped by historical forces—the term *sexuality* evolves in connection with the past as well as biblical views of sexuality and sexual behavior. Finally, from a *legal perspective,* certain sexual behaviors are identified as a social threat. Laws regarding criminal sexual behavior differ across time, place, and across federal, state, and local systems.

Sexual Deviance

The types of behaviors viewed as sexually deviant are, from sociological, criminological, and anthropological perspectives, socially constructed and change across time and place. For example, homosexual and bisexual behaviors have historically been included in texts on sexual deviance and sex crimes (Holmes, 1989). However, with changing conceptions of homosexuality in society, many no longer view such behavior as "deviant." This shift in thinking about homosexuality is reflected in the repeal of sodomy laws in most states across the United States as well as the removal of homosexuality from the *Diagnostic and Statistical Manual of Mental Disorders.* Furthermore, laws against adultery and fornication have existed throughout history based on the notion that adultery is a threat to the sanctity of marriage. However, today these laws have little public support, and they are rarely enforced even though they remain on the books in most states.

The amount of force with which sexually deviant behaviors are socially controlled and officially targeted is also dictated by social forces and factors such as politics and demographic shifts. For example, in his book *Moral Panic,* Jenkins (1998) argues that panics over sex crimes have historically occurred during periods in which the majority population is aging. Concern about sex crimes was at its lowest in the United States during periods of high tolerance for sexual experimentation (e.g., 1920s and 1960s) and highest in 1915, 1950, 1985, and post-1995. Following the sexual revolution of the 1960s, the increasing conservative stance on a range of issues during the 1980s Reagan era was associated with the aging of the baby boomers who supported get-tough campaigns on drugs, crime, and child abuse as a way to control their own children. According to Jenkins, "Preventing sexual acts *against* the young can be a way of regulating sexual acts *by* that population" (p. 225), and the post-1995 furor over sex predators and cyberstalkers is the result of a changing cultural landscape in which American culture is becoming increasingly feminized, with heightened sensitivity and concern over issues of sexual exploitation and violence.

Thus, the types of behaviors viewed as "normal" versus "deviant" change across time and place as do the formal and informal mechanisms of social control that target deviant sexual behavior. What's deviant and who we are willing to put in prison and for how long depend to a large extent on sociocultural and political forces. Sociology, specifically deviance theory, offers a lens through which to view the historical changes in definitions of normal and deviant sexual behaviors and the cultural dynamics of legislative changes such as sexual predator laws, three-strikes laws, sex offender registration, and civil commitment regarding sex crimes.

Sexual Disorders

From medical and psychological perspectives, sexual pathologies have long been recognized. A century ago, Krafft-Ebing (1906) published *Psychopathia Sexualis* documenting case studies of sexual disorders including fetishism, sadism, masochism, transsexualism, transvestism, nymphomania, sexual bondage, and lust murder. Today, sexual disorders are identified in the *Diagnostic and Statistical Manual of Mental Disorders, Fourth Edition, Text Revision (DSM-IV-TR),* including behaviors that are sexually deviant in the sense that they are associated with some form of individual or interpersonal distress. Some, but not all of the *DSM* sexual disorders are crimes.

The *DSM-IV-TR* classifies sexual disorders under the heading, *Sexual and Gender Identity Disorders.* This category includes gender identity disorders, sexual dysfunctions, and paraphilias.

Sexual Dysfunctions

Sexual dysfunctions involve a disturbance in sexual desire that causes distress and interpersonal difficulty. *Gender identity disorders,* a type of sexual dysfunction, are characterized by cross-gender identification and persistent discomfort with one's assigned sex. Other sexual dysfunctions include

- *Sexual desire disorders*—absent or markedly diminished sexual appetite
- *Sexual arousal disorders*—inability to achieve or maintain "lubrication-swelling response to sexual excitement" (in women) or "adequate erection" (in men)
- *Orgasmic disorders*—delay in or absence of orgasm (in men or women) or premature ejaculation (in men)
- *Sexual pain disorders*—genital pain before, during, or after intercourse

The behavioral symptoms of sexual dysfunctions and gender identity disorders are not crimes. These are sexual disorders associated with particular psychological, emotional, or behavioral symptoms that result in distress and interpersonal difficulty.

Paraphilias

Paraphilia literally means "abnormal love." In contrast with the sexual dysfunctions and gender identity disorder, symptoms of many paraphilias are criminal behaviors. *Paraphilias* are a group of persistent sexual behavioral patterns characterized by sexual fantasies, urges, or behaviors involving nonhuman objects (fetishism, transvestic fetishism), suffering or humiliation (sexual sadism, masochism), children (pedophilia), or other nonconsenting person (voyeurism, frotteurism, exhibitionism) (APA, 2000). All of the paraphilias involve a particular behavior associated with sexual arousal, urges, and fantasies:

- *Exhibitionism*—exposure of one's genitals
- *Fetishism*—the use of nonliving objects such as women's underwear, bras, etc.
- *Frotteurism*—touching and rubbing against nonconsenting persons
- *Pedophilia*—sexual activity with a prepubescent child
- *Sexual masochism*—being beaten, bound, humiliated, and/or made to suffer
- *Sexual sadism*—deriving sexual excitement from psychological or physical suffering of the victim
- *Transvestic fetishism*—cross-dressing by a male in women's attire
- *Voyeurism*—observing unsuspecting individuals who are in the process of undressing, naked, and/or engaged in sexual activity, sometimes referred to as *scoptophilia* (Hickey, 2002, 2006; Holmes, 1989), the "sexualization of the sensation of looking" (Meloy, 1988, p. 72)
- *Paraphilia not otherwise specified*—paraphilias that do not meet the criteria for specific categories

The *DSM-IV-TR* category *paraphilias not otherwise specified* includes behaviors that are sometimes considered nuisance sex behaviors, but may also be associated with extreme sex crimes such as sexual homicide. Many paraphilias that would be classified in this category have been found in sexual homicide cases (Hickey, 2002, 2006). Paraphilias exist on a continuum varying in degree of severity and dangerousness, and multiple paraphilias are often found in one person with one being dominant. The following is a noncomprehensive list of sexual behaviors that may be classified as a paraphilia not otherwise specified or are sexual behaviors engaged in by actual sexual homicide offenders at some point in their lives:

- *Animal torture*—torture, mutilation, and killing of animals for sexual gratification and experimentation (Physical cruelty to animals is one of the criteria for conduct disorder, which, in some cases, is the childhood precursor to antisocial personality disorder and psychopathy.)
- *Anthropophagy*—eating flesh and/or slicing parts of the body (i.e., cannibalism)
- *Autoeroticism*—sexual arousal through self-stimulation (e.g., masturbation to pornography, sexual asphyxia, or aquaerotic asphyxiation)
- *Coprophilia*—sexual interest in and gratification from touching feces
- *Coprophagia*—sexual arousal through eating feces (a variant of coprophilia) (See Wise & Goldberg, 1995, for an illustrative case study on coprophagia and its escalation.)
- *Erotophonophilia*—sexual arousal from killing
- *Gerontophilia*—sexual interest in elderly persons
- *Infibulation*—engaging in self-torture such as piercing genitals with sharp objects (e.g., needles, pins)
- *Klismaphilia*—sexual arousal through receiving or administration of enemas
- *Mixoscopia* or *triolism*—sexual arousal from seeing oneself in sexual scenes or sharing a sexual partner with another person and watching
- *Necrophilia*—engaging in sexual acts with dead bodies
- *Necrofetishism*—fetish for dead bodies that may involve keeping bodies or body parts in one's home
- *Partialism*—exclusive sexual focus on particular parts of the body
- *Piquerism*—sexual arousal through stabbing, wounding, or cutting
- *Pygmalionism*—sexual involvement with dolls or mannequins
- *Pyromania*—sexual arousal by firesetting[2]
- *Urophilia*—sexual interest in drinking or touching urine
- *Zoophilia* or *bestiality*—sexual activity with animals[3]

It is important to underscore that *sexual dysfunctions and gender identity disorder are mental disorders, not crimes.* Paraphilias (i.e., sexual sadism, sexual masochism, fetishism, transvestic fetishism) are not criminal unless the behavioral symptoms of these disorders cross over into acts that are harmful to nonconsenting second or third parties. For example, as the Meiwes-Brandes case illustrates, sexual masochism and sexual sadism may involve consenting or nonconsenting persons. Sadism and masochism (S&M) is widely practiced between consenting adults. Such behavior is generally seen by the larger society as sexually deviant, but engaging in S&M activities is not a crime, and in many cases, may not be a diagnosable paraphilia. An individual can be diagnosed with a paraphilia if the behavior causes marked distress or interpersonal difficulty. Individuals who consensually engage in S&M who are not distressed by the behavior are not likely to be diagnosed with sexual masochism or sexual sadism. To illustrate further, a person with a fetish for women's underwear who purchases the underwear for his own use or obtains undergarments from friends or acquaintances has not committed a crime. But, someone who steals women's underwear can be charged with burglary or theft. For example, 30-year-old Sung Koo Kim, a Brigham Young University student, was arrested in Portland in June 2004, charged with burglary and theft for stealing at least 3,000 pairs of women's underwear from college dorms, and sentenced to six years in prison ("Sung Koo Kim Gets Nearly Six Years for Underwear Theft," 2005). In Kim's case (as in the case of Armin Meiwes's sexually motivated manslaughter), his fetishism (a paraphilia) led to theft and burglary (criminal behavior), but the paraphilia itself was not a crime.[4] Police also found 40,000 pictures of women being tortured and raped on Kim's computer. But this, and even pedophiliac or sexual homicide fantasies (provided the pornography does not involve children), does not constitute a crime.

Sex Crimes

Sex crimes are differentiated from *sexual disorders* and *sexual deviance* in that they are behavioral acts that violate the law. As is true with all types of crimes, the legal terminology and laws regarding what is and is not a sex crime vary across states and the federal system. The lines between normal, deviant, and disordered sexuality and sex crimes are sometimes hazy. The same or similar acts may be designated as a sex crime or not depending on the law in particular times and places or whether the act has been reported/identified or not.

Legal Definitions of Sex Offenses

From a legal perspective, *sex offenses* are acts deemed both sexually deviant *and* a threat to individuals and public safety. Behaviors that generally fall into the category of sex crimes are those in which the offender engages in a sexual act with a nonconsenting victim. Sexual assault and rape, child molestation, child rape, sexual misconduct with a minor, indecent liberties, voyeurism, sexual violation of human remains, and custodial sexual misconduct are examples of sexual behaviors legally defined as sex offenses (RCW 9.94A.030, 2004). In Washington State, sex offense is defined as

- Any offense defined as a sex offense by RCW 9.94A.030 (listed in above paragraph);

- Any violation under RCW 9A.44.096 (sexual misconduct with a minor in the second degree);

- Any violation under RCW 9.68A.090 (communication with a minor for immoral purposes);

- Any federal or out-of-state conviction for an offense that under the laws of this state would be classified as a sex offense under this subsection; and

- Any gross misdemeanor that is, under chapter 9A.28 RCW, a criminal attempt, criminal solicitation, or criminal conspiracy to commit an offense that is classified as a sex offense under RCW 9.94A.030 or this subsection.

The U.S. Criminal Code lists sex offenses under Sexual Abuse (Title 18, Chapter 109A) and Sexual Exploitation of Children (Title 18, Chapter 110). Offenders convicted of a federal sex crime are those who cross state lines, kidnap their victims, or commit their offense within the jurisdictional boundaries of federal law. As in state laws, federal sex offenses involve sex acts or sexual contact with a nonconsenting person or sexual exploitation of children such as cases involving children in "sexually explicit behaviors" for pornographic enterprises. The U.S. Criminal Code defines *sexual contact* as "the intentional touching, either directly or through the clothing, of the genitalia, anus, groin, breast, inner thigh, or buttocks of any person with an intent to abuse, humiliate, harass, degrade, or arouse or gratify the sexual desire of any person." *Sex act* is defined as:

- contact between the penis and the vulva or the penis and the anus, and for purposes of this subparagraph contact involving the penis occurs upon penetration, however slight;
- contact between the mouth and the penis, the mouth and the vulva, or the mouth and the anus;
- the penetration, however slight, of the anal or genital opening of another by a hand or finger or by any object, with an intent to abuse, humiliate, harass, degrade, or arouse or gratify the sexual desire of any person; or
- the intentional touching, not through the clothing, of the genitalia of another person who has not attained the age of 16 years with an intent to abuse, humiliate, harass, degrade, or arouse or gratify the sexual desire of any person.

Sexually explicit conduct refers to actual or simulated

- sexual intercourse, including genital-genital, oral-genital, anal-genital, or oral-anal, whether between persons of the same or opposite sex;
- bestiality;
- masturbation;
- sadistic or masochistic abuse; or
- lascivious exhibition of the genitals or pubic area of any person.

Of the crime categories, sex crimes, especially those committed against children, are the most publicly abhorred and socially controlled. Sexual predators, pedophiliac priests, serial rapists, and child molesters are the targets of an enormous amount of news media attention and punitive measures. Public fear of sex crime and anger toward sex offenders has driven legislation such as sexual psychopath and sexual predator laws, two- and one-strike laws, and sex offender registration. Even in prison, sex offenders are the lowest on the offender hierarchy and, as a result, are victimized and aggressively targeted by other offenders (Sabo, Kupers, & London, 2001; see Box 6.1).

BOX 6.1

JOHN GEOGHAN

John Geoghan.

Photo credit: © John Mottern/AFP/Getty Images.

Catholic priest John Geoghan preyed on young boys in Boston parishes for 30 years before his crimes were uncovered in 1998. He was defrocked by the church after 150 victims came forward to say they had been raped or fondled by Geoghan. Geoghan was sentenced in 2002 to 9 to 10 years in prison for sexually molesting a 10-year-old boy, and the Boston Archdiocese paid $10 million in civil settlements to other victims. While in prison, Geoghan's attorneys said he was harassed by corrections officers and received numerous infractions for insolence. Geoghan was moved from a medium security prison to the new maximum security prison, Souza-Baranowski Correctional Center. A year later, while in the protective custody unit, Geoghan was brutally murdered by Joseph Druce, a convicted killer serving life without parole and with a known hatred of pedophiles, who got into Geoghan's cell, beat him, and used a bedsheet to bind and strangle him to death.

Sexual Psychopathy and Sexual Predator Laws

The terms *sexual predator* and *sexual psychopath* are legal terms used to impose civil commitment of dangerous sex offenders whose behavior is associated with mental illness and pathological tendency to reoffend. Sexual deviancy and psychopathy have been associated in the literature since the 1800s. Early writers (Karpman, 1954; Krafft-Ebing, 1906; and others) used the term *sexual psychopath* to refer to sex offenders whose behaviors were rooted in psychopathology. Individuals referred to as sexual psychopaths in the literature over the last two centuries would not necessarily be those considered psychopaths today (i.e., based on a high score on the Psychopathy Checklist-Revised). Although a subset of sexual offenders are psychopathic, most sex offenders are not psychopaths, most psychopaths are not sex offenders, and the legal definitions of sexual psychopathy and sexual predator in the past and today are not synonymous with traditional or contemporary psychological definitions of psychopathy (APA, 1999; Smith & Meyer, 1987). Of the civilly committed sexually violent predators housed in the Special Commitment Center in Washington State, only 27.5% exceed the PCL-R cutoff score of 30 to be classified as psychopathic and 41.1% have been diagnosed with antisocial personality disorder (Richards & Jackson, 2007a).

The intertwining of the terms sexual deviancy and psychopathy in the research literature made its way into law in the 1930s with the *psychopathic personality* and *sexual psychopath* laws. These laws were designed to civilly commit sex offenders whose behavior can be attributed to mental illness, with the idea that sexual psychopaths, unlike other types of offenders, were sick and could be treated. The sexual psychopath laws were based on six assumptions:

1. A mental disability exists called *sexual psychopathy*.

2. Persons suffering from sexual psychopathy are at higher risk of dangerously reoffending than are other types of offenders.

3. Sexual psychopaths can be identified by mental health experts.

4. The dangerousness of sexual psychopaths can be predicted.

5. Treatment is available for the sexual psychopath.

6. Large numbers of persons so diagnosed can be cured.

Even though virtually none of the six assumptions was supported empirically or otherwise, 25 states had enacted sexual psychopath laws by the 1960s. By the 1980s, most of these laws were repealed because treatment was ineffective, and it was determined that *sexual psychopathy* did not describe a homogeneous group of offenders whose behavior could be treated, predicted, or "cured." In urging the repeal of the sexual psychopath laws, the Group for the Advancement of Psychiatry (GAP) declared that:

> First and foremost, the sex psychopath and sexual offender statutes can best be described as approaches that have failed. The discrepancy between the promises in sex statutes and performances have rarely been resolved. . . . The notion is naïve and confusing that a hybrid amalgam of law and psychiatry can validly label a person a "sex psychopath" or "sex

offender" and then treat him in a manner consistent with a guarantee of community safety. The mere assumption that such a heterogeneous legal classification could define treatability and make people amenable to treatment is not only fallacious; it is startling. (cited in APA, 1999, p. 14)

The sexual psychopath laws illustrate the difficulties in using a clinical concept (psychopathy) to define a criminal behavior (sex offending) in such a way as to identify and predict dangerousness for the purpose of public safety.

Despite the troublesome history of the sexual psychopath laws, these laws were resurrected in the 1990s. The new laws replaced the term *sexual psychopath* with *sexual predator.* Washington State was the first to enact the sexual predator law under the Community Protection Act of 1990, which extended postrelease supervision for certain sex offenders, required sex offender registration, and established a new law for the civil commitment of "sexually violent predators." The law was revived in the aftermath of and public outcry in response to a number of high-profile cases including the 1989 rape of a 7-year-old boy by Earl Shriner, an offender who had previously served a 10-year sentence for kidnapping and assaulting two teenage girls. The case was particularly horrific because Shriner had cut off the boy's penis and because he had a lengthy previous history of sexual violence toward children.[5]

The sexual predator law differs from the old sexual psychopath laws by subjecting the offenders to civil commitment *after* they serve a full prison term, based on a process involving petition by the prosecuting attorney or attorney general, a finding of probable cause, a forensic evaluation, and trial. The broad definition of sexually violent predators under Washington's law may do no better than previous sexual psychopath laws in terms of designating a homogeneous group of offenders who are predictably dangerous with an identifiable (and treatable) mental illness. The law has been challenged since its inception for committing offenders deemed "untreatable" to indeterminant civil confinement for treatment. In recent years a series of state and U.S. Supreme Court rulings have pressured states that have sexual predator laws to prove they are working to treat and release civilly committed sex predators rather than indefinitely confine them (APA, 1999).

Understanding the history behind the sexual psychopath and sexual predator laws illustrates the need for meaningful offender typologies (in science and law) that identify homogeneous groups of offenders. It is crucial that legal concepts reflect and are consistent with clinical concepts that have an empirical basis and direct implications for treatment and management of offenders. It could be argued that sexual psychopath and predator laws represent clinical concepts sloppily applied by legislatures in the name of public safety. Jenkins (1998) notes that the term *sexual predator* was a media construction created, in part, by the Westley Dodd and Earl Shriner cases and Jack Olsen's 1991 book *Predator* (about a Washington State serial rapist) and the local appeal and familiarity with legislators and media (Box 6.2).[6] These laws, historically and at present, are an attempt to link personality and mental disorders with a criminal behavior and treatment with punishment—a longstanding and unresolved dilemma in criminal justice.

BOX 6.2

NOTORIOUS WASHINGTON STATE SEXUAL PREDATORS

Westley Dodd Execution, Washington State Penitentiary, Walla Walla Washington, 1993.

Photo credit: © Getty Images.

A Florida State University fraternity celebrates Ted Bundy's execution with a banner that says, "Watch Ted Fry, See Ted Die!" as they prepare for a cookout where they will serve "Bundy burgers" and "electrified hot dogs."

Photo credit: © Bettman/Corbis.

Washington State was the first state in the United States to enact legislation specifically directed at sex offenders. Washington State enacted the *Community Protection Act of 1990,* which required sex offender registration and civil commitment of sexually violent predators. The Washington legislation coincided with and was driven by public dissatisfaction over violent crime and an awareness of predatory crime. Under the law, sex offenders released to the community are required to register their address with law enforcement and those deemed sexually violent predators, on completion of their prison sentence, are civilly committed. The Washington State legislation, considered by some at the time and still today to be a draconian revival of the old habitual offender laws of the early 1900s, was fueled in part by anger, fear, and panic over high-profile offenders including

(Continued)

(Continued)

- **Ted Bundy:** One of the most notorious serial killers, from 1974 to 1978 Bundy murdered over 30 women. The exact number of Bundy's victims is unknown. Bundy's earliest victims were college students from the University of Washington and other universities in Washington State who he lured by wearing a fake cast or sling to get sympathy, asking for help, or posing as an authority figure. Bundy murdered most of his victims by hitting them in the head with a blunt object, and then took their bodies to remote locations where he had sex with their corpses and applied make-up to them. He confessed that he had decapitated some of his victims with a hacksaw. Eleven of Bundy's victims were from Washington State.

- **Kevin Coe:** Fredrick "Kevin" Coe committed rapes in Spokane, Washington's South Hill area in 1981. Coe served a 25-year sentence for one of the rapes but was said to have committed over 40 rapes that terrorized the city. Coe's case was the subject of Jack Olsen's book *Son: A Psychopath and His Victims* and a made-for-TV movie. Coe was released in 2006 and the state immediately filed a violent sexual predator action to detain Coe for a probable cause hearing to determine his status as a sexually violent predator. At the time of this writing he is housed at the Washington State Special Commitment Center on McNeil Island awaiting a civil commitment trial.

- **Charles Campbell:** In 1982 Campbell murdered Renae Wicklund, her 8-year-old daughter Shannah, and a neighbor, Barbara Hendrickson. Wicklund had testified in a rape case years earlier that Campbell had attacked and sodomized her and held a knife to her baby's throat. Campbell committed the murders while on work release after doing time for the rape. Campbell was executed by hanging in 1994.

- **Gene Raymond Kane:** In 1988 Diane Ballasiotes was raped and murdered in Pioneer Square in Seattle by a convicted sex offender, Gene Kane. Kane had served a 13-year sentence for attacking two women and was placed on work release in downtown Seattle. Ballasiotes's mother, Ida Ballasiotes, became a powerful force in Washington State as a state legislator.

- **Earl Shriner:** In 1989 Shriner raped and mutilated 7-year-old Ryan Alan Hade. Shriner had a 24-year history of sexual assaults against children and had served a sentence for murdering a 15-year-old classmate when he was 16. After his release from prison, he committed more crimes and was sent to prison for 10 years.

He was released in 1989, when he committed the heinous offense against Hade. He lured Hade out of sight with a doughnut when the boy was riding his bike in the woods near his home. Shriner was sentenced to life without the possibility of parole. Tragically, Hade later died in 2005 at age 23 in a motorcycle crash.

- **Westley Allan Dodd:** In 1989 Dodd murdered 10- and 11-year-old brothers William and Cole Neer and 4-year-old Lee Iseli in Vancouver, Washington. Dodd sexually assaulted and stabbed the Cole brothers to death and weeks later abducted Iseli from a park and sexually assaulted him in his home for 2 days and then hanged him with a rope in his closet. Dodd kept a journal of the assault and murders and took Polaroid pictures of Iseli before and after his death, including a photo of the boy hanging in the closet. Dodd was executed by hanging in 1993.

- **Gary Ridgway:** Although Gary Ridgway, the Green River Killer, was not caught and convicted until 13 years after the Community Protection Act of 1990 was enacted, bodies of the Green River Killer victims first began to be discovered in 1982, and the years of frustration and speculation surrounding the case likely influenced the enactment of the sex offender law. In November 2004 Gary Ridgway pled guilty to the sexual homicides of 48 women, including prostitutes and teen runaways. Ridgway strangled his victims after having sex with them and engaged in necrophilia with at least some of his victims' bodies. He was sentenced to life without parole after reaching a plea agreement with prosecutors.

Frustration over the legal inability to detain offenders that criminal justice officials had deemed too dangerous for release and the succession of horrific offenses committed by offenders with sexually violent criminal histories culminated in the Washington State 1990 sex offender registration and civil commitment legislation. Parents of murdered children, citizens, criminal justice officials, and legislators called for legal action that would enhance public safety by making the public aware of sex offenders in their midst and providing legal means to indeterminately incarcerate.

The civil commitment component of the Washington Community Protection Act involves end-of-sentence review petitioned by the prosecuting attorney or attorney general, consisting of a probable cause hearing to determine whether or not the offender meets the legal definition of "sexually violent predator." If probable cause exists, then a court will hold a full hearing to determine if civil commitment should be ordered. The legal definition of sexually violent predator in Washington State is "any person who has been convicted of or charged with a crime of sexual violence and who suffers from a mental abnormality or personality disorder which makes the person likely to engage in predatory acts of sexual violence if not confined in a secure facility"

(Continued)

(Continued)

(RCW 71.09.020). The length of civil commitment is indefinite, but an offender may be released from confinement to the community or to less restrictive community custody. Such release is based on a further finding that the offender participated in treatment and mental health staff determine that the offender has made treatment gains that reduce the likelihood of reoffense and risk to public safety.

The Washington State Community Protection Act set the stage for sexual violent predator legislation in another 20 states, driven by similar stories around the country including the murder of Polly Klaas by Richard Allen Davis, the 1990 abduction and disappearance of Jacob Wetterling in Minnesota, and the 1994 rape and murder of Megan Kanka in New Jersey by a convicted sex offender who lived across the street.

Photo Credit (Bundy, Coe, Campbell, Shriner, Dodd, and Ridgway photos): *The Seattle Times.*

Sex Offender Typologies

Sex crimes are committed by a heterogeneous group of offenders whose behavior reflects diverse offending patterns. According to Nicholas Groth, author of *Men Who Rape: The Psychology of the Offender,*

> One of the most basic observations one can make regarding men who rape is that not all such offenders are alike. They do not do the very same thing in the very same way or for the very same reasons. In some cases, similar acts occur for different reasons, and in other cases, different acts serve similar purposes. (Groth, 1979, p. 12)

The heterogeneity of sex offenders has made it difficult to draw conclusions necessary to deal with the population in the criminal justice system. Investigative practices, sentencing, correctional supervision, and treatment depend on clear understanding of who sex offenders are, the nature of their offending, the factors and developmental pathways that shape their behavior, and propensity for future offending.

Researchers have long attempted to develop meaningful typologies of sex offenders. Sex crimes and sex offenders have been classified based on factors such as motivation, victim type, modus operandi, nature of offense, and association with other criminal offenses. The most common sex offender typology is the distinction between the rapist and the child molester, based on age of victim. Many researchers have used this distinction as a starting point, developing more sophisticated subtypes of the two general categories including aspects of offender motivation and nature of offense (Danni & Hampe, 2000; Knight & Prentky, 1990; Looman, Gauthier, & Boer, 2001; Prentky & Burgess, 2000).

Sex offender typologies have been developed for the purpose of general understanding (Holmes, 1989), crime prevention (Miethe & McCorkle, 2001), victim outreach (Silverman et al., 1988), correctional supervision (Danni & Hampe, 2000), treatment (Knight & Prentky, 1990), and law enforcement investigation (Douglas et al., 1997). Holmes (1989) classifies sex crimes into three categories based on the nature of the offense: *nuisance sex behaviors, crimes against children,* and *dangerous sex crimes.* Miethe and McCorkle (2001) offer a multitrait typology identifying four sexual assault syndromes: *sexual homicide offenders, child molesters, adolescent sex offenders,* and *date rape and intrafamilial sexual assault.* Douglas et al. (1997) classify rape and sexual assault in terms of four motivational categories, with multiple subcategories including *criminal enterprise rape* (rape committed during the course of a felony), *personal cause sexual assault* (an act motivated by interpersonal aggression resulting in sexual victimization), *group cause sexual assault* (sexual assault involving three or more offenders); and *sexual assault not classified elsewhere.*

Knight and Prentky's (1990) typology, developed at the Massachusetts Treatment Center (discussed in Chapter 3), is one of the most reliable and valid sex offender typologies developed to date. The researchers developed separate typologies for child molesters and rapists. Their empirically based typology differentiates rapists into four motivational categories that yield nine types (see Chapter 3, Figure 3.2), and child molesters are differentiated by degree of fixation and amount of contact with the victim(s), with 24 possible types with offenders assigned to types along two axes (see Chapter 3, Figure 3.3). Their typology assimilates a vast body of theory and research on sex offender typologies and modes of aggression, and has been replicated within and outside the Massachusetts Treatment Center (Looman, Gauthier, & Boer, 2001).

The Massachusetts Treatment Center typologies illustrate the crucial factors associated with sex offending behavior and the features that differentiate types and subtypes. For example, a Type 1 rapist (opportunistic, high social competence) commits rape for very different reasons than the Type 5 rapist (sexual, sadistic, high social competence), requiring a different law enforcement strategy in terms of investigative direction. The Type 1 rapist is likely to be psychologically "normal," engaging in rape behavior if the opportunity arises (e.g., during the course of a felony for profit, in a date-rape or group/gang rape situation). A Type 5 rapist is likely to be psychopathologically disordered, possess highly developed fantasies, and engage in elaborate planning and predatory stalking of victims. The offense committed by the Type 5 rapist is more likely to involve signature aspects, with the rape leading to murder. Similarly, the Axis I/Type 2–Axis II/Type 3 child molester (low fixation, low social competence; low contact, low physical injury, nonsadistic) differs considerably from the Axis I/Type 0–Axis II/Type 1 offender (high fixation, low social competence; high contact, interpersonal meaning). These differences have important implications for mental health treatment and criminal justice policy and practice regarding sex offenders.

General Categories of Sex Crimes

For the purpose of understanding the similarities and differences between three major categories of sex crime, rape and sexual assault, child molesting, and sexual homicide are discussed here with attention to the heterogeneity of offenders and typologies developed within each category. Offenders in each group differ in motivation, victim selection, nature of sexual acts, and other characteristics. Understanding of the types of offenses as well as the subtypes within each general category is important in identifying the origins and development of sexual offending and in sorting through the varieties of sex offense behaviors.

Rape

Rape is commonly defined as *nonconsensual vaginal, oral, or anal penetration by force, or threat of force.* The *National Violence Against Women Survey* conducted in 1996 by the National Institute of Justice and Centers for Disease Control and Prevention found that 17.6% of the 8,000 women and 3% of the 8,005 men surveyed have been victims of a completed or attempted rape (Tjaden & Thoennes, 2000). In 2005, there were 93,934 forcible rapes in the United States (UCR, 2005), a 3.4% increase from 2001. However, since 1996, rape arrests have decreased 2.4%, with a rape rate for 2005 estimated at 62.5 per 100,000. (Rape data have been generally collected for female victims only; the UCR rape rate is based on estimates of the U.S. female population from census data.) Prior to the 1990s, the U.S. rape rate vacillated with increases in the 1940s, mid-1960s to early 1980s, and from 1985 to 1992 (Miethe & McCorkle, 2001). The following are a number of key findings regarding rape:

- Forcible rape comprises 91.4% of all reported rape offenses (UCR, 2005).
- An estimated 91% of rape and sexual assault victims are female and 99% of offenders are male (UCR, 2002).
- Three out of every four rape incidents are committed by offenders with whom the victim had a prior relationship (UCR, 2002).
- Women report being raped or sexually assaulted by a friend or acquaintance in 38% of rape/sexual assault victimizations (Catalano, 2006).
- On college campuses, during any given academic year, 2.8% of all women will experience a completed or attempted rape (Fisher, Cullen, & Turner, 2000).
- Most rapes occur between 6 pm and 6 am, in the victim's own home, by a single offender who is an acquaintance or a family member of the victim (Miethe & McCorkle, 2001).
- Stranger rapes account for 20% of single offender victimizations, but 76% of victimizations involving multiple offenders. Multiple offender rapes account for approximately 7% of all rapes (Greenfeld, 1997).
- Of all rapes committed from 1992 to 2000, 39% of attempted rapes and 17% of sexual assaults against females resulted in injury and most injured rape victims do not receive medical treatment for their injuries (Rennison, 2002).
- Most rapes (approximately 65%) are not reported to police (Rennison, 2002).
- Adolescents are responsible for 50% of sexual assaults on children and 30% of rapes of adolescent and adult women (Burk & Burkhart, 2003).

One of the most central issues in the literature on rape is the absence of the behavior from the list of paraphilias in the *DSM*. *Rape is a crime, not a sexual disorder.* Rape is not listed as a paraphilia in the *DSM-IV-TR*, in part, because it is a culturally reinforced behavior that is not fundamentally distinguished by psychopathology. In 1975, Brownmiller wrote *Against Our Will: Men, Women, and Rape,* which argued that rape is a culturally supported crime of violence used by men as a tactic of terror against women. In Brownmiller's view, rape is "nothing more or less than a conscious process of intimidation by which *all men* keep *all women* in a state of fear" (p. 5). Brownmiller and other feminist writers have argued that social and cultural forces (e.g., patriarchal ideology, hypermasculine values, rape myths, pornography, media depictions of women and the linking of sex and violence) work together to foster a rape-conducive climate, and the fear of rape that girls and women have to live with restricts their movement and their choices and serves the function of female subjugation (Prentky & Burgess, 2000). In her landmark work, *Intercourse,* Dworkin (1987) argued,

> The men as a body politic have power over women and decide how women will suffer: which sadistic acts against the bodies of women will be construed to be normal. In the United States, incest is increasingly the sadism of choice, the intercourse itself wounding the female child and socializing her to female status—early; perhaps a sexual response to the political rebellion of adult women; a tyranny to destroy the potential for rebellion. "I felt like I was being ripped up the middle of my legs all the way to my throat," one incest victim said. "I was sure that if I looked down, I would be on two parts of the bed." . . . Incestuous rape is becoming the central paradigm for intercourse in our time. Women are supposed to be small and childlike, in looks, in rights; child prostitution keeps increasing in mass and in legitimacy, the children sexually used by a long chain of men—fathers, uncles, grandfathers, brothers, pimps, pornographers, and the good citizens who are the consumers; and men, who are, after all, just family, are supposed to slice us up the middle, leaving us in parts on the bed. (p. 194)

Women see themselves as prey and men as predators, and are afraid to jog at night or take a walk to the corner store after dark, while men don't give such behaviors a second thought, attesting to the gender disparity that exists regarding fear of rape and sexual assault. Accepting rape as a paraphilia links rape behavior with psychopathology, negating the extent to which the behavior is culturally supported.

Sexual stereotypes about women (and men) fuel and facilitate rape behavior. Cultural norms about what is and is not humiliating for whom are expressed and reflected in particular acts committed by rapists (Darke, 1990). Rapists' thinking errors, neutralization techniques, excuses, and justifications are founded in and shaped by cultural stereotypes, rape myths, images in media and pop culture, and subcultural norms and values (Scully & Marolla, 1984). On the other hand, clinical interviews with rapists provide some support for the classification of rape as a paraphilia. Many rapists have recurrent and repetitive urges and fantasies to commit rape and a history of other paraphilias associated with their rape behavior (Abel & Rouleau, 1990), and extreme forms of rape behavior such as sadistic rape and sexual homicide are associated with personality disorder and mental illness. Thus, there appears to be a continuum of rape proneness within the general male population. Rape is a culturally reinforced behavior committed by individuals with Axis I mental illnesses and Axis II personality disorders, and by "normal rapists" who cannot be diagnosed with either (Laws &

O'Donohue, 1997). Those at the middle to higher end of the continuum hold more rape-prone attitudes and beliefs, which interact with other factors to produce rape behavior. Questions remain regarding what the critical interactive factors are and how they shape behavior in different types of rapists (Prentky & Burgess, 2000).

The issue of whether or not rape is an uncontrollable paraphilia versus a consciously chosen crime is intertwined with perspectives on rape as a sexual crime or a crime of violence. The argument that rape is a crime of violence, not sex, has been challenged on a number of levels. Feminist writers of the 1970s and 1980s such as Brownmiller (1975), MacKinnon (1983), and Dworkin (1987) argued that rape is an act of violence against women and that heterosexual sex itself is an act of violence and female subjugation. Others suggest that this sort of equating of sex and violence is a narrow and empirically baseless redefinition of the term *sexual* (Palmer, Thornhill, & DiBarri, 2002). Naffine (1996) offers an alternative feminist perspective on rape, suggesting that the notion that men can harm women through rape (and sex) must be deconstructed—"rape is a language, a particular expression of sexuality" (p. 103), a "masculine cultural construct" that pits male violence against female vulnerability. In other words, the cultural notion that any woman can be destroyed and terrorized by the male penis actually *reinforces* rape behavior, causing women (and men) to equate rape with death, providing the cultural framework within which rapists can use (and come to understand) sex as a means of violence. Research suggests that sexual and aggressive processes interact in sexual assault (Barbaree, 1990), that sexual arousal is crucial to sex offender behavior (Palmer, Thornhill, & DiBarri, 2002), and that rape is "neither an act of violence nor an act of sexual passion—it is a crime of *sexual violence*" (Vogelman, 1990, p. 61).

The extent to which rapists and rape events are similar or differ has been the subject of much research attention. Rape is often classified, based on the victim-offender relationship, into four types—*stranger rape, acquaintance rape, date rape,* and *partner/marital rape.* Other rapist types noted by Groth (1979) and others include *gang rape, male rape,* and *child rape.* Regardless of the victim-offender relationship, rape is a learned behavior that involves the use of cognitive distortions and neutralizations that all allow offenders to psychologically validate their behaviors. This is true for *all* types of rapists:

> Most rapists share the same belief system, regardless of whether they are convicted offenders or college students, whether they are raping a stranger or their wives, and whether they define themselves as rapists or believe they are "normal." These belief systems include beliefs that rape is justified and that women and men are sexual enemies. (Ryan, 2004, p. 20)

The culturally supported hypermasculine cognitions of rapists play a central role in instigating, sustaining, and defending rape. These cognitions include excessive sexual preoccupation, rape and seduction fantasies and scripts, rape-supportive belief systems, rape myth acceptance, and hypermasculine self-definition (Anderson et al., 2003; Buddie & Miller, 2002; Frese, Moya, & Megias, 2004; Murnen, Wright, & Kalunzy, 2002; O'Donohue, Yeater, & Fanetti, 2003; Ryan, 2004). Rape cultures and hypermasculine subcultures such as some fraternities and athletic teams create a context within which rape behavior is validated and reinforced (Humphrey & Kahn, 2000; O'Sullivan, 1993).

The relationship context appears to be associated with differences in the dynamics of rape and attributions of who is to blame. Studies suggest that the closer the relationship between the offender and victim, the less power tactics are used by the offender as a method of force and coercion and that alcohol and drug tactics are more likely to be used in date and acquaintance rape contexts (Cleveland, Koss, & Lyons, 1999). Perceptions of the cause of rape (male pathology, male hostility, victim precipitation) and who is to blame (offender, society, victim) also differ depending on type of rape, with the perception that female precipitation (blaming the victim) is most closely associated with partner and date rape whereas male pathology/hostility (blaming the offender) is least associated with rapes that involve known offenders (Cowan, 2000). McCabe and Wauchope (2005) found that rapists who attack strangers most commonly engaged in vaginal penetration and kissing/fondling, suggesting that even rapists who do not know their victims may be trying to convince themselves that their assaults are consensual and mutually enjoyable.

Types of rape behavior have also been classified based on motivational factors. Groth's (1979) work represents one of the first attempts to develop an empirical rape typology. Groth identified three motivational rape patterns: power, anger, and sadistic rape. *Power rapists* commit rape for the sexual conquest. Sexual desire is not the primary aim of the power rapist. Rather, the assertion of masculinity, power, control, strength, domination, and intimidation are the primary goals, and the behavior is associated with feelings of omnipotence and entitlement. *Anger rapists* commit rape as an expression of rage and retaliation. The anger rape is characterized by physical brutality and a surprise or blitz (sudden, immediate) attack. Sex is used as a weapon and rape an expression of anger, and the offender often engages in humiliating sexual acts to degrade the victim. Like the power rapist, the anger rapist does not commit rape for sexual arousal or satisfaction. For the anger rapist, satisfaction and relief come from the expression of anger, not sexual gratification. *Sadistic rapists* commit rape for pleasure and arousal. For the sadistic rapist, sexuality and aggression are linked and pleasure is achieved through bondage, torture, and ritualistic behaviors such as forcing the victim to behave in a particular way or through focus on and mutilation of particular parts of the victim's body. The sadistic rape is premeditated and instrumental and many sadistic rapists commit sexual homicide.

Groth's power-anger-sadistic typology has been expanded by a number of authors (Hazelwood & Burgess, 1987; Keppel & Walter, 1999; Knight & Prentky, 1990). The *power assertive, power reassurance, anger retaliatory,* and *anger excitation* typology (discussed in Chapter 3) is the expansion of Groth's original work and has become one of the best-known rape (and sexual homicide) typologies. The typology can be practically applied to law enforcement to provide information regarding the offender's behavioral parameters that offers informed direction for investigative practices (Keppel & Walter, 1999). Other researchers have noted differences with respect to the particular types of attack. For example, anger retaliatory rapists are noted for their blitz-style attacks whereas power assertive rapists are more likely to use the con approach. A study by Silverman et al. (1988) involving the analysis of 1,000 rape cases found that *blitz* and *confidence* styles of attacks are important categories of rape that have implications for victim services. Blitz rape victims are more likely to have been confronted with a weapon and to have been threatened with murder whereas confidence victims are more likely to have consumed alcohol or drugs and been subjected to a prolonged rape incident. Victims of confidence rapes are more likely to experience guilt and self-blame in the aftermath of the attack. These findings suggest that victim outreach strategies may need to be directed and modified to fit the type of attack a victim has experienced.

Returning to the Massachusetts Treatment Center rapist typology (which can be seen as a more complex empirically based extension of Groth's original anger-power-sadistic typology that assimilates multiple rape typologies in the academic literature), rape is classified into nine motivational types: opportunist–high social competence, opportunist–low social competence, pervasive anger, overt sadism, muted sadism, sexual–high social competence, sexual–low social competence, vindictive–high social competence, vindictive–low social competence (Table 6.1).

❖ Table 6.1   Features of Nine Types of Rapists in the Massachusetts Treatment Center Rapist Typology (MTC: R3)

Type 1: Opportunistic–High Social Competence	Instrumental aggression—no gratuitous violence or evidence of pervasive anger
	Moderate impulsivity, antisocial behavior in adulthood
	High level of social and interpersonal competence
	Offenses not typically sexualized—no history of paraphilias or evidence of sadism
	Offenses do not appear to be compulsive—minimal planning, little evidence of premeditation
Type 2: Opportunistic–Low Social Competence	Instrumental aggression—no gratuitous violence or evidence of pervasive anger
	Moderate impulsivity, antisocial behavior in adolescence and adulthood
	Low level of social and interpersonal competence
	Offenses not typically sexualized—no history of paraphilias or evidence of sadism
	Offenses do not appear to be compulsive—minimal planning, little evidence of premeditation
Type 3: Pervasive Anger	High level of affective aggression—gratuitous violence in most aspects of offender's life
	History of aggression toward men and women
	Moderate impulsivity, antisocial behavior in adolescence and adulthood

	Offenses not typically sexualized—no history of paraphilias or evidence of sadism
	Offenses do not appear to be compulsive—minimal planning, little evidence of premeditation
Type 4: Overt Sadism	High level of affective aggression—gratuitous violence and pervasive anger
	Sexual offenses marked by sadism with clear evidence of connection between sex acts and pain, suffering, and humiliation of victims
	Moderate impulsivity, antisocial behavior in adolescence and adulthood
	History of other paraphilias often present
	Offense planning and premeditation
Type 5: Muted Sadism	Instrumental aggression—no gratuitous violence or evidence of pervasive anger
	Impulsivity, antisocial behavior may be present but not critical feature of this type
	Sexual offenses marked by sadism with low level of violence and limited physical injury to victims, sexual acts symbolic and noninjurious, relative absence of affective aggression distinguishes from overt sadism type
	History of other paraphilias may be present
	Offense planning and premeditation
Type 6: Sexual–High Social Competence	Instrumental aggression—no gratuitous violence or evidence of pervasive anger
	Minimal impulsivity, antisocial behavior in adolescence
	Moderate impulsivity, antisocial behavior may be present in adulthood
	High level of social and interpersonal competence
	Offenses marked by high degree of sexualization, rape fantasy, and expressed interest in victim as a sexual object
	History of other paraphilias often present but no evidence of sadism
	Offense planning and premeditation
Type 7: Sexual–Low Social Competence	Instrumental aggression—no gratuitous violence or evidence of pervasive anger
	Minimal impulsivity, antisocial behavior in adolescence

(Continued)

❖ Table 6.1 (Continued)

	Moderate impulsivity, antisocial behavior may be present in adulthood
	Low level of social and interpersonal competence
	Offenses marked by high degree of sexualization, rape fantasy, and expressed interest in victim as a sexual object
	History of other paraphilias often present but no evidence of sadism
	Offense planning and premeditation
Type 8: Vindictive–Low Social Competence	High level of affective aggression and gratuitous violence directed specifically at women in sexual and other offenses
	Anger is misogynistic with no evidence of pervasive anger
	Minimal impulsivity, antisocial behavior in adolescence
	Moderate impulsivity, antisocial behavior may be present in adulthood
	Low level of social and interpersonal competence
	Offenses not typically sexualized—no history of paraphilias or evidence of sadism
	Offenses do not appear to be compulsive—minimal planning, little evidence of premeditation
Type 9: Vindictive–High Social Competence	High level of affective aggression and gratuitous violence directed specifically at women in sexual and other offenses
	Anger is misogynistic with no evidence of pervasive anger
	Minimal impulsivity, antisocial behavior in adolescence
	Although some impulsive, antisocial behavior may be present in adulthood, but not extensive
	High level of social and interpersonal competence
	Offenses not typically sexualized—no history of paraphilias or evidence of sadism
	Offenses do not appear to be compulsive—minimal planning, little evidence of premeditation

Adapted from Prentky & Burgess (2000). *Forensic management of sexual offenders.* New York: Kluwer/Plenum, pp. 64–65.

The MTC:R3 typology has the potential for practical utility at a number of points in the criminal justice system, including criminal profiling, correctional classification and risk assessment, treatment planning, and understanding the etiology and developmental pathways of offending behavior.

Child Sexual Assault

Sexual assaults against children are a major social concern that has influenced criminal justice legislation and policy and practice in social and health services. Results from meta-analyses of studies of the prevalence of child sexual abuse suggest that somewhere between 22 and 40% of women and 8 and 13% of men have been sexually abused at some point during their childhood (Faller, 2003). Others cite findings suggesting the numbers are higher—7 to 53% of girls and 3 to 37% of boys (Salter et al., 2003). Data from the UCR National Incident-Based Reporting System (NIBRS) shows that 67% of all victims of sexual assault reported to law enforcement agencies between 1991 and 1996 were juveniles, with more than half of the juvenile victims under the age of 12, and one of every seven (14% of all sexual assault victims) under age 6. The sexual crimes committed against juveniles include forcible fondling (84%), forcible sodomy (79%), assault with an object (75%), and forcible rape (46%) (Snyder, 2000). The perpetrators of sexual abuse of children tend to be male adolescents or adults known to the child and members of the same household (Salter et al., 2003).

Substantiated cases of child sexual abuse decreased 30% nationwide from a high of 149,800 in 1992 to 103,600 in 1998. Possible explanations for the decrease include actual decline in incidence due to public awareness, prevention programs, and increased sentence length and monitoring of sex offenders or changes in policies, practices, and attitudes that have reduced the amount of child sexual abuse reported and substantiated (Jones & Finkelhor, 2001). A survey sponsored by the *Center for Missing and Exploited Children* found that one in five youths received a sexual solicitation over the Internet in the past year, and one in 33 received an aggressive sexual solicitation. Only a fraction of these incidents were reported to parents or authorities (U.S. Department of Justice, 2001). Additional data from the NIBRS shows that

- The single age with the greatest number of sexual assault victims is age 14, and there are more sexual assault victims at age 2 than there are in any age group above 40.

- Juvenile victims of sexual assault were more likely to be male (18%) than adult victims (4%), and 27% of those under age 12 are male.

- Young juveniles are more likely to be sexually assaulted in the hours when meals are served and after school.

- Weapons other than the offender's hands and feet are rarely used in the sexual assault of young juveniles.

- Only 3% of sexual assaults of children under age 6 involved strangers, and such assaults are the least likely of all crimes to result in arrest or some form of clearance. (Snyder, 2000)

Child sexual assault can take many forms beyond the image that many conjure when they think of the typical child molester. Most child sex offenders do not fit the stereotype of the lurking dirty old man. This is one of the reasons why many sex offenders who harm children continue their behavior for long periods of time without being detected (Danni & Hampe, 2000). The following are case examples of sexual assaults against children reflecting a range of behaviors and victim-offender relationships:

- Mary Kay Letourneau, a 35-year-old high school teacher and married mother of four, pled guilty in 1998 to two counts of second-degree child rape for having sex with a 13-year-old student and giving birth to a daughter conceived in the relationship. Letourneau was sentenced to 6 months behind bars followed by sex-offender treatment. She was also ordered to disclose her "sexual deviancy" to any potential partners, avoid places where minors are known to congregate, and not initiate or prolong contact with children. Following the sentence, Letourneau quickly violated the terms of her supervision by again having sex with her victim, Vili Fualaau, and was sent back to prison to serve the full 7½ year sentence. In prison, it was learned she had become pregnant by Fualaau again, and she gave birth to a second daughter. In June 2004, her release date was postponed until she found a suitable address where neighbors were informed of her status as a sex offender. In May 2005, 9 months after she was released from prison, Letourneau and Fualaau married in a lavish media wedding for which the couple was reportedly paid $750,000.

- Sixty-one-year-old Wilburn Vernon Biggers of Charleston, South Carolina, was sentenced in 2004 to 5 years in federal prison after pleading guilty to using the Internet to entice a minor for sex. Biggers contacted someone in an Internet chat room he thought was a 15-year-old female and persuaded "her" to meet him for a sexual encounter. He rented a motel room and went to a restaurant for his meeting with the supposed teen. The person Biggers had chatted with was a law officer with the South Carolina Computer Crime Center. He was arrested on federal charges that led to his guilty plea.

- John Geoghan, a Boston Catholic priest, was found guilty in January 2002 of molesting a boy in a swimming pool a decade earlier and sentenced to 9 to 10 years in prison. More than 130 people accused Geoghan of sexual abuse during his 30-year career in six parishes. Geoghan was defrocked in 1998 and sent to prison in 2002. In 2003 he was murdered in prison.

- A Connecticut man, Donald Bailey, 52, was arrested in 2003 and charged with first-degree sexual assault and risk of injury to a minor. After receiving a complaint about the sexual abuse of a child, state police served a search-and-seizure warrant at his home seizing VHS tapes, 8-mm videotapes, a personal computer, and photographs. Police said one of the video tapes showed Bailey directing minors in compromising positions. Bailey was charged with first-degree sexual assault, three counts of risk of injury to a minor, employing a minor in an obscene performance, promoting a minor in an obscene performance, and possession of child pornography.

- A 41-year-old man was charged with statutory rape in San Francisco for paying to have sex with a 14-year-old. He pleaded guilty and was sentenced to 3 years' probation in exchange for testifying against the girl's pimp (Ryan, 2004).

- A 60-year-old Wisconsin man, previously convicted of incest in 1990 and placed on probation, pleaded guilty in 2004 to two counts of first-degree sexual assault of his two granddaughters. The girls, now age 6 and 9, were sexually assaulted between 1998 and 2003 ("Man, 60, faces prison in sex assault of grandkids," 2004).

- A 20-year-old woman was convicted of sexually assaulting her 3-year-old niece after she gave the child a bath and inserted her finger into the child's vagina. When questioned, the woman said she didn't know why she did it and didn't get any sexual feelings from the act (Groth, 1979).

As this list indicates, child sexual assaults take many forms and involve very different types of offenders and victims including incest, pedophilia, child rape, sexual exploitation of minors, and Internet child luring. Sexual acts involved in sex crimes against children range from fondling to sexual homicide (discussed in the next section).

Typologies of child sex offenders tend to group offenders into two general types: *situational* offenders, who sexually abuse children when the opportunity arises, and *preferential* offenders, who are sexually attracted to children (Dietz, 1983). Researchers have also classified child sex offenders in terms of high and low deviancy (Beech, 1998), passive and active offense pathways (Bickley & Beech, 2002), fixated and regressed types (Groth, 1979), and secure and insecure adult attachment (Marsa et al., 2004) with the primary distinction between types being severity of behavior and level of sexual preference for children. The Knight and Prentky (1990) child molester typology is, like their rape typology, one of the more sophisticated and empirically based classification systems for child sex offenders.

Common subtypes found in most child molester typologies include a type of offender with a longstanding sexual interest in/preference for children, a type that sexually offends under stress, and a type that sexually offends because they can (because children are easy targets for exploitation). These types are generally defined as follows:

- *Fixated type*—Longstanding, exclusive sexual preference for children. Few are married and there is minimal history of dating and peer interaction. Victim is generally known to the offender before sexual contact occurs. Sexual offense involves minimal force or aggression, including acts that are typically nongenital (kissing, caressing, sucking, fondling).

- *Regressed type*—Offender generally has established adult relationships and is likely to be married and have achieved a high level of social and sexual adaptation. At times of stress, the offender regresses, turning to an inappropriate sex object (a child) who is seen as a love object. The offense is likely to include genital sex. This type of offender may experience remorse, guilt, and shame in the aftermath of the offense.

- *Exploitative type*—Offender exploits weaknesses of the child to gratify his own sexual needs and will use aggression if necessary to get the child to comply. The offender is most likely to assault a stranger victim and does not care about the child's emotional or physical well being (Prentky & Burgess, 2000).

The Massachusetts Treatment Center Child Molester Typology is grounded, in part, on this more general typology. However, the researchers have identified additional features that more accurately differentiate homogeneous subtypes of offenders. Table 6.2 shows the subtypes of child molesters in this typology.

Recalling the diagram of the MTC child molester typology presented in Chapter 3, these six subtypes can be differentiated on Axis I of the MTC: CM3 typology with respect to low versus high fixation (enduring focus on children as sexual objects) and

❖ Table 6.2 Features of Six Axis II Subtypes of Child Molesters in Massachusetts Treatment
Center Child Molester Typology (MTC: CM3)

Type 1: Interpersonal	High contact with children Nongenital sexual acts (caressing, fondling, frottage) Known victim Long-term contact with victim Offenses show high degree of planning
Type 2: Narcissistic	High contact with children Primary motive self-centered sexual gratification Phallic sexual acts (victim used as masturbatory object) Stranger victim Single encounter with many victims Offenses spontaneous, low degree of planning
Type 3: Exploitative	Low contact with children Relatively little physical injury to victims with only enough force necessary to gain compliance Phallic sexual acts (sex gratification primary aim) No evidence of eroticized or sexualized aggression
Type 4: Muted Sadistic	Low contact with children Relatively little physical injury to victims Evidence of eroticized aggression (e.g., bondage, bizarre, ritualized acts, sadistic fantasy) Stranger victim Offenses reflect moderate degree of planning
Type 5: Aggressive	Low contact with children High degree of physical injury to victims Phallic sexual acts with no evidence of sadism or eroticized aggression Stranger victim Offenses reflect low degree of planning
Type 6: Overt Sadistic	Low contact with children High degree of physical injury to victims Offender aroused by subjecting victim to pain—evidence of force or threat of force to increase offender sexual arousal Evidence of eroticized aggression (e.g., bondage, bizarre, ritualized acts, sadistic fantasy) Stranger victim Offenses reflect high degree of planning

Adapted from Prentky & Burgess (2000). *Forensic management of sexual offenders.* New York: Kluwer/Plenum, p. 51.

low versus high social competence (mastery of interpersonal, social, and vocational skills). Thus, the MTC: CM3 typology yields 24 possible types of child molesters (e.g., high fixation/interpersonal, low social competence/narcissistic, low fixation/aggressive, high fixation/overt sadistic, and so on).

Danni and Hampe (2000) note that the Massachusetts Treatment Center typology is "the best example of research today in viewing sex offenders from a multidimensional perspective" (p. 492) but that it may be too complex and difficult to apply in practice for the average criminal justice professional. The Massachusetts Treatment Center typology draws on information regarding sexual acts committed, injury to victim, victim-offender relationship, and degree of premeditation and planning gleaned from diagnoses and information obtained by trained clinical professionals. This information may not be readily available to criminal justice agencies dealing with offenders. Danni and Hampe (2000) suggest that correctional supervision can be enhanced by more simply differentiating between pedophiles, hebophiles, and incest offenders. Analysis of presentence investigation report data from a sample of 168 child sex offenders under community supervision in Wyoming yielded the following types:

- *Pedophiles*—Engage in sexual activity with a prepubescent child. Pedophiles try to seduce their victims with gifts, trips, and so on. Many pedophiles have a history of being sexually victimized themselves in childhood. Motivation is sexual arousal/seduction. Their behavior is less likely to be discovered, and offenders are most difficult to supervise and treat. Treatment needs are lifelong and must be confrontative and probing.

- *Hebophiles*—Have sexual preference for children who have reached puberty and interpret sexual involvement with their victim as recipriocal.[7] Their behavior is episodic and impulsive. Motivation is a reciprocal sexual relationship. Behavior is more likely to be discovered because victims are older and may be more inclined to/capable of disclosure. They are able to recognize wrongdoing and more amenable to treatment.

- *Incest offenders*—Engage in sexual activity with their own children for their own selfish pleasure. Usually have successful sexual relationships with adults, and are motivated by anger. Behavior is less likely to be discovered because sexual abuse is within family unit and less likely to be disclosed. Supervision requires extensive collateral contacts.

The many typologies developed to explain and understand sexual offenders who assault children illustrate the complexity of the issue and the difficulties in merging research and practice to deal with sex offenders. If there are truly 24 possible types of sex offenders, the critical task for mental health and criminal justice is to employ appropriate investigative, treatment, and management practices that specifically address the risks, needs, and responsivity (Andrews & Bonta, 2003) of each type.

Sexual Homicide

Sexual homicide is the most severe form of sexual offending and the most complex in terms of offender psychopathology and developmental history. Sex offenders as a group have a higher likelihood to commit murder than nonsex offenders. The homicide rate among sex offenders is one per 400 sex offenders compared to one per 3,000 of the general population of nonsex offenders. Sex offenders who commit homicide are a subset of offenders who show histories of sadism, fetishism, voyeurism, early-onset criminal careers, firesetting, animal cruelty, antisocial personality disorder, pornography collection, learning disabilities, and alcohol and drug abuse (Langevin, 2003). The following are key findings in Meloy's (2000) review of the literature on sexual homicide:

- Most sexual homicide offenders are male and kill their first victim (usually a female stranger or casual acquaintance) prior to age 30.
- Sexual murderers usually have more than one paraphilia.
- Fantasy plays a central role in sexual homicide and can be inferred from offender productions (e.g., crime scene evidence, narratives, drawings).
- Sexual homicides usually evidence M.O. and signature.
- Sexual homicides are opportunistic rather than impulsive acts.
- Adolescents commit sexual homicide at the same rate as adults.
- Victim-offender relationships in sexual homicide are unusual in that they are *similar to paraphilias* in the selection of primarily stranger victims, but *dissimilar to other crimes of violence* that tend to involve known or related victims.
- Most sexual killers are not psychotic.
- All sexual killers evidence narcissistic and psychopathic personality traits.
- Not all serial killers may meet the criteria for antisocial personality disorder.
- Sexual murderers are less adaptive, more dysfunctional, and more schizoid and use more primitive defenses than other psychopaths.
- There is no evidence of biological anomalies, psychological factors, or social deviancies that predict sexual homicide.

In *Psychopathia Sexualis,* Krafft-Ebing wrote of *lust murder,* a special category of sexual behavior whereby sexual arousal is achieved through murder. Krafft-Ebing suggested that rape can be followed by three types of murder—unintentional murder, murder to destroy the witness, and murder out of lust. According to Krafft-Ebing (1906), who published his work around the time of Jack the Ripper, only the latter should be considered lust murder, presumed when "injuries of the genitals are found, the character and extent of which are such as could not be explained by merely a brutal attempt at coitus; and, still more, when the body has been opened, or parts (intestines, genitals) torn out and are wanting" (p. 527). Contemporary researchers define *sexual homicide* more broadly as the "intentional killing of a person during which there is sexual behavior by the perpetrator" (Meloy, 2000, p. 2) and the "killing of a person in the context of power, sexuality, and brutality" (Ressler, Burgess, & Douglas, 1992, p. 2). These definitions include rape-murders as well as murders in which sexual acts were committed after death involving overt and symbolic sexual behavior. Sexual motivation is inferred through victim attire/lack of attire, exposure of the sexual parts or sexual positioning of the victim's body, insertion of foreign objects into the victim's body cavities; evidence of sexual intercourse (oral, anal, vaginal); and substitute sexual activity, interest, or sadistic fantasy (Ressler, Burgess & Douglas, 1992).

Sexual homicide is a statistically rare phenomenon. The UCR does not collect data on sexual homicide, and the actual base rate of the crime is unknown (Meloy, 2000). It is estimated that fewer than 1% of all murders are sexual homicides (Meloy, 2000; Myers, 2002), most committed by males who kill their first victim before age 30. Victims of sexual homicide are most often children, adolescent girls, and women who are strangers or acquaintances of the offender. The following are case examples of sexual homicide offenses against children:

- Marc Dutroux, a 47-year-old Belgian electrician, raped and murdered several young girls with accomplices including his wife, Michelle Martin. Dutroux raped, drugged, and buried alive two teenage girls and kidnapped and left two 8-year-olds to starve in an underground cell while he was serving a 4-month sentence for car theft. Martin fed the couple's dogs upstairs while the girls starved to death. In 2004, Dutroux received a life sentence while Martin and another male accomplice received sentences of 30 and 25 years, respectively.

- Westley Allan Dodd, executed in 1993 at age 28, four years after he murdered three young boys. Dodd murdered 10- and 11-year-old brothers William and Cole Neer, whom he sexually assaulted and stabbed to death, and Lee Iseli, a 4–year-old whom he abducted and sexually assaulted in his home for two days and then hung with a rope in his closet. He kept a journal of the assault and murder and took Polaroid pictures of Iseli before and after his death, including one of the boy hanging in the closet.

- Jeremy Sagastegui, executed in 1998, stabbed, sexually assaulted, and drowned Kievan Sarbacher, a 3-year-old boy under his care. He then waited for Kievan's mother, Melissa Sarbacher, to return home. When she returned, he shot her and her friend, Lisa Vera-Acevado, who had accompanied Sarbacher home. Sagastegui confessed to detectives, telling them it "was a thrill" to watch the mother die, that he "anally raped the boy using a jar of Vaseline" and then wrapped him in a towel "so his guts wouldn't spill out all over the place." He told police the boy "was probably going to grow up to be a murderer."

Notorious serial killers such as Gary Ridgway, Ted Bundy, Jeffrey Dahmer, John Gacy, and Arthur Shawcross are examples of serial sexual homicide offenders. While all serials are not sexual homicide offenders, most sexual homicide offenders do not stop with one offense if they are successful at avoiding getting caught. There are few, if any, documented cases of sexual homicide committed by females, particularly involving male victims. However, some sexual homicide offenders use their consensual sex partners to assist them in the murder of female stranger victims (Meloy, 1992).

Cultural factors (such as pornography and gender stereotypes) play a strong role in the development of the sexual homicide offender. Most offenders who go to this behavioral extreme have complicated developmental histories of psychopathology, escalating paraphilias, highly developed fantasies, and experimentation. Many rapists, lust murderers, and sexually motivated murderers have histories of sexual behavior reflecting multiple nuisance paraphilias (Holmes, 1989) that have escalated through fantasy to experimentation (with dolls, animals, people),[8] and finally to the commission of acts of sexual homicide that often involve further experimentation and escalation in the nature and severity of wound infliction.[9] Serial sexual homicide offenders have significantly higher rates of paraphilias (particularly fetishism and cross-dressing); (Prentky et al., 1989), antisocial behaviors as youths, sexual sadism, psychopathy, personality disorders (primarily antisocial, borderline, and narcissistic personality disorders; see Myers, 2002).

Two of the best-known models explaining sexual homicide (and serial murder) are Hickey's (2002) trauma control model (discussed in Chapter 5) and the motivational model developed by Ressler, Burgess, and Douglas (1992), based on FBI Behavioral Science Unit interviews with 36 serial killers in the late 1970s and early 1980s. Arrigo and Purcell (2001) offer a model that integrates the two theories, with attention to the development and escalation of paraphilic behaviors. This integrative model suggests that sexual homicide is part of a paraphilic process, a cyclical system of behaviors. The authors suggest that sexual homicide is rooted in and maintained by the following features:

- *Formative development*—Predispositional factors interact with early childhood trauma to set the stage for paraphilic behaviors.

- *Low self-esteem*—Feelings of inadequacy and self-doubt, the outgrowth of predispositional factors and early childhood trauma, fuel patterned responses that take the form of fantasy. Fantasy operates as a stand-in for interpersonal relationships that the person is incapable of forming as a result of feelings of rejection and failure.

- *Early fantasy and paraphilic development*—Social isolation mobilizes paraphilic involvement. Fantasy, masturbation, facilitators, and paraphilic stimuli (fetishes, rituals) become part of a cyclical process. The particular paraphilic involvement is directly related to early childhood trauma (e.g., a fetish for a particular item is associated with some aspect of the offender's childhood or person the offender was closely involved with in childhood).

- *Paraphilic process*—The paraphilic process is cyclical, involving interacting elements including paraphilic stimuli and fantasy, orgasmic conditioning, and facilitators.

- *Stressors*—Feelings associated with early childhood trauma act as triggering mechanisms. Environmental, situational, or interpersonal events that generate strong feelings and reinforce early trauma are stressors that trigger a momentary loss of control that "feeds back" to the need to engage in paraphilic behavior. Response to stressors can include extreme behavior such as sexual homicide.

- *Behavioral manifestations*—The paraphilic behavior functions as a reinforcer, sequencing back to the fantasy, and escalating into more extreme behaviors.

- *Increasingly violent fantasies*—As fantasies become increasingly violent, paraphilic stimuli progress in intensity, duration, and frequency. Each time the individual engages in fantasy and paraphilic behavior, the need for increased stimulation and violent sexual arousal ensues, becoming part of the cycle or feedback loop.

The identification of an offense theme is particularly important in understanding sexual homicide. Because such offenses are so extreme, the behaviors committed within such acts reflect the psychopathology of the offender (Holmes & Holmes, 2002). The behavioral evidence found in sexual homicide reflects a continuum of organized-disorganized behaviors and related psychopathology. In sexual homicide, the offense themes and signature aspects of the offense are often strikingly salient and unusual. Behaviors such as evidence of planning, style of attack, type of weapon used, severity of wounds to victim's body, selection of victim, disposition or positioning of body, evidence of severe cruelty and torture offer insights into who the offender is. The unique sexual fantasy of the offender is acted out in sexual homicide. The offender's fantasy contains demographic, relational, paraphilic, situational, and self-perception components that are revealed through the offender's behavior (Hazelwood & Warren, 1995). Meloy (2000) offers the following example:

> . . . the perpetrator may imagine that a 15-year-old female (demographic) becomes his sex slave (relational), and he is able to anally and orally rape her at his whim (paraphilic) in his isolated mountain cabin (situational), thus enhancing his sense of omnipotence and gratifying himself sadistically (self-perception). (p. 8)

Thus, the victim's age, victim-offender interaction, nature of sex acts, location of offense, and evidence of offender self-perception (inferred through evidence of antemortem wounds and other crime scene evidence) contain key information regarding the offender's fantasy, way of relating, and psychopathology and the overall theme of the offense.

There are a number of well-known typologies of sexual homicide. Although not all serial murders are sexual homicide offenders, many serial murder typologies have been applied to sexual homicide with the belief that most serial killers are sexually motivated and most sexual homicide offenders will not stop their behavior if given the chance to continue. Typologies most often noted in discussions of sexual homicide include Holmes and DeBurger's (2004) motivational serial murder typology and Keppel and Walter's (1999) sexual homicide typology. The Holmes and DeBurger typology includes four types, each similar to one of the types in the Keppel and Walter power-anger typology:

- *Visionary killer*—Motivated by psychosis; auditory and visual hallucinations tell the offender to kill and engage in particular acts (Ed Gein is an example of a visionary killer). Similar to Keppel and Walter's power reassurance type.

- *Mission serial killer*—Motivated by revenge/retaliation against a particular group of people. Offender is in touch with reality and acts on a conscious, self-imposed duty to rid the world of a particular group of people (Gary Ridgway is an example of a mission killer). Similar to Keppel and Walter's anger retaliatory type.

- *Hedonistic serial killer*—Motivated by lust and thrill. Killing is an eroticized experience fueled by the linking of sex and violence in the developmental history of the offender (Jerry Brudos is an example of a hedonistic killer). Similar to Keppel and Walter's anger excitation type.

- *Power-control serial killer*—Motivated by power, omnipotence, entitlement, with sexual gratification from domination of the victim (Ted Bundy is an example of a power-control serial killer). Similar to Keppel and Walter's power assertive type.

Many sexual homicide offenders have a history of cruelty to animals involving sadistic experimentation. Merz-Perez and Heide (2004) suggest that three types of offenders can be explained by three motivational theories illustrating the links between animal cruelty and human violence. The first theory, *displaced aggression theory*, states that individuals hurt animals and people to control and express displaced anger. The authors suggest that Jeffrey Dahmer is an example of this type of offender because he experienced intense self-hatred and anger toward his parents. As a child, Dahmer dissected and mutilated animals, practicing techniques he would later use on victims including severing the head of a dog and impaling it on a stick. The second theory, *sadistic theory*, explains animal and human violence in terms of pleasure. Sadistic offenders, such as Leonard Lake, enjoy the process of killing and the shock and terror expressed by victims. The third theory, the *sexually polymorphous theory*, states that individuals harm animals and people for sexual pleasure. For these offenders, sexual homicide is necessary for sexual arousal. Henry Lee Lucas is an example of a sexually polymorphous type. Dahmer, Lake, and Lucas all had histories of animal cruelty in childhood, fantasy, and escalating propensity for violence. Their motivations differ, but all are sexual homicide offenders. Merz-Perez and Heide's (2004) typology suggests that, even within the small group of identified sexual homicide offenders, motives are heterogeneous.

Meloy's (2000) typology of sexual homicide offenders (presented in Chapter 3, Table 3.1) distinguishes between two types of offenders based on an integrative model of offense behavior. The model is particularly useful in that it integrates existing literature, taking into account biological, psychological, and developmental contributions to sexual homicide and behavioral manifestations reflected in crime scene evidence. Offenders are distinguished based on nature of offense (organized or disorganized), clinical diagnosis (*DSM* Axis I and Axis II), level of psychopathy (severe or mild/moderate), attachment pathology (chronically detached or attachment hunger), autonomic nervous system arousal (hyporeactive or hyperreactive), and presence or absence of early trauma. Based on this model, there are two types of sexual homicide offenders:

- *Compulsive*—characterized by organized offense characteristics, sexual sadism, antisocial or narcissistic personality, severe psychopathy, chronic detachment, and hyporeactivity (need high level of stimulation for arousal), early trauma often absent
- *Catathymic*—characterized by disorganized offense characteristics, mood disorder, various personality traits and disorders, mild-moderate psychopathy, attachment hunger, and hyperreactivity (need low level of stimulation for arousal); early trauma often present

This model is an important contribution to the literature on sexual homicide. The bimodal classification scheme is both practical (for use in the criminal justice system) and theoretically and empirically rich (developed through synthesis of research findings on the factors associated with sexual homicide).

Sex Offending and Gender

Sexual assault data are difficult to collect because many victims do not report the offense. Policies, practices, and public perception can influence reporting practices, and official statistics tend to underestimate the extent of sexual offenses. This is especially problematic in determining the extent of rape and sexual assault committed against males because masculinity norms make it difficult for many men to report rape. Furthermore, when females are the perpetrators of sexual assault and rape, the problem is compounded by legal definitions of rape, which define rape behavior in terms of male penetration of a female. However, many jurisdictions have made their legal definitions of rape and "sexual intercourse" gender neutral. For example, a person is guilty of rape in the first degree in Washington State when such person engages in sexual intercourse with another person by forcible compulsion by which the perpetrator or an accessory

- uses or threatens to use a deadly weapon or what appears to be a deadly weapon; or
- kidnaps the victim; or
- inflicts serious physical injury, including but not limited to physical injury, which renders the victim unconscious; or
- feloniously enters into the building or vehicle where the victim is situated.

Sexual intercourse is defined as follows:

(a) Has its ordinary meaning and occurs upon any penetration, however slight, and (b) Also means any penetration of the vagina or anus however slight, by an object, when committed on one person by another, whether such persons are of the same or opposite sex, except when such penetration is accomplished for medically recognized treatment or diagnostic purposes, and (c) Also means any act of sexual contact between persons involving the sex organs of one person and the mouth or anus of another whether such persons are of the same or opposite sex. (RCW 9A.44.010)

Female Sex Offenders

Sex offending has been viewed as a predominantly male behavior. And, in fact, female sex offending is rare in comparison with similar offenses committed by men. However, female sexual offenders have been identified in increasing numbers in recent years and it is likely that this number will continue to grow with changing perceptions of the gendered nature of crime. Cultural views of women as nonaggressive, nurturing caretakers have historically masked sexual abuse committed by females. The widely held belief that women are not capable of sex crimes has allowed many female sex offenders to go unnoticed, but there are documented cases of a heterogeneous group of female sex offenders who abuse children, other women, and men (Hislop, 2001).

Victims of female sex offenders tend to be child relatives or acquaintances. Female offenders account for 5% of female child molestation and 20% of male child molestation. Female sexual offenders report a higher incidence of sexual abuse in childhood than do male sexual offenders and a history of drug and alcohol abuse, poor coping skills, and depression and personality disorders (Vandiver & Kercher, 2004). Female sex offenders engage in many forms of sexual offending including sexual contact disguised as caretaking, sexual acts committed with a co-offender (usually a male), indirect participation in sexual assault by allowing victims to be assaulted with their knowledge and assistance, and indirect sexual acts (e.g., walking around nude in front of children for the purpose of sexual arousal, masturbating in front of children), ritual/group sexual abuse, and (in rare cases) rape of men (Hislop, 2001).

In many respects, acts of female sexual violence and assault resemble sexual behavior committed by men, with the exception that women do not force their penises into victims in the process of assault. Hislop (2001) asks the question on many people's minds regarding the notion of female sex offenders: *"What harm can be done without a penis?"* This question gets to the heart of the gendered nature of sexual offending and Naffine's (1996) call for the deconstruction of the harm associated with rape discussed previously. As long as sex offending and rape are viewed as exclusively male behaviors involving the use of the penis as a weapon, female sex offenders will remain undetected, male victims will be overlooked, and male offenders will use the social construction of the penis-as-weapon in the cognitive schemas that fuel and neutralize their rape behaviors.[10]

Research on female sex offenders is in its infancy. No psychological instruments currently available are specific to female sexual offending (Laws & O'Donohue, 1997), and much of what's known about female sexual offenders is based on case studies and small samples. The studies that have been conducted suggest that females commonly engage in the same sex acts with children as do male child molesters (including fondling, oral stimulation, and intercourse). Sexual penetration with objects may be more commonly engaged in by female sexual offenders and some studies suggest that the abuse committed by female offenders may be more severe than that committed by men. Female sexual abusers have been reported to use fingers or objects to penetrate their victims' vaginas and rectums including bizarre objects such as sticks, lit matches or candles, knives, metal toys, bottles, knitting needles, lit cigarettes, coat hangers, thorny rose stems, vacuum cleaner parts, goldfish, light bulbs, dildos, and vibrators. There are also documented cases in which females are penetrated by their male and female victims (Hislop, 2001, cites a case in which a woman was penetrated by a dildo she made her female child victim wear).

Little is known regarding the existence of female sexual sadists, lust murderers, or sexual homicide offenders. Cases of sexual sadism, sexual homicide, and serial murder committed by women have been documented, but again, much of what is known has been gleaned from case studies rather than empirical investigation. The problem with the lack of knowledge regarding female sexual offenders is twofold. First, many researchers apply theories and research developed from male offender samples to females. This "add women and stir" approach (Daly & Chesney-Lind, 1988) has hindered understanding of the nature and dynamics of female sexual offending. Much of what we know about female offenders in general, and female sexual offenders in particular, is shrouded in stereotypes and researcher bias. Second, even though there are documented cases of female sexual offending and the available statistics underreport the incidence and prevalence of female sexual offending, sexual offending is still predominantly a male offense. Because female sexual offending is such a rare phenomenon, it is difficult to conduct empirical research on such a low-base-rate behavior.

One question of interest is whether or not the definition of sexual homicide should be expanded to include female sexual homicide offenders, or if the motives of female serial murders have historically been misinferred. Despite documented cases to the contrary (Hickey, 2001), some researchers and law enforcement professionals continue to proclaim that there is no such thing as a female serial killer let alone a female sexual homicide offender. Aileen Wuornos is often (incorrectly) referred to as the "first female serial killer" by the popular press and some academics and members of law enforcement (Box 6.3). Some authors suggest that though her murders were not

BOX 6.3

AILEEN WUORNOS

Aileen Wuornos during a murder trial in 1992.

Photo credit: © Daytona Beach News Journal/Corbis Sygma.

Aileen Wuornos was convicted in 1992 for the murder of seven men in Florida. Wuornos committed the murders from 1989 to 1990 while engaging in prostitution. All of her victims were clients who she indicated at her trial she had murdered in self-defense after the men had become too rough. Several of her victims were found nude or partially dressed, all had been robbed, and most were shot in the torso. She claimed in an emotional testimony at her trial that one of her victims bound her hands to a steering wheel and poured alcohol in her anus, vagina, and eyes while raping her. After her trial while on death row, Wuornos recanted her claim that the murders were in self-defense. Aileen Wuornos was sentenced to death and was executed by lethal injection in October 2002.

Aileen Wuornos was born in 1956 in Troy, Michigan. Her parents were both teenagers when she was born and gave her up for adoption to her grandparents. Wuornos's biological father was imprisoned for kidnapping and raping a 7-year-old girl and committed suicide while incarcerated. Both of her parents were alcoholics. Wuornos claims she was raped at age 13, became pregnant,

(Continued)

(Continued)

and was sent to a home for unwed mothers and gave the baby up for adoption. She began living on her own at age 15 in the woods near her home and in an abandoned car, earning money through prostitution and panhandling. By all accounts, her childhood and teenage years were filled with abandonment, abuse, and social torment. She attempted to commit suicide at least six times, and her grandfather committed suicide when she was 20 years old. Shortly after, she married a 70-year-old man who she left because he was abusive. At age 25, she was arrested for robbery and did 14 months in prison. She moved to Daytona, Florida, where she became involved with a woman named Tyria Moore, who she claimed was the only person she ever loved.

Aileen Wuornos has been erroneously referred to as the "first female serial killer" in U.S. history. However, there have been many female serial killers throughout history in America and around the world. Hickey (2002) identified 68 female serial killers who committed their offenses between 1825 and 1995. Kelleher and Kelleher (1998) identified nearly 100 female serial killers since 1900, the majority of them in the United States. Wuornos likely became so notorious for two reasons. First, she committed her murders using a handgun, which is unusual for women who have historically used poison or other means to carry out their crimes. Second, Wuornos was a lesbian prostitute whose victims were men. From a feminist perspective, it could be argued that the Wuornos case reflects murders committed by a throwaway against members of society who mattered. In many respects, this is the flip side of the criticisms sometimes made regarding prostitutes murdered by male serial killers—that the police don't expend sufficient resources or pay enough attention in cases involving throwaway victims. In Wuornos's case, she was the throwaway and her victims were otherwise law-abiding, hardworking men with jobs and families. The victims of most female serial killers throughout history have tended to be children, spouses, or hospital patients, not male strangers. As a prostitute who killed her clients, Wuornos represented a violent social threat to men. The fact that Wuornos used a gun and killed male strangers when they were in the vulnerable position of soliciting a prostitute made her much more frightening and newsworthy than previous female serial killers.

Aileen Wuornos's story has been depicted in true crime books and movies including the made-for-TV movie *Overkill: The Aileen Wuornos Story* in 1992, starring Jean Smart, the 2003 film *Monster*, starring Charlize Theron who won an Oscar for her portrayal of Wuornos, and two documentaries by Nick Broomfield: *Aileen Wuornos: The Selling of a Serial Killer* in 1993 and *Aileen: Life and Death of a Serial Killer* in 2003.

sexually sadistic, they do meet the general definition of sexual homicide found in the forensic literature—"an intentional killing during which there is sexual activity by the perpetrator" (Meyers, Gooch, & Meloy, 2005), and that her behavior may represent a variant of serial sexual homicide by a female offender (Meyers, 2002). With the virtual absence of research and theory on female sexual homicide, examination of the possibility of a female variant of this behavior through analysis of the Wuornos and other cases is an important area for future research.

The most cited typology of female sex offenders (Matthews, Matthews, & Speltz, 1989) includes five categories of offenders: *teacher/lover, predisposed molester, male coerced, experimenter/exploiter,* and *psychologically disturbed.* Vandiver and Kercher (2004) developed an empirically based typology based on the unique motivational elements and power relationship between victim and offender in female sex offender cases. Cluster analysis using a sample of 471 female sex offenders yielded six types: *heterosexual nurturers, noncriminal homosexual offenders, female sexual predators, young adult child exploiters, homosexual criminals,* and *aggressive homosexual offenders.* Based on their research, the highest percentage of females were heterosexual nurturers—the typical female sexual offender is a 32-year-old White woman arrested for indecency or sexual assault of a male or female 12-year-old child who is an acquaintance or relative. This heterosexual nurturer group consisted of offenders who victimized only males comparable to many female sex offenders. This group is similar to the teacher/lover category and comparable to many such cases reported in the news media in recent years such as the well-known case of Mary Kay Letourneau (Box 6.4).

Male Rape and Sexual Assault Victims

An area that is perhaps just as underresearched as female sexual homicide is the rape and sexual assault of adult men. It would appear from the literature and statistics on sex offending that rape and sexual assault are rarely committed against men, except in prison settings (Groth, 1979). However, researchers have acknowledged that even though rape and sexual assault are predominantly crimes committed by men against women, there may be many more male victims than research and statistics reflect (Groth, 1979; Scarce, 1997). Male rape victims experience shame, stigmatization, and unique pressures to keep quiet about their victimization. Accounts of male rape victims also suggest that many do not report such crimes because they believe males can't be raped or they feel responsible in some way for their victimization (Pomeroy, 1991). Greater attention is beginning to be paid to the phenomenon of male rape committed by male offenders, but the phenomenon of male rape and sexual assault committed by female offenders (in particular cases in which women force adult males to engage in sexual intercourse) is barely mentioned in the literature beyond an occasionally anecdotal account in passing.

The popular perception of rape as a male crime of violence against women has resulted in the lack of attention to the phenomenon of male rape. As with the focus on female sex offenders, attention to male rape raises criticism that such focus distracts from the larger problem of sexual violence by men against women. However, the feminist writings of the 1970s and the attention to the power-violence elements of rape drew research attention to male rape, particularly in prisons and other correctional facilities (Scarce, 1997). Early writings on male rape include an essay by Brownmiller (1975) on the power dynamics of male-on-male rape in prison, and a section on male rape in Groth's (1979) work, which included accounts of rapes committed by heterosexual-, homosexual-, and bisexual-identified offenders who committed rapes outside of the prison setting (involving predominantly stranger or acquaintance rapes in cases where the victim was a hitchhiker picked up by the offender or assaulted in an outdoor setting).

BOX 6.4

MARY KAY LETOURNEAU

Mary Kay Letourneau in court 1997.

Photo credit: © *Seattle Times*.

Mary Kay Letourneau and Vili Fualaau May 2005.

Photo credit: © Ron Wurzer/Getty Images.

In 1989, 27-year-old elementary school teacher, wife, and mother Mary Kay Letourneau met second-grader Vili Fualaau when she was a teacher and he was a student at Shorewood Elementary School in a Seattle suburb. The two began a friendship that continued when Letourneau became Fualaau's teacher in the sixth grade. In 1996, at the end of Fualaau's sixth-grade year, Letourneau began having sex with the boy. At the time she was 34 years old, married, and a mother of four young children. Letourneau was arrested in 1997 for child rape. At the time of her arrest she was pregnant with Fualaau's child. After pleading guilty, she was sentenced to 7½ years in prison with all but 6 months of the sentence suspended provided she undergo treatment and not contact Fualaau. Soon after sentencing, she was caught with the boy, who she claimed she loved. After blatantly defying the court, she was sent to prison to complete her full sentence. While in prison she gave birth to a second child with Fualaau. During her time in prison, she violated her no contact order by sending Fualaau more than 20 letters and received disciplinary action that landed her in solitary confinement for 18 months. LeTourneau was released in 2004, when she was 42 and Fualaau was 21. The two have been together ever since, were married in 2005 in a ceremony that aired on *Entertainment Tonight*, and live with their two daughters in the Seattle area.

It is estimated that approximately 5 to 10% of reported rapes in the United States and the United Kingdom (where the bulk of the research has been conducted) involve male victims. Because male victims are much less likely to report having been raped, the prevalence of male rape is largely unknown. Male rape occurs in diverse contexts such as military organizations, in warfare, and in psychiatric institutions, prisons, and community settings. The typical male rapist is a young (mid-20s) heterosexual White man. Virtually every study conducted on the subject suggests the motivation for male rape is anger or attempt to overpower, humiliate, and degrade victims rather than lust, passion, or sexual desire. Homosexual men are victims at a much higher rate than heterosexual men, and Black victims are overrepresented in relation to their percentage in the communities in which studies have been conducted (Scarce, 1997).[11] Beauregard and Proulx (2007) conducted a case study analysis of 10 sexual murderers of adult male victims and proposed a typology of sexual homicide murderers of men (the authors avoid the term *homosexual homicide* because sexual murderers of men encompass those who kill both heterosexual and homosexual men), which yielded three distinct types: the avenger (motivated by anger and revenge), the sexual predator (motivated by sexual fantasies), and the nonsexual predator (instrumentally motivated robbery that turned into murder on victim resistance). Beauregard and Proulx's typology suggests that sexual murderers of men are more likely motivated by revenge and profit, which has not been found to be a primary motivation of sexual homicide murderers of women.

In his important and pioneering work, *Male on Male Rape*, Scarce (1997) notes that the reality of male rape "invokes a recognition of self vulnerability and homophobia" (p. 118). Whereas girls and women grow up learning about the possibility of rape and the normalization of sexual violence against women, male rape is rarely discussed, and when the images of male rape appear (in media, TV, film), the reaction is often mockery or malicious humor (e.g., "drop the soap jokes").[12] Male rape victims experience many of the traumatic effects of rape that female victims experience (e.g., post-traumatic stress, anger, stigma, shame, body image and self-esteem issues), but appear to experience other effects to a greater degree than female victims such as surprise, conflicting sense of sexual orientation (interpreting the experience as an act of sex), and heightened sense of vulnerability. Male rape victims also have difficulty seeking support and resources in the aftermath of rape. According to a male rape survivor,

> For years since this happened to me I have always read every word of newspaper stories on rape and not once has there been a man as the victim. Same goes for TV. I keep looking for someone out there like me and I know those guys exist. They're probably totally alone like I am and fumbling around in the dark too. (Scarce, 1997, p. 100)

Even rarer and perhaps more socially threatening/emasculating are images and accounts of male rape by females. As previously stated, such acts do occur, but there is little opportunity for open discourse on such behavior, let alone assistance, support, or acknowledgment for male victims who experience rape or sexual assaults by females. Thus, the deconstruction of the concept of rape and sexual assault has direct implications for understanding gender differences in offending patterns, social response to male and female victims of sexual violence, and the ways in which victims come to understand and deal with their victimization.

The Development of Sex Offending Behavior

The question *How does a person become a sex offender?* is of primary interest to those in the mental health and criminal justice systems who hope to understand these offenders in order to treat and manage their behaviors. Although most criminal behavior is understandable or at least imaginable, sex crimes, particularly the sexual homicide of children, are incomprehensible to the average person. For those who are not personally or professionally involved in the treatment or management of sex offenders, the question is often a matter of curiosity regarding what exactly would compel a person to engage in the most socially stigmatized and unconscionable of all criminal behaviors. For others, perhaps those who have been victims of sexual assault or who have a family member accused or convicted of a sex crime, answers may bring hope, understanding, or alleviation of anxiety and guilt. Some victims of sex crimes, both children and adults, blame themselves for many years in the aftermath of the offense. Family members of sex offenders often wonder what they could have done to prevent the behavior. Understanding what it takes to create a person who thinks he is entitled to rape any woman he sees on the street, who sexually preys on children, or who is sexually aroused by domination, torture, and mutilation offers hope that a social problem of such magnitude can be managed, dealt with, or controlled.

The complexity and ambiguity of the answers academics and clinicians are able to provide is far from satisfactory. Researchers have made gains in identifying developmental themes and risk factors for sex offending behavior, but as is true with most human behavior, the answers do not come in a convenient magic potion. In thinking about what makes a person a sex offender, the first step is to separate remote or developmental influences that contribute to deviant sexual preference, fantasy, urges, and aggression from factors that contribute to the behavioral act of committing a sexual offense. In other words, some people are diagnosed with pedophilia because they have a sexual preference for children involving urges and fantasies and do not act on these thoughts and feelings.[13] Such a person is a pedophile, but not a sex offender, until the fantasies are acted on. So the question "*How does a person become a sex offender?*" involves asking two subquestions: (1) *How does a person develop deviant sexual preferences, urges, and fantasies?* (2) *What is it that sends people with these fantasies, preferences, and urges over the edge?* Some types of sex offenders such as rapists and situational child molesters have developed "normal" sexual preferences. So the first subquestion applies differently depending on the type of offender. However, even rapists who have no history of mental disorder, paraphilia, or deviant sexual arousal patterns generally have urges and fantasies before they commit their crimes. So if we speak of urges rather than sexual preference, both questions can be asked of all types of sex offenders.

The literature on the development of sex offending consists of two distinct avenues of theory and research—etiological theories and risk assessment. Etiological theories attempt to explain the developmental processes that set the stage for sex offending behavior. The risk assessment explains sex offending behavior in terms of risk and protective factors that make a person more or less inclined to commit sex offending behavior. Beech and Ward (2004) integrate both approaches, offering an integrative model of sex offending behavior that explains sex offending in terms of

- *Developmental factors*—abuse, rejection, attachment problems

- *Static factors*—persistence and range of offending, psychosocial problems (antisocial history), historical risk factors not subject to change (e.g., never married, number of past offenses, etc.)

- *Stable dynamic factors*—offense-supportive cognitions, level of interpersonal functioning, self-regulation problems

- *Acute dynamic factors*—physiological arousal, deviant thoughts and fantasies, need for intimacy, affective states

- *Triggering events/Contextual risk factors*—victim access, social dislocation, substance abuse, relationship conflict, antisocial peers, noncooperation with supervision

How Does a Person Develop Deviant Sexual Preferences, Urges, and Fantasies?

No one decides what their sexual orientation will be—whether they will be attracted to males, females, adults, or children (Fagan, Wise Schmidt, & Berlin, 2002). Similarly, people have little say in whether they will develop a mental illness or personality disorder, or the sorts of environmental conditions in which they will be raised as children. Although "heterogeneity of developmental background and offense behavior is the rule with sexual offenders" (Burk & Burkhart, 2003, p. 493), factors such as sexual abuse in childhood, attachment disruptions in infancy, dysfunctional family environment, conditioning processes, social learning, biological predisposition to mental disorder, or particular personality traits appear to shape sex (and other) offending behavior. Studies of sex offenders reveal a long list of remote risk factors for sex offending behavior, many of which are also seen in violent offenders. As discussed in Chapter 2, explaining any criminal behavior requires attention to biological, sociological, cultural, psychological, routine activity/opportunity, and phenomenological factors. The sex offender develops the urge, fantasy, and/or sexual preference associated with the offense through cumulative misfortune. Biologically based sexual drive, misdirected through conditioning processes and reinforced by early childhood sexual victimization, is all it takes to create the urge or inclination to sexually offend. But it takes more than this to actually act on such urges.

Particular childhood risk factors appear to be associated with sex offending later in life including maternal neglect, lack of supervision, sexual abuse by a female, witnessing intrafamilial violence, and cruelty to animals. Being a male and a victim of sexual abuse in childhood are the most frequently cited risk factors for becoming a sex offender later in life (Salter et al., 2003). Factors that contribute to the development and expression of human sexuality also influence sex offending behavior. Genetic factors such as aggressiveness and impulsiveness, sex drive, neurotransmitters, and hormones play a role as do attachment processes and sociocultural factors. Childhood stressors such as poor child-parent bonds, low self-esteem, poor quality of relationships, inadequate emotional coping skills, and prior sexual abuse lead to reliance on sexualized coping (masturbation, sex acts) as an escape from difficult issues. Frequent pairing of sexual arousal through masturbation with inappropriate fantasy (particularly involving violence and control) leads to increased likelihood of using sex offense behavior (Burk & Burkhart, 2003) as a coping mechanism.

In recent years, research on the development of sex offending behavior has focused a great deal on early childhood attachment. Attachment theory (Ainsworth, 1989; Bowlby, 1969) is based on the universality of attachment processes in humans and primates. Bonding and attachment between infants and primary caregivers are universal needs in humans and primates. When primary caregivers are inaccessible, inconsistent, and fail to nurture or there is disruption in the bonding process, infants will fail to attach and may detach permanently. This theory has been applied to sex offenders (Burk & Burkhart, 2003; Marsa et al., 2004; Ward, Hudson, Johnston, & Marshall, 1997), psychopaths and predatory offenders (Meadows & Kuehnel, 2005; Meloy, 1988, 1992), and serial killers (Hickey, 2001; Shipley & Arrigo, 2004). Sex offenders have insecure/disorganized attachment styles that interfere with their ability to form close interpersonal relationships (Burk & Burkhart, 2003; Ward et al., 1997). Disorganized attachment refers to the lack or collapse of a strategy for dealing with the need for security and comfort under stress. Disorganized attachment styles are seen in children who have experienced neglectful, chaotic, abusive circumstances and perceive their parent simultaneously as a source of both comfort and distress (in the parent, mental illness, grief, extreme stress, substance abuse, and physical and sexual abuse are associated with disorganized attachment experiences; Burk & Burkhart, 2003). Sex offending is a distorted attempt by individuals who do not have the ability to form appropriate relationships to seek closeness (Marsa et al., 2004, p. 229), "one of several available external-interpersonally based self-regulatory strategies" (Burk & Burkhart, 2003, p. 492).

Individuals with insecure attachment styles have a particular vulnerability to sex offending when they are exposed to particular biological, sociocultural, and situational factors that reinforce or facilitate such behavior. Sex offenders experience more loneliness, interpersonal anxiety, external locus of control, and avoidance (Marsa et al., 2004) and engage in coercive sexual behavior to satisfy their emotional needs. Sex offending behavior is reinforced through a chain of conditioning (Laws & Marshall, 1990) and cognitive processes (Ryan, 2004; Segal & Stermac, 1990) that set the stage for an ongoing cycle of offending behavior:

> Once a sexual offense has been perpetrated, memories are established that may be elaborated into inappropriate sexual fantasies, thus leading to urges to reoffend. In addition, offenders employ a number of cognitive distortions such as minimization or victim blaming, to reduce feelings of guilt and fear of being caught, thus allowing the cycle of sexual offending to repeat. (Marsa et al., 2004, p. 229)

What Is It That Sends People With Deviant Fantasies, Preferences, and Urges Over the Edge?

The development of the urge to sexually offend is determined by biological, psychological, and sociological/environmental forces beyond the offender's control, but for those who do not have a clinically diagnosable psychosis (who have the potential to be declared legally insane), the decision to act on the urge to commit a sex crime falls more clearly within the bounds of free will and conscious choice. It is at this stage of the offending process that psychological, routine activity/opportunity, and phenomenological factors play a greater role. For example, proximate risk factors found to be associated with the behavioral expression of pedophilia include psychiatric disorders, substance abuse disorders, and psychosocial stress involving the loss of a relationship (Fagan et al., 2002). Sex offending occurs when vulnerable individuals experience stress, proximate risk factors (such as mental illness, substance use, exposure to pornography) and, from a routine activities perspective, are in close proximity to an available victim in the absence of guardians and social controls.

Cultural facilitators, though not the source of the desire to offend, are powerful situational/contextual factors that fuel fantasy development and facilitate sex offending behavior. Facilitators include alcohol and drug use, social climate, pornography, books, media, Internet chat rooms, computer images, films, and aspects of pop culture that validate (or are interpreted to validate) sex offending behavior. For example, Michael Briere pleaded guilty in June 2004 to the murder of Holly Jones, a 10-year-old Toronto girl. After his arrest, he told police that on the evening of the offense he had viewed child pornography on the Internet on his home computer and was overwhelmed by a desire for sex with a little girl. He then stepped outside his apartment, abducted Holly Jones, dragged her into his bedroom, sexually assaulted her, and then killed her. Her body, which Briere admitted dismembering, was found in parts in various places in Toronto ("DNA Helps Police Catch Molesters," 2004). The behavior of all types of sex offenders, from rapists to child molesters to sexual homicide offenders, is influenced by cultural facilitators in some way. Pornography appears to play a key role in the fantasy development that precipitates sex offending and sexual homicide (Hickey, 2002, 2006).

The role of the Internet in facilitating sex offending behavior has only begun to be empirically explored. Recent research by Quayle and Taylor (2003) suggests that viewing pornography on the Internet normalizes sex offending behavior in the minds of potential offenders and provides a social network for production and trade of child pornography and Internet seduction of children. According to one Internet pornography user, "I was finding more explicit stuff on the computer and I was looking at the computer and thinking oh . . . they're doing it . . . it can't be that bad . . . it's there you know" (Quayle & Taylor, 2003, p. 98).While the use of print pornography has long been linked to sexual violence (Murrin & Laws, 1990), Internet pornography may have a stronger normalizing effect. When potential sex offenders use pornographic magazines or videos, they tend to do so in isolation. The Internet offers a virtual community where deviant sexual interests and distorted cognitions are justified and validated within an online subculture. This "community" facilitates sexual offending by coaching users and justifying their behavior in isolation from the "real world" in which cognitive distortions and sex offending behaviors would be challenged. For potential sex offenders who are already socially and emotionally isolated, the Internet decreases social engagement with mainstream society while reinforcing sexually deviant fantasy. There is some evidence in this initial research to suggest that the particular experience of using Internet pornography may empower some potential sex offenders, facilitating an increase in actual contact offenses, but for others, it may promote a move to sexually exciting, but legal behaviors (e.g., sexual activity with adults).

Other facilitators such as use of drugs and alcohol (by the offender and/or the victim in the case of date and acquaintance rapes), media images linking sex and violence and depicting gendered cultural stereotypes, mental illness, involvement in hypermasculine subcultures, and stress such as the loss of a job or the dissolution of a relationship can be the "straw that broke the camel's back" for edge-sitters who have the urges and inclination to sexually offend, but haven't yet acted on them. For example, Gary Ridgway, the Green River Killer, began his career as a sexual homicide offender after his first divorce, and his offending behavior increased during problematic periods in his relationships with women (e.g., between his first, second, and third marriages; see King County Journal, 2003).

Sex offending behavior is associated with *static and dynamic risk factors* and a particular developmental history (Beech & Ward, 2004). The urge to sexually offend is rooted in biological forces and early childhood experiences that lead to sex offending as a coping strategy. This strategy is more likely and more often employed when particular stressors or disinhibiting facilitators are present. Burk and Burkhart (2003) offer a rich synopsis of biological, sociocultural, and attachment processes that explain how a person becomes a sex offender:

> Every person is equipped with a drive to survive, and so, even violent acts with socially devastating consequences can come to serve as a means for self preservation. . . . Any behavior, adaptive or maladaptive, can come to serve a self-regulatory purpose and assist the individual in re-establishing internal control. Empirical observations regarding the background of sexual offenders suggest that maladaptive strategies (substance use, interpersonal violence, sexual deviance, property crimes, impulsive behavior) are readily modeled in the environment and consequently, may be more likely to be adopted. Thus, this complex attachment system may serve as a diathesis which interacts with particular stressors (previous sexual victimization, exposure to misogynistic cultural/media stimuli, peer deviance) to potentiate controlling/abusive behavior. . . . processes other than attachment continue to influence the individual throughout their development, and factors such as conditioned sexual arousal, opportunity and chance likely play equal or greater parts in the maintenance of continued sexual offenses. (p. 503)

Thus, the ways in which particular biological, sociological/environmental, psychological, and cultural factors and forces play out in a person's life as well as the meanings attached to particular events and opportunities one encounters steer a person in one direction or the other. Sex offending becomes a deeply rooted and conditioned coping strategy, a deviant and socially destructive variant of the more benign strategies individuals with more fortunate life histories and developmental circumstances use.

Summary

To understand sex crime, it is important to understand the varieties of human sexual behavior, the processes by which certain types of sexual behaviors are deemed deviant and criminal, and the multiple perspectives from which the behavior is defined and controlled. Sexual behavior has been defined and explored in terms of *normal sexuality, sexual deviance, sexual disorder,* and *sexual crime.* Sex crimes are differentiated from *sexual disorders* and *sexual deviance* in that they are behavioral acts that violate the law *and* deemed both sexually deviant and a threat to individuals and public safety. Sexual dysfunctions and gender identity disorder are mental disorders, not crimes. *Sex crimes are crimes of violence. Sexual disorders and sex crimes sometimes overlap. Paraphilias* are a group of persistent sexual behavioral patterns identified in the *Diagnostic and Statistical Manual of Mental Disorders* characterized by sexual fantasies, urges, or behaviors involving nonhuman objects (fetishism, transvestic fetishism), suffering or humiliation (sexual sadism, masochism), children (pedophilia), or other nonconsenting person (voyeurism, frotteurism, exhibitionism) (APA, 2000). *Behaviors and paraphilias* that generally fall into the category of sex crimes are those in which the offender engages in a sexual act with a nonconsenting victim such as sexual assault, rape, child molestation, child rape, sexual misconduct with a minor, indecent liberties, voyeurism, sexual violation of human remains, and custodial sexual misconduct. Most states and the federal system have laws specifically targeting sex offenders. Sex offenders are required to register with law enforcement on release from correctional custody. The terms *sexual predator* and *sexual psychopath* are legal terms used to impose civil commitment of dangerous sex offenders whose behavior is associated with mental illness and pathological tendency to reoffend.

Major categories of sex crime discussed in this chapter include rape and sexual assault, child molesting, and sexual homicide. Offenders in each group differ in motivation, victim selection, nature of sexual acts, and other characteristics. Understanding the types of offenses as well as the subtypes within each general category is important in identifying the origins and development of sexual offending and in sorting through the varieties of sex offense behaviors. Sexual assault data are difficult to collect because many victims do not report the offense. Policies, practices, and public perception can influence reporting practices, and official statistics tend to underestimate the extent of sexual offenses. When females are the perpetrators of sexual assault and rape, the problem is compounded by legal definitions of rape, which define rape behavior in terms of male penetration of a female. Researchers have acknowledged that even though rape and sexual assault are predominantly crimes committed by men against women, there may be many more male victims than research and statistics reflect. No one decides what their sexual orientation will be—whether they will be attracted to males, females, adults, or children. Similarly, people have little say in whether they will develop a mental illness or personality disorder, or the sorts of environmental conditions in which they will be raised as children. The ways in which particular biological, sociological/environmental, psychological, and cultural factors and forces play out in a person's life as well as the meanings attached to particular events and opportunities one encounters steer a person in one direction or the other.

DISCUSSION QUESTIONS

1. Explain the difference between normal sexuality, sexual deviance, sexual disorder, and sex crime. For example, is pedophilia a crime? What's the difference between a married couple engaging in S&M sexual behavior and a clinical diagnosis of sexual sadism? Would most sexual behavior we tend to consider "deviant" be considered normal if we only knew what really goes on behind closed doors? Discuss.

2. Describe some of the better-known typologies in the sex crime literature (e.g., for rapists, child molesters, sexual homicide offenders, etc.). How are these typologies used in the mental health and criminal justice systems?

3. Discuss the historical origins of the sexually violent predator (SVP) laws. Explain the laws, who they target, and what they hope to achieve. Offer your views on the SVP laws—do you agree or disagree with this approach to dealing with sexually violent predators? Is there a better way to respond to sexually violent predators in our communities?

4. Most of the research on sex crimes has focused on male offenders and female victims. Theory and research on female sex offenders and male rape and sexual homicide victims have been almost completely ignored. Discuss some of the research that has been done in this area. What do we know about female sex offenders and (male and female) offenders who target male victims? If you were to design a study to examine this relatively untouched area, what research questions would you be interested in exploring?

5. How does a person become a sex offender? Explain.

On Your Own: Log on to the Web-based student study site at http://www.sagepub .com/helfgottstudy/ for the URL links in the Web Exercises, study aids such as review quizzes, and research recommendations including links to journal articles specifically selected for this book.

WEB EXERCISES

1. Go to the Legal Information Institute Web site to explore the legal definitions pertaining to sexual offenses listed in the U.S. Criminal Code (http://www.law.cornell .edu/uscode/html/uscode18/usc_sec_18_00003559——000.html) and your own state's criminal code at http://www.law.cornell.edu/topics/state_statutes2.html#criminal_code.

2. In 1993, Andrew Vachss published an article in the *New York Times* entitled "Sex Predators Can't Be Saved." The article discusses the execution of Washington State's Westley Dodd, sexual predator laws, and the notion of chemical castration. Read the article at http://www.vachss.com/av_dispatches/disp_9301_a.html and discuss the pros and cons of sex predator laws, the death penalty, and chemical castration as a way of dealing with sexual homicide offenders like Dodd.

3. Go to the BehaveNet Web site at http://www.behavenet.com/ and look up the *DSM-IV-TR* classification for sexual and gender identity disorders. Familiarize yourself with the diagnostic criteria for each paraphilia.

4. Go to the Washington State Institute for Public Policy Web site at http://www.wsipp.wa.gov/ and review reports on the impact of sex offender laws in Washington State.

7

Economic Crime ❖

I go to the mall almost every day and see stuff I want to buy. I do crime in order to buy nice stuff.

—14-year-old thief (Cromwell, Curtis, & Withrow, 2004, p. 232)

In September 2004, the largest chop shop on the East Coast was shut down by the FBI. The ring, led by real estate moguls Michael Pescatore and Sanford Edmonston, operated a $20 million illicit business involving theft of high-end cars ranging from BMWs to Land Cruisers, stripping and reassembly, and resale to innocent dealers and the public through the now defunct Astra Motor Cars. After more than a year-long investigation called Operation VIN City, federal agents arrested Pescatore and Edmonston on charges of mail fraud, money laundering, operating an illegal chop shop, illegal trafficking in motor vehicles, conspiracy, and tampering with, removing, or altering vehicle identification numbers (Smith, September 10, 2004). Astra Motor Cars was allegedly an "underground crime organization masquerading behind a front" that involved 11 defendants from six states (Davis, October 4, 2004) who acquired damaged, destroyed, or stolen vehicles and used parts to rebuild vehicles for resale to the public.

Violent and sex crimes tend to take the media spotlight and are at the forefront of most people's minds when they think about crime. However, the reality is that violent crimes represent only a small portion of all crime. Economic crime represents the bulk of crime in America and around the world. Of the Part I crimes reported in the Uniform

Crime Reports (UCR) for 2005, 12% were violent crimes and 88% were property crimes, with larceny-theft accounting for the largest part (62%) of all property crime (Figure 7.1).[1]

❖ **Figure 7.1** Comparison of Property and Violent-Crime—UCR Part I Offenses

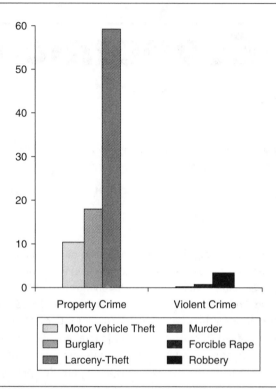

The National Crime Victimization Survey reported over 23 million crime victimizations in 2005, more than 18 million of which were property crimes (burglary, theft, motor-vehicle theft), accounting for 77% of all crime victimizations. While UCR data show that violent crime increased 2.3% from 2004 to 2005 and property crime decreased by 1.5% (UCR, 2005), National Crime Victimization Survey data show that violent crime has stayed the same since 2004 and property crime has declined primarily as a result of decreases in theft. Both violent and property crime victimization are at the lowest levels since 1973 (U.S. Department of Justice, 2003).

Major property crimes including burglary, larceny-theft, motor-vehicle theft, and arson fall within Part I of the FBI's Uniform Crime Report Crime Index. Other crimes that are economic, such as forgery and counterfeiting; fraud; embezzlement; buying, receiving, and possessing stolen property; vandalism; and prostitution and commercialized vice, are included in Part II of the UCR. According to the UCR, 10,166,159 property crimes were reported to police in 2005 with $16.5 billion in losses. Property crimes were committed in 2005 at a rate of 3,429.8 per 100,000 in the population, a decrease of 22.9% since 1996 and 6.2% since 2001. Of the property crimes reported, there were an estimated 299,835 arrests for burglary, 1,146,696 for larceny-theft, 147,459 for motor vehicle theft, and 16,337 for arson. For Part II offenses, there were 118,455 arrests for forgery and counterfeiting, 321,521 for fraud, 133,856 for stolen property (buying, receiving, possessing), 18,970 for embezzlement, 84,891 for prostitution and commercialized vice, and 11,180 for gambling (UCR, 2005).[2]

What Is Economic Crime?

The concept of economic crime has been less clearly articulated in the criminology/criminal justice literature than have the concepts of violent or sexual crime. Much of this is the result of distinguishing crime based on who commits the act rather than the nature of the offense and the underlying motivation and commonalities across different types of crime. Definitions of economic crime have historically been muddied by focus on the "who" and "why" rather than the "what" and "how" (Naylor, 2003). Criminal types such as *white-collar criminal*, *shoplifter*, and *professional thief* have dominated discussions of profit-driven crime with much less focus on the commonalities of economically motivated crime and the act itself. Only minimal attention has been directed to "how" economic crime is committed—with crime categories such as *computer-assisted crime* and *telemarketing fraud*, for example—and much less attention is given to the "what" question[3] (What is the essence or nature of economic crime?). Naylor (2003) argues that

> Ideally it should be possible to disaggregate the concept of profit-driven "crimes" through a typology that is functional, rather than sectoral, which is process- rather than offender-based, which is more general than any crime-related "script," and which is therefore applicable to all offences where profit is at least partially the motive. (p. 83)

Focusing on process and motivation (rather than on who commits the crime or how it is committed) allows us to conceptualize and understand economic crime as a distinct category of criminal behavior.

This focus raises a number of important questions critical to developing a meaningful definition of economic crime: *Are there similarities in motivation and process that allow offenses committed by very different types of offenders to be understood within a single crime category such as* economic crime? *Can criminal acts such as burglary and theft (property crimes) be understood and explained within the same general domain as acts such as insurance fraud, securities fraud, intellectual property crime (business, commercial, corporate, or white-collar crime), drug trafficking, extortion, illegal distribution of goods and services (often discussed within the context of organized crime), prostitution, and gambling (public order crime)? What is the relationship between street-level property crimes, commercial crimes, and criminal enterprise? Should crimes of economic need be distinguished from those motivated by economic greed?* Identifying its homogeneous features is critical to understanding the nature of economic crime.

It is important to note the distinction sometimes made between *economic crime* and *economic criminality*.[4] *Economic crime* refers to criminal behavior for the purpose of material gain, motivated by economic survival and disadvantageous economic circumstances. *Economic criminality* refers to dishonesty, criminal career, and the pursuit of material gain as a motivation for criminal behavior. Similarly, crime in general refers to an event in which the law is broken, while criminality refers to the propensity and motivation to engage in criminal behavior (Gottfredson & Hirschi, 1990). Although it is an oversimplification,[5] economic crime can be said to be motivated by need while economic criminality is motivated by greed. However, economic crimes can be motivated by both need *and* greed, and it is difficult to disentangle one from the other. Davies (2003) suggests that economic criminality is conflated with and inextricable from economic crime and "the effects of economic marginalization can combine with political disaffection and engender anti-social behavior" (p. 287).

This chapter focuses on economic crime as a distinct crime category. Economic crime is defined here as criminal behavior centrally motivated by the desire to obtain financial reward that does not also involve an act of violence against a person.[6] This definition acknowledges the convergence of economic crime and economic criminality, including behaviors motivated by need and greed, and focuses on the nature of the criminal act (acquisition of material gain through illegal means). Based on this definition, a wide range of offenses fall under the heading of economic crime: burglary, shoplifting, theft-larceny, motor-vehicle theft, many types of fraud, embezzlement, forgery, counterfeiting, money laundering, extortion, prostitution (from the prostitute's perspective), gambling, and arson.[7] The homogeneous element of economic crime is that the central motivation for the criminal act is financial reward.

The following are examples of economic crimes:

- Michael Phillip Morse, 57, a Toronto lawyer, was arrested for masterminding an international steal-to-order burglary ring. Morse allegedly coordinated a group of career criminals (also arrested) who burglarized homes and high-end antique and coin shops to steal $750,000 worth of items (sculptures, art, coins, carvings) for sale to art and antique collectors around the world who deal in underworld markets (Lamberti, October 26, 2004).

- A stolen vehicle was found abandoned by police after burglars used it to crash through the front door of the High Caliber Indoor Shooting Range and Training Center in St Louis. The burglars made off with 5 rifles, 15 handguns, and several knives (*St. Louis Dispatch*, October 25, 2004).

- An Escondido parolee was arrested and booked on suspicion of commercial burglary, grand theft, and forgery for financing a $42,000 Mercedes-Benz sedan from an Escondido dealership in someone else's name. The man allegedly used stolen identification to finance the car at Unique Automotive Ltd. (*San Diego Tribune*, July 29, 2004).

- Michael Morison, 39, of Boston was accused of shoplifting more than $315 worth of over-the-counter medication, all Aleve products (*Boston Herald*, November 7, 2004).

- A Milwaukee man used his children, aged 5, 6, 8, and 13, to steal clothes and bicycles from retail stores. The man taught the children how to remove the magnetic security tags from merchandise and they stole whole shopping carts of clothing and other items and four bikes at a time from Wal-Mart and Shopko stores (*Milwaukee Journal Sentinel*, November 4, 2004).

- A 29-year-old Oregon woman was arrested for stealing five cars parked in front of homes and in carports over a period of a month while on probation for an earlier robbery. When arrested, she told police, "Look at my record, that's how I buy drugs" (Danks, 2004, November 2, p. B02).

Within the general category of economic crime, subtypes vary by intensity and seriousness of the offense, style of transaction, type of expertise, and organizational and social context. These differences allow us to make inferences about the nature of the offense and the offender and an educated prediction about future offenses (Canter & Alison, 2000).

Economic Crime Typologies

There is little consensus in the literature on what crimes should be considered under the umbrella term *economic crime*. Clinard, Quinney, and Wildeman (1994) divide economic crime into five categories—*occasional property criminal behavior, conventional criminal behavior, professional criminal behavior, corporate criminal behavior,* and *organized criminal behavior*—the discerning factor being the offender's career pattern. Miethe, McCorkle, and Listwan (2006) classify economic crime into three categories, *residential and nonresidential burglary, motor vehicle theft,* and *occupational and organized crime,* with syndromes characterizing each. Other writers explain economic crime in terms of *white-collar* or *street-level* offenders (Kerley & Copes, 2004), apply the term *financial crime* to particular offenses such as corporate fraud (Croall, 2003), differentiate between *property crime* (burglary, arson, theft) and *enterprise crime* (white-collar, cyber, and organized crime) (Siegal, 2004), or employ subcategories such as *burglary* and *common property crime* (larceny-theft) (Dabney, 2004). Robbery is sometimes considered an economic crime with acknowledgment that it is both violent and economically motivated or considered a distinct category that is difficult to classify as either violent or economically motivated (Dabney, 2004; Miethe & McCorkle, 2001).

To be a meaningful crime category, *economic crime* must be homogeneous in the nature or essence of the criminal behavior. As was the case with violent and sex crime, it is important to ask, *What is it about economic crime that differentiates it from other criminal behaviors?* Is the nature, essence, or theme of economic crime best understood by classifications based on who commits the crime, the level of criminal career, or the level of offender sophistication, or is the offender motivation and drive for profit the central organizing feature that best differentiates it from other crime categories?

Canter and Alison (2000) suggest that the major premise for developing scientifically based offender typologies and profiling systems is that there are "psychologically important variations *between* types of crimes and also *within* any type of crime" (p. 7). This concept—that general and specific variations between and within crime categories can be ascertained by identifying offense themes—is known as the "Radex model" (Canter & Alison, 2000; Figure 7.2). The central question in understanding crime or a particular category of crime is therefore to identify the most useful behaviorally important aspects of offenses for determining their inherent salient psychological processes. *Is there a salient psychological process underlying economic crime? What are the important variations between economic crime and other types of crime and within categories of economic crime? Are there offense themes that distinguish economic crime from violent, sex, public order, and other types of crime and within categories of economic crime such as burglary, theft, arson, and fraud?*

One of the problems in classifying economic crime is the wide range of criminal behaviors motivated, or at least partially motivated, by profit. Burglary, shoplifting,

❖ **Figure 7.2**   The Radex Model Applied to Criminal Behavior

Source: Adapted from Canter and Alison (2000).

theft, arson, fraud, money-laundering, extortion, phony stock trade, tax fraud, and even murder can be profit driven. The shortcomings of traditional methods of classifying profit-driven offenses are highlighted by Naylor (2003):

> Indeed, on one level, the very term "crime" as a composite category is misleading. Ultimately what is important is not "crime" but "crimes," a term which automatically focuses attention onto what makes them different instead of forcing upon a wide range of offences an artificial unity. Applied to profit-driven offences the composite category of "crime" lumps together actions which, judged in terms of their inherent nature and/or consequences, are quite distinct—some involve force or fraud, and some free-market exchange; some have victims and some have clients; some occur by stealth at night and some take place in a normal business context by day; some are plotted by men with black eye-patches in smoky dives and some by people in the latest brand-name sportswear on the golf fairway. The only thing they have in common, apart from the motive of money (which may be only a partial explanation) is that they violate statutes which prescribe criminal sanctions for certain acts. (p. 83)

Returning to Canter and Alison's argument that offenses differ in terms of salient psychological themes, a typology of economic crime that focuses on motivation and process offers a central organizing principle with which to classify and understand economic crime. Crimes that can be classified as economic are those that are primarily motivated by profit. The central motivation is not always easily determined from the behavioral act itself. For example, a murder committed for the purpose of insurance fraud could be considered an economic crime whereas an arson that causes a great deal of property damage and economic loss committed for the purpose of sexual arousal would be considered a sex crime. The task in meaningful classification is to identify the behaviorally important facets of the offense that reveal the salient psychological processes underlying it (Canter & Alison, 2000).

Naylor (2003) offers an alternative typology of economic crime that is process- rather than offender-based and functional in that it applies to all offenses at least partially motivated by profit. This motivational typology divides profit-driven crime into three categories:

1. *Predatory offenses*—the involuntary transfer of property (e.g., purse-snatching, ransom kidnapping, extortion); the illegal redistribution of existing wealth

2. *Market-based offenses*—consensual market exchange of illegal goods and services (e.g., drug trafficking, prostitution, gambling, black market chains, fencing); the illegal earning of a new income

3. *Commercial offenses*—transfer of legal goods and services by otherwise legitimate entrepreneurs, investors, corporations by fraud and deception (e.g., telemarketing fraud, insider trading, commercial confidence tricks); the illegal redistribution of legally earned income

This typology is particularly useful because it preserves the essence of economic crime with attention to the ways in which offender subtypes (predatory offenders, market-based offenders, and commercial offenders) are connected and dependent on each other while coinhabiting and collectively defining the domain of economic crime. Focus on the nature of profit-driven crime helps us understand the modus operandi of the criminal economy that underlies economic crime. For example, in the case of intellectual property crime, the sale of bootleg software involves a predatory component (misappropriation of intellectual capital, which is a form of wealth), a market-based component (sale of illegal goods), and a commercial component (misrepresentation and sale of product as authentic/original). Another example would be the chop shop ring. Auto theft is a predatory crime, sale of auto parts from the auto theft is a market-based crime, and large-scale sale of original parts through auto dealers is commercial crime. Table 7.1 shows the primary distinctions between predatory, market-based, and commercial offenses within Naylor's typology of profit-driven crimes.

Similarly, economic crime can be viewed as a system of interactions between offenders involved in different aspects of a *stolen property system* (Walsh & Chappel, 2004). Based on research on patterns of criminal receiving in the northeast United States, Walsh and Chappel (2004) suggest viewing property crimes as a multistage

❖ Table 7.1   Naylor's (1993) Typology of Profit-Driven Crime

Offense Type	Method	Type of Profit Transfer	Essential Act
Predatory	Illegal—use of force or deception/con	Wealth	Illegal—theft
Market-Based	Legal—market-exchange	Illegal goods & services	Illegal—trafficking
Commercial	Illegal—fraud	Legal goods & services	Legal—market sale

Adapted from Naylor (1993).

process involving acts and actors spanning a broadly defined set of roles and behaviors. This stolen property system (SPS) is a "set of individuals and their interactions which locates, plans, facilitates, and its transfer to a new owner" (p. 195). The SPS has six functioning modes:

1. *Research and planning mode*—determining the demand for the item, its location, and how it can be acquired

2. *Extraction mode*—separating property from owner (theft, burglary)

3. *Exchange mode*—transferring item from extractor to marketer

4. *Marketing mode*—transporting and storing, demand analysis, packaging and advertising (any change to item before resale)

5. *Redistribution mode*—determining where, what price, and when item will be resold

6. *Evaluation mode*—analyzing system performance

Within this model, the thief and fence are interdependent, with the thief primarily involved in modes 1 and 2, the fence in modes 4 through 6, and the interaction between the thief and fence reflected by mode 3. No particular allocation of activities in the system is essential and the modes do not need to occur in a specific order. For example, the individual burglar who opportunistically burglarizes a home and sells the stolen items to a friend would skip mode 1, and act as both thief and fence, whereas the chop shop, which operates at a more sophisticated level of complexity, would involve all modes with multiple players and division of labor.

Using Naylor's typology of economic crime with acknowledgment that most profit-driven crime can be understood from the SPS model, we can classify economic crimes as predatory, market-based, or commercial offenses. This typology is comprehensive in that it includes street-level offenses as well as occupational, corporate, and organizational crime, and takes into account the central motivational drive for profit and the interconnections and reflexive relationship between the different players, offense modes, and opportunity structures that produce economic crime.

Predatory Offenses

Economic crimes that are predatory in nature involve intentional exploitation for the purpose of profit or gain, resulting in involuntary transfer of property. Predatory offenses tend to be committed by individuals or loosely formed groups of individuals. Further defined, predatory offenses involve

- Redistribution of legally owned wealth from one party to another
- Bilateral relations between offender and victim
- Involuntary transfer of property or wealth (cash, physical items, information, securities) through force, threat of force, or deception
- Identifiable victims (individuals, corporations, institutions)
- Use of a nonbusiness context or a business front purely to mislead
- Losses that are simple to determine (specific money or property stolen)
- An unambiguous morality (someone has been wronged by someone else)
- The need for compensation to the victim for losses (Naylor, 2003, p. 84)

Predatory offenses victimize private citizens, the public sector, or business institutions. Who the offender is (e.g., a street-level burglar versus a corporate embezzler) and who the victim is (private citizen versus business establishment or corporation) is not important. *The essential core of the definition of predatory economic crime is the nature of the act itself (the involuntary transfer of property) rather than the nature of the victim or the offender.* Property crimes such as burglary, theft, and arson are predatory in nature and thus fall under the heading of predatory crime.

Burglary

Burglary is *"the unlawful entry of a structure to commit a felony or theft"* (UCR, 2005). UCR data show that, in 2005, 2,154,126 homes, 2.6% of all households, were burglarized in the United States, with an estimated burglary rate of 750.2 offenses per 100,000. Burglaries accounted for 21.2% of all property crimes. The burglary rate decreased 14.1% from 1996 to 2005 (UCR, 2005). Victimization accounts of burglary are substantially higher, with 3,456,220 burglaries reported in 2005 at a rate of 29.5 offenses per 1,000 households. The burglary rate fell 49% from 1993 to 2005 (Catalano, 2006). Unlike violent crime, burglary rates are lower in the United States than they are in other developed nations such as Australia, England and Wales, Germany, and Canada (Dabney, 2004). Burglary is generally divided into two types— residential (targeting homes) and nonresidential (targeting businesses). In 2005, 65.8% of all burglaries were residential and most (62.4%) occurred during the day between the hours of 6 am and 6 pm, with an average loss of $1,725. Of the nonresidential burglaries, most (58%) occurred at night. A total of 298,835 burglary arrests were reported nationwide (UCR, 2005), 14% of all burglaries.

Burglary is commonly understood as an instrumental property crime committed by offenders who make rational choices for material gain (Cromwell & Olson, 2004; Merry & Harsent, 2000; Tunnell, 1992). Research suggests that the primary motivation for burglary is the need for money (Cromwell & Olson, 2004; Miethe & McCorkle, 2001; Tunnell, 1992). Many offenders commit the instrumental act of burglary to acquire money to satisfy and support more expressive needs such as drug addiction or a particular lifestyle—"to party" or to "live the fast, expensive life" (Cromwell & Olson, 2004, p. 16). Burglars indicate expressive factors as a secondary motivation including excitement and thrill, peer approval, intoxication, revenge (Cromwell & Olson, 2004; Merry & Harsent, 2000; Miethe, McCorkle, & Listwan, 2006), a game, or power and control (Tunnell, 1992).

A number of qualitative studies of burglars offer important insights into offender motivation and decision-making processes. The following quotes from offenders illustrate the range of primary and secondary motivations for burglary:

> "It doesn't take very long, the profit is quick. If I worked construction I would make in a week what I could make in fifteen minutes." (Tunnell, 1992, p. 40)

> "Once I got into the life, I liked it—a lot. I always liked to party and if you party you can't keep a job for any length of time. I like the ladies too. And the ladies like dudes with lots of folding money. You can't keep it up working for hourly wages. I've had some pretty good jobs before, but it was never enough. Not enough money, not enough time. Not enough freedom—when you work. Now I work for myself. I'm a self-employed thief. I can party all I want to and when I run out of green, I go get some more." (Cromwell & Olson, 2004, p. 17)

> "The excitement and the feeling of, you know, I fucked them, I mean I had got over on them. They put their best investigators on me and I fucked them, man, I sit back and laugh thinking. Really. Basically, and you know yourself, it's a sorry mother-fucker thing, but I mean it provides that damn challenge. Crime was a game . . . with a whole lot of reality to it." (Tunnell, 1992, p. 46)

Burglary is both a spontaneous and an opportunistic act (Miethe, McCorkle, & Listwan, 2006). Most researchers agree that the motivation and decision to commit burglary can be explained through the principle of *limited rationality*, which states that behavior, to be rational, does not have to be planned or the consequence of sequential decision making. When an offender decides to commit burglary, the decision is based on the individual's immediate perception of the risk and gains associated with the offense (Cromwell & Olson, 2004). Any offender who chooses to commit a burglary does so with limited knowledge of all of the information necessary to make an accurate cost-benefit analysis. Offenders may be superoptimistic, underestimating the likelihood of arrest, may overestimate the value of items inside a house they decide to burglarize and the gains that will come from committing the crime, or may have a particular orientation or personal philosophy that views an act as rational when it appears to be irrational. An offender in Cromwell and Olsen's (2004) ethnographic study of residential burglars stated:

I don't think about the future. Today is all that counts with me. You might be dead tomorrow, so live the best you can right now, today. I knew this dude that was always planning what he was gonna do someday—how he was gonna have a big car and a house and be rich and stuff—he got killed by some other dudes in a dope deal. All that planning didn't do no good for him. Wasted all that time, you know. I don't think that way. (p. 20)

The decision to commit burglary is heavily influenced by situational factors and opportunity. For a burglary to occur, there has to be a motivated offender, an absence of guardians, and a suitable target (Felson, 2002). "The motivation to commit a residential burglary is not itself sufficient to cause offenders to carry out the offense" (Wright & Decker, 1996, p. 34). Neighborhood ecology (neighborhood demographics, structure, and routine activities) is a factor associated with victimization risk (Capowich, 2003). The potential burglary target must be unoccupied, not easily observed, in an area where the burglar won't stand out, accessible, and contain items worth stealing. "Even a highly motivated burglar—who has immediate need for money—must still locate a vulnerable target and manage to effect entry without detection" (Cromwell & Olson, 2004, p. 18). Burglars pay attention to environmental cues that guide their decision to commit a crime. "The successful burglar is an up-to-date urban social psychologist" (David, 1974, p. 8) who knows when and how to strike. Common risk cues considered by burglars are *visibility* (the extent to which the house is overseen and observable to neighbors and passersby), *occupancy* (whether or not someone is in the dwelling), and *accessibility* (ease of access) (Cromwell & Olson, 2004; Miethe & McCorkle, 2001).

While committing burglaries involves some element of "skill" including having the nerve to commit the crime, "coolness," and the ability to make connections with criminal contacts (e.g., fences), burglars rarely mention having specialized mechanical skills (Åkerström, 1995). Most burglars are unsophisticated offenders who target easy access structures using some element of force. Approximately two-thirds of all robberies involve some form of forced entry (Dabney, 2004). Despite media and pop cultural accounts that tend to present burglars as much more ingenious than they actually are, 99% of all burglars don't have the ability to pick a lock or disable an alarm system (Cromwell & Olson, 2004). Box 7.1 provides examples of "botched burglaries" that are more the rule than the exception in residential burglary cases.

Burglars as a group do not specialize. Typical burglars are generalists with varied histories of violent, property, and public order crimes in their backgrounds. Rather than specializing in one type of crime, most burglars are "hustlers" who are constantly on the lookout for every opportunity to score or make connections for fencing, stealing, and drug deals (Åkerström, 1995). They are also thieves, assaulters, robbers, forgers, and drug dealers who have no special allegiance to burglary or any other type of crime. However, there is considerable evidence to suggest that burglars do specialize for short time periods, but that burglary is not an offense that tends to escalate to other, more serious crimes (Miethe, McCorkle, & Listwan, 2006).

Miethe, McCorkle, and Listwan (2006) identify two burglar types—*novice burglars*, who are motivated by financial need, easily deterred, and unsophisticated, and *professional burglars*, who are financially motivated, financial technically skilled,

BOX 7.1

BOTCHED BURGLARIES

One of the more prevalent myths about offenders is that they are more sophisticated than they actually are. Felson (2002) refers to this as the *ingenuity fallacy*. Burglars in particular tend to be unsophisticated and unskilled in the art of breaking and entering. The following are examples of some burglary bungles in the recent news:

- Mario Billings, a convicted thief, broke into Hale DeMar's house in Chicago for a second time in December 2003. Billings used stolen keys to enter the house and, in the process, set off the security alarm. During the burglary, Billings was confronted by DeMar who shot him. Billings escaped by crashing through a front window. Previously, Billings had burglarized DeMar's house by sneaking through a dog door and stealing DeMar's BMW sport utility vehicle, a television, and a ring of keys. He was arrested when he parked his car at a hospital. Billings received a sentence of 7 years.

- A 30- to 40-year-old man believed to be a day laborer looking for work attempted to burglarize the Amigo Express Drive-In Market in Fort Bend County, Texas, by climbing onto the roof and removing the exhaust vent cover. He lowered himself feet-first into the shaft, but got stuck near the bottom. He was found at 8:30 am the next morning dead in the shaft by a store employee who, when opening the store for business, noticed feet protruding from a ventilation exhaust duct. Police discovered the would-be burglar's body wedged in the 12-inch-wide shaft. Detectives believe he died from asphyxiation. Capt. Jerry Clements said, "It had to be an excruciating ordeal."

- In Hong Kong, unemployed 24-year-old Ngo Chi-Kong broke into the home of Leung Yau-Fun at night and stole a cell phone, a gold necklace, and a bag as Leung slept. After realizing he had woken Leung, Chi-Kong rushed to the balcony and fell as he tried to climb down, fracturing his pelvis, breaking his left hand, and cutting his left eye in the fall. After his release from the hospital, he was sentenced to 2 years and 4 months.

- In Escondido, California, three men in their late 20s were arrested for burglarizing a Payless Shoes store when police caught them hauling garbage bags of shoes from the store late at night. Shortly after, a woman said she heard loud noises, saw people breaking the store's window, and phoned police. Officers arrived at Payless Shoes and spotted the men with the bags. One man complied with police, but two tried to escape. One of the escapees injured his foot as he tried to flee and was taken to a hospital and treated.

organized, and engage in elaborate planning and division of labor. Tunnell (1992) differentiates between sporadic and persistent burglars. The sporadic burglar is a low-rate repetitive offender who is relatively uncommitted to crime and uses techniques of neutralization to aid in the decision to commit crime. The persistent burglar has been criminally active over a long period of time, sees him- or herself as a professional, and concentrates on planning the offense. The persistent offenders are not bothered by complex deliberations over whether or not to commit crime. Rather it is a given that crime is the route they will take to meet their needs. Similarly, Clinard, Quinney, and Wildeman (1994) distinguish between *occasional property offenders,* who do not make a career of their criminal behavior, and *conventional* and *professional* criminals, who engage in property offending as a way of life.[8] Box 7.2 offers insight into the world of offenders who engage in burglary as a way of life.

BOX 7.2

A DAY IN THE LIFE OF A BURGLAR

BY JON ROYAL FLEMING[1]

The sun is shining through the front of my living room window, smack dab into my face, MTV still playing softly on the TV.

Hey babe, we got any smokes left? I ask, as I roll over off the tangle of comforters . . . and try to start my day.

Last night we hit the clubs, Seattle's finest. Taxis, ¼ ounce of bud. Mixed drinks, cover charges, smokes, and a late night feeding frenzy, cleaned my pockets of my last $300.00, and change. . . . Plus rent's due in three days. Fucking got to go to work today. . . . I work only when I have to.

I guess my work day isn't too much different than the squares. My woman packs me lunch, I commute, work, get paid, and come home for dinner. Gotta pay the bills and survive somehow. . . . Everyone has to make a living, right?

The neighbor lets me use their Buick Skylark. Big car, big backseat, big trunk. I always fill the tank when I return it, and spot them $20.00 bucks. They just think I'm out hustling. They know that if anyone, say a detective, ever asks, they loaned it to a friend of a friend, to go to a job interview, "Bill" something. The car's a beater so no one would question loaning it out to a stranger.

Let's see? Do I have everything? Baseball cap to tuck my long hair up under, check. Extra pair of tube socks to use as gloves, check. Screwdriver to remove the front license plate, check. T-shirt to cover the back license plate, check. Sack lunch and a half pack of smokes, check.

It's time to go to work, 9:00 AM. "I'll see you tonight. . . . Maybe if you're good? Ill bring you home something pretty. A quick kiss and I'm out the door. Stop at Quickmart for a double latte, and it's onto I-5, north to the happy hunting grounds.

Pay attention, are there any detectives following me? Keep the eyes wide open. Never shit in your backyard. Always travel at least one county away to rob houses. The reason being, let's say you rob a house, and have a car full of loot, and get pulled over before you can get it to the fence. The cops only have a police report of stolen property from the county where it was stolen from, so if you make it one county over, you can tell them you are moving, and they will let you go. Same thing if someone saw your car near the house getting robbed, and they call it in. The call only

(Continued)

(Continued)

goes out to that county. So if you run for home, you're safe. You don't have to worry about getting pulled over. Gotta keep the odds on your side, you will not get caught. So today I have driven north of Seattle, to Snohomish County. This is an excellent area, a lot of work. See, let's say I travel to some rural area East of Everett. There is a big house, no close neighbors, a driveway with the house a ways away from the road, good cover. You have to figure, my working hours are 11:00 AM to 2:00 PM, a big house here, husband has to have a good job. Has to work in the city, Everett or Seattle. Big house, gonna have a wife and kids. 11:00 AM to 2:00 PM, she's out doing her daily chores, grocers, doing her hair, visiting with friends. All I need is 15 minutes with no one home to do my work. If I follow the rules, the odds are in my favor.

Finding the right house is just a feeling. It's a gift I have after years of experience. I can just *look* at a house or driveway, and *know* "this is it."

So here's a driveway, going into the trees, I can see a nice house set back a ways, no car in sight. I slowed down and checked the mailbox, the morning paper still there—good chance the owner left early for work. Before hunting in earnest, I pulled over and removed the front license plate with a screwdriver and placed the front license in the windshield on the dash. I pulled into the driveway all natural, heart racing. No one looks out the windows, I step out, car running and ring the door bell and knock. No answer. I repeat about five times. No one's home. A lot of times someone is home. So then I smile and ask to use their phone, saying I'm lost. I ask to get some water because my car's overheating. I explain that I am looking for "_____"'s house, as we had a party there last Friday and got wasted. I forgot what road it was on or any story that comes to mind. With a smile, always a smile, everything's okay. Relax my little sheep, there are no wolves amongst you. But right here an now, there is nobody home. Time to go to work.

I back the car in, facing the road. Turn off the engine, so it's quiet. Flip the license plate over on the front window, so no one can write it down. Hair tucked up under my hat, socks in pockets, T-shirt on hand, I step out, pop the trunk.

The T-shirt is stretched over the rear license plate. If anyone pulls up, I just jump in and drive away, licenses covered. If they try to block me in, I would aim for their front wheel well, smash it in, disable their car and get away.

I go up to the door, look close, listen. Do the doorbell and knock a couple more times, then "Pow," a swift kick to the front door, right next to the doorknob, and the 15 minute time starts ticking. Socks over hands, no fingerprints, I run into the house, yelling "Grandma and Grandpa, I broke the door, is anyone home?" I do this in the belief that if someone was home, they would say "who the fuck are you", instead of staying quiet or shooting me. I quickly run from room to room, making sure the house is clear. I open up the back door, always leaving an escape route, in case someone comes home. Time to work. First run to the bedroom, grab a pillow case, run back to the living room, unplug and disconnect the VCR or DVD, wrap the cords around it, grab the manual if it is handy, tuck the remote into the case, slide the pillowcase over it, set by the front door. Quickly appraise the TV and stereo, are they top notch? Yes, disconnect, set by door, if not, I plan on hitting at least 6 or 7 houses today and I would rather just leave them behind, as they fill up the space in the car. Next, back in the bedroom, I grab the other pillowcase, like a machine, methodical, done this thousands of times. First the jewelry, top of the dresser and nightstand, grab the jewelry box, necklace rack, change boxes. Next the dresser drawers, bottom of the underwear and sock drawers, grab all the ring and necklace boxes, into the pillowcase they go.

Quickly pull out each dresser drawer, jewelry, cash, pistols, into the sack, dump the rest onto the floor. Next, look under the mattress for pistols, then under the bed for rifles or shotguns. Next the closet, leather jackets, furs, guns leaning up in the corners of the closet, check the top shelf for pistols or cameras or camcorders . . . put the sack next to the front door. Go to the den, look for a gun rack or gun cabinet, empty it, roll them all up in a comforter, set them by the front door. Quickly scan the house, is the computer 486 or better? Is there a laptop, what kind of video game system is there? Grab all the games and all the CDs. Is there a safe, grab it, open it later. The phone answering machine, sports equipment, snow boards, roller blades, go to the garage, chain saws, nice tools, last, if there's room, see if there's anything nice for the neighbors. Grab several blankets or comforters to cover everything on the back seat and line the trunk. A quick look in the fridge — ahh, a cold beer, robbing houses is thirsty work. Oh, grab all the wine and hard alcohol. It's been 15 minutes, time to go. I open the trunk, lay out the comforter, quickly pack in what I can, guns and jewels *always* go in the trunk, in case I get pulled over. The rest goes in the back seat, carefully covered with a blanket. Remove the t-shirt off the back license plate, look for traffic and people walking and slowly pull out of the driveway. One house down. On average, the VCR is $50, the camcorder is $200. Computer is $400, video game is $50, TV is $100, camera is $50. The diamond rings are nice, get $250 each, sell the rest of the gold for weight after I smash it up. Save the thick gold necklace and one ring for my girl. I like to give her pretty things. The two pistols are $300 each, $100 for shotguns, $100 for rifles. So an average nice rural house will get me about $800 to $2700. But you never know when you'll hit the jackpot . . . an envelope with $5000 cash, old coins, a big gun collection, or best of all—a hidden grow room full of bud. I've gotten as much as $70,000 out of one house, or sometimes there has been nothing. It's like Christmas, the house is like a huge Christmas present with your name on it. You *never* know what you are going to get . . . Maybe $400, maybe $70,000, maybe more . . . But you know, if nobody is home and you follow the rules, it's *all* yours! The score is good and the car's already kinda full. I hit two more houses before 2:00 PM, and then it's back on I-5 south, going home. Back at the apartment I casually unload everything and sort it. Guns in one pile, electronics in one pile, jewels in one pile. First, I carefully go over each electronic item and peel off *all* serial number stickers as *all* stickers with numbers on them to prevent the item as being identified as stolen property. Any engraved numbers, I go over with my handy Dremel power tool, and grind off the numbers.

I wipe down each item to remove my fingerprints, then empty out the jewelry, quickly sort out the gold, silver, platinum, the rings and necklaces, toss *all* the boxes and junk jewelry and knickknacks, roll up the real stuff on paper towels and the it's time to dump it to the fence.

You can go two ways, three actually. First and fastest, you can go to *any* dope dealers, dump it all, a package deal, for a large amount of coke or crank, or bud, then resell the dope to get your money. Next, you can go to any group of outlaws as bikers and also get cash or dope,

(Continued)

(Continued)

last, find a real fence. . . . Spend some time before you go out robbing, there are fences in <u>any</u> city in America. Maybe a manager of a strip joint, or the owner of a used car lot, or a crooked pawn shop owner. Anyone with money and shady morals who is interested in a good deal and who can turn around and sell it all off piece by piece for a big profit. I'm in a hurry, so I just go to the Mexicans and trade everything for 14 oz of coke, turn around and drive to Rainier Ave., or Aurora Ave., stop at a few crack houses and sell off the coke cheap for $500 an oz. . . . With $7000 in cash in my pocket, I return home to my girl, pay my $750 rent, return the neighbor's car, break open a stolen bottle of vodka and Kahlua and mix up a White Russian, and roll a joint. I lay out my cash, and give my girl the necklace and the ring. You can bet I'm going to get something special tonight. We go out for Chinese food and hit the clubs again. . . . Just another day in the life. Whatever gets you by.

What? Do you actually believe I would waste my life away working eight hours a day at some measly job to barely pay the bills? I've seen how unhappy my parents and everyone else are. Hell no, not me. I choose to spend my days doing what I want to do. Going to the park or the beach, fishing or hunting, visiting with friends, lying around all day making love. We only have one life, we are only young once. Sure, you can lose the gamble and go to prison—but that's only if someone you chose to trust, tells on you. Deep inside, you know that if you follow the rules, you will get away with it. Don't do coke or crank, or you get stupid and the odds will not be in your favor. Just do what you do and try to enjoy life to its fullest.

[1]Jon Royal Fleming is currently serving time in Washington State.

A study by Mullens and Wright (2003) explored gender differences in residential burglary. Except for larceny-theft, female arrests for burglary exceed those of other serious index crimes. The authors found that when women engage in burglary, they generally become involved through their boyfriends whereas men become involved through same-sex peers. "Males, by and large, act as gatekeepers to the social world of residential burglary"(p. 821). Male and female burglars share similar motivations—to finance a party or drug lifestyle—with some minor differences; males tend to spend their proceeds on sexual conquests while women were more likely to spend part of their earnings on their children. Female participation in burglary is reduced (in the eyes of male burglars) to stereotypically sexualized roles (the belief that women need to use sex to acquire potential targets). Interestingly, male burglars noted a relationship as a reason for getting out of the business, whereas female burglars had to break off their relationships with their male partners to reduce their offending behavior. Similarly, female burglars expressed concern about how family members might perceive their criminality and male offenders did not express this concern or guilt (Mullins & Wright, 2003).

Larceny-Theft and Motor Vehicle Theft

Larceny-theft is the "unlawful taking, carrying, leading, or riding away of property from the possession or constructive possession of another" (UCR, 2005). Larceny-theft includes shoplifting, purse-snatching, pocket-picking, theft from motor vehicles, theft of motor vehicle parts, bicycle theft, and other crimes in which something is taken with no use of force, violence, or fraud. In 2005 there were an estimated 6.8 million larceny-thefts in the United States representing two-thirds of all property crime, at a rate of 2,286.3 offenses per 100,000 with economic losses estimated at $764 per offense, over $5 billion annually. This amount excludes thefts against businesses such as shoplifting, employee theft, and embezzlement,[9] which retail loss security professionals estimate costs retailers $10 billion a year (Dabney, 2004). Since 1996, the larceny-theft rate has dropped 23.3% (UCR, 2005). Victimization reports of theft show that 13,350,110 completed thefts occurred in 2005 at a rate of 114.6 per 1,000 persons or households (Catalano, 2006).

Motor vehicle theft is a separate category in the Uniform Crime Reports, defined as *"the theft or attempted theft of a motor vehicle"* (UCR, 2005), including theft of automobiles, motorcycles, buses, trucks, snowmobiles, and motor scooters. In 2005, there were an estimated 1.2 million motor vehicle thefts in the United States at a rate of 416.7 offenses per 100,000 in the population, a 20.7% decrease since 1996 (UCR, 2005). Most of the stolen vehicles are automobiles (73.4%; as opposed to trucks or buses). The average value of a stolen vehicle is $6,173 and the estimated total value of all vehicles stolen in the United States in 2003 was $7.6 billion. Law enforcement agencies cleared 13% of reported motor vehicle thefts in 2003, with 147,459 arrests nationwide (UCR, 2005).

As with burglary, most offenders who commit theft do so primarily for utilitarian purposes. However, expressive needs often also underlie instrumental motivation in crimes of theft. Theft, particularly *shoplifting,* is often associated with other motives such as mental illness or emotional need, but is primarily motivated by economic factors. People steal first and foremost as a means of satisfying material wants and needs and steal for different reasons at different times. Theft is widespread and committed by all types of people with different motives and using a broad range of methods. Teenagers steal to be popular with delinquent peers. Addicts steal to support a drug/alcohol habit. Some people steal items they don't need impulsively or when stressed or under the influence of drugs or alcohol. Others steal compulsively, feeling their behavior is out of their control (Cromwell, Curtis, & Withrow, 2004).[10] Even people with eating disorders have been known to steal to support the behavioral symptoms of their condition.[11] In a field study of shoplifters conducted in the 1970s, Walsh (1978) found that:

> There is little evidence to show that shoplifting is other than extremely widespread. People shoplift for luxury-type goods, most frequently for themselves. For some it's an "occupation," for others a "game," for yet others a "compulsion," or again "morally justifiable," and as one informant said, "some people want everything they can see." Apparently shop theft has emerged out of abundance and plenty as a "morality free" area for many, which is widely attractive to widely different groups of people. (p. 91)

It could be argued, then, that theft is morally justified (and easily neutralized) for many people. In other words, all types of people commit theft and use cognitive neutralization techniques that enable them to engage in the behavior guilt-free such as "insurance companies will cover it" or "everybody does it." Theft is committed in many forms from retail theft (shoplifting) to employee theft (embezzlement or stealing merchandise or other items from the workplace). Studies show that up to 90% of the general public admit to committing theft at some point during their lives (Gabor, 1994). The relative social acceptance of theft in conjunction with the ease with which offenders are able to neutralize the behavior increases the heterogeneity of this category of criminal behavior.

Motor vehicle theft is a specialized form of theft that can be understood as a distinct, less heterogeneous, crime subcategory. Research on motor vehicle theft shows that people steal cars for four reasons: transportation, commission of other crimes, commercial theft, and joyriding (Fleming, 2004); auto theft can be divided into two general types or "syndromes"—*joyriders* and *financially motivated vehicle thieves* (Miethe, McCorkle, & Listwan, 2006, pp. 103–104). Of these motives, joyriding, predominantly committed by teenage boys, is the only expressive motivation. Offenders who steal cars to joyride do so spontaneously to receive praise from their peers and excitement and thrill. On the other hand, the other three motivations are primarily instrumental (stealing a car for transportation or for profit). People steal cars because they don't have one and want one or because they need to get somewhere (fast) and don't have the time or money to acquire transportation through legitimate means. At the more sophisticated level, auto theft spans the three types of economic crime, involving the actual (predatory) theft of the vehicle to the fencing (marketing) of the stolen goods, and then resale of vehicle through legitimate (commercial) business enterprises.

Motor vehicle thefts tend to occur in the summer during evening hours, near the victim's home either in a parking garage or on the street. Victims tend to be strangers to the offender, who gains access to the vehicle through either an open door or by quick forced entry. Motor vehicle theft is usually committed by multiple offenders who are under the influence of alcohol or drugs in situations where there is low security, high target attraction (a desirable and accessible target), and low guardianship (Miethe, McCorkle, & Listwan, 2006). Auto theft is driven by supply and demand—instrumental motives are driven by the demand for certain cars and their parts (Fleming, 2004). Often older vehicles are stolen for their parts, which are no longer being manufactured and are difficult to obtain. Car thieves follow market trends, targeting vehicles that provide the best market for stolen parts. Following are the most common vehicles to be stolen, according to the National Insurance Crime Bureau (2004):

- Toyota Camry
- Honda Accord
- Honda Civic
- Oldsmobile Cutlass/Supreme/Ciera
- Jeep Cherokee/Grand Cherokee

- Chevrolet Full Size C/K Pickup
- Toyota Corolla
- Ford Taurus
- Chevrolet Caprice
- Ford F150 Pickup

There is some disagreement regarding whether or not auto thieves specialize and whether auto theft escalates into a more violent offense pattern. Some studies show that auto thieves are more likely than other types of offenders to specialize, and other research suggests that people who commit auto theft are criminally versatile. Offenders involved in professional auto theft and chop shop rings specialize whereas opportunistic auto thieves tend to be involved in a range of criminal behaviors, and there is no evidence that they escalate to violent crime (Miethe, McCorkle, & Listwan, 2006).

Motor vehicle thieves' accounts of their crimes suggest that money is the primary motivation for their criminal behavior. However, auto thieves are motivated by other things besides money. Qualitative research on auto thieves reveals that auto theft is the means by which offenders can maintain the street life in ways that are not purely financial. Stealing cars allows them to have "mobile parties," to travel to where they imagine the action is, and to acquire high-end status car accessories like rims and stereos. Furthermore, auto theft provides a thrill that lasts longer than other types of theft because the crime can last for hours or days, providing a thrill by seeing how long the offenders can push their luck while driving a stolen car. Most important, commission of auto theft carries with it a status and symbolism associated with a sense of power and prestige (Copes, 2003).

Though some heterogeneity exists within the concept of larceny-theft, in type of theft (shoplifting, pick-pocketing, bike theft, auto theft, stealing a range of items to support a drug, alcohol, food, etc.) and the rationales of offenders (joyriders, professional thieves, opportunists, etc.), three common features distinguish larceny-theft from other crime categories:

1. Theft is a property crime.

2. The act of stealing an object is qualitatively different from harming a living being.

3. Theft is predominantly financially motivated.[12]

Theft can be categorized as heterogeneous in terms of offender motives; it is predominantly economically motivated, with secondary expressive motives for some offenders, and dependent on situational factors and precipitators (e.g., target accessibility, absence of audience/onlookers, etc.). Auto theft is committed by a diverse group of offenders, but as a crime category is less heterogeneous than theft-larceny because the element of skill and increased difficulty in neutralizing commission of the behavior results in a smaller group of potential offenders than shoplifting.

Fraudulent Offenses

Fraud can be broadly defined as an offense of deception. Fraud is a predatory crime because it involves transfer of wealth from victim to offender by deception. *Fraudulent offenses* include forgery, counterfeiting, corruption, copyright offenses, and embezzlement (Dodd, 2000). Fraud and the various forms it may take are often considered *white-collar crimes* or *occupational crimes* because these offenses are frequently committed by individuals in occupational settings and many fraudulent offenses are not generally thought of as street-level property offenses. Though many researchers include a range of fraudulent practices under the heading of fraud, the FBI Uniform Crime Reporting System defines (and collects data for) fraud, forgery and counterfeiting, and embezzlement separately as follows:

- *Fraud*—The intentional perversion of the truth for the purpose of inducing another person or other entity in reliance upon it to part with something of value or to surrender a legal right. Fraudulent conversion and obtaining of money or property by false pretenses. Confidence games and bad checks, except forgeries and counterfeiting, are included. (UCR, 2003, p. 497)

- *Forgery and Counterfeiting*—The altering, copying, or imitating of something without authority or right, with the intent to deceive or defraud by passing the copy or thing altered or imitated as that which is original or genuine; or the selling, buying, or possession of an altered, copied, or imitated thing with the intent to deceive or defraud. Attempts are included. (UCR, 2003, p. 497)

- *Embezzlement*—The unlawful misappropriation or misapplication by an offender to his/her own use or purpose of money, property, or some other thing of value entrusted to his/her care, custody, or control. (UCR, 2003, p. 498)

In 2005, there were 321,521 arrests for fraud, 118,455 for forgery and counterfeiting, and 18,970 for embezzlement, at a rate per 100,000 of 106.4 for fraud, 40.1 for forgery/counterfeiting, and 6.5 for embezzlement (UCR, 2005).[13]

The term *occupational fraud* has been used as an umbrella term to refer to all fraudulent employee practices. Occupational fraud is "the use of one's occupation for personal enrichment through the deliberate misapplication of the employing organization's resources or assets" (Wells, 2005, p. 8). However, it is difficult to assess the true cost or actual amount of fraud committed by employees in businesses and corporations. Sometimes fraud involves multibillion dollar accounting misstatements, but it more likely takes the form of corruption or misappropriation, which is much harder to uncover. In most cases of occupational fraud, there is no direct evidence of the crime (Wells, 2005). Fraud is committed by individuals and businesses/corporations. When it is committed by an individual against an employer or one individual against another, it is a predatory crime.

Embezzlement is a common form of fraud, defined as the *fraudulent appropriation of money belonging to an employer or other party that has been entrusted to one's care* (Friedrichs, 2004). Embezzlement is a predatory crime involving transfer of wealth from a victim (business or corporation) to an offender (employee). In this sense, embezzlement is no different from other forms of theft except that the offender is a trusted employee and not a street-level offender. Another difference may be in how the context tends to make it easier for offenders to neutralize their behaviors. In the minds of employers, embezzlement is a crime, but often in the minds of the offenders, it is seen as "borrowing," "fiddling," or "fringing" (Friedrichs, 2004).

The essential feature of embezzlement and fraud is deception, but not all deception necessarily constitutes fraud. For an act to be considered fraud it must include the following:

- A false statement

- Knowledge that the statement was false when it was uttered

- Victim reliance on the false statement

- Damages incurred as result of victim's reliance on the false statement

Much of what is known about fraud comes from research of Edwin Sutherland in the 1930s on white-collar crime and elite deviance[14] and from Cressey's (1973) work, *Other People's Money,* on embezzlers and the nature of the violation of trust between employee and employer. Cressey's (1973) hypothesis came to be known as the *fraud triangle,* which explains embezzlement and fraudulent acts in terms of three points of a triangle: (1) opportunity, (2) pressure, and (3) rationalization. The employee who is willing to violate the employer's trust for financial gain is one who perceives an opportunity to commit the offense, has the technical skills to carry it out, is experiencing some sort of private (nonsharable) financial problem, and justifies and excuses the behavior by maintaining a self-view as a noncriminal. Taking Cressey's research further, Albrecht and colleagues developed the *fraud scale,* based on research that identified *personal characteristics* of the offender and features of the *occupational environment* that are red flags for occupational fraud. According to the fraud scale, when situational pressures and perceived opportunities are high and personal integrity is low, occupational fraud is more likely to occur than when the opposite is true (Wells, 2005).

Albrecht and colleagues identified personal characteristics and features of the organizational environment most likely to contribute to occupational fraud. The researchers identified 50 possible red flags of occupational fraud and abuse and asked internal auditors of companies that had experienced fraud to rank the factors that were present in the cases they had worked. The results revealed 10 personal characteristics and 10 aspects of the organizational environment contributing to occupational fraud (Albrecht et al., 1984, cited in Wells, 2005), further supporting the *Cressey Fraud Triangle* and theory that nonsharable financial problems, opportunity, and a way to rationalize or justify the act are the necessary components of occupational fraud. Table 7.2 shows the most highly ranked factors associated with personal characteristics and occupational environment. Other research supports these findings, suggesting that situational inducements and behavioral adaptations to the organizational environment are key elements in the decision to commit fraud (Dodd, 2000).

Identity theft is one of the fastest growing crimes in recent years. Identity theft involves using personal information such as Social Security and credit card numbers to steal people's money. Worldwide losses resulting from identity theft have been estimated in the billions. Identity theft is considered to be a hybrid form of crime—common theft by people in "white-collar" situations. Thieves often access victims' personal information through occupational settings and then pass the

❖ **Table 7.2** Factors Associated With Occupational Fraud

Personal Characteristics	Organizational Environment
Living beyond their means	Placing too much trust in key employees
An overwhelming desire for personal gains	Lack of proper procedures for authorizations and transactions
High personal debt	Inadequate disclosures of personal investments and incomes
A close association with customers	No separation of authorization of transactions from the custody of related assets
Feeling pay not commensurate with responsibility	Lack of independent checks on performance
A wheeler-dealer attitude	Inadequate attention to details
Strong challenge to beat the system	No separation of custody of assets from the accounting for those assets
Excessive gambling habits	No separation of duties between accounting functions
Undue family or peer pressure	Lack of clear lines of authority and responsibility
No recognition for job performance	Department that is not frequently reviewed by internal auditors

Source: Adapted from Wells (2005, pp. 22–23), review of Albrecht, Howe, & Romney (1984).

information on to others. Known identity theft rings have involved employees in software companies, credit card companies, and state motor vehicle licensing. Thieves are also able to obtain personal information in other ways. A relatively new scheme called *phishing* uses ruses to trick people into giving out Social Security numbers and other personal information. Box 7.3 describes how offenders use phishing to steal victims' identities.

The background and demographics of offenders who commit fraud differ in a number of respects from those committing other types of predatory crime. First, the gender disparity across these offenders is much smaller than it is in all other crime categories. The *2004 National Fraud Survey* found that the principle perpetrator was male in 53% of cases and female in 47% of the cases, though the losses caused by males were significantly higher. The median loss caused by a male employee was $160,000,

BOX 7.3

PHISHING

"Phishing" is a scheme identity thieves use to steal personal information. Identity thieves pretend to be someone they're not to trick people into giving them personal information such as Social Security numbers, mother's maiden names, PIN numbers, financial account numbers, and other information.

Phishing is done through e-mail or by phone. The most common method is to send an e-mail to a victim pretending to be from a legitimate retailer, bank, credit card company, state lottery agency, or governmental agency. The sender asks the victim to "confirm" personal information for a particular reason (e.g., "Someone has placed an order in your name," "Your account is about to be closed," "Your information has been lost due to a computer problem," "You have won the lottery and we need to deposit the money into your account," etc.). Ironically, a classic method of phishing involves the sender claiming to be from the fraud department of a well-known company asking to verify personal information because the recipient has been the victim of identity theft. E-mail phishers will spam large numbers of victims hoping that a percentage will take the bait. In a phishing scam in 2003, the offenders sent mass e-mails supposedly from eBay claiming that the user's account was about to be suspended unless he clicked on the provided link to update credit card information.

The National Consumer League's Internet Fraud Watch offers the following recommendations to avoid becoming a victim of phishing.

- *Don't click on the link in an e-mail that asks for your personal information.* It will take you to a phony Web site that looks like one from the real company it is claiming to represent. If you enter personal information into the Web site it will go right into the hands of identity thieves. To check on the legitimacy of the message, call the company directly or go to its official Web site on your own through a search engine.

- *If someone contacts you by phone or e-mail to say you've been the victim of fraud, verify the person's identity* before you hand over personal information. Generally, if you have been the victim of fraud credit card companies and law enforcement agencies won't ask you for personal information over the phone. If they do, call the main number of the agency to find out if the person is legitimate.

- *Be careful about listing yourself on a job search site.* Job seekers who list on Web sites are targets for phishers who pose as potential employers and ask for Social Security numbers and other personal information. Again, verify the person's identity before giving out personal information.

- *Be suspicious if you are contacted out of the blue by someone asking for your personal information.* Legitimate companies generally don't ask for personal information over the phone or by e-mail without warning.

- *If you've been "phished," report immediately.* Contact the agencies the phisher claimed to be representing and report to local law enforcement through the *National Fraud Information Center/Internet Fraud Watch* (www.fraud.org or 800-876-7060).

whereas the median loss caused by a female employee was $60,000. Second, most people who commit occupational fraud are first-time offenders. The National Fraud Survey found that 82.9% of offenders had never been charged with or convicted of a prior offense. Third, unlike other types of predatory offenses, there is a high level of trust between the victim and offender in occupational fraud cases. Offenders who caused the highest amount of economic losses to their employers in 2004 were those who had been with the companies the longest; employees for less than 1 year made away with a median amount of $26,000 and those employed for over 10 years made off with a median of $171,000 (Wells, 2005).

Arson

Arson is defined in the Uniform Crime Reports as "any willful or malicious burning or attempt to burn, with or without intent to defraud, a dwelling house, public building, motor vehicle or aircraft, personal property of another, etc." (UCR, 2005). The extent of arson crimes in the United States is largely unknown because of limited reporting of arson by law enforcement. In 2005, law enforcement reported 67,504 offenses and 12,012 arson arrests in the United States, at a rate of 5.5 per 100,000. The nationwide arson rate in the United States for 2005 was 26.9 per 100,000 and the average value loss was $14,910. In 2005, 16,337 individuals were arrested for arson offenses. Arson is largely a crime committed by juvenile males. In 2005, 48.6% of persons arrested for arson were juveniles, and of those juveniles, 59.4% were under the age of 15 (UCR, 2005).

Arson is a heterogeneous crime category. Individuals (and groups) who commit arson are a mixed bag ranging from profit-driven offenders who commit arson as insurance fraud to serial arsonists who are motivated by excitement, revenge, or a political agenda (Douglas et al., 1992). Arson is a legal term referring to *intentional* firesetting. The term *firesetter* is sometimes used to refer to individuals who set fires without intent. Arson is classified here as an economic crime because its nature or "essence" is *property destruction by fire* and it is a criminal behavior that results in financial loss. However, arson is a complex crime that does not fall neatly into a single overarching motivational category of criminal behavior. Arson can be classified as a violent crime in the case of arson-homicide or as a political crime in cases where arson and bombing are the modus operandi of terrorists.[15]

People intentionally set fires for all sorts of reasons—profit, revenge, arousal, to conceal a crime, to make a political statement, for developmental experimentation in childhood, to attract attention/recognition, to communicate a wish or desire.[16] Arson is sometimes committed for its own sake (e.g., arousal, vandalism, revenge) or as the modus operandi in the commission of another type of crime (e.g., insurance fraud, setting fire to evidence to cover up a homicide, or sending a particular message in an assault, homicide, or hate crime[17]). When arson is committed to cover up or as part of a homicide or as a form of revenge or retaliation resulting in physical harm to others, it is also (and best understood as) a violent crime. Motivational typologies of arsonists divide arson into the following general types. The FBI's Crime Classification Manual (Douglas et al., 1992) classifies arson as follows:

- *Profit-motivated arson*—committed, often by professionals, in order to make a fraudulent insurance claim

- *Excitement arson*—committed by pyromaniacs or paraphiliacs who derive pleasure, arousal, or release of tension from firesetting

- *Revenge arson*—committed as an act of revenge

- *Vandalism arson*—committed for "fun"

- *Crime-concealment arson*—committed to hide another crime

- *Extremist arson*—committed as a political act

- *Serial arson*—committed by socially inadequate underachiever with prior histories of nuisance offenses and substance abuse against unoccupied targets

Arson has also been classified as either "person-oriented" or "object-oriented," with underlying motivations that are either expressive or instrumental (Fritzon, 2000). Viewing arson in this way produces four arson themes:

1. *Expressive arson directed at a person* (attack directed inwards stemming from anxiety, depression, or suicidal thoughts)

2. *Instrumental arson directed at a person* (attack directed outwards toward another person as form of revenge)

3. *Expressive arson directed at an object* (attack a form of emotional acting out to release tension or result of fascination with watching fire; may involve targeting certain buildings that have symbolic value)

4. *Instrumental arson directed at an object* (attack directed at obtaining benefit by changing aspects of the object—e.g., to hide evidence from another crime such as homicide or burglary)

In a study applying this typology to juvenile firesetters, Santtila, Häkkänen, Alison, and Whyte (2003) found that depressed female youth were more likely to commit expressive arson whereas delinquent youth were more likely to commit instrumental arson, and classifying arson along these dimensions has implications for prevention, intervention, and investigation.

Arson committed for the purpose of arousal is a *DSM-IV-TR* Impulse Control Disorder called *pyromania*. Pyromania is characterized by multiple episodes of deliberate and purposeful firesetting that include the following diagnostic criteria:

- Deliberate and purposeful firesetting on more than one occasion

- Tension or affective arousal before the act

- Fascination with, interest in, curiosity about, or attraction to fire and its situational contexts (e.g., paraphernalia, uses, consequences)

- Pleasure, gratification, or relief from setting fires, or when witnessing or participating in their aftermath

- The firesetting is not done for monetary gain, as an expression of sociopolitical ideology, to conceal criminal activity, to express anger or vengeance, to improve one's living circumstances, in response to a delusion of hallucination, or as the result of impaired judgment (e.g., dementia, mental retardation, substance intoxication)

- The firesetting is not better accounted for by conduct disorder, a manic episode, or antisocial personality disorder (APA, *DSM-IV-TR*, 2000, p. 671)

Pyromania is a rare disorder occurring most often in males with learning difficulties and poor social skills. Pyromaniacs are fascinated with fire and experience release of tension, feelings of relief, and pleasure during or following the act of firesetting (Doley, 2003). A popular belief is that serial arsonists are pyromaniacs; however, evidence shows that this is not the case and true pyromania is an extremely rare phenomenon (Doley, 2003). Most fires that may appear to be set for the offender's satisfaction are more likely to be committed by juveniles with other disorders such as conduct disorder, attention-deficit/hyperactivity disorder, or adjustment disorder. In fact, pyromania is the least frequent diagnosis for firesetters, who are more likely to be diagnosed with conduct disorder (in children), antisocial personality disorder (in adults), or schizophrenia, mood disorder, mental retardation, or organic psychosis (Fritzon, 2000).

Some research attention has been given to the link between arson and sexual arousal. Focus on the sexual motives of firesetting originated in psychodynamic explanations of arson. Freud hypothesized that firesetting is connected to bedwetting and that setting fires represents a symbolic masturbation for the offender. Studies of juvenile firesetters have provided some support for this theory, and comprehensive review of research over the past 80 years has produced mixed findings. However, recent empirical research largely discredits the arson-sexual arousal theory (Fritzon, 2000). There are no data to support claims that sexual motivation is commonly involved in arson (Brett, 2004), and it appears that sexually motivated acts of arson are as rare, if not more so, than the true pyromaniac (Doley, 2003).

Recent research has compared arsonists with violent and property offenders. The results show that arsonists have a greater similarity to property offenders in personality, offense history, and sexual behavior (Brett, 2004). Other research shows that, although few child firesetters grow up to be adult arsonists, most adult arsonists began setting fires in childhood (Fritzon, 2000). Studies on child firesetters offer conflicting views—children set fires as a natural consequence of difficult progression through a developmental stage or as a result of environmental and family stressors. Studies show that adult firesetters are more socially isolated, less likely to be physically aggressive, and have more extensive psychiatric histories than other mentally disordered offenders (Fritzon, 2000).

Market-Based Offenses

Market-based crimes involve the consensual market exchange of illegal goods and services resulting in the illegal earning of a new income. Market-based offenses are primarily committed by groups ranging in complexity and sophistication from loosely organized gangs to organized crime networks. Crimes such as drug trafficking, prostitution, gambling, black market chains, fencing, criminal receiving, and the purchase, distribution, and resale portion of auto theft rings (e.g., the Astra Motor Cars example) are market-based crimes. Market-based crimes involve

- Production and/or distribution of goods and services that are inherently illegal
- Exchanges involving producers, distributors, money managers, and retailers on the supply end and willing consumers on the demand end
- An underground network
- Voluntary transfers
- Difficulty defining a victim other than "society"
- Income earned by suppliers
- An implicit notion of fair market value
- Transfers that take place primarily in cash
- Ambiguous morality subject to change (Naylor, 2003)

Market-based crime consists of both black market and hidden economy crimes, which differ in that the former involves the sale of prohibited items, activities, or services (e.g., drugs, gambling, prostitution) and the latter involves distribution and resale of illegally obtained, but otherwise legal, property. *Black market prices are much higher for inherently illegal goods and services* than they would be if the goods and services were legal. *In the hidden economy system, prices for illegally obtained goods are much lower.* The primary difference is in the nature of the contraband or property. *Relative contraband* are goods and services that are illegally obtained or legal in one place or situation but not another. *Absolute contraband* are goods and services that are illegal. *Fiscal contraband* involves tax evasion where the gains to the seller of goods and services are savings in taxes. So, for example, underground gambling (gambling in establishments that haven't paid the proper tax and licenses) would be relative contraband in Las Vegas, where gambling is not prohibited (a hidden economy offense), but in areas that ban gambling completely it would be absolute contraband (a black market offense). Market-based crimes can be divided into those involving evasion of regulations, taxes, and prohibitions, but the *norm for all market-based offenses is consensual market exchange* (Naylor, 2003).

The line between predatory and market-based crime is sometimes hazy. Predatory crimes such as burglary and theft often require market-based crimes (fencing, money laundering) to dispose of merchandise and to launder the money. The primary act in this case is predatory and market-based crime is a secondary aid in the involuntarily transfer of wealth. Market-based crimes can involve force (drug dealers settling accounts at gunpoint) or fraud (dealers altering merchandise before sale or conning customers). And although all market-based offenses operate underground, they often involve partial use of (or may be hidden within) legitimate businesses when illegal merchandise (knowingly or unknowingly) ends up for sale in a legitimate business.[18]

Manufacture, Distribution, and Sale of Stolen Goods

Most burglary and larceny-theft goes beyond an individual stealing a single item for its own sake (e.g., someone stealing a jacket, or a pair of shoes, or a car because he or she wants to own it). Street-level economic crime requires an outlet to sell stolen property. Offenders who provide this outlet are generally referred to as *fences* or *criminal receivers*. In 2005, there were 133,856 arrests for buying, receiving, or possessing stolen property (UCR, 2005). Offenders who purchase (and in some cases resell) stolen goods can be viewed on a continuum from the *professional fence,* who operates as a middleman to purchase and redistribute stolen goods in large-scale theft operations, to the *amateur receiver,* who is an ordinary person in a legitimate job who (knowingly or unknowingly) purchases stolen goods for personal consumption. As a result of the nature of this offense, the actual number of offenders who engage in buying, selling, and receiving stolen property is largely unknown.

The term *fence* has appeared in common language for over 200 years and refers to a professional dealer in stolen property. Klockars (1974), author of the classic work *The Professional Fence*, writes,

> First, the fence must be a *dealer* in stolen property; that is a buyer and seller with direct contact with thieves (sellers) and customers (buyers), not simply a member of a burglary gang charged with selling what is stolen, nor a thief hustling his own swag, nor an "in-between man" or a "piece man" trading on his knowledge of where certain types of property can be sold. Second, the fence must be *successful:* he must buy and sell stolen property regularly and profitably, and have done so for a considerable period of time, perhaps years. Third, the fence must be *public:* he must acquire a reputation as a successful dealer in stolen property among law breakers, law enforcers, and others acquainted with the criminal community. He must arrive at a way of managing the full significance of that reputation. (p. 172)

More recent research has focused on the range of offenders involved in the criminal receiving process and the role of criminal receiving more generally as it relates to the perpetuation and proliferation of property crime.

Economic crimes occur, in part, because there is a market for stolen goods. The criminal receiver can be viewed as a marketing mechanism (Walsh, 1977, p. 39). If burglars and thieves could not sell the items they steal, there would be little incentive to commit most forms of economic crime. Figure 7.3 shows the role of criminal receiving in property crime.

Professional fences tend to prefer to deal with professional thieves and not with juvenile property offenders or drug users, so much of the distribution and sale of stolen goods involves ordinary citizens who buy stolen property for their own use or to sell in legitimate businesses. A study by Cromwell, Olsen, and Avary (1996) found that over half of nonprofessional receivers are legitimate business owners who engage in fencing as a part-time enterprise to stretch the dollar or as a means of economic survival in communities that rely on an informal or "hidden" economy (Henry, 1978). These nonprofessional receivers view purchasing stolen property as a victimless crime and are able to dissociate themselves from the "theft" and "victim" aspects of the offense (Cromwell, Olsen, & Avary, 1996).

❖ **Figure 7.3** The Role of Criminal Receiving in Property Crime

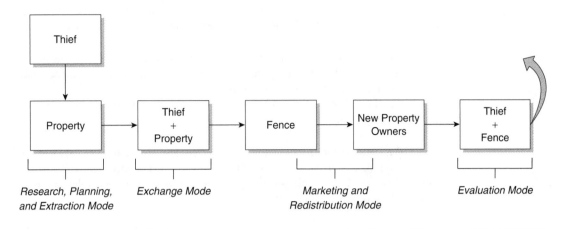

Source: Adapted from Walsh (1977).

Receivers are a heterogeneous group who, even more than shoplifters, are able to neutralize their behavior because they commit the crime at a distance. Receivers range from professional criminals with ties to organized crime to everyday people who buy stolen goods for personal consumption. Because fences and nonprofessional receivers are not the ones who engage in the *predatory* act of *planning* the offense and *extracting* the stolen item(s), they are able to easily rationalize or neutralize their behavior. As an informant in Cromwell, Olsen, and Avary's (1996) study who purchased a stolen VCR said,

> O.K., it's maybe too good a deal to be completely honest. I asked him if it was stolen and he said, "No," and I took his word for it. That's all I can do. I don't want to know either. (p. 51)

Cromwell, Olsen, and Avary (1996) propose a typology of receivers differentiated by the frequency with which they purchase stolen property, scale or volume of purchases, purpose of purchase (resale versus personal consumption), and level of commitment to purchasing stolen property. The typology includes the following six types of receivers:

1. *Professional fences*—High-frequency, high-volume purchase of stolen goods for resale with commitment to receiving as a primary occupation; may be involved in legitimate business as a front, but principle business is buying and selling stolen merchandise.

2. *Part-time fences*—Low-volume, low-frequency purchase of stolen goods. There are two types of part-time fences: (1) the *passive receiver,* who purchases the stolen item for personal use, and the *proactive receiver,* who buys for resale only, but on a smaller scale than the professional fence and does not depend on fencing as a sole source of income.

3. *Associational fences*—Legitimate occupational status puts in close association or interaction with thieves (e.g., defense attorneys, police officers, bail bond agents). These individuals "receive" stolen items as payment for professional services. In many cases, the fencing is justified by the view that their clients may have no other way to pay for their services.

4. *Neighborhood hustlers*—Engage in fencing as part of a lifestyle of "hustling," including small-time crimes and confidence games. These individuals may engage in many types of crimes and may act as a burglar, a fence, or a middleman (connecting the thieves to the fence) and purchase stolen goods for personal consumption and resale depending on the item and need.

5. *Drug-dealers* (who barter drugs for stolen property)—Take stolen items as payment for drugs and reselling to make a larger profit. Thieves who steal items to purchase drugs often go this route because, although they receive a lower price for the stolen goods, it is a time-efficient way to obtain drugs.

6. *Amateurs*—Purchase stolen items for personal consumption. There are two types of amateur fences: (1) strangers approached by the thief in a public setting who buy items for personal consumption, trying to take advantage of a deal, and (2) individuals with whom the thief has developed an ongoing relationship to sell items for personal use. Some amateur fences eventually become part-time fences as a result of the lure of financial gains and absence of sanctions.

Most stolen property is purchased by nonprofessional fences. Cromwell, Olsen, and Avary (1996) found that only 27% of stolen property is sold to professional fences. Thus, the bulk of criminal receivers are everyday people engaged in legitimate business who buy, sell, or barter in stolen goods on the side, drug dealers who fence as a form of bartering to enhance their drug dealing business, small-time criminals who dabble in whatever criminal opportunity presents itself, or otherwise law-abiding people trying to get a good price on items for personal consumption.

Most buying and selling of stolen goods is committed by nonprofessional receivers involved in a cultural network of *hidden economy trading* (Henry, 1978). Hidden economy trading is a "genuinely different phenomenon from either normal trade or normal crime" (p. 79), involving ordinary people in honest jobs who illicitly buy and sell cheap (usually stolen) goods. Hidden economy trading differs from black marketeering in that goods are sold for a lower (rather than higher) price in an environment of materialism rather than deprivation.[19] What is unique about nonprofessional receiving is that, although both professional and nonprofessional criminal receiving provide a market for stolen goods that instigates and perpetuates property crime, nonprofessional receivers do not view themselves as criminal and easily justify and excuse their behavior. An informant in Henry's (1978) study of property crimes committed by ordinary people said,

> You know you can talk a lot about what is legal and what isn't. To my mind this [receiving] is probably technically illegal. Morally it isn't because nobody is making money out of it . . . not real money. Well, alright, the person who's receiving the goods is saving money if you like, but he's not actually making anything. He's not going out selling the stuff . . . hawking it around, making a profit on it, not in actual money. And the bloke who

is selling, he's not making much out of it. He's getting favours more than anything. It's not a business . . . or a shady business deal as such. It's sort of a community action group. . . . it doesn't get any worse or any more rampant. It works well . . . very well, and it helps the people a lot. You know, from that point of view it is just not immoral. . . . I think in fact it's very, very moral. I think it's a good thing. (p. 78)

Another aspect of nonprofessional receiving is important to note. Although on the surface the motive for unprofessional receivers appears to be economic (getting a good price on a particular item), amateur receivers receive social rewards for engaging in the behavior. Depending on the circumstance, nonprofessional receivers enjoy the reciprocity and exchange within the trading network and feeling like they are involved in something "special." One receiver who purchased stolen cigarettes reflected on the experience, "It's not just because you got them cheap. There's something special about them. Somewhere along the line they've become special cigarettes" (Henry, 1978, p. 93).

Criminal receiving operates, then, within a context a social relations and fencing networks. *Fencing networks* are systems of relationships and functions that develop between producers or marketers in the theft and disposal of stolen goods. Walsh (1977) identifies three distinct types of fencing networks:

1. *Kinship network*—links consisting of familial relationships between thieves and receivers where manufacture, sale, and distribution of stolen goods are a family business

2. *Work-a-day network*—links established through a legitimate employer-employee relationship where the employee is a known thief or burglar and the employer acts as the receiver

3. *Play network*—links involving elite burglars and criminal entrepreneurs who connect through a recreational setting such as a private social club or association. Individuals within these networks acknowledge crime as their profession, are proud of and financially comfortable with it, and identify recreationally as a successful criminal.

These networks are sometimes interlinked to form *supranetworks* that constitute unique relationships between thieves, fences, and particular organizations and businesses. These fencing networks and the relationships among them enable and perpetuate economic crime. "There may be a little larceny in the heart of every man, but it is unlikely to be acted upon without the help, encouragement, and reinforcement of like-minded individuals. Neither is it likely to be as systematized, as rational or as 'safe' as that perpetuated by the fencing network" (Walsh, 1977, p. 146).

Drug Trafficking, Prostitution, Gambling, and Organized Crime

Drug trafficking, gambling, and prostitution can be considered both market-based and public order crime. *The sale and distribution component of drug offenses, prostitution, and gambling are market-based crimes.*[20] The perpetrators of market-based crimes range from loosely organized groups or gangs to *organized crime networks*. Most of the activities of organized crime networks (such as gambling, prostitution, drug distribution, and loan sharking) involve providing illegal services to individuals pursuing prohibited pleasures or people in financial need (Gabor, 1994). Drug trafficking and illegal gambling are also market-based offenses because the offenders obtain financial gain from distributing and selling illegal goods and services. Drug trafficking and underground gambling operations generally involve a black market network operated by groups ranging from small gangs to organized crime groups with links to prison gangs and governmental agencies.[21]

Historically, organized crime has been difficult to define (Abidinsky, 1985; Friedrich, 2004; Kennedy & Finckenauer, 1995). "There appear to be as many descriptions of organized crime as there are authors" (Albanese, 2000, p. 410). One of the major problems in defining organized crime is that it cannot be defined by criminal acts alone. Organized crime is not a criminal behavior; rather, the concept describes the nature and level of sophistication of the group to which individual offenders belong. The phenomenon (in both popular culture and scholarly discourse) is defined in terms of the attributes and characteristics of the offenders engaged in organized criminal behavior and the features or level of organization of the group to which the offenders belong. Albanese (2000) offers a definition of organized crime based on a consensus of researchers over the past 30 years:

> Organized crime is a continuing criminal enterprise that rationally works to profit from illicit activities; its continuing existence is maintained through the use of force, threats, monopoly control, and/or the corruption of public officials. (p. 411)

Organized crime is not considered here as a distinct crime category because the concept refers more to the level of sophistication of the group to which offenders belong than to the nature of the criminal behavior. With the focus on market-based economic crime, whether the group involved in the behavior is highly sophisticated (and organized) or a lower-level loosely organized street gang is less important than the nature of the offense itself.

Theories of organized crime include the alien conspiracy theory, cultural transmission theory, and enterprise theory. *Alien conspiracy theory* contends that organized crime is caused by a particular group of alien foreigners who invaded and infiltrated a law-abiding America, forming a structured, secretive, and nationwide criminal organization. This theory, which is now referred to as the *Mafia myth*, has little empirical support. *Cultural transmission theory* suggests that organized crime is a result of subcultural groups with shared norms, values, and beliefs that conflict with those of the larger culture. Organized crime is a product of cultural transmission and differential association. People engage in organized crime because they live in close proximity to areas where significant gambling, prostitution, drug trafficking, loan sharking, and so on occur and are exposed to a prevailing atmosphere of disregard and contempt for the law. *Enterprise theory* suggests that organized crime is the product of a legitimate marketplace that leaves certain populations unserved or unsatisfied. This creates an opportunity for a sprectrum of economic activities or enterprises including certain kinds of crime and legitimate businesses. New laws (e.g., prohibition, drug laws, gambling laws, etc.) that create a category of illegal goods and services open up illicit opportunities that reinforce and are reinforced by organized crime networks (Kennedy & Finckenauer, 1995).

Organized crime groups rationally work to profit from illegal activities that are in public demand. Organized crime activity falls into three categories:

- *Provision of illicit services*—attempts to satisfy the public demand for sex, money, gambling, or other service society does not fulfill

- *Provision of illicit goods*—attempts to satisfy the public demand for products that cannot be obtained through legal channels such as drugs and stolen property

- *Infiltration of legitimate business*—uses legitimate business to obtain money such as labor racketeering and takeover of waste disposal companies (Albanese, Parker, & Chapman, 2002)

The relationship between organized crime activity and market-based crime can best be explained by enterprise theory. It is commonly known that organized crime in America got its roots in the Prohibition era. High demand for illegal goods (alcohol) created an illegal market dominated by bootleggers turned organized criminals. A high level of demand for a particular good (drugs) or service (prostitution, gambling) combined with high profit and low risk of arrest to provide "ideal conditions for illicit business groups to enter the market to seek profits by organizing the supply" (Lodhi & Vaz, 1980, p. 145, cited in Kennedy & Finckenauer, 1995, p. 41). The nature of market-based crime lies primarily in the relationship between the offending group and the marketplace. A group of motivated offenders and the opportunity provided by a marketplace that restricts or underprovides certain goods and services is prime grounds for market-based crime. So, the nature of market-based crime is not the type of good or service at the heart of the enterprise, but rather the process by which the good or service is acquired, marketed, and distributed. According to Albanese (2000), "The precise type of crime or product is not as important as the use of illegal means for its use, acquisition, or exploitation" (p. 414). Upon deciding to engage in market-based crime and determining who the co-conspirators will be, offenders must decide what they will market:

> What products or services? To whom? Is there an existing demand for this product or service that is not being met, either in whole or in part? Can a demand be created or expanded? What is the competition? What is the territory? What are the risks and how can they be controlled? . . . Where will the investment capital come from? What about raw materials, supply, and distribution? . . . How will the profits be handled? Should they be laundered? Reinvested? Or invested in legitimate businesses? (Kennedy & Finckenauer, 1995, p. 44)

These decisions must be made to complete a successful criminal enterprise and lie at the heart of market-based crime.

Market-based offenses such as prostitution, drug trafficking, loan sharking, bootlegging, and sports fixing have come to be associated with what is known as organized crime (Kennedy & Finckenauer, 1995). However, rather than defining organized crime by explaining the types of behavior group members commit, market-based economic crime can be explained by examining what it is about organized crime that facilitates market-based criminal behavior. In other words, though market-based crime is a feature of most definitions of organized crime, the focus here is on organized crime as a feature of market-based offenses. Maltz (1976) offers a typology of organized crime consisting of six means by which organized crimes are committed: violence, theft, corruption, economic coercion, deception, and victim participation (taking advantage of people who want to purchase illicit goods and services; see Kennedy & Finckenauer, 1995). These criminal means span the range of economic crimes consisting of predatory, market-based, and commercial offenses and other major categories of crime (violent, public order, political). Thus, market-based offenses are one type of criminal enterprise in which organized criminals are involved. However, market-based offenses *rely* on a network structure organized crime groups provide.

Prostitution is one of the more difficult crimes to classify in a criminal behavior typology. Prostitution can be viewed as human trafficking, in which case it is an economic (or in some cases violent) crime in which the offenders are the "pimps" or human traffickers and the victims are the prostitutes. Viewed as the manufacture, distribution, and sale of an illegal service, where the offender is the prostitute, who obtains financial gain from selling an illegal service, prostitution is best defined as an economic crime.[22] Prostitution can also be viewed as a crime against public order, a crime with no clear victim or offender in which the behavior has simply been defined as criminal based on a history of legislating morality. Prostitution, like gambling, and drug trafficking, is simply a means through which market-based crime can occur because it is prohibited by law in most states. Whenever there is a good or service that the public wants and they can't get or can't get enough of (legally), market-based crime will occur and be supported by organized (and loosely organized) groups of individuals.

The work of Peter Reuter (1985, 2004), author of *Disorganized Crime: Illegal Markets and the Mafia*, explains the inherent connections between market-based crime and organized criminal groups in the United States and transnationally. Others further highlight the importance of social network analysis and state economic failure in understanding transnational organized crime (Bibes, 2001; Block & Griffin, 2002; Sung, 2004). There are particular circumstances under which some gangs acquire the defining characteristics of organized crime. From Reuter's perspective, adult gangs are primarily instrumental—they exist solely for economic purposes. There are many gangs in American cities, but only certain conditions will produce organized crime. These conditions are determined by supply and demand. Factors that affect the extent of organized crime include illegal market opportunities, the extent of recent migration of ethnic groups into the community, providing a recruiting base for organized crime, and the strength and corruptness of local government (Kennedy & Finckenauer, 1995). Violence and the threat of violence is a secondary tool that enables organized crime groups to form cartels incorporating many businesses and organizations and extort other entrepreneurs. This view of organized crime offers a broad theoretical framework that highlights the interconnections and interdependencies between market-based and organized crime.

Albanese (2000) asks, "Do criminals organize around opportunities for crime . . . or do criminal opportunities create new offenders?"(p. 410); he proposes a model for understanding the relationship between criminal opportunities, criminal environment, and skills necessary to carry out organized criminal behavior. Criminal opportunities include easy access types (illicit goods and services that are in high public demand such as gambling, pornography, and narcotics) and new types made possible by social or technological change such as the Internet, cell phones, or companies and banks for money laundering. Opportunity factors include economic conditions, governmental regulation, demand for a product or service, enforcement effectiveness, and new product or service opportunities. Based on the work of Reuter, Albanese, and others, clearly *the market place provides the means through which organized crime groups form and flourish, and organized crime groups facilitate and perpetuate market-based crime.* Large-scale drug trafficking, prostitution, illegal gambling, and other market-based criminal operations would not exist without organized criminals, and organized crime would not exist without the market-based need for illegal or illegally obtained goods and services.

Commercial Offenses

Commercial offenses are crimes committed by otherwise legitimate investors, entrepreneurs, and corporations. Commercial crimes involve

- Production/distribution of inherently legal goods and services using illegal methods
- Multilateral exchanges that seem voluntary, but include a fraudulent and thus involuntary aspect
- A normal business setting
- Identifiable victims
- Unmerited and illegally obtained earned income
- Income transfers through normal banking instruments
- Notion of unfair market value
- Unambiguous morality (in theory), since behavior involves fraud, which is clearly illegal
- Need for restitution/compensation (Naylor, 2003)

Crimes that fall under the heading of commercial offenses include bankruptcy fraud, consumer fraud, illegal dumping of toxic waste, violations of antitrust laws, price fixing, and false advertising. Much, if not all, commercial crime can be seen as a form of "elite deviance" involving acts of economic domination (Simon, 1996).

With commercial crime, it is often difficult to determine whether a crime has been committed and where the line is drawn between a shrewd business practice and fraud. The terms *white-collar crime, corporate crime,* and *enterprise crime*[23] are sometimes used to refer to commercial offenses. The distinction here is that some offenses that can be viewed as white collar are actually predatory offenses (embezzlement, occupational fraud). In contrast, *the corporation or business is the offender, not the victim,* in commercial crime, and the basic act committed is legal market sales using fraudulent methods to increase profit.

Commercial crime can be distinguished from predatory and market-based crime in that income is legally earned but illegally redistributed. In other words, it is a way of committing crime without engaging in an overt illegal act involving illegal goods and services. In fact, when asked to reflect on his life as a mobster and swindler, notorious organized crime leader Charles "Lucky" Luciano confessed that, if he could change just one thing, it would be to "do it legal." He said, "I learned too late that you need just as good a brain to make a crooked million as an honest million. These days, you apply for a license to steal from the public," Luciano said. "If I had my time again, I'd make sure I got that license first" (from Robert Lacey, *Little Man: Meyer Lansky and the Gangster Life,* 1991, p. 405, cited in State of New York, 1997).

Lucky Luciano is not the only one to recognize the crime committed by corporations and the difficulty in controlling it. In 1979, a survey of the American public showed that big business was next to Congress as one of the least trusted institutions. From the launching of the consumer movement by Ralph Nader to the Ford Pinto case in the 1970s to the more recent corporate scandals such as Enron and Martha Stewart's conviction for insider trading, the public has been aware of and concerned about crime committed by corporations (Box 7.4).

BOX 7.4

CORPORATE SCANDALS

A sign advertising a humorous website is pasted on the ENRON sign at the entrance of their headquarters in Houston, Texas, January 26, 2002.

Photo credit: © Hector Mata/Getty Images.

If you mention the words "corporate scandal" in the United States, most people think "Enron." The collapse of Enron, the second largest bankruptcy in U.S. history, resulted in thousands of employees losing their 401(k) life savings plans, which were tied to the energy company's stock.

Enron is an energy trading and communications company based in Houston, Texas. The company, formed in 1985 by Houston Natural Gas CEO Kenneth Lay through the merger of Houston Natural Gas and InterNorth, was originally involved in the transmission and distribution of gas and electricity across the United States and construction and operation of pipelines and power plants worldwide. The company expanded, becoming involved in commodities trading and broadband services and launching Enron Online, which generated over 90% of its income. Enron was named "America's Most Innovative Company" for four years from 1996 through 2000, was on *Fortune*'s list of "100 Best Companies to Work for in America" in 2000, and (as a result of fraudulent accounting) was listed as the seventh largest company in the United States before its demise. The Securities and Exchange Commission launched an investigation into the company and, in November 2001, the company announced it had overstated its earnings since 1997 by about $600 million. After a series of scandals involving irregular accounting procedures by the company's accounting firm, Arthur Andersen, Enron's stock plunged from $85 per share to 30 cents per share. Enron employed 21,000 people at the time of its bankruptcy in 2001. Following the company's bankruptcy, Enron CEO Ken Ley resigned and was charged with 11 counts including securities and wire fraud and making false statements. Arthur Andersen was charged and given the maximum sentence ($500,000 fine and 5 years probation) for obstruction of justice after shredding Enron documents. Former Enron CFO Andrew Fastow was charged with 98 counts including fraud and money laundering and eventually pled guilty to conspiracy to commit wire fraud and securities fraud, receiving a 10-year sentence. His wife, also charged, pled guilty to filing false tax forms and received a one-year prison term. As of January 2004, at least 14 Enron employees and executives had been indicted and seven pled guilty, and former Enron Vice President Clifford Baxter committed suicide in 2002 after making $22 million cashing in on Enron stock options before the stock dropped (Burke & Barnhart, 2002).

The Enron downfall was the result of "individual and collective greed born in an atmosphere of market euphoria and corporate arrogance" (Thomas, 2002). But apparently Enron is not a bizarre corporate anomaly. The Enron scandal was followed by a string of corporate scandal in 2002 (see Patsuris, 2002):

- *WorldCom* (formerly MCI)—Overstated cash flow by booking $3.8 billion in operating expenses as capital expenses and gave founder Bernard Ebbers off-the-books loans of $400 million. Publicized the $120 billion + merger between WorldCom and Sprint that never came to be and reaped benefits of fictitious profits. The investigation uncovered over $11 billion in accounting fraud. Ebbers was charged with securities fraud, making false statements to the U.S. Securities and Exchange Commission, and conspiracy resulting in the largest bankruptcy in U.S. history, with 25,000 WorldCom employees losing their jobs and huge investor losses.
- *Halliburton*—Improperly booked $100 million in construction cost overruns. An accounting fraud lawsuit was filed by Judicial Watch, a legal watchdog group, against the company and its CEO, Vice President Dick Cheney.
- *Kmart*—People claiming to be Kmart employees sent anonymous letters accusing the company of misleading investors about its financial health. The company was in the process of bankruptcy.
- *Global Crossing*—Shredded documents of accounting practices and engaged in "network capacity swaps" with other carriers to inflate revenue. The company filed for Chapter 11 bankruptcy.
- *Bristol-Myers Squibb*—Inflated revenue in 2001 by $1.5 billion by forcing wholesalers to accept more inventory than they could sell to get the products off the manufacturer's books.
- *AOL Time Warner*—Inflated sales by booking barter deals. After being ordered to preserve the documents, the company stated that it may have overestimated revenue by $49 million.
- *Adelphia Communications*—$3.1 billion in off-balance-sheet loans were given to the Rigas family, founders of the company, who inflated capital expenses and hid the debt. Three Rigas family members and two executives were arrested for fraud and the company sued the Rigas family for $1 billion for breach of fiduciary duties.

Corporate crime costs U.S. consumers an estimated $200 billion per year. This is approximately 40 times more than the losses from street crime; however, only 2% of corporate crime cases result in imprisonment (Simon, 1996). The following are examples of some of the most prevalent types of commercial crimes.

Consumer Fraud

Consumer fraud has occurred throughout the Western world since the first century AD in ancient Rome. Some even suggest that America's founding fathers engaged in various forms of fraudulent activities involving land. Today, there are many types of consumer fraud including stock market swindles, phony contests and lotteries, sales of useless merchandise and services, get-rich-quick scams, land swindles, medical quackery, weight-loss gimmicks, work-at-home scams, magazine subscription rackets, travel deceptions, charity scams, tax preparation shysters, bogus employment agencies, referral schemes, fraudulent contractors, deceptive credit offerings, credit repair scams, fraudulent sweepstakes and prize offerings, Nigerian money offers, and pyramids and multilevel marketing rip-offs. These various swindles and scams are committed by *contrepreneurs* (a term used in the literature to refer to white-collar cons) in small businesses or larger corporations who carry out swindles by appearing to be engaged in legitimate business.

Consumer fraud can occur through many methods. These scams are often operated through mail-order, telemarketing, and the Internet (technology's role in shaping consumer fraud is discussed in Chapter 10). These businesses prey on vulnerable victims—the elderly, people in unfortunate financial situations—human fantasy (phone sex scams), vanity (useless wrinkle creams or hair loss products), loneliness (phony Internet dating services), insecurity and fear (worthless home security gadgets) (Friedrichs, 2004). The following are some common examples of consumer fraud:

- *Home loan and equity fraud*—This type of consumer fraud is often referred to a *predatory lending*. It has become an enormous problem in the United States, resulting in people losing their homes and investments. Companies that engage in predatory lending work with appraisers and mortgage brokers to sell property for more than it's worth using phony appraisals, encourage borrowers to lie about their income and assets to get loans, knowingly lend more money than the borrower can afford to pay, charge high interest rates based on borrowers' race or national origin and not their credit history, pressure borrowers to accept high-risk loans, target vulnerable borrowers for equity loans or cash-out refinances, strip homeowners of their equity by convincing them to refinance again and again, and use high pressure sales tactics to sell loans, home improvement projects, or homeowners insurance, and then finance at high interest rates.

- *Home improvement fraud*—A large amount of consumer fraud is committed by contractors who are either outright con artists or bilk victims by doing shoddy or incomplete work. Fraudulent contractors prey on homeowners who are not knowledgeable about the work they are doing. Some will knock on people's doors to tell them they are doing inspections (e.g., on a furnace, or plumbing) and then report a large amount of work that has to be done at a high cost. Other types of contractor fraud are failing to complete a job after being compensated, purchasing/using inferior quality materials (and lying about it to the homeowner), and doing/charging for unnecessary work.

- *Time-share vacation resorts*—This type of fraud usually involves a phone call from someone saying the victim has "won" a trip to Disneyland or Disneyworld, Hawaii, Florida, or Las Vegas. If the "offer" is accepted, the free vacation will turn out to have all sorts of restrictions attached, including purchasing a travel club membership or buying into a time-share resort. In the end, victims commit themselves to expensive time-share plans that do not deliver as promised, the "free" vacation costs much more than it otherwise would have, or the free trip has so many restrictions that it's never used at all or, in some cases, is never awarded.

- *Educational scholarship and financial aid scams*—With the high cost of education and competition in getting into colleges and universities, there has been a rise in unscrupulous companies falsely guaranteeing or promising scholarships, grants, and other financial aid for a fee. Generally, little or none of the promised assistance is awarded. These companies inflate or misrepresent the amount they will award and often claim that they are the only ones who can award such a high amount or they may entice victims by saying they are finalists for a scholarship contest. Other educational scams involve companies falsely claiming to ensure placement in a particular school for a fee, or charging for bogus degrees.

- *Medicare fraud*—Medicare fraud is committed by companies (and sometimes individuals) in the medical field that falsely bill for services not furnished or not furnished as billed, misrepresent diagnoses to justify payments, overbill, or falsify certificates of medical necessity to justify payment. Examples are an ambulance company billing for nonemergency transports of patients who could travel by different means, hospitals making arrangements with private laboratories to do (and charge Medicare for) unnecessary lab tests, or medical supply companies billing for phony or inferior products (and charging for genuine ones) such as orthotic or prosthetic devices.

These are just a handful of the many types of consumer fraud in operation today. The common feature of all types of consumer fraud is that they are attempts by businesses and corporations to engage in legal market sales using fraudulent methods to increase profit.

Investment and Securities Fraud

Investment fraud is a type of consumer fraud, but rather than selling merchandise or services, it involves using fraudulent practices to sell securities and investments. Investment fraud involves companies that make fraudulent claims and misrepresentations to sell stocks, bonds, and commodities. More than half of all consumer dollar injury reported is the result of investment fraud. The average loss from investment fraud is over $15,000, with losses as high as hundreds of thousands of dollars for a single consumer. Like other types of consumer fraud, the targets of investment fraud are often the elderly who are past the income-earning years and looking for ways to increase their assets. Investment fraudsters use aggressive marketing strategies such as telemarketing or infomercials with "success stories" of real investors to advertise the fraudulent investments. In just two cases challenged by the Federal Trade Commission, the offenders took more than $100 million from thousands of consumers who were effectively lured by advertising campaigns on several national cable stations (Federal Trade Commission, n.d.). It is estimated that Americans lose over $2 billion annually as a result of investment fraud (Friedrichs, 2004).

Much of the losses from investment fraud are a result of the fraudulent sale of *penny stock,* also referred to as *microcap stock*—low-priced stock that typically sells for less than one dollar per share. Companies will sell the stock through a series of gross misrepresentations, use insiders to "pump up" the stock price, and then "dump" or sell the stock at its peak. From the 1940s to the 1970s, fraudulent sale of penny stocks was primarily confined to the western United States. In the 1940s, worthless shares of gold and silver mining stocks were sold to unsuspecting investors. In the early 1980s, brokerage firms specializing in penny stocks increased dramatically and spread across the country. Fraud and abuse in the penny stock market became rampant in the late 1980s, with penny stock companies targeting unsophisticated and first-time investors through major telemarketing campaigns (State of New York Attorney General, 1997).

Another common form of investment fraud is the *pyramid scheme.* Companies involved in pyramid schemes often call themselves *multilevel marketing operations* and can be disguised as motivational companies, buying clubs, mail-order operations, or investment groups. A typical pyramid scheme involves a small group of individuals on top who recruit participants, who in turn, recruit other participants, who contribute money to the organization. Recruits are told they will eventually earn large sums of money if they successfully recruit others to join (and pay into) the company. Usually there is no legitimate product being sold, though some companies, particularly those that refer to themselves as multilevel marketing operations, will involve selling some sort of product. Pyramid schemes are illegal because they are deceptive. They eventually collapse because it is mathematically impossible to recruit enough people to sustain the pyramid (a nine-level pyramid built when each participant gets six people to join would involve over 10 million people), the odds of actually earning anything are slim to none, and in the end many losers pay a few winners.

As a result of high-profile cases in recent years, including the Enron scandal in beginning in 2001 and the Martha Stewart scandal in 2003, *insider trading* has become one of the better-known forms of securities fraud.[24] In June 2003, Martha Stewart, CEO of Martha Stewart Living and Omnimedia, was indicted, along with her former stockbroker, Peter Bacanovic, in New York on charges of insider stock trading. Stewart was accused of selling 3,928 shares of stock in ImClone Systems, a biopharmaceutical company, for over $200,000 in 2001 after receiving an unlawful tip from Bacanovic—one day before the Food and Drug Administration rejected ImClone's application for a cancer drug. ImClone Systems stock plummeted immediately. Samuel Waksal, ImClone's

Photo 7.1   Martha Stewart holds up the poncho she wore when she left prison during a speech on March 7, 2005, in New York City to an audience of her employees and the media on her first day back to her offices after her release from prison. The poncho was made by a fellow inmate. Stewart was released from prison March 4, 2005.

Photo credit: © Stephen Chernin/Getty Images.

founder, pled guilty in 2002 to selling the stock before the FDA announcement. By selling the stock, Stewart and her companies avoided losses of $45,673. The Securities and Exchange Commission charged that both Stewart and Bacanovic lied to commission staff to try to cover up the crime by saying that they had planned, prior to receiving the tip, to sell the stock when it fell below $60 per share (U.S. Securities & Exchange Commission, 2003). In February 2004, the charge of securities fraud was dropped. On March 5, 2004, Stewart was found guilty of conspiracy, obstruction of justice, and two counts of making false statements. Both Stewart and Baconovic (also convicted) were sentenced to five months in prison, five months of home confinement, two years probation, and hefty fines ($30,000 for Stewart and $4,000 for Baconovic).

Is There an Underlying Theoretical Explanation for Economic Crime?

If it is homogeneous with respect to primary motive, what theoretical explanation best explains economic crime? With the range of subtypes of economic crime, does it make sense to think of economic crime in terms of a single meaningful crime category?

Rational Choice and Routine Activity Theory

Rational choice and routine activity theories have been the dominant theories applied to economic crime. From the routine activities perspective, crime occurs in the context of a willing offender, a suitable target, and the absence of guardians. Individuals, groups, and organizations who engage in economic crime base decisions about whether or not to commit crime on situational and opportunity factors and their perception of risk and gains associated with the offense. In contrast with violent or sex crime, *economic crime is largely instrumentally motivated. All economic crime involves some level of planning, purpose, and risk assessment, with resulting harm being economic loss to victims.* Some offenders obtain other forms of satisfaction by committing burglary, theft, or fraud (e.g., thrill, power/control) and/or appear to be expressively or spontaneously committed (e.g., arson, motor vehicle theft, shoplifting), but noninstrumental motives are secondary for most offenders who commit economic crimes.

This does not mean that economic offenders do not derive some emotional or personal benefit from committing economic crime. Katz's (1988) phenomenological theory of crime highlights the sensual, emotional, and personal meanings associated with criminal acts, including property offenses. For example, burglars sometimes defecate in the homes they burgle for no other reason than desecrating the property and insulting the victim. This is an act of power and humiliation that has little to do with the instrumental goal of economic gain. Although further research is needed to unravel the mysteries of this particular act and to determine the characteristics of offenders who engage in this behavior during the commission of a burglary, the thrill, power, of "fun" that is derived from leaving excrement behind for victims to discover is secondary to the act of burglary, which is a predatory economic crime involving involuntary transfer of wealth from victim to offender.[25]

Offenders are motivated to commit economic crime out of perceived need or greed, though the difference between the two is sometimes not clear. A teenager boy who burglarizes homes to obtain clothing and cash that others in his peer group have may appear greedy but feel needy. The employee who embezzles from her company because she's having personal financial difficulties and needs money to salvage her situation may appear greedy but feel needy. The homeless man who shoplifts a winter coat because he is cold obviously needs the coat. But the decision to commit the crime in each of these cases involves a decision-making process that requires a risk-benefit determination—for example, embezzling money is worth the risk and better than filing bankruptcy, stealing a coat is more advantageous than asking for one at a shelter or begging for money to buy one at a secondhand store. Regardless of whether the offense is predatory, market-based, or commercial, the essence of economic crime is that it is instrumentally motivated, shaped by opportunity factors, and involves risk-benefit determination even if the decision-making process has only a "bounded" rationality[26] based on the limited information available to the individuals or organizations committing the offense.

Another distinction between economic and other types of crime is that *economic crime is easy to cognitively neutralize.* Rational choice and free will theories of criminal behavior apply much more appropriately to economic crime than to violent and sex crimes that are shaped by much more complex emotional and developmental forces. It's less difficult to justify and excuse behavior that results in economic loss than behavior that results in physical harm. In other words, the "mental gymnastics" (Gabor, 1994, p. 167) necessary to commit a crime are less sophisticated in the case of economic crime. There are a number of obvious reasons for this. First, the materialism and greed that is so much a part of American culture offers a readily available justification for committing economic crime.[27] Second, though "victim blaming" in the case of violent offenses is highly controversial, this is not the case with economic crime. American culture puts high value on not being a "sucker." The "anybody that dumb deserves to be taken" mentality is alive and well to justify any burglar, robber, criminal receiver, occupational fraudster, or insider trader. Thus, the techniques of neutralization used to excuse economic crime are consistent with the values and beliefs of individualistic and capitalistic culture.

The literature categorizes the cognitive rationalizations of offenders as *justifications,* which are positive interpretations of behaviors ("it didn't hurt anyone"); *excuses,* which are defensive ("it was an accident"); *neutralizations,* which are explanations of future behavior; and *accounts,* which are explanations of past behavior (Friedrichs, 2004). Excuses involve admitting wrongdoing but denying responsibility, whereas justifications involve admitting the act but denying it is wrong. Techniques of neutralization are linguistic devices used to maintain a positive self-image despite conflicting evidence (criminal or deviant behavior; see Willott, Griffin, & Torrance, 2001). Research shows that average people use techniques of neutralization to engage in deviant behavior (e.g., cheating on college exams; see McCabe, 2003) and that white-collar offenders such as doctors engaging in Medicare fraud use rationalizations and justifications in much the same manner as convicted rapists (Jesilow, Pontell, & Geis, 1996).

A study by Willott, Griffin, and Torrance (2001) examined whether or not linguistic strategies offenders use are both constrained and facilitated by shared ways of speaking and looking at the world. The authors were specifically interested in how discourses of class and masculinity shape justifications and excuses of economic offenders. The study found that male economic offenders drew on the "man-as-bread-winner" discourse to account for their criminal behavior, though the more economically privileged (white-collar) offenders represented themselves as morally superior to both "real" criminals and criminal justice officials. Thus, male economic offenders' excuses and justifications are supported by cultural notions of masculinity (men as breadwinners) and class (professional elite risk takers).

Gabor (1994) argues that "criminality is merely an extension of everyday decision-making. . . . criminal activity represents a solution—occasionally a desperate and destructive one—to the perpetrator's problems or the attempt to achieve some fleeting objective" (pp. 237–238). Along these lines, economic crime can be viewed as an extension of everyday decision making that is much less a product of individual psychopathology or biological forces, and more the result of the confluence of personality, situations, and culture and of need, opportunity, skill, and attitudes favorable to criminal behavior. This does not mean that psychopaths or individuals with other mental disorders do not commit economic crime[28] or that personality or other psychological variables do not play a role in economic crime.[29] However, individualistic explanations of criminal behavior fall short of explaining crime that is understandable with goals (material wealth) closely connected to those of the larger society.

Is Economic Crime a Meaningful Crime Category?

A crucial question in discussing economic crime as a single crime category is whether or not the same theory or theories can explain all types of crime within the category. *Is economic crime a homogeneous crime category? Can burglary, theft, fraud, forgery, criminal receiving, identity theft, consumer fraud, securities fraud, illegal dumping, and insider trading be explained by the same theory? Is there a common feature shared by predatory, market-based, and commercial offenders that explains economic crime in some meaningful way?*

Researchers have historically disagreed on whether or not a general theory can explain both conventional property crimes and white-collar offenses. Some argue that only on a very high level of generality (such as the common motivation of the desire for personal gain) can one theory be applied to all times of economic crime. However, this level of generality does not advance understanding of the different patterns of involvement and complex circumstances that shape the many forms of economic crime (Friedrichs, 2004).

Economic crime is a general category of crime characterized by

- *Instrumental motivation*
- *Relatively simplistic (or "normal") cognitive neutralizations* supported by cultural norms and values rather than a product of psychopathology[30]
- *Modus operandi that involves some level of planning, purpose, and risk assessment*
- *Harm of economic loss to victims*

Within this broad category of crime are subcategories (predatory, market-based, and commercial) that further define the forms economic crime may take in terms of patterns and levels of involvement and context.

Returning to the Astra Motor Cars case presented at the beginning of this chapter, defining economic crime as a broad but distinct crime category offers a theoretical framework with which to make sense of the many forms of criminal behavior that occur in the world of large-scale crime rings organized for the purpose of economic gain. Naylor's typology of profit-driven crimes and distinctions between predatory, market-based, and commercial offenses help us isolate the primary force behind crimes such as auto theft. The world of auto theft is made up of predators, professional thieves and fraudsters, and occupational white-collar offenders that engage in auto theft for its own sake ("joyriders") or as part of an elaborate ring for larger economic gain ("jockeys") (Tremblay, Clermont, & Cusson, 1994). Naylor's model provides an understanding of the "modus operandi of the criminal economy" by deconstructing the criminal act into a series of constituents, chain of responsibility, and flow of command (Naylor, 2003, p. 99). In the Astra Motor Cars case, the auto thieves who originally stole the cars were engaged in predatory offenses driven by the market-based offense and facilitated and maintained by commercial outlets.

Summary

Economic crime involves a criminal act or acts resulting in financial loss and is centrally motivated by the desire to obtain financial reward. It can be understood broadly with Naylor's typology of profit-driven crime. This typology divides economic crime into three categories: predatory, market-based, and commercial offenses. Crimes such as burglary, arson, and occupational fraud are examples of predatory economic crime because they involve direct illegal transfer of wealth from one party to another. Market-based crimes such as criminal receiving and drug trafficking involve either a black market or hidden economy network made up of criminal groups ranging in sophistication from small-time gangs to organized crime networks. Commercial offenses are economic crimes committed by corporations involving fraudulent acts committed by legitimate businesses for economic gain. Economic crime can be committed by street-level or elite offenders and by individuals or groups who use a range of methods. The common feature of economic crime is that it is a primarily instrumentally motivated offense, facilitated by neutralization techniques and opportunity factors, that results in economic harm.

DISCUSSION QUESTIONS

1. It is suggested in this chapter that economic crime is a meaningful crime category that is homogeneous with respect to important elements. Define economic crime. What are the elements of economic crime? Discuss.

2. Explain Naylor's (2003) typology of economic crime and Walsh and Chappel's (2004) *stolen property system (SPS)* model. How do the works of Naylor and Walsh and Chappel help us better understand economic crime?

3. What differentiates economic crime from other criminal behaviors? Are there similarities in motivation and process that allow offenses committed by very different types of offenders to be understood within a single crime category such as "economic crime"? Can criminal acts such as burglary and theft (property crimes) be understood and explained within the same general domain as insurance fraud, securities fraud, intellectual property crime (business, commercial, corporate, or white-collar crime), drug trafficking, extortion, illegal distribution of goods and services (often discussed within the context of organized crime), prostitution, and gambling (public order crime)?

4. Is there a salient psychological process that underlies economic crime? What are the important variations between economic crime and other types of crime and within categories of economic crime? Are there offense themes that distinguish economic crime from violent, sex, public order, and other types of crime and distinguish among economic crime categories such as burglary, theft, arson, and fraud?

On Your Own: Log on to the Web-based student study site at http://www.sagepub.com/helfgottstudy/ for the URL links in the Web Exercises, study aids such as review quizzes, and research recommendations including links to journal articles specifically selected for this book.

WEB EXERCISES

1. Review the recent press releases of the *U.S. Securities and Exchange Commission:* http://www.sec.gov/news/press.shtml. Select a case that interests you, list and explain the crimes charged, and write a general summary of the case.

2. Go to *Reporting Economic Crime Online,* at https://www.recol.ca/fraudprevention.aspx, and review the different types of fraudulent scams. What are the recommendations for avoiding different types of scams?

3. Visit the Web site for the *Journal of Economic Crime Management:* http://www.jecm.org/. Read the articles in the current issue and discuss in class the latest research being conducted on economic crime.

4. The *PricewaterhouseCoopers Global Economic Crime Survey* reports results from many countries on the nature and extent of economic crime. Go to http://www.pwc.com/extweb/home.nsf/docid/29CAE5B1F1D40EE38525736A007123FD and compare and contrast the economic crime problem in the United States with those in other countries. What are the similarities and differences?

Public Order Crime

Crime and bad lives are the measure of a State's failure, all crime in the end is the crime of the community.

—H.G. Wells

Criminal behavior that violates the moral sentiment of society without a clearly identifiable victim is generally referred to as public order crime. Offenses that fall in this category are sometimes called "victimless" or "vice" crimes. Of the crime categories, public order crime is the largest in scope and number, including prostitution, gambling, pornography, substance abuse, public drunkenness, driving under the influence, disorderly conduct, trespassing, vagrancy, curfew and loitering law violations, runaways, carrying/possessing weapons, liquor law violations, and vandalism/graffiti.[1] These behaviors often result in harm to offenders themselves, with harm to others being less direct in most cases and perceived more as disruption of the public order.

In 2005, there were 279,562 arrests for vandalism, 193,469 for weapons violations, 84,891 for prostitution and commercialized vice, 1,846,351 for drug abuse violations, 11,180 for gambling, 1,371,919 for driving under the influence, 597,838 for liquor law violations, 556,167 for public drunkenness, 678,231 for disorderly conduct, 33,227 for vagrancy, 140,835 for curfew and loitering law violations, 129,128 for crimes against family and children (includes offenses such as failing to pay child support, child abandonment, child neglect, and custodial interference), 108,954 for runaways, and 3,863,785 for all other offenses (state and local offenses not listed elsewhere). Most public order crimes are committed by males, with the exception of prostitution (90% of offenders arrested for vandalism, driving under the influence, drunkenness, and gambling are male; 60% of prostitutes are female). African Americans are disproportionately arrested for public order offenses (Miethe, McCorkle, & Listwan, 2006).

Public order offenses are a distinct category of criminal behavior because they are predominantly motivated by addiction, mental illness, or other life problems (e.g., homelessness, domestic problems). Public order offenses contribute to the social disorganization of communities that perpetuate the cycle of offending (i.e., the *broken window theory*) and are deemed as crimes for this very reason. The following are case examples of public order offenses:

- Jorge Sanchez, 20, of East Boston wanted a $2.49 bag of Cheetos but was prepared to pay only 50 cents to a gas station attendant. Sanchez was drunk and his language got slightly salty.

- The Web site *World Sex Guide Forum* (wsgforum.com) provides a cyber forum for men seeking prostitutes. Johns use the site to trade tips on the best places to find hookers, where to be on the lookout for police, and when to go on the prowl.

- Ten prostitutes and johns were arrested in a Boston sting, in which undercover female officers posed as prostitutes and male officers pretended to be potential clients. Police said, "We're trying to improve the quality of life of people in this neighborhood."

- A Pennsylvania woman was charged with public drunkenness after she was found passed out on the street.

- A man was charged with driving under the influence of alcohol after a police officer said he noticed that the vehicle he was driving did not have its taillights turned on. The man smelled of alcohol and failed a field sobriety test and was charged with drunk driving, resisting arrest, disorderly conduct, and driving without his car lights on.

- A high school football and basketball player in Connecticut was charged with possession of less than 4 ounces of marijuana, possession of marijuana with intent to sell, possession of marijuana within 1,500 feet of a school, and possession of marijuana with intent to sell within 1,500 feet of a school.

- In 1995 British actor Hugh Grant was convicted of lewd conduct for soliciting Hollywood prostitute Devine Brown.

The essential feature of public order crimes is that they are prohibited by law because they are perceived as a threat to community life and social order. Whether or not particular behaviors are deemed threatening and made illegal depends on the time and place. For example, during prohibition it was a crime to manufacture, possess, or consume alcohol, which is not the case today. Prostitution is legal in some Nevada counties but illegal in other parts of the country. Laws against marijuana differ from state to state. In some it is a felony to possess a small amount of marijuana but no more than a misdemeanor or city ordinance violation carrying a fine in others.

Public order offenses share a number of characteristics. First, they are *mala prohibita* offenses. Unlike *mala en se* offenses, which are considered inherently wrong by society (e.g., murder, robbery), *mala prohibita* offenses are wrong simply because they are prohibited by some legal body. There is little consensus on the seriousness of these offenses or whether laws should be enacted against them or enforced (Miethe, McCorkle, & Listwan, 2006), and public order offenses are often targeted by moral entrepreneurs who see particular behaviors as harmful to the social order and evidence of moral decline (Box 8.1). For example,

BOX 8.1

SEATTLE TELEPHONE POLE POSTER BAN

Photo credit: © Z&Z/Boomdust Productions.

In 1995 a law was enacted in the city of Seattle prohibiting posting signs on utility poles. Prior to the law, local musicians and businesses relied on the free advertising and throughout the city most utility poles were covered in multiple layers of paper and staples. The law was enacted as a result of a moral entrepreneurial campaign declaring that the signs were harmful to the public order on a number of levels. Advocates of the law argued that the signs were dangerous to utility workers who could hurt themselves on the nails when scaling the poles (though most of the posters were attached with staples), that the paper buildup was a fire hazard, and that the signs increased pollution and were aesthetically distasteful (that contributed to the "visual blight and clutter and harmed the urban aesthetic").

Critics of the law argued that this was a citywide ban on low-cost advertising that significantly impacted small businesses and local musicians and an example of suburban aesthetics being imposed on urban artists and less well off businesses that had no other way to advertise their services. After the law was enacted in April 1995, it became illegal to post a sign on a utility pole, each sign posted carrying a $50 fine. By 1998, 729 violation notices were issued, carrying penalties of $85,000.

In 1999, the city of Seattle sued Mighty Movers, a local moving company, for $7,870.00 in removal costs to remove signs posted illegally by the company. A King County Superior Court Judge sided with the city. In response, Mighty Movers joined forces with the Joint Artists and Music Promotions Action Committee to get the decision reversed, arguing that the ban was a violation of First Amendment protections against governmental restrictions of free speech. In 2002, the Washington State Court of Appeals ruled that posting signs on utility poles and lamp posts is "traditional public forum" and there was no compelling governmental interest in banning it.

In 2004, the Washington State Supreme Court upheld the sign ban, stating that utility poles are not a traditional forum for public communication. Siding with the city, the court determined that the ban did not limit free speech and the law meets a reasonable governmental interest, stating:

The City enacted the ordinance to protect the safety of utility workers who must climb the poles, to enhance public safety by promoting unobstructed vision for drivers and pedestrians, to prevent damage to public property, and to enhance urban aesthetics. The Seattle City Council made the legislative determination that a prohibition against all private signs and posters on utility poles is the best way to protect worker safety and promote the other public interests at stake. *(City of Seattle v. Mighty Movers, 2004)*

Today, posting signs on utility poles in Seattle is a public order offense whereas it was not an offense in 1993 or in 2002, nor is it an offense in other cities. However, a similar campaign occurred in Portland, Oregon, and critics of the campaign there argued that the poster ban killed the music scene in Seattle and that the posters themselves were a historical art form.

This is just one of many examples of how a group of moral entrepreneurs identifies a particular behavior or group, labels it a threat to social order and public safety, and engages enough support to enact a law against it. Though the sign posting in this example is a very minor offense that carries a monetary fine, other behaviors deemed a social and moral threat that carry stiffer penalties such as prostitution, vagrancy, panhandling, gambling, and drug use were enacted into law through a similar moral entrepreneurial process for similar reasons.

some textbooks still list homosexuality under public order crime (Clinard, Quinney, & Wildeman, 1994). As recently as the 1960s, every state in the United States had an antisodomy law making homosexuality illegal. However, today most of these laws have been repealed, and homosexuality is no longer considered a crime against public order. Similarly, some public order offenses such as prostitution and gambling are illegal in some places but not others. Second, public order offenses are "victimless" crimes. Though some argue that there is no such thing as a "victimless" crime, since we are all harmed in some way by disruptions to public order, public order offenses tend to involve either a solitary act (e.g., public drunkenness, vagrancy) or a consensual act between two or more adults (e.g., prostitution, gambling).

The Nature of Public Order Offenses

People engage in public order offenses for instrumental and expressive reasons (Miethe, McCorkle, & Listwan, 2006). Public order offenses that are part of large-scale market-based operations motivated by economic profit are best understood as economic crimes (e.g., drug trafficking, prostitution, gambling). Drug abuse, soliciting a prostitute, and gambling addiction are best understood as public order offenses because they involve individual-level behaviors deemed illegal that result from addiction or an inclination toward engaging in behaviors the public sees as morally depraved and disruptive. These are victimless offenses committed by consenting adults that have been deemed wrong by law because they violate the norms or threaten the perceived well-being of society.

Public order offenders tend to have histories of involvement in a range of minor offenses. Public order offenders do not specialize in a particular type of offense, with the exception of prostitution, which for some is a purely economic endeavor. (The divergence in opinion regarding the motivation for prostitution is discussed in the next section.) Public order offense behaviors do not appear to escalate over time. Most public order offenses require little planning and are motivated by socioemotional needs such as peer acceptance, material gain, emotional need, anxiety, or addiction. People tend to commit public order crimes because they are homeless and have nowhere to go (vagrancy, panhandling); have substance abuse problems (drunkenness, drunk driving, narcotics possession, disorderly conduct) or other addiction (gambling, sex, pornography); are influenced by peers, group dynamics, or youthful inclination toward irresponsible and risk-taking behaviors (vandalism, trespassing); or simply disagree with a particular law making their offenses a crime or violation. (Depending on the situation, public order offenses such as trespassing or disorderly conduct committed in the context of a political protest can be considered a political crime; this is discussed in Chapter 9.)

Public Order Crime Typologies

Public order offenses involve acts that have a number of common features:

- Victimless
- Consensual
- Relative across time and place
- A violation of social norms
- Perceived as a threat to social order and the well-being of society
- Illegal
- The product of addiction and/or problems in living

A wide array of offenses can be included under the heading of public order crime: prostitution, gambling, illicit drug use, drunkenness, driving while under the influence, pornography possession, adultery, truancy, vagrancy, vandalism, trespassing, loitering, panhandling, littering, disturbing the peace, illegal possession of firearms, disorderly conduct, runaways, and even traffic violations. Most crime typologies include only major types, for the sake of brevity, to illustrate the common features of such offenses. Miethe, McCorkle, and Listwan (2006) divide public order offenses into four subcategories or "syndromes"—prostitution, pornography, substance abuse, and gambling—which are described in terms of offender roles (buyers/sellers) and degree of criminal involvement (professionals/novices, addicts/occasional-recreational users).

Clinard, Quinney, and Wildeman (1994) include homosexuality, exhibitionism, and traffic offenses. Dabney (2004) identifies drug offenses and prostitution as "the most pervasive and well documented of public order crimes," offering a comprehensive examination of each to illustrate the similarities and differences across public order offenses.

To provide an overview of the different types and defining nature of public order offenses, public order crime is divided here into the following subtypes:

- Sex-related offenses
- Substance abuse–related offenses
- Gambling
- Other public order offenses

Sex-Related Offenses: Prostitution, Commercialized Vice, and Pornography

Prostitution

The UCR defines prostitution and commercialized vice as "The unlawful promotion of or participation in sexual activities for profit, including attempts" (UCR, 2005). Prostitution is often referred to as the "world's oldest profession." The word *prostitution* literally means "up front" or "to expose" and is derived from the Latin word *prostitutes.* Many researchers classify prostitution into two categories—*indoor* (escort and high-end call girl services, massage parlors) and *outdoor* (traditional street prostitution). More detailed subtypes of prostitutes include *streetwalkers* (who work the streets in public view), *bargirls* (who work in bars), *brothel prostitutes* (who work in large established houses of prostitution often managed by a "madam"), *escort service prostitutes* (who work under the front of a legitimate escort service), *circuit travelers* (who move/work in groups to lumber, agricultural, and labor camps servicing an entire work crew and moving on), *skeezers* (who barter drugs for sex), *massage parlor* and *photo studio prostitutes* (who work in massage parlors and offer limited sexual services under the front of the legitimate business), and *cyberprostitutes* (who offer services from personal Web sites) (Siegal, 2006). Prostitution and commercial sex enterprises such as strip clubs, escort services, child and adult pornography, phone sex services, and massage brothels are part of a multibillion dollar global market. The commercial sex industry is entangled with other forms of criminal behavior including economic crime, human trafficking, drug and alcohol offenses, violence, and transnational and organized crime.

The actual extent of prostitution in America (and elsewhere) is largely unknown because most of the prostitution in the United States is not brought to the attention of police. Prostitution offenses are scarce in police reports. The only available source of uniformly collected and geographically diverse crime data on the nature of prostitution is the *National Incident Based Reporting System* (NIBRS). NIBRS data offer some information on the demographics of prostitution offenders and victims and the dynamics of the offense. From 1997 through 2000, NIBRS data show 14,230 recorded incidents of prostitution, 0.17 of all crime or 2 in 1,000 out of every incident known to police. Most (71%) prostitutes known to police are White, and police are more likely to encounter prostitutes in summer months in the hours between 6 pm and midnight (Finkelhor & Ormrod, 2004).

Large-scale economic motivations and gains of the commercial sex industry that benefit organized and transnational criminal networks are far removed from the motivations and dynamics of street prostitution. Prostitution is a crime in most parts of the United States, but it is not a crime in many places around the world. This makes it difficult to view prostitution as similar to other forms of criminal behavior that produce clear harm to an identifiable victim. In countries such as England, France, Denmark, Canada, the Netherlands, Germany, Greece, Portugal, Spain, Switzerland, New Zealand, and some states in Australia, prostitution is either legal and or has been decriminalized (Phoenix, 2004). Although prostitution is promoted through organized crime and transnational sex trafficking activities which are largely economic crimes, the act of prostitution itself can best be understood as a public order offense.

The nature of prostitution differs in important ways from that of a purely economic crime. First, there is disagreement about whether or not a victim exists and who the victim is. Some view prostitution as a purely consensual business exchange, others see the prostitutes themselves as victims, and still others recognize prostitution as a threat to the moral foundation of society that victimizes the community. Research and discourse have viewed prostitution as sexual exploitation and violence against women, occupational choice, domestic violence, sexual liberation and empowerment, human rights violation, and petty crime (Farley & Kelly, 2000). Whether prostitution is understood as criminal behavior (as opposed to criminal victimization or a career choice) is a matter of political perspective (Box 8.2). Second, prostitution is rooted in a host of social problems including poverty, addiction, and abuse. Girls and women involved in prostitution tend to have lives ravaged by the cumulative effects of poverty, "who often have been homeless, physically, sexually, and emotionally abused by parents, partners, and boyfriends, grew up in state care and in institutions and have had histories of absconding from foster placements and children's homes" (Phoenix, 2004, p. 292).

Prostitution has been viewed from two ends of the political spectrum—as violent victimization of women and as sex work. Some argue that "If prostitution becomes 'sex work,' then the brutal exploitation of those prostituted by pimps becomes and employer-employee relationship. And the predatory, pedophiliac purchase of a human being by the john becomes just one more business transaction" (Farley & Kelly, 2000, pp. 27–28). Others acknowledge that, for some, prostitution is a consciously and rationally chosen economic enterprise that is a means of both survival and empowerment. Prostitution can be viewed, then, along a spectrum with women who are forced into prostitution (e.g., sex trafficking, kidnapping, rape) at one end and women who decide to work as prostitutes, some for purely economic reasons and others because they enjoy sex and have no qualms about engaging in sex work at the other (Delacoste & Alexander, 1988).

A study by the London Home Office (2004) found that 70% of prostitutes started out as children or teenagers and 80 to 95% felt trapped and were involved in the business to support a serious drug habit. Other research shows that most female offenders have been involved in prostitution though it is unclear which came first, prostitution or other crime choices (Pollock, 1999). In the United States, a disproportionate percentage of prostitutes are women of color. Around the world, indigenous women are exploited in prostitution (Mayan women in Mexico City, First Nation women in Vancouver,

BOX 8.2

DECRIMINALIZING PROSTITUTION

Carol Leigh, aka Scarlot Harlot, and protestors for the decriminalization of prostitution.

Photo credit: © Carol Leigh/Tracy Mostovoy. Reprinted with permission.

The debate over the decriminalization of prostitution began in the 1970s and has gained force in recent years in California. In Berkeley, California, in 2004, *Angel's Initiative,* named after a prostitute who was murdered, was put on the ballots as Measure Q. In favor of the initiative were organizations such as COYOTE (Call Off Your Old Tired Ethics), SWOP (Sex Workers Outreach Project), and long-time feminist, sex worker, and decriminalization activist Carol Leigh, also known as the Scarlet Harlot. Opponents of the initiative argued that it would increase child prostitution and take a "look the other way stance" regarding a serious social problem. Supporters contend that making prostitution a low law enforcement priority would alleviate violence against women, improve public health for prostitutes who are too embarrassed or afraid to seek medical attention, help prostitutes transition out of street work, and encourage statewide reform.

Angel's Initiative

Shall the City of Berkeley help stop violence against women, demand that the State of California repeal laws that prohibit private consensual adult sexual behavior and that treat women unfairly, make enforcing those laws a low police priority, and cease wasting vital funds?

WHEREAS, Persons should never be forced into having sex or doing any other act against their will, whether by force or fraud, and whether they are adults or children;

WHEREAS, Laws that make criminals of adults for having consensual sex have a profound effect on the safety and well being of those adults, with all that imports for the dignity of the persons charged. When victims of such laws receive criminal convictions, collateral consequences always follow; and

(Continued)

(Continued)

WHEREAS, Such consequences include the marginalizing of those individuals, negatively impacting their safety and access to health education and services, and preventing them from obtaining other employment due to the stigma and status of a criminal conviction; and

WHEREAS, The American Law Institute promulgated a Model Penal Code and made clear that it did not recommend or provide for "criminal penalties for consensual sexual relations conducted in private." It justified its decision on three grounds: (1) The prohibitions undermined respect for the law by penalizing conduct many people engaged in; (2) the statutes regulated private conduct not harmful to others; and (3) the laws were arbitrarily enforced and thus invited the danger of blackmail; and

WHEREAS, Article I of the Constitution of California decrees that all people are by nature free and independent and have inalienable rights. Among these are pursuing and obtaining safety, happiness, and privacy; and

WHEREAS, The Supreme Court of the United States has recently lauded "emerging awareness that liberty gives substantial protection to adult persons in deciding how to conduct their private lives in matters pertaining to sex," that people "are entitled to respect for their private lives," and the "State cannot demean their existence or control their destiny by making their private sexual conduct a crime."

NOW THEREFORE BE IT RESOLVED by the City of Berkeley that a new chapter 12.27 is added to the Berkeley Municipal Code to read as follows:

12.27.010 Purpose

The unjust laws criminalizing consensual sexual activity among adults in private whether for money or any other consideration must be repealed.

Brutal hate crimes routinely perpetrated against prostitutes reveal how such laws disenfranchise and foster discrimination against persons, especially women, and do more to harm Berkeley citizens than protect them.

We demand the reform of sex laws, and the return of our basic freedoms of life, liberty, and the pursuit of happiness.

The ordinance codified in this chapter will:

A. Decrease tensions between the police and members of the community who are made to feel like criminals as a result of engaging in consensual adult sexual activity in private;
B. Require the police department to submit semi-annual reports on the amount of arrests made by law enforcement in Berkeley;
C. Instruct the city government to support efforts toward the statewide repeal of prostitution laws.

12.27.020 Definitions.

For purposes of this Chapter, "prostitution" means any consensual sexual activity among or between adults whether for money or any other consideration.

For purposes of this Chapter, nonconsensual sex acts, whether perpetrated by fraud, threat of force, or force, as well as any sex acts perpetrated against minors are not "prostitution," and are referred to instead as "criminal sexual acts," collectively.

For purposes of this Chapter, "prostitution laws" mean the portions of Sections 266, 266d, 266e, 266f, 266h, 266i, 315, 316, 318, 647, 653.20, 653.22, 653.23, and 653.28 of the California Penal Code which criminalize sexual activity among or between consenting adults whether for money or any other consideration.

For purposes of this Chapter, "prostitution laws" does not mean the portions of those Sections, or any other Sections of California law that prohibit criminal sexual acts as defined in this Chapter.

12.27.030 Efforts to decriminalize prostitution in California.
It is the desire of the people of Berkeley that laws prohibiting or regulating private consensual sexual activity between or among adults be repealed in California. In this context, the people of Berkeley fully support the present statewide efforts to repeal prostitution laws. The City Council is directed to lobby in favor of the repeal of these laws.

12.27.040 Law enforcement priority of prostitution statutes.
The City Council shall seek to ensure that the Berkeley police department gives lowest priority to the enforcement of prostitution laws. If other portions of the Berkeley Municipal Code require "lowest priority" enforcement levels, such as the enforcement of marijuana laws, this section shall not be construed to elevate enforcement efforts against those acts. Instead, this section shall be interpreted to require equally low priority for the enforcement of "lowest priority" acts.

12.27.050 Berkeley police department reporting requirement.
The city council shall ensure that the Berkeley Police Department reports semi-annually to it and the Berkeley Police Review Commission regarding all prostitution law enforcement activities, if any, engaged in by the Berkeley Police Department, and by county, state, and federal, and/or other law enforcement agencies within Berkeley.

12.27.060 Severability.
If any provision of this ordinance, or the application of such provision to any person or circumstance, shall be held invalid by any court, the remainder of this ordinance to the extent that it can be given effect, or the application of such provision to persons or circumstances other than those as to which it is held invalid, shall not be affected thereby, and to this end the sections of this ordinance are severable.

BE IT FINALLY RESOLVED, that the City Clerk is directed to transmit this resolution to all City departments, the courts, the Governor and the Attorney General of the State of California, to all members of the California Congressional delegation, the United States Attorney General, and the President of the United States of America.

Hmong women in Minneapolis) and African American women are arrested for prostitution at a higher rate (Farley & Kelly, 2000). Some suggest that what makes prostitution so dangerous is the simple fact that it is illegal (Delacoste & Alexander, 1988).

Prostitution cannot be explained by any single disciplinary or theoretical perspective. Following are some theories that have been offered to explain prostitution:

- Sexual and physical abuse in childhood contributes to the psychological development of life scripts that lead to choices supporting a life of prostitution.

- In a political and economic system with limited opportunity for unskilled or low-skilled women, prostitution offers an alternative and relatively lucrative occupation.

- The sexualization of women promotes and perpetuates prostitution through socialization processes that send the message that women exist to service male sexual needs.

Which explanation is applicable depends to some extent on the individual offender and circumstances of the offense. Speaking generally, it can be said that *prostitution is motivated by economic need within the context of a complex web of physical, sexual, and substance abuse perpetuated by socialization practices and social beliefs that reinforce the notion that sex is an economic commodity.* More often than not, prostitutes are portrayed as psychological victims of a risky family situation and an unequal market; however, this perspective has been increasingly challenged by feminist writers, prostitutes, and researchers who assert that prostitution is rationally chosen, economically motivated, sex work[2] (Carpenter, 1998; Delacoste & Alexander, 1988; Høigård & Finstad, 1992).

On an individual level, prostitutes experience their involvement in contradictory ways, as both a means of survival and a threat to survival—an act that is simultaneously rooted in poverty and contributes to an endless cycle of poverty, abuse, and social disorganization. In a study of British streetwalkers, Phoenix (2004) found that prostitutes construct a "prostitute-identity" to make sense of the paradox of prostitution:

> [T]he women claimed that involvement in prostitution alleviated their poverty, provided them with housing, helped them to live independently and gave them a means to fashion better lives for themselves. Yet, they *also* claimed that involvement in prostitution created their poverty, generated their housing difficulties, made them more dependent on men and/or families and jeopardized their social and material survival. But in their recollections, the women indicated that they could see no alternative to their current lifestyle, they had to live with the contradiction (i.e. they had to make sense of their lives within prostitution). (p. 297)

To make sense of this contradictory experience, the women constructed particular ways of viewing their involvement that helped reconcile the conflicting aspects of their roles as prostitutes.

The relationship between prostitution and drug use is particularly complex. Many female drug users are prostitutes and many prostitutes are drug users (Inciardi, O'Connell, & Saum, 2004). According to Cusick (2002), "Pre-prostitution drug use is as frequently experienced as pre-drug use prostitution"(p. 238), and most prostitutes have criminal records for offenses other than prostitution before they ever became involved in prostitution. Though some prostitutes use drugs to facilitate their behavior, others prostitute to support their drug habit. Furthermore, there is a category of women who prostitute specifically for drugs (e.g., crack) rather than for money to purchase drugs. Inciardi, O'Conell, and Saum distinguish between "crack whores," who exchange sex for crack in crack houses, and prostitutes who sell sex for money on the streets to buy crack. According to the authors, prostitutes have fewer sex partners, are more conscious of sexually transmitted diseases, and have friendships and peer relationships through which experiences are shared and meaning is communicated.

Many researchers note that prostitutes use drugs and alcohol to anesthetize themselves against the trauma of their work. A majority of prostitutes have been raped and physically assaulted by their customers and their pimps. One study in Oregon found that prostitutes were raped an average of once a week. Farley and Kelly (2000, p. 16) argue that "Women in prostitution are battered women" (p. 16). Prostitutes are proficient at dissociation. Many report having depression, posttraumatic stress disorder (PTSD), or a more severe dissociative disorder. Prostitutes have been said to suffer from the Stockholm syndrome, whereby captives come to identify with and bond with their captors, identifying and bonding with their pimps (their captors). Prostitutes suffer from chronic health problems similar to those found in people who have suffered severe torture and have a mortality rate 40 times higher than the general population (Farley & Kelly, 2000).

Research has focused predominantly on female prostitutes and male clients, but prostitutes and their clients can be of either sex, though in the words of former sex worker and author Carol Queen, "Whoredom is more gender-integrated, by far, than clienthood"(Queen, 2000, p. 106). Male prostitutes who serve predominantly male clients are generally referred to as *hustlers* or *rent boys* whereas male prostitutes who serve females are often referred to as *gigolos* or *escorts*. Until relatively recently, male prostitution was not the subject of scholarly research or popular discourse. It wasn't until the end of the 19th century that the phrase came to be consistently used to refer to men who sold sex[3] (Kaye, 2003). The proportion of male prostitutes grew considerably in the 1990s.[4] Recent research shows that 61% of juvenile prostitution offenders and 53% of the adult prostitution offenders are male (Finkelhor & Ormrod, 2004). This increase in male prostitution raises a number of questions: *Can male prostitution be understood within the same framework as female prostitution? How does gender (of the prostitute and client) shape the behavior and the meaning it holds and the identities of the offenders and clients?*

Kaye (2003) notes that conceptions of male prostitution have changed dramatically with changing views of homosexuality[5]—as homosexuality has become more socially and politically acceptable, the many forms male prostitution may take are becoming better understood. Clients of male prostitutes are predominantly male, though there are male prostitutes who operate through escort services with female clients. The sexual orientation of male clients of male prostitutes is mixed. Morse, Simon, Balson, and Osofsky (1992) found that 53% of customers of male prostitutes identified themselves as bisexual, 40% as heterosexual, and only 1 person identified himself as homosexual. The majority of clients (73%) stated that, in addition to having sex with male prostitutes, they also regularly had sex with female prostitutes.

The sociopolitical context within which male prostitutes operate is markedly different for men (versus women) who engage in the behavior:

[T]he meaning of what is purchased varies with the sex of the body. Men and women who prostitute do not share exactly the same experience in their work because the same set of socially ascribed meanings are not applied to both patterns of transaction: they do not sell the same thing. Though "sex" is sold in both cases, it is a sexual act whose meaning is distinctly gendered. Difference (and inequality) between women and men thus exists at the level of discourse, as well as within the material practices which ground the narrations. Similarly, the sex which is sold by "blacks" and "whites," or by "men" and "boys," carries different meaning, thereby producing different experiences and (potentially) different identities for both sellers and buyers. (Kaye, 2003)

Thus, being a male prostitute carries a very different meaning and experience from being a female prostitute. Some argue that the male who engages in prostitution is in a position of sexual power whereas the female who engages in prostitution is in a position of sexual victimization.[6] Regardless of the individual motivation of the person engaging in prostitution (whether male or female), the social construction of gender and the sexual power imbalance between males and females organizes the meaning and experience of prostitution. In prostitution, demand creates supply. For most women, "prostitution is the experience of being hunted, dominated, harassed, assaulted, and battered" (Farley & Kelly, 2000, p. 29), whereas men engaging in prostitution do not become positioned as, or take on the status of, women (Carpenter, 1998).

Juvenile prostitution represents 1.4% of prostitution incidents identified in NIBRS data. Juveniles can be categorized as either victims or offenders in NIBRS data, depending on whether they are pimped by an adult (in which case they tend to be classified as victims of statutory rape or other sex crimes) or engage in the activity on their own (in which case they tend to be classified as offenders). The following features of juvenile prostitution illustrate its nature and dynamics:

- Although the majority of juvenile prostitution incidents take place at an outdoor location, juvenile prostitutes are more likely than adult prostitutes to involve multiple offenders and to occur indoors in large urban areas (Finkelhor & Ormrod, 2004, p. 2).

- Girls engaging in outdoor prostitution are generally referred to as streetwalkers. It is estimated that 20% of all street prostitutes are juvenile girls. Juvenile streetwalkers have been identified in the literature as "part-timers" and "true prostitutes" (Flowers, 2001).

- Police are less likely to arrest juvenile prostitutes than adults, but are more likely to come in contact with and to arrest male than female juveniles involved in prostitution (Finkelhor & Ormrod, 2004, p. 2).

- Juvenile prostitutes in the United States come from every racial and ethnic persuasion and nationality—the majority are White, followed by Black, Hispanic, Native American, and Asian (Flowers, 2001).

- Police are more likely to categorize juvenile prostitutes as offenders than victims, but those categorized as victims are more likely to be female than male (Finkelhor & Ormrod, 2004, p. 2).

- The number of juvenile prostitutes in the United States ranges from hundreds of thousands to millions (Flowers, 2001).

- More girls than boys enter prostitution and most are homeless, abused runaways who engage in prostitution as a survival strategy or for drugs (Flowers, 2001).

- Boy prostitutes are known in the male prostitution subculture as *chickens* and their customers as *chicken hawks,* and types of boy prostitutes have been identified in the literature as *street hustlers, bar hustlers, call boys,* and *kept boys* (Flowers, 2001, p. 136).

- Prostituted juveniles face severe medical and heath hazards including physical injury, eating disorders, drug and alcohol addiction, mental disorders, sexually transmitted diseases, pregnancy, and attempted suicide (Flowers, 2001).

- Prostitution of young girls is largely controlled by pimps who charm, coerce, manipulate, and keep them in prostitution through use of violence, intimidation, drugs, pornography, pregnancy, fear, and love (Flowers, 2001).

- Between 1989 and 1995 in England and Wales, 10% of females arrested for prostitution were juveniles. It is estimated that one-third of juveniles engaged in prostitution in the United Kingdom are under age 16, the majority of adult prostitutes began their careers between age 12 and 15, and half of all juvenile prostitutes had no sexual experiences prior to prostitution (Cusick, 2002).

Juvenile prostitution illustrates the difficulty in determining the line between the view of the prostitute as victim versus the prostitute as offender. Many young people become involved in prostitution after running away from home, a period in state custody/care, becoming involved in drug use, and getting introduced through friends, partners, predatory adults, or others involved in the prostitution-drug-crime lifestyle. Cusick (2002) emphasizes that, although the term *sex worker* has become fashionable, implying rational choice and economic motivation for many involved in prostitution, the term should not be used to describe juveniles because juveniles engaged in prostitution is abuse and the client is a sex offender. Increasingly states are recognizing the juvenile prostitute as the victim and the client as a sex offender (though this has historically not been the norm). Cusick also notes that a more complete typology of entry models into prostitution is needed to show the range of ways juveniles become involved in prostitution.

Situational factors underlying the motivation for prostitution are numerous—family conflict, parental promiscuity, lower socioeconomic status, child abuse or neglect, poor work history, and a litany of other factors. Emotional states associated with the decision to engage in prostitution are the development of a strong independent personality, desire to gain attention and acceptance of adults, and desire to take control of one's life. The depiction of individuals involved in prostitution as victims appears to have some support with respect to both street (outdoor) prostitutes and those who work in indoor venues such as escort services and massage parlors. In a study of 222 Chicago-area prostitutes, Raphael and Shapiro (2004) found that both indoor and outdoor prostitutes experienced high levels of violence, which has a traumatic effect on their psychological well-being and ability to exit the lifestyle.

Solicitation

The demand side of prostitution has been largely ignored. This is true with respect to both arrests and the academic literature. For example, a study by the Seattle Women's Commission in 1995 found that there were 1,210 arrests of women on prostitution charges, and 62% of those arrested were charged and 42% were convicted. On the other hand, 228 men were arrested for solicitation, of whom 98% were charged and 8% convicted (Farley & Kelly, 2000). Similarly, what is known about the demographic characteristics, motivations, and interpersonal style of the clients of prostitutes constitutes a tiny fraction of the research on prostitution.

A recent British Columbia study by Kennedy, Gorzalka, and Yuille (2004) involving 734 men arrested for soliciting a prostitute who volunteered to participate in a Prostitution Offender Program in Vancouver, British Columbia, offers a demographic profile of male solicitors. The findings show that the typical male solicitor in Canada who selected to participate in the program is an educated, employed, middle-class, 38-year-old father who speaks a second language, is in a serious/committed relationship, and secretly engages in the offense in the evenings (preferably 9 pm to 12 am) or on weekends, uses a condom with the prostitute (but not with his wife), and has previously attempted to quit for fear of embarrassment or acquiring a criminal record. The study also found the following:

- A large proportion of the men lived in the region in which they were arrested.

- Most (58%) reported that they had previously had sex with a prostitute at an average age of 27 and average number of 42 times (ranging from 1 to 4,000 times).

- The average amount of money spent on prostitutes (over the offender's lifetime) was $1,964, with a range of $20 to $50,000.

- Most (60%) reported that they did not enjoy having sex with prostitutes.

- The most popular reasons given for initially engaging in prostitution were curiosity (27%), loneliness (19.4%), and being sexually frustrated (16.1%). Other reasons given were for sexual gratification, to relieve stress, being at a bachelor party, being drunk, being enticed by a prostitute.

- Offenders noted that the best part about having sex with a prostitute was no commitments/attachment (23.8%), a quick sexual encounter (22.1%), sexual gratification (14.3%), variety/different partners (11.7%), can request a specific sex act (10.8%), anonymity (4.3%), intimacy (3%), and being in control (0.9%).

- Most (62%) said the race of their ideal prostitute is Caucasian followed by "no preference" (23%), and East Asian (7%).

- In terms of the ideal appearance of prostitutes, most of the offenders said that their main interest was that the prostitute was attractive (35.8%), healthy (30.2%), slender (9.9%), blonde (5.6%), tall (3.5%), and busty (2.5%).

- Most of the offenders regularly asked for oral sex (52%), half oral and half intercourse (22.9%), intercourse (20.1%), manual stimulation (4.3%), and other (2.5%).

Based on these findings, men who solicit prostitutes are established members of their communities, in contrast with girls and women involved in prostitution, who tend to come from troubled and socioeconomically disadvantaged backgrounds.

The finding that clients of prostitutes are predominantly "normal" middle-class married men has received mixed support. Narratives of sex workers paint a picture of the client as a normal married man (Høigård & Finstad, 1992; Sycamore, 2000). One sex worker stated, "My johns were mostly upper-middle-class professional men, ages 35 and older—'yuppies and their dads.' They were lawyers and insurance executives, physicians and venture capitalists, well-to-do retirees and business owners, stockbrokers, and more lawyers" (Queen, 2000, p. 107). However, a large survey of johns in Oslo found that the majority of clients of prostitutes are single men. Høigård and Finstad (1992) hypothesize that, because prostitutes are aware that the traditional view of johns is creepy outsider-type men, they are more inclined to describe their clients as predominantly normal married men because they see a lot of them in their work even though many of their clients are also single men and the typical creepy outsider.

Though little attention has been devoted in the literature to the motivations of solicitors and the nature of their interactions with prostitutes, narrative accounts of sex workers offer some indication of who their clients are. Some such accounts differ quite markedly from the traditional view of the solicitor as a violent victimizer:

> I've never met a whore for whom money was irrelevant. But for all the talk of "selling our bodies" (which is ridiculous; we still have our bodies at the end of the transaction), the commodification of our time, our flesh, our actions, there's surprisingly little corresponding talk about the client's body, the client's role.
>
> When I say "client's role," I emphatically do not mean client as abuser: this is the first assumption of people who believe sex (at least when exchanged for money) is automatically abusive. This is not my experience at all; in fact, I've experienced many clients as much more pleasant and respectful than a lot of people in my past who wanted to have sex for free. Portraying all johns as abusive is like overlooking the difference between a bank customer and a bank robber because both stand at the same teller's window and make a withdrawal. Equating the purchase of sexual entertainment with abuse and misogyny is too simple, for one thing. It erases useful-to-consider differences between men who are hateful and those who are respectful, and it undermines the client's own experience as well as his motivation for treating whores with respect. (Queen, 2000, p. 106)

Although most prostitutes report experiences with clients who behave violently or unpredictably (Høigård & Finstad, 1992), and it is clear from the research literature on prostitution that the lifestyle involves violence perpetuated by both pimps and clients, the consensus appears to be that all types of people, primarily men, solicit prostitutes and most johns are average men who want sexual satisfaction (Sycamore, 2000).

Motivation for engaging in prostitution is varied. In understanding client motives, it is important to ask, *Why do men seek prostitutes?* and *What is it about sex with prostitutes that makes prostitution attractive?* The motivations identified in the literature tend to fall into one of two categories—solicitation of prostitutes as a means to fulfill *sexual need* and solicitation of prostitutes as a *sexual alternative,* though minimal research is available to explain why a man would choose to buy sex when other alternatives are available (Carpenter, 1998). (One suggestion for the lack of research in this area is that the view of solicitors as anomalous rather than normal maintains the look-the-other-way attitude regarding promiscuity of normal in contrast with disordered men.)

A number of authors have offered motivational typologies to explain male solicitation of prostitution. Queen (2000) suggests seven primary reasons why men solicit prostitutes:

- *Convenience:* Men solicit prostitutes because they can; sex is available for purchase and it's convenient and consistent with the "my-time-is-valuable" mindset.

- *Boundaries:* Purchasing sex offers space and clear boundaries that allow the client to engage in sex with no personal attachment.

- *Partner variety:* Sex with prostitutes offers an avenue through which men can engage in sexual relations with multiple partners.

- *Sexual variety:* Sex with prostitutes offers an opportunity to engage in sexual activities that the client may not feel comfortable engaging in or asking for with the person with whom he has a relationship, or that his partner is not willing to engage in.

- *Male role:* Being a client allows the man to have both the traditionally masculine control over the sexual exchange and the freedom to be in a more passive position not traditionally acceptable in sexual relationships.

- *Sexual growth and experimentation:* Beyond the motivation of sexual variety, some clients see sex with prostitutes as a means by which they can experiment and grow sexually.

- *Personal comfort and healing:* Some clients solicit prostitutes to be close to someone and want only to be touched, to talk with someone, or to use the sex as a form of sex therapy.[7]

Høigård and Finstad (1992), noting that client motives are so varied that "men's motives for going to prostitutes are as countless as grains of sand" (p. 92), classify them into five categories:

1. *Sex acts:* Many men want specific sex acts from prostitutes that they have seen in pornography. They want to live out a fantasy and to self-centeredly pursue their desire to engage in particular sex acts.

2. *Different and exciting experience:* Some clients engage in sex with prostitutes only once or on occasion out of curiosity or interest in a unique sexual experience.

3. *Easy and noncommittal:* Some clients solicit prostitutes because they want sex, but not a relationship. Married customers may find it an easy way to have additional partners, and unmarried clients may seek emotionless sex.

4. *One-sidedness:* Many men solicit prostitutes so that they can engage in one-sided sexual pleasure and avoid the mutuality that comes with sex with a regular partner in a relationship.

5. *Availability:* Men like to know that sex is available to them anytime when their needs and fantasies can't be met in everyday life. Availability brings a feeling of power for customers who see sex as something that women give and men take.

The client motivations identified in the literature suggest that male solicitation in prostitution is tied to both individual needs and cultural ideas about male and female sexuality and sex-role stereotypes.

Promotion

Promotion of prostitution or *pimping* has been called the "second oldest profession" (Reitman, 1931). The U.S. Federal Sentencing Guidelines defines promotion as *"persuading, inducing, enticing, or coercing a person to engage in a commercial sex act, or to travel to engage in, a commercial sex act"* (U.S. Sentencing Commission, 2004, §2G1.1). Some researchers suggest that 80 to 90% of prostitution is promoted and controlled by pimps who actively recruit girls and women, in particular runaways and women of color. The dynamic between prostitutes and pimps is much like that of the batterer and domestic violence victim. Pimps often use violence and other means as a mechanism of control, engaging in manipulative and elaborate schemes to control prostitutes including isolation, threatening to report to police, developing an intimate relationship, intimidation, degradation, and maintaining financial control (Giobbe, 1993). Much of the violence against prostitutes is perpetrated by pimps, who are significantly more dangerous than johns (Farley & Kelly, 2000).

In contrast with this traditional view and popular stereotype of pimps as violent men who live lives of luxury by casting girls and women onto the street, Høigård and Finstad's (1992) study of prostitution in Oslo, Norway, found that much of what is known about "the pimp" is based more on popular myth and stereotype than reality. Høigård and Finstad's research revealed five types of pimps:

1. *The nonviolent boyfriend-pimp:* This type of pimp is in an emotional relationship with the prostitute (married, living together, engaged). As a couple, both parties make the decision for the woman to engage in prostitution for the money.

2. *The violent boyfriend-pimp:* The largest category in the pimp data. This type of pimp is also in an emotional relationship with the prostitute; however, he engages in violence to force the woman into prostitution. The relationship between the prostitute and violent boyfriend pimp is much like any other abusive relationship in which the cycle of abuse repeats itself over and over again (he beats her, they make up, she leaves, she returns).

3. *The sex-pimp:* This type of pimp is in a casual sexual relationship with the prostitute and usually involves same-age drug-using youth who engage in fleeting sexual relationships.

4. *The "stable" pimp:* This type of pimp has a number of women who prostitute themselves for him, often having a relationship with one of them. This is the closest to the popular stereotype of a pimp.

5. *The sex club pimp:* This type of pimp also has a number of women who prostitute themselves for him, but does not have a relationship with any of them. The relationship between the pimp and the prostitutes is more of an impersonal employer-employee relationship/ business arrangement.

These different types of pimps can be reflected on multiple continua, illustrating the many different types of people and relationships that underlie the label of "pimp."

Figure 8.1 shows four continua or dimensions on which the prostitute-pimp relationship can be understood.

❖ **Figure 8.1**   The Prostitution-Pimp Continuum

Degree of Planning by Pimp When Meeting Potential Prostitute Spontaneous →→→→→→→→→→Conscious Strategies to Entrap
Emotional Content of Pimp-Prostitute Relationship Mutual Love →→→→→→→→→→→ Psychic/Physical Violence
Economics of Relationship Man Is Self-Supported →→→→→→→→→→→ Man Lives Off Woman
Number of Women "Working" for Pimp Relationship With One Woman →→→→→→→→→→→ Exploitation of Several Women

Source: Adapted from Høigård & Finstad (2000, p. 168).

Most of the prostitutes in the Oslo study did not view the men in their lives who economically benefitted from their prostitution as pimps. According to the researchers, asking women engaged in prostitution if they have a pimp is "making a fool of yourself and announcing that you're from another planet" (Høigård & Finstad, 1992, p. 134). For the prostitutes in Norway, the term *pimp* is a stereotype that has little relationship to the everyday lived realities.

This does not mean that pimps do not exist. The perception among prostitutes of who is and who is not a pimp does not necessarily correspond to the legal definition of promoting prostitution. Most of the individuals arrested for "promoting prostitution" are not viewed by prostitutes as "pimps." The degree to which prostitution promoters are viewed as pimps may be related to how prostitution is viewed in a community and whether it is decriminalized or legal. For example, prostitution in Norway differs from the picture internationally. Prostitution is legal in Norway and more prostitutes engage in the behavior on their own (Høigård & Finstad, 1992).

Female pimps, often referred to as "madams," are rarely discussed in the academic literature. One of the more notorious female pimps is Heidi Fleiss, aka the "Hollywood Madam." In1997, Fleiss was convicted and sentenced to 3 years in federal prison for conspiracy, money laundering, and tax evasion associated with running a high-priced prostitution ring serving the rich and famous. Other examples include

- Pasha Cowan was a former prostitute turned madam who admitted to providing prostitutes for University of Colorado football players in 2002–2003 (Herdy, 2005).

- Tamera Sue Florey, a Columbus, Ohio, woman, was convicted of operating a house of prostitution and sentenced to home detention (Cadwallader, 2005).

- Jenny Paulino, a New York madam, sent call girls to prostitution dens in Manhattan high-rises (Ross & Lemire, 2005).

- Julie Moya, 47, was charged with two counts of statutory rape and promoting prostitution at a series of brothels run out of Manhattan apartments. Moya kept meticulous records such as the names of johns, the time/date of visits, how much they paid, and their physical descriptions (Ross, 2005).

- Margaret McDonald, known as the "world's most successful madam," was arrested in Paris on suspicion of aggravated pimping in May 2002. At the time, her business was run from five mobile telephones and a laptop computer that held the names of 550 female and 60 male escorts. In France, she was the most notorious madam since Madame Claude, who ran a house of 50 call girls in Paris in the 1960s (Alderson, 2005).

- A lesbian couple, Kathy and Sharon Joyner, ran a massage/prostitution parlor called the Healing Touch, hiring three girls at a time who dressed in conservative outfits, had girl-next-door personas, and served high-end, high-profile male clients (Yang, 2005).

Thus, a wide range of individuals, male and female, engage in promoting prostitution, and the stereotype of the violent male street pimp is only a small part of the story.

Pornography

Pornography has been defined as a type of prostitution in which prostitution is documented (Farley & Kelly, 2000). The word pornography comes from the Greek word *porne,* which means prostitute, and *graphein,* which means "to write" (Siegal, 2006). Most criminal codes prohibit the production, sale, and display of obscene material. However, it has historically been difficult to define and agree on what is and is not obscene. In 1964, Justice Stewart made the now famous statement on obscenity, *"I know it when I see it,"* which has made the legal definition of obscenity morally ambiguous and difficult to enforce. Typically, pornographic materials involving adults is legal and constitutionally protected in the United States by the First Amendment.

Child pornography is a different story. Every year, over a million children are believed to be used in pornography or prostitution, much of it distributed through the Internet. Consumers of child pornography are typically child molesters and male pedophiles (Flowers, 2001). Though some consumers of child pornography do not act on their fantasies and are not active sex offenders, consumption of child pornography is best understood within the framework of sex offending and deviant sexual arousal.[8] Law enforcement agencies are in a constant struggle to protect children against the producers, distributors, and consumers of child porn as well as organizations, associations, and networks that promote child porn such as the *North American Man-Boy Love Association,* the *Pedophile Information Exchange,* and the *Child Sensuality Circle* (Flowers, 2001).

Pornography contributes to public disorder in a number of ways. First, pornography contributes to the objectification of girls and women and the normalization of sexual violence. Pornography is often used by pimps to induce and coerce girls and women into prostitution, to "teach" them what acts to perform, and in strip clubs to promote prostitution. Studies show that approximately half of all prostitutes have reported being involved in pornography. Some argue that pornography is a form of "cultural propaganda which reifies the notion that women are prostitutes," promotes rape myths, and normalizes sexual violence (Farley & Kelly, 2000, p. 30). Second, pornography is a facilitator for sexual violence and sexual homicide and serial murder

(Hickey, 2002, 2006). The empirical link between pornography and violence is modest, and not all consumers of pornography end up engaging in sexual violence. However, research on rapists, pedophiles, and serial killers shows that most have a long history of pornography consumption and that the use of pornography contributes to and exacerbates deviant sexual fantasy development.

As a result of concern over the effect of pornography on community standards of decency and the role of pornography as a facilitator in crimes of sexual violence primarily targeting female and child victims, the *United States Attorney General's Commission on Pornography* has made a concerted effort to aggressively target producers of pornographic materials, particularly adult films that portray sexual violence.

Substance Abuse–Related Offenses and Addiction

A large percentage of public order crimes are rooted in substance abuse or addiction. Addiction to drugs and alcohol is a major problem in the United States, Canada, and around the world. Drug and alcohol addiction contribute to a wide range of public order offenses including but not limited to possession, distribution, and manufacture of illegal drugs, driving under the influence, public drunkenness, disorderly conduct, vagrancy, and loitering. A significant number of offenders of all types are under the influence of either drugs or alcohol during the commission of their crimes, ranging from minor public order offenses to violent crimes and homicide.

The causes of substance abuse differ with respect to the individual user and the theoretical perspective. Some people use and abuse drugs and alcohol because it is readily available in the neighborhoods and peer groups within which they live and interact. Others abuse drugs and alcohol to mediate and (self) medicate psychological deficits such as personality disorders, depression, anxiety disorders, or a range of psychiatric afflictions. Some rationally and consciously choose to engage in substance abuse for "fun," to get high and to experience the effects (to relax, to increase sexual responsiveness, to increase energy, etc.). Some substance abusers begin with marijuana and move on to harder drugs (the *gateway model*, i.e., the view that most people get involved with drugs slowly, moving from marijuana or alcohol to more serious drugs to experience a better "high"). Others begin using powerful drugs such as heroin or methamphetamines without ever having used marijuana.

Substance abuse is a type of addiction. The term *addiction* refers to the compulsion to use drugs or alcohol (or to engage in a particular behavior such as gambling) regardless of adverse consequences. The term *chemical dependency* is used to differentiate addiction to an illegal substance from addiction to a particular behavior (gambling, sex). Though prostitution is presented in this chapter as a separate category, some clients of prostitutes are sex addicts and may be best understood from the addiction model. (*Sex addiction* is preoccupation with and compulsion to engage in sexual behavior to the extent that it has adverse consequences.)

Substance abuse is a criminal behavior when the substance consumed is illegal or illegally possessed. Determining which substances are legal and which are illegal is a moral entrepreneurial process. Some substances are illegal at one time and not at others. The most obvious historical example of this was the *Prohibition era* (1919–1933), during which time alcohol was illegal in the United States.[9] Throughout U.S. history, the notion that drugs are a social menace has waxed and waned from Prohibition to the wars against opium, marijuana, speed, PCP, LSD, and heroin culminating in the 1980s war on drugs, followed by the crusade against synthetic drugs such as ecstasy and methamphetamines (Jenkins, 1999).

Substance abuse is classified as a mental disorder in the *Diagnostic and Statistical Manual of Mental Disorders* (APA, 2000). The *DSM-IV-TR* category of *Substance-Related Disorders* includes the following:

> *Substance Use Disorders* (abuse of and dependence on substances taken voluntarily for their effect on the central nervous system or to prevent withdrawal symptoms)
>
> *Substance-Induced Disorders* (conditions such as anxiety, delirium, intoxication, sexual dysfunction, and amnesia that occur as a result of either the use of a substance or withdrawal after discontinuing its use)

The *DSM-IV-TR* defines *substance abuse* as repeated use of alcohol or drugs leading to problems, but not involving addiction or compulsion. The folowing are criteria for substance abuse:

A. A maladaptive pattern of substance use leading to clinically significant impairment or distress, as manifested by one (or more) of the following, occurring within a 12-month period:
   (1) Recurrent substance use resulting in a failure to fulfill major role obligations at work, school, or home (e.g., repeated absences or poor work performance related to substance use; substance-related absences, suspensions, or expulsions from school; neglect of children or household)
   (2) Recurrent substance use in situations in which it is physically hazardous (e.g., driving an automobile or operating a machine when impaired by substance use)
   (3) Recurrent substance-related legal problems (e.g., arrests for substance-related disorderly conduct)
   (4) Continued substance use despite having persistent or recurrent social or interpersonal problems caused or exacerbated by the effects of the substance (e.g., arguments with spouse about consequences of intoxication, physical fights)

B. The symptoms have never met the criteria for Substance Dependence for this class of substance.

Substance abuse of all drugs, legal or illegal (including alcohol, nicotine, and prescription medication), can be diagnosed as a *DSM-IV-TR* mental disorder. In other words, although there is some overlap in behavioral symptoms of substance-related disorders and substance-related criminal behavior, not all substance-related disorders are also crimes (i.e., nicotine addiction, alcoholism). As with the paraphilias and personality disorders, some symptoms of substance-related disorders are criminal behaviors (e.g., driving under the influence, substance-related arrests for disorderly conduct, assault, and other offenses) and, of course, the degree to which substance-related disorders and substance-related crimes overlap depends on whether or not the substance used is illegal.

Drug Offenses

A *drug* is a substance that has mood-altering, psychotropic, or psychoactive effects (Abidinsky, 2004). This includes substances ranging from caffeine, nicotine, and alcohol to prescription and over-the-counter medication to marijuana, crack cocaine, heroin, and methamphetamines. Drugs used to treat a medical condition are generally viewed as socially acceptable whereas recreational drugs that have a potential for abuse are not. *It is a crime to use, possess, manufacture, or distribute drugs classified as having abuse potential.* Illegal drugs are classified for medical and explanatory purposes based on their general effects. For example, there are *stimulants* (sometimes referred to as "uppers") such as methamphetamines and cocaine and *depressants* (sometimes referred to as "downers") such as alcohol and barbiturates. Another distinction sometimes made is between *hallucinogens* (mood-altering drugs) such as LSD and PCP and *narcotics* (drugs associated with physical dependency) such as cocaine and heroin. Illegal drugs (controlled substances) are classified based on their abuse potential into the following categories:

> *Schedule I:* high potential for abuse, currently no accepted medical use in the United States, lack of accepted safety for use under medical supervision
>
> *Schedule II:* high potential for abuse, currently accepted medical use in treatment in the United States; abuse may lead to severe physical or psychological dependence
>
> *Schedule III:* potential for abuse less than Schedule I and II substances; currently accepted medical use in treatment in the United States; abuse may lead to low or moderate physical dependence or high psychological dependence
>
> *Schedule IV:* potential for abuse less than Schedule I, II, and III substances; currently accepted medical use in treatment in the United States; abuse may lead to limited physical or psychological dependence compared with Schedule III drugs
>
> *Schedule V:* potential for abuse less than Schedule I, II, III, and IV substances; currently accepted medical use in treatment in the United States; abuse may lead to limited physical or psychological dependence in comparison with Schedule IV drugs

These categories are used in the federal system and (with some variations) across the states (in conjunction with other factors such as number of priors) to determine sanctions for the use and abuse of illegal substances.

Drug abuse violations are defined in the UCR as "laws prohibiting the production, distribution, and/or use of certain controlled substances and the equipment or devices utilized in their preparation and/or use. The unlawful cultivation, manufacture, distribution, sale, purchase, use, possession, transportation, or importation of any controlled drug or narcotic substance," including arrests for violations of state and local narcotics laws (UCR, 2005). In 2005, there were 1,846,351 arrests for drug abuse violations in the United States (UCR, 2005). In 2000, Americans spent $36 billion on cocaine, $11 billion on marijuana, $10 billion on heroin, $5.4 billion on methamphetamine, and $2.4 billion on other illegal substances. The projected overall cost of drug abuse to society was $160.7 billion in 2000 (Spiess, 2003).

The National Survey of Drug Use and Health (NSDUH) administered annually by the Substance Abuse and Mental Health Services Administration (SAMHSA) is a primary source of information about the extent of drug use in the United States. The NSDUH collects data on nine categories of illicit drug use: marijuana, cocaine, inhalants, hallucinogens, heroin, and nonmedical use of prescription pain killers, stimulants, sedatives, and tranquilizers. NSDUH findings for 2005 show the percentage of people in the United States over age 12 who reported illicit drug use during the month prior to the survey:

- An estimated 19.7 million people, 8.1% of the population, used an illicit drug.

- Marijuana is the most commonly used illicit drug, used by 14.6 million Americans, 6% of the population.

- 2.4 million people, 1% of the population, used cocaine.

- 1.1 million people, 0.4% of the population, used hallucinogens.

- 119,000 people, 0.1% of the population, used heroin.

- Over half (54.5%) of illicit drug users used marijuana only. Slightly less than half (45.4%) of all illicit drug users used illicit drugs other than marijuana (either in addition to or without using marijuana).

- Of the 9 million current drug users who used illicit drugs other than marijuana, 6.4 million were psychotherapeutic drug users (2.6% of the population). Of them, 6.4 million or 2.6% used psychotherapeutic drugs nonmedically—4.7 million used pain relievers, 1.8 million used tranquilizers, 1.1 million used stimulants, and 272,000 used sedatives.

- Over half of all Americans, 126 million people (51.8% of the population), reported using alcohol and 10.5 million people (4.3% of the population) reported driving under the influence of an illicit drug. (Substance Abuse and Mental Health Services Administration, 2006)

Drug abuse is a serious social and public health problem that has been the focus of moral entrepreneurial campaigns throughout the history of the United States:

> Drug 'wars,' antidrug crusades, and other periods of marked public concern about drugs are never merely reactions to the various troubles people have with drugs. These drug scares are recurring cultural and political phenomena in their own right and must, therefore, be understood sociologically on their own terms. (Reinarman, 2003, p. 137)

Laws have been enacted to control the "drug problem" in the United States for 200 years, targeting opium dens in the late 1800s, alcohol during the Prohibition era in the early 1900s, marijuana in the 1930s and 1960s, LSD in the 1970s, crack in the 1980s (Reinarman, 2003), and synthetic or designer drugs such as Rohypnol (the "date-rape drug") and ecstasy (the "rave drug") in the 1990s (Jenkins, 1999). In the 1980s, "drugs became the primary symbol of the hedonism so widely blamed for moral decay," and severe drug laws were enacted during the Reagan administration with slogans such as "zero tolerance" and Nancy Reagan's famous "Just say No" (Jenkins,1999). As a result of the drug wars, large numbers of offenders are now incarcerated in the state and federal systems for relatively minor drug offenses including many youth sentenced to long prison terms that resulted from single incidents or periods in their lives when they experimented with drugs. For example, over 2,000 Grateful Dead fans have been imprisoned as a result of charges of possessing small amounts of LSD on sugar cubes (Kelly & Bernstein, 2006; see Sullum, 1993, for discussion of the use of drug carrier weight in calculating federal drug crime sentences).

Photo 8.1   Deadheads in Prison

Deadheads at Federal Correctional Institution, Raybrook, NY. Photo Courtesy of Human Rights and the Drug War Photo Exhibit Project, www.hr95.org.

Part of the rationale for enacting such stiff penalties for drug use is the well-established association between drugs and crime. The Office of National Drug Control Policy classifies the drug-crime relationship in terms of three categories:

1. *Drug-defined offenses:* violations of drug laws, including possession, use, distribution, or manufacture of illegal drugs

2. *Drug-related offenses:* offenses that involve the influence of pharmacological effects or where the offender's addiction/need for the substance contributes to the commission of the crime

3. *Drug-using lifestyle:* a lifestyle that increases the chances of involvement in illegal activity because drug users may not participate in the legitimate market economy and are thus exposed to situational/contextual factors and criminogenic influences that make them more likely to be involved in a range of offenses

Drug-related offenses and drug-using lifestyles are major contributors to the crime problem in the United States (Spiess & Fallow, 2000). Research has shown that more prisoners are incarcerated for drug crimes than for any other offense, offenders are often under the influence of drugs during the commission of their crimes and test positive for drugs on arrest, drug trafficking contributes to violent crime, and many offenders engage in property crime to support a drug habit (Office of National Drug Control Policy, 2000). Among offenders on correctional supervision, 23.6% of the 1.6 million people on correctional supervision reported illicit drug use compared with 7.7% adults not under supervision (Substance Abuse and Mental Health Services Administration, 2006). The *Arrestee Drug Abuse Monitoring* (ADAM) program of the National Institute of Justice has collected the following national data about drug use, alcohol and drug dependency, and drug market participation in arrestees:

- Over 64% of arrestees had recently used one of five drugs (cocaine, marijuana, opiates, methamphetamines, or PCP) with marijuana the most common followed by cocaine.

- Few arrestees who both used drugs and were at risk for drug dependency had completed treatment in the year prior to arrest.

- A large percentage of women arrestees test positive for drugs, the largest percentage for cocaine, and the second largest for marijuana.

- Juvenile arrestees are more likely to test positive for marijuana than any other drug, with cocaine being the second most likely. Estimates indicate that for every 1,000 hardcore drug users, there are 750 arrests (Arrestee Drug Abuse Monitoring, 2000).

The drugs that account for the greatest proportion of drug addiction in the United States are morphine and heroin (Clinard & Meier, 2004). Both are white powdered substances derived from opium that users generally inject either directly into the veins or subcutaneously. These drugs must be prepared carefully because, if not diluted properly, they can produce toxic effects. The "high" that comes from morphine and heroin is an initial flushed or tingling sensation, followed by drowsiness, and then a state of euphoria. Each time a person uses the drug, more is needed to achieve the euphoric state as the user builds up a tolerance and physical dependency. As the tolerance increases, the addict becomes immune to the drug's effect and can tolerate doses that would be enough to kill a nonaddict. Addiction to heroin or morphine can occur over a very short time period, in some cases a matter of months. Addiction to the drug results in physical dependency and if the drug is not regularly used, severe withdrawal symptoms including nervousness, stomach cramps, running nose, vomiting, diarrhea, and shaking. Once the addict uses the drug, withdrawal symptoms will cease within 30 minutes.

Barbiturates, synthetic drugs that have a calming effect on the central nervous system, and *stimulants* such as cocaine, methamphetamines, and hallucinogens are generally not as addictive as heroin and morphine, but all are either psychologically or physically addictive (or both)[10] and illegal. Of the illicit drugs, marijuana is the most widely used in the United States. A large percentage of the population has tried marijuana at least once, and 7% are regular users (Clinard & Meier, 2004). Despite the popularity of the gateway theory—that marijuana facilitates experimentation with stronger and more addictive drugs—the overwhelming majority of marijuana users never progress to using harder drugs. Most continue to use marijuana or switch to alcohol and do not move on to harder drugs like heroin and morphine.

Although the correlation between drug use and criminal behavior has long been established, a cause-effect relationship has not. There is no convincing evidence that drug use causes crime, that crime causes drug use, or whether some third factor explains the drug-crime connection. Recent research has attempted to explore the drug-crime connection with a diverse range of methodologies. For example, employing *street ethnography*,[11] Knowles (1999) found that drug-using behavior is primarily a social learning experience that is part of a complex matrix of public order and other offenses (including prostitution, pornography, food stamp fraud, illegal gambling, and police corruption). The social learning of illegal drug use and abuse is facilitated by and symptomatic of a disordered social system. Yacoubian and Kane (1998) used an empirical approach to identify types of drug users to understand different patterns and trajectories of drug users. Using cluster analysis (a statistical technique used to identify groups that are similar with respect to particular variables/characteristics), the authors identified *six empirical clusters or types of illegal drug users:*

- *Dope fiends:* Highest rate of use of injectable and noninjectable drugs with need to be under the influence of drugs during commission of criminal offense. Crimes tend to be miscellaneous and property crimes. Most are male between the ages of 23 and 30. This type of drug user is highly physically dependent/addicted.

- *Zombies:* High rate of use of both injectable and noninjectable drugs. This type of user enjoys using drugs, but does not need to be under the influence while committing criminal offenses, which tend to be a mix of property and drug and alcohol offenses. Most are male between the ages of 30 and 37.

- *Converters:* High rate of sustained use of easily obtainable noninjectable drugs. Need to be under the influence of drugs during the commission of crimes, which tend to be property offenses and, to a lesser extent, drug and alcohol offenses. This type of drug user is addicted to noninjectable drugs and commits crime to support habit by converting stolen property into cash to obtain drugs. Most are male over age 37.

- *Injectors:* High use of injectable drugs and low use of easily obtainable noninjectable drugs. Moderately low rate of need to be under the influence during commission of crimes, which tend to be miscellaneous crimes (not property or violent). Most are male between the ages of 18 and 23.

- *Recreational users:* Moderately low use of injectable and noninjectable drugs. Do not need to be under the influence of drugs to commit criminal offenses, which are almost exclusively drug and alcohol offenses involving obtaining small amounts of drugs for irregular recreational use. Most are male between the ages of 30 and 37.

- *Enablers:* Low use of injectable and noninjectable drugs, but need to be under influence of drugs or alcohol when committing crimes. These offenders are not drug addicts, but rather engage in criminal behavior while under the influence of drugs or alcohol. Mixed gender (60% male, 40% female), with mean age of 37.

Based on findings from these creative approaches to understanding the drug-crime connection, it can be concluded that individuals who use illegal drugs are a diverse group of addicts, recreational users, and those who use drugs primarily to facilitate (other non–drug- and alcohol-related) criminal behavior. Illegal drug use, regardless of the type of user, is situated within a complex ecological framework in which drug use (as well as buying and selling) is intimately connected to public order, property, and other crimes.

Alcohol-Related Offenses and Driving Under the Influence

Although alcohol is not an illegal drug, *public drunkenness* and *drunk driving* are illegal. Alcohol is by far the oldest and most popular mood-altering drug used in the United States. (The two most popular legal drugs, alcohol and nicotine, cause more medical, psychological, physical, and social problems than any other drug; see Clinard & Meier, 2004). Alcohol consumption has long been associated with criminal behavior as well as a range of social and health problems including physical and psychological dependency, impaired social relationships, physical illness, and poor work performance (Clinard & Meier, 2004). Two-thirds of Americans have consumed alcohol, half of all Americans report that they drink alcohol regularly, and 18 million Americans (8.5% of the U.S. population) meet the diagnostic criteria for alcohol abuse or alcoholism (MADD, 2005). Heavy alcohol users aged 12 to 17 are more likely to participate in delinquent behavior than youth who are not heavy drinkers (U.S. Department of Health and Human Services, 2005), and at least 40% of all crimes (nonviolent and violent) are committed under the influence of alcohol (MADD, 2005). In 2005 there were 1,371,919 arrests in the United States for driving under the influence (DUI laws, though commonly associated with drinking and driving, apply to driving under the influence of any substance, e.g., illegal drugs, prescription drugs), 556,167 arrests for drunkenness, and 597,838 liquor law violations (UCR, 2005). This represents 18% of all arrests in the United States, not including disorderly conduct and other offenses that are typically alcohol related. Other authors report a higher percentage (31%) of alcohol-related offenses (e.g., Clinard & Meier, 2004), which likely includes other alcohol-related offenses.

Drunk driving is one of the most socially harmful substance-related criminal behaviors. A high percentage of drunk drivers are involved in traffic accidents, many with fatal outcomes (Karlsson et al., 2003). The following are findings regarding the nature, prevalence, and consequences of drunk driving in the United States:

- Motor vehicle crashes are the leading cause of death among youth age 16 to 20, and 29% of the young drivers killed in these crashes had been drinking alcohol (U.S. Department of Health & Human Services, 2004).

- Approximately 39% of the 42,800 total traffic fatalities in the United States in 2004 were alcohol related. An estimated 16,654 people were killed in these crashes—an average of one almost every half-hour. This is a decrease of 2% from 2003, when 17,013 people were killed in alcohol-related traffic crashes (40% of the 42,642 people killed in all traffic crashes; MADD, 2005).

- Of the 17,013 people who died in alcohol-related crashes in 2003, 86% had a blood alcohol concentration (BAC) of more than 0.08.

- In 2003, an estimated 13.6% of Americans aged 12 or older (32.3 million people) drove under the influence of alcohol at least once in the 12 months prior to the interview (a decrease of 14.2% or 33.5 million from 2002; U.S. Department of Health & Human Services, 2003).

- Among youth aged 16 to 20, 21% reported that they had driven under the influence of alcohol or drugs in the past year, with Whites more likely than other racial groups to report a DUI (U.S. Department of Health & Human Services, 2004).

- Of the 4.2 million youth age 16 to 20 who reported driving under the influence of alcohol or drugs in the past year, only 4% (169,000) had been arrested, with a higher percentage of males (6%) versus females (2%) (U.S. Department of Health & Human Services, 2004).

- Most drivers involved in fatal crashes are male age 21 to 24 (U.S. Department of Transportation, 2003).

- Young drivers prefer drinking at private parties whereas older drivers prefer to drink at bars and taverns.

- Many teens feel pressured to engage in drinking and careless driving on prom and graduation nights, which increases the teen crash rate (MADD, 2005).

- Social class is a consistently important predictor of both drunk driving and public drunkenness, with the working class more likely to report engaging in and to be arrested for public drunkenness and drunk driving (Karlsson & Romelsjö, 1997; study conducted in Sweden).

Clearly, drunk driving is both a prevalent and socially harmful criminal behavior. However, there is a long-standing ambivalence in America regarding alcohol consumption. On one hand, we believe that alcoholic beverages are a positive feature of our culture. Beer is sold on college campuses and at sporting events, wine is served at social gatherings, and all types of alcohol are sold at restaurants. Alcoholic beverages are a staple in the American diet and social landscape. On the other hand, the Puritan and temperance roots of American culture require self-control and restraint. The message is, have a little alcohol with your dinner, at your party, or every once in a while at your sporting event, but don't lose control. "Apparently there is a place for drunkenness in our culture, as long as it does no harm" (Jacobs, 1989, p. 193).

The problem with the cultural ambivalence over alcohol use is that people are left on their own to control themselves, with few policies and practices in place that acknowledge that alcohol is addictive and some individuals may be more affected (and have a harder time controlling themselves) than others. In recent years, initiatives such as free New Year's Eve taxi cab rides from bars, "designated driver" campaigns, public education on drunk driving, drunk driving crackdowns and checkpoints, stiffer penalties for drunk drivers, reduction of the BAC level to 0.08 in most states, and use of the interlock device (an apparatus affixed to the car's ignition to prevent a driver from starting a car without first breathing into the device and recording a BAC within the legal limit) for convicted drunk drivers have attempted to call attention to the problems associated with alcohol. However, the simple fact that alcohol is served in public places people will have to drive or walk away from ensures that public drunkenness and drunk driving will occur. Furthermore, public support and validation for alcohol consumption is a powerful facilitator for the cognitive neutralization techniques alcoholics, drunk drivers, and others who cross that self-control threshold and engage in alcohol-related criminal behavior use. In other words, many (if not most) drunk driving offenses can be explained within the context of routine activity theory. Ross, in his 1993 book, *Confronting Drunk Driving,* explains the "routine" nature of drunk driving:

American society combines a near-total commitment to private automobile transportation with a positive evaluation of drinking in recreational situations. Conventional and conforming behavior in these areas implies the likelihood of people driving while impaired by alcohol. Furthermore, in certain social categories, such as younger males, the norms regarding both drinking and driving appear to be extraordinarily favorable for the creation of impaired driving. Drunk driving can thus be seen as a routine, expected aspect of American life, supported by prevailing norms and institutions. (cited in Clinard & Meier, 2004, p. 329)

There is some disagreement in the literature regarding whether individuals arrested for alcohol-related DUI are mostly casual or chronic drinkers. Jacobs (1989) argues that one of the most common myths about drunk driving is that it is a crime virtually everyone commits, but when drinking and driving is differentiated from "drunk driving," this is not the case:

While practically everyone who drinks and drives necessarily engages in drinking/driving, drunk driving is qualitatively different, involving more than the mere combination of drinking and driving; it involves degraded and impaired driving capacities, the severe deterioration of judgment and control over the vehicle, and an endangering of one's own life and the lives of passengers, other road users, and pedestrians. (p. 43)

A study conducted by the Transportation Research Institute at the University of Michigan involving a case study of adolescent drivers convicted of felony drunk driving found that most of the fatal drunk drivers had poor driving histories, did not wear seat belts at the time of the accident, were drinking beer while in their vehicles, were driving at an excessive speed at the time of the crash, and took little responsibility for their actions (Eby, Hopp, & Streff, 1996). On the other hand, *Mothers Against Drunk Driving* (MADD), a long-time nonprofit agency devoted to fighting drunk driving and supporting victims of drunk driving, reports findings from a recent national survey that the majority of those who reported an alcohol-related DUI (in the prior 12 months) are not alcohol dependent or alcohol abusers (Caetano & McGrath, 2005).[12]

It is likely that, though many people drink and drive over the course of their lifetimes (and may become involved in alcohol-related accidents as a result), most do not engage in the pattern of substance abuse that is associated with and contributes to "drunk driving" offenses. Statistically speaking, individuals who are arrested for alcohol-related crimes tend to be problem drinkers or chronic alcoholics. On the other hand, alcohol can be a powerful facilitator for all types of criminal behavior because of its legality and availability and its potential to decrease inhibitions (regardless of whether the user is a one-time drinker or a chronic alcoholic).

Public drunkenness alone accounts for 4% of the total crime in the United States. Considering the range of criminal behavior and the fact that more serious alcohol-related offenses are not included in this category, this is a substantial amount of the overall crime. Most of the offenders arrested for public drunkenness are from lower-class minority groups. These offenders make up a group of offenders who have a high recidivism rate and experience a never-ending cycle of arrest, jail, release, and rearrest (Clinard & Meier, 2004). It is estimated that between 20 and 40% of the homeless population are heavy drinkers and a social solidarity component to drinking in skid-row populations makes alcohol use a routine activity for many who find themselves homeless. Furthermore, the simple fact that people who are homeless cannot drink alcohol behind closed doors accounts for the increased numbers of arrests for public drunkenness among this population.

Compulsive Gambling

Compulsive gambling is a pathological and uncontrollable urge to gamble despite adverse consequences. Because gambling is illegal in most states, compulsive gamblers often find themselves engaging in illegal gambling activities to meet the needs of their addiction. The UCR defines gambling as "to unlawfully bet or wager money or something else of value; assist, promote, or operate a game of chance for money or some other stake; possess or transmit wagering information; manufacture, sell, purchase, possess, or transport gambling equipment, devices or goods; or tamper with the outcome of a sporting event or contest to gain a gambling advantage" (UCR, 2005). Illegal gambling activities include but are not limited to conducting illegal lotteries, bookmaking, maintaining video gambling machines, pool selling, numbers games, Internet gambling, illegal Bingo, betting on sporting events (the National Football League's Super Bowl is the largest single occasion for legal and illegal sports betting; see Pavalko, 2000), and off-track horse and dog races. In 2005, there were 11,180 arrests for illegal gambling in the United States (UCR, 2005).

Much of the true picture of the extent of illegal gambling is masked by the view that illegal gambling is not a serious offense that should be formally sanctioned. Furthermore, illegal gambling is underreported (Pavalko, 2000). Because most illegal gambling is not identified and offenders are not arrested, the actual extent of illegal gambling activities is largely unknown. The bulk of the arrests for illegal gambling involve federal arrests in which illegal gambling is one of many charges against an organized crime member or members. Compulsive gambling more generally (legal and illegal) is a "hidden disease" that leaves few telltale signs.

Like alcohol consumption, gambling is legal in designated places in the United States. Gambling is a $550 billion-a-year industry. It is estimated that 80% of American adults gamble, and 10% become addicted. Like drug addicts, many compulsive gamblers engage in criminal behavior to support their habit. Research shows that 85% will commit a felony economic crime to support their addiction. Pathological gamblers have impaired social relationships and most experience poor work performance and physical symptoms as a result of their gambling behavior (Paul & Townsend, 1998).

A number of typologies have been developed to better understand compulsive gambling. Research suggests that, at the most basic level, it is meaningful to classify compulsive gamblers by gender. Male and female gamblers differ with respect to their underlying motivation and the types of gambling behaviors they engage in. Male gamblers tend to gamble for the excitement of it whereas female gamblers appear to engage in the behavior as a form of escapism (Paul & Townsend, 1998). McCown and Chamberlain (2000) classify gamblers into six types:

1. *Professional gamblers:* Gamble as an occupation. Professional gamblers are not addicted to gambling and can control and regulate when they play, the type of games they play, and how much money they spend. Professional gamblers are very rare today but were prevalent in the old West and the turn-of-the-century gambling parlors.

2. *Antisocial gamblers:* Also known as "rip-off artists," fix games or play with marked cards. They tend to have antisocial personality disorder, may develop an addiction to gambling, and tend to suffer from multiple addictions.

3. *Casual social gamblers:* Gamble for recreation and entertainment. Gambling is a harmless form of recreation that takes up a limited amount of leisure time and does not interfere with social or occupational obligations.

4. *Serious social gamblers:* Gambling is primary source of recreation and entertainment. Serious social gamblers manage to function on a daily basis, but devote a considerable (sometimes excessive) amount of leisure time to gambling. Casual and serious social gambling can be viewed along a continuum of time spent gambling from benign to extreme.

5. *Neurotic gamblers:* Gamble as a distraction from empty lives or dysfunctional emotional states. Neurotic gamblers use gambling as a drug to deal with low self-concept and a range of other emotional, psychological, and life problems. For neurotic gamblers, gambling is analgesic rather than euphoric and a way to deal with or avoid problems.

6. *Compulsive gamblers:* Gamble as a compulsion. Gambling and gambling-related activities are the most important thing in compulsive gamblers' lives. Compulsive gamblers experience euphoria not unlike that experienced by drug addicts. The hallmark of compulsive gamblers is that they become increasingly in debt and have to resort to extraordinary measures (i.e., crime) to get themselves out of their dire financial situations, with extremely high probability that they will resort to criminal behavior.

Like the substance-related disorders, gambling is also a disorder listed in the *DSM-IV-TR. Pathological gambling* is an *impulse disorder.* Impulse disorders (including intermittent explosive disorder, pyromania, kleptomania, and trichotillomania, i.e., a compulsion to pull out one's own hair) involve an inability to resist engaging in behaviors that may be harmful to the individual sufferer or others. The following are criteria for diagnosis of pathological gambling:

- Persistent and recurrent maladaptive gambling behavior as indicated by five (or more) of the following:

  (1) is preoccupied with gambling (e.g., preoccupied with reliving past gambling experiences, handicapping or planning the next venture, or thinking of ways to get money with which to gamble)

  (2) needs to gamble with increasing amounts of money in order to achieve the desired excitement

  (3) has repeated unsuccessful efforts to control, cut back, or stop gambling

(4) is restless or irritable when attempting to cut down or stop gambling

(5) gambles as a way of escaping from problems or of relieving a dysphoric mood (e.g., feelings of helplessness, guilt, anxiety, depression)

(6) after losing money gambling, often returns another day to get even ("chasing" one's losses)

(7) lies to family members, therapist, or others to conceal the extent of involvement with gambling

(8) has committed illegal acts such as forgery, fraud, theft, or embezzlement to finance gambling

(9) has jeopardized or lost a significant relationship, job, or educational or career opportunity because of gambling

(10) relies on others to provide money to relieve a desperate financial situation caused by gambling

- The gambling behavior is not better accounted for by a manic episode. (APA, 2000)

Although it is possible to be diagnosed as a pathological gambler and not engage in illegal gambling (e.g., someone who lives in Las Vegas who is addicted to roulette or the slots), most pathological gamblers find themselves engaging in some form of criminal behavior, either to support their habit, as part of their gambling activities, or through exposure to criminal networks that support legal and illegal gambling activities.

Robert Custer, a pioneer in the treatment of gambling addiction, developed a profile of the typical compulsive gambler. Although 20% of compulsive gamblers are female, the typical compulsive gambler who hits bottom is married, White, Catholic or Jewish, in his early 40s, began gambling in adolescence, comes from a lower-middle-class background with traditional values, has some college education, is in debt for approximately one year's salary, had minimal or no legal problems until his gambling progressed, is 15 times more likely to commit suicide than the general population, and has a 20% chance of also being addicted to drugs or alcohol.

Gambling enjoys an element of cultural support. Many who engage in compulsive gambling became involved in gambling as a form of risk-taking. The values of competition and risk-taking lie at the root of gambling behavior, particularly among men. Heineman (1992) suggests that team sports offer the opportunity to participate in competition, to engage in risk-taking behavior, and to try for the "big win." In adulthood, however, when there are fewer opportunities to participate in team sports, gambling offers the opportunity for vicarious participation in competition by wagering on who will win. This allows the gambler to participate in the action and the thrill associated with competitive risk-taking. This explanation of male compulsive gambling is consistent with findings suggesting that the motivation for male gamblers is excitement and risk.

The Nature and Dynamics of Addiction

The causes of substance abuse differ depending on the individual user and the theoretical perspective. Some people use and abuse drugs and alcohol because they are readily available in their neighborhoods and the peer groups within which they interact. Others abuse drugs and alcohol to mediate psychological deficits such as personality disorders, depression, anxiety disorders, or a range of psychiatric afflictions. Some rationally and consciously choose to engage in substance abuse for "fun," to get high, and to experience the effects (to relax, increase sexual responsiveness and energy, etc.). Some substance abusers begin with marijuana and move on to harder drugs (consistent with the gateway model); however, others begin using powerful drugs such as heroin or methamphetamines without ever having used marijuana.

Substance abuse is a type of addiction. The term *addiction* refers to the compulsion to use drugs or alcohol (or to engage in a particular behavior such as gambling) regardless of adverse consequences. Sometimes the term *chemical dependency* is used to differentiate addiction to an illegal substance from addiction to a particular behavior (gambling, sex). Addiction has been defined narrowly as physical dependence on a particular substance and broadly as powerlessness over a particular type of behavior. Thus, broadly speaking, a person can be addicted to work or sex. Clinard and Meier (2004) suggest that the disease model is largely responsible for the long list of "anonymous" groups such as Alcoholics Anonymous, Overeaters Anonymous, Narcotics Anonymous, Sex Addicts Anonymous, Workaholics Anonymous, and Gamblers Anonymous, and such expansive definitions of addiction may destroy the meaning of the term. Overcoming addiction requires "high resolve, a changed or changing personal identity, and a desire to reestablish conventional and social relationships" (Clinard & Meier, 2004, p. 276). Laws prohibiting drug use and abuse, public drunkenness, drunk driving, and gambling have been enacted largely based on the view that certain drugs are addictive and their use needs to be externally controlled and the belief that lack of self-control contributes to social disorder.

A number of explanatory models and perspectives on addiction exist. People can be physiologically, psychologically, socially addicted to a particular substance or behavior. *Physiological addiction* is characterized by progressive tolerance, withdrawal symptoms if the individual ceases the behavior, and craving especially during withdrawal. *Psychological addiction* is characterized by cognitive preoccupation with the behavior, use of neutralizing techniques (excuses and justifications), negative behavioral or physical consequences resulting from the addictive behavior, and negative emotions. *Social addiction* refers to the social basis of addiction; addicts cannot function without enablers or "codependents"—people who support, cover up, or otherwise facilitate the addict's addictive behavior (Vandenburgh, 2004).

Other Public Order Offenses: Disorderly Conduct, Vagrancy, Loitering, and Other Violations

Other offenses that are often viewed as disruptive to public order (and designated a crime for this reason) include disorderly conduct, vagrancy, loitering, trespassing, vandalism, and graffiti. In some cases (vandalism and graffiti), property is destroyed or damaged, so the offense might also be considered a property crime. However, these offenses are distinguished from other property crimes in that the motive of the offense is not economic gain, but is rather rooted in situational and routine activity factors (the opportunity to commit the offense), peer influence, addiction and substance abuse, and social disorganization. The primary harm in these offenses is public disorder, with no clearly identifiable victim (except in the case of property damage). The feature these offenses share is that they are rooted in substance abuse or social misfortune, have no clearly identifiable victim, and are perceived by the general public (and legislators) to be a menace to society and public order.

In 2005, there were 279,562 arrests for vandalism, 193,469 for carrying or possessing weapons, 678,231 for disorderly conduct, 33,227 for vagrancy, 3,764 for suspicion (arrested for no specific offense and released), 140,835 for curfew and loitering violations, 108,954 for runaways, and 3,863,785 for all other offenses (includes violations of state or local laws not included in categories of Part I or II offenses, other than traffic violations). All of these arrests combined account for 38% of the total number of arrests in the United States.

Is There an Underlying Theoretical Explanation for Public Order Crime?

Most public order crime can best be described as behavior deemed socially disruptive that is committed by individuals who are powerless, poverty stricken, and caught in a web of addiction and life problems. Unlike other types of offenders who specialize in a particular offense behavior or are attached to conventional norms and values, most public order offenders do not specialize in a single offense behavior and are caught up in a lifestyle and subculture in which offenses such as prostitution, drug use, gambling, drunkenness, and so on are part of the social landscape.

Public order offenses, from prostitution to substance abuse to gambling, are publicly perceived as an indication of weak social character (Dabney, 2004). However, public order offenders tend to perceive their situations as largely beyond their control or a product of a sociopolitical and economic system that enables, validates, and sustains their deviant and criminal behavior. From the perspective of the public order offender, he or she does not have a choice to participate in mainstream, conventional, legitimate behavior because of addiction or economic necessity, or in many cases both. Depending on one's view, this could be perceived as "a series of normative neutralizations in an effort to protect or defend their moral standing" (Dabney, 2004, p. 249) or a legitimate assessment of the situation of many individuals who engage in public order crime.

Several features distinguish public order crime as a homogeneous crime category. First, *the condition underlying most public order crime is addiction.* Substance-related offenses, gambling, driving under the influence, and soliciting prostitution are, for most, rooted in addiction. In fact, the foundation of the laws prohibiting public order offenses is the idea that engaging in these behaviors or use of these substances is physically or psychologically addictive and socially harmful. Second, *public order offenses are interrelated and rooted in and facilitated by an array of social problems,* including homelessness, poverty, and racism. Public order offenses thrive in an economic system that ensures that a segment of the population will be able to survive only by engaging in prostitution, buying or selling drugs, and committing other public order offenses. Third, *much public order crime is a young person's game that requires an element of risk-taking behavior* and attitude of nonconformity. Disorderly conduct, vandalism, and weapons violations tend to be committed by (male) youth fueled by bravado. The diagram in Figure 8.2 displays the interrelated features of public order crime.

❖ **Figure 8.2**   Features of Public Order Crime

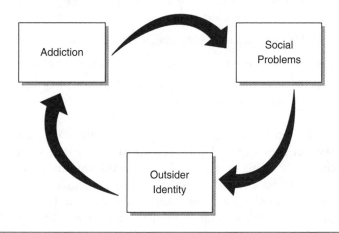

Dabney (2004) identifies a number of common features of public order crime:

- Most public order crimes require a baseline level of skill and organization.

- Most public order offenses take the form of one-on-one interactions between complete strangers or casual acquaintances.

- Most public order crimes occur in either open-air environments or private locales.

- Public order offenders display some of the most pronounced criminal careers of any category of perpetrator.

- Drug offenders exhibit considerable variation in their criminal activities, generally involving themselves in a variety of offenses.

- The pleasure principle tends to dominate the mindset of the public order offender.

- Public order offenders are driven by a host of instrumental and expressive motives.

- More often than not, persons in the production/distribution side of the public order crime equation are motivated by the promise of financial reward.

- Persons who play the client role in public order offenses tend to be motivated by self-gratification or self-enrichment.

- Public order offenses tend to be preceded by rudimentary exercises in planning and target selection.

- Persons who engage in these acts [public order offenses] usually invoke a series of normative neutralizations in an effort to protect or defend their moral standing.

- Public order offenders share an inextricable bond with what we know as the criminal subculture.

- Most offenders orient to one another as peers, colleagues, or team members.

- A great deal of scripted interaction and socialization takes place between the participants of public order offenses.

- The criminal justice system has a mixed statutory response to public order crimes.

- The clearance rates for public order offenses are woefully low.

- Society sends a mixed message in informal social control of public order crime (Dabney, 2004, pp. 252–553).

The most striking thing about public order crime is that it is the least discussed crime category but represents by far the largest single category of criminal behavior in terms of its prevalence and the amount of law enforcement resources devoted to its control. Taken together, substance-related offenses, prostitution, commercialized vice, gambling, and other public order offenses resulted in 9,426,270 total arrests for all public order offenses in 2005. With the total number of 14,094,167 arrests, public order offenses account for 67% of all arrests in the United States. Clearly, this suggests the need to develop policies and practices targeting the motivations, factors, and forces associated with public order crime to reduce, prevent, and control crime.

Summary

Criminal behavior that violates the moral sentiment of society without a clearly identifiable victim is generally referred to as public order crime. Such crimes include a broad range of offenses from prostitution and pornography to substance abuse, public drunkenness, driving under the influence, disorderly conduct, trespassing, vagrancy, and curfew and loitering law violations. The most commonly discussed public order offenses are prostitution and promoting and soliciting prostitution, substance abuse, driving under the influence, and gambling. A common theme running through most public order offenses (with the exception of prostitution when conceptualized as rational and purposeful sex work for economic gain) is that such offenses are largely rooted in addiction, opportunity, poverty, mental illness, and despair. Public order crime is designated as a punishable offense because the behavior is seen as disruptive in some way to the social and moral order. Laws against behaviors deemed to be a threat to public order change across time and place, and the public debate regarding whether the behavior should be seen as an offense at all is ongoing. Most public order offenders do not specialize in a particular criminal offense. Rather, they are immersed in a lifestyle and subculture in which offenses against the public order are a normalized part of the social landscape.

DISCUSSION QUESTIONS

1. Define public order crime. Is public order crime a homogeneous crime category? If so, what are the essential and interrelated features of this type of crime? Discuss.

2. Compared with other crime categories, what is the extent of the public order crime problem in America? In your opinion, what policies and practices should be implemented to better deal with public order offense?

3. Describe the prostitute-pimp continuum.

4. Can male prostitution be understood within the same framework as female prostitution? How does gender (of the prostitute and client) shape the behavior and the meaning it holds and the identities of the offenders and clients?

5. One of the most widespread public order offenses is driving under the influence. Identify some of the factors that influence and perpetuate DUI offenses from the different perspectives discussed in Chapter 2 (biological, psychological, sociological, cultural, opportunity, phenomenological). What factors ensure that DUI will remain a high crime problem in American society? What suggestions can you offer to reduce the incidence of DUI offenses? Discuss.

On Your Own: Log on to the Web-based student study site at http://www.sagepub .com/helfgottstudy/ for the URL links in the Web Exercises, study aids such as review quizzes, and research recommendations including links to journal articles specifically selected for this book.

WEB EXERCISES

1. Carol Leigh, otherwise known as the *Scarlet Harlot,* San Francisco-based prostitution activist and feminist and author of *The Unrepentant Whore* (Leigh, 2004), has fought for the rights of prostitutes since the 1970s. Go to the *Prostitution Education Network,* at http://www.bayswan .org/what_is.html, the Sex Worker's Outreach Project, at http://www.swop-usa.org/, and Leigh's Web site at http://www.unrepentantwhore.com/ to find out more about arguments in favor of decriminalizing prostitution. Contrast this view with information available on the *Prostitution Research & Education* Web site at http://www.prostitutionresearch.com/fact sheet.html that clearly paints a picture of the prostitute as victim. After reading arguments supporting these contrasting perspectives on prostitution, discuss whether or not prostitution should be considered (theoretically and legally) a "public order crime."

2. Read the Office of Juvenile Justice and Delinquency Prevention report on the prostitution of juveniles by Finkelhor and Ormrod (2004): http://ojjdp.ncjrs.org/publications/ PubAbstract.asp?pubi=11663. Discuss the issues raised in this report and the nature of, extent of, and legal issues pertaining to the prostitution of juveniles.

3. Read the 986 *Attorney General's Commission on Pornography:* http://www.afa.net/pornog raphy/attygenrpt.html. At the end of the report are questions regarding the extent of

pornography in the community. Using these questions, assess the nature and extent of pornography in your community and analyze/discuss the ways in which pornography contributes to public order or disorder in your local community.

4. Explore the Mothers Against Drunk Driving (MADD) in America Web site: http://www .madd.org/. Read through the site pages on MADD programs, research and statistics, activism, news, and so on, and identify what types of services the agency provides, its central priority issues, and future directions for research and policy on drunk driving.

5. Go to the National Institute of Justice Arrestee Drug Abuse Monitoring Program (ADAM) Web site: http://www.ojp.usdoj.gov/nij/adam/welcome.html. Go to the most recent *Arrestee Drug Abuse Monitoring: Annual Report* and determine the demographic characteristics of drug abuse arrestees. Using data available in the report, summarize and discuss the nature and characteristics of drug use among arrestees.

Political Crime ❖

*I am innocent of the charges the U.S. Government is trying to pin on me.
Just as many activists have experienced, I am being targeted by the U.S.
Government and the FBI, not because I am guilty, but because I have chosen
to challenge the status quo.*

—Michael Scarpitti aka Tre Arrow

Radical Environmental Activist,

Accused Eco-Terrorist, Political Prisoner

Not every value entails rebellion, but every act of rebellion tacitly invokes a value.

—Albert Camus (1956), *The Rebel*

Political crime is crime motivated by a particular ideological perspective. *Ideology* refers to "the distinctive belief systems, ideas, and abstract ideals that are perceived as providing the true meaning of life" (Hagan, 1997, p. 1). In the United States, there is no official category of criminal behavior called *political crime*. This is because the First Amendment of the Bill of Rights in the U.S. Constitution restricts the government from taking action against individuals for expressing their views, peacefully assembling, and redressing the government. The First Amendment reads,

> Congress shall make no law respecting an establishment of religion, or prohibiting the free exercise thereof; or abridging the freedom of speech, or of the press; or the right of the people peaceably to assemble, and to petition the government for a redress of grievances.

What this means is that citizens who disagree with governmental policies and viewpoints may do so publicly without threat of arrest or imprisonment. The more political freedom a particular state or country has, the greater the struggle to enhance and preserve it. In countries with little political freedom, there is no attempt to obscure that speaking out against the government is a punishable offense.[1] In the United States, a specific legal category of *political crime* would be in direct conflict with the First Amendment and the value placed in individual liberty in American culture.

Although it is not against the law in the United States to espouse political views contrary to those of the government, those who do are often targeted by law enforcement and sanctioned for violation of a range of offenses including violation of fire ordinances, loitering and trespassing, disturbing the peace, parading without a permit, and disorderly conduct. Some individuals and organized groups involved in political activism clearly cross the line engaging in more extreme offenses such as assault, murder, arson, and treason. In cases where an offense is not readily apparent, "the dominant sociopolitical forces are usually able to use existing or new legislation to suppress dissent and protest" (Clinard, Quinney, & Wildeman, 1994, p. 143).

The ways in which political offenders are defined, identified, and socially controlled make it virtually impossible to provide an accurate statistical figure to reflect the true extent of political crime in the United States and around the world. In the United States, at both state and federal levels, crimes that would be considered politically motivated may be recorded in any crime category from murder and arson to lesser offenses such as obstruction of justice. In the federal system, crimes that are explicitly political such as treason, espionage, sabotage, and sedition are included in the category of "national defense offenses" and civil rights violations are included under the category of "public order offenses." In 2004, there were 63 reported arrests for civil rights offenses and only 11 reported arrests for national defense offenses (U.S. Department of Justice, Compendium of Federal Justice Statistics, 2004). At the state level, as reflected in the UCR, crimes against the government are most likely recorded in arrest data under the categories of disorderly conduct, curfew and loitering violations, vandalism, "all other offenses," and to a lesser extent murder and arson. Thus, political crimes are imbedded in other crime categories, within the 14,062 arrests for murder, 16,337 arrests for arson, 678,231 for disorderly conduct, 140,835 for curfew and loitering, and 3,863,785 arrests for "all other" offenses (UCR, 2005).

Defining Political Crime

Political crime is a problematic concept. Data on political crime in research and course texts in criminology and criminal justice are sparse and there is considerable confusion about what constitutes a political offense (Ross, 2003). There are a number of factors that may contribute to this lack of consensus. First, all crimes can be viewed as political in that, by law, they have been deemed a threat to society. Some suggest that any attempt to categorize or classify "political crime" is itself a political act. Second, most ideologically motivated criminal behaviors fall under other categories of criminal behavior. Data are not collected through the UCR, the U.S. Department of Justice, or elsewhere specifically for political crime, so it is a very difficult phenomenon to study empirically. According to Hagan (1997), "It is not the crimes themselves that distinguish political criminals but rather their motivations, their views of crime as a necessary means to a higher goal" (p. 2). Political assassination is murder, destruction of property during a political protest is vandalism, bombing an occupied building as a terrorist act is arson, attempted murder, and (if those in the building die) mass murder, and so on. Yet, *political offenses have a distinct motivational nature that should not be overlooked. A typology of criminal behavior that omits political crime is incomplete, leaving out a distinct and homogeneous category of criminal behavior.*

Political crime differs from other types of crime in that its motivation is *ideological.* "An actor has committed a political crime if he or she has a political or ideological intention or motivation to cause harm" (Ross, 2003, p. 4). Political criminals engage in behaviors that violate the law for the primary purpose of opposing the ideas of an individual, group, or governmental power. Political crime has been defined in the literature as crime both by and against the government and committed in organizational, occupational, or individual contexts. When crime is committed by governmental agents for the purpose of maintaining power, it is called *state-organized crime* or *state crime.* Protesters who defy police orders to get out of the street, the animal rights activists who release animals from a laboratory, a militant who bombs a governmental building to protest a series of governmental actions, ideologically motivated suicide bombers who cause exorbitant harm to citizens of another country to further their message through fear, the government that maintains power by lying, stealing, violating the rights of or otherwise harming its citizens—all can be defined as political criminals.

In some contexts political crimes are committed simultaneously by both citizens and the state. For example, as has been the case in many riot situations throughout history (e.g., during the civil rights movement, Vietnam War protests, the LA riots), during the 1999 WTO riots in Seattle, both protesters and police were charged with committing offenses (Box 9.1). However, who gets convicted of a crime or defined as a political criminal is largely a matter of who has power. "Power and rhetoric typically are inseparable mechanisms by which the other is defined as political criminal" (Tunnell, 1993, p. x).

A point of contention in defining political crime in the literature deserves mention. Though most authors include crimes by the state in definitions of political crime (Clinard, Quinney, & Wildeman, 1994; Hagan, 1997; Ross, 2003), Turk (1982) argues that a distinction should be made between *political crime* and *political policing:*

> No matter how heinous such acts [political repression by police and governmental agents] may be, calling them political crimes confuses political criminality with political policing or with conventional politics, and therefore obscures the structured relationship between authorities and subjects. There is also the considerable danger that an empirical criterion (what the authorities do) will be abandoned for a nonempirical one (our application of our own interpretation of law). (p. 35)

This is an important distinction that is helpful in developing a meaningful and homogeneous concept of political crime. Broadening the concept of political crime to include repressive law or police policies and tactics draws focus away from criminal behavior to the origin and dynamics of law and society. Certainly, the behavior that

BOX 9.1

1999 WTO RIOTS

Police officers in front of downtown Seattle Starbucks during 1999 WTO Riots.

Photo credit: © Mike Nelson/Getty Images.

If democracy is to be robust and vigorous in our streets, we must all express our abhorrence for any action intended to cause injury to police, demonstrators, or bystanders. (Seattle City Council, Report of the WTO Accountability Committee, 2000, p. 10)

In responding as it did to the WTO protests, the City violated fundamentals of our free society which require that any governmental restriction on speech be as narrow as possible to accomplish its legitimate purpose and be "content-neutral"—that is, not favoring any particular view. The City ignored both these principles. (ACLU of Washington, 2000, ¶14)

The World Trade Organization (WTO) is a global international organization of 148 countries established in 1995 to deal with rules of trade between nations. The organization produces agreements negotiated and signed by the bulk of the world's trading nations to help the producers, importers, and exporters of goods and services conduct business (WTO, 2003). The WTO has come under attack from multiple groups, accused of bias toward wealthy nations and multinational corporations, in particular that the United States, Japan, and the European Union exert undue influence over less powerful nations. Some believe that WTO treaties have been adopted by member nations undemocratically or to the detriment of citizens or ecologies.

On November 30 through December 3, 1999, the WTO held their annual conference in Seattle. Foreign and trade ministers from 135 nations, including then President Clinton, attended the conference. Protestors (from Seattle and around the world) planned in advance to come to downtown Seattle to engage in public demonstrations such as marches, political theater, prayer vigils, teach-ins, and civil disobedience to express environmental, labor, religious, and human rights objections to the WTO (ACLU of Washington, 2000).[1] As promised, protesters showed up in force—many more than expected by the City of Seattle planners and police. An estimated 50,000+ demonstrators turned out, including labor unions, students, environmentalists, self-identified anarchists, and citizens speaking out against free trade. Protestors blocked streets, prevented WTO delegates from attending the meetings, formed human chains, chained themselves together with bike locks, and engaged in sit-ins expecting to be arrested for symbolic acts of civil disobedience.

The original plan of the City of Seattle was that the Seattle Police Department would arrest anyone committing criminal acts or conscious acts of civil disobedience. However, tensions escalated and the number of police was not enough to manage the large number of protesters (Seattle City Council, 2000). The police were unable to make mass arrests and turned to tear gas and other less-lethal methods to clear the streets. A riot ensued.[2] The police implemented a "no protest zone" and a curfew. The Mayor of Seattle, Paul Schell, declared a civil emergency that resulted in police activity throughout the week that, according to the ACLU, brought "unwarranted restrictions and outright assaults on citizens and on their basic American rights" (ACLU of Washington, 2000, ¶6). The National Guard was called in. Police and protesters engaged in multiple acts of violence. The police used tear gas, pepper gas, rubber bullets, clubs, and bean bag guns to control the crowds. When the riot spread to the nearby community of Capital Hill, just east of downtown, officers gassed and pepper sprayed residents on the streets and in cars. Officers wore riot gear that made them indistinguishable from each other, some taking advantage of the anonymity to assault protesters and refusing direct requests to provide names or badge numbers. Others tried to preserve their anonymity by targeting people carrying cameras (ACLU of Washington, 2000). Citizens, protesters, and self-proclaimed "anarchists" engaged in firesetting, assault, vandalism (including breaking windows of businesses such as Starbucks, Nike Town, and the Gap), and overturning police vehicles. Peaceful protesters tried to intervene when others became violent, but then became intermingled in the crowds—"legitimate protest activity by thousands on Seattle's streets became tangled with criminal acts of property destruction, vandalism, and assaults on police officers by a few persons in ways that may never be unraveled to everyone's satisfaction" (Seattle City Council, 2000).

---

[1] A *New York Times* article reported on October 13 that 300 groups vowed to bring 50,000 people to downtown Seattle to demonstrate, hold teach-ins, picket, and cause disruption and gridlock in the streets (ACLU of Washington, 2000).

[2] The disruption at the 1999 WTO conference in Seattle has been referred to by politicians, police, and media accounts as a "riot." However, the ACLU of Washington states that "Despite police and media descriptions to the contrary, the protests during the WTO conference did not constitute a riot. They were noisy and disruptive, yet demonstrators were overwhelming peaceful. Not so the police" (ACLU of Washington, 2000, ¶19).

(Continued)

(Continued)

In the end, over 500 protesters were arrested and many citizens, protesters, and police were injured. Damages amounted to over $7 million in property damage, $1.5 million in holiday sales, and $6 million for police force before the state of emergency ("World Trade Organization: Seattle Protests," 1999). More than 500 people submitted detailed reports of police misconduct to the ACLU of Washington before the end of the conference. The Seattle Police Department and the City of Seattle were heavily criticized for poor planning, underestimating the amount of police presence needed, inadequate and haphazard riot control training, and poor management. The curfew imposed by police during the riot was challenged in court, supported by District Judge Barbara Rothstein, and eventually partially overturned by the Ninth District Court, which determined that it was lawful for the City of Seattle to deem part of downtown off-limits during the WTO protests, but that the police violated citizens' First Amendment rights by going too far to enforce the curfew, targeting only those opposed to the WTO (O'Hagan, 2005). The Report of the WTO Accountability Committee (Seattle City Council, 2000) found that officers, accused of reacting out of fear and anger rather than professionally, were cut off from communication, enduring physical assaults with ball bearings, rocks, bottles, being squirted with urine, and taunted for long periods without rest, restroom use, food, or water. Had there been a sufficient number of police, and had police been able to make mass arrests, this would have eliminated the need for tear gas and other measures that exacerbated the situation. The ACLU of Washington reported that "brutality was not the norm" for the officers who reported for duty, but there were widespread reports of police using excessive force against citizens who posed no physical threat, were not resisting arrest, or were trying to leave the area.

In his book, *Breaking Rank: A Top Cop's Exposé of the Dark Side of American Policing*, Norm Stamper (Seattle Police Chief during the WTO riots) reflects:

I saw Technicolor images of bipods and tripods, looters, Dumpster fires, intersection bonfires. I saw cops being baited and assaulted. And I saw a cop kicking a retreating demonstrator in the groin before shooting him in the chest with a rubber pellet. That particular scene, caught by a television camera, was flashed around the globe, over and over, Rodney King-style. . . .

Then there was the cop who, spotting two women in a car videotaping the action, ordered one of them to roll down her window. When she complied, he shouted, "Film this!" and filled their car with mace. . . .

To this day I feel the pangs of regret: that my officers had to spend long hours on the streets with inadequate rest, sleep, pee breaks, and meals, absorbing every form of threat and abuse imaginable (including, for a number of officers, a dose of food poisoning, from eating vittles that had been sitting out all day); that Seattle's businesses were hurt during the rampaging; that the city and the police department I loved lost a big chunk of collective pride and self-confidence; that peaceful protestors failed to win an adequate hearing of their important anti-globalization message; and, yes, that Paul Schell's dream of a citywide "dialogue" had been crushed. (Stamper, 2005)

Turk refers to as "political policing" and other authors refer to as "state crime" (Ross, 2003), "state-organized crime" (Barkan, 2005), "governmental," or "patriarchal crime" (Hagan, 1997) is ideological in nature, involves power politics, and is motivated by the desire to maintain governmental power. However, "the concept of political crime by the government is more a sociological than political [or legal] entity" (Hagan, 1997, p. 25). To further complicate the matter, it is difficult (if not impossible) to sort out the roles of the individual and the state to identify responsibility and motivation. It is not always possible to discriminate between a crime committed on behalf of the state and one in which individuals use their governmental position to commit an offense for their own personal gain (Friedrichs, 2004).

According to Ross (2003), "You can identify a political crime through triangulating among existing laws, the individual's (or group's) motivations, the kind of victim/target attacked, the result, and the context of the action" (p. 5). Barkan (2005) suggests that it is best to take an eclectic view of political crime that encompasses many definitions of the term without being overly broad. He proposes that political crime be defined as, *any illegally or socially harmful act aimed at preserving or changing the existing political or social order* (p. 405). The difficulty with the concept becomes clear when questions arise such as the following:

– *With the disproportionate percentage of African Americans incarcerated in the United States who have lost their right to vote, and the large body of research supporting the historical institutional racism in the criminal justice system, should all incarcerated African Americans be considered "political prisoners"?*

– *If an environmental rights activist sets a building on fire to protest logging, construction, and forest destruction, isn't this best classified as arson—an economic/property crime?*

– *If an individual assassinates a political figure, is this just murder with an elaborate excuse?*

– *What's the difference between a terrorist act that results in thousands of deaths and mass murder?*

– *If an individual or group of individuals terrorizes, tortures, and murders someone because of their race or sexual orientation, is this political crime? Should hate crime be considered under the umbrella of political crime because such offenses are rooted in ideological agendas?*

– *If an individual engages in officially designated political offenses such as sedition, espionage, or treason for nonpolitical economic reasons, should the offense be considered a political or economic crime?*

Some crimes can be considered explicitly political, but most are not. Behaviors that involve real or alleged threats to public or social order or to national security have been codified in law. Treason, sedition, espionage, and political assassination are officially designated crimes. Crimes can be identified as political based on the affiliation of the offender or the effect of the criminal action on the public and the government (Ross, 2003). On the other side of the law, governmental reactions to citizen dissent (e.g., surveillance or harassment) are also criminal, though government agents are rarely charged and convicted for their offenses. The following are examples of a range of behaviors that could be defined as political crime:

- During World War II, the Nazis exterminated 6 million Jews (more than two-thirds of all Jews in Europe) and 5 million other people (including Slavs, Poles, Catholics, homosexuals, and gypsies).

- In September 1963, the Ku Klux Klan bombed the Sixteenth Street Baptist Church in Birmingham, Alabama, killing four little girls, spurring riots and galvanizing the civil rights movement.

- During the civil rights movement, a number of political leaders were assassinated including President Robert Kennedy in 1968, Martin Luther King Jr. in 1968, and Malcolm X in 1965.

- In 1998, 21-year-old Matthew Shepard, an openly gay University of Wyoming student, was found by two bikers severely beaten and tied to a rail post in near-freezing temperatures outside of Laramie, Wyoming. Shepard had been pistol whipped 18 times with a .357 caliber revolver. He suffered skull fractures, lacerations, and brainstem damage and died several days later in a Fort Collins hospital. Arthur Henderson, 21, and Aaron James McKinney, 22, were charged with first-degree murder for the offense. Their girlfriends, Chastity Vera Pasley, 20, and Krista Lean Price, 18, were charged as accessories after the fact of first-degree murder. At trial it was discovered that McKinney and Henderson had lured Shepard from a bar with the plan to rob him and specifically targeted him because he was gay.

- In 2002, Greenpeace protesters boarded a boat near Miami Beach that was carrying 70 tons of mahogany allegedly illegally harvested in the Brazilian rainforest. The protesters wore shirts that said "Greenpeace Illegal Forest Crime Unit" and carried a banner reading "President Bush, Stop Illegal Logging." The protesters were arrested and spent the weekend in jail on misdemeanor charges (Barkan, 2005).

- In 2002, the FBI added Tre Arrow, otherwise known as Michael Scarpitti, to the FBI Most Wanted list in connection with a series of 2001 Earth Liberation Front (ELF) arsons that caused hundreds of thousands of dollars worth of damage to concrete mixing trucks and logging trucks. Scarpitti, one of four activists charged, fled to Canada and was arrested there in 2004 for shoplifting a pair of bolt cutters. He is currently in prison in Canada awaiting extradition. ELF is the FBI's no. 1 domestic terrorism priority.

- In 1999, over 400 protesters were arrested during the WTO conference and resulting riots in Seattle. The demonstrators (including environmentalists, animal rights activists, individuals and groups protesting child labor and the treatment of workers in the Third World, and those generally protesting and expressing hostility regarding the domination of society by transnational corporations and banks and the social inequities of capitalism) sought to shut down the conference. Protesters engaged in a range of activities from peaceful prayer, marches, and forming human chains to more extreme behaviors such as occupying and barricading themselves in a vacant building, climbing a construction crane to hang a huge anti-WTO banner, spray-painting police cars, chaining themselves to manholes, setting fires, throwing objects at police officers, and breaking store windows.

- Also, during the 1999 WTO riots, police, who encountered 30,000 to 50,000 protesters, were charged with committing numerous civil rights violations including the implementation and enforcement of a "no protest zone," which violated the First

Amendment rights of free speech and assembly and inappropriate use of force such as using tear gas on heavily populated areas, spraying mace at peaceful protesters and non-protesting citizens, shooting rubber bullets at people who posed no threat, and making improper arrests and mistreating people in custody (ACLU Washington, 2000).

A meaningful and comprehensive conceptual definition of political crime must distinguish it from other types of offenses while offering additional insight into the nature and dynamics of the behavior not explainable within the framework of nonideologically motivated crimes.[2] Given the focus here on criminal behavior, and taking into account the (limited) consensus of researchers and writers on the subject, political crime is defined as *ideologically motivated behavior that is legally defined as criminal.* This definition includes crimes committed against the state as well as those committed by the state to the extent that they are in violation of a particular law. This includes civil and human rights violations committed by the police and governmental agents and agencies, but excludes individual and collective behaviors that may be immoral, questionable, or rooted in institutional racism, or practices that ensure that one group maintains power over another but have not (yet) been deemed illegal.[3]

Types of Political Crime

Political crime is generally classified into two categories: *oppositional crime* (crimes against the government) and *state crime* (crimes by the government; see Barkan, 2005; Hagan, 1997; Ross, 2003, Turk, 1982).[4] Oppositional crime includes nonviolent offenses such as dissent/political protest, sedition, espionage, and treason and violent offenses such as assassination and domestic and international terrorism. State crime includes political corruption, illegal domestic surveillance, human rights violations, state corporate crime, and state violence (genocide, torture, deadly force).

Oppositional Crime

Political offenders who engage in oppositional criminal behavior have strong ideological convictions that conflict with governmental interests. The behavior they engage in is intentional and directed toward affecting some form of change to the existing order. Political offenders can be viewed along a continuum of extremity of behavior from nonviolent and relatively straightforward (peaceful protest) to violent and complex in organization and sophistication (domestic and international terrorism). Political criminals can come from the political left (e.g., war protesters who violate curfews) or the political right (e.g., pro-lifers who target abortion clinics), or have an interest in advancing a particular cause (e.g., radical animal rights groups and environmentalists).

Dissent, Political Protest, Civil Disobedience, Riots, and Rebellion

According to Barkan (2005), the idea that political change has occurred in the United States as a result of the electoral system is a myth. Political rebellion, protests, riots, and mass violence have deep historical roots in the United States. Preindustrial peasant revolts, labor riots after industrialization, early U.S. agrarian revolts, violence against Native Americans and their reciprocal defensive violence, post–Civil War labor strife, riots during the civil rights movement and the Vietnam War—all are part of American cultural consciousness.

Many crimes considered political are nonviolent acts of dissent. Political dissent can be expressed in many ways—public political protest (picketing, sit-ins, forming human chains, blocking train tracks, logging roads, etc.), acts of civil disobedience (directly or indirectly disobeying a law and waiting to be arrested), or other expressions of opposition (e.g., circulating petitions, flag burning, wearing clothing with political statements). Political dissent is legal. Dissent becomes a crime when, during the course of the oppositional expression, a law is broken. Most forms of protesting and other expression of dissent are protected by the First Amendment. However, restrictions on where, how, how long, and how many citizens can protest often bring protesters into contact with law enforcement.

Civil disobedience is intentional violation of a law considered morally unjust. Acts of civil disobedience are generally public, nonviolent, and serve a symbolic function. For example, over the last two decades, radical environmentalists have organized massive civil disobedience campaigns, blocking logging roads and engaging in acts designed to threaten the livelihoods of adversaries (Taylor, 1998). Civil disobedience can be direct (violation of a law that is itself considered morally unjust) or indirect (violation of a law that is not considered unjust) (Barkan, 2005). One of the most famous acts of direct civil disobedience is Rosa Parks's 1955 refusal to sit in the back of the bus that ignited the civil rights movement. Other famous historical figures who protested through civil disobedience were Henry David Thoreau, who wrote his famous essay on civil disobedience after being jailed for failing to pay taxes to protest slavery and the Mexican War, Martin Luther King Jr., who adopted civil disobedience techniques as a leader of the civil rights movement, and Mohandas Gandhi, who brought world attention to the cause of India's independence from British rule with his philosophy of nonviolence and mass civil disobedience.

Sedition, Espionage, and Treason

Crimes that directly threaten national security are officially designated in the federal system as national defense offenses (U.S. Department of Justice, Compendium of Federal Justice Statistics, 2004). These crimes are rarely prosecuted. Only 11 arrests for national defense offenses were reported in 2004 (U.S. Department of Justice, Compendium of Federal Justice Statistics, 2004).

Sedition is the communication of information for the purpose of inciting governmental resistance, defamation, or treason. The Sedition Act of 1798 made it a crime to write anything scandalous about the Congress or the president. Sedition laws date back to early English history when it was against the law to say anything negative about people in power, a crime called *seditious libel* (Ross, 2003). The U.S. Code defines seditious conspiracy:

> If two or more persons in any State or Territory, or in any place subject to the jurisdiction of the United States, conspire to overthrow, put down, or to destroy by force the Government of the United States, or to levy war against them, or to oppose by force the authority thereof, or by force to prevent, hinder, or delay the execution of any law of the United States, or by force to seize, take, or possess any property of the United States contrary to the authority thereof, they shall each be fined under this title or imprisoned not more than twenty years, or both. (18, U.S.C., Section 2384, Legal Information Institute, 2005)

The seditious conspiracy law is rarely enforced because to do so would be an overt exertion of governmental power that often backfires, given the protections of the First Amendment. Generally speaking, individuals are free to express dissent and their ideological views up to the point of causing what is referred to in legal terms as "clear and present danger." For example, it is legally permissible to hold a large sign that reads "Impeach Bush." However, the Supreme Court draws the line at yelling "Fire!" in a crowded theater where people could get trampled as a result.[5]

The government has tended to use other acts to convict citizens who express dissent. For example, since the 1980s the U.S. Federal *Racketeer Influenced and Corrupt Organizations Act (RICO)*, originally enacted in 1970 to target organized crime, has been used to convict political protesters including animal rights activists (Second RICO Suit Filed Against Protesters, 1999) and pro-lifers (Racketeer Law Goes Too Far, 2002; Reversing Misuse of RICO Laws, 2003). In 2003, however, in *Scheidler v. National Organization for Women* (2003), the U.S. Supreme Court ruled that federal racketeering and extortion laws were improperly used in the prosecution of pro-life and other protesters (Supreme Court Rules RICO Law Doesn't Apply to Pro-Life Protesters, 2003).

Treason is an act or acts aimed at overthrowing one's own government (Ross, 2003). To be convicted of treason in the United States, an individual has to be a U.S. citizen or in the process of naturalization. Article III, Section 3, of the U.S. Constitution reads

> Treason against the United States, shall consist only in levying War against them, or in adhering to their Enemies, giving them Aid and Comfort. No Person shall be convicted of Treason unless on the Testimony of two Witnesses to the same overt Act, or on Confession in open Court.

> The Congress shall have Power to declare the Punishment of Treason, but no Attainder of Treason shall work Corruption of Blood, or Forfeiture except during the Life of the Person attainted.

Photo 9.1 John Walker Lindh.

Photo credit: © Getty Images News/Getty Images.

Historically, few (fewer than 50 cases in the United States) have been prosecuted for treason because the charge is so difficult to prove and the concept of treason itself is so slippery (Ross, 2003). Often, it is debatable whether or not an individual should be convicted of treason, with cases turning on a technicality of the law. For example, some argue that 21-year-old U.S. citizen John Walker Lindh should have been convicted of treason for joining the Taliban and fighting against the United States in Afghanistan in 2001 ("Did American Commit Treason?" 2001; Toensing, 2002). However, because (among other factors) prosecutors could not prove that Lindh was planning to overthrow the government, nor had the U.S. officially declared war against Afghanistan, Lindh was prosecuted and convicted of lesser charges. As a result of a plea agreement, Lindh was convicted for supplying services to the Taliban and carrying weapons while fighting against the Northern Alliance backed by the United States ("The Case of the American Taliban," 2001). He received a

20-year sentence, far less than the death sentence he could have received had he been convicted of treason.

Espionage, or spying, has a long history and many governments use it for national security purposes to obtain information about other governments perceived as threats. In 1917 Congress passed the *Espionage Act* (18 U.S.C., Section 2384), which was later extended by the *Sedition Act.* In 1996, President Clinton signed the *Economic Espionage Act* (18 U.S.C. 1831) into law, targeting individuals who steal trade secrets.[6] Espionage is not considered a crime by the government that employs the spy. In fact, governments themselves engage in international and domestic espionage. (Depending on whether or not it involves illegal surveillance, domestic espionage can be viewed as a form of state crime and is discussed in the next section.) However, spying for another government, particularly if the spy is a citizen of that country, is a crime that carries a severe penalty in most nations. When the citizen of one nation aids its enemy by spying and providing secrets, this is a form of treason. Espionage and treason are punishable by death in the United States.

One of the most famous cases of espionage and treason is the case of *Ethel and Julius Rosenberg,* American citizens who were members of the Communist party, who were tried, convicted, and executed for spying for the former Soviet Union during the Cold War. The Rosenbergs were executed by electric chair in New York's Sing Sing prison in 1953. They went to their deaths claiming innocence, leaving behind two young sons. To this day, a great deal of controversy remains regarding the case. Before their execution, the Rosenbergs issued the statement, "History will record . . . that we were victims of the most monstrous frame up of our country. . . . We die with honor and dignity—knowing we must be vindicated by history" (*National Committee to Reopen the Rosenberg Case,* n.d., ¶5).

Photo 9.2   Ethel and Julius Rosenberg.

Photo credit: © Bettmann/Corbis.

Terrorism, Hate Crime, and Political Assassination

Most people in the United States have come to associate the term *terrorism* with the events of September 11th, 2001, when Islamic terrorists, operatives of Osama Bin Laden, hijacked American Airlines Flight 11, United Airlines Flight 175, American Airlines Flight 77, and United Airlines Flight 93. American Airlines Flight 11 and United Airlines Flight 175 crashed into the World Trade Center Towers, American Airlines Flight 77 into the Pentagon, and United Airlines Flight 93 in a field in Shanksville, Pennsylvania. In the aftermath of the attacks, 2,948 people were confirmed dead, 24 reported dead, and 24 reported missing after the attacks (September 11th Victims, 2001) in what has been called the "single largest loss of life from an enemy attack on its soil" (National Commission on Terrorist Attacks in the United States, 2004).

Since the events of 9/11, other unprecedented terrorist attacks have occurred around the world including the 2005 bombings in London of three underground trains and a double-decker bus that killed 52 people and wounded 700 ("London Bomb Victims Identified," 2007; "Manhunt on as Toll Set to Rise," 2005; Van Natta & Johnston, 2005) and the 2004 train bombings in Madrid, Spain, dubbed "Spain's 9/11," that killed 191 people and injured over 1,500 ("Massacre in Madrid: Madrid Bombings One Year On," 2005).

There are two general types of terrorism: *domestic* and *international*. The FBI defines international and domestic terrorism as follows:

> International terrorism involves violent acts or acts dangerous to human life that are a violation of the criminal laws of the United States or any state, or that would be a criminal violation if committed within the jurisdiction of the United States or any state. Acts of international terrorism are intended to intimidate or coerce a civilian population, influence the policy of a government, or affect the conduct of a government. These acts transcend national boundaries in terms of the means by which they are accomplished, the persons they appear intended to intimidate, or the locale in which perpetrators operate.

(A)

(B)   (C)

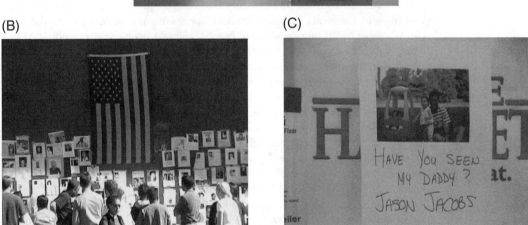

Photo 9.3 (A) The World Trade Center Bombing, (B) and (C) message boards to help locate missing people.

Photo credit: © Scott Helfgott and Bernard Whitman, 9-11-2001. Reprinted with permission.

Domestic terrorism is the unlawful use, or threatened use, of violence by a group or individual based and operating entirely within the United States (or its territories) without foreign direction, committed against persons or property to intimidate or coerce a government, the civilian population, or any segment thereof, in furtherance of political or social objectives. (Jarboe, 2002, ¶2–3)

The 9/11 attacks are an example of international terrorism. International terrorist activities have occurred throughout history in every region of the world. Following are other examples of international terrorist acts:

- 1972. *Munich Massacre,* when 11 members of an Israeli Olympic team were taken hostage and murdered by the Palestinian group Black September
- 1982. *Hyde Park and Regent's Park bombings* in London by the Provisional Irish Republican Army (IRA) that killed eight members of the British Army and seven horses
- 1982. *Sabra and Shatila Massacre* of at least 800 Palestinian civilians in the Shabra and Shatila refuge camps in (then) Israeli-occupied Beirut, Lebanon, by Lebanese Maronite Christian militias allied with Israel
- 1993. *World Trade Center bombing* by Islamist terrorists killing 6 people and injuring over 1,000
- 1998. *Bombing of Pan Am flight 103* over Lockerbie, Scotland, by two Libyans in which 259 people were killed

Following are examples of domestic terrorism:

- In 1972 the Provisional Irish Republican Army (IRA) planted 22 bombs in Belfast, Ireland. Nine people were killed and 132 seriously injured. The incident came to be known as *Bloody Friday.*
- Mail bombings by the *Unabomber,* Ted Kaczynski. Kaczynski, a Harvard university graduate with a PhD from the University of Michigan and former math professor at the University of California Berkeley, attacked universities and airlines (hence the name Un-A-bomber) with homemade mail bombs, killing 3 people and wounding 23 in a string of incidents from 1978 to 1995.
- The 1995 *Oklahoma City bombing* by Timothy McVeigh. McVeigh claimed the attack was a result of antigovernmental feelings he experienced while serving in the Gulf War as well as retaliation for governmental interventions in the Ruby Ridge, Idaho, incident in 1992 and Branch Davidian incident in Waco, Texas, in 1993.
- The 2004 *Beslan school hostage crisis.* Thirty male and female armed Chechen separatists wearing ski masks, led by Shamil Salmanovich Basayev and his principle deputy Magomet Yevloyev, took 1,300 people hostage, most under age 18. The terrorists' demands included withdrawal of Russian troops from Chechnya. In the end, 344 Russian civilians were killed, 172 of them children.
- Arsons, harassment, death threats, and other crimes allegedly and admittedly committed by the *Earth Liberation* and *Animal Liberation Front* (ELF and ALF; see Box 9.2; there is no particular rationale for these examples beyond highlighting relatively notorious terrorist acts; see Griset & Mahan [2003]; Martin [2003], Snowden & Whitsel [2005], White [2002] for comprehensive discussion of terrorism and review of terrorist case examples.)

ELF & ALF

The Earth Liberation Front (ELF) and the Animal Liberation Front (ALF) are environmental and animal rights extremist groups identified by the FBI as special interest domestic terrorists that represent a serious threat in the United States. The FBI lists ELF as the No.1 priority among domestic terrorist groups. It is estimated that ALF and ELF have committed more than 600 criminal acts in the United States since 1996 with damages exceeding $43 million (Jarboe, 2002). Many argue that individuals associated with ELF and ALF have been unfairly targeted by the FBI beyond proportion to the danger they represent (Taylor, 1998). ELF and ALF proponents argue that the damages caused by the organizations have been to property, not people, and that the risks posed by the behavior of the groups (e.g., tree spiking, power line sabotage, theft of animals from laboratories, destruction of a whaling processing station, graffiti, arson) have been overstated by authorities (Taylor, 1998).

ALF began in England with the hunt saboteur movement in the mid-1970s. The American branch of ALF began in the late 1970s (Jarboe, 2002) and its growth is strong (Newkirk, 2000). ALF "consists of small autonomous groups of people all over the world who carry out direct action according to ALF guidelines." The groups are called cells, which involve one or many individuals. Individuals in one cell do not know those in another because all activists are anonymous. Anyone who follows ALF guidelines can claim an action on behalf of ALF. ALF guidelines include the following:

Tre Arrow stayed on ledge of U.S. Forest Service building in Oregon protesting logging on Mount Hood.

Photo credit: © AP Photo/Don Ryan.

- To liberate animals from places of abuse, i.e., laboratories, factory farms, fur farms, etc. and place them in good homes where they may live out their natural lives, free from suffering.
- To inflict economic damage to those who profit from the misery and exploitation of animals.
- To reveal the horror and atrocities committed against animals behind locked doors, by performing nonviolent direct actions and liberations.
- To take all necessary precautions against harming any animal, human and nonhuman.
- Any group of people who are vegetarians or vegans and who carry out actions according to ALF guidelines have the right to regard themselves as part of the ALF. (Best & Nocella, 2004, p. 8)

Photo credit: © Stopecoviolence.com.

(Continued)

(Continued)

According to the ALF Primer, "Anyone in your community could be part of ALF without you know-ing. This includes PTA parents, church volunteers, your spouse, your neighbor, or your mayor" (Best & Nocella, 2004, p. 7).

In the early 1980s radical environmentalists such as Earth First! engaged in protests, civil dis-obedience, blockades, and more extreme tactics such as tree spiking,[1] power line sabotage, and hunt sabotage (along with ALF). ELF was formed in the early 1990s by Earth First! members who refused to abandon criminal acts (e.g., tree spiking) while members of Earth First! members wanted to remain mainstream and to leave criminal acts beyond unlawful protest to ALF. Some see Earth First! and ALF under the umbrella of "pagan environmentalism," a political ideology that some associate with far right millenarian movements and views shared by the likes of Ted Kaczynski (the Unabomber), Charles Manson, and the Nazis (Taylor, 1998). ELF advocates *monkey-wrenching* (sabotage and property destruction against industries and entities perceived to be damaging to the natural environment including tree spiking, arson, sabotage of logging or con-struction equipment) (Jarboe, 2002). The following are ELF guidelines:

- To inflict economic damage on those profiting from the destruction and exploitation of the natural environment.

- To reveal and educate the public on the atrocities committed against the earth and all species that populate it.

- To take all necessary precautions against harming any animal, human or nonhuman. (Rosebraugh, 2004, p. 18)

Craig Rosebraugh, media spokesperson for ELF, urges environmentalists and others who criticize ELF:

> To those within the movement who continue to disagree with the politics and strategies of the ELF, that is your choice. I only ask that you make a conscious effort to understand the historical role of diversity in political and social justice movements and the impor-tance of refraining from public condemnation of those efforts you disagree with. To those who now understand the necessary implementation of politically motivated prop-erty destruction to remove the profit motive from killing, I ask you to become involved. Look deep within your heart, find the fire that rages on for justice, form your own cell, and do what needs to be done to protect all life on this planet. (Rosebraugh, 2004)

ALF and ELF have proclaimed unity through speeches, Web sites, and publications.[2] ELF was listed for the first time along with ALF in a 1993 communique declaring solidarity in actions

---

[1] Tree spiking involves driving metal or hardened ceramic nails into trees to damage sawmill blades and deter log-ging. It is one of the most controversial tactics used by radical environmentalists because it can cause severe injury or death to loggers who unknowingly attempt to cut the spiked trees.

[2] Jonathan Paul and Craig Rosebraugh promoted unity of ALF and ELF at the 1998 National Animal Rights Conference held at the University of Oregon. In addition, ELF posted information on the ALF Web site until it began its own Web site in January 2001, and is listed in the same underground activist publications as the ALF (Jarboe, 2002).

between the two groups. The groups continue to be unified with crossover of leadership and membership. It is not uncommon for ALF and ELF to post joint declarations of responsibility for criminal actions on their Web sites. The groups have jointly claimed credit for a number of arsons including a 1997 arson attack on Bureau of Land Management wild horse corrals near Burns, Oregon, resulting in $450,000 in damages, and a 1998 arson attack of a U.S. Department of Agriculture Animal Damage Control Building near Olympia, Washington, resulting in damages exceeding $2 million. ELF claimed sole credit for the 1998 arson of a Vail, Colorado, ski facility, which exceeded $12 million, and a 1998 arson at the U.S. Forest Industries Office in Medford, Oregon, where damages exceeded $500,000. ELF has claimed a string of other arsons in Oregon, New York, Washington, Michigan, and Indiana. Crimes by ALF/ELF are well planned, involving preactivity surveillance and significant intelligence gathering against potential targets including review of trade publica-

Photo credit: © Layne Kennedy/Corbis.

tions, video/photographic surveillance, and posting information about potential targets on the Internet (Jarboe, 2002).

Individuals identified as leaders in one or both of the organizations and convicted and imprisoned for committing crimes on behalf of ALF and ELF include

- *Keith Mann*—A British animal rights advocate who is believed to be an early ringleader of ALF. Mann has been convicted and imprisoned for crimes including attacking the home of a fox hunter, possessing explosive substances, removing hundreds of mice from a research laboratory, and waging a terrorist-style sabotage against the meat industry (Bowcott, 2005). In 1994, at the age of 27, he was sentenced to 14 years in prison for explosives possession and other charges. After being paroled, he was again jailed for removing the mice from the research lab and contempt of court.

- *Douglas Ellerman*—At age 20, received the stiffest sentence against an animal rights activist in the United States. Ellerman, a confessed ALF follower and member of the Straight Edge Movement,[3] was convicted for attacking fur farms and releasing animals

(Continued)

(Continued)

(many of which died from stress from the attack or were killed on roads). Ellerman confessed to transporting pipe bombs to the scene of a 1997 arson at the Fur Breeders Agricultural coop in Sandy, Utah, and to setting fire to the facility ("Utah animal rights criminals sentenced to jail," 1997).

- *Michael Scarpitti (aka Tre Arrow)*—A suspected ELF recruit who allegedly groomed perpetrators for arson and other crimes. Scarpitti, now age 30, was on the FBI's Most Wanted list with a $25,000 reward for his capture until he was arrested in August 2004 in Canada for stealing a pair of bolt cutters from a Canadian tire store.[4] Scarpitti is wanted in connection with two 2001 Oregon arsons of logging and cement trucks committed by the Earth Liberation Front that caused $250,000 in damages. Scarpitti applied for asylum in Canada, but was ordered extradited back to the United States in July 2005 (Hainsworth, 2005). Scarpitti first gained notoriety in 2000 when he scaled a U.S. Forest Service building in downtown Portland and lived on a ledge for 11 days, protesting timber policies. In 2001, he suffered broken bones when he fell 60 feet from a tree where he was perched to protest logging in Oregon. Tre Arrow himself claims that he is dedicated to nonviolent activism and social justice and has been unfairly targeted by the U.S. government. He states:

  I am Tre Arrow, an innocent man imprisoned in Canada for almost a year and a half. I have become a target by the FBI, not because I am guilty of the charges in the US, but because I have become a threat to the powers that be. I am a threat because I stand in the way of corporate and government agendas. I am a threat because I cause corporations to lose precious profit from raping and pillaging earth-mother. I am a threat because I speak about the lies, cover-ups and atrocities committed by the hands of government and corporate figures. I am a threat because I speak the truth! The Powers That Be don't want us to know the truth! (Arrow, 2005)

---

[3] The Straight Edge movement is a youth movement in the United States that has proliferated in Utah. Members do not drink, smoke, use drugs or eat meat, and live by a philosophy of clean living. Law enforcement and others have referred to the movement as a "gang" or domestic terrorist group and members have been charged and convicted with a range of crimes including murder, arson, assault, and firebombing a McDonald's restaurant because it sells meat. Straight Edgers have been known to be coaffiliated with ALF and PETA (People for the Ethical Treatment of Animals).

[4] The Canadian security guard who caught him stealing the bolt cutters received the $25,000 reward from the FBI (Carnell, 2004).

In 2005 the National Counterterrorism Center (NCTC) released global terrorism statistics showing a sharp increase in significant terrorist acts from 175 incidents that killed 625 in 2003 to 651 attacks that killed 1,907 in 2004 (Glasser, April 28, 2005; criticism of the NCTC statistics suggests the comparison is not meaningful because data collection methodology changed from 2003 to 2004; see Glasser, May 1, 2005). In 2001, the U.S. Department of Justice published the 2000–2001 FBI Terrorist Report (U.S. Department of Justice, Terrorism 2000–2001). The report indicates that from

1980 to 2001, there were 345 acts of domestic terrorism, 136 acts of international terrorism, and 1 unclassified act (the 2001 anthrax mailings) of terrorism in the United States. Throughout the 21-year period, 14,047 people were injured and 2,993 people were killed, with a total of 17,040 casualties. (The FBI estimates 12,000 as the number of 9/11 victims; the actual number is unknown.) Of the 482 terrorist acts, 324 were bombings, 21 were assassinations, 19 were shootings, 19 were sabotage/malicious destruction, 15 were robberies, 10 were hostile takeovers, 6 were assaults, 6 were use of weapons of mass destruction, 3 were hijackings, 2 were kidnappings, 2 were rocket attacks, and 22 were other/unspecified.

Terrorist groups are generally stable entities that use a limited range of methods. Six tactics account for 95% of all terrorist attacks—bombings, assassinations, kidnappings, armed assaults, hijackings, and barricade and hostage incidents. Bombings are the most popular method of operation. Most terrorist groups exhibit remarkable stability and longevity. Some have been working for over a decade, replacing losses, preparing for attack, and turning into semipermanent subcultures (Ross, 2003).

Domestic terrorists account for 72% of the terrorist acts in the United States. In 2000–2001 there were 22 terrorist incidents. No acts of international terrorism were carried out in the United States in 2000, and the 9/11 attack was the first successful international terrorist attack since the 1993 World Trade bombing. Of the 22 terrorist incidents in 2000–2001, 20 were committed by special-interest domestic terrorists active in the animal rights and environmentalist movements, primarily targeting buildings and materials rather than persons. Three were committed by the *Animal Liberation Front (ALF)*, three by the *Earth Liberation Front (ELF)*, two by other environmental extremists—one by a group calling themselves Revenge of the Trees (ROTT) and the other by lone environmental extremist Mark Warren Sands (U.S. Department of Justice FBI Terrorism 2000–2001). Table 9.1 lists the terrorist incidents in the United States over 10 years of the 21-year period for which data have been collected.

Individuals and groups engage in terrorism because they hold a strong ideological belief and seek to forcefully attack a particular entity (individual, government, nation) to express their views with the goal of effecting political change. The term *terrorism* is inherently pejorative and involves making a moral judgment (Dingley, 1997). The argument is often made that what terrorists (and other political offenders) do is no different from what governments do, using the rationale that they must resort to extreme measures to convey their ideological message (Barkan, 2005; Clinard, Quinney, & Wildeman, 1994; Dingley, 1997; Hagan, 1997; Turk, 1982). "[O]ne man's freedom fighter is another man's terrorist" (Dingley, 1997, p. 26); however, governments that use terror (usually) have to answer to a larger constituency, whereas terrorists resort to *unsanctioned* violence to further their political aims (Dingley, 1997).

Research on characteristics of terrorists suggests that they lack overtly distinguishing features though they share common belief systems. Terrorism appears to attract people with aggressive, risk-taking personality styles who tend to project their own social and economic shortcomings onto others (individuals, institutions, governments, nations). Studies have shown that demographic characteristics of terrorists have changed over several decades. Findings from the 1980s and 1990s are generally consistent, with notable differences in the educational attainment and age of terrorists.

❖ Table 9.1   Terrorist Incidents in the United States 1990–2001

Date/Location of Incident	Group Responsible	Incident Type
1-12-90 Santurce, Puerto Rico	*Brigodo Internocionolisto Eugenio Moria de Hostas de los Fuerzos Revolucionories Pedro Albizu* Compos (Eugenio Maria de Hostas International Brigade of the Pedro Albizu Campos Revolutionary Forces)	Pipe bombing
1-12-90 Carolina, Puerto Rico	*Brigodo Internocionolisto Eugenio Moria de Hostas de los Fuerzos Revolucionories Pedro Albizu* Compos (Eugenio Maria de Hostas International Brigade of the Pedro Albizu Campos Revolutionary Forces)	Pipe bombing
2-22-90 Los Angeles, California	Up the IRS, Inc	Bombing
4-22-90 Santa Cruz County, California	Earth Night Action Group	Malicious destruction of property
5-27-90 Mayaguez, Puerto Rico	Unknown Puerto Rican group	Arson
9-17-90 Arecibo, Puerto Rico	Pedro Albizu Group Revolutionary Forces	Bombing
9-17-90 Veja Baja, Puerto Rico	Pedro Albizu Group Revolutionary Forces	Bombing
2-3-91 Mayaguez, Puerto Rico	Popular Liberation Army	Arson
2-18-91 Sabana Grande, Puerto Rico	Popular Liberation Army	Arson
3-17-91 Carolina, Puerto Rico	Unknown Puerto Rican group	Arson
4-1-91 Fresno, California	Popular Liberation Army	Bombing
7-6-91 Punta Borinquen, Puerto Rico	Popular Liberation Army	Bombing
4-5-92 New York, New York	Mujahedin-E-Khalq	Hostile takeover

Date/Location of Incident	Group Responsible	Incident Type
11-19-92 Urbana, Illinois	Mexican Revolutionary Movement	Attempted firebombing
12-10-92 Chicago, Illinois	Boricua Revolutionary Front	Car fire and attempted firebombing
2-26-93 New York, New York	International Radical Terrorists	Car bombing
7-20-93 Tacoma, Washington	American Front Skinheads	Pipe bombing
7-22-93 Tacoma, Washington	American Front Skinheads	Bombing
11-27/28-93 Chicago, Illinois	Animal Liberation Front (nine incidents)	Firebombing
3-1-94 New York, New York	Rashid Najib Baz convicted in November	Shooting
4-19-95 Oklahoma City, Oklahoma	Timothy McVeigh and Terry Nichols (Michael Fortier found guilty of failing to report to authorities of plot)	Truck bombing
4-1-96 Spokane, Washington	Spokane Bank Robbers	Pipe bombings/Bank robbery
7-12-96 Spokane, Washington	Spokane Bank Robbers	Pipe bombings/Bank robbery
7-27-96 Atlanta, Georgia	Eric Robert Rudolph, charged on October 13, 1998	Pipe bombing
7-2-97 Washington DC	Pending investigation—no claim of responsibility	Letter bomb (counted as one incident)
7-2-97 Leavenworth, Kansas	Pending investigation—no claim of responsibility	Letter bomb (counted as one incident)
7-6-97 Atlanta, Georgia	Eric Robert Randolph, charged on October 14, 1998	Bombing of abortion clinic
2-27-97 Atlanta, Georgia	Eric Robert Randolph, charged on October 14, 1998	Bombing of alternative lifestyle nightclub
2-29-98 Birmingham, Alabama	Eric Robert Randolph, charged on October 14, 1998	Bombing of reproductive services clinic
3-31-98 Arecibo, Puerto Rico	Claim of responsibility issued by *Las Macheteros*	Bombing of superaqueduct construction project
6-9-98 Rio Piedras, Puerto Rico	Claim of responsibility issued by *Las Macheteros*	Bombing of bank branch office

(Continued)

❖ **Table 9.1** (Continued)

Date/Location of Incident	Group Responsible	Incident Type
6-25-98 Santa Isabel, Puerto Rico	Las Macheteros suspected	Bombing of bank branch office
10-19-98 Vail, Colorado	Claim of responsibility issued by Earth Liberation Front	Arson fire at ski resort
3-27-99 Franklin Township, New Jersey	Claim of responsibility issued by Animal Liberation Front	Bombing of circus vehicles
4-5-99 Minneapolis, St. Paul, Minnesota	Animal Liberation Front	Malicious destruction and theft
5-9-99 Eugene, Oregon	Animal Liberation Front	Bombing
7-2/4-99 Chicago, Skokie, Illinois Northbrook, Bloomington, Indiana	Benjamin Nathaniel Smith	Multiple shootings
8-10-99 Granada Hills, California	Buford O'Neal Furrow	Multiple shootings
8-28/29-99 Orange, California	Claim of responsibility issued by Animal Liberation Front	Malicious destruction and theft
10-24-99 Bellingham, Washington	Claim of responsibility issued by Liberation	Malicious destruction
11-20-99 Puyallup, Washington	Animal Liberation Front	Malicious destruction
2-25-99 Monmouth, Oregon	Claim of responsibility issued by Earth Liberation Front	Arson
2-31-99 East Lansing, Michigan	Claim of responsibility issued by Earth Liberation Front	Arson
1-3-00 Petaluma, California	Animal Liberation Front	Incendiary attack
1-15-00 Petaluma, California	Animal Liberation Front	Incendiary attack
1-22-00 Bloomington, Indiana	Earth Liberation Front	Arson
5-7-00 Olympia, Washington	Revenge of the Trees	Arson
7-2-00 North Vernon, Indiana	Animal Liberation Front	Arson
7-20-00 Rhinelander, Wisconsin	Earth Liberation Front	Vandalism

Date/Location of Incident	Group Responsible	Incident Type
12-00 Phoenix, Arizona	Mark Warren Sands	Multiple arsons
12/9-30/00 Suffolk County, Long Island, New York	Earth Liberation Front	Multiple arsons
1-2-01 Glendale, Oregon	Earth Liberation Front	Arson
2-20-01 Visalia, California	Earth Liberation Front	Arson
3-9-01 Culpepper, Virginia	Earth Liberation Front	Tree spiking
3-30-01 Eugene, Oregon	Earth Liberation Front	Arson
4-15-01 Portland, Oregon	Earth Liberation Front	Arson
5-17-01 Harrisburg, Pennsylvania	Clayton Lee Wagner	Bank robbery
5-21-01 Seattle, Washington	Earth Liberation Front	Arson
5-21-01 Clatskanie, Oregon	Earth Liberation Front	Arson
7-24-01 Stateline, Nevada	Earth Liberation Front	Destruction of property
9-11-01 New York, New York; Arlington, Virginia; Stony Creek, Pennsylvania	Al-Qaeda	Aircraft attack
Fall-01 New York, New York; Washington DC; Lantana, Florida	Pending investigation; no claim of responsibility	*Bacillus anthracis* mailings
10-14-01 Litchfield, California	Earth Liberation Front	Arson
11-9-01 Morgantown, West Virginia	Clayton Lee Wagner	Bank robbery
11-21-01 San Diego, California	Animal Liberation Front	Burglary and vandalism

Source: Adapted from the 2000–2001 U.S. Department of Justice FBI Terrorism Report.

Findings in the 1980s presented a profile of the terrorist as a single male age 22 to 25 (40 to 50 if leaders), well educated, from a middle-upper-class background, and under-employed; current research suggests that educational level has increased among right-wing terrorists and that terrorists now tend to be older. Though terrorists are predominantly male, female participation has been higher than in other crime categories, ranging from 15 to 30% (Corley, Smith, & Damphouse, 2005; Dickey, 2005; Nacos, 2005), notable cases of female terrorists have occurred throughout history (Griset & Mahan, 2003), and female terrorist activity is widening regionally, logistically, and ideologically (Cunningham, 2003). Most notably, numbers of female suicide bombers have increased dramatically over the years, with a shift since 2000 from secular to religiously motivated attacks (Box 9.3).

BOX 9.3

FEMALE TERRORISTS

Layla Khaled at Guerilla Base in Jordan, one of two hijackers of American TWA jetliner in Damascus in 1969. A time bomb seriously damaged the jet.

Photo credit: © Bettmann/Corbis.

Women have participated as members of terrorists group throughout history and around the world—in Italy, Japan, West Germany, Sri Lanka, Iran (Cunningham, 2003), Israel, Palestine ("Female Arab Terrorism on the Rise," 2005), Chechnya, Turkey, Morocco, and Iraq ("Female Terrorists," 2005), the United States (e.g., Weather Underground and Patty Hearst and the Symbionese Liberation Army), and Russia/Chechnya, Uzbekistan, and Kashmir (Dickey, 2005).

Historically, "females have been among the leaders and chief ideologues . . . and followers in terrorist groups" (Nacos, 2005, p. 436). Approximately 20 to 30% of members in international and domestic terrorist groups are female. Some suggest that the heyday of female terrorism was during the Red Brigades in Italy and Red Army Faction in Germany, where the motivation was

Marxism rather than religion (Kassman, 2004). Palestinian militants are well known for employing female terrorists since the 1960s, and the number of female suicide bombers in the Arab-Israeli conflict has increased over time. Layla Khalid, carried out one of the first airline hijackings in 1969 to draw attention to the Palestinian cause. The first female suicide bombers appeared in Lebanon in the 1980s. In 1985, a 16-year-old girl killed two soldiers when she drove a car filled with explosives into an Israeli checkpoint in Lebanon. The girl was thought to be one of several hundred female suicide bombers trained in Ayatollah Khomeini's Iran (Foden, 2003). In 2002, Palestinian 27-year-old suicide bomber Wafa Idris killed an Israeli civilian and wounded 140 people. Chechen separatist militants have included females for many years—19 of the 41 Chechen militants in the 2002 siege of a Moscow theater, where more than 120 people were killed, were women who were part of a group called Black Widows, whose primary motive for terrorist acts is to avenge the death of husbands or loved ones slain in the Chechnyan conflict. Witnesses said that the female terrorists were crueler than the men (Foden, 2003). Black Widows wear veils and black from head to toe and a suicide or "martyr's" belt filled with explosives. Four female hostage-takers in the Beslan school massacre in 2004 were seen wearing suicide belts, also said to be Black Widows. After the spate of female suicide bombers in Russia since 2000, Russian reporters coined the term *shakhidka,* or female Islamist suicide bomber, combining the Arabic word for martyr—*shahid*—and the Russian female suffix *-ka* (Devine, 2004).

Prior to 2000, every suicide attack by women was secular. In recent years, religiously oriented Islamic militant organizations have begun to use female terrorists. Since 2000, more than two-thirds of the suicide bomb missions have been carried out by Islamists (Dickey, 2005). In September 2005, the first woman became a suicide bomber for Al Qaeda in Iraq, dressed as a man in a checkered scarf and long white robe with explosives strapped to her waist. The bomb killed five men and wounded 30. In January 2004, Reem Riashi, a mother of two from Hamas, made a videotape before she carried out her suicide bomb operation, in which she said she hoped her "organs would be scattered in the air" and her soul would "reach paradise" (Dickey, 2005, p. 34). The phenomenon of female terrorists appears to have spread dramatically to Iraq and Jordan, leaving counterterrorist experts concerned about female suicide bomber attacks in Western Europe and the United States (Dickey, 2005).

Female terrorists, including young girls and mothers, pose a special security challenge, blurring the profile of would-be bombers. A growing number of female terrorists are scientists, housewives, or teenagers educated in Europe and the United States, and many female bombers pose as pregnant women with explosives strapped to their bellies (Moore, 2006). According to journalist Michael Tierney, who has studied female terrorists in the Al-Aqsa teen brigade, "Previously, the suicide bomber fitted a stereotype: male, unmarried, immature, under-educated, aged between 17 and 23, and fanatically religious. Today, the martyr has evolved: he has become a she" (Foden, 2003, ¶6). There is evidence to suggest that terrorist groups make gender stereotypes a tactical advantage, using women because they are less likely to be identified by law enforcement (Nacos, 2005). The success of suicide bombers depends on accessibility to target populations and the element of surprise, and female terrorists have been particularly adept at

(Continued)

(Continued)

both (Zedalis, 2004). Counterterrorism experts say detection is more difficult because of social attitudes toward women and the hesitancy of security personnel to do invasive searches of girls and women. Russian terrorism expert Olga Oliker suggests that identification of female terrorists will require a significant psychological shift in the mindset of security forces to view women as potential adversaries, "People aren't used to looking at women as potential bombers. And you need to train people to pay attention to girls as well as boys and to see women as potential attackers" (Kassman, 2004, ¶17). In recent years, married suicide bombers (both long-time couples and those married for the purpose of the suicide mission) have become of increased concern for counterterrorism experts (Dickey, 2005).

The motivations for female terrorism are unclear. Media accounts of female terrorists are laced with gender clichés and gender stereotypes that leave a gap between the media image of the female terrorists and their lived reality (Nacos, 2005). There is no evidence that male and female terrorists differ in terms of ideological fervor, brutality, motivation, or methods. Motivations and circumstances of female terrorists likely span a wide range. Whether the terrorist act is international or domestic, the culture from which the terrorist is from, demographic characteristics of the terrorist such as age, economic background, and other characteristis all likely play a role in whether terrorist acts are acts of empowerment or patriarchal control. Some female terrorists are committed to a cause. Others become involved to personally avenge the death of a husband or loved one. Others become involved by being forced, manipulated, or sold by their families. There is evidence to suggest that young Chechnyan Black Widows in the Moscow theater siege were psychologically exploited or sold by relatives. Some female terrorists are likely deeply motivated by ideology whereas others, especially those in Middle Eastern cultures, are exploited and used as weapons in an ideological war dictated by men. Feminism plays a strong role in the philosophies and agendas of some domestic terrorist groups. For example, Jones (2004) suggests that the Animal Liberation Front is a "feminist project" that draws from the principles of ecofeminism, anarcha-feminism, radical feminism, and feminist ethics. "Speciesism and sexism are so closely related that one might say they are the same thing under different guises" (Jones, 2004, p. 139). *Asharq Al-Awsat,* a London-based Arabic newspaper, published an interview with a woman using the code-name Umm Osama, "the mother of Osama." She claimed to oversee the training of female mojahedin affiliated with al-Qaeda, and cited the success of female Chechen and Palestinian suicide bombers saying, "We are building a women's structure that will carry out operations that will make the US forget its own name" (Foden, 2003, ¶17).

A number of terrorist subtypes have been identified in the literature. Dingley (1997) suggests that terrorists can be meaningfully differentiated as separatist-nationalist or anarcho-ideological. *Separatist-nationalist terrorists* are well-adjusted, non–mentally disordered people with high education who suffer from low social status and project this suffering onto an external entity. *Anarcho-ideological terrorists* tend to be more behaviorally determined, showing more disruption in childhood and identity problems that involve a loner mentality and social marginalization. Terrorists "tend to represent the overeducated and underemployed middle and lower middle classes who externalize their problems" (Dingley, 1997, p.30). Martin's (2003) typology is most comprehensive in capturing the range of terrorist types. He offers five types of terrorism:

- *State terrorism* (committed by governments against perceived enemies)
- *Dissident terrorism* (committed by groups against governments)
- *Religious terrorism* (motivated by belief that a higher power sanctions and commands the use of violence in the name of the faith)
- *Criminal terrorism* (motivated by profit)
- *International terrorism* (committed on a global scale with targets selected based on their value as symbols of international interest)

Of these categories, the dissident, religious, and international types are most consistent with the definition of terrorism as ideologically motivated crime. Barkan's (2005) typology is similar to Martin's though he omits the criminal terrorism category and adds vigilante terrorism—*state terrorism* (by police and government), *vigilante terrorism* (by private groups against other private groups to maintain the status quo), *insurgent terrorism* (against governmental authorities to bring about radical change), and *transnational or global terrorism* (committed by residents of one nation against another nation). Similarly, Vasilenko (2004) proposes five types: *political terrorism* (struggle for power), *separatist terrorism* (right to territorial succession), *nationalist terrorism* (exclusion of other nationalities and ethnic groups), *religious terrorism* (recognition of leading role of own religion), and *criminal terrorism* (material profit). Tilly (2004) proposes four types—*militias, autonomists, conspirators, and zealots*—that differ with respect to degree of specialization and location of attack.

Arena and Arrigo (2005) identify three forms of terrorism similar to the categories presented by Martin (excluding criminal terrorism and state terrorism; based on the conceptual organization of this text, criminal terrorism is more meaningfully classified as an economic crime, and state terrorism is discussed in the section on state crime)—*national terrorism, religious terrorism,* and *revolutionary terrorism.* The *Provisional Irish Republican Army* (PIRA) exemplifies nationalist terrorism, *Hamas* (the Palestinian Covenant of the Islamic Resistance Movement) religious terrorism, and the *Tupamaros* (Uruguay revolutionary group) revolutionary terrorism. Applying identity theory and symbolic interactionism, Arena and Arrigo argue that the act of joining a terrorist group is an attempt to reconcile a fragmented identity. The terrorist's identity is shaped and behavior is influenced by the symbols and objects, social acts, meaning, role taking and role making, and "emergence of the self" (p. 32) associated with the terrorist group. "Identity can be seen as part of the reason why some countries have such a difficult time ridding themselves of terrorist threats" (p. 43).

The research on the causes of terrorism suggests, as with most types of criminal behavior, that no grand theory can explain who will become a terrorist and why individuals engage in terrorist behavior. Tilly (2004) argues,

> Properly understood, terror is a strategy, not a creed. Terrorists range across a wide spectrum of organizations, circumstances, and beliefs. Terrorism is not a single causally coherent phenomenon. No social scientist can speak responsibly as though it were. (p. 12)

Research on the relationship between mental illness and terrorism suggests that there is no causal connection between an individual's mental disorder and terrorist behavior; however, engaging in terrorist activity may increase the likelihood of developing a mental disorder (Weatherston & Moran, 2003). The type of offender, the target, the type of terrorist act, the country, the time period, and an unlimited number of situational and contextual factors and unique pattern of causation help explain the formation of a terrorist and terrorist behavior. Ross (2003) suggests that a "broad theoretical framework that can accommodate some of these ideas may be achieved through integrating both structural and psychological explanations" (p. 71).

Hate crime, also referred to as *bias crime,* is a form of domestic terrorism. For example, several terrorist incidents in the United States in the 1990s have been attributed to the American Front Skinheads, who committed a series of bombings in meeting places where Blacks, gays, and Jews gathered in California and Washington, including a gay bar and an NAACP office:

> Hate groups are now espousing the *leaderless resistance* model for fighting the people they view as their enemies. This doctrine advocates independent actions by individuals or small leaderless cells. The strategy seeks to prevent authorities from connecting illegal activities to the organization's command and control structure. Individuals acting on their own perpetrate acts of "resistance" that support the espoused philosophy of the larger group. (City of Seattle Emergency Management, 2005, ¶4)

What this means is that it is becoming increasingly difficult to distinguish terrorist acts committed by organized groups and lone individuals who adhere to (and have formed their psychological identities through) an ideological doctrine espoused by a particular hate or terrorist group. However, *not all terrorist acts are hate crimes and not all hate crimes are terrorist acts* (Martin, 2003). Some dissident terrorists target a state or system with no particular animosity toward a particular race, religion, or other group. Some hate crimes have little or no identifiable political agenda beyond having strong negative feelings toward a particular group.

It can be argued, however, that any criminal behavior legally defined as a hate crime is political in that animosity toward a particular racial, ethnic, or other group is in and of itself founded on a particular ideology. During "times of social distress and economic uncertainty, tensions between groups become acute and find expression in hate crimes" and the context and social climate in which hate crimes occur is relevant to their understanding (Kelly & Maghan, 1998). Furthermore, research shows that certain types of hate crime increase during periods when there is political and economic racial or ethnic conflict. For example, when African Americans have made the greatest economic and political gains in the United States, there have been more incidents of arson of Black churches—"it appears that the majority group attempts to repress or threaten the minority group by attacking an institution central to that group: the black church" (Soule & Van Dyke, 1999).

Hate groups engage in what has been called *vigilante terrorism* (Barkan & Snowden, 2001, cited in Martin, 2003). Many hate crimes are committed by "lone wolves" who identify with the Ku Klux Klan, the Aryan Nation, or other groups. *Are such acts by lone individuals acting on behalf of a cause with which they identify hate crimes or terrorist attacks? Given that some hate groups resemble gangs at one stage in their life cycle and paramilitary organizations at another, should all hate crimes be viewed as terrorist attacks? Should massacres of "enemy" civilians by paramilitaries, communal violence between religions or ethnonationalist groups, or genocidal campaigns by governments be considered hate crimes?* These are all important, yet unresolved, questions in conceptualizing hate crime.

Hate crime is a legal concept defined as crimes that manifest evidence of prejudice based on race, religion, ethnicity, sexual orientation, or disability (FBI, 2004). In 1990 Congress passed the *Hate Crime Statistics Act,* requiring the Attorney General to collect data about bias crime in the United States. The act was amended to include bias against people with disabilities as part of the *Violent Crime and Law Enforcement Act of 1994.* The FBI uses the terms hate crime and bias crime interchangeably defining *bias crime* as a criminal offense "motivated, in whole or in part, by the offender's bias against a race, religion, sexual orientation, ethnicity/national origin, or disability, and committed against persons, property, or society" (FBI, 2004, p. 3).

For crime to be considered a hate or bias crime there must be a *criminal offense* and evidence of *bias motivation.* In 2005, there were 7,163 reported hate crime incidents and 8,380 offenses involving 8,804 victims and 6,804 offenders. Of the 7,163 incidents, 7,160 involved single-bias incidents with 54.7% involving racial bias,[7] 17.91 religious bias, 14.2 sexual-orientation bias, and 0.7 disability bias. Most (5,190 or 62%) were offenses against persons, 3,109 (35%) were crimes against property, and the remainder directed at multiple or unknown targets (UCR, 2005). National Incident-Based Reporting System Data on bias incidents from 1997 to 1999 (U.S. Department of Justice, Bureau of Justice Statistics, 2001) provide a more comprehensive look at the situational and contextual characteristics of hate crime offenses:

- In 60% of incidents, the most serious offense was a violent crime, most commonly simple assault or intimidation.

- Most (61%) incidents were motivated by race: 14% by religion, 13% by sexual orientation, 11% by ethnicity, and 1% by victim disability.

- Racially motivated hate crimes most frequently targeted Blacks whereas religiously motivated hate crimes more frequently targeted Jews.

- Young offenders under age 18 are responsible for most hate crimes (31% of violent offenders and 46% property offenders are under age 18).

- The majority of hate crime offenders are White males (60%). Of those remaining, 21% are Black males, 10% White females, 6% Black females, 2% other male, and 1% other female.

- In terms of offense location, 32% of hate crimes occurred in a residence, 28% in an open space, 19% in a commercial/retail establishment, 12% in a school or college, and 3% in a synagogue, church, or temple.

- The targets of hate crimes are predominantly individuals (84%). Businesses represent 6% of victims, governments 4%, religious organizations 2%, and society or the general public 2%.

The NIBRS data represent the first attempt to provide accurate statistical information regarding the nature and extent of hate crime in the United States. However, it is likely that the numbers do not reflect the extent of the problem. Hate crime victims may be more inclined to hide their victim status than non–hate crime offenders and research on other data collection methods suggests higher estimates for serious hate offenses than are reflected in victimization reports (Rayburn, Earleywine, & Davidson, 2003).

Several particularly heinous incidents, including Matthew Shepard's murder in 1998, have increased public attention to hate crime:

- In 1993, Colin Ferguson shot 25 people on a Long Island commuter train, killing six. Notes found on his person and testimony during his trial indicated that he selected his targets because they were White. During his trial, his defense attorney argued that the mass murder was the result of "black rage" and that he was driven to mental illness through a lifetime of racial oppression. Ferguson was convicted of six counts of murder and received six consecutive life sentences without the possibility of parole.[8]

- In 1994, Brandon Teena was raped and murdered by two men who discovered that she was a woman who had been passing as a man while she awaited a sex change operation. Teena was forcibly outed by the local police department and newspapers after she was arrested for a misdemeanor check-forging charge. Although the authorities in the case did not prosecute the murder as a hate crime, there was substantial evidence that the offenders were enraged at finding out that Teena was a woman passing as a man. Brandon Teena was the subject of the 1999 film *Boys Don't Cry.*

- In 1998 James Byrd, an African American, was savagely murdered in a hate crime in Jasper, Texas. Byrd was tied to a pickup truck with a chain and dragged three miles. An autopsy showed that he was alive for much of the dragging and died when his arm and head were severed. Three White supremacists (Shawn Berry, Lawrence Brewer, and John King) were convicted for the crime. Brewer and King were sentenced to death. Berry was sentenced to life.

An estimated 500+ hate groups are operating in the United States. These include groups such as the Aryan Nation, The White Patriot Party, White Aryan Resistance (WAR), The Order, Posse Comitatus, neo-Nazis, and the Christian Conservative Church. Membership in these groups is growing at an alarming rate, particularly with the ability for interested individuals to become involved anonymously via the Internet (Anderson, Dyson, & Brooks, 2002).

A central issue in evaluating whether or not an offense can be considered a hate crime is identifying factors that reflect hate bias. *What type of evidence does law enforcement use to support bias motivation?* In most cases, the presence of *hate speech* establishes ideological motivation. For example, a recent case in Seattle involved a Black teenager accused of randomly murdering a White man, a popular tennis coach, as he sat in his car. The offender was transferred to adult court and will likely be charged with a hate crime after stating to neighbors that he had a grudge against White people. One neighbor told police, "He always say that he (was) gonna kill all the white people in the world." Another neighbor said he "had, like, some sort of complex against

Caucasian people. And he said he wanted to kill them all and told me I could watch" ("Documents, Neighbors Reveal Possible Murder Motive," 2005).

In general, law enforcement agencies record hate crimes when the investigation reveals evidence to support a bias motivation including written statements, graffiti at the scene, and verbal statements or gestures made by the offender (U.S. Department of Justice, Bureau of Justice Statistics, 2001). Dunbar (2003) suggests that in addition to hate speech, other valid signifiers (that may reflect a more enduring form of bias motivation than hate speech) include offenders' articulated beliefs about in-group superiority, affiliation with social cohorts who espouse a hate-based worldview, display of symbols that communicate a hate-based worldview (e.g., clothing, art, iconography), and a history of perpetrating bias-motivated aggression.

McDevitt, Levin, and Bennett (2002) conducted a study of 169 hate crime cases in Boston to develop an empirical typology of hate crime offenders. The study provides empirical grounding for a typology of hate crime offenders consisting of *four motivational types*:

- *Thrill*—offenders who commit hate crimes for excitement or thrill
- *Defensive*—offenders who commit hate crimes to defend their turf
- *Mission*—offenders who commit hate crimes to rid the world of groups they view as inferior or evil
- *Retaliatory*—offenders who commit hate crimes in reaction to and retaliation for an actual hate crime incident or rumor of a hate crime incident, whereby the offender seeks revenge against the group to which the perpetrator of the original offense belongs

Thrill offenders account for 66% of hate crime offenses, defensive offenders for 25%, retaliatory 8%, and mission less than 1%. Of the four types, individuals who commit hate crimes for thrill are the least likely to be viewed as political offenders and perhaps are best understood as marginally ideologically motivated violent offenders. The defensive, mission, and retaliatory types (34% of all hate crime offenders in this study) can be seen as politically motivated in that their actions are based on a particular ideology and interest in gaining power and control over a particular group (who are protected by the existing government).

Research on the developmental, behavioral, and ideological characteristics of hate crime offenders suggests that these offenders are unique in the force of their ideological motivation and there is significant within-group variability in the degree of bias motivation in hate crime cases. Hate crime offenders who have a higher level of bias motivation (as signified by prior bias criminality, membership in hate groups, blatantly expressed hate speech, and symbolic representation of hate beliefs) engage in significantly more instrumental, predatory, and premeditated aggression than do hate crime offenders with a lower level of bias motivation. Hate crime is a "special case crime" reflecting a "special class of violence" (Dunbar, 2003, p. 203). Hate crime offenders are more likely than other offenders to be criminally versatile, more likely to use drugs or alcohol during the commission of the crime, and more likely to seriously injure the victim (Messner, McHugh, & Felson, 2004). Findings suggest that they are volatile individuals with low self-esteem who want to belong to a group and are seeking a place in the world and will take such acceptance wherever they can find it even if it means engaging in criminal behavior. Hate crimes appear to increase during tough economic times. Those who become members of hate groups are socialized and indoctrinated into the group's norms and lifestyle. This indoctrination is a powerful force in the neutralization and devaluation of victims by hate crime offenders (Anderson, Dyson, & Brooks, 2002).

Gerstenfeld (2004, p. 77) asks, *"In the space of less than two decades, how does a person change from an accommodating toddler into a violent bigot?"* The development of prejudice is a central component in the development of a hate crime offender. Gerstenfeld identifies stages in the development of prejudice that may offer at least a partial answer to this question. The following are the stages in the development of prejudice that set the stage for hate crime:

- Ability to engage in social categorization (to divide the world up into categories of people—male/female, Black/White, Christian/Jewish/Muslim, etc.)

- Self identification—ability to learn which groups they belong to and which groups they do not

- Stereotyping—learning to associate stereotypes with particular groups of people, a "mental picture" attached to a particular group

- Internalization of prejudice—resulting in aversive behavior

These common developmental states in conjunction with family values that support bigotry, parents with authoritarian personality styles, situational forces such as peer influences and social support for particular belief systems, economic difficulties, and sociocultural environment all contribute to the formation of a hate crime offender.

Political assassination is the murder of public figures for political reasons (Barkan, 2005). Sometimes political assassination is committed by a lone individual with a political grudge. If a public figure such as the president of the United States is assassinated by someone for a nonpolitical reason (e.g., mental illness), then it is not considered a political crime. For example, John Hinckley's attempted assassination of Ronald Reagan in 1981 was not politically motivated and perhaps best classified as a copycat crime (discussed in Chapter 10). Hinckley attempted to assassinate Reagan after seeing the movie *Taxi Driver* more than 15 times to impress Jodi Foster, an actress in the film whom he had formed a fictional relationship with. Hinckley was determined to be not guilty by reason of insanity and committed to Saint Elizabeth's Hospital in Virginia. However, most political assassinations are not committed by individuals who are mentally ill. The list of political assassinations and attempted assassinations since the 1960s is a long one:

- Medgar Evers, civil rights leader

- Martin Luther King Jr.

- Malcolm X

- Yitzhak Rabin, Israeli prime minister

- Anwar Sadat, president of Egypt

- Joseph Yablonski, United Mine Workers activist

Five types of political assassins have been noted in the literature (discussed by Clarke, 1982) and named by Hagan (1997):

1. *Political assassins*—who (believe they) commit their acts selflessly for political reasons

2. *Egocentric assassins*—who have an egocentric need for acceptance, recognition, and status and commit their crimes to achieve notoriety and attention

3. *Psychopathic assassins*—who are emotionally unattached to others and transfer their emotional resentment onto the victims of their crimes

4. *Insane assassins*—who have documented histories of organic psychosis (e.g., schizophrenia)

5. *Atypical assassins*—who defy classification (e.g., James Earl Ray, who assassinated Martin Luther King Jr., was an unsuccessful career criminal who appeared to be primarily motivated by the $50,000 payment for the assassination)

Of these types, only insane assassins would be legally classifiable as out of touch with reality for the purposes of the insanity defense. Thus, for most assassins, assassination is an instrumental/goal-oriented criminal behavior committed for a particular purpose, though only political assassination (and perhaps atypical assassination depending on the circumstances) is ideologically motivated and best understood as political (rather than violent) crime.

State Crime

In his classic book *On the Take,* William Chambliss explores the corruption in police, governmental, and commercial establishments in Seattle in the 1960s. Chambliss's work was one of the first to highlight lawlessness and corruption committed by individuals, groups, and organizations in power for the purpose of maintaining that power (Chambliss, 1978, 1988). Research and writing in the overlapping areas of state-organized and state corporate crime has brought additional attention to political scandals highlighting crimes (and possible crimes) committed by governmental officials including the following:

- The CIA and FBI cover-up of the crimes of former employee and Cuban exile Ricardo Morales, who, following CIA orders, bombed a Cuban airliner in Venezuela that killed 73 people (Simon, 1996).

- Unanswered questions surrounding CIA involvement in the assassinations of John F. Kennedy, Malcolm X, and Martin Luther King Jr. (Simon, 1996).

- The 1972–1974 Watergate scandal when the Democratic Party's Watergate Headquarters in Washington was illegally burgled and bugged by individuals hired by the Republican power structure. The Watergate scandal led to the resignation of President Richard Nixon, who accepted full responsibility but denied personal involvement. The scandal was leaked by an insider source given the moniker "Deep Throat." In 2005, former Associate Director of the FBI W. Mark Felt confirmed, on his deathbed, he was Deep Throat.

- The 1983–1988 Iran-Contra scandal when the U.S. government, under the direction of Lt. Colonel Oliver North, sold arms to Iran. The United States diverted proceeds from the sale to the Contras fighting a guerrilla war against the leftist Sandanista government in Nicaragua. Funding the Contras and the sale of weapons to Iran violated administrative policy and legislation.

- The abuse of Iraqi prisoners by U.S. Army personnel, CIA agents, and contractors at Abu Ghraib Correctional Facility in Bahgdad in 2003–2004. Prisoners were bound, hooded, and photographed while being tortured and interrogated using various methods including being forced to strip naked and stacked on top of each other in a pyramid formation, being sexually ridiculed by being forced to simulate sexual positions, and threatened with dogs and electrical shock. Some reports indicated that some prisoners were raped and sodomized and one detainee was killed during an interrogation involving a particularly brutal torture technique and then packed in ice and placed in a shower. Six soldiers were convicted of charges including conspiracy, cruelty to prisoners, assault, maltreatment of detainees, dereliction of duty, indecent acts, and obstruction of justice.

Photo 9.4 U.S. Army PFC Lynndie England arrives at Ft. Hood, Texas, Monday, May 2, 2005, for the arraignment phase of her court martial trial for alleged prisoner abuses at Abu Ghraib prison in Iraq. England, one of nine reservists convicted of abuses of prisoners at Abu Ghraib was convicted and is now serving time in military prison.

Photo credit: © Corbis.

Over the last 20 years, attention to this phenomenon of governmental corruption and state crime at local, national, and international levels has increased.

State crime has been defined as "harmful activities carried out by the state or on behalf of some state agency" (Friedrichs, 2004), including political acts and political omissions that involve illegal surveillance, imprisonment, harassment, violations of First and Fourth Amendments, drug and arms trafficking, air piracy, terrorism, and other abuses of state power (Barak, 1998). State crime serves to protect the existing order. State crime includes offenses such as political repression, genocide, war crimes, illegal secret police operations, human rights violations, and unethical or illegal experimentation (Barkan, 2005; Hagan, 1997). Some authors (Clinard, Quinney, & Wildeman, 1994; Ross, 2003) include political corruption under the heading of state crime, though others argue that corruption and other acts committed for personal gain are best understood as an economic crimes (Friedrichs, 2004).[9]

Ross (2003) defines the "state" as "the political entity that holds a legitimate monopoly on the use of force, law, and administration" (p. 82). Government is the political and administrative apparatus of the state. The balance of power is shifted toward the state in any political conflict because the state has a disproportionate share of the resources. Furthermore, the state has the power to define what is criminal and what is not. Given this power imbalance, the concept of state crime is conceptually hazy. If the state has the power to define what's criminal, certainly the acts it engages in itself (in the form of state-employed individuals engaging in corrupt, immoral, unethical, or illegal behavior to further organizational state goals) will not be defined as criminal. Turk (1982) suggests that state crime is best understood as a separate category altogether, as *political policing* because of the conceptual difficulty in referring to governmental behavior as "criminal" because "crime is what the state says it is, and governments are not inclined to prosecute themselves" (Clinard, Quinney, & Wildeman, 1994, p. 145). This presents a problem in defining state crime because, without the aid of an inside whistleblower, much of the behavior the state engages in is either legal or undetected.

State crime can be divided into two general categories of offenses: (1) political repression, human rights violations, and state violence and (2) domestic espionage, illegal surveillance, and other tactics of state control. Most of the offenses committed by government and state agencies can be classified in one of these two categories—the former involving direct nonviolent and violent tactics that blatantly violate basic human rights and the latter involving indirect tactics aimed at maintaining existing state power that violate citizen civil rights. Though each category represents a different method and expression of state criminality, both are committed by agents of the state for the ideological purpose of maintaining state power.

Political Repression, Human Rights Violations, and State Violence

Political repression can involve tactics and *human rights* violations ranging from nonviolent acts to extreme acts of *state violence*. There are numerous examples throughout history of governments and governmental agents who have used illegal and violent means to repress dissent. Acts of political repression are most evident in nations with totalitarian regimes. However, all governments engage in repressive and even violent tactics to maintain power including democratic nations. Methods of political repression range from nonviolent use of law to imprison dissenters to violent state terrorism using assassination and genocide to eliminate the threat of a particular group of people and ideology. Examples of nonviolent human rights violations include restrictions on political participation; restrictions on freedom of expression, association, assembly, and religion; violations of due process; and racial, gender, religious, or ethnic discrimination.

State violence is an extreme "form of political criminality that generally consists of illegal, physically harmful actions committed by a country's coercive organizations (i.e., police, national security agencies, and military) against individuals and groups" (Ross, 2003, p. 138). Victims of state violence tend to be actual or suspected criminals, ethnic or religious groups, political dissidents, immigrants, or people of color. Examples of violent tactics of political repression that violate human rights include torture (such as the previous example of torture of Iraqi detainees), assassination of political figures or special threat dissenters, execution of dissidents, commitment to mental hospitals, disappearances or kidnappings, death squad activity, police violence and use of excessive and deadly force, deaths in custody, and genocide (Ross, 2003). When governments resort to rule by terror, their actions are referred to as *state terrorism* (Barkan, 2005).

Of the types of extreme state violence used as a tool of political repression, *police violence* is the most prominent in advanced industrialized countries. The literature on police violence focuses to some extent on individual-level factors that contribute to police violence (e.g., the bad apple theory), but *organizational norms, institutionalized policies and practices, and laws support and reinforce the use of violence against certain individuals and groups of people.* Organizational norms, policies, and practices fuel and support rationalizations used to target people from certain groups. These organizational norms work in conjunction with the established policies, practice, and laws to help maintain the dominant political order (Garland, 1990; Ross, 2003).

One of the most infamous acts of state violence was the 1989 massacre at Tiananmen Square in China. Thousands of unarmed demonstrators gathered at Tiananmen Square, China's capital in Beijing, to demand democratic reforms. They were met with open fire by the military, who slaughtered several hundred demonstrators and arrested, imprisoned, and later executed others, many of whom were students. Other examples include police violence used against protesters in the United States during the civil rights movement and the Vietnam War, including the 1970 shootings of students protesting the American invasion of Cambodia at Kent State University by the National Guard, in which four students were killed (only one of whom had participated in the protests) and nine wounded, and the police violence against protesters at the WTO riots in Seattle and the Port of Oakland antiwar protests in 2003, in which Oakland police opened fire with wooden dowels, concussion grenades, tear gas, and "sting balls" (Hull, 2003).

The most severe act of political repression is genocide. *Genocide* is the "deliberate extermination of a group because of its race, religion, ethnicity, or nationality" (Barkan, 2005, p. 406). Genocide may also be committed against a group of people for their politics.[10] *Genocide is a crime against humanity and a form of state terrorism and mass murder.* The term genocide was coined from the Greek word *genos* (race) and the Latin root *-cide* (killing) by Raphael Lemkin, a Polish lawyer, during World War II after the Nazi slaughter of over 6 million Jews and approximately 5 million other people in one of the most infamous acts of genocide in world history. According to Rummel, (1996, Chapter 1, ¶1), "Somewhere around 170,000,000 people have been murdered by their own governments, aside from war," since 1990, and "the more democratic a nation the less it murders its own people."

Genocide is a crime under international law defined as such by the *International Criminal Court.* The International Criminal Court has identified a number of elements of genocide to evaluate acts fitting the definition of genocide. This is an important step in clarifying an internationally accepted legal definition of genocide (Table 9.2). Since World War II, genocide has been a crime under customary and conventional international law. Thus, though difficult to prosecute, most of the nations in the world have agreed that the act of genocide is fundamentally wrong and should be punished. Genocide is generally associated with totalitarian governments, but acts by democratic governments have also been referred to as genocide. Historians and scholars have referred to the killings of American Indians when the Europeans first settled in North America and the wartime slaughter of 2 million Vietnamese, many of whom were civilians. Since the Nazi Holocaust, there have been many other acts of genocide around the world (examples taken from Barkan, 2005):

- In the early 1990s, ethnic conflict led to the deaths of tens of thousands in a region known as Bosnia-Herzegovina. In 1992, the region declared its independence from Yugoslavia. At the time there were three nationalities in Bosnia—Croats, Serbs, and Muslims. The Croats and Muslims voted for independence but the Serbs boycotted the referendum. The conflict led to a civil war, and by the end of 1992, the Serbs controlled

❖ Table 9.2   Elements of the Crime of Genocide

Act	Genocide by Killing	Genocide by Causing Serious Bodily or Mental Harm	Genocide by Deliberately Inflicting Conditions of Life Calculated to Bring About Physical Destruction	Genocide by Imposing Measures Intended to Prevent Births	Genocide by Forcibly Transferring Children
Conduct	The perpetrator killed one or more persons.	The perpetrator caused serious bodily or mental harm to one or more persons.	The perpetrator inflicted certain conditions of life on one or more persons.	The perpetrator imposed certain measures on one or more persons.	The perpetrator forcibly transferred one or more persons.
Note	The term *killed* is interchangeable with the term *caused death.*	This conduct may include, but is not necessarily restricted to, acts of torture, rape, sexual violence, or inhuman or degrading treatment.	The term *conditions of life* may include, but is not necessarily restricted to, deliberate deprivation of resources indispensable for survival, such as food or medical services, or systematic expulsion from homes.		The term *forcibly* is not restricted to physical force, but may include threat of force or coercion, such as that caused by fear of violence, duress, detention, psychological oppression or abuse of power, against such person or persons or another person, or by taking advantage of a coercive environment.
Consequences and Circumstances			The conditions of life were calculated to bring about the physical destruction of that group, in whole or in part.	The measures imposed were intended to prevent births within that group.	The transfer was from that group to another group.

(Continued)

359

❖ Table 9.2 (Continued)

Act	Genocide by Killing	Genocide by Causing Serious Bodily or Mental Harm	Genocide by Deliberately Inflicting Conditions of Life Calculated to Bring About Physical Destruction	Genocide by Imposing Measures Intended to Prevent Births	Genocide by Forcibly Transferring Children
					The person or persons were under the age of 18 years.
					The perpetrator knew, or should have known, that the person or persons were under the age of 18 years.
	Such person or persons belonged to a particular national, ethnic, racial, or religious group.	Such person or persons belonged to a particular national, ethnic, racial, or religious group.	Such person or persons belonged to a particular national, ethnic, racial, or religious group.	Such person or persons belonged to a particular national, ethnic, racial, or religious group.	Such person or persons belonged to a particular national, ethnic, racial, or religious group.
Intent	The perpetrator intended to destroy, in whole or in part, that national, ethnic, racial, or religious group, as such.	The perpetrator intended to destroy, in whole or in part, that national, ethnic, racial, or religious group, as such.	The perpetrator intended to destroy, in whole or in part, that national, ethnic, racial, or religious group, as such.	The perpetrator intended to destroy, in whole or in part, that national, ethnic, racial, or religious group, as such.	The perpetrator intended to destroy, in whole or in part, that national, ethnic, racial, or religious group, as such.

Act	Genocide by Killing	Genocide by Causing Serious Bodily or Mental Harm	Genocide by Deliberately Inflicting Conditions of Life Calculated to Bring About Physical Destruction	Genocide by Imposing Measures Intended to Prevent Births	Genocide by Forcibly Transferring Children
Context	The conduct took place in the context of a manifest pattern of similar conduct directed against that group or was conduct that could itself effect such destruction.	The conduct took place in the context of a manifest pattern of similar conduct directed against that group or was conduct that could itself effect such destruction.	The conduct took place in the context of a manifest pattern of similar conduct directed against that group or was conduct that could itself effect such destruction.	The conduct took place in the context of a manifest pattern of similar conduct directed against that group or was conduct that could itself effect such destruction.	The conduct took place in the context of a manifest pattern of similar conduct directed against that group or was conduct that could itself effect such destruction.
Note	The term *in the context of* would include the initial acts in an emerging pattern; the term *manifest* is an objective qualification.	The term *in the context of* would include the initial acts in an emerging pattern; the term *manifest* is an objective qualification.	The term *in the context of* would include the initial acts in an emerging pattern; the term *manifest* is an objective qualification.	The term *in the context of* would include the initial acts in an emerging pattern; the term *manifest* is an objective qualification.	The term *in the context of* would include the initial acts in an emerging pattern; the term *manifest* is an objective qualification.

Source: Table replicated from Prevent Genocide.com: http://www.preventgenocide.org/genocide/elements.htm.

70% of Bosnia and engaged in forced expulsions of Muslims called *ethnic cleansing*, massacres of unarmed Muslims and Croats, and the rape by troops of an estimated 20,000 Muslim women (termed by some as "gynocide").

- In 1994 a civil war took place in Rwanda between the two major groups, the Hutu and the Tutsi. A plane carrying the Rwandan president, a Hutu, crashed and the government blamed a Tutsi rebel group for shooting the plane. In reaction, governmental troops killed an estimated 1 million Tutsis in the following months. By July that year, the Tutsis fought back, captured the Rwandan capital, and 1 million Hutus fled.

- The 2004 the Janjaweed, an Arab militia group, committed mass murder of Africans in Sudan. The Sudanese government paid the Janjaweed to quell political unrest in the western region of Darfur. The Janjaweed used mass terror tactics including rape, torture, arson, and murder, killing between 300,000 and 1 million people.

Genocide is state-sanctioned mass murder. Are perpetrators of genocide any different from perpetrators of mass murder? How is it that human beings employed as governmental agents are cognitively, emotionally, and behaviorally able to execute large groups of people? These are important questions to explore in understanding the nature and dynamics of genocide.

Stanton (1998) suggests that the genocide process involves eight stages, and that it is important to understand these stages to intervene:

1. *Classification:* People are divided into "us" and "them."
2. *Symbolization:* Hate symbols are associated with pariah groups.
3. *Dehumanization:* Members of pariah groups are dehumanized.
4. *Organization:* Governmental units, militias, armies are trained, organized, and armed.
5. *Polarization:* Hate groups broadcast polarizing propaganda.
6. *Identification:* Potential victims are identified based on affiliation with particular group and symbols of association.
7. *Extermination:* Mass murder of members of target group is carried out.
8. *Denial:* Perpetrators deny that any crime has been committed.

Components of this process are very similar to the borderline primitive defenses used by psychopaths and the techniques of neutralization used by all offenders to rationalize criminal behavior.

Domestic Espionage, Illegal Surveillance, and Other Tactics of State Control

The term *domestic espionage* refers to governmental spying, information-gathering, and domestic surveillance of dissident groups by police and state agents (Theoharis, 2004). Other terms used to refer to the activities involved in domestic espionage are *secret policing* (Hagan, 1997), *political policing* (Turk, 1982), and *illegal domestic surveillance* (Ross, 2003). *Domestic espionage* is distinguished here from espionage discussed in the previous section in that this form of spying is conducted by governmental agents to obtain information from its citizens to repress dissident groups and maintain state power, in contrast with *international espionage*, which involves surveillance of a foreign government, spying, and treason by citizens against their own country for enemy intelligence, and *economic (or industrial) espionage,* which involves corporate spying for trade secrets. Targets of domestic espionage can be citizens, organizations, businesses, or foreign governments. Surveillance and information gathering tactics are a legitimate law enforcement activity; however, these tactics cross the legal threshold of acceptability in the eyes of the public when they violate citizen civil rights.

Intelligence gathering operations generally involve collecting information from open sources. However, undercover domestic surveillance tactics have been a part of law enforcement since its inception, despite the changes over time in the constitutional protections of citizens against illegal surveillance, search, and seizure (i.e., selective incorporation of Bill of Rights, specifically the First and Fourth Amendments, to the states). Undercover operations involving domestic espionage including wiretapping and other forms of state-sponsored deception are widespread, institutionally condoned, part of the organizational fabric of policing (Marx, 1988). Domestic surveillance is an ongoing practice in democratic states, with historical evidence supporting its use in the United States, Canada, and Great Britain (Ross, 2003), and all countries require some type of secret police (Hagan, 1997).

The use of repressive illegal surveillance tactics is particularly salient during times of social strife and cultural crises. For example, a number of groups seen as a political threat were investigated by COINTELPRO, an FBI counterintelligence program aimed at investigating and disrupting political radical dissident groups that operated from 1956 to 1971. The Socialist Workers Party, the Students for a Democratic Society, the Black Panther Party, the Nation of Islam, the American Indian Party, and the Weather Underground were targets of COINTELPRO, whose methods included deception and infiltration, psychological warfare, legal harassment, and excessive force. Some suggest that the post-9/11 environment, the Patriot Act, the power of the political right, and public fear of both international and domestic terrorism may bring a return of something like COINTELPRO and increased tolerance for undercover surveillance activities that violate civil rights ("Going Undercover/Criminalizing Dissent?" 2004).

The most common technique used in domestic espionage in the United States is wiretapping. Wiretapping was illegal in the United States from 1937 to 1968. In 1968 it was ruled permissible if authorized by court order when probable cause is established. Despite the long period in American history during which wiretapping was completely illegal, its use as well as the burglaries committed to install the devices has continued to this day. Former FBI Director J. Edgar Hoover officially condoned illegal burglaries and the planting of bugs throughout his tenure, illegal wiretapping was the mainstay of the Watergate scandal, and even today police are known to go "judge shopping" for a sympathetic judge who will issue a court order based on questionable evidence to support probable cause (Ross, 2003, p. 111).

In addition to the use of state violence, domestic espionage, and illegal surveillance, governmental agents and law enforcement engage in other tactics to control dissident groups and individuals. Hagan (1997) identifies additional tactics used to repress political dissidents:

- Litigation against leaders of political movements
- Disinformation campaigns

- Administrative harassment
- Informants and agents provocateurs
- Support of counter or alternative groups
- "Snitch jacketing" (falsely accusing innocent individuals of being informants)

The Nature and Dynamics of Political Crime

What causes political criminality? What are the factors and forces that contribute to its manifestation? How do political criminals differ from other types of offenders in terms of motivation, cognitive processing, modus operandi, psychopathology, environment, and upbringing? Do certain contextual/situational factors influence the occurrence of political crime? Does it make sense to ask the same questions about political crime as are asked about other types of crimes? Can political crime be understood within the context of the instrumental/expressive framework? Are all political criminals alike along a primary and meaningful dimension? These are some of the questions that are important in making sense of political criminality.

The following are common features of political criminality:

- Ideological motivation
- Willingness to take action that violates law to further an ideological objective
- Ability to easily cognitively neutralize criminal behavior (i.e., if a person believes strongly that their behavior appeals to a higher loyalty, it is difficult to think of oneself in a negative light)

Beyond these three characteristics, political offenders are a heterogeneous group. Socrates, Sir Thomas More, Mahatma Gandhi, Martin Luther King Jr., and Malcolm X all were political criminals (Barkan, 2005). So were Adolf Hitler, Lee Harvey Oswald, Timothy McVeigh, and Saddam Hussein. Add to the list Marie Antoinette, Benedict Arnold, Ethel and Julius Rosenberg, Richard Nixon, Oliver North, and Aldrich Ames, and you get a mixed bag of offenders, some who, though condemned for their behavior, were later considered heroes and key political figures who honorably suffered to facilitate positive and powerful social change.

Political criminals are unique in that, unlike other types of offenders, they are motivated by a powerful and particular ideological agenda. This provides them with a stronger than average framework for neutralizing criminal behavior. In some ways, this framework resembles the defensive organization of the primary psychopath, who cares little about the norms and values of society because he or she is narcissistically attached and unable to empathize or attach to others, let alone to behave in ways consistent with others' views.[11] However, most political offenders are not psychopaths at all. And, in fact, political offenders with strong ideological stances and willingness to sacrifice their own lives and freedoms are the antithesis of the psychopath. Rather, the values and beliefs of political criminals result in antiestablishment (not necessarily antisocial) behavior for the purpose of changing the existing power structure. Political offenders tend to see their behavior as morally acceptable despite the existing laws providing them with a psychological framework that makes their behavior very easy for them to cognitively neutralize, and as a result, their behavior very difficult to control.

There is a big difference, however, between the antiwar protester who violates a temporary curfew or an animal rights activist who releases animals from a vivisection laboratory and political assassins, political leaders and soldiers who commit genocide, or military personnel who engage in torture and murder in violation of international human rights agreements. Clearly, political criminals share the common feature of ideological motivation but are differentially influenced by a range of psychological, environmental, cultural, situational, and phenomenological factors and forces that shape the behavior they engage in.

Summary

Political crime is motivated by a particular ideological perspective. Though it is not against the law in the United States to espouse political views contrary to those of the government, people who do are often targeted by law enforcement and sanctioned for violating a range of laws. The ways in which political offenders are defined, identified, and socially controlled make it virtually impossible to provide an accurate statistical figure for the true extent of political crime in the United States and around the world, though available data suggest that political crime has existed throughout history and is prevalent around the world. Some crimes can be considered explicitly political; most are not. Political crime can be classified in terms of two general categories: *oppositional crime* (crimes against the government) and *state crime* (crimes by the government). Oppositional crime includes nonviolent offenses such as dissent/political protest, sedition, espionage, and treason and violent offenses such as assassination, international and domestic terrorism, and hate crime. State crime includes *political repression, human rights violations, and state violence* and *domestic espionage, illegal surveillance, and other tactics of state control. Common features of political criminality* include ideological motivation, willingness to take action that violates law to further an ideological objective, and the ability to easily cognitively neutralize criminal behavior.

DISCUSSION QUESTIONS

1. Can political crime be considered a homogeneous category of criminal behavior? How do political criminals differ from other types of offenders in terms of motivation, cognitive processing, modus operandi, psychopathology, environment and upbringing, and other traits? Discuss.

2. What causes political criminality? What are the factors and forces that contribute to its manifestation? Do certain contextual/situational factors influence the occurrence of political crime? Discuss.

3. Does it make sense to ask the same questions about political crime as are asked about other types of crimes? For example, can political crime be understood within the context of the instrumental/expressive framework? Are all political criminals alike along a primary and meaningful dimension?

4. Based on what we know to date about female terrorists, how do male and female terrorists differ? Can female terrorists be understood from the same perspectives and theories as male terrorists? Discuss.

5. Does it make sense to include hate crime under the heading of political crime? Discuss.

On Your Own: Log on to the Web-based student study site at http://www.sagepub .com/helfgottstudy/ for the URL links in the Web Exercises, study aids such as review quizzes, and research recommendations including links to journal articles specifically selected for this book.

WEB EXERCISES

1. Review arrest data reported in the UCR at http://www.fbi.gov/ucr/ucr.htm and *Compendium of Federal Criminal Justice Statistics* at http://www.ojp.usdoj.gov/bjs/pub/ pdf/cfjs02.pdf. If you were to do a study on the extent of political crime in the United States, what crime categories would you include? Is it possible to do any sort of descriptive study of the extent of political crime using existing data? What sort of additional data are needed to conduct such a study?

2. Go to the section on "situations and cases" on the Web site for the *International Criminal Court* at http://www.icc-cpi.int/home.html&1=en. Explore the cases currently under investigation. Given the definition of political crime presented in this chapter, what types of political offenses are being investigated by the United Nations?

3. The case of Julius and Ethel Rosenberg continues to be one of the best-known and contro-versial espionage cases throughout history. Read about their case and access original doc-uments from the Eisenhower Library at http://www.eisenhower.archives.gov/dl/ Rosenbergs/Rosenbergsfiles.html and the Crime Library at http://www.crimelibrary .com/rosen/rosenmain.htm. Discuss the issues associated with the case and why groups such as the *National Committee to Reopen the Rosenberg Case* (http://www.rosenbergtrial .org/comitfrm.html) persist after over 50 years.

4. The *Earth Liberation Front* (ELF) and *Animal Liberation Front* (ALF) have been identified as spe-cial-interest domestic terrorist groups of high priority to the FBI. Read the 2002 congressional testimony by James Jarboe, Domestic Terrorism Section Chief of the *FBI Counterterrorism Division on the Threat of Eco-Terrorism:* http://www.fbi.gov/congress/congress02/jar boe021202.htm. After reading the testimony, visit Web sites supporting ELF: http://www.earth liberationfront.com/; and ALF: http://www.animalliberationfront.com/index.html. Discuss both sides of the issue. Based on your review of the materials, are ELF and ALF justifiably viewed as violent extremist groups that deserve a place on the FBI most wanted list?

5. Go to the U.S. Department of Justice/FBI Report *Terrorism 2000/2001:* http://www .fbi.gov/publications/terror/terror2000_2001.pdf. Review the complete list of terrorist incidents since 1980. How have terrorist incidents changed over time? Discuss the motiva-tions and nature of terrorist incidents.

6. Visit R.J. Rummel's Web site: http://www.hawaii.edu/powerkills/. Rummel coined the term *democide* and has claimed that over 170,000,000 people have been murdered by govern-ments, a far greater number than were killed in war. Explore the site and some of Rummel's claims. Discuss whether or not democide is a useful concept.

The Influence of Technology, Media, and Popular Culture on Criminal Behavior

Copycat Crime and Cybercrime

Life is like a video game. Everybody's got to die sometime.

> —18-year-old Devin Moore, to police after he was apprehended for fatally gunning down two police officers and an emergency dispatcher

In 2003, 18-year-old Devin Moore was arrested for suspicion of auto theft in Fayette, Alabama. Moore, who had no prior criminal history, was cooperative with police when they brought him to the police station. Once inside the station and booked,

Moore lunged at an officer, grabbed his .40-caliber Glock automatic, and shot the officer twice. When another officer came running, Moore shot him three times and walked down the hallway toward the emergency dispatcher doorway where he shot a 9-1-1 dispatcher five times. Then he grabbed police car keys, walked out the front door, and drove off in a police cruiser. All three victims—Officer Arnold Strickland, Officer James Crump, and Emergency Dispatcher Ace Wheeler—were shot in the head and pronounced dead at the scene. Moore was captured shortly after ("Can a Video Game Lead to Murder," March 6, 2005).

Following his capture, Moore's comments to police suggested that he had been playing the video game *Grand Theft Auto—Vice City* for hours on end before the murders. Later, at trial, it was revealed that he was a compulsive violent video game player who suffered from childhood abuse-related posttraumatic stress disorder. Moore's defense attorneys argued the "*GTA* defense"—that he was not guilty by reason of insanity and that he had lost touch with reality and was acting out in real life the virtual violence in *Grand Theft Auto*. Despite his attorney's efforts, the *GTA* defense was unsuccessful and Moore was convicted on August 10, 2005, of capital murder ("Jury Convicts Video Game Defense Killer," August 11, 2005) and sentenced to death (Farrell, 2005).

Did playing Grand Theft Auto cause Devin Moore to murder? Did hours of engagement in virtual violence impair Moore's ability to distinguish fantasy from reality? The influence of films, television, music videos, song lyrics, and computer games on criminal behavior is a popular topic and political issue raised by media watchdogs. A long list of research findings, particularly with respect to television, shows that viewing violent media has an imitative influence on aggressive behavior and contributes to the development of the *mean world syndrome*—a view of the world as more hostile and dangerous than it actually is (Jhally, Kilbourne, & Gerbner, 1994). Many people consume violent media every day and do not mimic the violent media images they see. However, for some individuals, violent media play a key role in the criminal behavior they engage in.

Determining whether or not there is an empirical relationship between violent and criminal is a complex endeavor given the many factors and forces that shape criminal behavior on an individual level. We are all influenced on some level by our daily surroundings. Peer groups, TV shows, books, news media, personal experience, hobbies, education, habits, the community and culture in which we live, and the cultural artifacts that populate that culture make their way into our thinking and behavior. Criminal behavior is dictated by the interplay between static factors that are unchangeable (e.g., genetic predisposition, personality) and dynamic or changeable factors largely shaped by aspects of an offenders' environment and culture (e.g., antisocial attitudes, delinquent peers, situational triggers; Andrews & Bonta, 2003, 2006). Continuous playing of a violent video game can be seen as one of many dynamic risk factors that shape behavior. However, the question of causation is more complicated.

It is virtually impossible to isolate a single stimulus such as a violent video game as a causative factor amid the many influences and risk factors that contribute to criminal behavior. Atkinson (1999) suggests that "the precise psychological role media played [in documented media-mediated crimes] is never clear—nor can it be, until we are able to 'map a brain like a computer hard drive'" (¶8). Millions of people play violent video games and do not go out and steal cars or murder police officers. People are differentially impacted by all sorts of cultural artifacts—books, TV shows, video games—and many people alter their behavior in a positive, not a negative, way in response to watching TV or playing a video game. These issues make the media- and technology-mediated crime very difficult to empirically study and causation virtually impossible to establish.

We may not yet be able to "map a brain like a computer hard drive," but integrating criminological theory with research in cognitive psychology can help explain the process by which chronic exposure to a game like *GTA* can influence individual behavior. When an individual engages in criminal (or any) behavior, he or she does so within a sociocultural context and in a *cognitive script* that is dictated and inhabited by whatever populates that context. A script is a "simple, well structured sequence of events—in a specified order—that are associated with a highly familiar activity" (Matlin, 2005, p. 275). It is a type of schema referring to a prototypic series of events that occur over a period of time and share an underlying similarity. People have scripts for all kinds of everyday events and activities from going to the grocery store or a party or purchasing a pair of shoes to breaking off a relationship or dealing with conflict.

Scripts are cultural products. Children learn complex social scripts (e.g., rules on how to interpret, understand, and handle situations) and schemas (e.g., beliefs, attitudes) from role models they see around them. Parents, teachers, peers, fairy tales, toys, books, songs, magazines, billboards, TV shows, films, video games—all help teach the scripts a person is expected to follow in any given culture. Adolescents have "a limited repertoire of 'cultural scripts' or 'strategies of action' that they can draw on to resolve their social problems" (Newman et al., 2004, p. 148). Once scripts are learned (often on an automatic, nonconscious level), they serve as guides or tools for future behavior, and repeated priming and use of a set of schemas eventually make them chronically accessible (Anderson et al., 2003). Aspects of events, experiences, and event sequences become the content of a broader *cognitive schema* that are encoded in memory and provide the basis for attributions, judgments, and behavioral decisions (see Walsh & Gentile, *Sex, Murder, and Video Games*, 2003, for a discussion of the impact of violent computer games on worldview, gender stereotypes, and criminal behavior).

People are often influenced as much by artistic, media, and pop cultural representations as they are by personal experiences. Most of what is known about the world comes from symbolic rather than experienced reality, particularly in advanced media-saturated societies like the United States. According to Ray Surette (1998), foremost researcher in the area of media and crime, what you know comes from "all the events you didn't witness but believe occurred, all the facts about the world you didn't personally collect but believe to be true, and all the things you believe to exist but haven't personally seen" (p. xvi). Youth (and adult media junkies) tend to be more influenced by pop culture, are more technologically savvy, and are more likely to weave information from media sources into their worldview than older people. Children and adolescents largely rely on symbolic reality they draw from popular culture to form their cognitive scripts.

Criminal behavior is the complex product of the convergence of biological, psychological, sociological, routine activity/opportunity, phenomenological, and cultural factors at a particular time and place for a specific individual. People are influenced by static factors, which stay the same over time (e.g., gender, personality), and dynamic factors, which change over time (e.g., setting, cognitive scripts). Different people are more or less influenced by different factors and forces that can either decrease or increase the likelihood of criminal behavior. For some people, exposure to media violence may be a risk factor that increases their likelihood of engaging in criminal behavior. For others, violent media may be a protective factor that decreases the likelihood of criminal behavior by providing a harmless cathartic outlet. Depending on the individual and range of other influences, some risk factors are more "risky" for certain types of people, and in some cases, factors that have been empirically determined to increase the likelihood of criminal behavior in most people may, for some individuals, actually reduce the likelihood of criminal behavior.

Consider a hypothetical example. An individual who has many psychopathic personality characteristics (static factor) is raised in an abusive family in a lower-scale environment on the East Coast in the 1930s (dynamic factor). He learns at a young age that people will leave him alone if he uses aggression and violence. His idols, based on what he sees around him in popular culture and neighborhood lore, are famous organized crime gangsters like Lucky Luciano and Al Capone (for detailed information on Luciano, Capone, and other mob bosses go to http://www.crimelibrary.com/gangsters_outlaws/mob_bosses/index.html). As a teenager, he becomes involved with low-level thugs who, because he is known to use violence

Photo 10.1 Computer hacker Kevin Mitnick.

Photo credit: © Dan Callister/Getty Images.

when necessary, introduce him to members of organized crime groups looking for an "enforcer." He becomes a successful hit man and murders dozens of people during the course of his life. In contrast, consider a person with the same static factors—psychopathic characteristics, high intelligence—except he is brought up in the 1990s in an upscale environment with a loving family on the West Coast. He is educated in computer science and Web development, acquires knowledge about stocks and bonds and idolizes famous cybercriminals such as Kevin Mitnick aka Mafiaboy, and Mark Abene aka Phiber Optik. His environmental (dynamic) factors contribute to a cognitive schema that fosters involvement in Internet securities fraud rather than violent criminal behavior. These are overly simplistic examples, but they illustrate the basic process in the development of cognitive scripts—people's beliefs, perceptions, and actions are largely dictated in obvious and not so obvious ways by who and what they see around them.

Technology-Related Risk Factors for Criminal Behavior

Technology, the application of science to human endeavors, involves the use of tools, knowledge, and ideas to make the world better and tasks and activities more manageable, efficient, enjoyable, and entertaining. "Technology changes everything, crime included" (Clarke, 2004). It breeds new and enhances old forms of criminal behavior. With every technological advance, the potential emerges for criminal behavior to change. *Technological advances have impacted criminal behavior in three ways:*

1. *Mass communication technology* has transformed media and popular culture into a powerful influence on offender behavior.

2. *Computer technology* has created new avenues and different opportunities for criminal behavior.

3. *Investigative technology* has altered methods offenders use and the types of crimes they engage in.

Criminologists, psychologists, and others studying criminal behavior have barely begun to explore the nature and dynamics of media- (and technology-) mediated criminal behavior (Black, 1991; Ferrell, 1995). Pop culture, television, and film are contemporary forms of myth (Hill, 1992), in which stories about good/evil, right/wrong, and love/hate are told on movie screens or computer monitors by strangers rather than around campfires by elders. Today more than ever before, the influences of technology play a powerful role for most people in the development of cognitive and behavioral scripts. With respect to criminal behavior, technology, media, and popular culture shape offender choices in unique ways—from the decision to commit a crime, the type of crime, and the manner in which it is committed to providing a ready-made script for rationalization techniques to neutralize offense behavior.

It is important to recognize the interrelationship between technology, media, and popular culture in thinking about the role of technology in criminal behavior. *Technology breeds false familiarity, blurs fantasy and reality, and provides a virtual realm that mediates conscience.* This has important implications for the study of criminal behavior. Technological advances have all but guaranteed that the boundary between an event and media representation of an event has

> increasingly become a dotted line through which the real and the simulated share a mass bank of visual references. Within this complex matrix of narrative/visual relationships, images are hyper—and often confused with one another—and in the mass replication of visual texts, the electronic representation of an event often becomes embedded within the event itself . . . the large-scale dissemination of electronic images leads to a saturated state of hyperconsciousness in which real and simulated events are increasingly determined/ defined in mimetic relation to each other. (Tietchen, 1998, ¶17)

Computer technology has enhanced mass communication beyond anything imaginable just 30 years ago. Mass communication systems are now cybercrime targets. Offenders have become more sophisticated in their MOs in an effort to stay one step ahead of law enforcement technology, and learn crime commission and avoidance techniques from watching *CSI* and *Forensic Files*. All of these influences converge in cases in which offenders are inspired by hi-tech images of crime and violence that blur the line between fantasy and reality, enjoy hearing their crimes disseminated through the news media immediately and globally, use the news media to communicate with police, learn the latest forensic techniques on the Internet to avoid detection, and become better at what they do to stay ahead of law enforcement and investigative technology.[1]

Technology has dramatically influenced the study of crime, criminal behavior, and criminal justice. Clarke (2004) argues that, with the new technology, criminologists "must no longer imagine themselves engaged in 'pure' science . . . and must embrace the role of 'applied' scientists" (p. 57) by focusing less on theory and more on how to prevent and control crime. The traditional focus of criminology on explanations rather than solutions, theory without application, and methodological rigor over creativity and real-world relevance is particularly problematic when it comes to technology-related criminal behavior. Technology-related (or hi-tech) crime is often committed by individuals from backgrounds that do not fall neatly into the traditional theories of crime that emphasize the role of socioeconomic status and deprivation as primary crime correlates. Since the 1970s, criminology has slowly been supplanted by applied criminal justice programs in universities. The influence of technology on crime and criminal behavior may now be moving even further toward application, with new "crime science" programs being developed that focus on understanding crime (rather than criminals), rational choice (rather than criminal dispositions), how (rather than why) crime is committed, specific crime and disorder problems (rather than general crime and delinquency), crime as normal (rather than pathological), and so on.

The pace at which technology is advancing and the unprecedented exposure to and influence of media and popular culture calls for empirical examination of the unique role *technology-related factors* play in motivating and shaping criminal behavior. *How have technological advances such as radio, TV, the Internet, video and computer games, networked violent role-play communities, MTV, online banking, check cards, chat rooms, Netflix, Napster, real-time news reports, reality TV, video poker, online bingo, cell phones, and investigative advances such as DNA, GPS tracking, LoJack vehicle recovery systems, and geographical profiling influenced criminal behavior? Has the convergence of culture and technology created a criminogenically lethal set of pop cultural artifacts that have the potential to motivate or lay the blueprint for criminal behavior in ways the world has never seen before?* Criminologists can no longer ignore the ways in which mass media and computer technology shape criminal behavior. With the unprecedented exposure to technology, it is increasingly important to examine the unique role that technology-related factors play in motivating and shaping criminal behavior.

The Criminogenic Effects of Mass Culture and Media Violence

There is no shortage of anecdotal evidence regarding crimes inspired by media and pop cultural sources, but little empirical evidence exists to explain the complex ways in which technology, media, and popular culture influence criminal behavior on an individual level. Most researchers agree that mass media technology presents special challenges for criminology because of its powerful influence on behavior. Surette (1990) suggests that the electronic media present greater concerns than print media because they can criminally influence a larger at-risk pool of individuals. Similarly, Black (1991) argues that the dramatic rise in the number of political assassinations in the 1960s and 1970s and other senseless murders attributed to mental illness in the 1980s are attributed to the cultural impact of television and must be understood within the "historically unprecedented context of hyperaestheticized mass-culture" (p. 136). This suggests that the imitative effects of violent mass media may be much stronger than a story about violence presented in a book or in narrative form from person to person.

Children and adolescents today develop in an environment saturated with technology and mass media imagery. Toddlers are exposed to TV, computers, and the Internet. Kindergartners have Game Boys, cell phones, and iPods. By the time they are preteens, they tote cell phones with digital and video cameras, laptops with wireless Internet access, and communicate with each other via e-mail, text messages, MySpace, FaceBook, and YouTube. With the click of a button, an 8-year-old can find out instantly how to build a birdhouse or a bomb. Youth depend on media as a source of information. With parents spending more and more time at work, away from their children, to make ends meet, the media have become a more powerful socializing agent than ever before. The forms and amount of media violence in the United States are particularly extreme relative to that in other countries, and American children receive mixed messages about the meaning of violence (e.g., parents tell kids they can't play violent video games and then sit on the sofa to watch the evening news filled with stories about war) (Wooden & Blazak, 2001).

Criminological theory and research in the 21st century has to be concerned with how cultural technological changes such as video gaming, the Internet, television, and film influence criminal behavior. As technologies become more relevant to targeted audience members, more dominant as an information source, and more entertaining, adolescents become much more lilkely to use this information as a tool to understand themselves and others (Lloyd, 2002). Determining whether or not a violent computer game, a film, or access to the Internet contributed to a particular criminal act is less a question of whether or not technology or a particular media form *causes* the behavior than one of how the influence *motivates* and *shapes* the behavior in a particular individual:

> It is not simply that the mass media report in certain ways on criminal events or provide fashionable fodder out of which criminal subcultures construct collective styles. For good or bad, postmodern society exists well beyond such discrete, linear patterns of action and reaction. Rather, criminal events, identities, and styles take life within a media-saturated environment, and thus exist from the start as moments in a mediated spiral of presentation and representation (Ferrell & Sanders, 1995, p. 14).

Exploration of how technology serves to motivate criminal behavior requires interdisciplinary analysis of the socializing properties of technology, media, and popular culture. According to Lloyd (2002):

> Mass communications, particularly the Internet and television programming, including music videos, can be reconceptualized as opportunities for adolescents to identify cues for social behavior among their peer group as well as cognitively rehearse their own approaches to certain interactions. . . . Without appreciation for the specific "cultural competencies" of

the adolescent culture, mass media influences are likely to be overlooked as a significant socialization agent for this population in the new millennium (p. 88).

This is even more important to consider in light of findings reported by Anderson and coworkers (2003), from three nationally representative surveys[2] and other studies that found the following:

- Virtually all families with children have a television set.
- Most have at least one VCR or DVD player.
- Most (approximately 75%) subscribe to cable or satellite TV.
- 7 in 10 families with children have a video-game system.
- 7 in 10 families own a computer.
- The majority of American children have a TV in their bedroom (including 30% of children age 3 and under).
- 33 to 39% of children age 2 to 17 have a video-game player in their bedroom.
- 30% of children have a VCR in their bedroom.
- 6 to 11% of children have Internet access in their bedrooms.
- The percentage of families with on-line connections has risen in recent years from 15% in 1996 to 52% in 2000.
- Children spend more time consuming entertainment media than engaging in any other activity besides sleeping and school.
- Children average approximately 4 hours per day in front of a TV or computer screen.
- 25% of 6th graders watch more than 40 hours of TV per week.
- On any given Saturday morning at 10 am, 60% of American 6- to 11-year-olds are watching TV.

One of the most researched areas in communications and criminology is the relationship between television violence and antisocial and aggressive behavior. The effects of TV violence, in the 1960s and 1970s, was one of the most well-funded and extensively studied areas in the social sciences (Sparks, 1992). In the 1980s and 1990s, the research on the effects of TV violence (known as the "effects literature") shifted to focus on the effects on the general public's fear of crime and perceptions of the criminal justice system. Research on the influence of TV violence on aggression has consistently shown that TV violence increases aggression and social anxiety, cultivates a "mean view" of the world, and negatively impacts real-world behavior.

More than 1,000 studies have been conducted on the effects of TV and film violence over the past 40 years, and in the last decade the *National Institute of Mental Health,* the *American Academy of Pediatrics,* the *American Academy of Child and Adolescent Psychiatry,* and the *American Medical Association* have reviewed these studies and concluded that TV violence leads to real-world violence (Senate Committee on the Judiciary, 1999). More recent research has further clarified the role media violence plays in creating real-world violence, suggesting that media violence produces short-term increases in aggression by triggering an automatic inclination toward imitation, enhancing autonomic arousal, and priming existing cognitive scripts (Anderson et al., 2003). Other researchers suggest that the attack on television violence by politicians, scientists, parents, and others is unwarranted and TV violence actually performs an innate human function by serving as "the most recent and least damaging venue for the routinized working out of innate aggressiveness and fear" (Fowles, 1999, p. 119).

Media effects research in the literature has focused on a number of key theoretical areas of the effects of mass media technology on criminal behavior. Sparks and Sparks (2002) identify six theoretical mechanisms that have formed our understanding of the influence of violent media:

1. *Catharsis:* Media violence provides a cathartic outlet that allows viewers to engage in fantasy aggression that reduces the need to carry out aggressive behavior.

2. *Social learning:* Media characters serve as role models. If people see aggressive characters being rewarded rather than punished for the behavior, they will be more likely to imitate the behavior.

3. *Priming:* Exposure to violent media images plants aggressive and violent cues in people's minds making them easily cognitively accessible. These cues interact with the viewers' emotional state and can increase the likelihood of aggressive behavior.

4. *Arousal:* People become physiologically aroused when they view media violence, in a way that intensifies the emotional state of the viewer.

5. *Desensitization:* The more violent media a person consumes, the more dulled the person's sensitivity to violence becomes. This can contribute to aggressive behavior by reducing the recognition that aggression and violence are behaviors that should be curtailed.

6. *Cultivation and fear:* Viewing violent media cultivates a particular social reality and induces high levels of fear that can persist for days, months, or years after initial exposure.

All six of these theoretical areas have been explored at length in the media effects literature. All but the catharsis theory have received empirical support.[3]

Many questions remain regarding the factors that mediate media violence effects and its influence on criminal behavior. Though the "scientific debate over whether media violence increases aggression and violence is essentially over" (Anderson et al., 2003, p. 81) with the conclusion that no one is immune to the powerful effects of media violence, the underlying psychological processes and magnitude of media-violence effects on extreme forms of violence is still unexplored. The bulk of the literature on the effects of violent media is based on studies that have investigated the impact of media violence on aggression. Review of the studies that have specifically focused on *criminal* aggression yield very different results and do not provide empirical evidence that viewing violent portrayals causes crime (Savage, 2004). To date, findings are inconsistent regarding the factors that mediate the extent to which media violence influences real-life violence. Factors such as viewer characteristics, social-environmental influences, nature of media content, and level or interaction with media source are all likely to play a role in whether or not and how violent media influences criminal behavior:

> After 50 years and over 1,000 studies . . . there is . . . not a single research study which is even remotely predictive of the Columbine massacre or similar high school

shootings ... as for making the explicit connection between on-screen mayhem by the bodies of Sylvester Stallone and Arnold Schwarzenegger, the minds of Oliver Stone and Wes Craven, and real-life singular, serial or mass murder, scientific psychology, albeit noble and earnest in its tireless efforts, has simply not delivered the goods. It asserts the causa nexus but doesn't actually demonstrate it. (Fischoff, 2004, p. 31)

Sparks and Sparks (2002, p. 277) ask, "If most scholars agree that the research evidence tends to converge on the conclusion that exposure to media violence causes aggressive behavior, then why has scholarly and public debate on this topic produced so much controversy?"

The media effects research has consistently showed that violent media accounts for 10 to 15% of the variance in aggressive behavior in any given study. However, this means that 85 to 90% of the variance is attributable to something else. On the other hand, in statistical terms, for one factor to account for 10 to 15% of the explanation for aggressive behavior is impressive. Critics of the media violence research also note that, if only one person out of millions who watch a violent film is inspired to mimic the violence, then this small statistical effect is virtually unpreventable given the diversity of viewers. On the other hand, very small statistical effects can translate into large social problems with tragic consequences. If one person out of thousands watching a violent film is inspired to mimic the violence and ends up murdering one or more people, then it is imperative that researchers continue to examine the influence of violent media to be able to explain what happened with that individual in the hope of someday being able to develop predictive models or preventive measures.

The Criminogenic Effects of Computer Technology

Computer technology has also had a major influence on criminal behavior. Computer technology, particularly the Internet, has created a virtual space to commit a new type of crime called *cybercrime*, that is

> activities in which computers, telephones, cellular equipment, and other technological devices are used for illicit purposes such as fraud, theft, electronic vandalism, violating intellectual property rights, and breaking and entering into computer systems and networks. (Speer, 2000, p. 269)[4]

This virtual space has been referred to as "the place between places" known as *cyberspace* (Britz, 2004). Cyberspace has become an underworld marketplace for criminal contraband such as drugs, weapons, and child pornography and a hi-tech means of committing crime ranging from low-level predatory offenses to highly sophisticated security breaches and information theft.

Law enforcement and the courts face investigative and legal challenges unique to cybercrime—in particular, the investigative challenge of locating an offender who is not physically present at the crime scene. Crimes such as *phishing*, identity theft, Internet insider trading, online child pornography rings, and Internet stalking reflect new, essentially invisible, methods of engaging in old crimes. Technology has had an unprecedented impact on globalization that has created vast opportunities for economic crime, organized crime, and terrorism. As a result, law enforcement must be technologically sophisticated to stay one step ahead of offenders and the criminal law has had to deal with new questions regarding what sorts of virtual behaviors constitute a punishable criminal act. New crime control technologies such as global positioning devices, facial recognition software (Speer, 2000), computer software applications for criminological research (e.g., the new PC_Eyewitness program for laboratories to conduct research on eyewitness memory and law enforcement to administer lineups; see MacLin, Meissner, & Zimmerman, 2005), video image processing, animation software, surveillance systems, and image databases for fingerprints, handwriting, shoe prints, drugs, cartridge cases, toolmarks, and so on (James & Nordby, 2005) have been introduced with radical implications for criminology, criminal justice, and forensic science.

Technology-Related Crime Subtypes

Technology plays a central role in two types of criminal behavior that have received an increasing amount of attention in recent years—*copycat crime* and *cybercrime*. Copycat crime and cybercrime are likely to become a significant part of the crime landscape in the 21st century. They are *subtypes* that can cut across all of the major crime categories while maintaining distinct features. In some respects, copycat and cybercrime represent more the process by which criminal behavior occurs than a type of crime. Both copycat and cybercrime can be violent, sex, economic, public order, or political crimes. Copycat and cybercrime are unique in that technology shapes their nature and presentation.

Copycat Crime

Copycat crime is crime inspired by another crime that has been publicized in the news media or fictionally or artistically represented in which the offender incorporates aspects of the original offense. To be a copycat, a crime "must have been inspired by an earlier, publicized crime—that is, there must be a pair of crimes linked by the media" (Surette, 1998, p. 137). Imitated crimes have occurred after intense media coverage of workplace violence, product tampering, hate crimes, mass murder, hijacking, and terrorism and after fictional depictions of robbery, murder, arson, carjacking, rape, and other types of crimes on TV, in film, and in video games. The copycat effect is also sometimes referred to as the *contagion effect, imitation, mimesis,* and *clusters* and generally refers to the "power of mass communication and culture to create an epidemic of similar behaviors" (Coleman, 2004, p. 1). Identifying copycat crimes can be problematic because the media can quantitatively and qualitatively influence individual criminal behavior in subtle and not so subtle ways (Surette, 1990). It is often difficult to know when an offense is linked to an earlier offense; crimes are also sometimes characterized as copycats when they are not.

Early references to the copycat phenomenon in the 1800s involved behaviors thought to be inspired by books. For example, Johann Most's book *Revolutionary War Science* published in 1885, a how-to terrorist manual, was associated with the 1886 Chicago Haymarket Square bombing (Surette, 1998). Gabriel Tarde was the first to offer a theoretical discussion of copycat crime in the early 1900s. He coined the term *suggesto-imitative assaults* to describe sensational violent crimes that appeared to spur similar incidents (Surette, 1990, p. 93). Sociologists in the 1970s examined the copycat phenomenon with respect to suicide, suggesting that the suicide rate increases with the level of media coverage of a suicide of a famous person. In 1974, sociologist David Phillips coined the term the *Werther effect* referring to the copycat phenomenon in response to Johann Wolfgang von Goethe's 1774 novel, *The Sorrows of Young Werther*. In the years following publication of the book in Europe, so many men shot themselves while sitting at their desks with an open copy of the book in front of them, that the book was banned in Germany, Denmark, and Italy (Coleman, 2004). Another well-known example of suicide contagion and the copycat effect occurred following publicity surrounding Marilyn Monroe's 1962 suicide. In the month after her death, the overall suicide rate in the United States increased by 12%, and 197 primarily young blond women appeared to use Monroe as a role model in their own suicides.

There is no shortage of contemporary examples of the copycat effect producing criminal behavior. A growing body of anecdotal evidence suggests that copycat crime is a very real phenomenon exacerbated by the central role of media and popular culture, particularly in the lives of youth. Box 10.1 lists some of the most notable copycat cases.

- **CATCHER IN THE RYE (1951)**—Mark David Chapman believed himself to be Holden Caulfield, the main character in the book. He murdered John Lennon in 1980 after years of fixation on both Lennon and Caulfield. He is believed to have murdered Lennon because he viewed him as a "phony," a term Caulfield used to refer to people.

- **CLOCKWORK ORANGE (1971)**—film associated with rape of a 17-year-old girl by male youths singing "Singing in the Rain" and string of brutal rapes and murders in Britain by men dressed similarly to the characters attributed to either the film or the book. Kubrick pulled the film in Britain in 1972 and it wasn't re-released there until 2000.

- **TAXI DRIVER (1976)**—John Hinckley's 1981 assassination attempt on Ronald Reagan was associated with the film. Hinckley was found not guilty by reason of insanity after his attorneys argued he was fixated on the film, its characters, and actors (Jodi Foster), and that his obsession with the film was evidence that he had lost the distinction between reality and fiction. Hinckley was said to have used *Taxi Driver* as a primary script and John Lennon's murder by Mark David Chapman as a secondary script in his assassination attempt. The film was played for jurors at his trial.

- **NATURAL BORN KILLERS (1994)**—Linked to a dozen murders in the U.S., Canada, and Europe and to school shooter cases including Columbine. Three copycats involved male/female pairs who went on murder sprees including the 1995 robbery/murder spree of 18-year-old Benjamin Darras and Sarah Edmondson that led to a civil suit against *NBK* director Oliver Stone that went to the U.S. Supreme court before it was dismissed in 2001; four murders committed by 19-year-old Florence Rey and 22-year-old boyfriend Audry Maupin dubbed "France's Natural Born Killers"; and 1998 case involving Veronique Herbert and Sebastien Paindavoine who murdered a 16-year-old boy in a sex set-up right out of the film.

- **THE MATRIX (1999, 2003)**—Associated with a half a dozen murders. In several of the offenders' trials (including D.C. Sniper shooter John Malvo), *The Matrix* was woven into the defendant's insanity defense. In at least two cases (Lynne Ansley in Ohio in 2002 and Vadim Mieseges San Francisco in 2003) the "matrix defense" resulted in a finding of not guilty by reason of insanity.

BOX 10.1

ANECDOTAL EVIDENCE OF COPYCAT CRIMES

- **BASKETBALL DIARIES (1995)**—Scene in the film, based on the book of the same name by Jim Carroll, is claimed to have partially inspired Columbine shooters Dylan Klebold and Eric Harris. In the scene, the character played by Leonardo DiCaprio has a dream where he walks into a school with a long black trenchcoat and automatic weapon and begins firing. The videotaped images of Klebold and Harris during the Columbine murders were strikingly similar to the scene in the *Basketball Diaries* (Coleman, 2004; Segal & Enos, 1991).

- **BEAVIS AND BUTT-HEAD (1993–1997)**—Blamed for inciting children to start fires, some of which were fatal (Surette, 1998).

- **CATCHER IN THE RYE (1951)**—Mark David Chapman believed himself to be Holden Caulfield, the main character in the book. He murdered John Lennon in 1980 after years of fixation on both Lennon and Caulfield. He is believed to have murdered Lennon because he viewed him as a "phony," a term Caulfield used to refer to people (Black, 1991).

- **CHILD'S PLAY 3 (1993)**—Film allegedly influenced two 10-year-old boys (Jon Venebles and Robert Thompson), who abducted 2-year-old James Bulger from a shopping mall, took him on a 2 ½ mile walk to a railway, and tortured and murdered him. The murder was similar to a scene in the film and the father of one of the boys was said to have rented the film in the week before the murder (Segal & Enos, 1991).

- **CLOCKWORK ORANGE (1971)**—Film associated with the rape of a 17-year-old girl by male youths singing "Singing in the Rain" and a string of brutal rapes and murders in Britain by men dressed similarly to the characters attributed to either the film or the book. Kubrick pulled the film in Britain in 1972 and it wasn't re-released there until 2000 (Carruthers, 2001; Coleman, 2004).

- **COLUMBINE SCHOOL SHOOTING (1999)**—The Columbine incident, and news coverage of the event, itself inspired copycats including a school shooting in Toronto, Canada, by a 14-year-old diagnosed with conduct disorder and said to be bordering on a diagnosis of psychopathy who was fixated on the Columbine shootings. Other school shooters have allegedly been inspired by media, including Barry Loukaitis in the Moses Lake, Washington, shooting in 1996, who was inspired by the Pearl Jam video *Jeremy*, and Michael Carneal in the West Paducah, Kentucky, shooting influenced by the *Basketball Diaries*. Most recently, Seung-Hui Cho, the gunman in the Virginia Tech massacre, specifically referred to Columbine in videotapes he made of himself on the day of the shootings.

- **DOOM I & II (1993, 1994)**—Violent computer role-playing game associated with Columbine shooting and a number of the school shootings and other crimes. Dylan Klebold and Eric Harris were avid players of *Doom* and were members of a community of *Doom* players who played the game on the Internet.

- **DOOMSDAY FLIGHT (1966)**—Bomb threats were reported by airlines after this TV movie aired (Surette, 1998).

(Continued)

(Continued)

- **EASY E AND NWA (1991)**—A group of kids in Texas were put in prison for a string of robberies and claimed they "got hyped" by their music (Surette, 1998).

- **GONE IN 60 SECONDS (2000)**—Film reportedly incited a number of car theft sprees in the United States and Canada.

- **GRAND THEFT AUTO VICE CITY (2002)**—18-year-old Devin Moore allegedly played the game for hours before stealing a car and gunning down two police officers and a 911 dispatcher in 2003. When captured he said, "Life is like a video game. Everybody's got to die some time." At trial, it was revealed that he was a compulsive violent video game player who suffered from childhood abuse-related posttraumatic stress disorder. Moore's attorney's argued the "*GTA* defense"—that he'd lost touch with reality and was acting out the virtual violence in *GTA*. Despite his attorney's efforts, the *GTA* defense was unsuccessful and Moore was sentenced to death in 2005 ("Can a Video Game Lead to Murder?" 2005).

- **HEATHERS (1989)**—Film inspired a 15-year-old girl in Seattle to lace a peanut butter sandwich with poison intending to kill an 11-year-old playmate (Surette, 1998).

- **HIT MAN: A TECHNICAL MANUAL FOR INDEPENDENT CONTRACTORS (1983)**—Book written under the pseudonym Rex Feral influenced a man who hired a professional hit man to murder his paraplegic son and ex-wife to obtain the insurance money. After the offender's trial and conviction, it was discovered that he had ordered and purchased a copy of the book *A Technical Manual for Independent Contractors*, which offered graphic instructions on how to murder someone. In court it was determined that the book was not protected speech because the publisher intended it as a how-to manual (O'Neil, 2001).

- **HORROR FILM GENRE**—Relationship was suggested between horror films (in general) and specific serial murder or violent crime cases, including the case of Armin Meiwes the German cannibal killer ("German Cannibal tells of Fantasy," December 3, 2003).

- **ICE-T'S "COP KILLER" (1992)**—Ice-T's music and lyrics accused of inciting violence against police and other crimes. In Virginia a record store owner was arrested for selling the CD *Body Count*, which contains the song. Many record stores reacted by removing the album from their stores (Surette, 1998).

- **IN COLD BLOOD (1967)**—Film version of the 1966 novel by Truman Capote is said to have influenced Jesse Carl McAllister, age 21, and Bradley Charles Price, age 22, in the execution-style murder of a young couple watching the sunset on a beach in Seaside, Oregon, in 1997. McAllister and Price shot the couple in the head and then fled to Mexico.

- **JACKASS (2002)**—A number of copycats of crimes (stolen golf carts) and stunts (jumping off buildings) occurred after release of the film (Coleman, 2004).

- **JAMES BYRD MURDER (1998)**—The brutal pickup truck dragging murder of James Byrd in Jasper, Texas, in 1998 was mimicked around the country within days of Byrd's murder. Separate cases in Illinois and Louisiana involved White men who dragged a Black man while yelling racial slurs ("A Third Car Dragging Incident Is Reported," 2001).

- **MAGNUM FORCE (1973)**—Film starring Clint Eastwood. Scene in the film where a woman was killed by pouring drain cleaner down her throat was modeled by murderers William Andrews and Dale Selby Pierre in what became known as the 1974 Ogden, Utah, "Hi-Fi murders." The pair robbed a stereo store and during the robbery mimicked the scene in *Magnum Force* by forcing five victims to drink Drano before they shot them all in the head (Douglas & Olshaker, 1999). Two of the victims survived, including then 16-year-old Cortney Naisbitt, whose experience was depicted in the book *Victim* (Kinder, 1982).

- **MAPPELTHORPE (1946-1989)**—Photographer's work was criticized for encouraging pedophilia and homosexual sadomasochism (Ferrell & Sanders, 1995).

- **MARILYN MANSON (1969-Present)**—Musician and pop culture icon. His music, style, artwork, and aesthetic has been linked to a number of crimes including the Columbine shootings and the 2003 murder of a 14-year-old girl in Scotland ("Jury Shown Manson Video," December 23, 2004; Poling, 2007). He's been accused of encouraging a cultlike following, and many of his followers are said to be involved in deviant and criminal activity. He was recently featured in a TNT documentary called *Faces of Evil* in which people who "celebrate evil" were profiled (Moore, 2002).

- **MARQUIS DE SADE**—De Sade's writings have been associated with sadism, pornography, and sexual violence throughout history (Black, 1991; Danner, 1984) in particular in the writings of prominent feminist writers.

- **MENACE II SOCIETY (1993)**—Motivated two youths who killed and robbed a motorist and four teens to steal a car, wound a man, and kill another (Ferrell & Sanders, 1995).

- **MONEY TRAIN (1995)**—The film including a scene where a man douses a subway token booth with a flammable liquid, lights a match, and demands money. When the clerk inside tries to hand him a bag of cash, the man throws the match through the coin slot at the clerk saying that he isn't in it for the money and sets the booth on fire. In the film, the clerk escapes before the booth explodes. Three days after the film opened, two Brooklyn men (19-year-old Thomas Malik and 18-year-old Vincent Ellerbe) squirted gasoline into a subway booth, setting 50-year-old clerk Harry Kaufman on fire. Kaufman subsequently died 2 weeks later after succumbing to burns over 80% of his body. In the two weeks following the film's opening a total of eight such subway booth attacks occurred (Segal & Enos, 1991; Surette, 1998).

- **NATURAL BORN KILLERS (1994)**—Movie linked to a dozen murders in the United States, Canada, and Europe and to school shooter cases including Columbine. Three copycats involved male/female pairs who went on murder sprees, including the 1995 robbery/murder spree of 18-year-old Benjamin Darras and Sarah Edmondson that led to a civil suit against *NBK* director Oliver Stone that went to the U.S. Supreme court before it was dismissed in 2001; four murders committed by 19-year-old Florence Rey and 22-year-old boyfriend Audry Maupin dubbed "France's Natural Born Killers"; and the 1998 case involving Veronique Herbert and Sebastien Paindavoine, who murdered a 16-year-old boy in a sex set-up right out of the film (O'Brien, 1999).

- **OLDBOY (2003)**—Korean revenge film said to have inspired Virginia Tech gunman Cho Seung-Hui, who murdered 32 students and professors at Virginia Tech in April 2007. Seung-Hui mailed photos and a videotape of himself to NBC news in which he posed with a gun to his head and

(Continued)

(Continued)

holding a hammer similar to images in this film. Images were so similar to those in the film that a Virginia Tech film and video professor noted links and Cho was said to have watched the film many times (Coyle, 2007; Hendrix, 2007; Sragow, 2007).

- **SET IT OFF (1996)**—Film influenced a bank robbery in Aberdeen, Washington, in the mid-1990s, committed by a woman, her teenage daughter, and friend. The trio watched the film prior to the robbery and witnesses said they counted off exactly like the characters in the film (Segal & Enos, 1991).

- **ROBOCOP II (1990)**—Influenced Nathaniel White, who committed multiple murders in New York. White said in a police interview that he got the idea for how to commit the crime in the first of his six murders from a scene in the film (Segal & Enos, 1991).

- **SEVEN (1995)**—Andrea Yates is said to have watched this film in the week before she murdered her five children by drowning in Texas in 2001 (Denno, 2003; Sweetingham, 2006).

- **SOPRANOS (1999–2006)**—In Riverside, California, in 2003, two brothers strangled their 41-year-old mother and then chopped off her head and hands to hide her identity (storing her head and hands in their bedroom in the family's apartment). The two, Jason Bautista a 20-year-old California State University biochemistry major and his 15-year-old half-brother, told investigators they'd gotten the idea for the dismemberment to foil identification of the body on an episode of the television show *The Sopranos* (Segal & Enos, 1991).

- **SLAYER (1983-Present)**—Heavy metal band whose music is said to have influenced three teenage boys to murder a 10th-grade girl in California in 2001. All three boys were said to be devotees of the band and in court one of the boys said Slayer's music influenced the way he looked at things (O'Neil, 2001).

- **STARSKY & HUTCH (1970s)**—TV series allegedly motivated a boy in Canada to extort $50,000 from a local mayor (Surette, 1998).

- **TAXI DRIVER (1976)**—John Hinckley's 1981 assassination attempt on Ronald Reagan was associated with the film. Hinckley was found not guilty by reason of insanity after his attorneys argued he was fixated on the film, its characters, and actors (Jodi Foster), and that his obsession with the film was evidence that he had lost the distinction between reality and fiction. Hinckley was said to have used *Taxi Driver* as a primary script and John Lennon's murder by Mark David Chapman as a secondary script in his assassination attempt. The film was played for jurors at his trial (Black, 1991; Low, Jeffries, & Bonnie, 1986).

- **THE BURNING BED (1984)**—After viewing this TV movie a man poured gasoline on his wife and said he was trying to frighten her. There have also been a number of similar crimes, though it is unclear if the perpetrators saw the movie.

- **THE GIFT (1998)**—Japanese TV show that depicted characters carrying butterfly knives. The show is claimed to have inspired a 13-year-old boy to stab his teacher to death with a butterfly knife. Two years later this alleged copycat murder fueled the fire over the film *Battle Royale*, an extremely violent film involving teenagers who are forced to kill each other on an island until the last (or best) is standing (Sparks & Sparks, 2002).

- **THE LAST SEDUCTION (1994)**—Prosecutors in the Mechele Linehan murder trial argued that Linehan, a former Alaskan exotic dancer turned Olympia, Washington, soccer mom, was influenced by the film to conspire with then boyfriend John Carlin III to kill her ex-fiance Kent Leppink in a 1996 murder-for-insurance plot. Prosecutors argued that Linehan committed the crime after viewing the film and used her sexuality to manipulate men, just like the film's main character played by Linda Fiorentino. Linehan, who in the 11 years since the crime married a doctor and had a daughter, was convicted of first-degree murder on October 22, 2007 (Holland, October 5 2007, October 22, 2007).

- **THE MATRIX (1999, 2003)**—Associated with a half dozen murders. In several of the offenders' trials (including DC sniper-shooter John Malvo), *The Matrix* was woven into the defendant's insanity defense. In at least two cases (Lynne Ansley in Ohio in 2002 and Vadim Mieseges in San Francisco in 2003) the "matrix defense" resulted in a finding of not guilty by reason of insanity (Coleman, 2004; Stern, 2003).

- **THE SECRET AGENT (1907)**—Federal authorities believe Ted Kaczynski, aka the Unabomber, was influenced by this novel written by Joseph Conrad. Kaczynski, a former math professor, was a fan of author Joseph Conrad and was believed to have read the book a dozen times before committing his crimes (Kovaleski, 1996).

- **THELMA & LOUISE (1991)**—Film said to have influenced a number of female pairs to commit a variety of crimes including bank robbery (Segal & Enos, 1991).

- **TV NEWS**—Has been said to motivate copycat terrorist activities (Surette, 1998).

- **TV PRISON MOVIES**—Motivated several girls in California to rape a 9-year-old girl after watching a movie about a girl who was raped in a juvenile institution (Surette, 1988).

- **TV WRESTLING (1999)**—In 1999 12-year-old Lionel Tate said he was mimicking wrestling moves he saw on TV when he murdered his 6-year-old playmate ("Lionel Tate Released," 2004).

- **TYLENOL POISONINGS (1980s and 1990s)**—In 1982 the parents of a 12-year-old Illinois girl complaining of a sore throat and runny nose gave her one extra-strength Tylenol capsule. Within an hour, the girl was found lying on the bathroom floor and was rushed to the hospital where she later died. That same day in a nearby Illinois suburb, a 27-year-old postal worker died from an unexplained heart attack. On the night of his death, his brother and sister-in-law took Tylenol they found at his home and collapsed and died shortly after. It was eventually discovered by the Cook County Medical Examiner's Office that all four had died as a result of cyanide poisoning and that the Tylenol capsules were filled with 65 milligrams of cyanide—10,000 times more than the amount needed to kill a person. Before the word got out and the Tylenol was recalled, three more deaths occurred in Illinois. From the first mention of the Tylenol murders, copycat tamperings occurred. The FDA identified 270 incidents, 36 of which were labeled hard core true tamperings. In the late 1980s and early 1990s there were copycat tampering murders in New York and in Washington State involving Tylenol, Excedrin, and Sudafed. Perpetrators were arrested in many of the tamperings that resulted in murders, including the arrest of Stella Nickell, who murdered her husband and another woman in Washington State. Nickell had

(Continued)

(Continued)

wanted to make her husband's murder look like a serial tampering homicide. Police identified Nickell after finding prints on a library book she had checked out called *Deadly Harvest*, specifically on pages dealing with cyanide poisoning. To date, the original Tylenol terrorist has never been caught (Bell, 2005).

- **WARRIORS (1979)**—Film about a Coney Island gang that was the subject of a 1989 liability suit. The case was brought by the parents of a teenager who was stabbed to death on a subway car by an offender who had just seen the film, which depicted a similar murder.

These cases are just a handful of the ever-growing list of anecdotal accounts of copycat crimes that illustrate the powerful role of media, popular culture, and art in influencing and shaping criminal behavior. Box 10.1 presents a comprehensive list of copycat cases.

Criminal behavior can be inspired by all sorts of events and cultural artifacts, including novels published well before the information age such as Goethe's *The Sorrows of Young Werther*. However, the unprecedented role technology and mass media play in modern society raises timely questions: *Are imitative acts of crime and violence increasing? Do youth today have a unique relationship with media and popular culture that mediates (contributes to or detracts from) the potential for copycat violence? Has elevation of the status of "star" and "hero" in contemporary times exacerbated the copycat effect? Is copycat crime a distinct criminal subtype characterized by a blurring of boundaries between fantasy and reality or a need for media publicity?*

In some respects, the copycat effect of criminal behavior is no different from the copycat effect of prosocial behavior. It can be explained in part through learning theory. People, in particular children, imitate what they see. A child may watch an episode of *Power Puff Girls* and then go off to imitate knocking out her own stuffed replica of the evil Monkey Mojojo. Or a teenager or young adult may watch an episode of *Law & Order* or *CSI* on TV and decide to pursue a career in law or forensic science. What is the difference between these imitative acts and the car theft and murder committed by a teen who plays *Grand Theft Auto* for hours on end? We are all influenced to some extent by popular culture. The extent to which technology has made media and popular culture such an enormous part of everyday life exacerbates the powerful influence of media images. However, imitation is too simplistic a process to fully explain copycat crime (Surette, 1990, p. 93). *There is something about the combined forces of technology and media's salient roles in contemporary life, the elevation of the criminal (specifically serial and mass murderers) to star status, and the value placed on public recognition reinforced by American popular culture that create the particular phenomenon of copycat crime.*

The crime and violence in film, television, computer games, true crime novels, and music videos have the potential to increase the copycat effect, not because of the violence itself, but as a result of the glorification of extreme violent crime and the message that committing violence is one route to fame and notoriety. According to Surette (1998), "The news media's emphasis on drama, violence, and entertainment and the entertainment media's emphasis on themes of violent criminality appear to work together to foster copycat crimes . . . simply for notoriety" (p. 139). There is an enormous disparity between the number of murders and extreme forms of criminal behavior such as serial murder displayed in popular culture and the actual extent of the phenomenon in real life (Jenkins, 1994). There are serial killer board games, trading cards, and serial killer art. In the 1980s and 1990s, dozens of serial killers were featured on popular magazine covers,[5] and films about them were instant box office smashes (Campbell, 2002). Some suggest that the serial killer film has replaced the Western in American genre fiction and the serial killer has become the "new mythic monster." This elevation of the serial killer to mythical figure has made the serial killer a supernatural being and blurred the boundaries between fantasy and reality for the general public, policymakers, and criminal justice professionals. Even police have been known to release offenders because they did not fit the media stereotype of a serial killer (Epstein, 1995).

An increasing number of documented cases show that actual serial murderers and school shooters have mimicked or altered their behavior based on media stories of actual or fictional killers. For example, in police interviews two of the most notorious serial killers in history, Gary Ridgway, the Green River killer, and Dennis Rader, the BTK killer, referred to following other serial killers in the media.[6] Similarly, Columbine school shooters Eric Harris and Dylan Klebold boasted on video about inflicting "the most deaths in U.S. history" in an attempt to one-up other school shooters and Timothy McVeigh's actions in the Oklahoma bombing (Cullen, 2004). The 2002 DC sniper shootings by John Muhammad and Lee Malvo inspired a series of sniper attacks around the world, and Lee Malvo himself was said to have watched the film *The Matrix* over 100 times to prepare himself for the sniper attacks (Malvo Trial CNN Transcripts, 2003). And just days before the eighth anniversary of the Columbine murders, Seung-Hui Cho mailed a video of himself to NBC News ranting about Columbine killers Klebold and Harris before going on to murder 32 students and professors on the Virginia Tech campus later that day (Cullen, 2007), committing the ultimate one-up of his Columbine predecessors. Clearly, the behavior of the most extreme serial killers and mass murderers in recent times has been shaped by media and popular culture.

The Nature and Mechanisms of Copycat Crime

The copycat effect influences crime in two ways: Images presented in media and popular culture can *trigger* criminal behavior or *shape* the form criminal behavior may take (Surette, 1998). Media images may send a would-be offender over the edge or give someone who was planning to commit a crime anyway ideas about how to commit it. For example, would Devin Moore have murdered Arnold Strickland, James Crump, and Ace Wheeler had he not been an avid player of *Grand Theft Auto*? Or did the video game simply give him ideas about how to carry out such a brutal act? It is virtually impossible to definitively answer this question and just as difficult to design an empirical study to test whether or not there is a causal relationship between virtual and actual violence, given the number of factors and forces that contribute to the criminal behavior on any individual in the real world.

Individual, environmental, situational, and media-related factors interact in a unique way to influence whether or not individuals will mimic criminal behavior they see in the media and popular culture (Figure 10.1). *Individual-level criminogenic factors*

❖ Figure 10.1   Factors That Influence Copycat Crime

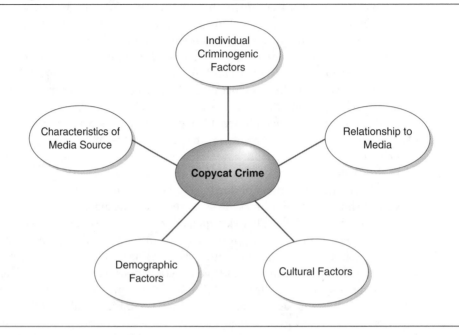

such as emotional development, personality and mental state, cognitive schema, social alienation, use/abuse of facilitators (drugs, alcohol, pornography), history of abuse or family dysfunction, and social/physical isolation increase or decrease the likelihood of mimetic violence and influence the extent to which an individual psychologically connects to a particular media source. A person's *relationship to media* such as trust in media as a source of information, level and extent of interaction with media, media literacy, artistic literacy, identification with perpetrators in media depiction, susceptibility to *mean world syndrome* influence the extent to which a particular media form will affect a person's cognitive scripts and, in turn, behavior. *Cultural factors* including the value placed on fame and notoriety, the relationship of crime and violence to the culture, extent to which others support or reject media as a legitimate source of information, social-cultural acceptance of particular media source, and moral panics can decrease or increase the importance of media for the individual. *Demographic factors* such as age, sex, socioeconomic status, race/ethnicity play a role in the type of media a person may use and the characters and images a person is likely to identify with. *Media-related factors* such as media (over- or under-) attention to certain crime stories, "language of violence" (Newman, 1998) that glorifies and legitimizes violence, presentation that blurs boundaries between fantasy and reality, media looping (showing and reframing an image in another context; see Manning, 1998), and a wide range of content factors related to the specific media source such as genre confusion, special effects, instant reincarnation/spawning, lack of consequences for violent acts, presentation of crime as fun, depiction of criminals as superhuman, and appeal of offender character all play a critical role in whether or not a particular media source is likely to influence a specific individual.

The copycat effect can be best understood along a continuum of influence. On one end of the continuum, media and pop cultural influences may play only a minor role in criminal behavior, for example, an offender who picks up an idea from a movie that makes its way into the modus operandi during the commission of a crime. On the other end of the continuum are individuals who may have a severe psychopathological disturbance and experienced a loss of boundary between fantasy and reality that becomes a major trigger for criminal behavior. At this extreme end of the continuum are isolated, personality disordered media junkies for whom pop cultural imagery plays a critical role in the formation of violent fantasy and resulting criminal behavior (Figure 10.2).

❖ Figure 10.2   Continuum of Influence of Media and Popular Culture
on Criminal Behavior

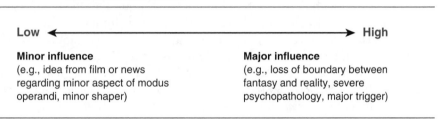

Cases in which an offender seeks to become both celebrated and a celebrity are examples of the extreme end of the continuum of media influence. John Hinckley and Mark David Chapman are often cited as classic examples of copycat criminals (e.g., Black, 1991; Surette, 1998). Black (1991) suggests that John Hinckley, who attempted to assassinate Ronald Reagan in 1981, and Mark Chapman, who murdered John Lennon in 1980, were both "frustrated middle-class youth engaged in a desperate quest for social identity and recognition" (p. 144) who operated "under the influence of mass media" (p. 138):

> In the world of the hyperreal, identity is contingent upon image, and individuals exist insofar as they are able to identify themselves with an image generated by the mass media. The individual who lacks a sense of identity may seize upon the image of a public figure that can serve him as a model. Such behavior is quite innocuous when the celebrity-model is already dead. . . . The problem arises when an anonymous individual tries to appropriate the image of a living celebrity as his own. The progress from celebrity qua model to celebrity qua double culminates in celebrity qua victim. This is to be expected in an age of mass-(re)production when uniqueness seems impossible to achieve: the anonymous individual tries to appropriate the celebrity's unique aura for himself. It takes a violent act of self-creation to transform the anonymous individual from a Nobody to a Somebody. (Black, 1991, p. 144)

In the 1980s, Hinckley and Chapman represented a relatively new phenomenon. Black argues that this 1980s form of violence was "historically unprecedented hyper-aestheticized violence" (p. 136) and that Chapman and Hinckley were "celebrity assassins" immersed in popular culture and the cultural values of fame and notoriety conveyed through media images. Chapman and Hinckley were consumed by the media, lacked identities, and needed to do something big to someone big in order to matter. Twenty-five years later, the rapidly growing list of copycat crimes and criminals of all types inspired by news stories, films, TV shows, music lyrics, computer games, Web sites, and so on suggests that *hyperaestheticized violence may be the crime wave of the future and that technological advances and cultural changes may increase the number of individuals on the extreme end of the copycat continuum.*

There has been a very limited amount of empirical research on copycat crime. Surette (2002) surveyed 68 incarcerated serious and violent male juvenile offenders and found that 26% indicated they had committed a crime they had seen or heard about in the media. The most common copycat practice is borrowing media crime techniques. Peterson-Manz (2002) compared homicides from 1990 to 1994 (9,442 cases) with news reports of murder and found that the numbers of homicides were significantly greater in the two weeks following front page news coverage of homicides. These studies are creative attempts at empirically examining copycat crime.

Important questions remain unanswered—*How does technology specifically alter or exacerbate the potential for mimetic crime? If, as evidence suggests, human beings have mimicked behaviors they've read about in books or heard about around campfires throughout history, what makes the 21st-century copycat offender different? Has the nature and extent of media imagery and technology exacerbated the copycat phenomenon to the point that a growing number of people are influenced by mass media? What is the difference between the* Catcher in the Rye *copycat (Mark Chapman) and the* Grand Theft Auto *copycat (Devin Moore)—is a computer game, film, or TV news story more instigatory or copycat-worthy than a book?* Given the difficulty of empirically investigating the phenomenon, theoretical analysis of actual cases provides a starting point for future research.

Characteristics of Copycat Offenders

Who are the people likely to commit copycat crime? What characteristics do copycat offenders possess? What do Sarah Edmondson and Ben Darras, Florence Rey and Audry Maupin, Veronique Herbert and Sebastien Paindavoine, Dylan Klebold and Eric Harris, Devin Moore, and John Hinckley have in common? Is it possible to predict who will and who will not become a copycat offender? Returning to the essential question—if external factors such as cultural emphasis on notoriety, the notion of crime as art, and media technologies that blur the boundaries between reality and fantasy play such a powerful role in creating copycat offenders, why is copycat crime such a rare phenomenon? Certainly there's more to it than this.

This question lies at the heart of the media violence debate and is the reason why legal challenges to violent media such as the lawsuit against Oliver Stone/*NBK* have not been successful against the First Amendment protections from free speech restrictions. If films like *Taxi Driver, Natural Born Killers,* and *The Matrix;* games like *Doom* and *Grand Theft Auto;* or music by *Marilyn Manson, Ice-T,* or *Slayer* interact with cultural forces to create copycat offenders, then there should be an epidemic of copycat crimes. The courts have consistently held that violent art is not the same thing as yelling "Fire!" in a crowded theater. Not everyone who has watched *NBK* or *The Matrix* has gone out and murdered someone. Regardless of the evidence suggesting media had a powerful influence on the behavior of known copycat offenders and the empirical evidence supporting a relationship between violent media and aggressive behavior, no causal relationship has been established between cultural or media factors and copycat crime. As with all types of criminal behavior, individual characteristics as well as situational and phenomenological factors interact with environmental and cultural influences to create a copycat offender. Research from cognitive psychology coupled with phenomenological perspectives (e.g., Ferrell, 1997; Katz, 1988) enable researchers to understand the meaning of behavior to a particular individual.

What is it about the offenders themselves that exacerbates the copycat effect? Answers to this question must be drawn from the more general research literature on criminal behavior pertaining to the specific type of offense. Oliver (2002) notes individual-level factors that influence the effects of media violence including individual affinities, readiness to respond, personality traits, disposition toward characters in media, selective attention, avoidance, perception, and memory and suggests that "unexplained variance can be appreciated as representing the opportunity for researchers to explore the importance of individual differences in the media effects process" (p. 520). As discussed in previous chapters, individual-level factors interact with media factors and environmental cultural influences to produce different types of criminal behavior. The question here is, *What are the particular individual-level factors that uniquely contribute to the copycat phenomenon?*

A synthesis of the research literature on the effects of violent media, the psychology of mimetic criminal behavior, and analysis of case studies of known copycat offenders reveals a number of factors that appear to play a role in copycat crime. These factors can be organized into three categories:

- Demographic Characteristics
  - Age
  - Sex

- Criminogenic Factors
  - Mental disorder (Axis I/conduct, bipolar, substance-related, psychotic, delusional, paraphilia)[7]
  - Personality disorder (*DSM* Axis II/Cluster B)
  - Developmental failure in attachment/human bonding/lack of identity
  - Cognitive schema of viewer/extremist beliefs
  - Social isolation and alienation
  - Aggressive traits/use of aggression as approach to conflict resolution

- Relationship to Media
  - Trust in media as a source of information
  - Media literacy

– Artistic literacy

– Identification with perpetrators featured in media source (with respect to gender, age, ethnicity, lifestyle, personal aesthetic, beliefs, habits, experiences, characteristics, etc.)

– Extent to which viewer uses media as a source of information

– Forms of media sources used and level of interaction with source

These individual-level factors interact with media characteristics and cultural-environmental factors such as:

- Media Characteristics
  – Imagery and storyline that blurs boundaries between fantasy and reality
  – Demographics of characters
  – Appeal an physical attractiveness of characters
  – Positive response to violence and crime (e.g., happy ending for criminals)
  – Media loops
  – Language of violence—how crime and violence is contextualized, weapons, validation, and tolerance for antisocial behavior

- Cultural-Environmental Factors
  – Cultural values placed on fame and notoriety
  – Cultural relationship to crime and violence
  – Extent to which others support or reject media as a legitimate source of information
  – Social-cultural acceptance of particular media source
  – Moral panics

Although age, sex, and criminogenic factors are associated with criminal behavior more generally (some more than others), it is the particular interaction between these factors and the individual's relationship to media that is critical in creating the propensity for copycat criminal behavior. Other individual and demographic factors such as race/ethnicity and socioeconomic status may play a role in which characters, themes, and media forms an individual is likely to identify with.

Research on the effects of violent media suggests that age and emotional development play a role in an individual's reaction to violent media content (Lloyd, 2002). The younger and less emotionally developed, the greater the likelihood of a relationship between violent media and aggressive behavior. This finding is supported by anecdotal evidence. The majority of known copycat offenders were under age 25 when they committed their offenses. Research on criminal behavior, particularly media-related crimes such as celebrity stalking (Meloy, 1998), suggests that failure in developmental bonding, formation of disordered identity, diagnosis with Axis I mental disorders and Axis II/Cluster B personality disorders, social isolation and alienation, disordered cognitive schema, and aggressive traits interact with media-related influences to produce copycat criminal behavior. Critical media factors include the degree to which an individual trusts and uses media as a source of information about the world, the extent to which the individual identifies with characters depicted in the media source (Gerbner, 1994; Katz in Jhally, 1999), artistic illiteracy (Black, 1991), media illiteracy (Gerbner, 1994), and the nature of the media content and presentation (Manning, 1998; Newman, 1998). The unique interaction between these demographic, criminogenic, and media-related factors determines the propensity for copycat criminal behavior.

Crime as Art

One issue that is rarely discussed in the criminological literature is the notion of crime as art. The view of crime as art, both in culture and in the minds of individual offenders, is a critical piece in understanding copycat crime. Black (1991) argues that "our custom-ary experience of murder and other forms of violence is primarily aesthetic" (p. 3)—we live today in a world of *aestheticized hyperreality.* This aestheticized hyperreality has an impact on all of us. Violent crime is a rare event that few people have to experience first-hand. What most of us know about violent crime comes from exposure to television, film, the Internet, books, magazines, visual art, and photographs. America and many other cul-tures have become so media-saturated that media-mediated violence has taken on a life of its own. Film, news media, the Internet, and popular culture are contemporary creators of myth. Instead of sitting around campfires listening to family lore from their grandparents, children of today (and those of the past two generations) learn about the world through the media. TV stars, rappers, pop divas, celebrity starlets, sports icons, and video game characters are the familiar faces whose words and actions dictate right and wrong. Most people's experience with violence is media-mediated, and offenders are no exception; the overattention to media portrayals of crime and violence (to the exclusion of the far from glamorous reality of crime) is critical in the production of copycat offenses.

This *media-mediated relationship to violence* is problematic on both cultural and individual levels. Media-mediated violence is related to the "unprecedented role played by the media in contemporary society as a mimetic mechanism" (Black, 1991, p. 144). When crime and violence are presented as entertainment on a wide scale, the potential to blur the boundary between fantasy and reality is high. This blurring of boundaries occurs on a cultural level whenever media and popular culture make their way into pol-icy and practice in the form of legislation, jury decision making, and law enforcement practice. Every day, people base decisions about violence in the home, school, and com-munity on what they see on TV, not on real life. Glamorization of crime and violence in media and popular culture sends the powerful message that crime matters, that crim-inals are worthy of attention, and that the more horrific and extreme the offense is, the more notoriety the offender gains. On an individual level, repeated exposure of certain types of individuals to certain types of media violence in a culture where violence and violent offenders have superstar status can be a particularly volatile mix.

The aesthetic-critical approach is necessary to make sense of copycat crime in which the media have played a major role. In the age of mass communication technology, for most people, *reality is media mediated.* Disciplines and perspectives through which crime and violence have been traditionally explored—law, philosophy, sociology, psy-chology, criminology—fall short in their ability to understand the offender's viewpoint because they are not morally neutral. Black suggests that the aesthetic-critical approach offers an alternative lens through which to understand murder and violent crime—one that offers a phenomenological description rather than a prescriptive assessment of the process underlying copycat or media-mediated crime (Black, 1991).

Celebrity Obsession

Mass media technology has altered the public relationship to celebrities. Celebrities seem familiar because of the amount of time we spend watching them in various forms of media. This voyeuristic relationship between the public and celebrities is culturally supported and reinforced. Obsessional following, stalking behavior, and surveillance activities are sanctioned in American popular culture through TV, films, music, comics, jokes, visual art, and advertisements (Marx, 1995).[8] How many times have you heard regular people sitting around discussing the latest drama in the lives of celebrities they've never met? The Brad Pitt–Jennifer Aniston–Angelina Jolie love triangle or the latest Jolie-Pitt adoption; Paris Hilton's LA County jail sentence; David Letterman's late-life baby, Britney Spears's shaved head, Tom Cruise's bizarre couch jumping extravaganza, Lindsay Lohan's bathroom cocaine scandal, and so on. The fact that popular magazines pay thousands of dollars for photos of celebrities going grocery shopping to paparazzi (sometimes referred to as "stalkerazzis")[9] willing to engage in risky behaviors, with sometimes fatal consequences, tells us something about our relationship to celebrity and the public interest in entertainment voyeurism. Cultural obsession with celebrity plays a powerful role in the dynamics of copycat crime.

Despite known cases of harm and death resulting from obsessed fans and paparazzi, little research attention has been given to the ways in which mass media technology creates new targets for criminal victimization. Media technology creates a false familiarity with strangers, and the more visible and accessible a person is, the more likely he or she is to be a target of crime. From a routine activities perspective, "Any activity that separates those who are prone to violence from each other, or from potential victims, is likely to decrease the incidence of violence" (Felson, 1996, p. 116). TV and other forms of media have the potential to reduce crime *if potential offenders stay at home watching, and away from potential victims,* and vice versa. However, media technology figuratively brings individuals we would otherwise not know into our worlds, and this overexposure to media celebrities and the pseudofamiliarity many people experience with them adds an entirely new dimension to the notion of routine activity. *Though media technology physically separates people, it also reduces virtual distance and increases virtual accessibility, thus creating a new type of victimization target.* Most victims are selected because they are familiar and accessible. The pseudofamiliarity with strangers created by celebrity culture creates the potential for an increased number of stranger-victims.

Individuals who suffer from attachment pathology take the usual familiarity with celebrities many steps further, developing elaborate fantasies about a particular celebrity—a "narcissistic link" between themselves and the object of their admiration that can turn into dangerous or deadly stalking behavior (Meloy, 1992, 1998). There are generally three types of stalking perpetrators: simple obsessionals, love obsessionals, and erotomaniacs. *Simple obsessionals* have some prior (usually intimate) relationship with the victim and are the most common; *love obsessionals* have no existing relationship with the victim and usually target celebrities; *erotomaniacs*, the rarest type, delusionally believe that the victim loves them (Zona, Palarea, & Lane, 1998). Stalking perpetrators are likely to have criminal, psychiatric, and drug abuse histories and show evidence of a range of *DSM* Axis I and Axis II (primarily Cluster B) disorders, though most are not psychotic at the time of their offense. (Early research assumptions suggested that the majority of stalkers suffered from delusional disorders, the erotomanic subtype in particular; however, recent research indicates that this is an unlikely primary diagnosis; Meloy, 1998).

The list of celebrity stalking victims is long, most notably the following:

- Actress *Theresa Saldana*, who was brutally stabbed multiple times by a fan in 1982. Saldana survived the attack and founded the Victims for Victims Organization. Her case led to the California Driver's Policy Protection Act because the perpetrator found her home address through driver's license records.

- Actress *Rebecca Schaeffer*, who starred in the 1980s sitcom *My Sister Sam*, who in 1989, at age 21, was shot dead at her own front door by obsessed fan Robert Bardo. Schaeffer's case indirectly led to stalking laws and specialized stalking units within law enforcement agencies (Harvey, 2002; Orion, 1997).

- Actress *Jodie Foster*, who has long been the subject of John Hinckley's fantasies and whose attention he sought when he attempted to assassinate President Ronald Reagan in 1981. Hinckley sent detailed letters to Foster while she attended Yale and indicated to authorities after the assassination attempt that his primary motivation was to win Foster's affection.

- Musician and former Beatle, *John Lennon*, who was murdered at his home in 1980 by Mark David Chapman, an obsessed identity disordered fan who, after reading Salinger's *Catcher in the Rye*, became angry with Lennon for becoming a "phoney" (Black, 1991).

Add to this list, Madonna, Brad Pitt, Jennifer Aniston, Steven Spielberg, Gianni Versace (Harvey, 2002), Whitney Houston, Sharon Gless, Janet Jackson, Suzanne Sommers, Paula Abdul, Justine Bateman, Cher, Olivia Newton-John, Vanna White, Kathie Lee Gifford (Orion, 1997), Avril Lavigne (Sullivan, 2004), and Sandra Bullock (Therolf, 2007), all of whom have been the victims of celebrity stalkers or, in some cases, multiple stalkers who formed obsessive media-mediated pseudo-relationships with them. David Letterman was the victim of two serious celebrity-related offenses, one involving a female stalker (Margaret Rey, aka the David Letterman stalker, was mentally ill, served time in a mental institution as a result of convictions for trespassing on Letterman's property, and committed suicide at age 46 in Colorado in 1998 by kneeling in front of a train), and the other involving the attempted kidnapping for ransom of his son ("Heartfelt Thanks from Letterman," 2005; Wolf, 2005). Sandra Bullock was also the victim of two stalkers, a man from Michigan in 2003, and in 2007, a woman who tried to run her husband, *Monster Garage* producer and motorcycle mogul Jesse James, over multiple times with her car in the couple's driveway. The woman was charged with assault with a deadly weapon.

The role of celebrities in the age of mass technology is an important consideration in exploring the dynamics of copycat crime. David Harvey, television producer, radio broadcaster, and author of the book *Obsession: Celebrities and Their Stalkers*, observes that modern society promotes, and has adopted, a world of celebrity culture. In this world, people such as pop stars, sports stars, television and film stars and even football managers, achieve status and become "New Gods" to be followed and worshiped by each generation. For those with obsessive characteristics, ranging from simply obsessed persons to persons suffering advanced paranoid disorders, these "New Gods" continue to supply new targets for harassment, stalking, and even death. (Harvey, 2002, p. xiv)

Celebrities, and to a lesser extent anyone (famous or not) who makes it onto the TV news, Internet, or other media form, have an increased exposure that brings with it an increased likelihood of being victims of celebrity stalking or a range of other offenses potential offenders are drawn to.

The celebrity obsession phenomenon helps us better understand copycat crime in two ways. First, media play a central role in crime involving celebrities and copycat crime. Both find inspiration in a media source and are driven by and dependent on the cultural power of fame and notoriety. Second, technology gives potential copycats wide access to information that validates and can be used to mimic the behavior of notorious offenders and well-publicized cases, particularly those involving celebrities. For example, tribute Web pages devoted to celebrity stalkers such as Mark David Chapman and Andrew Cunanan that detail their methods and beliefs are available for anyone who may be an aspiring celebrity stalker (Harvey, 2002). Copycats of celebrity stalking incidents are perhaps the crimes that most clearly and blatantly reveal the role of media and the quest for notoriety. Harvey (2002) describes the case of Sarah Lockett, a news reporter for Meridian Television in England who was stalked by Jeremy Dyer, a fan who sent her over 80 letters from 1998 to 1999 and was sentenced to prison for 2 years for harassment. The letters included numerous references to the well-publicized celebrity murder of BBC news reporter Jill Dando. Dando was shot in the head at close range at her doorstep in 1999 by Barry George, a media-obsessed celebrity stalker who had a history of obsession with a number of celebrities (including Princess Diana and Freddie Mercury, lead singer from the band Queen). Dyer's letters to Lockett specifically referenced the Dando murder with threatening passages such as the following:

> You looked a bit miserable on the Monday show. I suppose you would be considering Jill Dando just got her brains blown out by a probable stalker. (Harvey, 2002, p. 149)

> If I had murdered Jill Dando I'd have kidnapped her or done something else to her rather than shooting her in the head . . . It seems a waste of a victim to me. He could have used her before killing her eg, by raping or assaulting her, getting his money's worth as it were . . . . (Harvey, 2002, p. 151)

Dyer used the Dando murder to threaten his victim and to validate and reinforce his own stalking behaviors. Visibility made both Dando and Lockett targets of celebrity stalkers whose fantasies and behaviors were influenced by the cultural emphasis on fame and celebrity voyeurism and facilitated by media technology. The cultural forces that make it appealing to become a notorious celebrity killer are crucial to understanding copycat crime.

NBK *Copycats: A Case Study in Media-Related Factors That Enhance the Copycat Effect*

The string of copycats inspired by the 1994 film *Natural Born Killers* (dubbed in the media as the "*NBK* copycats") are worth exploring in some depth to examine media-related factors that enhance the copycat effect. *Natural Born Killers* has inspired the largest number of lethal copycat crimes of any other cultural artifacts. *Natural Born Killers*, loosely based on the real-life 1958 Charles Starkweather and Caril Ann Fugate murder spree, is a story of Mickey and Mallory Knox, a young, attractive, visually eclectic couple who embark on a fast-paced, fun-loving, road-trip-serial-mass murder spree across the Southwest that results in over 50 murders. The film is shot in multiple film formats, with heavy metal music and a range of visual genres including animation, sitcom, and newslike sequences including a depiction of childhood sexual abuse to the theme of "I Love Lucy," acts of female aggression to the tune of female metal band L7, psychedelic mushroom trips, and "psychological landscapes" (Kiselyak, 1996). The characters' backgrounds are presented through old TV clips, superhero/villain animation, old news footage, and background music by the industrial metal band Nine Inch Nails. The film ends with a brutal prison riot scene (with images strikingly similar to horrific real-life images of the 1980 New Mexico Prison riot) shot in the famous (and very real) Illinois Stateville Prison in which (in the Director's cut edition) the prison warden (played by Tommy Lee Jones) is attacked by rioting inmates who thrust his severed head in the air on a broom stick. The couple escapes from prison, taking hostage TV reporter Wayne Gayle (played by Robert Downey Jr.), and then in the final scene execute Gayle while he begs for his life. The postcredit images show Mickey and a pregnant Mallory riding off into the sunset in a motor home with a bunch of kids.

What was it about Natural Born Killers *that inspired so many copycat murders?* Was it the psychedelic psychological background landscapes? The use of multiple types of film formats? Genre confusion? Gratuitous violence? The presentation of serial murder as fun? The love story? The justification for violence in the childhood histories of the main characters? The use of violence as a form of feminist empowerment? (At numerous points throughout the film, Mallory Knox [played by Juliet Lewis] lashes out at men who sexualize and mock her by shooting them dead while hollering phrases such as, "How sexy am I now flirty boy?") The happily-ever-after ending? Excessive media looping? Retrospective speculation of the many aspects of the film that make it distinct is of little help in establishing and empirical link between media characteristics and the copycat effect, yet examination of films like *NBK* and others (e.g., *The Matrix*) that have resulted in a disproportionate number of copycats is a first step in developing hypotheses and a theoretical framework for future research.

The film *Natural Born Killers* and the *NBK* copycats illustrate the power of technology and popular culture to exacerbate the copycat phenomenon. A number of factors are likely to have played a role in the film's mimetic potential—all minimizing the distinction between fantasy and reality for viewers. First, the film was full of media loops. A media loop involves showing and reframing an image in another context—such as an instant replay, a clip of a real-life event within a fictional film, or footage from an original news story replayed within the context of another form of entertainment or news program (e.g., *20/20* or *60 Minutes*; Manning, 1998). *NBK* includes a barrage of images of past criminal events including the Charles Whitman killing spree at the University of Texas in 1966, the Rodney King beating, the Menendez brothers, Richard Ramirez, O.J. Simpson's trial, the Manson murders, and so on. Furthermore, the film contained a complex sort of media loop that might best be called a *copycat loop* (the term is not used in Manning's article but coined here). A copycat loop can be thought of as a type of media loop that involves showing and reframing an image of a copycat crime in another context—such as reference to a real-life copycat crime in a television show, film, or computer game. An example of a copycat loop is the scene in *Natural Born Killers* where Mickey Knox (played by Woody Harrelson) asks reporter Wayne Gayle if coverage of his murderous rampage would get higher ratings than Ted Bundy or Charles Manson, suggesting that he admired and may have been emulating these murderers in his own crimes. Another example is the detective, Jack Scagnetti (played by Tom Sizemore), who claims that his mother was a victim of the (real-life) Charles Whitman mass murder and depicted as sexually aroused by Mallory, eventually mimicking the couple's behavior by murdering a prostitute in his hotel room. In fact, and most important, the entire film itself is a copycat loop. *NBK* was one in a string of many film depictions of the 1958 Charles Starkweather and Caril Ann Fugate murder spree.[10] Copycat loops, even more than other types of media loops, distort and blur the boundary between reality and fantasy while glorifying mimetic violence. This is double trouble, so to speak, because the media loops themselves confuse the audience while the glamorization and normalization of copycat crime provides a convenient and appealing cognitive distortion for media junkies who already have difficulty locating the line between fantasy and reality. For people who are not necessarily media junkies, copycat looping creates cognitive confusion that may have the potential to make crime and murder look appealing to individuals who do not have violent inclinations or risk factors, particularly young people at various levels of rebellion.

Second, the most appealing characters in *Natural Born Killers* are Mickey and Mallory Knox, who are hip, physically attractive, and make murder look like fun. Films and media images that ask the audience to identify with violent characters by making them likable while glamorizing and making excuses for the violence they engage in increase the potential for copycat violence. For example, one of the most grotesquely violent films in history is the 1986 film, *Henry: Portrait of a Serial Killer,* based on the story of serial killers Henry Lee Lucas and Otis Toole. To date, no known copycat crimes have been inspired by this film. In contrast to *NBK*, the murderous characters in *Henry* are depicted as despicable, unlikeable, and physically unattractive. Furthermore, the violent aftermath of the murders is shown in close-up fashion in a manner that is uncomfortable for viewers because it forces the audience to sit and look at death scenes that include a raped, bound, and mutilated woman with a bottle broken into her face and a home invasion murder (depicted as if it could happen to anyone) in which a husband, wife, and son are tortured and viciously killed while the killers laugh and videotape the event. Unlike *NBK*, the murders in *Henry* are not depicted as fun or funny, and the characters are extremely unappealing and difficult to identify with (for anyone, including viewers who may be just as despicable themselves).

Third, *NBK* depicts female violence in a manner that is contradictory and confusing, empowering and infantilizing. Mallory Knox is portrayed as a victim of sexual assault and incest who is rescued by bad boy Mickey, who murders her parents (with her help), and is taken off into the sunset. Mallory Knox evolves into a killer with fragmented emotions who, if sexually harassed or devalued, responds with violence. What is so contradictory about her character is that she is physically small, emotionally vulnerable with Mickey, and simultaneously portrayed as a victim and predator. In theaters during the opening night of the film, audiences raved and cheered as Mallory broke necks and shot dead men who humiliated or sexualized her. Like her character, her violence both horrified and empowered audiences, and became the inspiration for a string of unprecedented violent female copycats (Box 10.2).

BOX 10.2

NBK COPYCATS

NBK's Mickey and Mallory Knox.

Photo credit: © Corbis.

The 1994 film *Natural Born Killers* by Oliver Stone has been linked to over a dozen copycat crimes. To date, no other film has been linked to so many real-life criminal cases.

The film depicts two young lovers, Mickey and Mallory Knox, who, after murdering Mallory's abusive parents, set out on a murder spree killing over 50 people. Oliver Stone says (in the Director's Cut) that the star of the film is "chaos" and that, though the film is graphically violent, its main point and his main objective in making it, was to hold a mirror up to American culture to reflect the cultural fascination and media glorification of serial and mass murderers. The film is shot in 18 different formats, including animation, 16 mm and 35 mm cameras, back projection, and High 8 with approximately 3,000 rapid-fire cuts. The backdrop of the film is what the film's animator refers to as a "psychological landscape" depicting Mickey and Mallory's flashbacks to childhood at various points of the film.

(Continued)

(Continued)

In addition, the film interjects media footage of real-life events such as the Charles Whitman mass murder, the Rodney King beating, and the O.J. Simpson, Lorena Bobbitt, and Menendez trials, moving back and forth from the fictional characters' storyline to real-life violent media events. According to one commentator, "Even to a generation raised on MTV and Sega games, this is the cinematic equivalent of staring into a strobe light for two hours" (Patten, 1997, p. 3).

In November 1994, 19-year-old Florence Rey and 22-year-old Audry Maupin killed five people during a car chase in Paris that also left Maupin dead. Rey described the shootings as "fate" (a line from the film) and the pair was dubbed "France's Natural Born Killers." Rey was sentenced to 20 years in prison, though there was no evidence that she'd ever watched the film, nor that she had fired any of the lethal bullets.

Soon after the Rey case came to trial, another couple—18-year-old Veronique Herbert and Sebastien Paindavoine—were also tried in Paris for the murder of 16-year-old Abdeladim Gahbiche. Herbert was said to be obsessed with *Natural Born Killers*. In trial it was uncovered that she had lured her victim to his death with the promise of sex just like the scene in the film where Mallory Knox murdered a gas station attendant. Herbert was accused of being the ringleader in the case and received a 15-year sentence while Paindavoine received a 12-year sentence.

In March 1995, teenagers Benjamin Darras and Sarah Edmonson went on a robbery/murder spree after watching *Natural Born Killers* multiple times over a period of days while consuming hallucinogenic drugs. By the end of their spree, they had killed Bill Savage and seriously wounded Patsy Byers, whose injuries resulted in her becoming a paraplegic. They were caught soon after and convicted and sentenced to 35 years each for the Beyers shooting. Darras was also sentenced to life for Savage's murder. Edmondson was the daughter of an Oklahoma district court judge and granddaughter of a former U.S. congressman who had a history of drug abuse and psychiatric problems. Darras was the son of divorced parents. His father was an alcoholic father who committed suicide. Darras had a history of psychiatric treatment and drug abuse.

In 1996 Patsy Beyers filed a lawsuit against Oliver Stone, Warner Brothers, Ben Darras and Sarah Edmondson and their families and insurance carriers. Patsy Beyers and her family claimed that Stone, the film's producers, and the movie theaters that showed the film were all liable for producing a film that glorified violence and for distributing a film that they knew or would have known would incite some individuals to commit a crime such as shooting Patsy Beyers. The case was heard by a Louisiana trial judge who concluded that the law does not recognize such a cause of action. The family appealed, and by the time the case landed in the Louisiana Court of Appeals, more than a dozen copycat shootings had been linked to *Natural Born Killers*. A source for the plaintiff's counsel was author John Grisham, who had been a friend of Edmondson and Darrus's first victim, Bill Savage. Grisham wrote a scathing article attacking Stone and accusing him of intentionally producing a film that would cause copycat violence. The court of appeals ruled that the case had to go to trial because the plaintiff alleged that Stone had intentionally created a film that would cause impressionable viewers to mimic the violence depicted in the film. The Louisiana court was influenced by a previous case in which a professional hit man was recruited to murder his paraplegic son and ex-wife so he would obtain the insurance money. After the offender's trial and conviction, it was discovered that he had ordered and purchased a copy of the book *A Technical Manual for Independent Contractors*, which offered graphic instructions on how to murder someone. This case was thrown out on First Amendment grounds and because the book had been in print for over 10 years before the offender ordered it and the crime occurred 13 months after the offender had received the book in the mail. However, on appeal, the verdict was reversed, the court determining that the publisher had acknowledged a degree of intent in a preliminary court proceeding, conceding that the book had been written for the purpose of aiding and abetting murder. This and other cases were brought into the legal wrangling in the *NBK* court case. The case made it all the way to the U.S. Supreme Court in 1999. The U.S. Supreme Court remanded it back to the Louisiana Court of Appeals. In 2001, the Louisiana Court dismissed the case, finding that there was no evidence to indicate that Stone had intended for the film to incite violence.

While the Darras and Edmondson case is the best known of the *NBK* copycats in the United States and the Rey/Maupin and Herbert/Paindavoine cases the most notorious in Europe, a number of other cases have also been linked to the film:

- In 1994 a 14-year-old boy was accused of decapitating a 13-year-old girl. The boy told police he wanted to be famous "like the natural born killers."

- Twenty-one-year-old William Sodders of Rock Point, New York, was turned in by his father for killing a local firefighter. His father told police that the son was obsessed with *Natural Born Killers* and that he shot the firefighter with a stolen 9 mm for the thrill.

- In Salt Lake City, Nathan Martinez wore tinted round sunglasses and shaved his head like Micky Knox and then shot his stepmother and 10-year-old sister. When arrested, he told police how much he loved *Natural Born Killers*.

- In 1995, four individuals in their 20s were accused of killing a truck driver in Georgia after seeing *Natural Born Killers* 19 times.

- One of the codefendants in a Massachusetts murder case in 1995 bragged to his girlfriend that he and his accomplice are "natural born killers."

- School shooters including Michael Carneal in Paducah, Kentucky, Barry Loukaitis in Moses Lake, Washington, and Columbine perpetrators Klebold and Harris had all seen and made reference to *Natural Born Killers*. According to the prosecutor in the Loukaitis case, Loukaitis, a 15-year-old who killed a teacher and two classmates with a high-powered rifle in a junior high school algebra class in 1996, got ideas to plan and carry out the murders from Stephen King's book *Rage* (written under a pseudonym) and the film *Natural Born Killers*.

So, what is it about this film that inspired so many copycats? Was Grisham correct in his accusation that Stone intentionally created the film to incite violence? The central issue in the Beyers's lawsuit was a statement made by Oliver Stone about the film at its premier. He said, "The most pacifist people in the world said they came out of this movie and wanted to kill somebody" (O'Neil, 2001, p. 157). Clearly, there was something about this film that set it apart from others in terms of its potential for copycat violence. Identifying what made this film so influential in the minds of these copycat offenders, and whether or not a causal role can be attributed to the film, is an empirical question of great importance for future research.

Boyle (2001) argues that the way in which Mallory Knox is depicted in *NBK* is consistent with the way female violent offenders are presented in real life. When a man commits a violent act, in fantasy or reality, he is much more likely to be presented as a violent "natural born killer" than a female counterpart. According to Boyle (p. 315), "Mickey fills a recognizable (male) space in Western culture," wheras Mallory must be explained and understood. Interestingly, Oliver Stone says he chose Woody Harrelson for the part of Mickey Knox because Harrelson's real-life father is in prison for murder. Stone suggests in the Director's cut interview that Harrelson himself knows violence because it is in his blood. The masculinization of violence in the film serves to make male violence normal and invisible. The *NBK* copycats were unique in that, though violent copycat crimes have been perpetrated by boys and men, *NBK* inspired a string of female offenders to commit murder. However, as Boyle suggests, in the film and real life, even though the female perpetrators were just as instrumentally aggressive and violent as their male counterparts, they were depicted as expressively motivated and their crimes were explained away in ways that the male offenders' crimes were not.

Oliver Stone has said that his purpose of making the film was to hold up a mirror to American society—to get people to stop and think about the absurdity that's gone on in society around the glorification and glamorization of murder and murderers. In the film, Mickey and Mallory have followers—fans who hold up signs with statements such as "Murder me Mickey," and interviews with adoring fans who say things like, "If I were a murderer, I'd want to be Mickey and Mallory." According to Stone, *Natural Born Killers* is about cultural chaos in American society and the human extremes that produce it. Stone suggests that American culture is in a culturally bankrupt "age of absurdity," and "Many people think that Mickey and Mallory could happen tomorrow" (Kiselyak, 1996). The film is also about the fine lines between fact and fiction and between the criminal and crime voyeur. Woody Harrelson says about his experience playing the role of Mickey,

> I don't know where the make believe leaves off and the reality begins sometimes. . . . I think most people can make that claim, that they've been angry enough in their lives they would have killed somebody. So, where's the line? Where's the line between you and Mickey or you and Mallory—I mean where is it? It's a very thin line I think. (Kiselyak, 1996)

Harrelson's words echo those of his character who, in a televised interview from the state penitentiary, responds to a question asking him how he could shoot an innocent person to death:

> Innocent? Who's innocent? . . . It's just murder man. All God's creatures do it in some form or another. I mean, you look in the forest, got species killing other species and our species killing *all* species, including the forest, and we just call it industry, not murder. (Kiselyak, 1996)

This blurring of boundaries between fantasy and reality throughout the film is a critical factor to consider with respect to the number of real-life offenses the film is said to have inspired.[11]

The film *Natural Born Killers* might be thought of as what Reiber and Green (1989) call a *social dream*—a distinctive cultural product that so closely captures an aspect of the impulses and conflicts of society that its content, though quite fantastic, passes without reflection or comment by the general public. The social dream (like an ordinary dream) stirs little reaction because it reflects an everyday phenomenon. The graphic violence of *Natural Born Killers did* evoke reaction and comment by the general public, film critics, and politicians, but its central theme *did not* evoke a reaction (though several weeks following its release, Republican Senator and 1996 presidential candidate Bob Dole implied in a nationally broadcast speech about the impact of Hollywood violence on the American family that it and another film, *True Romance,* should be banned; the film was banned in Ireland, its release was delayed in Britain, and it was a box-office smash in America). Perhaps this is largely what made *Natural Born Killers* so appealing to would-be copycat criminals. On its surface, the film was a glorious display of unabashed violence. Less overtly, it was a virtual reflection of the bizarre cultural glorification of both celebrity and infamy—a message that directly appeals to and validates the psyches of known copycat offenders who, like many of the film's critics, were not inclined or able to process the deeper substantive message Stone intended to convey.

Cybercrime

Cybercrime involves activities in which computers and other technological devices are used for illicit purposes.[12] There are four major elements of cybercrime—location, victim, offender, and action taken to eliminate threat (Speer, 2000):

1. *Location* of the offender in relation to the crime: The offender is generally not present at crime scene. This distinguishes cybercrime from other types of offenses and defies Locard's exchange principle (the hallmark of crime scene investigation) that, in every crime scene, the offender leaves something behind and takes something away. In addition to the difficulty in locating a cybercrime offender, it is often difficult to determine the law enforcement jurisdiction charged with responding to the offense.

2. *Victim:* Primary victim is usually a government, corporation, or organization. Individuals are also victims, but fewer resources and less focus are given to individual victims because of their limited influence and power. Victim concerns regarding invasion of privacy have hindered cybercrime legislation. Potential targets have internal security enforcement measures in place and often use vigilante tactics (counteroffensive computer programs) to combat hackers.

3. *Offender:* Cyberoffenders are a heterogeneous group including teenagers experimenting for fun, adults attempting to steal sensitive information, individuals and groups engaged in software pirating and illegal transfer who are not aware they are committing cybercrime. Furthermore, cybercriminals possess the same skills and abilities as corporate and governmental professionals, making it difficult to identify or monitor individuals with the propensity to commit cybercrime.

4. *The action taken* to eliminate the threat (Speer, 2000): Summits held in the United States and Europe have identified steps needed to combat the threat of cybercrime

including modifying domestic regulations and developing international cooperation and standards, new legislation, and a classification system for cybercrime.

Cybercrime is distinct in that the offender is not present at the crime scene, the primary victim is most often an institution, offender characteristics and motive are heterogeneous, and control involves global, technologically sophisticated, and political and indirect strategies. Cybercrime is harder to detect than traditional crime, and as a result most cybercriminals are never caught. Furthermore, cybercrime more than any other crime category moves faster than legislation and law enforcement budgets can keep up with, thus presenting enormous challenges for law enforcement, institutions, and governments charged with responding to the threat such crimes represent.

Like copycat crime, cybercrime cuts across other crime categories, and may be considered a subtype of criminal behavior characterized by the process by which the crime is carried out. Some types of crimes referred to as cybercrime can be best understood within the context of a more traditional crime category based on the nature of the offense. For example, a kidnapping/murder in which the offender uses the Internet to communicate with the victim's family to extort ransom is first and foremost a violent crime, a sexual predator using the Internet to lure a victim is first and foremost a sex crime, and a phishing scam in which an offender fraudulently obtains personal information through a phony Web site to steal the individuals' funds is first and foremost an economic crime. All of these offenses involve technology, however, and it is important to also consider the elements of the offenses that could be (sub)categorized and understood as cybercrime. The following examples reflect the range of offenses that can be considered cybercrimes:

- In one of the best-known cases of cybercrime, two Cisco Systems accountants broke into parts of the company's computer system and issued themselves nearly $8 million in company stock (Tedeschi, 2003).

- In 1998 five people from Manhattan and the Bronx, New York, were arrested for an innovative theft of telephone calling card numbers. The offenders used an electronic device called a "dial number recorder" to obtain calling card numbers that unknowing victims had entered into airport public phones. The offenders would call airport pay phones, wait for people to answer, and the device would record the tones associated with the calling card numbers that the victims had punched in and translate them back into numbers. Offenders then used the numbers to make a profit on the black market (Blair, 1998).

- For two decades Nigerian fraudsters have been sending out polite letters, and more recently e-mails, inviting potential victims to participate in bogus real estate deals and shady financial schemes for a cut of the money in return for "advance fees." The offenders are estimated to make hundreds of millions of dollars annually with Americans losing millions each year (Catan & Peel, 2003) with an annual median loss per victim of $5,000 (National White Collar Crime Center, 2005).

- During the holiday shopping season in 2005, police arrested 23 people from New Jersey on charges of scamming Internet auction site shoppers and theft by deception. The offenders advertised merchandise including baseball cards, designer handbags, Rolex watches, Xbox video game systems, laptop computers, and BMW automobiles for sale on Internet auction sites and collected payment from winning bidders without sending the merchandise ("Cops Arrest 23 in Online Shopping Scams," 2005).

- In 2004, the chief executive officer of an online payment processing company called Protx received an e-mail signed by "John Martino" threatening to attack the company's servers for one month if the company did not pay $10,000. The executive ignored the e-mails and two months later the company's system was knocked off-line by thousands of "zombies" (computers hijacked by hackers to flood and knock down a system with e-mails), disabling the company for days. During the attack, "Martino" e-mailed again asking for $10,000, and then several months later asking for $10,000 per month as a "protection plan." As the last e-mail extortion came through, the hacker crashed the company's system again with 70,000 zombies (Ratliff, 2005).

- Two men and a woman from California and Arizona were indicted for conspiring to engage in the business of sending spam e-mails for their own personal gain. The defendants embedded pornographic Internet advertisements in the e-mails to earn commission for directing Internet traffic to the porn Web sites. The three sent e-mails to tens of millions of America Online customers during a 6-month period in 2004 and were reported by Spamhaus, an international nonprofit organization that collects data on spammers worldwide, to be one of the 200 largest spamming operations in the world ("Three Defendants Indicted, Fourth Pleads Guilty in Takedown of Major International Spam Operation," 2005).

- A 35-year-old graphic designer from Chattanooga, Tennessee, arranged online to have sex with two children, ages 4 and 6, then drove to Marietta, Georgia, to meet them with whips, knives, and two stuffed animals. He was arrested by undercover FBI agents who posed online as the children (Ahmed, 2005).

This diverse list ranges from low-level predatory crimes to sophisticated economic offenses using computer technology in very different ways. Regardless of the motivation for the offense and primary type of crime (e.g., economic, violent, sex, public order, political), these offenses involve the use of computer technology to carry out the offense.

What essential features distinguish cybercrime from other types of offenses? Though some argue that the use of computer technology as a modus operandi does not sufficiently characterize the offense to help understand or explain its motivation, the role of technology in all of the preceding offenses distinguishes these crimes from those that involve more traditional methods. In addition to changing the method with which crime is committed, technology has shaped the environments within which crime operates. What distinguishes cybercrime above and beyond other features is the *intangible environment* within which such offenses are committed, creating unlimited opportunities for offenders. Offenders can commit multinational crime with little fear in a virtual environment without jurisdictional demarcations (Britz, 2004):

For the first time, criminals can cross international boundaries without the use of passports or official documentation. Whereas traditional criminal activity required the physical presence of perpetrators, cybercrime is facilitated by international connections that enable individuals to commit criminal activity in England while sitting in their offices in Alabama. In addition, electronic crime does not require vehicular transportation, physical storage capability, or labor-intensive practices, all of which increase the potential for discovery and enforcement. (Britz, 2004, p. 5)

Computer technology as modus operandi and the intangibility of the environment are essential features of cybercrime.

Categorizing Cybercrime

Cybercrimes can be categorized into two general categories of offenses (Britz, 2004, identifies three offense categories—computer as target, computer as means, and computer as incidental—but for the sake of brevity, these categories are combined here into two general types):

1. *Computer as target:* theft of computer hardware and software copyright infringement

2. *Computer as instrument or incidental:* computer used as means to commit crime or for storage for crime-related activities that involve technology only to the extent that information is digitalized and contained within a computer

Cybercrimes range from nuisance offenses such as spreading viruses and spamming to predatory offenses such as Internet child luring to economic offenses such as wire transfers and fraud. These offenses share the essential features of use of *computer technology as modus operandi* and *intangibility.* In some cases the categories overlap. For example, hacking (unauthorized intrusion into a computer system) used a computer to target another computer. An example of the use of a computer as target, instrument, and incidental would be the use of a computer to access information (incidental) that is then used through another computer (instrumental) to breach a computer security system (target).

Computer as Target

There are three general ways in which computers themselves can be targets of crime. First, computer systems can be targeted through *hacking* activities, which involve attacking a system to steal or destroy information. Second, computers and their components are extremely vulnerable to theft. Laptops, computer chips, portable hard drives, and other computer components are small, movable, and valuable, making them a prime target for *hardware theft.* Third, *software piracy* is one of the most prevalent forms of cybercrime.

The best-known type of crime involving computers as targets is *hacking.* Hacking involves breaking into a computer system. The word *hacker* (originally a Yiddish term referring to an inept furniture maker) has taken on a range of meaning from the person who benignly enjoys learning about the ins and outs of computer systems to one who maliciously, deceptively, and illegally uses this ability to acquire information (Schell & Dodge, 2002). Hackers operate in virtually every country at a high economic cost to the global marketplace. Some reports indicate that computer hackers cost businesses 6 cents per every dollar of revenue—billions of dollars with the figure climbing steadily as the number of offenders engaged in hacking activities soars with thousands of new computer viruses created every year (DeLong, 2001). *Phreaking* is an early precursor to hacking that involves telecommunications fraud through the illegal manipulation of PBXs, access codes, access tones, or switches (and many hackers started their careers as phreakers). Hackers use similar though more sophisticated methods to attack computer systems for the information they contain, for retribution/retaliation, or in some cases for no reason other than curiosity or challenge.

Computer hackers vary in their motivation. Kovacich and Boni (2000) categorize hackers into three types—the "curious" who break into computers to learn more about them; the "meddlers," juvenile delinquents who break into systems for the challenge and peer acceptance; and the "criminals" who break into systems to steal, damage, or destroy information (Kovacich & Boni, 2000). Britz (2004) classifies hacker motivation into six categories—boredom, intellectual challenge, revenge, sexual gratification, economic, and political—and suggests that boredom and intellectual challenge are the most common motivators and revenge by insiders is one of the most overlooked cyberthreat. Some security experts suggest that up to 80% of hacking incidents are committed by the meddlers or *scriptkiddies,* another term used for less sophisticated "teenage kids out to be challenged and to be recognized for their exploits by their peers" (Schell & Dodge, 2002, p. 5). Thus, whereas the act of hacking (breaking into computer systems) is the same regardless of the offender motivation, the types of offenders who engage in the behavior and their reasons for doing it can differ considerably, with direct implications for investigations and understanding of offense behavior.

Many computer hackers do not use the term *hacker* in a pejorative sense and divide hackers into two subtypes: *White Hats* (good hackers) and *Black Hats* (bad hackers). Some use the term *cracker* to refer generally to criminal hackers or to a specific type of Black Hat. From this perspective, the act of breaking into a computer system is not inherently criminal. In fact, some suggest that hackers should be seen as enthusiastic, passionate, creative, and artistic programmers rather than dangerous criminals. White Hats generally are seen as individuals motivated by creativity, self-exploration, and the desire to push the envelope for the betterment of society. White Hats operate from an ethical perspective or "hacker paradigm," believing that any and all information that teaches individuals about the way the world works should be free. Black Hats are motivated by revenge or greed and come in many forms. Schell and Dodge (2002) subdivide Black Hats into the following categories:

- *Crackers:* Individuals who break into computer systems without authorization, flooding Internet sites and resulting in denial of service to legitimate users, making a copy-protected program run by digging into the code, deliberately defacing Web sites for fraudulent purposes.

- *Phreakers:* Individuals who exploit telecommunications companies by fooling company switches to connect for free using methods ranging from unsophisticated replication of dial tones to sophisticated reprogramming of telephone company switches.

- *Destructive hacktivists:* Individuals who target Internet sites for political purposes to disrupt but not destroy normal operations. Destructive hacktivist activity ranges from nuisance activities such as Web sit-ins, virtual blockades, automated e-mail bombs, and URL redirection to computer break-ins, computer viruses and worms, and Web defacement.

- *Cyberterrorists:* Individuals or groups who engage in unlawful attacks or threats of attack against computer networks and the information contained within them to intimidate or coerce a government or its people to further a political objective. Cyberterrorist activity is distinct from destructive hacktivism in that it involves violence or psychological harm through the threat of violent attack against persons or property if specific demands are not met.

- *Cyberstalkers:* Individuals who gain online access to information about a target for the purpose of intimidation or physical harm. Information such as financial information, personal letters, or blog journal entries is used for the purpose of eventually harming the person. Cyberstalking can result in assault, kidnapping, or murder.

Hacking presents special legal and law enforcement challenges. On one hand, "The hacker notion that all knowledge should be shared is liberating" (Schell & Dodge, 2002, p. 296), and governmental, law enforcement agencies, and the rest of us can benefit from the knowledge and expertise of White Hats. On the other hand, information is a powerful weapon in the hands of Black Hats, who are motivated by anger, desire for power, or greed. Computer hacking is an expertise that, like many talents, can be used to achieve both criminal and noncriminal goals.

In terms of MO, most hackers prey on systematic vulnerabilities or careless uninformed employees who leak or fail to adequately protect passwords to steal information. A common method of computer intrusion is *confidence scams* in which the offender poses as a representative from the vendor's security system or IT department to persuade unknowing employees to reveal privileged information. Another common method is simply uncovering personal passwords by *gathering personal information from employees* who often create passwords using the name of their pets, birthdates, and other personal data. Hackers are aided in this endeavor because most companies do not invest a large amount of resources in security training and employees are a company's biggest liability in terms of security threat. More sophisticated approaches to gaining secure information include using lists of default passwords (and banking on system administrator negligence—not changing passwords) and targeting backdoors created when vendors allow remote access to maintain and update their systems (Britz, 2004).

Computer as Instrument or Incidental

In addition to being targets of crime, computers are used as a *means* to commit traditional forms of crime such as theft, fraud, terrorism, phony stock trading, stalking, and sex offenses. In these cases, the computer is simply a hi-tech tool to commit a traditional type of crime. Criminal offenses in all categories can be committed through the use of the computer.

Violent crime. One of the most prevalent forms of computer-facilitated violent crime is cyberstalking (discussed in the previous section). Cyberstalking can involve a computer as target (when information within a computer is illegally obtained) or as a tool with which to taunt, threaten, and intimidate victims over the Internet. The computer can also be used to intimidate victims and witnesses. E-mail threats and Web postings that harass or intimidate are examples of this type of offense. Some also argue that prisoners may use personal Web sites to further harm and intimidate victims even from behind bars (in some cases on death row). Prisoner Web sites have also been used to meet people outside of prison who then become involved in illegal activities on behalf of the prisoner. In one case, a woman who met her death row husband on the Internet attempted to break him out of prison. Both she and the inmate were shot to death during the attempted escape (Box 10.3).

Sex crime. Computers are used to facilitate Internet sex trafficking, child luring, and child pornography trafficking. Media and law enforcement attention has been directed toward these offenses in recent years, particularly against pedophiles who seek, groom, and lure young victims over the Internet. The popularity of Web space and use of the Internet as a social venue for teens has made Web communities such as MySpace.com hunting grounds for predatory pedophiles looking to lure young victims (Auchard & Li, 2006). An even more widespread offense is the circulation of child

BOX 10.3

PRISONER WEB SITES

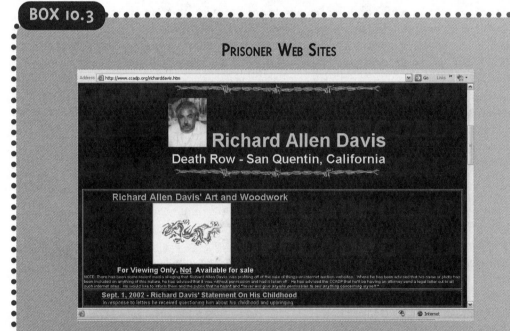

Richard Allen Davis's Web Site: http://www.ccadp.org/richarddavis.htm. Reprinted with permission.

Prisoner Web sites are a growing phenomenon that offers prisoners a bridge to the outside. Notorious prisoners such as Susan Smith and death row inmates, such as Cecil Davis on Washington's death row who raped and suffocated Yoshiko Couch in 1996 with rags soaked in Gum Out (a fuel line cleaner) in front of her disabled husband, and Richard Allen Davis in San Quentin in California (who abducted and murdered Polly Klaas in 1993), have Web sites.

(Continued)

(Continued)

An excerpt to illustrate from Cecil Davis's Web site:

Hello, my potential pen-friend, "How Goes?", You don't know me, so allow me to introduce myself. My name is Cecil E Davis, also known as K.C. Please feel free to call me that . . . I have a ready smile for anyone. I'm honest, trustworthy and fun to be with. In my spare time I enjoy body building, writing poems, and reading. I love listening to music, especially jazz and R&B. I am a hard worker. By trade I am a carpenter. I enjoy working with and training animals of all kinds. I also enjoy throwing horseshoes and playing pool, dominoes, checkers, chess, pinochle, and any game of poker. I love children and I have six of my own; I have spent over ten years in the military. My greatest strengths are my ambition, my optimism, and my persistence in passion for life. . . If you are interested please reply with a photo of yourself as soon as you are able. . . I am looking forward to a everlasting correspondence relationship with you! Shalom and peace! KC

In some cases, these sites have triggered outrage. In Arizona in 1997, a woman who met her death row husband on the Internet, attempted to break him out of prison. Both she and the inmate were shot to death during the escape. Some inmates have taunted victim's families by writing details about their crimes and making reference to their victims. Jack Trawick, an inmate on Alabama's death row who confessed to kidnapping 21-year-old Mary Kate Gach from a shopping mall in 1992, beating her with a hammer, strangling her, stabbing her through the heart and throwing her body off an embankment says on his site, "Was it really worth it? It was for me [a smiley face is included]. I would do the whole thing again knowing death row was waiting for me. Watching you die was (is) worth it all."

The Canadian Coalition Against the Death Penalty sponsors many of these prisoner Web sites. The organization posts on Richard Allen Davis's site:

We find it regrettable that most American media is more interested in looking at or hearing about the one or two high profile cases on our pages, in order to upset and inflame victim's families at the expense of the hundreds of other prisoners for whom we have set up websites; many of whom are wrongly convicted, have issues in their cases, were juveniles at the time of the offense, are victims of endemic racism and or corruption in the judicial system etc. We invite journalists to look over our pages to see what horrifies human rights activists worldwide. To view some of these other cases, visit ccadp.org.

Richard Allen Davis, San Quentin Death Row. Photo posted on his Web site.

Organizations That Sponsor or Feature Prisoner Web Sites:

PrisonerLife.com: http://www.prisonerlife.com/

Canadian Coalition Against the Death Penalty: http://www.ccadp.org/

PrisonZone.com: http://www.prisonzone.com/prison.html

CellPals.com: http://www.cellpals.com/paypalhome.htm

pornography, which is readily available and easily accessible online. Child pornography has heavily circulated through the Internet dating back to the late 1980s and mid-1990s and continues on a large scale today. Early well-known child porn cases include a 7-year-old girl named "Helena" who was shown having sex with an adult man and a boy named "Gavin" of the same age (the images are known to child porn collectors as "hel-lo," which stands for "Helena/Lolita"), the 1990s KG "Kindergarten" photos depicting hundreds, possibly thousands, of nude images of young girls aged 3 to 6, and the more hardcore KX series depicting the girls performing oral sex and masturbation on adult men (Jenkins, 2001). According to Jenkins (2001), the Internet child porn market is a "bandit culture" of child porn suppliers and consumers that sustains an unprecedented worldwide market. "This underworld represents a new type of social organization, made possible by novel forms of technology and characterized by types of interaction that would have been inconceivable only a few years ago" (p. 7).

Economic crime. The computer can be used as a tool to commit theft through sophisticated Internet scams. A wide range of Internet fraud scams include phishing (sending victims a phone Web site or other ruse to acquire Social Security numbers and other personal information for fraudulent use; see Box 7.2), Nigerian Advance Fee Scam Letters,[13] and Internet auction scams. Internet auction scams constitute the majority of Internet fraud offenses, representing 71% of all complaints of Internet fraud referred to the FBI (National White Collar Crime Center, 2005). Internet auction scams use an Internet auction site such as eBay to defraud a buyer of goods or services. In these scams, the buyer will "win" the online auction and send money to the seller, who does not follow through in sending the purchased item. Other types of economic offenses include counterfeiting and forgery involving the use of high-level graphic software, *data diddling* (computer program manipulation to redirect/reroute data representing economic exchanges) (Britz, 2004), securities fraud involving phony stock traders who provide false information to promote stocks in which they hold interest, or insider trading in which chat rooms operate as an information forum.

Public order crime. Internet gambling, Internet pornography, Internet prostitution and escort services, and Web sit-ins are examples of public order offenses committed with the use of computers. The Internet opens up new social contexts that interact with a range of user vulnerabilities resulting in large-scale Internet public order offenses. Individuals who may not gamble or use pornography in public settings, may be less inhibited about engaging in the same activities over the Internet. Mentally disabled or disordered individuals are particularly vulnerable to overuse of the Internet. A Survey of Internet Mental Health Issues (SIMHI) administered to 1,504 mental health professionals on their clients' Internet use found that the majority (61%) of clients reported excessive Internet use particularly viewing pornography and visiting sexual chat rooms. Harassment was reported in 10% of client cases and gambling and role-playing was reported as problematic in 15% of cases (Mitchell, Becker-Blease, & Finkelhor, 2005). Although much of this Internet activity cannot be criminally prosecuted (and in many cases does not involve a clearcut violation of the law), the Internet provides a convenient and anonymous forum for nuisance behavior, some of which crosses the line between deviant behavior and public order crime. For example, Internet sports betting businesses and bookmakers have been prosecuted through the Wire Wager Act, and Internet gambling is seen as perpetuating compulsive gambling and gambling by minors, with potential for fraud and organized crime activity (Malcolm, 2003).

Political crime. Cyberterrorists often attack computer systems themselves to threaten and intimidate (in which case the computer is the target), but terrorists also use computers simply as a means to communicate and intimidate. Domestic terrorist groups such as ALF and ELF have Web sites devoted to recruiting new members and spreading information about their cause. Insurgent terrorist organizations such as the IRA and PLO have used the media to gain identity, notoriety, and spread messages of intimidation and threat (Paletz & Schmid, 1992). In the years since 9–11, Al-Qaeda chiefs communicate primarily by courier. However, their underlings have made wide use of computers to communicate—joining chat rooms, sending e-mail, and Web surfing to keep apprised of events. U.S. intelligence agencies have gathered enormous quantities of data captured on computers. Militants in Afghanistan have used Microsoft Front Page and other software to create graphics and to assemble text, audio, and video content for display on the Web, enlisting confederates in China, Pakistan, and Britain to assist with technical tasks and uploading (Higgins, 2002). Computer technology clearly offers terrorist groups the means to recruit new members, communicate, gather information, and convey information.

Crimes of the Future—How Technology Shapes Criminal Behavior

In some respects, technology has done little to change the nature of criminal behavior. As Emile Durkheim has said, "There is no society that is not confronted with the problem of criminality. Its form changes; the acts thus characterized are not the same everywhere; but everywhere and always, there have been men who have behaved in such a way as to draw upon themselves penal repression" (Adler & Adler, 2006, p. 57). Violent, sexual, economic, public order, and political crime have and will continue to remain (from a Durkheimian perspective) a normal and necessary part of social life. In this sense, crime can be considered a static social phenomenon. However, technology has changed the modus operandi of criminal elements throughout history, and current technological advances have changed the physical environment in which crime occurs (Britz, 2004). Furthermore, media and computer technology have changed the nature of social life in such profound ways that no behavior is immune to its influence.

Technology shapes MO behavior, exacerbates some types of offenses, and creates entirely new motivational influences and categories of criminal behavior. Hackers make safe crackers obsolete. Celebrity stalkers have fewer targets in times and places where little value is placed on "stars" and there are no TV, film, or Webcast to simultaneously blast millions of images (and notions) of a person into living rooms worldwide. Teenagers who derive their identity through online gaming communities while being shunned in their own physical communities are developmentally frozen in a distinct space between their actual and virtual worlds. Technology breeds false familiarity, a blurred line between fantasy and reality, and a virtual realm within which rationalizations and feelings of guilt (that normally help to mediate criminal action) are absolved. What does this mean for the study of criminal behavior? Criminologists can no longer ignore the ways in which media and computer technology have and will continue to shape crime. On the individual level, technology shapes offender motivation and modus operandi and the development of deviant identity. Socially and culturally, technology has changed the nature of social life, which in turn has a profound effect on the nature and dynamics of criminal behavior.

Technological influences on criminal behavior exist along a continuum. In some cases, technology plays a minor role (e.g., using a computer to make contact with a potential victim or to store information, getting an idea from a movie that makes its way into a real-life crime); in other cases, technology drives the motivation, the MO, and the very nature of the offense (e.g., Black Hat hackers who break into systems for the thrill, creativity, and greed; copycat murderers are psychologically and culturally immersed in and act on a pop cultural script).

Compare, for example, the *Natural Born Killer* or the Devin Moore's *Grand Theft Auto* copycats with another well-known murder case in which the offenders were said to have been influenced by media. In 1974, a mass murder in Ogden, Utah, came to be called the Hi-Fi Murders. The offenders, Dale Pierre Selby and William Andrews, shot five people during a robbery of a Hi-Fi stereo shop while a third offender, Keith Roberts, waited in the getaway car. Three of the victims were murdered and two were gravely wounded.[14] This crime became well known for a number of reasons. First, it was an extreme mass murder committed in a small quiet town. Second, the offenders were Black men enlisted in the Air Force and stationed nearby, and the victims were White longtime members of the community. However, the notoriety of this case is perhaps more likely the result of the method Selby and Andrews used to commit the crime. Prior to shooting the victims in the head, Selby raped one of the victims (18-year-old Michelle Ansley), and then the pair forced all five of the victims to drink drain cleaner. The investigation revealed that Pierre and Andrews had gotten the drain cleaner idea from the Clint Eastwood movie *Magnum Force* in which a pimp murdered a prostitute by forcing her to drink drain cleaner. In the film, the victim died immediately. In the Hi-Fi case, the victims choked, vomited, coughed, and wretched after being forced to drink the cleaner. The offenders then shot them (the medical examiner who testified in the case indicated that the victims would have eventually died from the drain cleaner, but the process would have taken up to 12 hours). Douglas and Olshaker (1999) argue that "these two sadistic creeps would have committed this crime regardless of what they had seen or heard. What the media influenced was the details" (p. 107). Douglas contends that if he were to have profiled this case as an unsolved crime, the behavior speaks for itself and it would have made little difference that the offenders had seen *Magnum Force*. Selby and Andrews had seen *Magnum Force* two times during the course of making detailed plans to commit the robbery, including renting a storage space for the stolen merchandise. Pierre had a history of and previous conviction for auto theft, and after his execution in 1987, Kinder said, "It did not bother me at all when they executed [Selby]," "Pierre Dale Selby was a psychopath. The other two men were terrified of him."

This offense differs from the *NBK* and *GTA* copycats, the John Hinckley case, and the *Matrix* cases in that a particular aspect of the offenders' MO was inspired by the film. Selby and Andrews did not commit the offense under the influence of mass media in a Hinckley-style offense. In his study of self-reported copycat crime among juvenile offenders, Surette (2002) found that the most common copycat practice is borrowing media crime techniques. Thus, Selby and Andrews's film-inspired use of drain cleaner as a murder/assault weapon is not unlike the 26% of offenders in Surette's study who indicated they had committed a crime they had seen or heard about in the media.[15]

Understanding the level of influence of technology on criminal behavior in general and individual offenses in particular has important implications for the development of criminological theory and criminal justice practice. Lloyd (2002) offers four suggestions to guide future research on the criminogenic influence of mass media technology:

1. *Psychometrically sound instruments that quantify media influences.* These measures should be used to assess a range of media technology such as film, music videos, and the Internet to assess the nature and extent of criminogenic influence.

2. *Identification of individual and ecological variables predictive of consumption patterns and differential views of media.* Individual factors such as gender, age, ethnicity, and ecological factors such as peer culture are likely to play key roles in the perception of media images and their integration into an individual's personal identity.

3. *Increased precision in conceptualizing media influences on specific developmental tasks* (such as risk taking behavior, maladaptive cognitive processing)

4. *Examination of individuals (specifically adolescents) who identify with prosocial media messages to understand the range of positive and negative outcomes*

Although Lloyd's suggestions for future research pertain primarily to media influence on adolescent identity, these are important and logical steps in working to develop an empirical framework to test hypotheses and provide research findings to support or refute mounting anecdotal evidence that have suggested links between technology and criminal behavior.

Summary

Today more than ever before, the influences of technology play a powerful role for most people in the development of cognitive and behavioral scripts. With respect to criminal behavior, technology, media, and popular culture shape offender choices in unique ways—from the decision to commit a crime, the type of crime, and the manner in which it is committed to providing a ready-made script for rationalization techniques to neutralize offense behavior. It is impossible to ignore the role that media and computer technology play in shaping offender motivation and modus operandi, neutralizing guilt, and providing justification for offenders' actions. Given its power to influence criminal behavior, it is important to consider technology as a potential risk factor for some individuals. Copycat crime and cybercrime are two distinct subtypes of criminal behavior. Both can be considered methods of committing crime that cut across all major crime categories. Technological influences on criminal behavior exist along a continuum. Depending on the particular offense, media and computer technology play more or less of a role in the centrality of their influence on the nature or essence of the offense. Understanding the level of influence of technology on criminal behavior has important implications for the development of criminological theory and criminal justice practice.

As media and computer technology continue to advance rapidly and play an increasingly central role in people's lives, the importance of developing a theory and conducting empirical research on the relationship between technology and criminal behavior becomes greater. Research on technology and criminal behavior is virtually nonexistent, with the bulk of the empirical studies focusing on the relationship between violent media and general aggression, and much of the research literature consists of anecdotal accounts or armchair theories and typologies that have yet to be empirically validated. Important questions are left unanswered:

– *Are children who are born and grow up with mass media technology in the 21st century more or less likely to be negatively criminogenically influenced by it? Will children who grow up in a world where media technology is a normal part of everyday life have a healthier relationship to media than individuals who grew up in the 20th century (e.g., such as John Hinckley, who committed his copycat offense in what Joel Black has referred to as the 1980s aesthetic age of hyperreality)?*

– *Is there empirical support for the technology-criminal behavior continuum proposed in this chapter? Does technological influence on criminal behavior exist along a continuum of severity? If so, what individual, social, cultural, and other characteristics distinguish the low- versus high-technology influenced offender?*

– *As computer technology becomes more sophisticated and video and other virtual reality games more realistic, is there more or less potential for cathartic versus criminogenic effects of virtual violence?*

– *With the methodological difficulties in empirically studying the link between violent media and criminal behavior, it is unlikely that a direct causal link will be ever be established. However, is there an empirically identifiable cluster of factors that constitute an individual, culture, or context at high risk for copycat or cybercrime?*

The intersection of technology and criminal behavior is uncharted territory in criminological research. The development and empirical validation of theory in the area of technology and criminal behavior is a critical area for future exploration. With the degree to which mass media and computer technology have altered social conditions and cultural landscape, technology will play an increasingly salient role in influencing offender motivation and modus operandi in a segment of offenses. Additionally, it will become increasingly important to understand the influence of technology more generally on all types of offenses and the ways in which media, computer, and other technologies interact with other individual, social, and cultural factors to produce a web of criminogenic influence.

DISCUSSION QUESTIONS

1. It is suggested in this chapter that mass media and computer technology can be thought of as a dynamic risk factor for criminal behavior. Explain how technology influences criminal behavior and discuss whether you agree or disagree that it is important for criminologists to focus attention to the role of technology in shaping crime in the 21st century.

2. Are copycat crime and cybercrime meaningful (and homogeneous) crime categories? Are these types of crime best viewed theoretically as subtypes or supertypes of criminal behavior? Discuss.

3. Review the different cultural artifacts that have been linked to copycat cases in Box 10.1. What, if any, conclusions can be drawn from examining this list of anecdotal evidence? If you were asked to design an empirical study to examine the copycat phenomenon, how would you design such a study? In other words, how can criminologists move beyond anecdotal accounts of copycat crime to study the phenomenon empirically?

4. As indicated at the end of the chapter, one interesting question to consider is whether children who are born and grow up with mass media technology in the 21st century are more or less likely to be negatively criminogenically influenced by it. Do you think children who grow up in a world where media technology is a normal part of everyday life have a healthier relationship to media than individuals who grew up in the 20th century (e.g., such as John Hinckley who committed his copycat offense in what Joel Black has referred to as the 1980s *aesthetic age of hyperreality*)? Discuss.

5. As computer technology becomes more sophisticated and video and other virtual reality games more realistic, do you think there will be more or less potential for cathartic versus criminogenic effects of virtual violence? How would you design a study to examine this research question? Discuss.

 On Your Own: Log on to the Web-based student study site at http://www.sagepub .com/helfgottstudy/ for the URL links in the Web Exercises, study aids such as review quizzes, and research recommendations including links to journal articles specifically selected for this book.

WEB EXERCISES

1. Read the Senate Judiciary Committee Report, "Children, Violence, and the Media: A Report for Parents and Policymakers": http://judiciary.senate.gov/oldsite/mediavio.htm. Do you agree or disagree with the report's conclusion that "a steady diet of television, movie, music, video game, and Internet violence plays a significant role in the disheartening number of violent acts committed by America's youth. We must now devote ourselves to reducing the amount and degree of violence in our media and to shielding our children from such harmful depictions"? Does sufficient research exist to make the claim that the effects of media violence are no longer open to debate? Is there research that contradicts this claim? What policy initiatives would you support to deal with the problem of media violence in society?

2. Watch the film *Natural Born Killers* and then visit http://www.mediaknowall.com/violence/nbknotes.html, a Web site devoted to the *NBK* copycats; the Guardian Unlimited article describing the copycats at http://film.guardian.co.uk/interview/interviewpages/0,6737,862931,00.html; and the Childcare Action Project Summary analysis of the film at http://www.capalert.com/capreports/naturalborn.htm. Discuss the controversy and identify components of the film that you think contribute to the copycat effect.

3. Explore the range of Nigerian Advanced Fee scams in operation: http://internet-fraud.com/internet-fraud/nigerian-scams.htm. Discuss the nature and range of these scams and the types of people who may be more or less susceptible to being victimized by this type of offense. How has the Internet changed the nature and extent of fraudulent activity? How can law enforcement stay one step ahead of offenders who engage in these types of offenses? What sorts of crime prevention, victim advocacy/information, and security measures have and should be implemented to address these offenses?

4. Review the range of cybercrime cases reported on the U.S. Department of Justice Cybercrime Web site: http://www.cybercrime.gov/. What are the current investigative and legal issues pertaining to cybercrime? Based on the cases and other information provided on the Web site, speculate on how the nature of cybercrime and its response might change 10, 20, 50, or 100 years from now.

5. Go to the *Stalking Resource Center* and read the article, "Cyberstalking: Dangers on the Information Superhighway" and additional resources on the Web site http://www.ncvc.org/src/main.aspx?dbID=DB_Cyberstalking814. How have both mass media and computer technology shaped this form of criminal behavior? How does the phenomenon of cyberstalking intersect with cultural factors that contribute to copycat crime? Discuss.

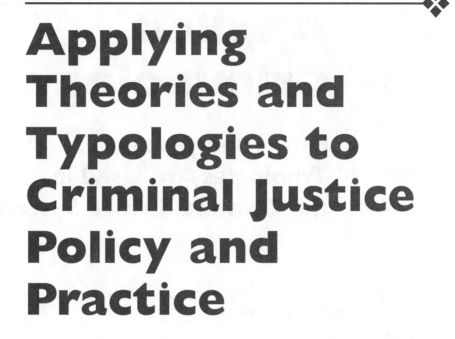

PART III

Applying Theories and Typologies to Criminal Justice Policy and Practice

Applied Criminology

How Theories and Typologies Are Used in the Criminal Justice System

> *. . . criminology is almost wholly assignable as an applied science to the given objectives of criminal policy.*
>
> —Keiser (1992, p. 41)

In the early morning hours of March 25, 2006, 28-year-old Kyle Huff was invited to an after-hours party following a Rave dubbed "Better off Undead" on Seattle's Capital Hill that featured ravers in costume with ghoul make-up and fake blood. Huff, a 6-foot 5-inch, 280-pound former pizza deliverer and art student, had moved to Seattle 5 years earlier from Whitefish, Montana, with his twin brother. Huff was invited to the party because some said he looked different, edgy, and like a wallflower. Huff arrived at the party after 4 am, stayed for a few hours, and then left the house to go to his car parked a couple blocks away. He returned minutes later with a shotgun and handgun, sprayed the word "NOW" on several steps along the way, walked up to the house and opened fire. He killed six partygoers ranging in age from 14 to 32, wounded two others, and when confronted with a lone police officer approaching the scene, he put a gun in his mouth and pulled the trigger.

The Capital Hill murder-suicide was the worst mass murder the city of Seattle had seen in 23 years, and with the killer dead, the victims, their families, and the community were left with no motive to help process the aftermath of the offense.

Seattle Police Chief Gil Kerlikowske acted quickly to provide the community with a way to process the horrific crime by setting up a blue ribbon panel led by well-known mass murder expert Dr. James Alan Fox to examine the evidence and identify a motive for the offense. *Families & Friends of Violent Crime Victims* Executive Director Jenny Wieland noted that some of the families of the victims had already contacted her agency for assistance and emphasized the importance of identifying the cause and motive for the offense. "Murder is so hard to comprehend in the first place, the question of why comes naturally" (Martin, 2006).

The Seattle Capital Hill murder case illustrates a practical application of criminological theory and crime typologies. In this case, Dr. Fox, coauthor of *The Will to Kill: Making Sense of Senseless Murder, Extreme Killing: Understanding Serial and Mass Murder, Overkill: Serial Killing and Mass Murder Exposed,* and other works was brought in to help analyze and explain the behavior of a suicide-homicide perpetrator where few clues were left regarding motive and rationale for the offense. The purpose of this application of theory to practice was to help the victims and their families and the community process this extreme offense. This is an important example of the many ways in which criminological theory and criminal typologies (in this case of mass murder) are used in the criminal justice system. *At all stages of the criminal justice process, from arrest to adjudication to corrections to victim services, theories and typologies are employed to answer investigative, legal, and correctional questions and to provide research support for programs, policies, and legislation.*

The term *applied criminology* refers to the application of criminological theory to criminal justice practice.[1] Linking theory to practice is central to the discipline of criminal justice and crucial at all stages of the criminal justice process. Criminal justice theory and research are used to inform policy, legislation, and practice. However, criminal justice/criminological theory and research and criminal justice practice differ considerable in terms of the nature of the roles and tasks associated with science versus practice, which limits the degree to which empirical research and theory can be practically applied to criminal justice practice (Keiser, 1992).

Crime prevention policy depends on knowledge about situational and opportunity factors that increase and decrease the likelihood for an offense to occur. Police strategy is informed by theories about offender motivation and offense patterns. Juries and attorneys rely on expert testimony involving social science research on the nature and types of criminal behavior in reaching adjudication and sentencing decisions. Development of effective correctional management and treatment is based on theory and knowledge about the needs and risk levels of different types of offenders in correctional populations. Victim services can be enhanced and improved with attention to offender typologies and theory and research on victim-offender dynamics and the ways in which offense characteristics influence victim impact and recovery in the aftermath of crime. Determination of when and in what situation juvenile offenders should be adjudicated as adults is guided by theory and research in developmental psychology and life-course criminology. At all stages of the criminal justice system—from arrest to release, from crime prevention strategy to victim services—theory and research play primary roles in the administration of justice.

It has long been recognized that criminal justice practice must be informed by theory and research, but empirical research on criminal behavior accumulated in the last 50 years has given new meaning to the term *applied criminology*. One notable example is in the area of psychopathy and violent risk prediction. The advent and standardization of the Psychopathy Checklist–Revised (Hare, 1991, 2003) made it possible to conduct research using a common definition. Prior to the 1990s, the term *psychopath* was considered a wastebasket category with minimal utility in the criminal justice system. The concept of psychopathy has been discussed in the criminal justice and mental health literature since the early 1800s, but lack of empirical research and consensus on its meaning made applying the concept to criminal justice practice problematic (the concept of psychopathy, however, has been part of the discourse in criminal justice for over 200 years, as the dividing line between insanity and criminality and as the basis of old and new habitual offender and civil commitment laws). Today, a vast and growing body of research links psychopathy to violent recidivism (Blair et al., 2005; Gacono, 2000; Hare, 2007; Patrick, 2006) and this has led to the beginnings of a *minitheory of crime of human predatory violence* (Scottish Executive, 2000). Psychopathy is now recognized as the "single most important clinical construct in the criminal justice system" (Hare, 1998). Theory and research on psychopathy is used by law enforcement agencies in hostage negotiation training (Greenstone, Kosson, & Gacono, 2000), criminal profiling (Turvey, 1999, 2002), crime scene analysis (O'Toole, 2007), adjudication and sentencing decisions (Freeman, 2001; Edens, 2001), and in correctional classification, management, treatment, and release decisions (Wong & Hare, 2005).

Psychopathy research is just one of many lines of criminological inquiry that has been applied on a wide scale to criminal justice practice. Theories and research from all areas of criminology (psychological, sociological, biological, routine activity, etc.) have been applied to criminal justice practice more frequently with the accumulation of methodologically sound and theoretically rich research and closer nexus between academics and practitioners. Criminal typologies play a role in law enforcement, judicial, and correctional response to specific types of offenders and offense situations.

Police and Public Safety

When law enforcement officers respond to crime, they have to know something about the dynamics of different types of offense situations. Most law enforcement work involves service and order maintenance functions that bring officers into contact with a wide range of types of people and criminal behavior. Experience is the most important tool in understanding the nature and dynamics of these different offense situations. However, theory and research is a valuable aid to law enforcement in developing policy and practice. Criminal behavior research and offender typologies are often used to guide law enforcement interaction with offenders in the investigation process. Theory and research on criminal behavior is used to develop crime prevention strategies and public education, to develop policy regarding law enforcement response to particular types of offenders and offense situations, to guide investigation strategy and interrogation techniques, and to help protect the public. Theory and research is important in police investigations. For example, law enforcement officers and detectives have to know something about the dynamics of rape, burglary, arson, and other types of offenses to be able to interview victims and make decisions regarding investigative directions. Many criminal investigation textbooks include specific chapters on rape, burglary, homicide, arson, and other types of offenses that address theory and research on crime types and offense dynamics (Fisher, 2004) and/or focus entirely on a specific type of offense (Geberth, 1996).

Criminological theory and criminal behavior research has been increasingly applied in recent years in two notable areas—*criminal profiling* and *crime prevention/ public safety*. Criminal profiling involves the application of research on criminal behavior and criminal typologies to law enforcement investigations in extreme cases. Law enforcement agencies often bring in consultants or rely on detectives trained in the behavioral sciences to offer investigative suggestions. In the area of crime prevention and public safety, theory and research has been used in a range of capacities including city planning, community crime prevention strategies, and victim services.

Criminal Profiling

One of the best-known applications of criminal behavior theory and research to law enforcement practice is in criminal profiling. *Criminal profiling is the inference of offender traits from physical and behavioral evidence.* Criminal profiling applies social science research on criminal behavior to law enforcement investigations. The process of criminal profiling is the reverse of clinical assessment and risk prediction, using theory and research to reach backward in time to determine what occurred at the scene and make inferences from crime scene evidence about the characteristics of an unknown offender. In contrast, clinical assessment and risk prediction uses theory and research to reach forward in time to predict a known offender's future behavior. Douglas and coworkers (1992) refer to the profiling process as a "form of retroclassification" whereby, rather than classifying a known entity into a particular category (e.g., *DSM* diagnosis), characteristics are inferred from crime evidence to categorize the unknown offender.

Another way of understanding profiling is as a branch of forensic science that applies social science to law enforcement investigations. As in other areas of forensic science, *criminal profiling involves identifying class and individual characteristics (of the offender) from crime scene evidence*. Identification of class characteristics requires understanding crime typologies—what factors, characteristics, conditions, and dynamics are associated with specific types of criminality. For example, if a footprint is found at a crime scene, forensic scientists would identify class and individual characteristics to try to come up with a statistical "match" to link a particular offender to the scene. Class characteristics of a footprint include outsole shape and markings that distinguish the particular class of shoes (e.g., Nike running shoes, Frye boots) that made the print. Individual characteristics include wear patterns such as evidence of pronation or supination. With profiling, identifying class characteristics involves making inferences about features of a crime scene that are consistent with particular offender types, for example, classifying an unknown offender as a particular type of sexual homicide offender (e.g., power assertive, power reassurance, anger retaliatory, anger excitation). Identifying individual characteristics in profiling involves identifying (through a comprehensive forensic assessment) characteristics likely to belong to only one individual through statistically based assertions that would link a particular individual to a scene (e.g., DNA profile, hair and fiber evidence). Profiling alone cannot help identify individual characteristics, but it can be used as part of a comprehensive forensic investigative strategy.

Traditional investigative techniques often fall short in extreme cases. Profiling is used to supplement other investigative and forensic science techniques based on the idea that *a small group of psychopathologically distinct offenders are responsible for a disproportionate amount of social harm.* Offenses and offenders considered most suitable for profiling include serial murderers, rapists, sexual predators, spree killers, mass murderers, family annihilation murderers, bombers, terrorists, stalkers, and arsonists, because crime scenes in these cases are said to reflect the offender's psychopathology (Holmes & Holmes, 2002), and cases where the offense appears to be motiveless (Douglas, Ressler, Burgess, & Hartman, 2004). In cases of suicide-homicide such as the Kyle Huff mass murder in Seattle, profiling is sometimes used to retrospectively piece together the offender's motivation and behaviors prior to the offense.

Criminal profiling has had a long history, beginning in the 1880s when Thomas Bond and George Phillips tried to profile Jack the Ripper. In the 1940s, during World War II, psychiatrist Walter Langer was commissioned to construct a psychodynamic profile of Hitler. Psychiatrist James Brussel followed, in 1957, working with the NYPD to construct a profile of the Mad Bomber. In the 1970s and 1980s the FBI (Howard Teten, John Douglas, Robert Ressler, Roy Hazelwood, and others) became involved in psychological profiling and popularized the technique. Since the 1990s, there has been an attempt (by David Canter, Maurice Godwin, Ron Holmes, Robert Keppel, Brent Turvey, and others) to "scientize" profiling and move the practice beyond the purview of the FBI (Egger, 1999).

Many terms are used to describe profiling, and a range of approaches to profiling and the general process of profiling have been extensively reviewed (Annon, 1995; Cook & Hinman, 1999; Daéid, 1997; Davis, 1999; Egger, 1999; Godwin, 1998; Homant & Kennedy, 1998; O'Toole, 1999; Pinzotto & Finkel, 1990; Wilson, Lincoln, & Kocsis, 1997). Other terms and variants of profiling include investigative profiling, crime scene assessment, criminal investigative analysis, psychological profiling, criminal personality profiling, sociopsychological profiling, offender profiling, behavioral evidence analysis, investigative process management, crime scene analysis, crime scene profiling, geographical profiling, equivocal death analysis, and applied criminology. There are five general approaches to profiling:

1. *Personality profiling:* Personality theory and clinical diagnostic categories used to construct a *personality profile* representing the type of offender most likely to have committed the crime. Generally conducted by psychiatrists, psychologists, academic criminologists.

2. *Criminal investigative analysis:* Crime scene patterns, crime scene indicators, victimology, and data collected from interviews with offenders used to determine type

(organized/disorganized) of offender who committed the crime. Generally thought of as the method developed by the FBI. Done by law enforcement officers trained in profiling.

3. *Investigative psychology:* Techniques and theories from psychology, psychiatry, and criminology to develop a profile based on statistical probability. Conducted primarily by academic psychologists and criminologists with no investigative training who use typologies and empirical studies to construct profiles. Term is used primarily in reference to the work of David Canter and the Investigative Psychology program at the University of Liverpool.

4. *Behavioral evidence analysis:* Method of criminal profiling involving deductive reasoning and critical thinking, focusing on hypothesis testing through analysis of forensic evidence. Approach was proposed by Brent Turvey (1999, 2002). In contrast with other methods, it emphasizes integrating forensic psychology and forensic science in the profiling process.

5. *Geographic profiling:* Aids investigations by predicting a serial offender's probable location. A mathematical model uses information from a series of related crimes to analyze the locations of the crimes and characteristics of local neighborhoods and produce a map showing the areas in which the offender most likely lives, works, and entertains and the offender's travel routes. Developed by Detective Inspector Kim Rossmo, author of *Geographic Profiling.*

All of the profiling approaches involve the attempt to infer characteristics and patterns of an unknown offender from crime scene evidence using theory and research in the social sciences, though each differs slightly in emphasis and process. A number of authors have discussed the differences between approaches in their use of "deductive" versus "inductive" reasoning. For example, criminal investigative analysis, the FBI approach, is often called "inductive" because it involves applying theory and typologies from data gathered from known offenders and then classifying crime scene evidence to create a profile based on these data. In contrast, Turvey (1999, 2002) argues that his approach is "deductive" because it involves developing and testing a hypothesis from forensic evidence. Most profiling approaches, however, can be said to involve both inductive and deductive reasoning in that inductive methods help to identify the *class* characteristics of the offender (by narrowing the suspect pool based on statistical probability rooted in research on known offenders) while deductive methods help to identify the offender's *individual* characteristics (by further narrowing the suspect pool to identify an individual offender through hypothesis testing based on physical/ behavioral evidence—*forensic individuation*).

Fundamental Assumptions and the Profiling Process

Criminal profiling is based on a number of assumptions rooted in personality theory. The first assumption is that the crime scene reflects the *personality* of the offender. The second assumption is that the *method of operation (modus operandi or MO)* remains similar. The third assumption is that the offender's *signature* (unique behaviors the offender had to engage in to meet psychological needs—the offender's "own personal stamp"; Keppel & Birnes, 1997, p. 5) will remain the same. The fourth assumption is that the offender's *personality will not change* (Holmes & Holmes, 2002). The primary goal of profiling is to determine the what, why, and who from crime scene information. Following are other benefits:

- Further understanding of the case or the offender

- Reassurance of officers' conclusions

- Information for interrogation and interviewing

- Information for defense or prosecution

- Information for psychological autopsies in equivocal death investigations

Criminal profiles are used at the investigative and trial stages of the criminal justice process. In the investigative stage, the crime is known and the offender is unknown. In investigations, profiling is used to reduce suspect pool, link cases, assess offense escalation potential, identify investigative leads and strategies, keep the investigation on track, and prevent future crimes (Cook & Hinman, 1999). At trial, the crime and the offender are known and profiling can be used to assist in evaluating the value and nature of forensic evidence and developing interview/interrogation strategies, to offer insight on the offender's state of mind before, during, and after the crime, and to clarify case linkage issues (Turvey, 1999, 2002).

A criminal profile is a report that provides investigative suggestions based on a thorough analysis of crime scene evidence. A criminal profile typically includes the following:

- *List of case material examined and background/timeline of case:* All available case material including crime scene photos, police reports, media coverage, interviews conducted, and timeline

- *Victimology: Background information* (name, sex, age, height, weight, family, friends, acquaintances, education, employment, residence, neighborhood, etc.); *lifestyle risk* (personality, personal, professional, social habits); and *incident risk* (factors associated with victim and offender risk present at the moment the crime took place—e.g., victim lifestyle, victim state of mind, location, victim drug/alcohol use, number of victims, offender MO risk—high planning = low risk)

- *Scene characteristics: Location type* (indoor, vehicle, outdoor, primary/secondary scenes); *use of weapon* (type, who it belongs to, where it came from, where it was found, when/how it was used); *victim resistance* (victim compliance, passive resistance, verbal resistance, physical resistance); *method of approach* (surprise, con); *method of attack* (blitz, use and type of force); *method of control* (control-oriented force, verbal threat, presence of physical threat); *sexual acts* (nature/sequence, planning/preparation); *verbal behavior/scripting* (what the offender says to victim and asks victim to say back— usually unknown in murders, often available in nonhomicidal rapes); *evidence of planning/precautionary acts* (level of planning, steps taken to stage/throw off investigation); *motivation* (identified through convergence of evidence—MO, signature, trophies taken, scripting, type of weapon, method of attack, control, etc.)

- *Review/analysis of physical evidence:* Focus on principles central to forensic investigation such as *corpus delicti* (the "body of the crime" or all the facts that show a crime has taken place); *Locard's exchange principle*—the transfer of evidence between offender to victim with specific attention to *MO* (manner in which the offender committed the crime); *signature (*the "theme of the crime," behaviors the offender needed to engage in to meet psychological/fantasy needs); *wound battern analysis* (examination, reconstruction, and analysis of physical injuries to determine type and origin of wound)

- *Offender characteristics:* Knowledge of/familiarity with victim, knowledge of/familiarity with location, skill level/background, mode of aggression/motivation, personality style, demographic characteristics (sex, age, intelligence, education level, cultural background, ethnic background, social class)[2]

- *Investigative suggestions:* Narrow suspect pool, linkage analysis, interview/interrogation suggestions, geographical location, etc.

The ultimate purpose of the profile is "to produce a behavioral composite, combining social and psychological assessment of the offender" (Egger, 1999) for use in the investigative and trial stage of the criminal justice process.

Key Criminological Concepts Central to the Profiling Process

The fundamental process of criminal profiling involves applying research and theory in criminal behavior to law enforcement investigations. Although different approaches to profiling involve different theories, lines of research, and methodology, a number of concepts are of central importance in making inferences about offender characteristics from crime scene evidence:

- *Psychopathy/psychosis:* Psychopathy is a personality disorder consisting of a particular constellation of characteristics including lack of attachment, defect in affect, absence of anxiety, antisocial behavior, and capacity for reality testing, and it is generally measured through the Psychopathy Checklist–Revised (PCL-R) and associated with *DSM-IV-TR* Axis II personality disorder; Psychosis is a clinical mental illness (e.g., schizophrenia), *DSM-IV-TR* Axis I diagnosis, may meet legal definition of insanity, has lack of capacity for reality testing. Though clinical diagnoses of these disorders must be done by licensed psychologist or psychiatrist and the psychopathy-psychosis dichotomy tends to be oversimplified when applied in the profiling process, inferences about whether an offender is psychopathic or psychotic have historically been part of the profiling process and are a component of other typologies.

- *Organized-disorganized typology:* Developed by FBI profilers (Douglas et al., 1992; Ressler, Burgess, & Douglas, 1992). Whether the crime scene is left organized or disorganized is said to provide information about the offender's criminal sophistication and personality. An organized crime scene reflects an offender who commits crime out of a need for power. Motivation is associated with psychopathy. A disorganized crime scene reflects an offender who commits crime out of passion, compulsion, frustration, or anxiety. Motivation is associated with psychosis. Although recent findings have questioned whether the organized-disorganized typology reflects distinct subsets of offense characteristics (Canter et al., 2004) and the typology has been criticized as too simplistic (Turvey, 1999, 2002), it is a primary component of the FBI profiling method, remains a starting point for classifying crime scene evidence, and is the most widely cited classifications of violent, serial offenders.

- *Predatory/affective aggression:* Aggression is shaped by emotional states—most commonly anger. Aggression can be motivationally categorized into two broad categories: *affective* (or expressive, defensive) and *predatory* (or instrumental, appetitive). Predatory aggression is characterized by lack of perceived threat, planned/purposeful violence, goal orientation, lack of conscious experience of emotion, increased self-esteem, and unimpaired reality testing. Affective aggression is characterized by a goal of reducing perceived threat, conscious experience of emotion, reactive/unplanned violence, decreased self-esteem, and possible loss of reality testing (Meloy, 1988). Predatory aggression is stereotypically associated with masculinity whereas affective aggression is stereotypically associated with femininity.[3]

- *MO and signature:* Modus operandi (MO) is a Latin term meaning *method of operation.* MO reflects *how* the offender committed the crime, what he or she had to do to successfully complete it, and it tells about the experience/state of the offender and situational/contextual factors involved in the crime. *Signature* is the *psychological calling card* (Keppel & Birnes, 1997), consisting of behavior/expression of violent fantasy the killer *must* leave at the scene to satisfy emotional/psychological needs. Signature goes beyond what's necessary to commit the crime and *tells about the offender's emotional/psychological needs and motivation for committing the crime.*

- *Sexual homicide typologies:* A number of well-known sexual homicide typologies are often applied in the criminal profiling process including the power assertive, power assurance, anger excitation, anger retaliatory (Keppel & Walter, 1999), the power/control, visionary, hedonistic, mission typology (Holmes & Holmes, 2002), and Meloy's (2000) compulsive/ catathymic typology.

These and other concepts and typologies are crucial to the profiling process because they offer a *language* with which to discuss, explain, and classify. This language provides a foundation on which *inferences* can be made. A *profile* is then constructed based on inferences as an aid in investigation, interrogation, risk assessment, and case linkage. Research shows that criminal profiling is operationally useful, particularly in terms of furthering officers' understanding of a case and providing the reassurance of having an expert confirm officer judgment (Copson, 2004).

Crime Prevention, Public Safety, and Victim Services

Routine activity theory tells us that *potential offenders are more likely to commit crime when temptations are high and controls are low* and that all crimes include three elements—a likely offender, a suitable target, and the absence of a capable guardian against the offense (Felson, 2002). Certain crimes are more likely to occur when facilitators (e.g., drugs, alcohol, weapons) are present, when there is an audience present (e.g., bar room brawl where drunk patrons are cheering), or when some sort of camouflage is available to help the offender avoid being noticed (e.g., familiarity, population density, Internet). Some products are stolen more than others because they are "hot products" that are "craved," because they are concealable, removable, available, valuable, enjoyable, and disposable (Clarke, 1997). Studies show that access and visibility are key factors in burglars' selection of particular targets. Robbers are more likely to select victims who they perceive to be vulnerable. Violent stranger crimes are statistically rare because it takes an extremely bold offender whose temptation has superseded the high controls present in a stranger offense.

Many police departments and private security firms make recommendations to communities through block watch programs and consultation with neighborhood groups based on concepts drawn from routine activity theory and research on environmental and situational crime prevention. Theory and research on situational and opportunity dynamics of crime and offender typologies that offer insight regarding the MO, motivation, and victim selection of different types of offenders provide critical information for preventing crime and enhancing public safety. Crime prevention strategies are often explained in terms of two converging lines of research and theory development—*environmental crime prevention* and *situational crime prevention.*

Environmental crime prevention refers to (re)constructing or rearranging aspects of the environment with attention to the ecological aspects of crime and its prevention. Environmental crime prevention is rooted in the early work of Jane Jacobs's (1961) *The Life and Death of Great American Cities,* which dealt with how the sterile high-rise public housing of urban renewal were designed for crime while old urban neighborhoods with high pedestrian traffic and close community bonds protected people against crime; Oscar Newman's (1970) classic book *Defensible Space,* which focused on designing safer public housing; and C. Ray Jeffrey's (1971) *Crime Prevention Through Environmental Design* (CPTED). This early work has been extended by Paul and Patricia Brantingham (1991) in their book *Environmental Criminology* and other works and George Kelling and Catherine Coles's (1996) *Fixing Broken Windows.* A central principle of environmental crime prevention is the Crowe-Zahm mixing principle (Crowe & Zahm, 2004), which states that crime can be reduced by placing safe activities in unsafe locations and unsafe activities in safe locations (Felson, 2002).

Situational crime prevention refers to altering situations to make crime targets less rewarding while increasing risks, effort, and guilt to reduce temptation to commit crime. Based on the work of Clarke (1997) in *Situational Crime Prevention* and earlier work, situational crime prevention involves practical focus on the here and now, with attention to situational features of potential crime opportunities such as making objects more difficult to steal (e.g., steering wheel locks, alarm systems, computer passwords, etc.). Some consider situational crime prevention to be a more holistic approach than environmental crime prevention, which focuses on altering environmental features to design out crime (Sorensen & Walsh, 1995).

Many law enforcement, public housing, college campuses, and other agencies have applied the principles of situational and environmental crime prevention. Today, C. Ray Jeffrey's *crime prevention through environmental design* (CPTED) concept is a problem-solving approach to crime prevention involving a comprehensive crime reduction strategy (Travis, 1996) that encompasses principles of routine activity theory and environmental and situational crime prevention. This application of theories of rational choice, situational and environmental crime prevention, and routine activity has been termed *alternative criminology, alt-criminology*, and *applied crime analysis* (Vellani & Nahoun, 2001). The following examples show the range of the applications of CPTED principles and routine activity and rational choice theories:

- In response to high incidence of campus parking garage crime, in 1999, the Ohio State University changed some aspects of the existing parking structure to reduce incidence of crime. Changes included increased lighting, installation of black chain-link in lower-level wall openings to reduce outside access while maintaining visibility, trimming trees and shrubs to reduce hiding places, and painting ceilings with white reflective paint. Crime in the garage was reduced by half of what it was in the 4 years prior (Tseng, Duane, & Hadipriono, 2004.

- A U.S. Department of Justice grant funded a study conducted by Metro Atlanta Pact and a private Atlanta-based firm, MXD Collaborative in Atlanta's Liberty Heights community to do a CPTED analysis. The community, characterized by below-average income levels and higher than average crime rate, had a problem with vandalism and nuisance crimes in particular. The CPTED analysis recommended that the community install speed bumps to reduce speeding in neighborhoods, add sidewalks to increase pedestrian traffic, reduce shrubbery to prevent hiding places, increase lighting for greater visibility, and remove abandoned cars throughout the neighborhood (Fernandez, 1996).

- Brindleyplace in Birmingham, England, is the largest ongoing development of office, leisure, and residential buildings in Europe and fully designed using CPTED principles. The development (which will eventually be the size of a small town of 33,000) features strengthened door panels, closed-circuit TV cameras, 17 in-house security officers who patrol 24 hours a day, bright and effectively utilized lights, and open spaces. In comparison with a nearby community that had 2,400 crimes in 18 months, Brindleyplace had only 202 in 34 months. Metropolitan Police Commander Bill Griffiths says of the experience, "Designing out crime is no longer merely a concept. . . . It's a proven formula out there working successfully" (Arnot, 1998).

- In Dallas, Texas, a $41 million hi-tech school called the Townview Magnet Center was built based on CPTED principles. The colorful brick building sits next to the Dallas County Probation Department and has six metal detectors, five full-time police officers, 37 surveillance cameras, and a security-conscious configuration (Applebome, 1995).

These examples illustrate the application of CPTED principles and routine activity and rational choice theories and the notion that offenders commit crimes largely as a result of opportunity. If the opportunity to commit crime is physically removed from a community, crime will be less likely to occur. But this is only part of the story.

An underlying assumption of opportunity/routine activity theory is that offenders make a series of rational decisions in committing a crime, enabled or disabled by situational and environmental factors. This notion of the rational offender is more or less accurate depending on the type of crime committed (Miethe, McCorkle, & Listwan, 2006). The presence or absence of certain types of opportunities, potential victims, audience, and other factors is highly dependent on types and subtypes of crime. For example, the homicide-suicide committed by Kyle Huff in Seattle is a very different sort of crime from a series of car thefts committed by a theft ring. Reducing opportunity for one type of offense may create an opportunity for another. For example, living in a penthouse suite on the 45th floor of a high-rise building may reduce accessibility for a predatory rapist seeking to break into a residence to assault a stranger victim. On the other hand, lack of visibility may create an opportunity for a date rape or a domestic violence incident. Measures taken to reduce temptation and increase controls for identity theft (e.g., public education, fingerprints on bankcards, passwords, and Internet security) differ from those necessary to reduce the likelihood of a barroom brawl (presence of capable guardians, limitations on alcohol consumption). Knowledge about the dynamics, motivation, and MO of particular types and subtypes of offenses dictates law enforcement response and crime prevention strategy.

Theories and typologies of crime can assist in developing and improving victim services. Research shows that the response of victims in the aftermath of crime depends on the nature of the offense and the subtype of offender responsible for the crime. Family members of homicide offenders and violent crime victims have different needs from victims of property and public order crime. Victims of sex crimes require services that specifically address the nature of the harm resulting from the particular offense. Victims of child abuse, family violence, and elder abuse greatly benefit from targeted support and continuity of services from charging through sentencing (International Association of Chiefs of Police, 1999). Crisis intervention, advocacy, support throughout the investigative process, and counseling services are informed by research and theory on how different types of crime and the dynamics of offenses impact victims (U.S. Department of Justice, Office of Victims of Crime, n.d.).

One example of an application of typologies of crime in victim services involves victims of different types of rapists. Rapists differ with respect to their motivation and MO. Power assertive rapists are more inclined to use what's called a "confidence" approach, whereas power reassurance rapists may assault the victim using a "blitz" attack. Bowie, Silverman, Kalick, and Edbril (1990) found that the psychological impact of rape differs with type of rape/rapist. Rape victims attacked by a confidence offender have different needs than a blitz offense victim in the aftermath of the offense. The immediate concerns of blitz rape victims include feeling safe and dealing with fear that the rapist may return whereas confidence rape victims tend to feel guilt and self-blame. Blitz rape victims may respond with flashbacks, nightmares, sleep and appetite disturbances, anxiety, heightened startle responses, and depression and usually seek treatment soon after the rape whereas confidence rape victims often delay seeking help. Mental health services must specifically target the special concerns of victims. Treatment for blitz rape victims may include psychotherapy, medication, and behavioral desensitization. Confidence rape victims need assurance that they deserve help and clarification of the definition/meaning of rape, and may have doubts about their ability to judge who is and who is not trustworthy. The importance of understanding offense dynamics and offender type in delivering services to victims of crime cannot be overstated. Victimology (the study of victimization and victims) and criminology (the study of crime and criminals) cannot be understood independently.

Research on domestic violence differentiating types of spouse abusers also has important implications for public safety and victim services. Studies show that batterers who stalk their victims are much more dangerous than batterers who do not stalk. Stalking behavior implied an added level of dangerousness, suggesting a different psychopathology. Stalking behavior and predatory fantasy is associated with repetitive and escalating domestic violence, and batterers who stalk tend to create increased victim fear (Burgess, Harner, Baker, Hartman, & Lole, 2001). Studies revealing different types of spouse abusers suggest that preventing further victimization depends on best practices that target specific subtypes of spouse abuse offenders (Dixon & Browne, 2003). Understanding subtypes of batterers has important implications for victim services. Victim advocates and law enforcement need to be able to evaluate the danger presented by different types of batterers and to respond to the special needs of victims.

The Courts

Theories and typologies of criminal behavior are used to answer legal questions in civil, criminal, and juvenile courts, to assist prosecutorial, judicial, and jury decision making, and to inform sentencing policy. Criminal behavior theories in ancient times and today have recognized the intentionality of a criminal act in adjudication and sentencing. From the 1800s until today discourse on the relationship between psychopathy, mental illness, criminality, and insanity has influenced the law of insanity and notions of who can and who cannot be legally defined and sanctioned as criminal. Theory and research on crime and criminals has influenced laws designed to selectively incapacitate dangerous offenders. Theory and research on special offender populations is the foundation for the development of special jurisdiction courts such as drug and mental health courts.

Criminal Law and the Insanity Defense

The roots of criminal law go back at least to ancient times in Rome, biblical Israel, and classical Athens. In all three of these ancient societies, the harshest sanctions were against intentional offenders with lesser penalties for diminished intent (Shelden, 2001). For a behavior to be legally defined as a crime, two features must be present—*mens rea* (a "guilty mind") and *actus reus* ("guilty act"). To be convicted of a crime a person must have intentionally (*mens rea*) committed an act that is defined by society as criminal (*actus reus*). If the court establishes that a defendant charged with a crime did not intend to commit the criminal act or that the defendant was not able to appreciate the wrongfulness of the act, the individual cannot be held responsible for the crime. Juveniles and individuals with some forms of mental impairment and mental illness are not held responsible for their criminal behavior.

Science has been used to make legal decisions in the civil and criminal courts, legislation, and policy since the scientific revolution, from 1543 to 1789 (see Faigman's

(1999) *Legal Alchemy for* a comprehensive discussion on the use and misuse of science in the legal system),

> from the DNA profile of O.J. Simpson and the drug induced stupor that "compelled" Richard Allen Davis to kidnap and kill Polly Klaas to the assortment of forensic evidence that was found and lost in the Jon Benet Ramsey investigation. And in a wide variety of less publicized cases, science is offered to prove a "myriad" of syndromes as well as the toxicity of substances too numerous to count and too scary to contemplate. Rarely does a case, criminal or civil, go to trial today without the presence of experts, most of whom lay claim to a scientific basis for their testimony. (Faigman, 1999, p. x)

Discourse, theory, and research on criminal behavior in the physical and social sciences inform legal decisions regarding criminal culpability, levels of responsibility, and insanity. Science enters and influences law and criminal justice in interaction with politics and cultural sentiment. Today, actuarial risk assessment instruments and the "new criminologies of everyday life"[4] appeal to politicians and have made their way into law and the "new culture of crime control" (Garland, 2001).

What we know about the nature of different types of violent crimes has important implications for criminal law. The courts recognize situations in which a violent crime is committed with diminished levels of intent. For example, research on *battered woman syndrome* drawn from the literature on domestic violence and female offenders has played a role in trials involving battered women who kill (Faigman, 1999). Research on infanticide and postpartum depression has been referenced in cases involving women who kill their children (Hyman, 2004). Furthermore, the classification of motivation into predatory/instrumental and affective/expressive drawn from the aggression research has been used in the courts through expert testimony in determining intent, premeditation, diminished capacity, and liability (Beck, 1998).

However, the relationship between law and science has always been conflicted. Nowhere is this conflict more pronounced than in the legal contexts of the *insanity defense* where the science of mental illness and criminal behavior must be applied to make a legal determination of criminal responsibility. *Insanity* is a legal concept referring to diminished mental ability at the time of a crime that precludes criminal responsibility (Smith & Meyer, 1987). On average, the insanity defense is used in less than 1% of felony cases (one-third or fewer of which are murder cases) and is successful only 15 to 25% of the time (Borum & Fulero, 1999). An acquittal by reason of insanity involves a legal question that requires a scientific answer. The law assumes human beings have free will, whereas science assumed human behavior is determined by a range of biological, individual, and social forces. Law seeks justice, science seeks truth. Law is an adversarial process that must work within a finite time frame, depending on precedent. Science is a cooperative process that progresses slowly, depending on future advances. The insanity defense raises questions about the meaning of free will and criminal responsibility—the foundation of criminal law.

The legal determination of insanity as a criminal defense hinges on the reconciliation of definitions of the law of insanity with what is known about the nature of a range of mental conditions. How the law of insanity should be formulated has always been a controversial issue fueled by difficulties in communication between the law and mental health disciplines:

> The law needs science to help it know about the facts of the world in which legal policy must operate. Without such knowledge, legal policy is literally blinded . . . the law's version of science often has very different starting assumptions than science's version of science. There is no clearer example of this than the law's assumption that people have free will and science's assumption that behavior is determined by some combination of nature and nurture. . . . The law assumes that people are "responsible" for their actions. . . . Science assumes that people are affected by their biology and their experiences. . . . While these differing starting principles serve the two professions well in their separate capacities, they create intellectual chaos when the two fields must work together. This chaos is especially well illustrated by the context known in the law as "insanity" and in science as "mental illness" (Faigman, 1999, pp. 26–27).

Study of the psychology of criminal behavior is concerned with diagnosis and treatment. In contrast, criminal law is charged with determining moral responsibility traditionally without concern about whether or not a person is too sick to be bad. Theoretical concepts central to the psychology of criminal behavior are difficult to reconcile with the practice of criminal law. The concept and nature of "disease" (and which conditions should be considered as such and where lines should be drawn), the controversy over whether psychological disorders should be viewed from a dimensional versus a categorical perspective, and the fact that all criminal (and other) behavior can be explained by motivational forces are issues that are problematic for the criminal law (Low, Jeffries, & Bonnie, 1986).

The first recorded case of acquittal by reason of insanity was in 1505, but the defense did not formally take hold until the mid-1800s when, in 1838, Isaac Ray published his treatise on the *Medical Jurisprudence of Insanity*, a first effort of psychiatry to influence law. Then in 1843, the *M'Naughten case* became the rule by which insanity was judged in Britain and in the United States for over 100 years and the origin of modern formulations of the insanity defense. Daniel M'Naughten killed Sir Robert Peel's secretary and said he had meant to kill Peel, and he had delusions of persecution (which would today be called paranoid schizophrenia). The decision from this case came to be known as the *M'Naughten Rule,* which said a person cannot be held accountable for a criminal act if the defendant

1. Has a mental disease or defect

2. Has the ability to "know" the "nature and quality of the act" and that the act "was wrong"

Most states have used variations of the M'Naughten Rule ever since, including the Durham Rule, the irresistible impulse defense, the American Law Institute's Model Penal Code, and Guilty But Mentally Ill (GBMI) (Box 11.1).

BOX 11.1

LEGAL TESTS FOR INSANITY

Insanity is a legal term that excuses individual responsibility for committing a criminal offense. The insanity defense, or the determination of "not guilty by reason of insanity" (NGBRI), is based on the historical belief that crime can be committed only by rational persons and that those who commit a criminal offense who are not aware of what they are doing do not possess criminal intent, and therefore deserve treatment rather than punishment. Although psychological conceptions of mental illness are considered in determining insanity (e.g., in determining the mental state of a defendant, what type of mental illness the defendant possesses), insanity is a legal standard, not a psychological or medical concept or classification. Like all legal standards, the insanity defense has changed over time and differs across cultures and jurisdictions. In the United States, versions of insanity defense differ in the federal and state systems and in various states. The following are the variations of the insanity defense that have been used over time and are currently in use.

The M'Naughten Rule

The historic origin of the insanity defense is the 1843 case of Daniel M'Naughten. Daniel M'Naughten shot and killed British Prime Minister Sir Robert Peel's secretary, Edward Drummond. The jury in the case acquitted M'Naughten with a finding "not guilty by reason of insanity." The ruling was controversial at the time and resulted in the establishment of an official process by which insanity was to be determined. This process, developed by the English common law judges, came to be known as the M'Naughten Rule. The M'Naughten Rule required evidence that at the time of the offense, the defendant's actions were committed under a defect of reason, a disease of the mind, resulting in the defendant's *inability to know what he or she was doing or that what he or she was doing was wrong*. The M'Naughten Rule, sometimes called the "right/wrong" test, is the historical foundation of the insanity defense in Britain and the United States.

The Durham Rule

The M'Naughten Rule was criticized because it did not take into account individuals who knew the difference between right and wrong when committing an act, but who could not control their behavior to stop themselves from committing the act. As a result of this dissatisfaction with the M'Naughten Rule, the District of Columbia Federal Court of Appeals formulated a new rule called the Durham Rule in 1954, in the case *Durham v. United States*. The Durham Rule, also known as the "Irresistible Impulse Test" required that to be determined "not guilty by reason of insanity" the defendant's act must be the *product of a mental disease or defect that rendered the accused incapable of controlling his or her behavior*. The Durham Rule was criticized because of concerns over the interpretation of "mental disease or defect." Critics argued that the Durham Rule left open the possibility of a broad range of minor mental disorders in the *Diagnostic and Statistical Manual*

(Continued)

(Continued)

of Mental Disorders to be considered under the rule and gave psychologists and psychiatrists too much power in the courtroom. The Durham Rule was abandoned by the DC Federal Court of Appeals in the 1972 case of *United States v. Brawner.*

The American Law Institute Model Penal Code

The Model Penal Code was adopted in the 1972 case of *United States v. Brawner* that dealt with the murder trial of Archie Brawner. The Model Penal Code combined the principles of the M'Naughten and Durham Rules with specification of the type of mental disease or defect that could be considered to establish insanity. The Model Penal Code excluded a specific type of mental disease or defect—antisocial personality disorder or any abnormality manifested only by repeated criminal or antisocial conduct. Under the Model Penal Code, a defendant could be considered not guilty by reason of insanity if at the time of the conduct, as a result of mental disease or defect, the defendant lacked the substantial capacity to appreciate the wrongfulness of the conduct or conform to the requirements of the law. The Model Penal Code included a major caveat—that the mental disease or defect could not be solely manifested by antisocial or repeated criminal conduct. The Model Penal Code can be seen as an attempt to exclude antisocial personality disorder and psychopaths from the insanity defense. However, because the law requires that the mental disease or defect be manifested only by antisocial or criminal behavior and most psychopaths and antisocial personality disordered individuals behaviorally manifest their personality disorder in other types of conduct, some question whether or not this caveat can technically ever apply to anyone (Smith & Meyer, 1987).

The Insanity Reform Act of 1984

Public outrage over the 1982 acquittal of John Hinckley prompted a barrage of legislation at the federal level and throughout the country intended to abolish or severely restrict the use if the insanity defense. John Hinckley was tried in federal court in the District of Columbia, which at the time used the Model Penal Code as the test of insanity. Critics of the Model Penal Code and Hinckley's acquittal argued that Hinckley clearly knew what he was doing when he plotted to assassinate then President Ronald Reagan and that the current formation of the insanity defense allowed offenders to get away with murder. The Insanity Reform Act of 1984 was a compromise between insanity defense abolitionists and legal and psychiatric professionals who argued for modification rather than abolition. The Insanity Reform Act of 1984 removed the volitional prong of the ALI test that excused a defendant who could not control his or her behavior and narrowed the definition of mental disease or defect to include only severe mental disease or defect. In addition, the Insanity Reform Act shifted the burden of proof to the defendant, limited the scope of expert psychiatric testimony, and established procedures for the hospitalization and release of acquittees. The Insanity Reform Act of 1984 was essentially a return to a test more closely resembling the original M'Naughten Rule.

Guilty But Mentally Ill

As a result of public reaction to the acquittal of John Hinkley in 1982, a number of states developed an alternative to the determination of "not guilty by reason of insanity." The "guilty but mentally ill" (GBMI) alternative required that *defendants deemed mentally ill at the time of their offense would be treated in a psychiatric facility until they are determined to be no longer mentally ill and then would be transferred to a correctional facility to serve the remainder of their sentence.* The states that allow for the GBMI verdict provide GBMI as an alternative to NGRI, giving the jury four verdict options: guilty, not guilty, guilty but mentally ill, and not guilty by reason of insanity. Thus, the defendant is given a criminal sentence, but mental health and correctional professionals determine if treatment is needed and where the offender will reside during the course of his or her sentence. To date, 12 states have established the GBMI. Research on the GBMI option shows that GBMI does not appear to enhance public safety or increase treatment effectiveness. Additionally, research shows that the GBMI option has not decreased the number of NGRI acquittees, but rather those found GBMI tend to come from the group of defendants who previously would have been found guilty (Borum & Fulero, 1999).

The fundamental question at issue in the variations of the insanity defense is what criteria should be used to determine the line dividing those who are and those who are not criminally responsible. For example, in the 1800s and much of the 1900s, the terms *criminality, psychopathy,* and *insanity* were confounded in scholarly discourse. However, the American Law Institute's (ALI) Model Penal Code contains a clause that specifically excludes conditions of abnormality manifested by repeated criminal or antisocial conduct. This clause represents a purposeful effort to bar psychopathy from the insanity defense (Smith & Meyer, 1987).

The M'Naughten and irresistible impulse tests for insanity have been criticized because they do not recognize that mental processes are interrelated and interdependent (Goldstein, 1967). The insanity tests "unscientifically abstract out of the mental make-up but one phase or element of mental life, the cognitive, which, in this era of dynamic psychology, is beginning to be regarded as not the most important factor in conduct and its disorders" (McCord & McCord, 1964, p. 178). Thus, though there is considerable debate over the bases for the insanity defenses, individuals who do not exhibit cognitive defect must be held responsible for their acts. Of the mental disorders, psychopathy is the disorder most likely to produce instrumental and predatory criminal behavior. Yet, because psychopaths are cognitively intact, psychopathy represents the antithesis of insanity. "Everyone recognizes that the present [legal] definition of insanity has little relation to the truths of mental life" (Cordozo, 1930), but it has been, and remains, extremely difficult to resolve the issues involved in the opposing objectives of the criminal justice system's demand for responsibility in the law, and the mental health system's desire to treat mental illnesses that manifest in criminal behavior.[5]

The importance of theory and research on criminal behavior in cases involving the insanity defense is illustrated by two historic insanity defense cases in the United States—*United States v. John W. Hinckley, Jr.*, in 1982 and *Texas v. Andrea Yates* in 2002, and the subsequent retrial in 2006 (a complete review and analysis of these cases is beyond the scope of this discussion; see Low, Jeffries, & Bonnie, 1986, for a comprehensive analysis of the Hinckley case and Slobogin, 2003, Hyman, 2004, and Denno, 2003, for review and analyses of the Yates case). Both the Hinckley and Yates trials involved testimony by prosecution expert witness psychiatrist Park Dietz, who testified that both defendants were not psychotic at the time of their offenses. The decisions in both of these cases clearly depended on the legal definition of insanity at the federal level at the time of the Hinckley case (Model Penal Code) and in Texas (M'Naughten) in the Yates case, and the psychiatric testimony provided by defense and prosecution experts. Of relevance to the application of criminology and criminal behavior theory is the ways in which understanding of the nature of the offenders was brought into the trial in the form of expert testimony and whether or not advances in criminological research will have an impact on similar cases in the future.

At issue in the Hinckley case was whether or not Hinckley suffered from personality disorder or psychosis, and testimony on the nature of both conditions was given. In the Yates case, the primary issue was establishing whether or not she had engaged in a conscious act of predatory aggression and the contributory role of postpartum depression and history of hospitalization for psychiatric illness including schizophrenia and depression. Additionally, both cases involved the copycat effect. Both Hinckley and Yates referenced a fictional film in explaining the motivation for their offenses. In Hinckley's case it was the 1976 film *Taxi Driver* and in Yates's case it was the 1995 film *Se7en* (Denno, 2003).[6]

In the Hinckley trial, Park Dietz testified that Hinckley met criteria for dysthymic disorder, narcissistic personality disorder, and schizoid personality disorder—diagnoses that were less serious than schizophrenia, which the defense experts had determined Hinckley to have. Ultimately, the Hinckley trial came down to the question of whether or not Hinckley's fascination with the movie *Taxi Driver*, adoption of the identity of the film's main character Travis Bickle, and fixation on Jodie Foster, the actress who played the character Iris in the film, were evidence that he had lost touch with reality and was unable to appreciate the wrongfulness of his conduct when he attempted to assassinate Ronald Reagan. In the Yates trial, the test for insanity in Texas was the M'Naughten Rule, so the central issue was whether or not Yates knew the difference between right and wrong at the time she killed her children. The defense argued that her behavior was the result of postpartum psychosis, a long history of psychiatric illness, and the belief that she was inhabited by Satan and that God had told her to kill her children to ensure their safety from her bad influence (Hyman, 2004). The prosecution argued that Yates knew what she was doing when she killed her children and that behavior she engaged in before and during the offense showed she had systematically and methodically committed a predatory crime that she planned in advance and knew was wrong. In her interview with Dietz, Yates indicated that she was thinking about the film *Se7en* the day of the murders and how the "Seven deadly sins" fit in, and that she had committed all of the sins but murder and the drowning would be her seventh and last sin.[7]

Research and theory on the role and nature of (different types of) psychopathology in violent crime, predatory/affective aggression (and the behaviors and cognition associated with each), and the copycat effect played a role in the Hinckley and Yates trials. A primary issue in the Hinckley case that led to reform of the insanity defense was whether the concept of mental disease was properly defined in the law. To whom the insanity defense can be extended depends on how mental disease is defined. In the Hinckley trial, experts for the prosecution and defense agreed that Hinckley was mentally ill—the prosecution arguing he had personality disorders and the defense arguing he was psychotic. Ultimately, the jury had to decide whether or not his criminal behavior was, based on the legal definition of insanity at the time, the product of a mental disease or defect. Arguably, the jury had no choice but to find that Hinckley suffered from a mental disease or defect (Low, Jeffries, & Bonnie, 1986). In the Yates case, jurors indicated that their guilty verdict was heavily influenced by the premeditated and methodical manner in which she had committed the offense ("Jurors," 2002). At the time of the Hinckley trial, there was no literature on the copycat effect; however, the role of the film in the offense played a substantial role in the trial. Future cases are likely to rely more heavily on research on the copycat effect, as can be seen in more recent cases in which attorneys have used media-mediation as a defense (e.g., *Grand Theft Auto* defense, *Matrix* defense).

These and other cases illustrate the ways in which research and theory on criminal behavior helps to answer legal questions—in this case whether or not a defendant should be held criminally responsible for committing a violent act. Criminal behavior research is critical in answering questions that have been raised in the past and are likely to arise in future cases such as the following:

- *Can a person engage in behaviors associated with predatory aggression and be psychotic at the same time?*

- *What is the extent and nature of comorbidity of Axis I mental disorders and Axis II disorders? Is psychopathy incompatible with psychoticism? If Axis I and Axis II disorders co-occur (specifically psychopathy and schizophrenia) in some cases, how reasonable is it to make legal decisions based on attempts to separate Axis I and Axis II disorders? (See Blackburn et al., 2003, for a discussion of comorbidity of Axis I mental disorders and Axis II disorders and Hare, 1996a, p. 47, for discussion of the debate regarding whether or not psychopathy and schizophrenia can co-occur.)*

- *Are offenders whose behavior is influenced by the copycat a homogeneous group? Does the blurring of boundaries between reality and fantasy associated with copycat crime play a central contributory role that should be considered in determinations of criminal responsibility?*

- *What is the relationship between gender, sexuality, mental disorder, and criminal behavior? What is the nature of sex-specific disorders such as postpartum psychosis and sex-typed disorders such as psychopathy, and what role do sexual stereotypes play in jurors' understanding and decision making in cases involving these disorders?*

These are questions that have arisen in insanity defense cases and that will likely arise in the future. Legal decisions must be based on what's available in the research literature. Empirical research conducted in these and other areas will likely play an important role in legal decisions in cases in which these questions arise. As science evolves and new findings in criminal behavior research emerge, new answers about the nature of criminal behavior and mental illness will influence where the line is drawn between free will and deterministic forces in law and legal policy and the insanity defense.

Selective Incapacitation:
Habitual Offender and Sexual Predator Laws

It has long been recognized that a small number of offenders commit a disproportionate share of criminal behavior. These offenders are often referred to as *career criminals, persistent offenders, chronic offenders, sociopaths*, or *psychopaths*. Although most people commit crime during short periods (e.g., adolescence, in particular situations) and approximately 30 to 50% of the general population is involved in crime in some capacity at some point in their lives (DeLisi, 2005), career offenders engage in criminal behavior across the lifespan. The notion of the career criminal has dominated discourse on criminal justice policy probably more than any other single criminological concept. "Nearly every federal agency concerned with research on crime, delinquency, or criminal justice assumes the existence of the career criminal" (Blumstein, Cohen, Roth, & Visher, 1986, p. 68).

The notion of the career criminal can be traced to before the turn of the 20th century, when governmental agencies commissioned special committees to devise methods to control the behavior of habitual offenders. This idea was revived in the 1970s with what came to be known as the *6% solution*—the hypothesis that incarcerating a small number of dangerous offenders will significantly reduce the crime rate and protect public safety. The 6% solution was based on the landmark study *Delinquency in a Birth Cohort* (Wolfgang, Figlio, & Sellin, 1972) that found that 6% of a cohort of 10,000 young men in Philadelphia born in 1945 was responsible for over 50% of total crime. Wolfgang's research has been referred to as the most important piece of criminal justice research in the last quarter century (Blumstein, Cohen, Roth, & Visher, 1986).

In the 1980s, career criminal prosecution programs were established with more than a hundred jurisdictions around the country adopting some form of priority prosecution of career offenders. However, jurisdictions were not uniform in their understanding or definition of habitual offenders. In 1990, the National Institute of Justice published a report titled *Redefining the Career Criminal* (Chaiken & Chaiken, 1990), which underscored the need for identifying a dangerous subgroup of career criminals given resource concerns demanding targeted prosecution focused on offenders who present the greatest public threat. The report noted three overlapping types of career offenders:

- *Persistent offenders,* who commit crimes over a long period of time (at least one-third of their lifetimes)

- *High-rate offenders,* who commit numerous crimes per year during periods when not incarcerated or when the opportunity arises

- *Dangerous offenders,* who commit violent crimes often resulting in victim injury

Some offenders fit in only one category—for example, a middle-aged offender who has committed low-level burglaries since his teenage years would be considered a persistent (but not high-rate or dangerous) offender. Other offenders fit in more than one category—for example, a serial rapist who commits a string of violent rapes over a year-long period would be classified as a high-rate and dangerous offender. The findings of the NIJ report suggested that it is more confusing than productive to think of offenders in terms of habitual or persistent criminal behavior and that it is the high-rate dangerous offenders who should be the priority target for prosecution. Following are indicators of high-rate dangerous offense behavior:

- Prior adult conviction for murder, robbery, kidnapping, sex crime involving a child, forcible rape, or burglary

- Absconding while under correctional supervision

- Arrested while on parole or pretrial release

- History of drug problem

- Use of a knife in instant offense

- Female victim of instant offense

- Instant offense occurred in outside public location

- One or more juvenile convictions for robbery

Research over the past 30 years in psychology and criminology, particularly in the areas of life-course criminology and psychopathy, continue to support this notion that a small subgroup of offenders commit a large amount of crime. In the life-course criminology literature, a subgroup of *antisocial persistent* offenders (Moffit, 1993) has been identified as a distinct subgroup characterized by chronic offending patterns across the life course. Research on the empirical link between psychopathy and violent recidivism suggests that psychopathic criminals are chronic offenders at unusually high risk for reoffense (Douglas, Vincent, & Edens, 2006) and has answered important questions regarding the static/personality factors associated with violent criminal behavior.

The notion of the career criminal is appealing to policymakers and legislators because it isolates the problem of crime to a distinct subgroup of offenders. According to Gottfredson and Hirschi (2001), "Discovery of the career criminal by criminologists stimulated the idea of selective incapacitation. To implement the idea of selective incapacitation, one need only identify career criminals" (p. 71). However, there are theoretical problems with the concept of the career criminal that have yet to be worked out, making it an appealing yet fundamentally flawed basis for crime control policy. For example, *what characterizes a career criminal—criminal mindset, personality disorder, nature and type of criminal behavior, quality or quantity of crime committed? How do we detect a career criminal before rather than after he or she is already at the later stages of a criminal career?* Research shows that criminals who make careers of offense behavior are those who specialize in a particular type of offense whereas there is no evidence of offense specialization in the life cycle of ordinary offenders.

The age-crime effect is well established in the literature. Crime is an activity highly concentrated among youth, and regardless of offense type, criminal behavior statistically declines with age. Criminal behavior tends to peak at age 25 and then rapidly decline. However, a number of researchers contend that they have identified a subgroup of offenders whose behavior is constant across age. Hare, McPherson, and Forth (1988) found that the criminal behavior of psychopaths remains high until age 40 and then drops dramatically whereas the criminal behavior of nonpsychopaths is relatively constant over the years. The authors suggest that the commonly held notion that criminal behavior decreases dramatically at middle age may be accounted for by the inclusion of psychopaths in study samples. But this suggests that psychopaths are a subgroup that may have an intense period of offenses with a rapid decline at middle age, whereas lower-level chronic nonpsychopathic offenders continue their careers across the life course.

Three Strikes Legislation

In the 1990s, laws known as *Three Strikes You're Out* were enacted in more than half of the states, requiring long-term sentences for repeat offenders. The laws, a revival of the old habitual offender laws of the early to mid-1900s, were said by proponents to reduce crime by deterring and selectively incapacitating the most dangerous and criminally active offenders. Washington State was the first jurisdiction to enact three strikes legislation in December 1993. California followed in 1994, and by the late 1990s over 26 states and the federal government had also introduced similar laws (Clark, Austin, & Henry, 1997). Before the introduction of three strikes legislation, habitual offender statutes had existed in most states, but were rarely applied.

The impetus for the change in sentencing practices arose, in part, from public outrage over cases in which offenders with prior felony convictions committed heinous violent crimes. *The public and politicians recognized through a series of high-profile heinous cases a dangerous subtype of violent offender that represented a substantial threat to public safety.* In Washington, the 1988 murder of 29-year-old Diane Ballasiotes by a sex offender on work release, and in California the murders of 18-year-old Kimber Reynolds in 1992 and 12-year-old Polly Klaas in 1993 by repeat violent offenders were cited as reasons to enact the three strikes legislation (Moore, 1999). Politicians and lawyers argued that the public had come to believe existing laws did not protect them. This concern, whether accurate or not, led to the expansion of three strikes across the nation and its adoption as federal sentencing policy.

Despite similar terminology, three strikes legislation is defined differently across the states and federal system. All of the laws require longer periods of incarceration for offenders convicted of violent crimes. Crimes that count as strikes (the "strike zone"), the number of them required to be "out," and the meaning of "out" vary across the states. California's legislation is the most expansive, allowing the third strike to be any felony and doubling the sentence for two strikes offenders. Washington has a narrower strike zone but includes nonviolent offenses such as treason, promoting prostitution, drug-related felonies, and attempts. To be called "out" can mean an enhanced sentence with a set minimum or maximum, life with the possibility of parole, or life without the possibility of parole. "Out" in Washington is life without the possibility of parole whereas in California it is 25 years to life. Georgia, South Carolina, and Montana mandate life without the possibility of parole after two violent felony convictions, and Washington added a two strikes sentencing provision for sex offenders in 1996. Other variations of the law include states with four strikes provisions and a range of sentencing options left to the discretion of the courts.

Since 1993, over 7,000 offenders have been sentenced under California's three strikes law, the widest sweeping and most used in the country. Other states have sentenced far fewer under the law and many have not applied the legislation to any significant extent. As of August 2002, for example, just 206 offenders had been sentenced under Washington's (the nation's oldest) three strikes law. Differences in the laws have resulted in different types of offenders being sentenced across the states. In Washington, few (7%) three strikers have been nonviolent offenders whereas in California most (60%) have been sentenced for property and drug offenses (Clark, Austin, & Henry, 1997).

Studies on the impact of three strikes on the criminal justice system show that the legislation has disrupted the efficiency of the courts with increased trial rates, clogged dockets, and divergent prosecutorial policies (e.g., differential interpretation and application of the law by prosecutors across counties within states). Findings suggest that the sentencing policy may actually increase the homicide rate and contribute to a growth in offender suicides, escapes, assaults, and attempted murder of law enforcement officers because offenders have nothing to lose. Three strikes laws have been found to disproportionately target nonviolent and minority offenders and studies show no measurable effect on crime rates. With the exception of California, the laws have not had a significant impact on prison populations because many violent offenders sentenced under three strikes would have received lengthy prison sentences prior to the law. However, the cost of caring for the aging prison populations resulting from three strikes, particularly in California, is projected to increase dramatically in the future, leading some to suggest that "we may be incarcerating ourselves into an epidemic" (King & Mauer, 2001, p. 12).[8]

Because three strikes legislation has not significantly impacted a large number of offenders, prison systems, recidivism, or crime rates, many critics and researchers consider the law symbolic, with little instrumental value. According to Austin, Clark, Hardyman, and Henry (1999), three strikes is "much ado about nothing and is having virtually no impact on sentencing practices" (p. 271). Studies on the origins of public support for three strikes suggest that even the source of support for the law is symbolic, founded on social distance, lack of understanding, and perceived lack of moral and social cohesion rather than on the instrumental goal of crime control. Politicians and victims rights advocates who promoted three strikes relied on public fear of crime and frustration over not being able to protect children and others from *violent recidivists*.

Poster-boy superpredators like Richard Allen Davis were the law's target in the minds of voters, who saw three strikes as a way to gain control over an out-of-control situation. In practice, however, particularly in California where the range of strikeable offenses is so broad, the law is applied to far too few Davises and too many nonviolent offenders who citizens did not originally expect would be sentenced under three strikes. Studies in the years following enactment of the legislation show that when citizens learn details of three strikes laws and hear about cases in which nonviolent offenders are sentenced to life or life without parole, they are less supportive of the sentencing policy (Zimrig, Hawkins, & Kamin, 2001).

Numerous constitutional challenges to three strikes have been raised on grounds that the laws violate Fifth Amendment protection against double jeopardy, Eighth Amendment protection against cruel and unusual punishment, the 14th Amendment's equal protection clause, and *ex post facto* constitutional provisions. In California, a number of cases have highlighted how the laws may penalize relatively minor offenders. Controversial cases in which nonviolent individuals have been sentenced under three strikes include Jerry Williams whose third strike was grabbing a slice of pizza from some children. Likewise, Gregory Taylor, a homeless ex-convict who tried to pry open the kitchen door of a church where he had been fed in the past to steal some food, was also sentenced to 25 years to life. Critics argue that the inability of courts to incapacitate selectively the most dangerous offenders is fundamentally at odds with the intent of the law.

Given the research suggesting that criminal behavior of most offenders declines after age 30 (known as the *burnout phenomenon*), it makes little sense to incapacitate offenders from age 38, the average age of three strikers, given that this is the stage of their life cycle in which most will naturally desist from committing crime. Finally, there is little evidence that the law is an effective deterrent to violent crime, since the causes of such crime are many and varied. Even with the foreknowledge of the new legislation, it is unclear whether individuals would be put off from committing a violent act, given the subjective and emotional nature of some crimes.

Significantly fewer women are sentenced under three strikes laws than men. As of March 2007, in Washington State, only 4 (1.6%) (State of Washington Sentencing Guidelines Commission, June 2007) and, in California, 81 (1%) women had been sentenced under the law (California Department of Corrections and Rehabilitation, June 2007). Feminist criminologists argue that three strikes laws were not intended for, and should not apply to, female offenders who generally do not commit the violent predatory crime for which the law was intended. Some also suggest that because women tend to be the primary caregivers of children and many children with incarcerated mothers end up in the foster care system, that sentencing women under three strikes laws has harmful effects that go well beyond the sentenced offender. This view that three strikes should not apply to women based on their different needs and circumstances suggests that gender-neutral sentencing guidelines casts too wide a net, including women without considering their unique place in society, the nature of their crimes, their greater amenability to rehabilitation, and the totality of the circumstances of women's lives.

In November 2002, the U.S. Supreme Court heard two California cases involving three strikes offenders (Leandro Andrade and Gary Ewing) who received sentences for minor thefts (of videotapes in one case and golf clubs in the other). At issue was whether the California three strikes law was cruel and unusual punishment when it "struck out" offenders for nonviolent crimes. On March 5, 2003, the Supreme Court ruled on the Ewing case and upheld Andrade concluding that three strikes does not violate the Eighth Amendment and recidivism is a serious public safety concern that has long been recognized as a legitimate basis for increased punishment. Justice Sandra Day O'Connor wrote in her opinion that the U.S. Supreme Court does not sit as a "superlegislature" (p. 15) and that "Ewing's sentence is justified by the State's public-safety interest in incapacitating and deterring recidivist felons, and amply supported by his own long, serious criminal record" (*Ewing v. California*, 2003, p. 17). Citing evidence that California's recidivism had been reduced by 25% and that for the first time since the 1970s there are more parolees exiting California than entering, the court acknowledged that legislatures enacting three strikes laws made a deliberate policy choice to enhance public safety by incapacitating habitual offenders.

The U.S. Supreme Court's landmark decision resolves a primary legal question that is likely to make future challenges beyond state legislative systems much more difficult. The court's decision to uphold three strikes on the basis of public safety underscores the original intent of the legislation and the right of individual states to enact sentencing policy that balances defendants' constitutional rights with public safety interests. The decision may close the door to further federal challenges and open it for further expansion of three strike laws (and other variants of the habitual offender laws) to a greater number of states and to a broader class of offenders. In the views of three strikes advocates, and now the U.S. Supreme Court, three strikes laws reflect a focused state strategy necessary to control career criminals, ensuring public safety through long-term incarceration of habitual offenders.

Sexual Predator Laws

Sexual predator laws are a variant of the habitual offender laws in that they involve identifying the worst of the worst habitual offenders, those who engage in predatory sex offenses whose criminal behavior is determined to be the product of a mental disease or defect. Sexual predator laws have a long history. Current laws, referred to as *sexually violent predator* or SVP laws are a revival of the old *sexual psychopathy* laws of the early 1900s.[9] Like the habitual offender laws, the purpose of sexual predator laws is to protect the public by identifying the subtype of offenders deemed most dangerous. However, sexual predator laws take habitual criminal legislation a step further in that they apply after an offender has served his or her sentence. Sexual predator laws involve civil commitment on completion of a sentence of confinement.

Washington State was the first state to revive the old sexual psychopath laws. The current Washington law, enacted as part of the *Community Protection Act of 1990,* is called the *Sexually Violent Predator* (SVP) statute (RCW 71.09.020). The way the law works is that the prosecuting attorney or attorney general will petition the court for an end-of-sentence review of an offender and probable cause hearing to determine whether or not he or she[10] meets the legal definition of sexually violent predator. The legal definition of sexually violent predator in Washington State is *"any person who has been convicted of or charged with a crime of sexual violence and who suffers from a mental abnormality or personality disorder which makes the person likely to engage in predatory acts of sexual violence if not confined in a secure facility"* (RCW 71.09.020). If there is probable cause that the offender meets the legal definition, the offender is civilly committed for an indefinite length of time. An offender may be released from confinement to the community to less restrictive community custody after participating in treatment and when mental health staff determine the offender has made treatment gains that reduce the likelihood of reoffense and risk to public safety. Approximately 16 other states have similar civil commitment laws for sexual predators.

In 1994, Kansas enacted a sexual predator law that was patterned after the Washington State law. Prior to this, the state had a civil commitment law pertaining to the mentally ill. Like the Washington SVP law, the Kansas sexual predator law defines sexual predators as *"any person who has been convicted or charged with a sexually violent offense and who suffers from a mental abnormality or personality disorder which makes the person likely to engage in the predatory acts of sexual violence"* (Kan. Stat. Ann. §59–29a01 [1994], cited in *Kansas v. Hendricks,* 1997). Both the Washington and Kansas laws draw on theory and research regarding the nature of sexual violence and treatment amenability for predatory offenders. According to the Kansas state legislator:

> [A] small but extremely dangerous group of sexually violent predators exist who do not have a mental disease or defect that renders them appropriate for involuntary treatment pursuant to the [general involuntary civil commitment statute]. . . . In contrast to persons appropriate for civil commitment under the [general involuntary civil commitment statute], sexually violent predators generally have anti social personality features which are unamenable to existing mental illness treatment modalities and those features render them likely to engage in sexually violent behavior. The legislature further finds that sexually violent predators' likelihood of engaging in repeat acts of predatory sexual violence is high. The existing involuntary commitment procedure . . . is inadequate to address the risk these sexually violent predators pose to society. The legislature further finds that the prognosis for rehabilitating sexually violent predators in a prison setting is poor, the treatment needs of this population are very long term and the treatment modalities for this population are very different than the traditional treatment modalities for people appropriate for commitment under the [general involuntary civil commitment statute]. (Kan. Stat. Ann. §59–29a01 [1994], cited in *Kansas v. Hendricks,* 1997)

Moral and constitutional challenges have been made to the habitual offender and sexual predator laws throughout history (Jenkins, 1998). Opponents of the three strikes laws argue that they exacerbate racial disparity in sentencing, overburden the courts and corrections, result in disproportionate sentences for nonviolent offenders, do not deter, and are infrequently applied to those dangerous and violent offenders for whom they were originally intended. The sexual psychopath laws in the early and mid-1900s were heavily criticized (Kittrie, 1971; Sutherland, 1950) and the contemporary SVP laws in Kansas and Washington have been constitutionally challenged and upheld by the Supreme Court in *Kansas v. Hendricks* (1997) and *Seling v. Young* (2001). At issue in the *Hendricks* case was whether or not pedophilia could be considered a "mental abnormality" under the act and whether or not it is constitutional to civilly commit an individual for a condition for which there is no known treatment. Hendricks was diagnosed as a pedophile who could not control his urge to molest children when under stress and was likely to reoffend. In the *Hendricks* case, the court considered Hendricks's pedophilia as "mental abnormality" and determined that, in situations where there is no known treatment for a particular disorder that produces sexually predatory and violent criminal behavior, incapacitation is a legitimate end of civil commitment law. In *Seling v. Young*, Andre Brigham Young, a civilly committed resident of the Washington State Special Commitment Center (SCC) for sexually violent predators challenged Mark Seling, then superintendent of the SCC, for failing to provide adequate treatment and for the punitive nature of civil confinement. The court upheld Young's civil commitment but remanded the case for the District Court to determine whether the conditions at the center rendered the act punitive as applied to Young.

One difference between the old and the new laws is that the tools used to make the determinations of probable cause in states that currently have SVP laws are based on a large body of theory and research on the relationship between antisocial personality disorder, psychopathy, sexual aggression, and sexual deviancy. Research conducted to date suggests that offenders who meet the sexually violent predator criteria are at higher risk for reoffense than other types of violent offenders. A study of 89 released sex offenders recommended for civil commitment under the Washington law, but for whom no petition was filed, found that these offenders had a high violent recidivism rate. Over half (57%) were convicted of new felony offenses, 40% with an against-person offense, and 29% with a felony sex offense (Milloy, 2003). Although science was used to both support and refute the old laws, and some predict the new laws will meet the same fate (Jenkins, 1998), the courts have the benefit of a large body of research and forensic assessment tools to make the determination of probable cause. For example, in Colorado, a sexually violent predator screening instrument is used presentence. The instrument "combines empirical research conducted by the Division of Criminal Justice with additional criteria specified by the Colorado Sex Offender Management Board" (Box 11.2). Not all sexually violent predators meet the criteria for primary or prototypical psychopathy (i.e., PCL-R score above 30), but many do, most have a high number of psychopathic personality traits, and the combination of psychopathy, sexual deviancy, and predatory behavior puts this group at extremely high risk for reoffense.

BOX 11.2

TO BE COMPLETED ONLY ON INDIVIDUALS CONVICTED OF FELONIES

COLORADO SEXUALLY VIOLENT PREDATOR ASSESSMENT SCREENING INSTRUMENT

Pursuant to 18-3-414.5, C.R.S.

This assessment must be completed for all adult cases convicted on or after July 1, 1999 for specific sex crimes committed on or after July 1, 1997. The completed assessment must accompany the pre-sentence report and the mental health sex offense specific evaluation submitted to the court/parole board. According to 18-3-414.5(2) and (3), C.R.S.: "Based on the results of such assessment, the court/parole board shall make specific findings of fact and enter an order" concerning whether the defendant is a sexually violent predator. This assessment instrument combines empirical research conducted by the Division of Criminal Justice (Part 3) with additional criteria specified by the Colorado Sex Offender Management Board (Part 2).

Assessment Summary:

Probation Officers or SOTMP Therapists, based on the information provided on the following pages, please check the boxes that apply. Checks in boxes I, II, III and IVa or IVb indicate that the person satisfies the legislative criteria for the definition of sexual predator pursuant to 18-3-414.5(1), C.R.S.

- ❑ (I) The defendant is 18 years of age or older or has been tried as an adult, and has been convicted of one of the five crimes defined in Part 1, pursuant to 18-3-414.5, C.R.S.
- ❑ (II) The conviction occurred on or after July 1, 1999 for a crime committed on or after July 1, 1997, pursuant to 18-3-414.5, C.R.S.
- ❑ (III) The victim was a stranger to the offender (Part 2A), **or** the defendant established a relationship primarily for the purpose of sexual victimization (Part 2B), **or** the defendant promoted a relationship primarily for the purpose of sexual victimization (Part 2C), pursuant to 18-3-414.5, C.R.S.
- ❑ (IVa) The defendant scores 4 or more on the Sex Offender Risk Scale (SORS, Part 3A), pursuant to 18-3-414.5 and 16-11.7-103(4)(c.5), C.R.S., **or**
- ❑ (IVb) Meets mental abnormality criteria (Part 3B), pursuant to 16-11.7-103(4)(c.5), C.R.S.

Court/Parole Board Finding:

18-3-414.5(2), C.R.S. states: "Based on the results of such assessment, the court/parole board shall make specific findings of fact and enter an order concerning whether the defendant is a sexually violent predator." Probation Officer or SOTMP Therapist, based on the court's/parole board's decision, please check the box that applies.

❑ The court/parole board finds this person to meet the criteria specified in 18-3-414.5, C.R.S., sexually violent predator.

❑ The court/parole board finds this person to meet the criteria specified in 18-3-414.5(1), C.R.S., but the court does NOT find the person to be a sexually violent predator.

❑ The court/parole board finds this person does NOT meet the criteria specified in 18-3-414.5, C.R.S., sexually violent predator.

PLACEMENT DECISION	Following the court finding, *Probation Officers* must mail or fax *all completed pages* within one month to:	Following the parole board's finding, *SOTMP Therapists* must mail or fax *all completed pages* within one month to:
❑ Probation ❑ DOC ❑ Community Corrections ❑ Parole	**Chris Rowe** **Division of Probation Services** **1301 Pennsylvania Street, Ste 300** **Denver, CO 80203** **Fax: (303) 837-2340**	**Pat Lounders** **Division of Criminal Justice** **700 Kipling Street, Ste 1000** **Denver, CO 80215** **Fax: (303) 239-4491**

Background

Probation officers and sex offender evaluators listed on the Sex Offender Management Board (SOMB) provider list or SOTMP therapists will complete this instrument on every sex offender that meets the following criteria:

(I) Is 18 years of age or older at the date of the offense, or who is younger but is tried as an adult pursuant to section 19-2-517 or 19-2-518, C.R.S.

(II) Has been convicted* on or after July 1, 1999 of one of the following offenses committed on or after July 1, 1997:

○ Sexual assault, in violation of section 18-3-402, C.R.S. or sexual assault in the first degree in violation of section 18-3-402, C.R.S. as it existed prior to July 1, 2000;

○ Sexual assault, in the second degree in violation of section 18-3-403, C.R.S. as it existed prior to July 1, 2000;

○ Unlawful sexual contact, in violation of section 18-3-404(1.5) or (2), C.R.S. or sexual assault in the third degree, in violation of section 18-3-404(1.5) or (2), C.R.S. as it existed prior to July 1, 2000;

○ Sexual assault on a child, in violation of sections 18-3-405, C.R.S.; or

○ Sexual assault on a child by one in a position of trust, in violation of section 18-3-405.3, C.R.S.

(Continued)

(Continued)

    (III) Whose victim was one of the following (per 18-3-414.5(1)(a)(III), C.R.S.):

        ○ A stranger to the offender (See Part 2A on page 4 of this form), **or**

        ○ A person with whom the offender established a relationship primarily for the purpose of sexual victimization (See Part 2B on page 4 of this form), **or****

        ○ A person with whom the offender promoted a relationship primarily for the purpose of sexual victimization (See Part 2C on page 5 of this form).

    (IV) Pursuant to 18-3-414.5(1)(a)(IV), C.R.S. and 16-11.7-103(4)(c.5), C.R.S. is likely to subsequently commit one or more of the offenses specified in 18-3-414.5(II)(a), C.R.S. under the circumstances described in 18-3-414.5(III)(a), C.R.S., according to the scores derived from the SOMB's actuarial risk assessment instrument (Part 3A or Part 3B of this form) (specifically pursuant to 16-11.7-103(4)(c.5), C.R.S.).

    (V) Once the form is completed by the probation officer and the evaluator or SOTMP therapist, it should be forwarded to the court/parole board, pursuant to 18-3-414.5(2) and (3) C.R.S. Based on the results of the assessment (included on the following pages of this form), the court/parole board shall make specific findings of fact and enter an order concerning whether the defendant is a sexually violent predator.

An offender found to be a sexually violent predator is required to register with the local law enforcement agency in the jurisdiction in which they reside within five days of becoming a temporary or permanent resident, and on a quarterly basis thereafter, for the remainder of his or her natural life, pursuant to Section 16-22-108(1)(d), C.R.S. Offenders found to be sexually violent predators will also be subject to placement on the internet listing of sex offenders maintained by the Colorado Bureau of Investigations (CBI) and linked to the State of Colorado's homepage, pursuant to Section 16-22-111, C.R.S. and may be subject to community notification pursuant to Section 16-13-903, C.R.S.

*Convicted includes having pleaded guilty or nolo contendere.

**The members of the Sex Offender Management Board determined that the three relationship categories are mutually exclusive. This document reflects the Board's decision.

INSTRUCTIONS: Overview

*This instrument requires information from **both** the Pre-Sentence Investigation writer and the SOMB-listed sex offender evaluator. For **Department of Corrections** cases, a Sex Offender Treatment and Management Program therapist must complete the entire form and forward it to the parole board when the offender is considered for release. All completed forms for **Probation** must be faxed or mailed to the **Division of Probation Services**, and those from the **Department of Corrections** should be mailed or faxed to the **Division of Criminal Justice** (see cover page). Pursuant to 16-22-108(1)(d)(I), C.R.S., the **parole board** "shall make specific findings concerning whether the offender is a sexually violent predator" based on the results of this assessment conducted by DOC. If the parole board finds an offender meets the criteria defined in this instrument, the offender is required to register pursuant to 16-22-108(1)(d)(I), C.R.S.*

The Probation Officer completes **Part 1** and **Part 3A items 1 through 6**. The Probation Officer then forwards the instrument to the SOMB-listed sex offender evaluator *along with police reports and victim statements*. If either police reports or victim statements are NOT forwarded with this instrument to the evaluator, please indicate why here: _____

_____

Sections of this instrument to be completed by the Probation Officer are designated with : P

The Evaluator completes **Part 2, Part 3A items 7 through 10**, and **Part 3B, including the Instrument Summary**. The evaluator then returns the completed instrument to the Probation Officer, along with the completed mental health sex offense specific evaluation, pursuant to C.R.S. 16-11.7-104(1).

Sections of this instrument to be completed by the mental health Evaluator are designated with: E

The SOTMP Therapist must complete the **entire** form **(Parts 1, 2, 3A, and 3B)**.

Data Sources used to complete this instrument must be identified:

Please choose from the following data sources when completing the following sections of this instrument.

1 - Criminal History
2 - Pre-Sentence Investigation Process
3 - Police Report
4 - Mental Health Evaluation
5 - Official Record/Documentation
6 - Child Protection or Social Service Records
7 - Demographic Information
8 - NCIC
9 - Education Records
10 - Victim Report (self report or from any data source)
11 - Sexual History (official record, self report)
12 - Sex Offense Specific Mental Health Evaluation
13 - Prison Record
14 - Self-Report
15 - CCIC
16 - Results of a Plethysmograph Examination or an Abel Screen (SOMB Standards)
17- Polygraph
18- Other _____

(Continued)

(Continued)

| P | *Probation Officer or SOTMP Therapist Please Complete Part I* |

CLIENT INFORMATION

Offender Name:	CC#: (Court Case Number)		
SS#:	SID#	ML#	DOB:
Gender: ❑ Male ❑ Female	Ethnicity: ❑ Anglo ❑ Black ❑ Hispanic ❑ Other		
PO: *(Does not apply to DOC cases)*	PO Telephone Number: *(Does not apply to DOC cases)*		
Date Forwarded to Evaluator: *(Does not apply to DOC cases)*			
Judicial District: *(Does not apply to DOC cases)*			
SOMB Evaluator/SOTMP Therapist:	Evaluator/Therapist Telephone Number:		
Date of Evaluation:	Date Returned to PO: *(Does not apply to DOC cases)*		

Defining Sexual Assault Crimes (18-3-414.5(1) C.R.S.)

The offender is 18 years of age or older as of the date the crime was committed or is tried as an adult pursuant to 19-2-517 or 19-2-518, C.R.S. Also, the offender has been convicted on or after July 1, 1999 of one of the following crimes committed on or after July 1, 1997. Attempts, conspiracies, accessories and deferred judgments *do not* apply. Conviction includes pleas of guilty and nolo contendere.

Please check the box indicating which of the five *felony* crimes qualifies the offender for this assessment.

- ❑ Sexual assault, or sexual assault in the first degree, in violation of section 18-3-402, C.R.S. as it existed prior to July 1, 2000;
- ❑ Sexual assault, in the second degree in violation of section 18-3-403, C.R.S. as it existed prior to July 1, 2000;
- ❑ Unlawful sexual contact, in violation of section 18-3-404(1.5) or (2), C.R.S. or sexual assault in the third degree, in violation of section 18-3-404(1.5) or (2), C.R.S. as it existed prior to July 1, 2000;
- ❑ Sexual assault on a child, in violation of section 18-3-405, C.R.S.; or
- ❑ Sexual assault on a child by one in a position of trust, in violation of section 18-3-405.3,

Meets **DEFINING SEXUAL ASSAULT CRIMES** Criterion:

❑ Yes
❑ No

| E | *Evaluator or SOTMP Therapist Please Complete Part 2* |

The following criteria were developed by representatives of the Sex Offender Management Board, the Judicial Department and the Department of Corrections to assist the court and the state board of parole (per 16-11.7-103(4)(e), C.R.S.) in the identification of "undue risk." For purposes of this document, undue risk includes the designation of sexual predator as outlined in 18-3-414.5(III) C.R.S.

THE OFFENDER MUST MEET ONE OF THE FOLLOWING THREE SEXUALLY VIOLENT PREDATOR RELATIONSHIP DEFINITIONS: 1) STRANGER, 2) ESTABLISHED A RELATIONSHIP, OR 3) PROMOTED A RELATIONSHIP.

A. STRANGER
Pursuant to 18-3-414.5(1)(a)(III), C.R.S. the victim is a **stranger** to the offender when the victim has never known or met the offender, or has met the offender in such a casual manner as to have little or no familiar or personal knowledge of said offender, prior to the current offense.

Please select the appropriate data source from the list on page 3.

Data source(s):

Meets **STRANGER** Criterion:
  ❏ Yes
  ❏ No
If yes, go to Summary on page 6. If no, continue in Part 2.

B. ESTABLISHED A RELATIONSHIP
(Consider only when stranger does not apply). Pursuant to 18-3-414.5(1)(a)(III), C.R.S., the offender **established a relationship** primarily for the purpose of sexual victimization when **any two of the following criteria** are present *(check all that apply). List all data sources used in the box below.*

  ❏ The offender has a history of multiple victims and similar behavior.
  ❏ The offender has actively manipulated the environment to gain access to this victim.
  ❏ The offender introduced sexual content in the relationship (introduction of pornography, inappropriate discussion of sexual relations with child).
  ❏ The offender persisted in the introduction of sexual contact or inappropriate behavior of a sexual nature despite lack of consent or the absence of the ability to consent.

(Continued)

(Continued)

Please select the appropriate data source from the list on page 3.

Data source(s):

Meets **ESTABLISHED A RELATIONSHIP** Criteria: *(Offender must meet at least two of the above items to meet established criteria).*
- ❑ Yes
- ❑ No

If yes, go to Summary on page 6. If no, continue in Part 2.

C. PROMOTED A RELATIONSHIP

(Consider only when stranger or established a relationship criteria above do not apply.) Pursuant to 18-3-414.5(1)(a)(III), C.R.S., the offender **promoted an existing relationship** primarily for the purpose of sexual victimization when **the first item below is present and any other item is present** *(check all that apply). List all data sources used in the box below.*

- ❑ The offender took steps to change the focus of the relationship to facilitate the commission of a sexual assault such as but not limited to planning, increased frequency of contact, introduction of inappropriate sexual contact, stalking, seduction or drugging of the victim,

And

- ❑ The offender engaged in contact with the victim that was progressively more sexually intrusive, or
- ❑ The offender used or engaged in threat, intimidation, force or coercion in the relationship, or
- ❑ The offender engaged in repetitive non-consensual sexual contact, or
- ❑ The offender established control of the victim through means such as but not limited to emotional abuse, physical abuse, financial control or isolation of the victim in order to facilitate the sexual assault.

Please select the appropriate data source from the list on page 3.

Data source(s):

Meets **PROMOTED A RELATIONSHIP** Criteria: (*The promoted criteria are met when the first bullet and at least one of the bottom four bullets apply*).
- ❑ Yes
- ❑ No

SUMMARY OF PART 2 RELATIONSHIP INFORMATION:

A. Meets **STRANGER** Criterion:
- ❏ Yes
- ❏ No
- ❏ NA because "B" or "C" is Yes

B. Meets **ESTABLISHED A RELATIONSHIP** Criteria:
- ❏ Yes
- ❏ No
- ❏ NA because "A" or "C" is Yes

C. Meets **PROMOTED A RELATIONSHIP** Criteria:
- ❏ Yes
- ❏ No
- ❏ NA because "A" or "B" is Yes

SOMB SEX OFFENDER RISK SCALE (SORS)

*Pursuant to 16-11.7-103(4)(c.5), C.R.S. the Division of Criminal Justice worked in consultation with the Sex Offender Management Board (SOMB) to develop an actuarial risk assessment scale to be used in the identification of an offender's risk to fail. Data on demographic, index crime, criminal/juvenile history, sexual history and therapy/attitude characteristics were studied. Failure was measured at 12 and 30 months. **Two-thirds of convicted male sex offenders scoring 4 or more on the 10-item scale below were nearly four times as likely (371%) to fail supervision or treatment as someone scoring below 4. Nine studies of sex offenders have found supervision or treatment failure to be correlated with the subsequent commission of a new sex crime. Women who score 0-3 are considered low risk. Women who score 4-8 are considered high risk but the probability for revocation is unknown due to the small number of women in the study.** Please refer to the "Handbook: Sexually Violent Predator Risk Assessment Instrument Background and Instruction, June 2003" for additional information (available at http://dcj.state.co.us/ors/docs.htm).*

Each item is scored 1 (YES) or 0 (NO). Missing information must be coded 0. Please indicate data sources.

| P | *Probation Officer or SOTMP Therapist Please Complete Items 1 through 6*

NA   YES   NO

- ❏   ❏   1. **The offender has one or more juvenile felony adjudications.** (Include attempts and conspiracies but not deferred judgments).
  Data Source(s) _____

(Continued)

(Continued)

☐ ☐   2. **The offender has one or more prior adult felony convictions.** (Include attempts and conspiracies and deferred judgments/sentences).
Data Source(s) _____

☐ ☐ ☐   3. **The offender was employed less than full time at arrest.** *This does not apply to women.* (Part-time, sporadic, or day labor is not considered full-time. Multiple, concurrent, stable part-time jobs are considered full-time employment. Full time work refers to 35 or more hours per week).
Data Source(s) _____

☐ ☐   4. **The offender failed first or second grade.** (Whatever the reason, if the offender failed these grades in elementary school, and was held back or repeated the grade, this item scores "yes". Probation Officers may need to work closely with the SOMB evaluator and polygraph examiner to obtain this information).
Data Source(s) _____

☐ ☐   5. **The offender possessed a weapon during the current crime.** (A weapon is defined as a gun, knife, or object that could be used to intimidate or harm a victim. The offenders need only to possess the weapon during the crime, not use the weapon. If the victim was led to believe that a weapon was present, regardless if it was, score this criterion "yes").
Data Source(s) _____

☐ ☐   6. **The victim had ingested or was administered alcohol or drugs during or immediately prior to the current crime.**
Data Source(s) _____

| E | *Evaluator or SOTMP Therapist Please Complete Items 7 through 10* |

NA YES NO

☐ ☐ ☐   7. **The offender reports that he was NOT sexually aroused during the current crime.** *This does not apply to women.* (Sexual arousal refers to an erection. The erection must have been sustained throughout the sexual assault. Data sources include self-report and/or corroborating documentation such as the victim report and police report).
Data Source(s) _____

☐ ☐   8. **The offender scored 20 or above on the COLORADO-SOMB Denial Scale.**

☐ ☐   9. **The offender scored 20 or above on the COLORADO-SOMB Deviancy Scale.**

☐ ☐ 10. **The offender scored 20 or below on the COLORADO-SOMB Motivation Scale.**

The last three items on this scale are scored from the Colorado Sex Offender Management Board (SOMB) Checklist (attached).

TOTAL
Add number of "Yes" responses

Meets **DCJ SEX OFFENDER RISK SCALE** Criteria: *(Total score of 4 or more "Yes" responses for both men and women)*
❑ Yes
❑ No

E *Evaluator or SOTMP Therapist Please Complete Part 3B*

3B MENTAL ABNORMALITY
Mental abnormality is referenced in 16-11.7-103(4)(c.5), C.R.S. The criteria defined below were found to be empirically linked with failure in the study described in Part 3A. Individuals who meet the following criteria are statistically more likely to fail treatment or supervision. The offender suffers from a **mental abnormality** if one of the following testing instruments indicates psychosis, or personality disorder that makes the person more likely to engage in sexually violent predatory offenses.

The offender meets this criterion when he or she scores:
❑ 18 or more on the Psychopathy Check List Short Version (PCL-SV), **OR**
❑ 30 on the Psychopathy Check List Revised PCL-R, **OR**
❑ 85 or more on **each** of the following Millon Clinical Multiaxial Inventory (MCMI-III) scales: narcissistic, antisocial, and paranoid.

Please indicate the score of the appropriate test below.

Psychopathy Checklist
PCL-SV SCORE: ⟶
OR
PCL-R SCORE: ⟶

– OR –

Millon Clinical Multiaxial Inventory (MCMI-III)

Narcissistic: ⟶
AND
Antisocial: ⟶
AND
Paranoid: ⟶

(Continued)

(Continued)

Meets MENTAL ABNORMALITY Criterion:
- ☐ Yes
- ☐ No

INSTRUMENT SUMMARY

To be identified a sexually violent predator, the offender must have yes on Parts 1 + 2 + [3A or 3B].

Defining Sexual Assault Crimes Criterion **(Part 1)**
- ☐ Yes
- ☐ No

Meets Date Requirement **(Per Statute)**
- ☐ Yes
- ☐ No

Meets Relationship Criteria **(Part 2)**
- ☐ Yes
- ☐ No

Scored *4 or more* on DCJ Sex Offender Risk Scale **(Part 3A)**
- ☐ Yes
- ☐ No

Meets Mental Abnormality Criterion **(Part 3B)**
- ☐ Yes
- ☐ No

SOMB CHECKLIST

Please endorse each of the following items as they apply to the client: "0" means "does not apply at all" to a "5" meaning "applies very much". **Please complete the entire form and fax it to DCJ at 303-239-4491.**

Date _____ CR# _____ SS# _____

Client Name _____

SOMB Evaluator _____ Referring Probation Officer _____

	Not at all . . . Very Much
DENIAL	
Denies actual facts of offense.	0 1 2 3 4 5
Denies wrongness of actions.	0 1 2 3 4 5
Minimizes prior offenses.	0 1 2 3 4 5
Portrays self as victim.	0 1 2 3 4 5
Blames others for the crime.	0 1 2 3 4 5
Holds grudges against "system".	0 1 2 3 4 5
Says victim "wanted it".	0 1 2 3 4 5
Says therapy is unnecessary.	0 1 2 3 4 5
DEVIANT SEXUAL PRACTICES	
Has no socially appropriate sexual outlet.	0 1 2 3 4 5
Engages in many forms of deviant sexuality.	0 1 2 3 4 5
Obsessed with deviant sexual practices.	0 1 2 3 4 5
Engages in bizarre sexual practices.	0 1 2 3 4 5
Poor control of sexual behavior.	0 1 2 3 4 5
Talks constantly about sex.	0 1 2 3 4 5
Nothing seems "off limits" sexually.	0 1 2 3 4 5
Masturbation is compulsive or excessive.	0 1 2 3 4 5
MOTIVATION	
Verbalizes desire for treatment.	0 1 2 3 4 5
Agrees with court order for intervention.	0 1 2 3 4 5
Pays attention to evaluator.	0 1 2 3 4 5
Arrives for appointments on time.	0 1 2 3 4 5
Is positive about evaluator's testing.	0 1 2 3 4 5
Actively participates in evaluation.	0 1 2 3 4 5
Completes evaluation requirements.	0 1 2 3 4 5
Seeks additional help.	0 1 2 3 4 5
SOCIAL SKILLS	
Socially appropriate.	0 1 2 3 4 5
Appropriate social connectedness.	0 1 2 3 4 5
Pleasant in conversation.	0 1 2 3 4 5
Non-hostile interaction.	0 1 2 3 4 5
Dresses appropriately.	0 1 2 3 4 5
Forms genuine bonds with others.	0 1 2 3 4 5
Appropriate social network.	0 1 2 3 4 5
Appropriately helpful to others.	0 1 2 3 4 5
	Not at all . . . Very Much

(Continued)

(Continued)

Not at all . . . Very Much

POSITIVE SOCIAL SUPPORT

Has many pro-social friends.	0	1	2	3	4	5
Has close friends.	0	1	2	3	4	5
Interacts with friends regularly.	0	1	2	3	4	5
Has healthy family.	0	1	2	3	4	5
People are interested in his progress.	0	1	2	3	4	5
People have offered to help him.	0	1	2	3	4	5
Has friends/family he could live with.	0	1	2	3	4	5
Has lived in same community for years.	0	1	2	3	4	5

READINESS TO CHANGE

Verbalizes desire to change.	0	1	2	3	4	5
Sees other ways of behaving.	0	1	2	3	4	5
Appears tired of old ways.	0	1	2	3	4	5
Shows detrimental effects on victim.	0	1	2	3	4	5
Has plan for change.	0	1	2	3	4	5
Willingness to discuss sexual history.	0	1	2	3	4	5
Can see future in changing.	0	1	2	3	4	5
Eliminates deviant sexual behavior.	0	1	2	3	4	5

TAKING CARE OF BUSINESS

Work/school stability.	0	1	2	3	4	5
Keeps up on financial obligations.	0	1	2	3	4	5
Maintains stable family life/living situation.	0	1	2	3	4	5
Completes homework.	0	1	2	3	4	5
Takes responsibility for life incidents.	0	1	2	3	4	5
Reports/journals about stressful situations.	0	1	2	3	4	5
Reports/journals about anger.	0	1	2	3	4	5
Reports/journals about high risk situations.	0	1	2	3	4	5

Not at all . . . Very Much

Although only three of these items are used in the SORS Risk Scale, all of these items were found to statistically correlate with revocation/treatment failure. Because scores can change over time, this checklist may be used by therapists or supervising officers as a set of dynamic indicators of supervision/treatment outcome.

Jenkins (1998) notes that the term *predator* originated in popular writings of Jack Olsen and Andrew Vachss and made its way from popular culture into the habitual offender and civil commitment laws with the help of high-profile and heinous cases such as Earl Shriner and Westley Dodd in Washington State and Richard Allen Davis in California. This transfer of the use of the term predator from pop culture to law coincided with the exponential accumulation of research in the area of psychopathy, sexual deviancy, and violent crime.

Criminological theory, typologies of crime, and notions of the nature and dynamics of particular types of offenders have played a sidelining role in the historical wax and wane of habitual offender legislation. Public fear, limited resources, and community intolerance for persistent criminal behavior have kept habitual offender legislation and the more general notion of selective prosecution and incapacitation alive for over a century. The community protection approach to dealing with sex offenders that has developed in the United States and Canada since the mid-1980s has been primarily influenced by advocacy-group pressure, public fear, and political expedience rather than by a solid body of social science research. However, theory and research on the nature and dynamics of career criminality, predatory violence, sex offending, paraphilia, and treatment amenability for certain types of offenders has made its way into Supreme Court decisions and legislation.

Recent U.S. Supreme Court rulings have supported habitual offender, civil commitment, and sex offender registration legislation, giving attention to the ways in which certain types of offenders (persistent, predatory, sex offenders) differ from other types of offenders. In response to the 2003 U.S. Supreme Court rulings that upheld persistent offender, civil commitment, and sex offender registration legislation, legal analyst Andre Cohen commented, "This is a ruling that recognizes that there is a difference between sex offenders and other criminals and that there is a need to treat offenders differently AFTER they have served time for their crimes in comparison to other convicted criminals" ("Court Allows States to Throw the Book," 2003).

However, an attempt to pass a severe "one strike" law against habitual sex offenders in Washington State failed when proponents were unable to obtain the necessary 225,000 signatures (organizers obtained 203,000 signatures, 85% from eastern Washington, with little support in western Washington and Seattle) (Sims, 2006). The law was named "Dylan's law" after Dylan Groene, who was abducted, raped, and murdered by Joseph Duncan in May 2005 in the Pacific Northwest. Duncan, who had previously served 14 years in prison for sexually assaulting children in Washington State and had been diagnosed in 1980 as a sexual deviant with antisocial personality, abducted and raped Shasta and Dylan Groene after murdering the children's mother, brother, and mother's boyfriend in their Idaho home. Dylan was murdered and Shasta was found alive with Duncan in Montana 6 weeks after the abduction. The founder of the Citizen's for One Strike Law in Washington argued:

> We can not rehabilitate evil like those who make a living in the predator industrial complex want to convince us to believe is possible—NO! We must take dominion over this evil! Evil by its very nature can not be rehabilitated and it must be controlled otherwise it runs wild and controls us. That is exactly why we are now facing an epidemic of sexual terrorism.

This means we must continue this battle until we have pushed evil back into the pit it so rightfully belongs! (Oetting, 2006)

Dylan's law called for life without the possibility of parole for violent and predatory sex crimes including rape, kidnapping, child molestation, and sexual homicide.

Though Dylan's law as well as other current and previous habitual offender legislation draw on theory and research on the nature and dynamics of predatory sex crimes to support the need to incarcerate and civilly commit sexual predators, habitual offender laws in the past have fallen short of meeting their goal of containing the worst of the worst. Sherman et al. (1997) concluded, in a National Institute of Justice report to the U.S. Congress, that "It is not yet possible to predict who will be the high frequency offenders in the future; therefore targeting them for increased prison sentences is impossible." The problem hinges on the ability to identify and select the most dangerous offenders among the large number of offenders who leave prison to return to society every day.

Predicting Dangerousness and Violent Risk Assessment

Sexually violent predator/civil commitment laws represent an attempt to use both criminal history and psychological assessment to determine whether or not an individual meets the definition of a sexually violent predator. Habitual offender laws are loosely rooted (and often politically justified) by discourse, theory, and research on career criminality and criminal behavior. The ultimate goal of civil commitment and habitual offender legislation is public safety. However, attempts to selectively incapacitate the "right" offenders have historically been unsuccessful. The laws have resulted in the long-term incapacitation of habitual felons who commit crimes of minor social consequence but are easily caught. Some argue that the laws impose life terms for unsuccessful low-level persistent felons, which some have called a "progressive tax on stupidity" (Zimring, Hawkins, & Kamin, 2001, p. 4) rather than a public safety mechanism. The horrific crimes committed by Joseph Duncan against the Groene family after he had been released from a lengthy period of incarceration for sex crimes against children illustrate the need for a means to accurately predict who will and who will not be a danger to the public in making release decisions. Even with civil commitment and one, two, and three strikes legislation, 93% of all prison inmates will eventually be released (Petersilia, 2003).

The term *prediction of dangerousness* generally refers to (1) the prediction of general and violent recidivism and (2) the identification of conditions under which an offender is likely to commit a crime or to behave aggressively or violently. Theory and research on criminal behavior and offender types play an important role in determining which individual offenders will and will not recidivate. A primary assumption at the root of social policy regarding offenders and public safety is that certain characteristics of an individual offender are related to future criminal conduct—"if all the variance in criminal conduct were attributed to measurement error and the environment, and none of the variance were accounted for by individual characteristics, the occurrence of crime could never be affected by decisions about the institutionalization of individual offenders" (Quinsey, Harris, Rice, & Cormier, 1998, p. 27). This notion that individual offenders and types of offenders differ in their risk for future dangerousness forms the basis on which the courts rely on research, theory, and expert testimony of psychologists, psychiatrists, criminologists, and other behavioral scientists to assist in determining who is and who is not dangerous.

Dangerousness prediction comes into play in a range of criminal justice decisions from pretrial release, juvenile transfers to adult court, sentencing, civil commitment, and capital sentencing to correctional classification and treatment and parole or offender reentry. The following are examples of cases that have involved dangerousness assessment by the court:

- After leading officers on a 7-mile chase and nearly running over two officers, a 69-year-old Marshfield man was arrested and charged with his seventh drunken driving offense, assault and battery of a police officer with a dangerous weapon, and resisting arrest. A judge ordered the man held without bail to await a dangerousness hearing ("Repeat Offender Arrested for the 7th Time," 2006).

- A 16-year-old high school student was arrested for setting a fire that damaged a strip of businesses. The student was arraigned on counts of burning a building and injuring a firefighter during commission of a crime. The youth, who had a long history of similar offenses, was held without bail pending a dangerousness hearing (Block, 2006).

- Ohio prisoners can be transferred to supermax prison facilities based on past misconduct and a determination of future dangerousness. In 2005, the state law was challenged based on failure to provide prisoners adequate notice and explanation. In a U.S. Supreme Court decision upholding the law, Justice Sandra Day O'Connor protested: "I mean, this is a prison classification, for goodness' sake!" (McGough, 2005, A6).

- A repeat sex offender raped an elderly woman at a railway station one month after he was released from confinement. The offender has prior sex offenses dating back over 20 years, including rape, attempted rape, and false imprisonment. At adjudication, the judge weighed the offenders risk of future dangerousness against the deprivation of the offender's liberty and determined there was evidence to suggest that the offender's recidivist behavior could be broken and imposed a sentence in which the offender would be released in his 50s as opposed to an indefinite sentence in which the offender would be unlikely to ever be released (Giles, 1995).

- A 25-year-old offender was convicted of murder in Texas in 1986 for killing a man in a gunfight as the offender was trying to kidnap the victim's girlfriend. An expert witness testified that the offender presented substantial risk of further violent acts. The Texas capital punishment statute requires that risk for future dangerousness be established for imposition of the death sentence. The offender was sentenced to death as a direct result of psychiatric testimony on his future dangerousness. Years later, his attorneys appealed his sentence, arguing that the psychiatric testimony was wrong using the offender's prison record of minor infractions to show that he is not dangerous. However, the sentence was upheld and the offender was convicted (Liptak, 2004).

States differ in how and where prediction of dangerousness may be introduced to the court (e.g., some states do not allow dangerousness evaluations to be made as part of the bail/pretrial detention decision process or in capital sentencing decisions); however, since the 1970s, the courts have increasingly relied on expert testimony on an offender's likelihood for future dangerousness in a range of decision points in the criminal and civil justice process.

The use of expert testimony in imposing the death penalty has been consistently upheld by the courts. In the landmark case *Barefoot v. Estelle* (1980), the U.S. Supreme Court rejected the defendant's claim that psychiatrists as a group are incompetent to predict dangerousness to a degree of scientific certainty. This decision has been much criticized. Ewing (1983) calls for a ban on psychological and psychiatric predictions of dangerousness in capital sentencing proceedings. Regnier (2004) suggests that current standards of scientific admissibility do not support the inclusion of expert predictions of future dangerousness and argues, "If 'due process' means anything it should mean that one may not be put to death based on speculation about his future conduct, no matter how reasonable the speculation" (p. 502).

Attempts to clinically predict dangerousness began in the 1970s in response to deinstitutionalization of the mentally ill. Predictions of dangerousness have predominantly been based on clinical evaluation, but in recent years actuarial predictors have been developed and are considered more accurate than clinical prediction. Studies show that clinical prediction is still prevalent despite development and standardization of actuarial predictors of risk and recidivism. Actuarial risk assessment tools developed by Canadian researchers have shown great promise. In the last decade, risk assessment has made significant strides and the tools available, based on a large body of theory and research, can predict the likelihood of a new offense with a degree of accuracy that cannot compare to clinical judgment. These new risk assessment tools have important implications for policy because they offer policymakers a tool with which to effectively, realistically, and cost-effectively distinguish among offenders based on level of risk (Lieb, 2000).

Risk Assessment Instruments

Since the 1980s, researchers have directed their attention to the development and standardization of risk assessment instruments. Initial success of risk prediction instruments was used to justify risk-based legislation in the United States and Canada (Hanson, 2005), and the 1990s habitual offender and civil commitment laws in the United States and dangerous offender designations in Canada were driven by the notion that tools existed that could accurately predict who would and who would not reoffend. Some researchers argue that clinical judgment should be completely replaced with actuarial methods of predicting dangerousness and criminal risk (Quinsey et al., 1998), in other words, that violence prediction based on assessing an individual for factors that have been statistically associated with recidivism is far superior to the long-used method of clinical judgment, which is fraught with flaws and human error.

Progress in violence risk assessment can be attributed to actuarial instruments that are now used on a wide scale in the United States and Canada developed by three groups of Canadian researchers—Robert Hare and his colleagues at the University of British Columbia; Don Andrews and James Bonta from Ontario; and Vern Quinsey, Grant Harris, Marnie Rice, and their colleagues from the Mental Health Centre Penetanguishene, Ontario. These researchers are responsible for the development of the *Psychopathy Checklist–Revised* (1990, 2001),[11] *Level of Service Inventory–Revised* (LSI-R) (Andrews & Bonta, 1995), *Violence Risk Appraisal Guide* (VRAG), and *Sex*

Offender Risk Appraisal Guide (SORAG) (Quinsey et al., 1998). Robert Hare's research on the PCL-R produced the first big successes in violence risk prediction; Harris, Rice, and Quinsey documented how common clinical variables could be used to empirically predict recidivism; and Andrews and Bonta's work emphasized the need to differentiate between different types of risk factors (Hanson, 2005).

The LSI-R, VRAG, PCL-R, and variations of these instruments are currently being used by the courts and departments of corrections in Canada and the United States to make critical pretrial detainment, correctional management, and release decisions.[12] The *Self-Appraisal Questionnaire,* an empirically based, theoretically and rationally derived risk assessment tool that is self-administered (and easier and less costly to use) and shows adequate predictive validity has also recently been developed (Loza & Green, 2003). Other instruments have been developed in the last 15 years including the *Historical, Clinical, Risk-20 (HCR-20)* developed by Webster, Douglas, Eaves, and Hart (1997) and instruments developed for use with specialized populations such as wife assaulters, young offenders, and sex offenders (Hanson, 2005; Table 11.1). These instruments represent a new wave of theoretically derived and empirically validated risk assessment tools that have important implications for criminal justice practice.

❖ Table 11.1   Actuarial Instruments Used in the Forensic Assessment of Future Dangerousness

Psychopathy Checklist–Revised (PCL-R) (Hare, 1991, 2003)	20-Item Checklist designed to measure the clinical construct of psychopathy. Consists of Factor 1 items reflecting interpersonal/affective features and Factor 2 items reflecting antisocial/lifestyle features. Each of the 20 items is scored on a 0- to 2-point scale. The score is the sum of the 20 items with total score range from 0 to 40 points. Items scored based on interview with offender and institutional file information.
Violence Risk Appraisal Guide (VRAG) (Quinsey, Harris, Rice, & Cormier, 1998)	12-Item scale for male offenders who have committed serious, violent (including sexual) offenses. Items include lived with both biological parents, elementary school maladjustment, history of alcohol problems, marital status, criminal history score for nonviolent offenses using, failure on prior conditional release, age at time of offense, victim injury, female victim, meets *DSM-III* criteria for personality disorder, meets *DSM-III* criteria for schizophrenia, PCL-R score. Scored based on review of a comprehensive psychosocial history including information gathered from third parties and review of records. Give statistical probability from 0 to 100% that an offender will violently or sexually violently recidivate.

(Continued)

(Continued)

Sex Offender Risk Appraisal Guide (SORAG) (Quinsey, Harris, Rice, & Cormier, 1998)	14-Item scale for male offenders who have committed sexual offenses. Includes items on the VRAG + phallometric test results, number of previous convictions for sexual offenses, history of sex offenses only against girls under 14. Scored based on review of a comprehensive psychosocial history including information gathered from third parties and review of records. Give statistical probability from 0 to 100% that an offender will violently or sexually violently recidivate.
Level of Service Inventory-Revised (Andrews & Bonta, 1995, 2001, 2003)	54-Item instrument that includes a range of risk factors associated with criminal conduct. The 54 items on the LSI-R are answered with a Yes/No or 0–3 rating and measure offender risk, needs, and responsivity factors. The content of the LSI-R reflects the recidivism literature, professional opinions of community corrections officers, and the social learning theory of criminal behavior.
Historical, Clinical, Risk-20 (HCR-20) (Webster, Douglas, Eaves, & Hart, 1995, 1997)	20-Item instrument that includes 10 historical items (e.g., severity and frequency of previous violence, young age at first violent incident, history of serious, acute mental illness, psychopathy assessed by the PCL-R, prior supervision failure), 5 clinical items (e.g., lack of insight, negative attitudes, active symptoms of major mental illness), and risk management items (lack of personal support, stress, exposure to destabilizers).
Sexual Violence Risk-20 (SVR-20) (Boer, Hart, Kropp, & Webster, 1997)	20-Item scale developed specifically for assessing risk of sexual violence. Variant of the HCR-20. Items include psychosocial adjustment items (e.g., sexual deviation, victim of child abuse, psychopathy, major mental illness), sexual offense items (e.g., multiple sex offense types, physical harm to victim in sex offenses, escalation in frequency or severity of sex offenses), and future plans items (lacks realistic plans, negative attitude toward intervention).
Rapid Risk Assessment for Sexual Offender Recidivism (RRASOR) (Hanson, 1997)	4-Item instrument designed to measure sex offender recidivism. Items include prior sex offenses, age at release from period of incarceration, victim gender, and relationship to victim. The score is the sum of the 4 items with total score range from 0 to 6 points.

Structured Anchored Clinical Judgment-Minimum (SACJ-Min) (Thornton, see Prentky & Burgess, 2000)	9-Item clinical rating scale including male victim, never married, noncontact sex offenses, stranger victims, any current sex offense, any current nonsexual violent offense, any prior nonsexual violent offense, and four or more prior sentencing occasions.
Minnesota Sex Offender Screening Tool (MnSOST-R) (Epperson et al., 2003)	16-Item scale developed for the Minnesota Department of Corrections. Items include number of sex-related convictions, length of sex offending history, number of different age groups victimized, age at release from institution, drug/alcohol abuse, sex offender treatment while incarcerated, chemical dependency treatment while incarcerated.
Static 99 (Hanson & Thornton, 1999)	10-Item scale combining items from the RRASOR and SACJ-Min. Items 1 to 5 are coded using archival data. Items 6 to 10 are coded using all available information including self-report, collateral reports, and victim statements.
Sex Predator Risk Assessment Screening Instrument (English, 1999)	Composed of 4 Parts: defining sexual assault crimes, relationship to victim, sex offender risk scale, mental abnormality (as measured by a 30+ score on the PCL-R or 18+ on the Psychopathy Checklist: Screening version or 85+ on MCMI-3 narcissistic, antisocial, and paranoid scales).
Self-Appraisal Questionnaire (Loza & Green, 2003)	A 72-Item self-report risk-need measure designed to cover predictive content areas demonstrated to be reliable and valid for the assessment and prediction of postrelease offending. Items are true/false and make up eight subscales: Criminal Tendencies, Antisocial Personality Problems, Conduct Problems, Criminal History, Alcohol and/or Drug Abuse, Antisocial Associates, Anger, and Validity subscales. The number of items used in the prediction of recidivism is 67 out of the total number of the 72 SAQ items. The Validity subscale can be used to validate offenders' truthfulness in responding to the SAQ's items.
Abel Assessment for Sexual Interest (Abel et al., 1994)	Computerized test used to identify sexual interest by presenting slides of nude people in different age ranges.

Level of Service Inventory–Revised (LSI-R)

The *LSI-R* (Andrews & Bonta, 1995, 2001) is an objective offender assessment instrument designed by Canadian researchers Don Andrews and James Bonta to identify dynamic areas of offender risk and needs that may be addressed in programming and to assist in the implementation of least restrictive criminal sanctions. The LSI-R is the most widely used and best validated measure of general criminal recidivism (Hanson, 2005). The instrument systematically compiles risk and needs information important to offender treatment planning. The LSI-R is composed of 54 items that sample a range of risk factors associated with criminal conduct supported by theory, empirical research, and professional opinion. The 54 items on the LSI-R are answered with a yes/no or 0–3 rating. The content of the LSI-R reflects the recidivism literature, professional opinions of community corrections officers, and the social learning theory of criminal behavior (LSI-R, 2001).

The LSI-R is based on theory and research reviewed in detail in Andrews and Bonta's (2003, 2006) *The Psychology of Criminal Conduct,* which forms the basis of a general personality and social psychology of criminal conduct. This psychology of criminal conduct (PCC) acknowledges the complexity of human behavior and the variation in criminal behavior. Different offenders have different backgrounds, experiences, and needs and the number, nature, and interaction of these characteristics produce different levels of offender risk. According to Andrews and Bonta (2003),

> there are substantial individual differences in criminal conduct. People differ in their frequency of criminal activity and in the number, type, and variety of criminal acts in which they engage. In addition, while accounting for a disproportionate amount of total criminal activity, the more criminally active offenders tend not to be specialists. (p. 428)

The large body of theory and research on which the LSI-R is based has led to a consensual understanding of the concepts in the analysis of criminal conduct and the correlates of criminal behavior.

Key criminal behavior correlates have been identified, and empirical research has shown that certain factors play a larger or smaller role and have weaker or stronger predictive validity. Based on this research, major and minor factors are associated with criminal behavior:

- *Major factors* (characteristics strongly correlated with criminal behavior):
  - Antisocial attitudes, beliefs, values
  - Procriminal associates/interpersonal supports for crime (and the absence of prosocial support/isolation from individuals who do not condone criminal behavior)
  - Personality factors conducive to criminal behavior (e.g., psychopathy, below-average verbal intelligence, impulsivity, weak self-control, propensity for risk-taking/thrill-seeking, etc.)
  - History of antisocial behavior from childhood involving a number of types of antisocial acts in different settings

- Familial factors (criminality, mental illness, poor parental supervision, neglect and abuse, low levels of affection, etc.)

- Low levels of personal educational, vocational, and financial achievement and unstable employment

- *Minor factors* (characteristics that have a weaker association with criminal behavior):

  - Lower-class origins

  - Personal distress

  - Biological/neuropsychological factors

These factors are measured through the 54 items of the LSI-R and are grouped into the following subcomponents (with the number of items listed in parentheses):

- Criminal History (10)

- Education/Employment (10)

- Financial (2)

- Family/Marital (4)

- Accommodation (3)

- Leisure/Recreation (2)

- Companions (5)

- Alcohol/Drug Problems (9)

The LSI-R is administered through an interview and review of institutional file information. The lowest possible score is 0 and the highest is 54. A score of 41+ is associated with high risk/need, 34–40 with medium risk/need, 24–33 with moderate risk/need, 14–23 with low to moderate risk/need, and 0–13 with low risk/need.

A meta-analysis of predictors of adult offender recidivism conducted by Gendreau, Little, and Goggin (1996) found that the LSI-R was the most useful actuarial measure compared with other popular offender risk and antisocial personality scales (e.g., MMPI) and the PCL-R in particular (Gendreau, Goggin, & Smith, 2002). However, several states that have used the LSI-R have found that the instrument is a moderate predictor of recidivism (and a weak predictor of sex offense recidivism) that can be enhanced by using a more succinct version such as the LSI-R Screening Version (LSI-SV; Austin, Coleman, Peyton, & Johnson, 2003) or by adding other measures of offender risk that specifically measure recidivism of violent felonies (Washington State Institute for Public Policy, 2003, February 2006).

Violence Risk Appraisal Guide (VRAG) and Sex Offender Risk Appraisal Guide (SORAG)

The *Violence Risk Appraisal Guide (VRAG)* and the *Sex Offender Risk Appraisal Guide (SORAG)* are actuarial instruments that predict violent recidivism based on the statistical probability (from 0 to 100%) that an offender will violently (or sexually violently) reoffend. The VRAG is for male offenders who have committed serious, violent (including sexual) offenses. The SORAG is for male offenders who have committed sexual offenses. The VRAG was developed based on 25 years of research at the Oak Ridge Division of the Mental Health Care Center, a maximum security psychiatric hospital in Penetanguishene, Ontario. The instrument has been touted as the most accurate risk assessment instrument available (Quinsey et al., 1998), which predicts violent recidivism better than the LSI-R.

The VRAG and SORAG are scored based on review of a comprehensive psychosocial history including information gathered from third parties and review of records. The VRAG consists of 12 variables found to be highly independently correlated with violent recidivism:

1. PCL-R score

2. Elementary school maladjustment score

3. Meets criteria for DSM personality disorder

4. Age at time of index offense

5. Separation from either parent (except by death) under age 16

6. Failure on prior conditional release

7. Cormier-Lang Criminal History score for nonviolent offenses

8. Never married

9. Meets DSM criteria for schizophrenia

10. Most serious victim injury

11. Alcohol abuse score

12. Female victim in index offense (Quinsey et al., 1998, p. 147)

The SORAG was developed specifically for use with sex offenders, to predict the likelihood of sexual recidivism. Research suggests that the SORAG predicts sexual recidivism with the same accuracy as, if not better than, the VORAG predicts violent recidivism (Quinsey et al., 1998). The SORAG consists of the following 14 factors:

1. PCL-R score

2. Elementary school maladjustment score

3. Lived with genetic parents until age 16 (except separation by death from natural causes)

4. Cormier-Lang Criminal History score for nonviolent offenses

5. Cormier-Lang criminal history score for violent offenses

6. Number previous convictions for sex offense

7. History of sex offenses against male children or adults

8. Never married

9. Age at time of index offense (negatively scored)

10. Failure on prior conditional release

11. Phallometrically determined sexual deviancy score

12. Meets criteria for DSM criteria for any personality disorder

13. Meets DSM criteria for schizophrenia (negatively scored)

14. Alcohol abuse history score (Quinsey et al., 1998, p. 157)

The items on the VRAG and SORAG are scored from −5 to +5, representing ±5% above/below the base rate or mean overall violent recidivism rate. The VRAG and SORAG are not commercially available instruments (as are the PCL-R and the LSI-R); however, the scoring criteria are presented in detail in Quinsey, Harris, Rice, and Cormier's (1998) *Violent Offenders: Appraising and Managing Risk*. Additionally, the ability of the VRAG and SORAG to predict violent recidivism in female offenders remains questionable since studies have not yet validated the instrument with female populations.

Research on the VRAG and SORAG has shown that the tools are much more accurate predictors of violent and sexual recidivism than clinical judgment. The VRAG and the SORAG are based on theory and research that has empirically identified factors statistically linked to criminal behavior. These instruments represent the application of theory and research to the practice of actuarial prediction. Quinsey, Harris, Rice, and Cormier (1998) reflect on their work since the 1970s in violent offender research:

> It never occurred to us then that solutions to the etiological problems associated with violent offending might actually be found, not in the distant future, but within our own lifetimes. We now think of theories of violent offending not as things that one gathers data "about" but as things that can be put to a definitive test. (p. 235)

Psychopathy Checklist–Revised (PCL-R)

The *PCL-R* (Hare, 1991, 2003) is a 20-item checklist developed by Robert Hare to measure the construct of psychopathy. The PCL-R is the first reliable and valid measure of psychopathy offering researchers a long-awaited tool with which to empirically study and clinically assess psychopathy (Hare, 1993). Each item of the PCL-R is scored on a 0 to 2–point scale based on information obtained through interview and review of an offender's institutional file. Particular items on the checklist represent Factor 1 (personality traits) and Factor 2 (behavioral symptoms). A score of 30 to 40 is generally associated with primary psychopathy, a score of 20 to 29 with secondary psychopathy, and 0 to 19 with the absence of psychopathy, though there has been extensive discourse and debate regarding whether or not psychopathy is a taxon or a dimensional construct (Edens & Petrila, 2006).

The 20 PCL-R items measure the behaviors and personality traits central to the construct of psychopathy. The PCL-R is composed of two factors that are correlated with each other (0.56 in prison inmates and 0.53 in forensic patients; see Hare, Hart, & Harpur, 1991). Factor 1 reflects core personality features of the condition and is considered to infer interpersonal style. Factor 1 is positively correlated with clinical ratings of psychopathy, prototypicality ratings of narcissistic and histrionic personality disorder, and self-report measures of Machiavellianism and narcissism, and is negatively correlated with measures of empathy and anxiety (Hare, 1991; Harpur, Hare, & Hakstian, 1989; Hart & Hare, 1989). Factor 2 reflects chronically unstable and antisocial lifestyle and is considered to be a measure of social deviance. It is positively correlated with criminal behaviors, socioeconomic background, self-report measures of socialization and antisocial behavior, and diagnosis of APD (Hare, 1991; Harpur et al., 1989). Items 11 and 17 are not included in the definition of the factors. Following are the 20 PCL-R items:

1. Glibness/superficial charm (*Factor 1*)
2. Grandiose sense of self-worth (*Factor 1*)
3. Need for stimulation/proneness to boredom (*Factor 1*)
4. Pathological lying (*Factor 1*)
5. Conning/manipulative (*Factor 1*)
6. Lack of remorse or guilt (*Factor 1*)
7. Shallow affect (*Factor 1*)
8. Callous/lack of empathy (*Factor 1*)
9. Parasitic lifestyle (*Factor 2*)
10. Poor behavioral controls (*Factor 2*)
11. Promiscuous sexual behavior
12. Early behavioral problems (*Factor 2*)
13. Lack of realistic, long-term goals (*Factor 2*)
14. Impulsivity (*Factor 2*)
15. Irresponsibility (*Factor 2*)
16. Failure to accept responsibility for actions (*Factor 1*)
17. Many short-term marital relationships
18. Juvenile delinquency (*Factor 2*)
19. Revocation of conditional release (*Factor 2*)
20. Criminal versatility (*Factor 2*; added in the second edition of the PCL-R; Hare, 2003)

The construct of psychopathy reflects the relationship between personality traits and behavioral symptoms and the importance of understanding the condition as a unitary syndrome composed of two distinct underlying mechanisms. The factor structure of the PCL-R has been referred to as the most important example of factorial studies of assessment measures that has contributed to great progress in science and practice. Specifically, the decomposition of psychopathy into two factors—affective/ interpersonal and impulsive/antisocial—has led to an "explosion of meaningful external correlates," and evidence is growing that the risk for reactive violence is related to low levels of restraint associated with impulsivity factor (Kamphuis & Emmelkamp, 2005, p. 171).

Recent research conducted by Hare and his colleagues supports a four-factor model of psychopathy with items representing four distinct dimensions of the psychopathy construct. Based on this research, the construct of psychopathy reflects the covariation of the four factors—interpersonal, affective, lifestyle, and antisocial (Hare & Neumann, 2006).

1. *Interpersonal:*

    Item 1—Glibness/superficial charm

    Item 2—Grandiose sense of self-worth

    Item 4—Pathological lying

    Item 5—Conning/manipulative

2. *Affective:*

    Item 6—Lack of remorse or guilt

    Item 7—Shallow affect

    Item 8—Callous/lack of empathy

    Item 16—Failure to accept responsibility

3. *Lifestyle:*

    Item 3—Need for stimulation/proneness to boredom

    Item 14—Impulsivity

    Item 15—Irresponsibility

    Item 9—Parasitic lifestyle

    Item 13—Lack of realistic, long-term goals

4. *Antisocial:*

    Item 10—Poor behavioral controls

    Item 12—Early behavioral problems

    Item 18—Juvenile delinquency

    Item 19—Revocation of conditional release

    Item 20—Criminal versatility

Individuals who score high on the set of items that make up one factor, but not other factors, would not score high enough on the checklist as a whole to be considered a psychopath.

A large body of research has accumulated to support the use of the PCL-R as a risk prediction instrument. The PCL-R is a valid and reliable measure of psychopathy that is a strong predictor of general and violent recidivism (Gacono, 2000; Hare, 1991, 2003; Harris et al., 1991; Hart, 1998; Hemphill et al., 1998, Hodgins, 1997; Laurell & Dåderman, 2005; Litwack & Schlesinger, 1998; Salekin, Rogers, & Sewell, 1996; Serin & Amos, 1995) and a determinant of high criminogenic offender risk/needs (Simourd & Hodge, 2000). The PCL-R has gained widespread attention and is now used at various stages of the criminal justice system in Canada and the United States (Hare, 1998). As discussed in Chapter 4, the relationship between psychopathy and violent risk is so empirically strong that psychopathy has been referred to as the most important construct in the criminal justice system and unparalleled as a risk assessment tool (Hare, 1998). Although debate and discussion continues over whether the LSI-R or PCL-R better predicts general recidivism, and use of the PCL-R as a risk assessment tool has been criticized given it was not developed for this purpose (Gendreau, Goggin, & Smith, 2002), the PCL-R has a "well deserved reputation as the most reliable and valid measure of the clinical construct of psychopathy" and "one aspect of its validity is the ability to predict violence in an unusually wide variety of populations and contexts" (Hemphill & Hare, 2004, p. 237). In one of the most recent literature reviews of the research on psychopathy and criminal recidivism Douglas, Vincent, and Edens (2006) state:

> With some disclaimers, it is fair to state that psychopathy is an important and meaningful risk factor for subsequent antisocial behavior of many types, across many contexts, by many different types of people. In fact, the field may have reached asymptote in terms of novel information to be gleaned from studies that simply address the question whether an association exists between psychopathy and recidivism. (p. 548)

Issues in Violence Risk Assessment

There are a number of issues to consider in violence risk assessment. First, *it is more accurate to identify the predictors of behavior than to predict whether or not a behavior will occur in the future.* Actuarial violence risk instruments determine statistical probability of risk based on identifying risk factors that are known to be statistically associated with recidivism. If Offender A comes from an unstable family background, has a low level of education, possesses an antisocial attitude, is unemployed and homeless, has antisocial friends, and so on, he is more likely to reoffend than Offender B, who comes from a stable background, has a high level of education and predominantly prosocial friends, is employed, and owns a house. However, just because Offender A possesses a high number of risk factors for future dangerousness it does not mean he will reoffend, nor does the lack of such risk factors mean Offender B will not reoffend.

The ultimate goal in offender risk assessment is predictive accuracy. Judges, juries, correctional administrators and staff, and parole/indeterminate sentencing review boards are charged with making decisions based on accurate determination of the likelihood of reoffense for individual offenders and groups of offenders at every stage of the criminal justice process, from pretrial detention to sentencing to releases. Wrong decisions can have disastrous and tragic consequences when parolees violently reoffend, enormous personal consequences for offenders who are confined for longer periods or in a more restrictive custodial environment than necessary, and economic impact (e.g., cost of incarceration, settlements in civil wrongful death cases) on governmental agencies that over-incarcerate low-risk offenders or under-incarcerate high-risk offenders.

Recidivism prediction can result in one of four possibilities:

True Positive: Offender predicted to reoffend and does—**CORRECT**

True Negative: Offender predicted not to reoffend and does not—**CORRECT**

False Positive: Offender predicted to reoffend and does not—**INCORRECT**

False Negative: Offender predicted not to reoffend and does—**INCORRECT**

The goal of risk prediction is to maximize true positives and true negatives and minimize false positives and false negatives. False positives and false negatives are called *decision errors* (Figure 11.1).

Risk assessment involves a tradeoff between false positives and false negatives. The more stringent the criteria used to predict dangerousness (e.g., a score of 30+ on the PCL-R, 41+ on the LSI-R, 28+ on the VRAG), the greater the chance of being right when predicting an offender will reoffend (true positive) and of being wrong when predicting an offender will not reoffend (false negative). However, the lower the criteria used to predict dangerousness, the greater the chance of being wrong when predicting an offender will reoffend (false positive) but right when predicting an offender will not reoffend (true negative). Ultimately, then, risk prediction is a balancing act between false positives and false negatives that pits due process (offenders' rights) against crime control (public safety) objectives (see Hart, 1998; Serin & Brown, 2000, for discussion of decision errors associated with use of PCL-R cutoff scores) and

❖ **Figure 11.1**   Decision Errors in Violence Risk Prediction

research suggests that we cannot yet predict violent recidivism without a high false positive rate (Martinez, 1997) that would be unacceptable to most civil libertarians.

Furthermore, even though research has shown that violence risk instruments predict violence with moderate accuracy, we do not know exactly what they are measuring. Furthermore, some argue that actuarial prediction may be counterproductive to crime reduction goals, aggravate social disparities, and distort conceptions of just punishment (see Harcourt, 2007, for review and analysis of problems with actuarial approach and impact on civil liberties, racial disparity, crime, and public safety). One view is that the instruments differentiate a high-risk criminal subgroup or antisocial taxon from normal offenders. Another position is that the instruments identify correlated, but conceptually distinct, risk factors that reflect a continuum of risk potential (Hanson, 2005). Which position an evaluator takes has important implication for conditional release, management, and treatment of offenders. If the view is that the instruments differentiate a high-risk criminal subgroup, this provides rationale for habitual offender legislation that restricts the liberty of offenders designated by the instruments as "dangerous." In contrast, if the view is that the instruments identify where an individual currently sits on the continuum of risk, the assessment may be used to determine an appropriate treatment strategy with promise for change. Reconciling these contrasting positions is important, particularly in sorting out ethical objections to the use of violence prediction instruments that assess static factors that essentially designate a high scorer as being incapable of change.

Research on violence risk assessment has led to the recognition that no single variable or constellation of variables can be said to be the cause of violence. In civil cases involving clinicians who have treated individuals who have gone on to commit violent acts, the courts have generally held that impulsive acts of violence are unforeseeable (Beck, 1998). According to Monahan et al. (2001), who conducted the *Macarthur Study of Mental Disorder and Violence,* the accumulation of risk factors produces the propensity for violence and no one risk factor is necessary or sufficient for a person to behave aggressively toward others. People will be violent by virtue of the presence of different sets of risk factors. There is no single path in a person's life that leads to an act of violence:

> Actuarial assessments of risk can be used to identify the most dangerous sex offenders. Criteria can be set in such a manner that very few false positives occur. It must be recognized, however, that actuarial instruments (or any other method) cannot identify all dangerous sex offenders without an unacceptably high false positive rate. (Monahan et al., 2001, p. 142)

However, the reality of the criminal justice system is that decisions have to be made every day to ensure public safety and administer justice. Though science may not be at a point where it can say, with 100% (or even 50%) certainty, that dangerousness can be predicted, the law is charged with administering justice and protecting the public with whatever information science can provide in the here and now.

Factors that predict dangerousness differ with respect to offense types (Beck & Shipley, 1989; Schwaner, 1998). Schwaner found that predictors of violent recidivism in a cohort of parolees differed across offense type and other key variables. The study made the following findings:

- Violent offenders are less likely to recidivate than nonviolent offenders (20.6% to 25.7%).

- Of the violent offender recidivists, 43.7% return for another violent offense.

- Predictors of violent recidivism include race, prior felony conditions, younger age at arrest, past parole/probation revocations, past violent commitments, release before age 25.

- Factors related to violent specialization are race, county of commitment, time served, age at release, prior felony convictions, prior probation/parole revocations.

- The profile of a violent repeat offender is a young Black male from an urban area, younger than 25 at time of release with history of parole failures.

- Time served appears to be a factor in violent reoffending—the more time, the more likely to reoffend (contrary to deterrence theory).

Although a large body of research supports the use of actuarial predictors of recidivism over clinical judgment, Schwaner's research suggests that contextual factors that cannot be explained by existing statistical models appear to better explain violent reoffense and interdisciplinary theories of criminal behavior and multiple methods, including qualitative assessment of the context of recidivism, should be used in conjunction with actuarial predictors.

Another issue to keep in mind in thinking about the application of criminological theory to risk assessment is that *causation and explanation are not the same as prediction.* Factors that have been identified as causes of or explanatory factors for criminal behavior (biological, psychological, sociological, situational, phenomenological) help explain, but do not predict criminal behavior. However, research from the various disciplinary perspectives that has shown the statistical association between specific factors (e.g., psychopathy, substance abuse, low socioeconomic status, male gender, antisocial peers, prosocial support, etc.) and criminal behavior is the theoretical and empirical foundation for the actuarial instruments currently in use (e.g., VRAG, LSI-R, PCL-R, HCR-20).

Specialized Courts and Deferred Prosecution: Drugs, Mental Health, DUIs

Specialized courts have been established in recent years to address the needs of offenders whose criminal behavior is the product of substance abuse or mental illness. These courts are based on the notion that mental illness and substance abuse play significant roles in the commission of crime for some offenders and that reducing offense behavior for these offenders requires addressing the underlying substance abuse or mental illness at the root of offending patterns. Drug and mental health courts are based on a *medical model,* rather than a crime control/rational choice model, and the view that these offenders do not freely choose to commit criminal behavior, but their substance abuse or mental illness and the inadequacy of community-based treatment services play primary roles. The medical model views criminal behavior as an illness that requires treatment. If the illness is treated, then offending is likely to be reduced (Grudzinskas et al., 2005).

In recent years there has been a widespread implementation across the United States of specialized criminal courts for defendants with substance abuse and mental health problems. Some jurisdictions have specialized courts for domestic violence offenders and people who are homeless (Tyuse & Linhorst, 2005) and diversion programs targeting persons with mental health, substance abuse, and homelessness issues (Grudzinskas et al., 2005). While substance abuse and mental illness can play a facilitative role in all types of criminal behavior, the offenses committed by offenders with substance abuse and mental health problems tend to be public order crimes. Specialized courts were developed to protect public safety, prevent incarceration, and facilitate community-based treatment for offenders whose criminal behavior is the product of a disease/illness, recognizing that traditional punishment practices have little effect on drug offenders who have an addiction or mentally ill offenders who can't help themselves. Through drug and mental health courts, the offender is diverted or sentenced to treatment rather than incarceration.

Specialized courts operate in different ways in different jurisdictions and can serve offenders presentence as a diversion program or postsentence as an alternative to incarceration. The first drug court was opened in 1989 in Miami, Dade County, and the first court to focus solely on mental health issues was opened in Broward County, Florida, in 1997. The Dade County drug court diverted nonviolent drug offenders at the presentence stage of the criminal justice process to a treatment/ supervision program involving drug testing, close supervision and monitoring, sanctions, and incentives. In some jurisdictions specialized courts are held postsentence with drug court graduates to avoid incarceration or give reduced probation sentences. As of 2002, 1,238 drug courts existed in all 50 states, Washington, DC, Guam, and Puerto Rico; in tribal courts in 14 states; and (based on the U.S. model) in Canada, Great Britain, and Australia. And as of 2004, 98 mental health courts were identified in 33 states (Tyuse & Linhorst, 2005). Research shows that treatment administered through drug courts significantly reduces recidivism compared with other kinds of programs. To date, findings on mental health courts do not show a significant reduction in recidivism (Washington State Institute for Public Policy, January 2006).

In some jurisdictions, deferred prosecution is an option for some types of offenders, such as those charged with driving under the influence (DUI) or driving while intoxicated (DWI); the offender's conviction is deferred for a period of time and will be dismissed if the offender successfully completes treatment. The drug court model has also been applied to DWI offenders. In 1995 in Las Cruces, New Mexico, Municipal Court Judge Stephen Ryan adopted the drug court model for DWI offenders—a court-supervised treatment program for nonalcoholic first- and second-time offenders, alcoholic first- and second-time offenders, and chronic alcoholic DWI offenders, one of the first of its kind in the country (Winfree & Giever, 2000).

Corrections

Classification, Management, Supervision, and Treatment

Theories and research on criminal behavior play an important role in the classification, management, and treatment of offenders in institutional and community corrections. As of 2004, there were 6,996,500 under some form of correctional supervision, with over 2 million incarcerated (1,421,911 in prison, 713,990 in jail, 4,151,125 on probation, and 765,355 on parole). This nearly 7 million people under correctional supervision represents 3.2% of the adult population in the United States—1 in every 31 adults (Glaze & Palla, 2005). Offenders under correctional supervision are a heterogeneous group with a range of needs, risk levels, motivations, support networks, and so on. Correctional agencies classify offenders to ensure that the least restrictive supervision is used, that offenders' needs are met, and that the public is protected, and they rely on classification models grounded in theory and research.

The terms correctional *rehabilitation, treatment, counseling, classification, management,* and *supervision* are often intermixed in research and discourse on offender interventions. Bartol and Bartol (2004) define *correctional rehabilitation* as programs and interventions that encourage prosocial functioning (e.g., anger management, substance abuse treatment, conflict resolution, victim awareness) and *correctional treatment* as therapeutic interventions that target mental health issues and disorders. Schrink (2000) defines *correctional counseling* as "an intensive, purposeful, interactive process between a counselor who is professionally prepared to deal with the special problems posed by a correctional environment and a client who has been found guilty of committing a crime or act of delinquency and placed in a correctional institution, facility, or agency" (pp. 41–42). *Correctional classification* refers to the process by which offenders are matched with the appropriate level of security, supervision, programs, and services (Silverman, 2001). The term *correctional management* generally refers to administrative strategies in housing and supervising offenders, and *correctional supervision* refers to surveillance methods in institutional and community settings (that may or may not be coupled with therapeutic interventions).

Correctional interventions are implemented in institutional and community settings. In prisons, jails, and other custodial settings (e.g., civil commitment facilities), interventions are facilitated by correctional counselors, psychiatric social workers, education specialists, psychologists, psychiatrists, and residential counselors (the title *residential counselor* is used in civil commitment facilities because it is not a correctional setting). In community settings, interventions are administered by community corrections officers, transition counselors (e.g., in work release and halfway houses), and therapists who may be social workers, psychologists, psychiatrists, or master's-level therapists. Most correctional treatment in institutional and community settings is administered by master's-level therapists (Van Voorhis, Braswell, & Lester, 2000) and many counselors in prisons and in community corrections have a bachelor's degree. PhD-level psychologists in prisons are often charged with assessment and evaluation or administrative duties whereas the duties of treatment delivery go to well-trained paraprofessionals. A major problem with administering treatment in correctional settings is maintaining program integrity (Boothby & Clements, 2000).

Correctional Rehabilitation in the United States

Reform and rehabilitation have been a correctional goal since the birth of the prison in the late 18th century. However, rehabilitation was not a primary correctional goal until the 1960s, when the *medical model* was officially implemented in correctional policy and practice. According to the medical model, criminal behavior should be seen as a disease or illness that can be cured through identification and treatment of individual-level characteristics such as social immaturity, psychological disorder, drug or alcohol abuse, illiteracy, and other characteristics and conditions associated with antisocial and criminal behavior. However, throughout most of the 1950s and 1960s, the correctional goal was rehabilitation, with correctional treatment programs showcased in all but the most secure correctional facilities (Van Voorhis et al., 2000). The rehabilitation movement in corrections was an outgrowth of the scientific criminology and penology that emerged in Europe and North America at the end of the 19th century and the focus on social engineering and adjustment in the early 1900s (Garland, 1990). The birth of psychology and psychiatry, the influence of psychodynamic theory in the 1930s, 1940s, and 1950s (e.g., Aichorn, *Wayward Youth*, 1935), publication of the first edition of the *Diagnostic and Statistical Manual of Mental Disorders* in 1957, and the influence of the medical model played roles in the shift in American corrections from the Big House era of the 1930s and 1940s to a focus on rehabilitation and offenders' right to be treated. With advances in psychological theories of criminal behavior, psychologists were eager to apply theory to practice in correctional settings (Hollin, 2004).

Despite the notion of the 1960s as the heyday of correctional rehabilitation, rehabilitation did not flourish even during this time and was abandoned before significant gains could be made, leading some to contend that there has never been a true rehabilitative era in corrections (Gendreau, 1996). By the late 1970s, prisoners' rights advocates and social critics began to question the amount of power psychologists and psychiatrists held and the legal and ethical issues associated with treating offenders in correctional settings. Tensions grew between psychological and criminological schools of thought and between psychological models of offending, rehabilitation through treatment, and the theoretical underpinnings of criminal justice (Hollin, 2004; Van Voorhis et al., 2000). Now classic works such as Kittrie's (1971) *The Right to Be Different,* Szaz's (1974) *The Myth of Mental Illness,* Rothman's (1971) *Discovery of the Asylum,* and Foucault's (1977) *Discipline and Punish* raised concerns regarding the use of the prison as a mechanism of social control, the social construction of mental illness, and the shift of power in corrections from correctional to mental health professionals.

No single work is more responsible for the demise of the correctional rehabilitation era than Martinson's (1974) famous "What Works? Questions and Answers About Prison Reform," published in *The Public Interest.* Robert Martinson was a coinvestigator in a study that reviewed findings of 230 correctional treatment studies (Lipton,

Martinson, & Wilkes, 1975). The Lipton et al. study actually revealed that correctional treatment does work for some offenders under some conditions; however, liberal and conservative politicians took hold of the research findings to argue against rehabilitation as a primary goal of corrections, using powerful antirehabilitation themes (Andrews & Bonta, 2003), with liberals generally arguing that treatment infringed on the rights of offenders and conservatives arguing that rehabilitation was a waste of resources and a soft stance on crime. Martinson himself, ironically, believed that the "nothing works" conclusion would empty most prisons, since they could not be reformed (Sarre, 1999). In 1979, a year before he died, he recanted the "nothing works" conclusion and restated the findings, saying that some treatment programs do show an effect on recidivism (Martinson, 1979).[13]

What Works? Applying Contemporary Theory and Research to Correctional Interventions

In the more than 30 years since the findings of Martinson and his colleagues were published, a large body of research has accumulated on the effectiveness of correctional rehabilitation. A paradigm shift has replaced the nothing works doctrine with *evidence-based corrections,* which emphasize empirically correctional initiatives that are firmly grounded in science, methodological rigor, and focus on what works and what doesn't (Cullen & Gendreau, 2001; Sherman et al., 1997). Results from systematic reviews and meta-analyses have contributed a great deal to our understanding of what works in corrections (Farrington, Petrosino, & Welsh, 2001). Sophisticated meta-analyses conducted since the Lipton, Martinson, and Wilkes's study show that punishment does not reduce recidivism, and when correctional interventions target criminogenic needs and offender risk, and are focus on the relationship between staff and offenders, treatment is effective with many offenders in a range of contexts, reducing recidivism from 40 to 80% (Andrews & Bonta, 2003; Cullen & Gendreau, 2001; Gendreau, Cullen, & Bonta, 1994; Gendreau, Little, & Goggin, 1996; Gendreau & Ross, 1987). Findings from the substantial body of research on prediction and influences of criminal behavior suggest that offending behavior can be substantially reduced through preventive and treatment interventions and that correctional rehabilitation strategies targeting offender risk, need, and responsivity are far superior to variations in official punishment practices (Andrews & Bonta, 2003; Andrews & Dowden, 2006; Dowden & Andrews, 2000, 2004; Dowden, Antonowicz, & Andrews, 2003; Phipps, Korinek, Aos, & Lieb, 1999).

Research on what works and what doesn't work in correctional classification, management, supervision, and treatment has been based on recidivism studies of correctional programs targeting different types of offenders under a range of conditions and correctional contexts. The theoretical foundations of successful correctional interventions draw from different perspectives such as social learning theory, psychoanalytic theory, cognitive-behavioral theory, person-centered/existential-phenomenological approaches (Van Voorhis et al., 2000; Shrum, 2004), with recognition that the strongest approaches in correctional contexts tend to be highly structured cognitive-behavioral approaches. The consensus in the correctional treatment literature is that treatment interventions should be based on a "risk, need, responsivity principle" that acknowledges both the general psychology of criminal conduct and individual differences that contribute to criminal behavior (Andrews & Bonta, 2003; Serin & Kennedy, 1997). Research also shows that identification of risk factors can operate as a correctional classification and programming tool (Clements, 1996) and in correctional management of violent offender populations, reducing the risk for and incidence of violence (Belfrage, Fransson, & Strand, 2004).

Understanding the unique characteristics of some types of offenders such as sex offenders, psychopathic offenders, stalkers, serial killers, spouse abusers, and mentally ill and substance abusing offenders has important implications for correctional supervision and treatment. Successful treatment strategies with these types of extreme and exceptional offenders require targeting one or two variables in treatment such as sexual arousal or predatory aggression. Violence can originate from diverse psychopathological constellations and motivational contexts. For example, effective interventions for narcissistic stalkers are likely to differ from those that would be effective with stalkers with delusional disorders (Kamphuis & Emmelkamp, 2005). Offenders with co-occurring mental health and substance abuse disorders have specialized needs that can be effectively met through evidence-based treatment approaches (Chandler, Peters, Field, & Juliano-Bult, 2004). Spouse abusers are a heterogeneous group including subtypes whose risk characteristics need to be differentially targeted in treatment (Burgess et al., 2001; Dixon & Browne, 2003). Similarly, treatment for sex offenders must target the specific needs of different types of offenders with the understanding, for example, that situational child molesters will have different treatment needs than sadistic rapists. Anger management programs that seek to reduce anger and increase self-control will be more effective with offenders who have low self-control than they will with offenders who have high self-control. Treatment strategies that seek to develop empathy in offenders will not likely be effective with offenders who score high on measures of psychopathic traits. In fact, studies show that such programs can produce the opposite results with psychopaths who tend to show higher rates of recidivism.

Research on sex offenders has accumulated considerably over the last 15 years, with 12,858 academic journal articles published from 1987 to 2001 (Prentky, 2003). Stalans (2004) reviewed recent developments in sex offender assessment and treatment in the community, noting that specialized treatment targeting the risk and needs of different types of sex offenders is the most promising direction in sex offender treatment research. Researchers and clinicians recognize that treatment approach must be directed toward the type of offender (e.g., incest offenders, extrafamilial child molesters, rapists) and different behavioral pathways. Different behavioral pathways addressed in treatment include:

- *Disinhibition:* Sexually deviant urges resulting from stress, anxiety, low self-esteem, and chance contact with potential victims

- *Misregulation:* Sex crimes resulting from maladaptive strategies to control sexually deviant urges such as masturbating to deviant fantasies and the use of pornography, drugs, and alcohol

- *Purposefulness:* Carefully planned, predatory sex crimes facilitated by cognitive distortions such as the view that women deserve or want to be raped

In recent years, research on treatment of sex offenders has switched from focusing on what works to which groups of sex offenders are more likely to benefit from treatment and supervision strategies that have been found to be effective (with some offenders in some contexts). For example, mentally ill, psychopathic, and sadistic sex offenders are not deterred by increased surveillance and monitoring. However, with specialized (intensive) supervision programs, community corrections officers can better detect new sex offenses when they occur, to identify which offenders are best placed in custodial settings (Stalans, 2004).

Cognitive-behavioral therapy for sex offenders in prison and in the community significantly reduce recidivism; however, programs targeting domestic violence victims have not produced success in reducing recidivism (Washington State Institute for Public Policy, February 2006). Prentky (2003) argues that, with this accumulation of research on risk factors for sexual abuse and the pervasive social problem it represents, the problem of sexual coercion should be reframed as a public health issue, with implementation of risk-relevant interventions and risk management (see Prentky, Janus, & Seto, 2003, for comprehensive collection of articles on sex offender theory, research, and public policy).

One of the most important areas of theory and research on criminal behavior with implications for treatment has been the bimodal classification of aggression into predatory and affective categories (Geen & Donnerstein, 1998; McEllistrem, 2004; Meloy, 1988). Raine et al.'s (1998) findings that affective murderers lack prefrontal control over emotion regulation and aggressive impulses, whereas predatory murderers have good prefrontal functioning (Raine et al., 1998), and Woodworth and Porter's (2002) research linking psychopathy and predatory aggression are examples of important work in this area that highlight the need for different treatment strategies for predatory and affectively motivated offenders. A common application of the bimodal classification of aggression to treatment is anger management programs that target offenders with high anger and low self-control and reduce recidivism in impulsively aggressive offenders (Wang & Diamond, 1999). Anger management treatment is less successful with offenders who are instrumental, predatory, or psychopathic, because their violent behavior is generally not emotionally reactive. On the other hand, violent offenders who have low anger control and high anger show the greatest gains from anger management programs (Howells et al., 2002).

The instrumental/predatory–expressive/affective dichotomy is used on a wide scale and has a long history in the psychology and criminology literature. However, Bushman and Anderson (2001) suggest that this dichotomy is a first-generation paradigm that is problematic when applied to real-life situations and need to be replaced. The authors use the Columbine high school murder-suicides committed by Dylan Klebold and Eric Harris to illustrate the difficulty in categorizing aggressive acts as either predatory/instrumental or affective/expressive. Klebold and Harris had been taunted and provoked by athletes in their school yet methodically planned the massacre (on April 20, 1999, the 110th anniversary of Adolf Hitler's birthday) for a year prior to the event. This crime and many others are difficult to categorize using a dichotomous model of aggression.

Bushman and Anderson (2001) note two major conceptual problems with the instrumental/predatory–expressive/affective dichotomy:

1. *It is confounded with the automatic-controlled information processing dichotomy:* Expressive/ affective aggression is by definition automatic, reactive, impulsive, and spontaneous. Instrumental/predatory aggression is by definition controlled, reasoned, calculated, and planned. The authors ask, "How should one classify an instance of anger-based aggressive behavior that would occur when the intended target is unarmed but that would not occur if the target was carrying a handgun?" (p. 276). In other words, they suggest that the dichotomy can't explain many instances of human aggression because some expressive/affective aggression has controlled features and some instrumental/predatory aggression has automatic features.

2. *It excludes aggressive acts arising from multiple motives:* The same motives can drive either type of aggression, different motives can drive the same aggressive behavior, and many behaviors are mixtures of instrumental/predatory and expressive/affective aggression. For example, a man whose masculinity has been insulted might impulsively react by punching the antagonist or may instead plot an act of revenge to restore his self and social image (same motive, different type of aggression). A child who pushes another child off of a bike may be angry at the child or may be pushing him off to get the bike (different motives, same behavior). In the case of the insulted man, his immediate goal served the goal of repairing his self-image and in this and other instances behaviors that appear automatic may be the result of a well-rehearsed decision with a quick cost-benefit calculation (mixed motives).

Bushman and Anderson propose a second-generation paradigm—the *knowledge structure approach* to deal with the difficulties that arise with the dichotomous model of aggression that acknowledges cognitive scripts and schemas as important mediators of aggression.[14] Based on this important intersection of the expressive/affective versus instrumental predatory aggression dichotomy with the automatic/controlled information processing model, any attempt to modify an offender's aggressive behavior must target cognitive scripts and schemas—beliefs about the costs and benefits of carrying out the behavior (outcome beliefs) and beliefs about one's ability to carry out the behavior (efficacy beliefs). This more sophisticated theoretical framework offers a promising approach for the future that may help to explain findings from evaluation studies of anger management programs that show minimal to no success at reducing violent recidivism by targeting anger (Loza & Loza-Fanous, 1999).

Community Supervision and Offender Reentry

What works in community corrections are carefully designed rehabilitation/treatment strategies that identify/attend to the risk, need, responsivity principle used in conjunction with increased surveillance or intensive rehabilitation supervision (Bonta,

Wallace-Capretta, & Rooney, 2000; Bralley & Prevost, 2001; Gendreau, Cullen, & Bonta, 1994). Criminological theory and empirical research on offender reentry suggest that swift, certain, graduated responses coupled with immediate offender accountability enhance offender compliance with supervision conditions (Reentry Policy Council, 2006). Intensive supervision of offenders without a treatment component have not been effective in reducing recidivism (Petersilia & Turner, 1993; Turner & Petersilia, 1992) and show particularly negative results for drug offenders (Martin & Scarpetti, 1993; Turner, Petersilia, & Deschenes, 1992) and chronic offenders (Schwaner, McGaughey, & Tewksbury, 1998).

The effects of community supervision depend on offender characteristics. Different types of offenders have different recidivism rates and respond differently to supervision practices.[15] Research shows that many individual-level factors such as offense type, age at first offense, personality disorder, self-efficacy, gang membership, and use of an alias are associated with recidivism (Benda, 2001; Benda, Corwyn, & Toombs, 2001; Martinez, 1997), and that offender desistance is a gradual process involving a complex interaction between individual and social factors (Haggard, Gumpert, & Grann, 2001).

Recognizing the characteristics of offender types and subtypes and the fit between the individual and the environment (Helfgott, 1997a; McMurray, 1993) are important tools in community supervision. For example, offenders with a history of disciplinary infractions in custody appear to do no better on parole than they do on unsupervised release on expiration of maximum sentence (Gottfredson, Mitchell-Herzfeld, & Flanagan, 1982). Drug offenders (particularly hard-core users) need intensive supervision combined with intensive, long-term, and comprehensive substance abuse treatment with coordinated care and cooperation between drug treatment and criminal justice agencies (Prendergast, Anglin, & Wellisch, 1995) that surveillance goals (constant technical violations for dirty urine analyses) often hinder treatment success (Hanlon, Nurco, Bateman, & O'Grady, 1999; Vito & Wilson, 1990). Chronic offenders tend to abscond when supervision becomes too strict because they feel their opportunities are stifled by probation and parole officers who tie them to an identity they can't change (Schwaner, McGaughey, & Tewksbury, 1998).

Summary

The term *applied criminology* refers to the application of criminological theory to criminal justice practice. The application of theory to practice is crucial at all stages of the criminal justice process. Theory and research on criminal behavior is applied in policing and public safety through crime prevention initiatives, criminal profiling, and victim services. In the courts, theory, research, and discourse on criminal behavior is imbedded in and continues to influence the law of insanity and has had a major influence on habitual offender and sexual predator legislation, prediction of dangerousness, and specialized courts including drug, mental health, and DUI/DWI courts. In corrections, research on criminal behavior and offender types, offender rehabilitation and the risk, need, and responsivity principle has had a major impact on correctional classification, management, and treatment in institutional and community corrections contexts.

Understanding the connection between criminological theory and criminal justice practice is an essential component of criminal justice education and the foundation of theoretically grounded evidence-based initiatives. Although identifying and understanding the factors and forces that influence criminal behavior is a worthy endeavor in and of itself, explaining and discussing criminal behavior in a textbook, college classroom, or academic article or to an audience does little to ensure that criminal justice initiatives do not repeat past mistakes or expend tax dollars on interventions that have no theoretical or empirical basis. A number of authors have noted the wasted efforts that throughout the history of criminal justice have occurred when policy and practice is blindly initiated without attention to theory and empirical research (Clements, 1996; Gendreau, 1996; Hengeller, 1996; Van Voorhis, Cullen, & Appelgate, 1995). Societal response to criminal behavior at all stages of the criminal justice process, from law enforcement and public safety to courts and law to corrections and offender reentry, depend on what is known about the causes, nature, extent, types, and subtypes of criminal behavior.

DISCUSSION QUESTIONS

1. Define the term *applied criminology.*

2. Explain how criminological theories and typologies have been used at different stages of the criminal justice process. Offer specific examples of the application of theory and typologies in law enforcement/public safety, courts/law, and corrections/offender reentry.

3. How has the predatory/affective aggression typology been applied in criminal justice practice? What are some of the problems in applying a theoretical model like this to real-world criminal behavior?

4. Oftentimes, criminology and victimology are seen as completely separate areas of theory and research, as if the study of crime and criminals has little or no connection to the study of victims and victimization. Discuss how theories and typologies of crime and criminals have been or could be applied to the study of victims, victimization, and the provision of victim services.

5. Academic criminologists and criminal justice practitioners spend much of their everyday activities in very different realms. Many academics and practitioners actively collaborate and seek ways to incorporate theory and research into criminal justice practice. However, for practical reasons much theory and research sits on the shelves of libraries and big ideas are discussed only in academic circles but never make their way into

criminal justice practice. Similarly, there are many policies and practices implemented in the criminal justice system that persist without ever having been empirically tested or situated within a historical or theoretical context in assessing effectiveness or practices that are effective, but have not been empirically evaluated and therefore do not have the proper backing for funding and continued success. Offer your thoughts on how connections between academic criminology and criminal justice practice can be strengthened and improved. What are some of the major hindrances to widespread application of criminological theory and research to criminal justice practice? Discuss.

 On Your Own: Log on to the Web-based student study site at http://www.sagepub .com/helfgottstudy/ for the URL links in the Web Exercises, study aids such as review quizzes, and research recommendations including links to journal articles specifically selected for this book.

WEB EXERCISES

1. Go to the *Frontline: Crime of Insanity Web site* at http://www.pbs.org/wgbh/pages/ frontline/shows/crime/. Review the history of insanity, the differences in laws across the United States and the federal system, and issues related to mentally ill offenders. How has the law of insanity changed over time? Can advanced knowledge, theory, and research on criminal behavior from an interdisciplinary framework reconcile the historic conflicts between the criminal justice and mental health systems that have created so much controversy around the insanity defense? Based on what you've read in the text, how should the law of insanity be changed to meaningfully incorporate empirical research on criminal behavior?

2. Explore the legislation enacted in Washington State dealing with sexual predators. Visit the Web site for the *Washington State Special Commitment Center:* http://www1.dshs.wa.gov/hrsa/scc/default.htm. Explore the links, including the "civil commitment process," "public safety and security measures," "treatment program," and "less restrictive alternative." Explain the process of civil commitment in Washington State and then compare it to the SVP process in other states. Go to the *Dylan's Law* Web site at http://www.citizensforaonestrikelaw.org/index.htm, which calls for a one strike law for sexually violent offenders in Washington State. Review the law and information (research, statistics) used to support it. Explain how criminological theory and research on predatory sex crime and persistent offenders have been used to support this legislation.

3. Visit the *Violence Risk* Web site: http://www.violence-risk.com/risk/instruments.htm. Review the range of actuarial risk assessment instruments now available. Describe and discuss the different instruments available. How do they compare and contrast? What specialized subgroups do they target? Which measure historical/static versus dynamic

risk factors? If you were in charge of selecting one or more of these tools for use to make release decisions for offenders who have served a period of incarceration, which would you select and why?

4. The *Reentry Policy Council* was established in 2001 by the Council of State Governments to assist government officials in responding to the number of people leaving jails and prisons to return to communities. The council, whose members include professionals with extensive expertise in areas such as victim services, legal barriers to reentry, family issues, and physical health produced a comprehensive report on the state of offender reentry with policy statements recommending actions necessary to increase the likelihood of offender success in transitioning from incarceration to community. Read the *Reentry Policy Council Report* at http://www.reentrypolicy.org/ and discuss the ways in which theory and research on criminal behavior have influenced the council's policy statements.

12

Challenges for the Future

Things that are out of your control, you just do what you can do. . . . It's like an earthquake.

> —Michael Owens, father of a student in the aftermath of the 2006 Platte Canyon High School hostage taking in which 16-year-old student Emily Keyes was murdered before the gunman killed himself. ("Student Describes Colorado Gunman's Takeover," September 28, 2006)

. . . society's fear of violent crime should be accompanied by a social outrage over the fact that most of what is known to work is not currently in practice; and in many instances, little to no interest is being shown for whether current practices are working.

> —Van Voorhis, Cullen, & Applegate (1995, p. 25)

In the middle of the day on September 27, 2006, a middle-aged man in a dark blue hooded sweatshirt with a backpack and two handguns walked into a small-town high school, through hallways amid students going to and from classes, and entered a college-prep English classroom that had been in session for 30 minutes. The man ordered the students to line up facing the chalkboard and one-by-one allowed the teacher and all but six female students to leave the room. He kept the six girls in the second-story classroom for 4 hours while groping and sexually assaulting them and forcing them to relay information in communications with police. He let four of the six students go at different points during the ordeal, but in the end, as SWAT officers busted in, the gunman used 16-year-old Emily Keyes as a human shield and then shot her in the back of the head as she tried to escape. The gunman, 53-year-old Duane Morrison, a transient with an arrest record for property and public order crime who lived in his yellow Jeep Wrangler that had been seen parked outside the school earlier in the day, shot himself. Emily Keyes, a volleyball player who was on the school debate team, communicated through text message to her family, "I love you guys," less than 2 hours before her murder.

Photo 12.1 Emily Keyes Memorial, September 30, 2006, in Baily, Colorado.

Photo credit: © Getty Images.

In the hours following the event, the question on most people's mind was the same—*"What would make a person do something like that?"* For many who witnessed and tried to process the events of that day, the answer was simple. Duane Morrison was an evil out-of-control sexual predator whose behavior defies explanation. Most, including the sheriff who led the hostage negotiations, were left looking sickened, lowering and shaking their heads. A father waiting outside the school told reporters the event was out of control, like an earthquake. The next day police discovered that Morrison had written a rambling 14-page letter delivered to his brother who lived in the area apologizing to his family for what would occur but with no information yielding motive or why the particular high school was targeted. Rumors surfaced that he had found information about the girls on My Space.com ("Police: School Shooter Asked for Girls by Name," September 29, 2006), though these rumors were discounted by police. Morrison's arrest history revealed that he had, only months earlier, been arrested, booked, and had his mugshot taken for an outstanding warrant for telephone harassment, leaving messages at city businesses, including a Harley-Davidson store that he threatened to show up at with guns if they didn't stop sending him catalogs. Prior to this, he had arrests for minor crimes in 1973 and no history of arrest for sex crimes. Morrison's stepmother told reporters, "We don't know why . . . We don't know how." The only indicator of any sort of sexual deviancy was a comment from a former landlady who described Morrison as "a nice guy, with a dark side" who made sexual comments to her about clothing she was folding in the apartment laundry room and who she said came off as though he "thought he was a ladies' man or that he was God's gift to women or something—that everybody would just fall at his feet" (Ngyuen, Harrison, & Armstrong, 2006).

Two days later, the principal of a K–12 school in rural Cazenovia, Wisconsin, was shot dead by a 15-year-old 9th grader with a .22 caliber pistol. Fellow students said the shooter was "just weird in the head" and the dean of students said, "I don't think there was any way of predicting this" ("Principal Shot in Wisconsin School, 9th Grader in Custody," September 29, 2006). Three days after the Wisconsin shooting, an even more shocking crime occurred. Charles Roberts, a 32-year-old milk deliverer, family man, and father of three with no criminal record, walked into a one-room Amish schoolhouse in Lancaster, Pennsylvania, with a shotgun, semiautomatic pistol, and a rifle. He let the 15 male students, a pregnant woman, and two adult women with infants go and ordered the remaining 10 female children ages 6 to 13 and a teenaged teacher's aide to line up in front of the chalkboard. He boarded up the doors with two-by-fours he had brought with him, bound the girls with zip ties, and shot them all in the back of their heads execution style. Three of the girls died immediately, one died in the arms of a state trooper, one the next day in the hospital, and five were critically wounded. Roberts left suicide notes for his children and wife and called his wife from the scene just before the murders to tell her he loved her, he wasn't coming home, and that 20 years earlier he had molested two family members, aged 3 and 5, and had been recently having molestation fantasies ("Fourth Girl Dies After Amish School Shooting," October 3, 2006). Evidence found at the scene and in Robert's truck included K-Y Jelly, a stun gun, and various hardware items suggesting he may have had plans to sexually assault and torture the children over a long period of time but became disorganized when police arrived. A neighbor who lived across the street from the school told reporters before

Photo 12.2 Funeral procession for 12-year-old Anna Mae Stoltzfus, a victim of the Amish school shooting October 6, 2006, in Nickel Mines, Pennsylvania. Four other victims were buried October 5th.

Photo credit: © Timothy A. Clary/AFP/Getty Images.

starting to cry, "I'm a World War II veteran . . . I've never seen anything like that" (Hambright, October 3, 2006). The method of the Amish schoolhouse shooting led many to speculate that this was a copycat crime because of the similarities with the Morrison hostage-taking in Colorado only days before.

Just weeks before all of this, 24-year-old Tiffany Hall was charged in Illinois with the deaths of her pregnant cousin, 23-year-old Jimella Tunstall, and Tunstall's fetus and her three children aged 1, 2, and 7. Hall allegedly knocked Tunstall unconscious, cut out her fetus with scissors, stole the baby, and then called police to come to a park where she reported she had given birth to a stillborn. It wasn't until the baby's funeral that Hall confessed to her boyfriend what she had done and was arrested. Tunstall's other children were later found dead in the washer and dryer in their apartment (Corum, 2006; "Kids of Woman Slain in Fetus Theft Found Dead," September 24, 2006). A year earlier, the same thing had happened in Kittanning, Pennsylvania, when a woman hit her pregnant neighbor over the head, took her out to a wooded area and sliced her abdomen with a razor knife ("New Twist in Fetus Theft Try," October 14, 2005). In 2004, a similar crime occurred in Skidmore, Missouri, when a young woman 8 months pregnant was strangled to death and her child cut from her body and stolen by a woman who tried to pass the baby off as her own ("Baby Found Alive, Woman Arrested," December 18, 2004). These are three of a half a dozen such crimes that have occurred over the past 20 years in which a pregnant woman was attacked and the fetus cut out by a female perpetrator (Meadows, 2005).

Then on April 16, 2007, 23-year-old Seung-Hui Cho, a college English major, stormed the Virginia Tech campus with two handguns and multiple clips of ammunition and went on a shooting rampage that left 32 fellow students and professors dead, and many wounded before he turned the gun on himself. Cho had a history of mental illness, but no criminal history. In retrospect, former professors, family members, and students offered insight into Cho's mental state by sharing anecdotal accounts of unusual behavior such as avoidance of others, inability to make eye contact, an imaginary supermodel girlfriend named "Jelly," and frightening writings in an English class ("Virginia Tech Shooter a Self-Described 'Question Mark,'" April 18, 2007). Prior to the event, however, Seung-Hui Cho was a Virginia Tech student in good standing who, in most respects, looked very much like any college students at any university.

The Science of Criminal Behavior

The Colorado, Amish school, and Virginia Tech shootings and the fetus theft murders are clearly extreme and baffling crimes, crimes that make the most experienced criminal behavior scholars and law enforcement professionals wince. Unfortunately, there is no shortage of examples of such extreme offenses. Fortunately, compared with other more usual types of offenses, these are anomalous crimes that occur so rarely

Photo 12.3   Virginia Tech Community Mourns Day After Deadliest U.S. Shooting.

Photo credit: © Scott Olson/Getty Images.

some may equate them with natural disasters. The job of criminal behavior scholars, criminologists, and forensic psychologists who study criminal behavior, however, is to make sense of both rare and everyday crimes through the scientific method. Like seismologists who study earthquakes, criminologists attempt to find answers that will help *prevent, explain*, and *predict* future criminal behavior. A great deal is known about where earthquakes are likely to occur, but there is currently no reliable way to predict exactly when an earthquake will occur in any specific location. Similarly, criminologists know a great deal about the factors that increase and decrease the probability that a particular individual will engage in criminal behavior in any given situation, though few say with confidence that criminal behavior can be predicted with any degree of scientific certainty.

But is it meaningful to compare criminal behavior to natural disasters? The interdisciplinary knowledge base that has accumulated from the biological, psychological, sociological, cultural, phenomenological, and opportunity/ecological perspectives provides an empirical foundation with which to make sense of crime and individual criminal acts. We know that some people commit crime because they are genetically predisposed to do so and because they see their peers or family members or people they identify with commit crime and they learn from and mimic what they see. Or they have personality traits that are behaviorally expressed in the form of criminal behavior. Or they develop elaborate fantasies that they are compelled to act out. We know that criminal behavior is determined by genetic predisposition, neurotransmitter imbalance, hypoglycemia, low autonomic reactivity, amygdala dysfunction, frontal lobe impairment, parental neglect, delinquent peers, social disorganization, lack of social bonds, deviant identity, antisocial characteristics, personality disorder, low self-control, psychopathology, deviant fantasy, antisocial cognitive scripts, social learning, hypermasculine subcultures, cultural norms and values, and situational and environmental opportunity.

We know that some individuals are more or less afflicted by any one of these variables and all or many of these variables may converge and interact in any given individual and situation to produce criminal behavior. We know that certain risk and protective factors make it more or less likely that any given individual will commit a criminal act. We have actuarial tools that help us "predict" who will and who will not reoffend, and we have identified preventive strategies that can be employed to reduce the likelihood that a child will grow up to become an offender. We can employ crime prevention techniques to build entire cities that "design out" certain types of crime. We know that types of crimes differ in offender motivation, offense characteristics, situational context, and sociocultural influence and each crime type has essential features that provide us with a language to explain and categorize offenses and offense-specific information that can be used to better respond to particular types of offenses. We know a lot.

But, on October 2, 2006, after over two centuries of discourse, theory development, and scientific study of criminal behavior, all of the sociologists, psychologists, and criminologists in the world couldn't stop the execution of 10 little Amish girls in a Pennsylvania schoolhouse. This simple horrific fact is worth holding on to as we think about future directions for the study of criminal behavior.

All too often, advances in criminology and criminal justice research go unnoticed—lost in the pages of academic journals, quashed by politics, abandoned from lack of funding or institutional support. Many of the most brilliant and applicable theoretical and empirical articles are read and discussed only by academic criminologists and students of criminology/criminal justice in college classrooms and academic conferences. Those educated in criminology/criminal justice who go on to careers in law enforcement, court services and law, corrections, and victim services generally find little opportunity in their daily work to apply the theory and research they've learned in the classroom. When research does make its way into practice, it is often quickly abandoned or distorted because the ideas and findings aren't adequately relayed to or supported by practitioners who work on the frontlines with offenders. The application to criminal justice practice of theory and research that has been accumulated by social and behavioral scientists is hindered by lack of time and resources, the nature and demands of the professional role, inaccessibility of research, inadequate background to understand statistical results, and inability of researchers to convey information in straightforward terminology.[1]

The notion that science matters less in a field like criminal justice than it does in other fields such as medicine, mental health, engineering, or astrophysics seriously hinders crime prevention and control. To use a medical analogy, most of us would not want to undergo major surgery for a serious illness conducted by a surgeon who disregarded advances in medical science and instead, say, used surgical techniques and instruments that were popular 50 years ago. We hope and expect that a doctor who will be operating on us has read the latest medical journals. However, policies and practices in the criminal justice system are, more often than not, implemented with disregard to research conducted by social and behavioral scientists. To make progress in understanding and responding to crime in the future, theory and empirical research conducted by social scientists who study criminal behavior must be embraced by criminal justice professionals and viewed as more than intellectual exercise confined to university classrooms. At the same time, criminal behavior scholars must reach out to criminal justice agencies and practitioners by making their work accessible, engaging in training, and presenting at conferences and events that do not just cater to fellow academics.

Remembering the Past to Inform the Future

There is nothing more meaningless or dangerous than policy and practice that focuses solely on the present with no connection to the past or sense of duty to future generations. We all have a responsibility to future generations to reflect on and critically evaluate past experiences, engage in systematic theory development and empirical research, and make sure that the accumulated knowledge bases on criminal behavior make their way into policy and practice. Fishbein (2001) argues that inquiry and policy in criminal justice must be informed by science—that "we need to be more creative, innovative, and scientific than approaches used in the past" (p. 97). However, this requires knowledge about what has gone on in the past. Many reactive criminal justice policies and legislation have been hastily pursued in a swirl of moral panic and initiated as if they were innovations, when a look back just a few decades would show that history repeats itself over alarmingly shorter cycles as time goes by.

In the history of criminology and the study of criminal behavior in the social sciences, the pendulum has swung back and forth, from the social eugenics movement in the early 1900s to the habitual offender and sexual psychopath laws of the 1930s and 1940s to the hysteria over juvenile delinquency in the 1950s to the emphasis on the social disorganization roots of crime and violence in the 1960s to the rehabilitation research that influenced the rise and fall of correctional rehabilitation in the 1970s to the movement to the "just deserts" model of the 1980s to the "get tough" movement of the 1990s and focus on risk assessment, situational, and environmental crime prevention of the late 20th and early 21st centuries. Though criminal justice professionals often have a difficult time seeing the direct impact of theory and research on criminal behavior in their everyday responsibilities, theory and research has in fact made its way into criminal justice policy and practice (albeit filtered through politics), shaping political direction and top-down initiatives and resource allocation. Criminal justice practices have always been influenced by, or at least coincided with, changes in thinking about crime and theoretical developments.

The late modern theoretical orientation reflected in Garland's (1990, 2001, 2002) work offers a useful framework with which to reflect on the future of criminological theory and criminal justice practice. Kraska (2004) outlines five key themes that characterize the criminal justice theory of late modernity:

1. *Actuarial justice: risk, safety, and control*—Hyper-concern with safety and control, focus on collecting and analyzing quantitative data, thinking about people in terms of statistical aggregates, basing decisions on statistical analysis, continual assessment of risk, harm, danger and maximizing safety/minimizing risk

2. *Neo-liberal and neo-conservative politics*—Loss of usefulness of the notions of "left" and "right" politics, attack on state-centered governance and assault on welfarism supported by traditional liberalism, view that the welfare state has created a culture of dependency, advocacy of the free market as model for social order, value placed on state-enforced law and order

3. *Contradiction and incoherence in criminal justice policy*—State of ambivalence between actuarial justice and emotive delivery of pain, state-centered versus private crime control, preventative versus proactive measures, and reactionary/punitive policies

4. *The decline of state sovereignty*—Redistribution of crime-control responsibilities to community organizations, private sector, partnerships with public and private social service agencies, and citizens. Blurring of traditional distinction between private and public and criminal justice and military efforts; shift based on perception that the state cannot control crime/protect public

5. *The socially exclusive society*—Exclusive society created through preoccupation with fear, danger, and risk guided by a neo-liberal free-market ideology in which members of society who don't fit into new economy and therefore pose potential danger are excluded as "other"; view that bifurcated society is a permanent state of affairs that has to be carefully managed; criminal justice system maintains the barrier between the included and excluded to ensure that certain populations remain excluded and others remain protected and segregated

The late modernity perspective on crime control offers a historical, cultural, and contemporary context within which to make sense of how advances in criminological theory and research on criminal behavior have meaningfully shaped criminal justice policy and practice and can shape them in the future. Based on this perspective, *crime control in the 21st century in America and Britain is characterized by actuarial justice, blurred boundaries between liberalism and conservatism, ambivalent and incoherent policies, redistribution of criminal justice functions to community and private sector, and a culture of fear that perpetuates the us versus them mentality.*

Garland (2001) argues that criminal justice in late modernity is characterized by the desire for security, orderliness, and control and the taming of chance with two new competing criminologies—the *criminology of everyday life* and the *criminology of the other*—replacing the official thinking of the previous modern and premodern eras. The criminology of control says crime is a normal part of everyday life that we have to realistically respond and adapt to and protect ourselves from, stressing rationality, technology, moral neutrality, and knowledge-based pragmatic solutions. The criminology of the other says crime is a catastrophe for which someone must be blamed, emphasizing the view of the dangerous other, the evildoer who must be controlled at all costs. Though different, *both are criminologies of control:*

> The characteristics of these new criminologies are different in most respects, as are their constituencies and sources of social support. But they share a focus upon control, an acknowledgement that crime has become a normal social fact, and a reaction against the criminological ideals and penal policies associated with penal-welfarism. The one is late-modern, taking the amoral social science approach even further than correctionalism did, viewing crime as the predictable outcome of normal social routines rather than of skewed dispositions. The other is anti-modern and anti-social science, adopting an absolutist, moralizing approach to crime, and insisting that criminal actions are voluntary, the bad choices of wicked individuals. (p. 185)

Garland suggests that the new criminologies that reject the social criminologies of the 20th century seem, on the surface, to be a "puzzling return to the naïve criminology of Jeremy Bentham and his utilitarian followers." However, the new criminologies are set at a time when the criminal justice system seeks to control criminals in much the same way they control themselves, through managerial and auditing processes. Harcourt (2007) echoes Garland suggesting that technical advances (in particular, the actuarial prediction of dangerousness) have "tamed punishment" with little attention to collateral consequences (p. 33).

It is critical that criminological theory be applied in a manner that is conscious of historical successes and failures as well as the impact of policies and practices on public safety and due process and individual liberty. For example, the current three strikes and sexually violent predator laws are a reincarnation of the old sexual psychopath laws from the early 1900s. These laws were heavily influenced by the rise of positivist criminology and the shift away from classical criminology (criminal behavior is a product of free will) to the idea that criminal behavior is determined by biological, psychological, and sociological factors and forces. Each disciplinary perspective has had its historical heyday—all with disastrous consequences for offenders whose rights were violated, victims who were not protected, or communities that lost resources to policies and practices founded on bad science or good science that was politically distorted.

One of the most pervasive applications of research in the criminal justice system has been the incorporation or prediction and classification methods into criminal justice decision making (Gottfredson & Tonry, 1987). This is what Garland refers to as *actuarial justice.* Many of the forensic assessment tools used today to classify offenders and predict dangerousness are standardized and validated based on years of empirical research. We are perhaps closer to the mark when we civilly commit a particular offender who we say has a high likelihood of reoffense than we were in 1910 when we proposed sterilizing a particular offender identified as a habitual criminal to prevent the birth of future criminals. However, it is worth noting that critical discussion of today's classification and prediction tools is eerily similar to the discourse of the past. It is imperative that criminal behavior scholars step outside of their disciplinary perspectives to think about the impact of their theories and research on issues of crime control and due process (see Harcourt, 2007, for critical discussion of the consequences of actuarial prediction). Biological and personality theories may enhance understanding of criminal behavior, but they have frightening effects on individual liberty. Ecological/opportunity theories provide practical solutions for crime prevention, but can potentially backfire by creating fear and isolation with overfocus on crime to the exclusion of community. Cultural and phenomenological perspectives can tell us something about the nature of subcultural style and aesthetic, but may be used by moral entrepreneurs to criminalize certain groups for political purposes. Sociological perspectives may correctly identify the social roots of criminal behavior while operating too slowly to protect the community from harm.

In 1959, Francis Allen wrote an article titled "Criminal Justice, Legal Values, and the Rehabilitative Ideal" (Allen, 2004), criticizing the changing conceptions of criminal behavior and the rise of the rehabilitative ideal. Allen argued that the shift in notions of crime as a product of free will to the notion of crime as a disease to be treated gave psychologists and psychiatrists great power over individual liberty. Allen offered a story about a man in his 80s who killed his wife while drunk and was indeterminately committed during the rehabilitation era under a statute that required automatic commitment of individuals acquitted on grounds of insanity in a criminal trial. He had been confined for over 30 years when staff at the institution determined that he was not psychotic, had probably never been psychotic, and at age 80 was ready to be released. However, the director of the institution said he could not be sure the man would never again reoffend and that the man would probably be better off staying in the institution. This story is worth thinking about almost 50 years later, in the current era of civil commitment in which offenders deemed "sexually violent predators" are being indefinitely committed based on forensic evaluation by mental health practitioners. Today's evaluations, using standardized and validated actuarial predictors, are a vast improvement over clinical prediction of the past. However, these tools are far from 100% accurate, which means many offenders in the United States who may or may not reoffend continue to be involuntarily incarcerated, after already serving long prison sentences, and will not be released until a psychologist or psychiatrist is able to say with certainty that they will not reoffend.

So returning to the questions—*What does it mean to be "creative, innovative, and scientific" in preventing and responding to criminal behavior? How can we apply advances in criminological theory and criminal justice practice to better understand and respond to criminal behavior in the 21st century?*—most criminology/criminal justice and legal scholars recognize that, in the history of societal responses to crime, few theoretical and empirically based initiatives have been given the chance they need to show positive gains. Historically, societal responses to criminal behavior have been characterized by impatience, frustration, politics, and fear. A creative, innovative, and scientific approach to preventing and responding to criminal behavior requires placing contemporary theory, research, and initiatives in historical context and focusing on the obstacles that have plagued the successful application of theory and research to practice. We have to ask ourselves what has historically stood in the way of our ability to adequately and successfully prevent and respond to crime and what changes and new directions we need to pursue in the future.

Crime scholars and criminologists have identified directions for the future and historical obstacles to successful implementation of theory to practice, offering the following suggestions:

- Major obstacles need to be removed before behavioral technology can be successfully translated and transferred to criminal justice policy and practice (Gendreau, 1996).

- The current criminal justice system was produced through political manipulation of public anxieties and racial tensions and moral panic. "What needs to be done now is to figure out how to undo unnecessary damage and lessen the chances that similar excesses will occur" (Tonry, 2004, p. 199).

- The origins and modulators of individual differences, the interactions of these differences with social variables, and interdisciplinary research that integrates the physical and social sciences will "yield answers to questions that have eluded the field of criminology for decades" (Fishbein, 2001, p. 108).

- "The most fundamental lesson of the twentieth century is not a political one but a structural one"—we need to recognize the limitations of the state and the importance of sharing the work of social control with local organizations and communities (Garland, 2001, p. 205).

- Crime and violence is a public health problem that needs to be addressed through the identification of at-risk populations, with the goal of decreasing risk factors and increasing protective factors (Fishbein, 2001; Prentky, 2003).

- Future research must focus on incorporating and integrating qualitative and qualitative methodologies and the full range of criminal behaviors across the lifespan (Piquero & Mazerolle, 2001).

- The field of criminology has failed to recognize the heterogeneity of adolescent delinquency. "Delinquency theories are woefully ill-informed about the phenomenology of modern teenagers from their own perspective" (Moffit, 1993, p. 134).

- Future research and practice must be informed by a general theory of crime that integrates and organizes the major crime theories into a unified whole (Agnew, 2005).

- Attention must be directed to the relationship between mass consumption of American cultural values and crime and crime control (Barak, 1998).

- "There are fundamental differences in offenders, victims, and situational elements within and across different types of crime. . . . An understanding of this diversity is essential for developing realistic programs of crime control" (Miethe, McCorkle, & Listwan, 2006, p. 150).

- Crime is a part of nature that can be understood through the life sciences. Nature's realities should inform crime prevention, tailoring interventions to the "fine points of particular offenses, narrowly specified but broadly conceived," taking into account that people have a natural capacity to enjoy doing what they're not supposed to do (Felson, 2006, p. 357).

These perspectives and suggestions offered by prominent crime and justice researchers highlight some of the challenges for the future. It is important to keep these ideas in mind in developing new directions for future research and practice in the study of and response to criminal behavior. In addition, we need to think beyond the traditional variables, analyses, and explanations that have been used to examine criminal behavior and give attention to cultural forces that shape criminal behavior and contemporary changes and challenges such as media and technology, globalization, and (in addition to quantitative methods) existential-phenomenological approaches to understanding criminal behavior and the ways in which personal meaning influences behavior, desistence, and persistence.

Challenges and Innovative Directions for the Study of Criminal Behavior

Review of the criminal behavior research literature suggests five considerations for future directions in criminal behavior research and its application to criminal justice practice:

- *Applied criminology*—Address obstacles to successful application of theory and research to criminal justice practice.

- *Interdisciplinary perspectives and theory integration*—Synthesize and integrate perspectives, theories, and empirical research.

- *Technology*—Develop theories and conduct empirical research on the role of mass media and computer technology in shaping criminal behavior.

- *Imbedded stereotypes*—Identify the ways in which gender, race, class, and age stereotypes continue to be imbedded in criminological theory and applied to criminal justice practice.

- *Methodological creativity*—Incorporate traditional and nontraditional methods into research designs in new ways to capture data areas missing in current literature.

Applied Criminology: Removing Obstacles

Criminology/criminal justice is a discipline that cannot be understood outside the framework of professional practice and application. However, the realities of the criminal justice system often make it difficult for the most well-intentioned practitioners and policymakers to keep up on the latest research and lack of resources, politics, and public fear of crime often make it impossible to implement the most innovative or promising initiatives. Gendreau (1996) identifies three major obstacles that need to be removed before behavioral technology can be successfully translated and transferred to criminal justice policy and practice: theoreticism, technology transfer, and training.

Theoreticism refers to the tendency of researchers to accept or reject knowledge on the basis of personal values and experiences; or rather, the inclination to ignore or disparage knowledge bases and entire disciplines outside of one's own affiliation or framework. This is nowhere more pronounced than in the study of criminal behavior, where the historical gap between psychologists and sociologists has characterized much of the academic discourse and the divide in criminological theory for nearly a century.[2]

Technology transfer refers to the process by which knowledge and information gets into the hands of those who need it. Many clinicians and practitioners do not read or keep up with the academic literature and recent research findings that have direct and profound implications for criminal justice practice and interventions. Fault for this research-practice gap does not lie solely with practitioners. Criminal justice scholars need to make their research findings accessible by publishing in newsletters, presenting at practitioner conferences, and appearing in the media.

Training programs in criminal justice specifically devoted to correctional treatment and responses to criminal behavior are sparse and often administered by individuals who do not have academic credentials or adequate knowledge of the research literature. As a result, the information disseminated to criminal justice practitioners is often outdated by as much as several decades. It is costly and time-consuming for criminal justice agencies to bring in researchers to train practitioners or to support collaborative initiatives, unless an agency is fortunate enough to receive grant funding such as the National Institute of Justice.

It is illustrative to compare societal responses to criminal behavior with responses to other social and public health problems such as auto accidents, cancer, obesity, and AIDS—all of which have been approached with the understanding that combating these problems requires a range of strategies and interventions that are influenced by a nearly unlimited multitude of variables and forces. It is considered malpractice in the medical field to withhold treatment known to be effective to a patient who needs it (Fishbein, 2001). Research on auto safety is used to make vehicles safer; billions of dollars are spent on obesity and weight loss research that has produced gastric bypass surgery, Nutra Systems, and Splenda. However, despite the important theories and research conducted on criminal behavior, the common view persists that we don't need research to combat crime. It costs too much and takes too long. We need to control crime immediately the best way we know how—*incarcerate* offenders and measure effectiveness of this strategy with the single outcome variable of *recidivism.*

In an article published in 2004 in *Corrections Today* reviewing progress in corrections over the past 30 years, Dana Wilks, a probation supervisor from Colorado, suggested that corrections must redefine success to include the acceptance of recidivism:

> When considering the offender's release from supervision, the question should not be "How can we equip this person to successfully reintegrate into society?" Rather, the corrections field should ask, "What contributions can this offender make before possibly reoffending, and what can our field do to decrease his risk of significantly harming the victim(s) when and if he recidivates?" (p. 110)

This is a daring recommendation. Recidivism reduction has been the primary outcome variable of interest in criminal justice research since the beginning of the discipline. The notion that recidivism rates should not be viewed as the sole measure of correctional success is not favorably received in the criminal justice community.[3] With this redefinition of success in the criminal justice system, Wilks suggests that a "successful" program may then become one that significantly increases the length of time from supervision termination to reoffense.

It could be argued that this redefinition of correctional success reflects a Durkheimian view of crime as normal,[4] a tendency toward "defining deviance down,"[5] or a defeatist perspective promoted by a burned out correctional professional. Or, the suggestion could be seen as a reasonable, hopeful, realistic, theoretically grounded, and evidence-based framework with great promise for the future of criminal justice practice. The evolution of criminal justice as an academic discipline, the emergence of interdisciplinary criminology, and the advances in theory and empirical research on criminal behavior and criminal justice practice have brought a more sophisticated understanding of criminal behavior and the need for creative and diverse responses to crime. The idea that correctional success should be thought of in terms of personal and interpersonal growth of the offender, reduction in community fear of crime, contributions of the offender to the community, length of time from release until reincarceration, reduction of victim harm, and so on is just one of the many examples of innovative thinking that offer hope for the future of criminal justice.

Theory and research on criminal behavior and crime types have direct implications for all stages of the criminal justice process, from law enforcement to the courts to corrections to victim services and juvenile justice. The more we know about criminal behavior, the nature of different types of crime, and the individual-situational dynamics that influence the extent and nature of criminal offending, the more information we have to guide criminal and social justice responses to crime. Removing the barriers to successful application of theory and research so that criminal justice is on par with other institutions and public services is a critical step toward improving the criminal justice system.

Interdisciplinary Perspectives and Theory Integration

There are so many different theories of crime and criminal behavior that it's difficult to organize them all into any coherent whole. The approach here has been to organize the perspectives into six general categories—*biological, psychological, sociological, ecological, cultural,* and *phenomenological.* This is an imperfect classification given there are perspectives and theories that overlap or evolved from other disciplinary perspectives. However, each of these perspectives represents a distinct knowledge base and contribution to our understanding of crime and criminal behavior.

The call for interdisciplinary theory and research on criminal behavior does not mean all research should integrate theory to answer all research questions. Some questions will require adherence to a particular discipline or knowledge base. Rather, what is needed in the study of crime and criminal behavior is (as noted by Gendreau, 1996) to rid the crime and justice studies of the theoreticism that keeps researchers closed off from the important and complimentary work being done in other disciplines. *Questions need to be asked, connections need to be made, and insights need to be synthesized to pull the best works together into a cohesive megatheory of crime.* For example, how does theory and research in the area of primitive borderline defenses of psychopaths connect with theory and research on techniques of neutralization? How does the psychopathy literature and notion that psychopathy is a minitheory of crime fit within the more general theoretical frameworks such as the general (self-control) theory of crime or life-course criminology? How can insights and methods from existential/phenomenological perspectives be integrated with traditional biological theories of crime? There is much to be done to connect all of the common, divergent, and critical dots in the study of criminal behavior.

It is important that future research incorporate the theory and research on typologies of crime and criminal behavior. *Not all crimes are alike*—for example, serial murder, spousal abuse, sadistic rape, child molestation, burglary, bank robbery, phishing, hacking, cracking, prostitution, sex trafficking, drug smuggling, drunk driving, insider trading, espionage, domestic terrorism, hate crime, celebrity stalking. *The study of criminal behavior can be greatly enhanced by integrating general theories of crime with research on crime types.* Crime typologies offer insight on the distinct nature of different types of crime. Although many offenders commit a range of offenses, each crime category has distinct essential features. Information about these crime type features, in conjunction with general theories of crime, help us understand offender motivation, modus operandi, situational dynamics, and the nature and dynamics of specific offense.

Technology

Much of the important research findings in criminology are based on secondary datasets that are decades (or in some cases a half century) old. Old or aging datasets are not problematic if we are studying human phenomena we expect remain constant across generations. But, as Moffit (1993) suggests, criminologists have ignored the phenomenology of modern teenagers. Can we really expect to learn about criminal behavior in 2010 from the Wolfgang birth cohort of children born in 1945? In 2010, Wolfgang's subjects will turn 65 years old! Similarly, can the FBI serial killer study of the 1970s that included Edmund Kemper (born in 1948) and John Wayne Gacy (born in 1942) tell us about serial killers born 50 years later? Certainly with a low base rate behavior such as serial murder, we need to use samples from all time periods, and there are offense characteristics that are timeless and universal. But researchers have given much too little attention to the ways in which large-scale cultural and global change such as technology influences the extent and nature of criminal behavior.

Technology has the potential to change the nature and extent of criminal behavior across crime categories as well as the criminal justice response to crime. Many questions remain unexplored regarding the ways in which technology may influence and shape criminal behavior:

- *Does instant access to global criminal events have the potential to increase or decrease the extent of crime or to change how offenders engage in criminal behavior?*

- *Do Internet Web sites and chat rooms for neo-nazi skinheads, Ku Klux Klan members, sexual predators, terrorists, escorts and prostitutes, and drug users who need to pass drug tests provide a virtual community that reinforces deviant identity and exacerbates the potential for criminal behavior such as hate crimes, violent crimes, sex crimes, political crimes, and public order crimes?*

- *Do the increasingly realistic opportunities to engage in virtual violence have more or less criminogenic influence than the TV shows and films of the mid-1900s? Will children who are born in 2006 be more or less technologically savvy than those born in the 1950s, 1960s, 1970s, and 1980s and thus less likely to be criminogenically influenced by media images?*

- *Do Internet Web sites provide offenders a vast arena for victim selection that changes the geography of crime?*

- *Has the access to information and inundation of media images of crime exacerbated the copycat effect on criminal behavior?*

- *What is the potential for media images to shape fear of crime and, in turn, reduce criminal behavior that results from lack of community, human barriers, and disconnection?*

- *What is the potential for technology to blur the boundaries between fantasy and reality in the minds of certain individuals in ways that fuel deviant fantasies that lead to criminal behavior?*

The relationship between mass media technology has been downplayed by many criminologists with little empirical research to provide scientifically based answers. Minimization of the role of technology on criminal behavior and lack of empirical research on the technology-crime relationship leave a blind spot in the criminology knowledge base. Technology has markedly influenced every area of life, from how children learn, to the ways in which people socialize and meet their spouses, increasing opportunities for disabled individuals to lead normal lives, organ and face transplants, and GPS tracking systems for Alzheimer's patients and children's cellphones. The Internet, wireless communication, cell phones, and other technologies have changed the nature of business, education, medicine, aviation, and virtually every aspect of social life on a global scale. Criminologists would be irresponsible to discount and devalue the role technology may play in shaping criminal behavior.

The small number of scholars whose work has focused on the intersection of mass media technology, culture, and criminal behavior (e.g., Anderson & Dill, 2000; Anderson et al., 2003; Black, 1991; Ferrell & Sanders, 1995; Rafter, 2000; Surette, 1990, 1998, 2002) have made important contributions to the criminology literature by advancing ideas and producing research that begins to answer questions about technology's role in criminal behavior. Given the roles of computer and mass media technology in accessing information about crime, we need research that builds on the work of these researchers. In the 21st century, most people will continue to use mass media and computer technology as the primary means of obtaining crime information. A number of authors have highlighted the power of film in generating understanding and perception of crime (Rafter, 2000) and the function of film in modern myth making (Hill, 1992). This notion can be extended in the 21st century to mass media generally, as the new medium for the mythology through which people learn about good, evil, and the boundaries of human behavior. In this century, our understanding of criminal behavior depends on the development of theoretical models and empirical research that takes into account the central role of mass and computer media technology in shaping criminal behavior and its response.

Imbedded Stereotypes

Feminist criminologists have said that there is one thing that would significantly reduce crime—to socialize little boys as if they were little girls and to "make men think and act more like women" (Pollock, 1999). In most law enforcement jurisdictions well into the 1990s, there was no official category for female gang members, so there was no such thing (Sikes, 1996). Until Aileen Wuornos was arrested and convicted in 1992 for the murder of seven men, FBI profilers and serial murder researchers commonly contended that there was no such thing as a female serial killer. Similarly, it was commonly believed there were no African American serial or spree killers until Wayne Williams was arrested in 1981 for the Atlanta child murders, Jack Olsen's (1995) book *Charmer* (about the Northwest serial killer George Russell convicted in 1991 for murdering three women) was published, and Lee Boyd Malvo and John Allen Muhammad were captured for the DC sniper shootings.

Stereotypes about gender, race, social class, and age are historically imbedded in law and in theories and typologies of crime and criminal behavior. Many laws are created with a particular image or stereotype in mind. For example, in most jurisdictions, a woman cannot legally rape a man by forcing the man to penetrate her.[6] Discussion of stereotypes imbedded in law is beyond the scope of this book, but it is important to recognize the connections between legal control and definition of certain groups of people and theories of criminal behavior. Both law and theory have defined how we view certain groups of people around issues of gender, class, race, ethnicity, and age.

Criminologists have historically viewed crime as a male phenomenon. As a result, female criminality is understood on male terms. Beyond a handful of feminist criminologists (e.g., Adler, 1975; Campbell, 1994; Chesney-Lind, 1997; Daly, 1995; Daly & Chesney-Lind, 1988; Kirsta, 1994; Naffine, 1996), criminologists and social scientists who study criminal behavior have done very little to move beyond the notion of men as perpetrators and women as victims. In the area of psychopathy, serial murder, and sex crimes, substantive discourse, theory development, and empirical research were virtually absent until the 1990s. This offender as male/victim as female dichotomy is imbedded in legal definitions of crime, and the result is that crime statistics do not accurately reflect the nature and extent of female crime and male victimization. This is particularly so with respect to instrumental crimes. According to Naffine (1996), author of *Feminism and Criminology*:

> Instrumental aggression in women, both of a legitimate and illegitimate nature, lacks a place in our culture. . . . The man who is the target of female violence is unmanned and positioned as a woman, as is the man who is raped by a man. The position of victim, especially the victim of sexual violence, is culturally sexed as female while the assailant is sexed as male. (Naffine, 1996, p. 147)

This view of women as incapable of engaging in instrumental criminal (and noncriminal) acts has resulted in major blind spots in our understanding of female criminality. It is interesting to note that redefining serial murder to be inclusive of female offenders reveals a long list of instrumentally motivated female serial killers (Hickey, 2002) long before Aileen Wuornos. Furthermore, even when there is ample evidence in male-female team killer situations that the female was the initiator of the offense, the media tends to portray the female of the pair as the follower and the male as leader (Boyle, 2001).

The fetus theft murders provide a good example of just one of many crimes that appear to be committed predominantly (if not solely) by women. This is a crime that, on the surface, appears to be committed by women who want to steal a baby to pass as their own—a motivation that is perhaps the end result of psychosis or deviant fantasy that has evolved over a long period of time. However, we know virtually nothing about this type of offense beyond the occasional media report. It's common to hear the argument that resources and energies are best spent studying male offenders and traditionally male offenses because so few women commit crime. However, taking note of the amount of attention and resources that have been directed to the study of (the very rare male) serial murder, it is worth thinking about why more attention isn't directed to crimes traditionally committed by women and why, when women commit traditionally male crimes, their behaviors are often redefined.

Racial, ethnic, class, and age stereotypes are also imbedded in criminological theories. If researchers believe there is no such thing as an African American serial killer, or an Asian outlaw motorcycle gangster, or an upper-class crack abuser, or an elderly graffiti artist these stereotypical assumptions will guide theory and research, with direct implications for criminal justice policy and practice. Because of the blunders of the past, criminal profilers caution against making inferences about gender, age, or race from crime scene evidence (Turvey, 1999, 2002). Other stages of the criminal justice process where blind spots resulting from stereotypes can impact policy and practice include law enforcement omitting individuals from suspect pools; widespread use of forensic assessment measures that have been standardized and validated from predominantly male offender samples, with little attention to how gender, race, and ethnicity shape manifestations of personality characteristics; and use of *battered woman syndrome* and *postpartum depression* as a criminal defense. The study of criminal behavior has a long way to go to systematically uncover the many stereotypes that cloud the reality of criminal behavior.

Methodological Creativity

Simply put, much of the criminal behavior research is boring. Who really wants to read another study that regurgitates old data from the Wolfgang cohort, the FBI serial killer study, or one after another of the studies reporting a test of this or that other theory through secondary analysis of data from a large-scale national social survey, or another study validating the PCL-R or the LSI-R? These studies are certainly important and by all means need to continue. However, *if researchers of the future were to try to match each of the more traditional research designs with more creative attempts to collect primary data from difficult to obtain samples, using both qualitative and quantitative data collection strategies, we might come closer to capturing some of the nuances of criminal behavior* that will help answer questions about individual-situation interactions, differences in criminal behavior across time periods, gender, race/ethnicity, cultures, subcultures, and other factors and findings that are more rooted in and relevant to real-life and real people in the here and now.

Several issues stand in the way of methodological creativity. First, researchers are lazy, overextended, or too resource-challenged to do innovative quality research. It takes an enormous amount of time and energy to collect primary data, especially in criminal justice settings that require the lengthy process of human subjects review, agency-research trust, political dealings, and logistical constraints. Academics often feel compelled to take shortcuts when possible to produce a greater number of publications.

Second, creative research is costly and time-consuming. The more creative research designs may be rejected by funding agencies and institutional review boards because they are less traditional and based on marginalized perspectives. Qualitative research is more time-consuming than traditional quantitative approaches and qualitative components of research designs may be discarded out of practicality. Third, creative research that matters requires collaboration between academic institutions and criminal justice agencies. There is often a lack of connection between academics who study criminal behavior and criminal justice agencies charged with responding to crime, or between researchers and their subjects of study. The most meaningful, creative research designs involve or are informed through close connection between the researcher and real-world offenders and criminal justice practitioners.

Criminologists need to improve their theories and make research accessible to real people and situations. In her 2005 Presidential Address to the American Society of Criminology, Julie Horney urged criminologists to be cautious about using simple models that don't reflect reality. She argued that advances in interdisciplinary criminology would be greatly enhanced by focusing on the situational specificity of behavior crime and proposed the development of an alternative psychology of criminal behavior that acknowledges individual-environment interaction and the power of situations as the impetus for criminal behavior. Most important, she said that the study of criminal behavior needs *details* that better capture the complexity of human behavior (Horney, 2006). To illustrate this point Horney suggests that

> it is worth noting that some people who overuse alcohol do so only in the evenings and never during the workday, some only in social situations but never when alone, and some only when they go out of town to conferences. And lest we think that those who have been involved in crime must be those who lack self control in every arena, it is important to observe that many who have committed serious offenses have also held steady jobs, getting themselves to work on time every day, and many have supported families. Many whose supposed lack of control has led to legal sanctions possess much more self control than I when it comes to diet and exercise. Many drug dealers don't use drugs because they know the negative consequences the drugs would have for them. The dependence of our behavior on particular situations frequently makes us all appear to be walking contradictions. Yet, if we accept situational specificity of behavior as a natural product of learning that is shaped by context, the supposed contradictions in self-control can be seen instead as examples of stimulus control that reflect complex learning environments. (p. 8)

This notion of relevance of individual-situation interaction in the study of criminal behavior calls for situational data in longitudinal studies that would allow researchers to examine change across different types of situations. Furthermore, acknowledgment that the situation plays an important role in when and whether an individual will commit a criminal act can (and should) be extended to analysis of cultural-individual interactions and the ways in which societal changes such as technology, economics, shifts in power, and so on interact with individual-level characteristics.

It is worthwhile to return again to the medical analogy. Recent findings in cancer research show a promising treatment called *chronotherapy*. Chronotherapy is the practice of coordinating medical treatment with biological rhythms based on the notion that the body's biological rhythms in fighting disease depend on gender, age, genetics, and other factors. A person's biological clock influences how the person's body changes throughout the day, affecting a range of functions such as blood pressure, blood coagulation, and blood flow. Biological rhythms come in different forms—ultradian (less than a day), circadian (24 hours), infradian (over 24 hours), and seasonal (months)—and biology varies predictably based on these cycles. The most advanced application of this concept is drug chronotherapy in which drugs (e.g., chemotherapy) are administered according to an individual's cycles to minimize their negative side effects. In addition to cancer treatment, drug chronotherapy has been used in asthma and arthritis treatment. Research also suggests that it is applicable to surgery—for example, in timing surgery for certain types of cancer (Stehlin, 1997).

What does chronotherapy have to do with criminal behavior? If drug effects vary in relation to a body's biological rhythms, then the body's clock potentially influences behavior—or if not behavior, then perhaps treatment for behavioral problems. A parallel theory in criminology to chronobiology is life-course criminology, which suggests that the potential for criminal behavior changes across the life course. Applying the concept of chronotherapy to criminal behavior from the framework of life-course criminology, we could hypothesize that interventions may work at some times but not others, and that knowledge of an individual's "biological clock" or the nature of crime across the life course will provide information to guide the timing of interventions.

One last point—this is not an attempt to revive the medical model of crime (though it already has been revived to some extent in the civil commitment legislation). Rather, the comparison is meant to stimulate thinking about other (perhaps more meaningful) analogies. It should be completely unacceptable to the general public when criminal justice practice is not guided by a theory and research as it is in other areas of life. We will never be able to completely eradicate criminal behavior, just as we will probably never completely eradicate illness and disease. But that does not mean we cannot use the information we have to implement historically reflective, theoretically guided, and empirically informed practices. There is no reason why criminal justice interventions should be any less informed by theory and research than interventions in other fields. In fact, if the relationship between theory and empirical research and criminal justice practice were as accepted as it is in other arenas, we might be able to stick with a policy or practice long enough to measure its effectiveness, build on its strengths, and work through the weaknesses. This has never occurred in the history of criminal justice. If there is a single final hope to be expressed here, it is that the future brings greater acknowledgment of crime as a natural part of life and patience to stick with scientifically informed policies and practices long enough to see them work.

Concluding Comments

Let's take a minute to dream a little bit. It is the 22nd century, year 3008. All of the suggestions for future directions in the study of criminal behavior have been implemented. Academic criminologists, psychologists, and sociologists work with criminal justice practitioners with a free flow of information. Criminal justice professionals read the academic journals and academics ground their work in the realities of crime and criminal justice in ways that make their work accessible. All criminal justice policy and practice is based on empirical findings. There are no ego/territorial issues and a purely integrative theory of crime has developed. Our theories and typologies of crime have changed with the times and can explain, predict, and prevent crime. Criminologists have discovered the formula for criminal behavior—the complex set of variables that produces criminal behavior across all types of people, situations, time periods, and so on. In fact, they have completely designed crime out of society by devising a special intervention system that computes each individual-situation crime formula so that individuals are programmed to avoid the point in time, space, and mental and physical life at which crime could potentially occur. Those individuals who are highly susceptible to extreme forms of criminal behavior as a result of personality or genetic predisposition are identified in early infancy and placed into a special program that guides and redirects their criminogenic tendencies to prosocial behavior. Pharmacological interventions have eradicated drug and alcohol addiction.

Sound absurd? If so, then *what can we reasonably expect in terms of the gains that might be made in the future study of criminal behavior? Can we at the very least expect that a century from now we will be able to identify a person in our midst who is so disturbed or frustrated or lost in fantasy early enough to intervene before the person walks into a school, lines up all the little girls, and executes them? Can we expect to know enough about the power of mass media to redesign our computer games, refocus our news media, and reevaluate the images we consume in ways that promote prosocial behavior and reduce fear of our neighbors? Might we redesign our criminal justice practices to reflect a more realistic view of crime as a part of everyday life, and of criminals who could just as easily be us? Can we revive correctional rehabilitation and give it a chance to systematically, scientifically, and ethically address the real needs and risks of offenders in ways that would allow them to be productive citizens when they are released? Can we improve our forensic assessment tools so that we have a better chance than in rolling dice to make decisions about indefinitely removing high-risk offenders from society in the name of public safety?*

Let's return one last time to some of the more extreme crimes discussed at the beginning of this chapter. The Platte Canyon Colorado High School and Amish school hostage incidents are examples of criminal events that cut across crime categories. These crimes are unusual in that they do not fall neatly into traditional types or subtypes. However, theory and research on the nature and dynamics of the different types of offense behaviors help us understand the events in terms of a combined offense. Both of these offenses were violent crimes incorporating features of violent crime subtypes (homicide-suicide, mass murder). They also appear to include elements of sex crimes (sexual assault, deviant sexual fantasy). In addition, the Amish murders occurred only days after the Colorado hostage/murder and incorporated with shocking similarity the method of lining little girls up facing a chalkboard. The similarities raise the possibility that the modus operandi of the offender in the Amish murders was shaped by the copycat effect. This also raises the issue of technology. The Colorado hostage incident was all over the news in minutes. Fifty years ago, a murder in one city would not have been known in real-time in a city on the other side of the country.

Instant access to all of the extreme criminal acts that the news can manage to cover has an impact on public fear of crime and offender behavior.

One final point—Virginia Tech shooter Seung-Hui Cho referred to Columbine killers Klebold and Harris and sent videotapes of himself to NBC News in which he posed in various ways holding weapons similar to scenes in movies. The crime was referred to in news accounts as the worst mass murder in American history. Mass murder expert James Alan Fox said repeatedly in news interviews after the Virginia Tech murders that we need to stop talking about mass murder and other crimes in terms of *Guinness Book of World Records:*

> It serves no purpose to focus on "mass murder trivia." Instead, we should focus on what responses may be appropriate based on the fact that seven of the eight largest mass shootings in US history have occurred over the past 25 years—during which access to high-powered weapons has become far too easy. (Fox, April 18, 2007)

If our culture didn't celebrate serial and mass murder and homicide-suicides in the news media, would Morrison, Roberts, and Cho have chosen to go about these crimes in the way they did? Would these offenders have chosen to quietly kill themselves or perhaps engage in violent acts on a smaller scale if murderers weren't treated like media superstars? Would Tiffany Hall and the other women who have committed fetus theft murders and assaults have thought this up on their own without the wide media coverage of the small number of such bizarre offenses? Even if these crimes could not have been prevented, could the harm have been minimized in some way? Could some of these victims' lives have been spared?

Summary

How can we apply advances in criminological theory and criminal justice practice to better understand and respond to criminal behavior in the 21st century? What does it mean to be "creative, innovative, and scientific" in preventing and responding to criminal behavior? These are critical questions in thinking about the future of theory and research on criminal behavior. Obstacles to applying criminological theory to criminal justice practice include barriers to interdisciplinary perspectives and theory integration, acknowledgment and examination of the ways in which technology shapes criminal behavior, imbedded stereotypes, and methodological creativity. A large, rich, interdisciplinary knowledge base has accumulated with contributions from the biological, psychological, sociological, cultural, phenomenological, and opportunity/ecological perspectives as well as theoretical and empirical research on crime types.

The job of criminal behavior scholars, criminologists, and forensic psychologists who study criminal behavior is to make sense of crime through the scientific method, with the goals of prevention, explanation, and prediction. It is important that contemporary theory and research on criminal behavior be cognizant of the past. Many current theories and practices are modernized versions of those of the past, yet few theoretical and empirically based initiatives have been given the chance they need to show positive gains. The future of theory and research on criminal behavior must fill in the gaps to improve theories and make research accessible to real people and situations and with attention to the changing nature of crime in the 21st century.

DISCUSSION QUESTIONS

1. If, as this chapter suggests, it is the job of criminal behavior scholars, criminologists, and forensic psychologists who study criminal behavior to make sense of both rare and everyday crimes through the scientific method, what can criminologists offer in response to extreme crimes like the Colorado, Nickel Mines, and Virginia Tech school shootings? Do you agree or disagree with the father who commented, after Emily Keyes's murder, that crimes like these are like earthquakes—is it meaningful to compare criminal behavior to natural disasters? And what about the more benign crimes discussed in this text, such as public order and lower-level property crimes? What can criminologists offer to help us understand and respond to everyday and extreme forms of criminal behavior?

2. Why do you think history keeps repeating itself when it comes to responding to crime and criminal behavior? If medical science were to rely on methods of treating diseases that were used in the early 1900s, would be as accepting as they seem to be when contemporary criminal justice practices are throwbacks to 100 years ago (e.g., habitual offender legislation)? Discuss.

3. Feminist criminologists have said that one thing would significantly reduce crime—to socialize little boys as if they were little girls and to "make men think and act more like women." Do you agree or disagree with this suggestion? How has theory and research on criminal behavior led researchers to this conclusion? What can be done in the future to respond to issues of gender and crime?

4. As discussed in this chapter, much theoretical and empirical research is read and discussed only by academic criminologists and students of criminology/criminal justice in college classrooms, and graduates who go on to careers in law enforcement, court services/law, corrections, and victim services find little opportunity to apply the theory and research they've learned in the classroom in their daily work. What hinders the application of theory and research to criminal justice practice? If you are planning a career in criminal justice, what can you do to ensure that this changes in the future? Discuss.

5. Review/discuss the five considerations for future directions in criminal behavior research discussed in this chapter. Can you offer additional suggestions and ideas to further theory, typologies, and application of and research on criminal behavior in the future?

 On Your Own: Log on to the Web-based student study site at http://www.sagepub .com/helfgottstudy/ for the URL links in the Web Exercises, study aids such as review quizzes, and research recommendations including links to journal articles specifically selected for this book.

WEB EXERCISES

1. There are a number of national and local sources of criminal justice research and resources, including the *National Criminal Justice Reference Service* (NCJRS) at http://www.ncjrs.gov/ whatsncjrs.html and the *Justice Research and Statistics Association* (JRSA) at http:// www.jrsa.org/, a nonprofit organization devoted to conducting and publishing policy relevant research on justice issues. Go to these Web sites and review some of the current research that has been published on criminal behavior and criminal justice. Identify studies that address some of the issues raised in this chapter and discuss some of blind spots you see in terms of areas that appear to remain unaddressed.

2. Go to the *360 Degrees: Perspectives on the U.S. Criminal Justice System* Web site: http://www.360degrees.org/360degrees.html. Click the "timeline" and spend some time getting a sense of the dominant theories of criminal behavior in the different time periods. Discuss the impact of these theories on the criminal justice practices of each era.

3. Also on the *360 Degrees: Perspectives on the U.S. Criminal Justice System* Web site (http://www.360degrees.org/360degrees.html), go to the "dynamic data" pages and take the online test, "What's your theory?" Discuss how your theoretical perspective could be enhanced by integrating additional perspectives.

4. Read Jeff Ferrell's (1995) "Culture, Crime, and Cultural Criminology" in the *Journal of Criminal Justice and Popular Culture:* http://www.albany.edu/scj/jcjpc/vol3is2/culture .html. Discuss how his ideas can be incorporated into suggestions for future research on criminal behavior.

5. Visit the U.S. Department of Justice Web page on Technology and Crime: http://www .ojp.usdoj.gov/topics/technology.htm. Discuss the types of research you find. How do you think the new science of criminal justice will influence criminal behavior of the future?

6. Read the classic article by Hazelwood and Warren (1990), "The Criminal Behavior of the Serial Rapist": http://www.holysmoke.org/fem/fem0126.htm. Using this article as a starting point, design a "methodologically creative" follow-up study to further explore the serial criminal behavior of the rapist in ways that will tap into some of the "blind spots" identified in this chapter.

7. As suggested in the concluding comments, one possibility for change in the future would be to redesign computer games and other media to encourage prosocial rather than antisocial behavior. In fact, this has already been done in a new computer game recently released by Rockstar Games for Playstation 2 (and soon to be released for Xbox 360 and Wii) called *Bully* (see: http://www.rockstargames.com/bully/home/). Read about how this game works at http://www.earthtimes.org/articles/show/9439.html, compare and contrast it with other games such as *Grand Theft Auto*, and offer your thoughts on whether you agree or disagree this is a promising idea for reducing some types or incidents of criminal behavior.

8. Review the news articles on the Virginia Tech shooting at http://topics.nytimes.com/top/ reference/timestopics/organizations/v/virginia_polytechnic_institute_and_state_university/ind ex.html?excamp=GGGNvirginiatechshooting. Discuss the biological, psychological, sociological, phenomenological, opportunity, and cultural factors that likely contributed to this event. Given what we know now, after the fact, and with the state of the research on criminal behavior, what can be done to prevent a crime like this from occurring in the future?

Notes

Notes for Chapter One

1. In *Lawrence et al. v Texas* (2003) the U.S. Supreme Court ruled that sodomy laws in the United States are unconstitutional. Before this ruling, 14 states, Puerto Rico, and the military had sodomy laws. In many countries around the world, homosexuality is criminalized. See http://www.sodomylaws.org/.

2. Burglary is the only crime category in which the NIBRS rate can be lower than the UCR's. This is because of the expansion of the hotel rule to include mini-storage units. If a burglary occurs involving two units of a property owned under the same management, the UCR counts this as two burglaries, whereas the NIBRS counts it as one burglary.

3. For example, in a number of studies I have conducted involving both offender self-report and corroboration with prison institutional files, offenders who have committed crimes involving rape and murder were willing to verbally report the murder but not the rape or would leave out particular details of the event that cast the offender in a particularly negative light in the mind of the offender.

4. Eagan (August 10, 1999) expressed concerns about Levitt's research in *The Boston Herald* and asked, "How are we supposed to feel about this? Grateful to these women? Glad that their criminal offspring never drew breath? Or nervous about the spectre of abortion as social engineering, as underclass population control, or about new opportunities for coercion of women?" (p. O22).

5. Historically, a distinction has been made between *criminology* and *criminal justice*, with criminal justice programs focusing on the criminal justice process and criminology programs focusing on the study of crime. The distinction is rooted in the origin of criminology as a subfield of sociology and the development of separate criminal justice programs in the 1970s that benefited from federal funding and focused on higher education for law enforcement practitioners (Adler, 1995). However, this distinction is becoming less clear as a greater number of academic programs encompass both the study of crime and its response. According to Cullen (1995), "The fact that a sociology department was the first to teach criminology on a campus, or that a criminal justice department was once affiliated with a sociology department, or that sociology has contributed much to our understanding of crime may be interesting for historical purposes. These facts however are largely irrelevant to the reality that criminal justice has now evolved as a distinct discipline with its own scholarly and educational mission" (p. 3) Undergraduate and graduate programs use titles such as Criminology and Criminal Justice, Criminal Justice, Administration of Justice, Crime, Law, & Justice, Justice Studies, Law & Society, Law, Society, & Justice, and are so similar in their curricula that they can be said to represent a single field of study. This text considers Criminology/ Criminal Justice as a single field of study that is inherently and uniquely interdisciplinary. In his presidential address to the Academy of Criminal Justice Sciences, Clear (2001) said that "Academic criminal justice has come of age . . . it must sharpen its self image as the champion of issues related to criminal justice higher education and professional preparation . . . This is our greatest challenge, for which we are now ready" (p. 726).

Notes for Chapter Two

1. See *Seattle Times'* coverage of the Baranyi and Anderson case: http://archives.seattletimes.nwsource .com/cgi-bin/texis.cgi/web/vortex/search?searchType= date&period=archive&maxReturn=20&skip=0&source= search&sectionID=&spg=hi&query=alex+baranyi+and+ david+anderson.

2. This text addresses the range of criminal behaviors from the most benign to the most extreme, with the notion that the dynamics involved in the commission of

minor criminal behaviors (and most human behaviors) are on many levels similar to those involved in the commission of the most extreme crimes. The term *criminal behavior* is confined here to behaviors that violate the criminal law. Noncriminal antisocial acts and deviant behavior are discussed at many points of theoretical overlap between sociology and criminology in the study of deviance and psychology, biology, and criminology in antisocial personality disorder and psychopathy. However, noncriminal antisocial behavior and deviance are not the primary focus of this text and are left, respectively, for abnormal psychology and deviance texts.

3. For example, many scholars who approach crime from the routine activity, cultural, and phenomenological perspectives are sociology-trained criminologists, and some texts address these perspectives under the heading of *sociological theories.* Some criminology/criminal justice–trained scholars engage in psychological or biological-based research, and many sociological and psychological theories arrive at similar conclusions, predictions, and policy implications, using their own disciplinary jargon.

4. For a detailed overview of criminological theories, readers should consult comprehensive criminology texts (e.g., Brown, Esbensen, & Geis, 2001; Hagan, 1997; Schmalleger, 2004; Siegal, 2004; Vold, Bernard, & Snipes, 2002; Walsh & Ellis, 2007).

5. See Raine (1993), Fishbein (2001), Rowe (2001), and Walsh (2002) for thorough coverage of the research and theory on biology and crime.

6. See Walsh (2002, pp. 49–74) for detailed discussion and examples of evolutionary psychology and evolutionary criminology and Fishbein (2001), Jones (1999), and Walsh (2002) for a more comprehensive discussion of evolutionary theories of criminal behavior.

7. Antisocial personality disorder is characterized by regular disregard for and violation of the rights of others through aggressive or destructive acts. Histrionic personality disorder is characterized by exaggerated emotion and attention seeking. Both are *DSM-IV-TR* Axis II, Cluster B, personality disorders. See APA, *DSM-IV-TR* (2000) for complete criteria, or visit BehaveNet for an online version of the *DSM-IV-TR*: http://www.behavenet.com/. These disorders are also discussed in Chapter 4.

8. Research empirically linking psychopathy and violence warrants a separate discussion of the role of psychopathy in criminal behavior, which is discussed in depth in Chapter 4.

9. Sykes and Matza's Techniques of Neutralization theory is generally viewed as a sociological theory. The theory, though sociological, is discussed here because it focuses on the ways in which cognitive processes enable criminal behavior.

10. Mass media effects on criminal behavior and the phenomenon of copycat crime are discussed in depth in Chapter 10.

11. Black (1991) offers a comprehensive analysis of media-mediated violence and the criminogenic and cathartic effects of depictions of violence in art, literature, film, TV, and pop culture in his book *The Aesthetics of Murder: A Study in Romantic Literature and Contemporary Culture,* including case study examples of copycat offenders such as John Hinckley and Mark David Chapman. However, for most people, rather than providing role models for criminal behavior, violent media primes violent events, exacerbates fear of crime, and creates and reinforces a "mean world" view (Gerbner, 1994).

12. See Henry and Milovanovic's (1996) *Constitutive Criminology: Beyond Postmodernism.*

13. For an anthology of readings in critical criminology, see Arrigo's (1998) *Social Justice/Criminal Justice: The Maturation of Critical Theory in Crime, Law, and Deviance.*

14. See Ferguson et al. (1984), the feminist sexuality debates for comparison of radical and liberal feminism, and Daly and Chesney-Lind (1988) for discussion of different schools of feminist thought. See Wolf's (1994) *Fire With Fire: The New Female Power and How to Use It,* for discussion of power feminism. See Potter (2006) for discussion of Black feminist criminology and critical race feminist theory.

15. Routine activity theory is commonly viewed as a sociological theory of crime. However, because of its the focus on opportunity and situational and contextual factors, rational choice, and the convergence of individual, situational/contextual, and environmental factors to increase or decrease the likelihood that crime will occur, and the popularity of this theory for its practical applicability in the criminal justice system, it warrants attention as a distinct criminological perspective.

16. This connection between symbols, style, and aesthetics has made its way into situational crime prevention strategies such as the use of classical music as a crime deterrent at transit stations and bus stops in the United States, Canada, Australia, and the United Kingdom (Burgard, 2006; Classical music on West Palm corner deters crime, 2001; Morris, 2005; Murray, 2005; Santos, 2007; Timberg, 2005). Composer Rob Kaplow suggests that people bring their associations with classical music into their experience

of it: "They listen to this sound, and what comes with it is this whole association of its packaging, which is unpleasant. . . . 'We don't want to be part of that elitist, white-tails, concert-going kind of world'"(Timberg, 2005, 26). For people who see themselves as aggressive, violent, or antisocial, certain types of music do not go along with their self-images. Music historian Robert Fink speculates that, "If people feel like they're sitting around in a cognac ad or a BMW commercial, it ruins the movie of themselves, it wrecks their soundtrack. It's tough for people to lounge around feeling 'hard' if the music is sending the wrong cultural message" (Timberg, 2005, 28).

17. Existentialism is an outgrowth of phenomenology found in the writings of 19th- and 20th-century European philosophers including Kierkegaard, Nietzsche, Sarte, Camus, and Frankl. Sufficient discussion of the broad range of definitions of existentialism is not possible here. Readers should consult the work of these authors or an introduction to philosophy text for a more complete definition and discussion of existentialist thought.

18. After writing *In the Belly of the Beast* and getting paroled from prison with the support of author Norman Mailer, Jack Henry Abbott murdered Richard Adan, an aspiring actor and New York waiter. This passage from his book was used in his murder trial. He was convicted, sent to prison, and committed suicide in prison in 2002.

19. Gottfredson and Hirschi's general theory of crime and life-course criminology are not generally classified as "integrated theories" in criminological texts because they are primarily sociological theories. I include them here because they integrate psychological and sociological concepts such as *self-control* and *antisocial propensity* (though they do not specifically address the psychological literature encompassing these concepts).

20. Description of these theories is beyond the scope of this text. See Cullen and Agnew (2006) and Vold, Bernard, and Snipes (2002) for detailed review of these theories.

21. This information was obtained from news articles in the *Seattle Times* and *Seattle Post-Intelligencer* between 1997 and 2001 and from court documents including review of appellate documents decided in 2000 (Baranyi) and 2002 (Anderson).

Notes for Chapter Three

1. This research is discussed in Chapter 4. For a recent overview article reviewing the research on psychopathy and violent crime, see Porter and Porter (2007).

2. *The Mask of Sanity* is now out of print but is available online at http://www.cassiopaea.org/cass/sanity_1.PdF.

3. The third edition of *Crime Profiles* was published in 2006. See Miethe, McCorkle, & Listwan (2006).

4. The term *compulsive* is a somewhat confusing label for the sexual homicide offender who is organized, antisocial and narcissistic, psychopathic, detached, and hyporeactive in contrast with the *catathymic* offender, who is disorganized, attached, hyperreactive, and so on. Meloy likely uses the term *compulsive* because this type of offender needs to commit the behavior, but is not out of control or out of touch with reality.

5. Chapter 6 presents narrative descriptions of the different types in the MTC:R3 and MTC:CM3 typologies.

6. This typology is consistently discussed in the offender profiling literature. It is also often referred to by law enforcement experts in news interviews and appears in many court documents in which expert testimony regarding crime scene evidence and case linkage is provided. While some in law enforcement contend that the typology is no longer regularly applied or respected, it continues to appears in the academic literature and narratives of law enforcement personnel and other experts in the media and court documents.

Notes for Chapter Four

1. Davis's Web site is provided through the *Canadian Coalition Against the Death Penalty* and has generated much controversy. It is available at http://www.ccadp.org/richarddavis.htm.

2. A large body of research on psychopathy and the prediction of violent recidivism has emerged in recent years. Studies linking psychopathy and violent recidivism are too numerous to review here. For specific findings and review of the research, see Gacono (2000), Harris, Rice, and Cormier (1991), Hare (2001, 2003), Hemphill et al. (1998), Hodgins (1997), Litwack and Schlesinger (1998), Salekin, Rogers, and Sewell (1996), Serin and Amos (1995), and Porter and Porter (2007).

3. Psychological characteristics in individuals cannot be directly observed. Psychological tests are used to make inferences about an individual's level of a characteristic. Psychologists use psychometric tests such as the PCL-R to make inferences about characteristics associated with a particular psychological condition. IRT is a psychometric model used to measure performance on a test item in relation to other items on a test; it enables

psychologists to measure individuals on the latent trait defined by the set of items while simultaneously scaling each item on the very same dimension.

4. While the PCL-R (Factor 1) measures personality features distinguishing between psychopathic and nonpsychopathic antisocial personality disordered (APD) individuals, but Factor 1 ratings depend on clinician inferences about the motives and accuracy of patient self-reports and interpersonal style (Kosson, Gacono, & Bodholdt, 2000). Because of the subjective nature of Factor 1 ratings, aspects of the interpersonal style of the psychopath can be lost. With this in mind, the Interpersonal Measure of Psychopathy (IM-P) was developed as a supplement to the PCL-R to assess the core personality of the psychopath by identifying and coding interpersonal behaviors (Kosson, Gacono, & Bodholdt, 2000).

5. See *International Classification of Diseases, 10th Edition* (World Health Organization, 1992). The ICD-10 classification *Dysocial Personality* is considered to represent the classic concept of psychopathy (Coid, 1993).

6. The amygdala is an almond-shaped structure located in the middle of the brain. The amygdala regulates behavioral expression of emotional reactions (See Blair, Mitchell, and Blair, 2005, for discussion of amygdale dysfunction in the psychopath).

7. Farrington explains the scarcity of longitudinal research focusing on psychopathy by the low prevalence of psychopathy in community samples and the fact that the PCL-R was designed for use with prison samples. The development of the PCL Screening Version (PCL-SV) has enabled researchers to use the tool in community samples in longitudinal research that treats psychopathy as a dimension rather than a category.

8. Academic discourse on the relationship between psychopathy and culture appeared to peak in the 1970s and 1980s (beginning in 1941 with Cleckley's attention to noncriminal psychopaths in the *Mask of Sanity*). Much of this early attention did not involve empirical research but represents an important synthesis of theory and research in psychology, criminology, sociology, anthropology, and philosophy that offers a theoretically rich foundation for future and much needed research in this area.

9. Noncriminal psychopaths have been referred to in the literature by many terms including *successful, adaptive, extrasocial, subclinical, nonincarcerated, industrial,* and *corporate.*

10. Diane Downs, subject of Ann Rule's (1987) book *Small Sacrifices,* is an example of a female psychopath.

Downs was said to have a histrionic personality disorder and was also referred to as an antisocial personality and a psychopath. Downs shot her three children—one died, one was paralyzed, and the other was seriously wounded—because she believed her lover didn't like kids. Downs saw one of her talents as being able to bear children and believed she could replace her children by getting pregnant again. She was a charming, seductive, dramatic person who held a job and had no criminal history until the day she shot her children.

11. For example, when rewards are used in experimental studies, women may respond more positively to visitation privileges than to small monetary rewards that are often used in studies involving incarcerated male psychopaths.

12. See Campbell (1994) for a discussion of the socialization of aggression in girls who must behave in such a way to survive (e.g., runaways, female gang members, girls who have never fit the social stereotype of femininity).

Notes for Chapter Five

1. This figure represents the percentage of homicides in which the offender was identified as a stranger out of the overall number of homicides for 2005. It is important to note that there were 6,724 homicides in which the offender was reported as "unknown."

2. Simple assaults are not included as a UCR Part 1 crime and are not included in the number of violent crimes. In 2005, there were 1,301,392 arrests for "other assaults" (Uniform Crime Reports, 2005).

3. Meloy (1988) and Weinshenker and Siegel (2002) refer to "predatory" and "affective" aggression. Geen (1998) refers to *instrumental* and *affective* aggression. Campbell (1990) uses the terms *instrumental* and *expressive,* and Black (1983) and Cooney and Phillips (2002) classify aggression as *predatory* and *moralistic.* These bimodal classifications are consistent in that they divide aggression into two general types (with some variation across authors)—aggression that is instrumental, predatory, and proactive and aggression that is expressive, affective, reactive, and moralistic.

4. Cooney and Phillips (2002) suggest that the concept of *moralistic violence* (p. 84) in the predatory-moralistic typology is broader than the concept of expressive violence in that the concept of moralistic violence can be applied to groups and nations. Moralistic violence is

defined as a conflict management strategy—an attempt to right a wrong rather than to inflict injury.

5. It is worth noting that some authors, depending on their perspective, suggest that all violence is motivated by one or the other type of aggression. For example, Felson (2002) argues that all violence is instrumental and emotional violence can be a rational act to get others to comply, restore justice, or protect one's self-image. According to Felson (2002, p. 45), "Violence requires neither a unique theory nor an elaborate one and can be explained with the three instrumental explanations above. Unfortunately, many of the people who write about violence are so upset that they cannot calm themselves down enough to analyze it well." This is a rational choice perspective based on the idea that all acts are the products of some level of rational choice. On the other hand, from a psychodynamic perspective, it could be argued that all violence is expressive/affective in that all decisions are fundamentally rooted in emotion or have psychodynamic/developmental origins.

6. Cornell et al. (1996) use the terms *instrumental* and *reactive* rather than *predatory* and *affective*. The authors define instrumental aggression as purposeful and goal directed and reactive aggression as an emotional response to frustration.

7. There may also be situations when predatory aggression appears affective. However, this would likely involve an offender who is motivated to intentionally make a violent act look affective. For example, an offender may do this to throw the police off or as part of his or her legal defense. In terms of physiological features of the actual offense behavior, however, it is difficult to mistake predatory for affective aggression.

8. Contemptuous delight is a feeling of pleasure and exhilaration as a result of putting another person down—one of few emotions that psychopaths appear to experience. See Meloy (1988), pp. 99–106.

9. The FBI Uniform Crime Report does not include simple assault under the category of violent crime. Arrests for simple assaults are included in the category "other assaults," which are not part of the crime index (the measure of serious crime including murder and non-negligent manslaughter, forcible rape, robbery, aggravated assault, burglary, larceny-theft, motor vehicle theft, arson).

10. Miethe, McCorkle, and Listwan (2006) summarize crime types in terms of *syndromes*. Syndromes are defined as combinations of offenders, victims, and situational characteristics (p. 15) that indicate the amount and nature of the diversity in behavioral patterns within each crime category.

11. Day, Gough, and McFadden (2003) suggest that it is not just masculine environments that produce the expectation of violent response to insult and dishonor. In their study of working-class cultural contexts in Britain, the authors found that violence plays a role in working-class femininities and women engage in violence in drinking situations in public settings to publicly demonstrate aggressive prowess, to defend themselves and their group in an atmosphere of surveillance, and to promote hard reputations.

Notes for Chapter Six

1. Schizoid personality disorder is an Axis II Personality Disorder in the *DSM-IV-TR*. Like antisocial personality disorder and psychopathy, this disorder is not an Axis I clinical disorder and does not meet criteria for legal insanity because persons so diagnosed are in touch with reality. However, in some cases schizoid personality disorder is a precursor to schizophrenia, a clinical condition that does meet the definition of legal insanity.

2. Pyromania is not classified as a paraphilia in the *DSM-IV-TR*. Rather, this disorder is included in the section Impulse Disorders Not Elsewhere Classified and is characterized by deliberate and purposeful firesetting, tension and affective arousal before setting a fire, fascination and curiosity about fire and firesetting, pleasure and release of tension after setting a fire, lack of material gain or instrumental motivation for setting the fire, and absence of cognitive impairment. Firesetting is also one of the criteria for conduct disorder.

3. Some researchers distinguish *zoophilia* from *bestiality*, suggesting that the term *zoophile* be used to refer to an emotional attachment to/sexual preference for animals and *bestiality* to sexual contact between humans and animals resulting in human sexual arousal. See Beetz (2004) for a thorough review of the bestiality/zoophilia literature.

4. Sung Koo Kim was a person of interest in the disappearance of a 19-year-old Oregon college student, Brooke Wilberger, until another individual, Joel Patrick Courtney, was charged with the crime.

5. Tragically, the boy (Ryan Alan Hade) died in a motorcycle accident on June 9, 2005, at age 23 ("Victim of 1989 rape mutilation dies in motorcycle crash," June 22, 2005).

6. Jack Olsen's book *Son: A Psychopath and his Victims*, published in 1983, was likely another powerful influence on the historical development of the sexually violent predator legislation in Washington State. Kevin Coe, the subject of the book, is one of Washington State's most notorious serial rapists. At the time of this writing, he is awaiting trial after having completed his prison sentence to determine whether or not he meets the criteria for civil commitment under Washington State's Sexually Violent Predator law.

7. This term comes from the word *ephebophilia*, an obscure word rarely used today referring to the sexual preference for boys at puberty (*epi hebe*). Hebophiles such as priests who sexually abuse boys in their teens are commonly referred to as pedophiles for lack of a better term. According to Jenkins (1996), in his book *Pedophiles and Priests*, the distinction between pedophilia and hebophilia may seem purely semantic, but it has important implications for treatment of offenders. Fagan et al. (2002) note that the pedophile often does not make the rational distinction between pedophilia and epehophilia or hebophilia. Many pedophiles prefer children in a particular age range (e.g., 9–14); thus, the age distinction may have little actual relevance in the offender's mental life.

8. Ressler, Burgess, and Douglas (1992) cite cases of sexual homicide offenders who have engaged in experimental "play" in childhood that served as a precursor to behaviors committed in the act of sexual homicide: For example, an offender who pulled off Barbie doll heads who later decapitated his victims, another who chased a friend around with a hatchet who later used a hatchet in his murders, and many offenders with histories of animal torture. Sexual homicide offenders have also been known to experiment with consensual sexual partners. For example, a former wife of Gary Ridgway told police that during their marriage Ridgway had, on two occasions, tied her up to wooden stakes in the ground for sex outdoors, getting the idea from a pornographic movie they watched, and sometimes inserted grapes and bananas into her vagina (King County Journal, 2003).

9. Turvey (1999, 2002) uses the term *experimental force* to refer to behaviors that fulfill psychological and fantasy-oriented needs. Behaviors reflecting experimental force include postmortem evisceration, postmortem biting of the victim's breast, postmortem removal of the victim's breasts, perimortem stab wounds of varying depth and symmetry, postmortem insertion of objects into victim's bodily orifices, and violent antemortem sexual

activity with a chemically unconscious victim. Serial sexual homicide offenders often engage in experimentation on human victims, seeking heightened forms of sexual arousal.

10. Many feminists do not agree with this view. Gender deconstruction of rape and sexual assault and focus on female sexual offending have been criticized for shifting attention away from the more prevalent and dangerous problem of male sexual assault against females. Some express legitimate concern that attention to female sexual offenders will distract focus away from male sexual offenders, who are the primary social problem, with fear that resources will also be redirected and used as just another tool to further subjugate women. Even more problematic is the possibility that if females are perceived to be capable of raping males (by forcing them to have sexual intercourse), this could be used against female rape victims of male offenders. This is a serious and legitimate concern that has worked to maintain the lack of research on female sexual offending. Some researchers who have focused on female sexual offending have reported receiving hostile professional reactions to their work (see Hislop, 2001, p. 44, for a more complete discussion of this important issue).

11. Scarce (1997) uses the term *hate rape* to refer to rapes motivated by racism and homophobia. The higher incidence of victimization of homosexual and Black men suggests that this is an important area in need of empirical exploration.

12. For a fascinating account of the experience of the actors involved in the male rape scene in the 1972 film *Deliverance*, starring Burt Reynolds and Ned Beatty, see Scarce (1997, pp. 114–119). In addition to the intensity of filming the scene and the actors' experience of blurred boundaries between reality and fiction, the actor (Beatty) who played the rape victim in the scene experienced taunting and verbal abuse for over two decades.

13. Fagan et al. (2002) note that pedophiles who try to satisfy their sexual urges by using child pornography are committing a crime even though they do not commit physical sex acts against children, but that a recent U.S. Supreme court case (*Ashcroft v Free Speech Coalition*, (00–795) US 198 F3d 1083, affirmed, 2002) declared unconstitutional criminal sanctions for pedophiles who view computer-generated sexualized images of children. Thus, technically, a pedophile who views digitally created sexualized images of children would not be committing a crime.

Notes for Chapter Seven

1. In June 2004, the FBI's UCR approved discontinuing the use of the Crime Index used since 1960. The rationale for elimination of the Crime Index was the inflation of the Index by the offense with the highest number. Larceny-theft makes up a majority of reported crime, thus the volume of these economic offenses overshadows more serious, but less frequently committed crime.

2. Prostitution and gambling are often considered *public order crimes* but are included here because they are also profit-driven crimes. Gambling can be considered both an economic crime (when it is for profit) and a public order crime (when it is an addiction). On the other hand, vandalism is an offense against property that is not included here because it is a nuisance criminal behavior without a primary economic motivation and best categorized as a public order offense.

3. Naylor (2003) suggests that the concept of "computer-assisted crime" is about as informative as "pen-and-paper assisted crime" would have been a couple of generations ago and that grouping crimes according to the method by which they are conducted has little use. For example, classifying crimes committed by phone as "telemarketing" crimes "makes as much sense as calling burglary through a second-floor window, 'ladder fraud'" (p. 83).

4. The distinction between crime and criminality, discussed in previous chapters, is at the heart of most discussions of criminal behavior. In economic crime, the boundaries between crime and criminality are less clear because economic need can produce behavioral patterns through which criminality is often inferred (e.g., antisocial personality, criminal career patterns, habitual offending). This is particularly important when race/ethnicity, social class, and gender issues are taken into account. For example, economic crimes committed by female offenders have been largely underexplored, misunderstood, and explained in male terms (Davies, 2003). Prostitution has come to be understood as a public order offense explained in sexual terms as rooted in promiscuity rather than economic necessity. Thus, a comprehensive definition of economic crime must attend to the complex relationship between economic need and criminogenic propensity.

5. Comparing crime (a behavioral act that violates a law) to criminality (propensity to commit crime) confounds social deviance with personality deviance. In most cases, crime is committed by those with a propensity to commit it, except when situational need arises that, despite the absence of criminality/propensity, compels an individual to commit crime. However, those who find themselves in circumstances conducive to economic crime are often influenced by a host of factors (subcultural style, antisocial peers, minimal social support, etc.) that foster the propensity to commit it.

6. Robbery, murder-for-hire, kidnapping, and murder resulting from burglary when the offender is caught by surprise can also be viewed as economic crimes in situations where profit is the central motive of the offense. However, these offenses are best classified as violent crime because an act in which an offender harms another person is qualitatively different in nature from acts involving inanimate objects. Though some authors argue that property crimes such as burglary have interpersonal components (Merry & Harsent, 2000), in most cases the offense of burglary is profit driven.

7. Arson (that does not result in homicide or physical harm to a person) can be classified as an economic, sex, or political crime depending on offender motive and the nature of the act. Arson committed by an individual whose motive is insurance fraud can be classified as an economic crime, whereas arson committed for the purpose of sexual arousal is a sex crime. Arson committed as political protest (e.g., arson of logging trucks or construction sites by environmental activists) can be classified as a political crime.

8. There are parallel literatures in sociology and psychology that describe chronic persistent offenders. Sociologists refer to the *career criminal* who is influenced by sociocultural factors and psychologists explain persistent offending in terms of *antisocial personality disorder*, *criminal personality*, and level of *psychopathy*. Regardless of where the emphasis is (on sociological or psychological factors) or the exact class of offenders, psychologists, sociologists, and interdisciplinary criminologists alike agree that a subset of chronic offenders commit a disproportionate amount of crime.

9. Embezzlement is not included as larceny-theft in the UCR and it is not reported as theft in the NCVS because the NCVS sample is made up of households only, not businesses.

10. For example, *kleptomania* is an impulse disorder recognized in the *Diagnostic and Statistical Manual of Mental Disorders*. Criteria for the disorder include recurrent failure to resist impulses to steal items not needed or for monetary value; increasing tension before committing theft; relief, gratification, or pleasure while committing theft; theft not committed out of vengeance or anger or in

response to delusion or hallucination; and stealing is not better explained by other disorders such as antisocial personality disorder or conduct disorder (APA, 2000).

11. Studies show that girls and women with eating disorders, specifically bulimia, sometimes shoplift. Some shoplift nonfood items, but most steal food, diet pills, and laxatives to support and maintain the secrecy of a costly habit of binge eating and purging (Goldner, Geller, Birmingham, & Remick, 2000).

12. Even joyriding, which is motivated by thrill, excitement, and peer pressure, can be seen as a financially motivated crime. Joyriders usually dump their car as soon as the ride is over; however, the unlawful taking of an item from another person, if only momentarily, is financially rewarded. A person who steals a car to impress peers or for quick transportation is still engaging in a crime that is momentarily economically advantageous in the mind of the offender. Stealing a car to have some fun or acquire transportation is in lieu of renting a car, which is financially burdensome.

13. The rate reported here is based on data from 10,843 agencies (204,034,545 of total population). The rate based on data for 7,898 cities (population 139,498,658 of total population) differs slightly—89.6 per 100,000 for fraud, 43.0 for forgery/counterfeiting, and 6.4 for embezzlement.

14. Joseph Wells, author of *Principles of Fraud Examination,* fittingly states, "Sutherland is to the world of white-collar criminality what Freud is to psychology" (Wells, 2005, p. 12).

15. For example, groups such as the *Earth Liberation Front* (ELF) and *Animal Liberation Front* (ALF) have been known to set fires to property such as forest ranger stations (in the case of ELF) and animal experimentation laboratories (ALF). The groups have also claimed to jointly commit arsons including that of a U.S. Bureau of Land Management horse barn, chutes, pens, and equipment in which 400 horses were released in 1997. Other examples of terrorist use of arson as an MO are the Oklahoma City bombing by Timothy McVeigh in 1995, the World Trade Center bombing in 1993, and the 9–11 use of jets as bombs in the attacks on the World Trade Center and Pentagon in 2001. Because terrorism is a qualitatively different type of crime that uses arson as a tool to incite terror for the purpose of asserting political views, it is discussed in the context of political crime in Chapter 9.

16. The term *communicative arson* is used in the *DSM-IV-TR* to refer to individuals with mental disorders

who set fires to communicate a need, wish, or desire directed at changing the nature or location of services (APA, 2000).

17. Mutilation by burning is commonly associated with *hate-arson* assaults. Arson-homicide, its relationship to paraphilias, and the symbolic role fire plays in homicidal attacks on homosexual, bisexual, and transexual victims are little researched areas currently being explored by Donald Drake and colleagues at the *University of Minnesota Center for Homicide Research* (see: http://www.chronline.org/index.html).

18. Naylor (2003) provides examples of radically different types of underground networks that interact with legitimate business in different ways. For example, illegal wildlife starts with poachers, is then traded (alive or dead depending on its use) to underground traffickers, and then the product is turned over to smugglers and eventually sold in pet stores or respectable Chinese pharmacies. Guns, however, start with legal suppliers (licensed dealers or gun shows) and then enter underground market chains to be sold on the street. Jewelry starts in a legal manufacturing operation (though materials may be smuggled) and is traded through regular channels and sold through respectable jewelry stores, where the store owner avoids taxation by engaging in off-the-book trades and cash deals.

19. Black markets generally operate in situations where a particular item is scarce (such as during wartime or periods of prohibition) and thus the price is driven up. In contrast, even in situations where a particular item is not readily available, hidden economy trading provides them at a cheaper price (Henry, 1978).

20. The consumption side of these offenses—use of drugs and engagement in prostitution and gambling, often referred to as "victimless crimes"—is addressed in the next chapter as public order offenses Historically and legislatively, these crimes have been deemed socially immoral and a threat to social order. The nature of these crimes as consensual but morally and legally impermissible puts them in a special category of offenses that on one level are economically motivated, but on another are addictive and socially destructive. Vice trafficking of any kind is best understood as an economic crime, whereas the addiction is best understood and addressed in the context of public order crime.

21. Organized crime networks often include a spectrum of individuals and subgroups from low-level "street" offenders and prison gangs to political figures and

governmental agencies. Thus, market-based crimes are perpetuated by individuals and groups ranging in sophistication. According to Simon (1996) in his book *Elite Deviance*, "In fact, the crime problem in the United States is actually rooted in a system in which lower-class criminals, the Mafia, a corrupt public sector, and deviant corporations cooperate for profit and power" (p. 12).

22. Davies (2003) notes that traditional criminological discourses on economic offending "slip into antifeminist explanations" (p. 289), suggesting that though men do crime for money, women do crime because they are mad, bad, or whores. Traditional theories present obviously economically motivated offenses such as prostitution as rooted in promiscuity rather than economic gain. Davies argues that, though a feminist critique of the traditional theories of economic crime is now well established, women continue to appear in the literature to do crime because they are victims pushed or driven into it through poverty, abuse, and hardship, leaving little room for the view that women are capable of committing instrumental, rational economic crime.

23. The term *enterprise crime* has been used to refer to a hybrid of white-collar crime, organized crime, professional crime, occupational crime, and corporate crime, taking into account the interconnections and interrelated dealings among legitimate business people, politicians, and syndicated racketeers. Research on corruption and organized crime such as Chambliss's (1978, 1988) classic work, *On the Take: From Petty Crooks to Presidents,* suggests that crime networks are connected to national businesses and political interests. Thus, enterprise crime is an umbrella term incorporating crime produced through large networks of offenders from a range of backgrounds and affiliations whose offenses cut across predatory, market-based, and commercial offense categories.

24. Naylor (2003) questions whether or not insider trading can clearly be considered a commercial crime (or a crime at all). Insider trading was first defined as a crime in cases involving officers of corporations about to merge who took advantage of knowledge about the merger to advance their own profit. It was then extended to many other situations including employees of law firms planning mergers, financial newspaper reporters who got leaks, and janitors who used information found in discarded memos to play the stock market for their own gain. Naylor argues that the crime of insider trading blurs the issue of breach-of-fiduciary-duty with the simple act of obtaining a profit that other people think belongs to them. With

insider trading there is no victim or victim-offender relationship. Rather there is a conflict between two sets of investors over who the profit belongs to. Insider trading is not a predatory crime because it does not involve forced transfer of property, a market-based crime since securities exchange is legal, or a clearcut commercial crime because trade based on privileged information does not involve actually rigging the market. According to Naylor, "This tendency to seek an ever-expanding mandate while blurring the central moral issues seems a danger inherent in all attempts to use the criminal code for purposes of economic regulation" (p. 100).

25. Defecation on someone else's property committed for its own sake would not be considered an economic crime. Rather it would be an act of vandalism or a nuisance offense, which would be considered a public order offense.

26. The concept of a "limited" or "bounded rationality," discussed earlier in the chapter in relation to burglary, was introduced in 1976 in a text by Herman Simon titled *Administrative Behavior* (Friedrichs, 2004).

27. Speaking to a graduating class at the University of California in the 1980s, Ivan Boesky, Wall Street financier convicted of insider trading that earned him tens of millions, said to the graduates, "Greed is all right, by the way. I want you to know that. I think greed is healthy. You can be greedy and still feel good about yourself" (*Newsweek*, 1986, cited in Gabor, 1994, p. 116).

28. Psychopaths are criminally versatile—they will engage in all types of crime when the opportunity arises if it benefits them in some way. Depending on background and opportunity factors, some psychopaths may limit their criminal behavior to economic crime because they have been able to acquire power through the behavior. The difference, however, between a psychopath who commits economic crime and a nonpsychopath who commits economic crime is that the goal for the psychopath is power (achieved through money or property) whereas the goal for the nonpsychopath is the money or property itself.

29. Alalehto (2003) found that "personality matters" in economic crime, with at least three personality types that are associated with white-collar economic crime: the positive extrovert, the disagreeable, and the neurotic.

30. The reference here to cognitive neutralizations as "simplistic" and "normal" suggests that there is a qualitative difference between what could be called "surface" or "higher-level" rationalizations that we all use and the more primitive defenses (discussed in Chapters 2 and 4) used by psychotics, psychopaths, and other individuals

with borderline personality psychopathology. In other words, commission of an economic crime does not require the same sort of defensive structure that would be found in individuals who suffer from severe personality or psychotic disorders. While disordered and nondisordered individuals use rationalizations to engage in deviant and criminal behavior, the justifications and excuses used to cause economic harm are much less extreme in the content of their cognitive schema and embedment within the individual's personality and psychodynamic development.

Notes for Chapter Eight

1. Vandalism can also be considered an economic crime because the harm caused is destruction of property resulting in economic loss. However, vandalism/graffiti is a public order crime because it is a nuisance behavior that contributes to the downward spiral of community deterioration (i.e., broken window theory). Arson was discussed in the previous chapter as an economic crime, but some instances of arson may also be considered vandalism (e.g., setting trash cans on fire). Like arson, vandalism is an offense that does not fall neatly into a single crime category. Vandalism/graffiti is discussed in this section as a public order offense because, though it does result in economic loss, it is rarely profit driven and is predominantly a crime against the public order.

2. Some prostitutes also argue that prostitution serves a social function by providing sex to sexually deprived men, and therefore helps to prevent rape. This is offered by some as an argument for legalized prostitution.

3. In fact, the phrase *male prostitute* originally referred to a man who either seduced married women and extorted money from them, or had sex with, or pimped for, a female prostitute.

4. This may be the result of a number of factors including increased attention of law enforcement to male prostitution, the disinclination for police officers to view male prostitutes as victims, or that male prostitutes are more likely than females to engage in the behavior outdoors, where they are more vulnerable to detection.

5. Male prostitutes identified in the 1800s were known to dress like female prostitutes. Much of the early discourse on male prostitution centered on whether the prostitutes were homosexual or heterosexual and whether the behavior was sexually or economically motivated. Though discourse in the 1900s viewed male prostitution

within the context of homosexual communities, today, it is recognized that many male prostitutes are heterosexual or bisexual males who engage in prostitution with other males (who identify as both homosexual and heterosexual).

6. Kaye (2003) quotes John Rechy's (1977) *The Sexual Outlaw*, "There is a terrific, terrible excitement in getting paid by another man for sex. A great psychological release, a feeling that this is where real sexual power lies—not only to be desired by one's own sex but to be paid for being desired, and if one chooses that strict role, not to reciprocate in those encounters; a feeling of emotional detachment as freedom—these are some of the lures; lures implicitly acknowledged as desirable by the very special place the malehustler [*sic*] occupies in the gay world, entirely different from that of the female prostitute in the straight. Even when he is disdained by those who would never pay for sex, he is still an object of admiration to most, at times an object of jealousy. To 'look like a hustler' in gay jargon is to look very, very good" (p. 153).

7. Queen (2000) offers an account of a client who was a pedophile who hired her to wear pigtails and engage him in a fantasy that would be strong enough to diminish his desire for girls, another of a client who was very shy and had gynecomastia (enlarged breasts) and a negative body image, and a third of a man who wanted to be held while he talked about his deceased wife.

8. Pornography is discussed here as public order crime and certainly child pornography can be defined as an offense against public order; however, the production, distribution, and consumption of child pornography is most meaningfully understood as a sex crime. Individuals who abduct or otherwise coerce children into engaging in sex acts for pornography or any other reason are engaging in a sex crime and must be understood within the framework used to understand motivations and offense dynamics in other types of sex offenders. The use of the Internet as an outlet for child pornography is discussed in Chapter 10.

9. In 1919 the 18th Amendment to the Constitution passed prohibiting the manufacture, transportation, and sale of intoxicating liquors. In 1920 the Volstead Act (named after prohibition sponsor Congressman Andrew Volstead of Minnesota) strengthened the language of the act and provided for its federal enforcement. By 1933 the 18th Amendment was repealed by the 21st Amendment when Prohibition brought violence, corruption, organized crime, and a 78% increase in the homicide rate instead of the drop in poverty and crime and increased sobriety its supporters had predicted.

10. There is controversy over whether long-term use of marijuana is physically or psychologically addictive. Much of the research on long-term use of marijuana suggests that marijuana is not physically addictive, but may result in psychological dependency.

11. *Street ethnography* is a qualitative method that involves entering the natural habitat of the subject of study (i.e., studying drug users on the street rather than in drug treatment centers) and learning about a phenomenon from the inside out (i.e., from the users themselves rather than from treatment providers, official statistics, or empirical methods).

12. This study found that in 2000, 37% of the Blacks, 38% of the Hispanics, 29% of Whites, 44% of the Native Americans/Alaskan Natives, 39% of Native Hawaiians/Pacific Islanders, 22% of the Asians, and 28% of those of mixed race who reported committing DUI in the past year are alcohol abusers or alcohol dependent; all the others who drove under the influence are not (MADD, 2005).

Notes for Chapter Nine

1. One of the best-known examples of intolerance for the expression of an ideological perspective in conflict with the established governmental powers is the case of Salman Rushdie in Iran. In 1989, Rushdie wrote and published a novel deemed by Ayatollah Khomeini's Iranian government as offensive to Islam, and Rushdie was sentenced to death with Khomeini urging all Muslims to execute Rushdie and his publishers.

2. As with other categories of criminal behavior, there is overlap. For example, if a corporation engages in fraudulent practices to maintain (economic) power and this corporation is connected in some way to governmental agents or agencies, is this crime best understood as an economic or political crime? In this case, since the primary motivation is economic rather than ideological, it is best understood as an economic crime. On the other hand, if law enforcement agencies violate the rights of citizens to keep certain groups in power (groups that have an economic interest), it is best understood as political crime because those engaging in the behavior are governmental agents. The agents themselves may not have an ideological motivation for engaging in practices that violate citizen rights. However, the state organization to which they belong provides them with the power and authority to deprive individuals of certain rights. The nature of acts that occur within this sort of power relationship, make such acts political.

3. This focus on legally defined criminal behavior is admittedly problematic with respect to political crime. Certainly, laws differ across time and place, are driven by political forces, and devised to maintain the power and social control of the government in power (and, in democratic nations, of the collective will). The facts that police and governmental agents actively engage in ideologically motivated behavior that maintains the status quo and most "political criminals" are charged and convicted for committing nonpolitical crimes make the conceptual definition of political crime even more ambiguous. However, discussion of the sociological, political, and economic forces that underlie and shape law and criminal justice policy and practice are beyond the scope of this text. For a comprehensive analysis and application of social theory to law and criminal justice policy and practice, see Garland's *Punishment and Modern Society* (1990), *The Culture of Control* (2002), and *Mass Imprisonment* (2001) and Garland and Sparks's *Criminology and Social Theory* (2000).

4. Turk discusses crimes against the government and crimes by the government, but (as previously discussed), prefers the term *political policing* for what others refer to as state or state-organized crime. Ross uses the terms *oppositional* and *state crime,* which will be used here because they are less cumbersome terms than "crimes by/against the government."

5. This is an example given by Justice Holmes in the 1919 U.S. Supreme Court case *Schenck v. United States.* The case involved the question of whether or not an incriminating document circulating information influencing men to obstruct the draft was seized from the headquarters of a Socialist party illegally. The court decided that "Words, which, ordinarily and in many places, would be within the freedom of speech protected by the First Amendment may become subject to prohibition when of such a nature and used in such circumstances as to present a clear and present danger that they will bring about the substantive evils which Congress has a right to prevent. The character of every act depends upon the circumstances in which it is done" (*Schneck v. the United States*, 249 U.S. 47 (1919), Legal Information Institute [Case Syllabus] ¶3). In Canada, citizens do not have the same degree of free speech protection as in the United States. For example, in 2005, a retired Native leader was convicted of a hate crime when he made

derogatory statements regarding Jews, telling a local newspaper that Jews were a disease and Hitler was trying to "clean up" when he "fried six million of those guys" (Brass, 2005).

6. The *Economic Espionage Act* targets trade secret theft and, on the surface, is a response to an economic rather than a political crime, targeting domestic and international theft of trade secrets. However, the line between political and economic espionage is sometimes hazy since some acts of espionage may appear political but are economically motivated, and political and economic interests are so intimately connected, that economic espionage could be politically motivated.

7. Of the racially motivated offenses, 66.3 were associated with antiblack bias, 21.2 antiwhite, 6.1% anti-Asian/Pacific Islander, and 4.7% directed against individuals representing more than one bias (U.S. Department of Justice, Hate Crime Statistics, 2003).

8. Although Ferguson was not specifically convicted of a hate crime, Kelly (1998) argues that his case is a particular "species of hate crime where the offender is literally driven to acts of indiscriminate violence because, we may suppose, of entanglements and cultural conflicts on a personal level" (p. 23).

9. There does not appear to be a clear consensus on whether or not the concept of state crime should include political corruption or crimes committed for personal gain. Some writers argue that, because individuals working for governmental agencies have power that others do not, and the power of the state provides them the opportunity to commit the offense, all offenses committed by governmental officials should be considered political or state crimes. However, other authors acknowledge that political corruption for personal economic gain is a qualitatively different type of offense in that it is not ideologically motivated. In this text, political corruption for personal gain and other offenses committed for economic motivation are considered economic crimes. Friedrichs (2004) uses the term *political white-collar crime* to refer to offenses by governmental officials for personal gain that violate the public trust. The distinction between economically and politically motivated offenses is a useful one, but the term *political white-collar crime* may contribute to even more conceptual confusion.

10. Some authors distinguish between *genocide* (state mass murder because of racial, ethnic, religious group membership) and *politicide* (state mass murder of people for their political views). In his book *Death by*

Government, Rummel (1996) coined the term *democide* to refer to the murder of any person or people by a government, including genocide, politicide, and mass murder.

11. There has been some interesting research in this area applying psychodynamic concepts and psychological diagnoses to nations, groups, and political offenders—see Lachkar's (2002) psychological analysis of the suicide bomber. Much of this research is theoretically rich but not empirically supported.

Notes for Chapter Ten

1. Perhaps one of the best recent examples of this convergence of influences is the BTK killer, Dennis Rader. Here is someone who tortured and murdered 10 people over a 30-year period, all the while watching his own crimes in the media. Driven by deviant sexual fantasy, sadism, psychopathy, and narcissism, and some might say the cultural lore of the brilliant serial killer, he followed his own crimes in the news, studied criminal justice to stay a step ahead of investigators, and was caught only because he decided to contact the media himself because there was too long a lull in media attention to his crimes. Even at his sentencing, when he received 10 consecutive life sentences, he gave a 30-minute speech that sounded like an acceptance speech for an academy award.

2. The surveys include two conducted by the Kaiser Family Foundation in 1999 (with a sample of 1,090 children ages 2 to 7 and 2,065 students in grades 3 to 12) and 2003 (with a sample of 1,065 parents of children age 6 months to 6 years) and one by the Annenberg Public Policy Center (with a sample of 1,235 parents of children age 2 to 17 and 416 children between the ages of 8 and 16); see Anderson et al., 2003.

3. A large number of studies have produced findings directly counter to the catharsis hypothesis, which has resulted in a "virtual abandonment" (Sparks & Sparks, 2002, p. 278) of the catharsis theory by the research community. However, most of these studies have been laboratory studies focusing on aggression in children (as opposed to juvenile or adult criminal behavior) in response to viewing a violent TV program or film. Research involving virtual violence and catharsis (in particular with first-person shooter games) is just beginning to be explored.

4. Speer (2000) distinguishes *information warfare* from cybercrime, suggesting that it is a related but distinct activity. Information warfare includes war-related activity implemented against the computer systems and

infrastructures of other governments/organizations using the same skills as are involved in cybercrime. However, the important difference is that information warfare involves a threat to national or international security whereas cybercrimes do not, and using the terms synonymously "sensationalizes crimes that are unimportant on levels of national or international security" (p. 260).

5. As a case in point, in 1988 James Wilson of Greenwood, South Carolina, went on a shooting spree in an elementary school. Police discovered in his room a photo of the *People* magazine cover of his hero Laurie Dann who had committed a similar crime a few months before in Winnetka, Illinois. These shootings were said to have inspired a string of copycat mass killings in the early 1990s (Fox & Levin, 2005).

6. In videotaped interviews with police (*State of Washington v. Ridgway*, 2004), Gary Ridgway mentions having followed other serial killers in the media such as Ted Bundy. Dennis Rader specifically mentions the Green River killer and Son of Sam in interviews regarding how he embraced the acronym BTK because it was like the "Green River Killer" and "Son of Sam . . ." ("Secret confessions of BTK," August 12, 2005).

7. Axis I mental disorders are not in and of themselves criminogenic factors. However, Axis I disorders appear to play a role in the commission of some types of criminal behavior for some individuals and are an important consideration with respect to the manifestation of copycat crime.

8. Marx (1995) offers examples such as Sting's song *Every Breath You Take,* the Santa Christmas song *"He knows when you are sleeping, he knows when you're awake. . . ."* Meloy (1998) suggests that films such as *Fatal Attraction, Play Misty for Me,* the *Peanuts* comic where Sally is always following Linus, the perfume *Obsession,* and so on offer cultural support for stalking as the "dark heart of the romantic pursuit" (p. 6). Other examples of pop cultural images of surveillance and stalking include the films *Sliver, Taxi Driver,* and *The Fan.*

9. The paparazzi who pursued Princess Diana when she died in the fatal car accident in 1997 have been referred to as "stalkerazzis" for engaging in a car chase to photograph her and then continuing to snap photos of her and her companions after they were injured and near death inside their severely damaged car (Meloy, 1998).

10. Other films that have depicted (some more loosely than others) the Starkweather-Fugate murder spree include the 1963 film, *The Sadist,* the 1974 film

Badlands, the 1993 films *Kalifornia* and *True Romance,* and the 2004 film *Starkweather.* See Sargeant's (1996) *Born Bad: The Story of Charles Starkweather and Caril Ann Fugate* for an overview of the Starkweather-Fugate murders and the cultural impact of their story.

11. *The Matrix* film trilogy, which is a close second to *NBK* in terms of the number of copycat offenses associated with the films, also involves a central theme that makes the viewer question the line between fantasy and reality.

12. This is a broad definition of cybercrime. There is debate over the semantics of computer-related crime. Some authors suggest that the term *cybercrime* should be used in reference to abuses and misuses of computer systems and networks that result in direct losses whereas the term *computer crime* has been traditionally defined as any criminal act committed against a computer and *computer-related crime* defined as any criminal act in which a computer is involved (Britz, 2004; James & Nordby, 2005). The term cybercrime is used broadly here for simplicity, with recognition that different definitions exist.

13. Nigerian Advance Fee scam letters (also known as 4-1-9 schemes after the section of the Nigerian penal code that addresses fraud schemes) involve unsolicited e-mails from fraudsters posing as officials from a foreign government or agency (usually Nigeria) who offer to transfer funds to the recipient's bank account. Recipients are usually told they are the beneficiary of a will, have won an award or prize, or the sender is in a disadvantaged state and in need of assistance and the target will need to transfer an advance fee and travel to Nigeria in order to receive the larger amount promised. See the U.S. Secret Service Web site: http://www.secretservice.gov/alert419.shtml.

14. The story of the Hi-Fi Murder case has been described in detail in books and a TV movie including Kinder's (1982) *Victim: The Other Side of Murder,* which was made into a TV movie in 1991 called *Aftermath: A Test of Love,* Douglas et al.'s (1992) *Crime Classification Manual,* and Douglas and Olshaker's (1999) *Anatomy of Motive.* Kinder's book details the aftermath of the crime for the most severely wounded living victim, 16-year-old Cortney Naisbitt. Naisbitt was shot in the head and paralyzed and debilitated for the rest of his life. He died in 2002 at age 44 in Seattle, Washington, from an undisclosed illness. Selby and Andrews were sentenced to death and were executed in 1987 and 1992, respectively. Incidentally, Andrews was executed after being the person to have served the longest sentence on death row.

15. Media influences may make their way into criminal behavior in an even more peripheral way. For example, in 2002 a man in England murdered his wife while saying, "You are the weakest link, goodbye," like the line in the British game show of the same name ("Husband 'Admitted Weakest Link Killing,'" January 28, 2002). This is an example of media influence on criminal behavior that would not be considered copycat crime but falls on the low influence end of the continuum of media influence. The question in a case like this is, what role did media play in producing the behavior? Is the media influence completely irrelevant or is it important to include cases like this to make sense of the copycat effect on criminal behavior?

Notes for Chapter Eleven

1. Some use the term a*pplied criminology* to refer to the application of criminological theory to law enforcement practice. This is likely rooted in the FBI's use of the term as a title for a course in the Behavioral Science Unit since the 1970s. The term has a long history in the general application of criminological theory to criminal justice policy and practice, but there is little consistency in how the term is used today. For example, some academic programs that emphasize the intersection of theory and practice use the term as a program or department title whereas others apply it to programs that focus on emergency management and security-oriented areas.

2. Inclusion of specific demographic characteristics such as IQ, sex, and age in a profile is controversial. Often, particularly when relying on existing databases of known offenders, characteristics inferred prove to be incorrect once the actual offender is identified.

3. Sex-typing is not limited to the predatory-affective dichotomy. Other classifications associated with masculinity-femininity relevant to analysis of criminal behavior include antisocial personality disorder and histrionic personality disorder. It is important to recognize the sexual stereotypes associated with these theoretical concepts because the stereotypes have made their way into clinical diagnoses, correctional case files, and criminal profiles.

4. Garland (2001) argues that the "new criminologies of everyday life" are based on a set of theoretical frameworks such as routine activity and rational choice theories that have reframed criminal behavior in terms of choice and free will, leading to policies and practices that he terms the *new iron cage* of crime control in late modernity.

5. Although several of the quotes cited in this section are decades old, these issues are not relics of history. For more recent reviews of the insanity defenses and discussion of the incompatibility of the criminal justice and mental health systems regarding the issue of insanity, see Low, Jeffries, and Bonnie (1986) and Linder (2002).

6. Another example of the copycat effect in the Yates case is Park Dietz's testimony that she was influenced by an episode of *Law & Order* depicting a crime similar to her own. However, it was determined on appeal that no such episode ever aired—a primary basis for granting her the 2006 retrial.

7. The film *Se7en* depicts a serial killer who uses Thomas Aquinas's *seven deadly sins* as a blueprint to commit murder. The sins (gluttony, greed, sloth, lust, pride, envy, wrath) do not include murder per se. Published accounts of Yates's reference to the film do not offer information to explain exactly how Yates incorporated the film into her own cognitive script before, during, and after the murders.

8. Since the inception of three strikes, situations have arisen in which prosecutors, judges, and juries have been unwilling to prosecute and convict because of perceived unfairness of the law. This has primarily been an issue in California, because of the breadth of the law. In a California case in 2000, two jurors, who had no problem finding the defendant guilty of burglary, said they could not live with themselves if they complied with the judge's order to validate two prior convictions. Both jurors were replaced with alternates and the defendant (37-year-old Steven Bell) was convicted and sentenced to 25 years to life for bicycle theft.

9. *Sexual psychopath* is (like *sexually violent predator*) a legal term used to impose civil commitment. The definition and adoption of the laws between 1937 and 1957 reflect the historical conceptual connection between psychopathy and sexual deviancy. Some states (e.g., Minnesota) still refer to "sexual psychopathic personalities" and "sexually dangerous persons" in the modernized version of the older sexual psychopath laws. However, *sexual psychopathy* and *sexually violent predator* as used in civil commitment statutes are legal, not psychological terms. The terminology and definitions used in civil commitment legislation in different states may not correspond to the scientific conceptualization of psychopathy, antisocial personality, pedophilia, and other disorders. In fact, the U.S. Supreme Court noted (in *Kansas v. Hendricks,* 1997) the distinction between law and science,

stating that the two need not always agree: "States have, over the years, developed numerous specialized terms to define mental health concepts. Often, those definitions do not fit precisely with the definitions employed by the medical community. The legal definitions of 'insanity' and 'competency,' for example, vary substantially from their psychiatric counterparts. . . . Legal definitions . . . need not mirror those advanced by the medical profession" (*Kansas v. Hendricks*, 1997).

10. Most offenders civilly committed under this law are male, but some female offenders have been deemed sexual predators and have been civilly committed. At the time of this writing, there is one female offender who has been civilly committed currently serving time at the Washington State Special Commitment Center.

11. The PCL-R was not developed as a risk assessment tool. However, a large body of research has accumulated over the past decade showing that high scores on the PCL-R are empirically associated with general and violent recidivism (see Chapter 4).

12. The LSI-R has been used in Canada for 17 years and in provincial prisons for 7 years as a matter of policy (Girard & Wormith, 2004). The LSI-R is also used by some departments of corrections in the United States. The PCL-R is administered to all prison inmates in Canada prior to release from custody.

13. Martinson suffered from manic depression and committed suicide in 1980 by jumping from the window of his Manhattan apartment in front of his teenaged son (Sarre, 1999).

14. According to Bushman and Anderson (2001), knowledge structures are "organized packets of interrelated information stored in semantic (long term) memory" (p. 276). Cognitive scripts and cognitive schemas are knowledge structures. Scripts contain information about how people and objects behave under different circumstances and schemas contain information about a concept, its attributes, and relations to other concepts. Cognitive schemas and scripts are key mediators of instrumental/predatory and expressive/affective aggression. See Anderson and Dill (2000) for discussion of the *general affective aggression model,* and an example of a second-generation paradigm. For example, as discussed in Chapter 5, the Green River Killer, Gary Ridgeway, committed several murders during his 20-year career as an instrumental killer that could be categorized as expressive/affective because they were committed in angry reaction to victims who didn't adhere to Ridgeway's cognitive script.

15. For example, although a study conducted in Finland found that murderers released from prison are 10 times more likely to commit murder than the general population (Tiihonen, Hakola, Nevalainen, & Eronen, 1995), murderers have lower recidivism rates than all other types of offenders except sex offenders (Beck & Shipley, 1989; Lee, 2001; Miethe & McCorkle, 2001; Soronsen & Pilgrim, 2000; Tennessee Statistical Analysis Center, 1997; Washington State Department of Corrections, 2001). A study of 658 long-term offenders who had served time for murder and been released to the community found that the offenders in the study had a low rate of recidivism, with only 5 of the 658 committing a second murder—a less than 1% recidivism rate (Weekes, 1992).

Notes for Chapter Twelve

1. Whenever I have the opportunity, I ask criminal justice professionals what role they think criminological theory plays in their work. I've asked this question of many state and federal law enforcement and corrections officers over the years, as well as former students in a wide range of criminal justice positions. The reply is almost always the same—theory and research play a minimal role in everyday criminal justice practice. When I ask why, the answer is usually that there isn't enough time, that the research just doesn't apply or isn't accessible, or that research does make its way into practice but very slowly and in small ways through special training sessions and presentations. Even when research is supported by grants and agency interest, once the research is done and the report is written, it is likely to sit on a shelf. I recently had a conversation with a former student, also with a graduate degree, who had gone on to work as a corrections officer. The former student called to tell me that he had left his position in corrections to pursue other career directions because he had wanted to make a difference with offenders but had found it impossible to apply any of what he'd learned in his work at the prison. Every time he expressed his desire to help offenders or to apply some of his knowledge about human behavior in his correctional work, he was viewed with disdain by other officers.

2. Gendreau (1996) notes that psychologists have expressed puzzlement as to why anyone would want to read sociological journals, completely disregarding major sociological contributions to criminology. In my own experience at the beginning of my career, soon after receiving my PhD, which was a study of psychometric

assessment of psychopathy, a sociologically trained criminal justice scholar congratulated me on receiving my degree but then said, "I wish you had chosen a different topic for your dissertation."

3. I once gave a presentation entitled "A restorative approach to intensive supervision programs" at a continuing legal education event in which I suggested considering alternative outcome measures of success in evaluating correctional interventions. A judge in the back of the room shook her head through the entire presentation. After the presentation, I approached her to ask if she had a concern about something I said. She responded, "If you can't tell me how to reduce recidivism and reduce the cost of incarceration, then you have nothing of value to say."

4. This view of crime as normal is, of course, not new and was articulated by Emile Durkheim in his 1895 work, *The Rules of Sociological Method,* and developed further by Erickson (1966) in his book *Wayward Puritans.* Based on this view from the consensus school of thought, deviance is socially functional in all cultures across all time periods as a mechanism of social solidarity.

5. The term *defining deviancy down* was coined by Moynihan (1993) to refer to the cultural tendency to tolerate, normalize, and choose not to notice deviance at times when the amount of deviant behavior rises above the level a community can afford to recognize and control. Garland (2001) uses the term to describe a bureaucratic strategy employed when high crime rates, caseloads, and demands give way to implementation of devices that filter complaints out of the system or lower the degree to which criminal behaviors are criminalized and punished. Karmen (1994) argues that Moynihan ignored examples of defining deviancy up in which crime previously not defined as such has become criminalized (e.g., child and spousal abuse, sexual harassment, police brutality).

6. This is not a hypothetical scenario. A detective once gave a guest lecture in one of my classes describing a situation in which several women tied up a man and penetrated him anally with bottles and other objects so he would involuntarily achieve an erection. A student writing a paper about female rapists found a Web site about how to rape a man, complete with instructions on how to force an erection.

Glossary

Acquaintance Homicide: Homicide of someone known to the offender, including spousal murder, parricide, infanticide, matricide, patricide, and family annihilation murder.

Actuarial Risk Prediction Instruments: Standardized measures used to forensically evaluate offender risk, including empirically derived factors associated with risk for criminal, violent, and/or sexually violent behavior. Examples include the *Level of Service Inventory-Revised* (LSI-R), the *Violence Risk Appraisal Guide* (VRAG), the *Sex Offender Risk Appraisal Guide* (SORAG), and the *Psychopathy Checklist-Revised* (PCL-R).

Actus Reus: Act of violating the law; guilty act.

Addiction: The compulsion to use drugs and/or alcohol, or to engage in a particular behavior (e.g., gambling, smoking) regardless of adverse consequences.

Adolescent-Limited Offender: Offender who engages in criminal behavior during adolescence, with the behavior tapering off into adulthood.

Aesthetic-Critical Approach: An alternative lens through which to understand murder and violent crime proposed by Joel Black in the book *The Aesthetics of Murder*—one that can offer a phenomenological description rather than a prescriptive assessment of the process underlying copycat or media-mediated crime.

Aestheticized Hyperreality: A condition of contemporary culture in which reality is media-mediated and the boundary between fantasy and reality is blurred, which helps explain and contributes to the copycat effect on criminal behavior.

Affective Aggression: A form of expressive and reactive aggression characterized by a physiological alarm state, reaction to a perceived threat with the goal of threat reduction, defensive posturing, and reduced self-esteem; also referred to as expressive or reactive aggression.

Aggregate-Level Factors: Factors statistically associated with criminal behavior across large groups of offenders.

Aggression: A component of normal behavior with a neural basis that is similar in animal and humans. Biological, psychological, sociological, cultural, contextual factors play a role in shaping how aggression is behaviorally displayed in humans. Modes of aggression may include acts of violence, but not necessarily.

American Civil Liberties Union (ACLU): National organization advocating individual rights, by litigating, legislating, and educating the public on a broad array of issues affecting individual rights.

American Law Institute Model Penal Code: Legal test of insanity adopted in the 1972 case *United States v. Brawner*. The Model Penal Code combined the principles of the M'Naughten and Durham Rules with specification of the type of mental disease or defect that could be considered to establish insanity, excluding antisocial personality disorder or any abnormality manifested only by repeated criminal and/or antisocial conduct. Under the Model Penal Code, a defendant could be considered not guilty by reason of insanity if at the time of the conduct, as a result of mental disease or defect, the defendant lacked the substantial capacity to appreciate the wrongfulness of the conduct or conform to the requirements of the law.

Amygdala: An almond-shaped structure located in the middle of the brain that regulates behavioral expression of emotional reactions.

Anarcho-Ideological Terrorists: Individuals who engage in behaviorally determined terrorist activity who show disruption in childhood and identity problems that involve a loner mentality and social marginalization.

Anger Excitation: Applied to rape and sexual homicide offenders, describes an offender motivated by anger and fueled by fantasy who engages in prolonged torture, exploitation, and mutilation of his victims.

Anger Retaliatory: Applied to rape and sexual homicide offenders, describes an offender motivated by anger/revenge who may select symbolic victim.

Anomie: State of normlessness.

Anthropophagy: Eating flesh and/or slicing parts of the body (i.e., cannibalism).

Antisocial Behavior: Behavior that involves acting out against other people or society.

Antisocial Personality Disorder: An Axis II, Cluster B personality disorder in the *Diagnostic and Statistical Manual of Mental Disorders (DSM-IV-TR)*. Criteria for the disorder include a pervasive pattern of and disregard for, and violation of, the rights of others that begins in childhood or early adolescence and continues into adulthood. Antisocial personality disorder is distinguished from criminal behavior undertaken for gain not accompanied by the personality features characteristic of this disorder; often associated with psychopathy and sociopathy; however, most people diagnosed with antisocial personality disorders are not psychopaths.

Applied Criminology: The application of criminological theory to criminal justice practice.

Arrestee Drug Abuse Monitoring (ADAM) Program: National Institute of Justice program that collects national data about drug use, alcohol and drug dependency, and drug market participation in arrestees.

Arson: Any willful or malicious burning or attempt to burn, with or without intent to defraud, a dwelling house, public building, motor vehicle or aircraft, personal property of another.

Assault: An intentional behavioral expression of aggression directed at another person. Aggravated assaults generally involve premeditated, intentional acts that result in serious injury and/or use of weapons. Simple assaults typically do not involve a weapon and result in minimal or no injury.

Attention Deficit/Hyperactivity Disorder: *DSM-IV-TR* Axis I childhood clinical disorder characterized by problems with attention, hyperactivity, and impulsiveness.

Autoeroticism: Sexual arousal through self-stimulation (e.g., masturbation to pornography, sexual asphyxia, or aquaerotic asphyxiation).

Avoidant Personality Disorder: *DSM-IV-TR* Axis II, Cluster C personality disorder characterized by a pervasive pattern of social inhibition, feelings of inadequacy, and hypersensitivity to negative evaluation.

Battered Woman Syndrome: Defense used to establish diminished capacity in cases involving a woman whose criminal act is the product of a history of abuse by the victim.

Behavioral Evidence Analysis: Method of criminal profiling involving deductive reasoning and critical thinking with focus on hypothesis testing through analysis of forensic evidence. In contrast with other methods, emphasizes integrating forensic psychology and forensic science in the profiling process.

Biological Theories of Crime: Biological theories explain crime in terms of the interaction between biological predisposition and environmental conditions on behavioral outcomes.

Bipolar Disorder: *DSM-IV-TR* Axis I clinical disorder characterized by dramatic "mood swings" or episodes of mania, hypomania, or major depression.

Black Hats: Computer hackers who use hacking skills to engage in destructive or criminal behavior motivated by revenge or greed (also called *criminal hacker* or *cracker*).

Black Widow: Term used to refer to female terrorists whose primary motive for terrorist acts is to avenge the death of husbands or loved ones. This term is also used to refer to female serial killers who murder their husbands for insurance purposes.

Body Type Theory: Biological typology developed by William Sheldon based on embryology and the physiology of development composed of three body types—*endomorph*, *mesomorph*, and *ectomorph*.

Borderline Personality Disorder: *DSM-IV-TR* Axis II, Cluster B personality disorder characterized by a pervasive pattern of instability of interpersonal relationships, self-image, and affects and marked impulsivity.

Borderline Personality Organization (BPO): Theory proposed by Otto Kernberg suggesting that personality exists along a continuum from psychotic to borderline to neurotic. Psychotic personality organization is characterized be the use of primitive defenses and lack of capacity for reality testing; borderline personality organization is characterized by the use of primitive defenses and capacity for reality testing; and neurotic personality organization is characterized by use of higher-level defenses and capacity for reality testing.

Broken Window Theory: Theory of crime that says that when disorder exists (i.e., broken windows) there will be more crime. Repairing disorder will reduce crime because people will be more invested in a community that is in good repair.

Burglary: The unlawful entry of a structure to commit a felony or theft.

Burnout Phenomenon: The notion that criminal behavior of most offenders declines after age 30.

Career Criminal: Term used to refer to an offender who engages in criminal behavior across the life-span (also called *chronic offender, persistent offender,* and *habitual offender*).

Catathymic Sexual Homicide Offender: Characterized by disorganized offense characteristics, mood disorder, various personality traits and disorders, mild to moderate psychopathy, attachment hunger, and hyperreactivity (need low level of stimulation for arousal), and early trauma is often present. One of two types in Meloy's (2000) compulsive/catathymic sexual homicide typology.

Celebrity Obsession: Cultural phenomenon characterized by obsession with celebrities.

Cheater Theory: Evolutionary theory that holds that, in some species, alternative reproductive strategies have evolved in some males. In these species, at least two types of males have evolved—"dads" and "cads." Dads reproduce by accommodating female preferences for males who are prone to provide parental care for their offspring. Cads reproduce by using force or deception to mate without providing adequate care for their offspring. According to this theory, chronic offenders are "human cads."

Chemical Dependency: Addiction to an illegal substance.

Chop Shop: A building, place, facility where stolen cars are disassembled for parts that are then sold.

Chronotherapy: The practice of coordinating medical treatment with biological rhythms based on the notion that the body's biological rhythms in fighting disease depend on gender, age, genetics, and other factors. A parallel theory in criminology to chronobiology is life-course criminology, which suggests that the potential for criminal behavior changes across the life course.

Civil Commitment: Detainment in a psychiatric or forensic facility on legal determination that mental disorder or illness is a threat to safety of the public or self.

Civil Disobedience: The intentional violation of a law considered morally unjust. Acts of civil disobedience are generally public, nonviolent, and serve a symbolic function.

Classical ("Pavlovian") Conditioning: The increase or decrease of behaviors through pairing and removal of stimuli, based on the work of Ivan Pavlov.

Classical Criminology: The school of thought originating in the eighteenth century that viewed criminal behavior as the product of free will and rational decision making. Classical theorists such as Cesare Beccaria and Jeremy Bentham saw crime as a product of free will committed by people who made cost-benefit analyses regarding the pleasure crime would bring.

Cluster Analysis: A statistical technique used to identify groups (clusters) that are similar in particular variables/ characteristics.

Cognitive Schema: Aspects of events, experiences, and event sequences that are encoded in memory and provide the basis for attributions, judgments, and behavioral decisions.

Cognitive Script: A schema referring to a prototype or a series of events occurring across a period of time that share an underlying similarity.

Cognitive Thinking Errors: Term coined by Yochelson and Samenow in their three-volume *Criminal Personality* referring to errors in thinking of individuals with *criminal personalities.* Term is now used more widely to refer to cognitive distortions that are criminogenic and lead to criminal behavior.

COINTELPRO: FBI Counterintelligence Program.

Commercial Offenses: Crimes committed by otherwise legitimate investors, entrepreneurs, and corporations (sometimes called *white-collar crime, corporate crime,* and *enterprise crime*).

Community Protection Act of 1990: Washington State law enacted in 1990 that extended postrelease supervision for certain sex offenders, required sex offender registration, and established a new law for the civil commitment of *sexually violent predators.* The law was the first in the country to impose civil commitment of sexually violent predators.

Compulsive Gambling: *DSM-IV-TR* Axis I impulse disorder characterized by uncontrollable urge to gamble despite adverse consequences.

Compulsive Sexual Homicide Offender: Offender with organized offense characteristics, sexual sadism, antisocial or narcissistic personality, severe psychopathy, chronic detachment, and hyporeactivity (needs high level of stimulation for arousal); early trauma is often absent. One of two types in Meloy's compulsive/catathymic sexual homicide typology.

Conduct Disorder: *DSM-IV-TR* Axis I childhood clinical disorder characterized by a repetitive and persistent pattern of behavior in which the basic rights of others or major age-appropriate societal norms or rules are violated, including destruction of property, physical cruelty to people and animals, deception, rule violation, and other antisocial behaviors.

Confidence Scams: Method of fraud by which the offender gains confidence and trust of the victim to gain access to information, finances, or material items for the purpose of economic gain.

Conflict Model: Broad sociological view of society as the product of conflicting views, opinions, and forces that shape norms, values, and laws.

Conflict Theory: Argues that crime is defined by those in power and is used as a mechanism of control to maintain the interests of the economically and politically powerful. Locate the cause of crime in the incompatible interests of multiple groups in society.

Consensus Model: Broad sociological view of society as the product of consensus of views, opinions, and forces that shape norms, values, and laws.

Consumer Fraud: Deception of consumers for profit including a range of fraudulent acts such as stock market swindles, phony contests and lotteries, sales of useless merchandise, get-rich-quick scams, land swindles, medical quackery, Medicare fraud, weight-loss gimmicks, work-at-home scams, magazine subscription rackets, travel deceptions, charity scams, tax preparation shysters, bogus employment agencies, referral schemes, fraudulent contractors, and deceptive credit offerings, credit repair scams, fraudulent sweepstakes and prize offerings, Nigerian money offers, and pyramid schemes.

Contrepreneur: A term used in the literature to refer to white-collar cons.

Coprophagia: Sexual arousal through eating feces (a variant of coprophilia).

Coprophilia: Sexual interest in and gratification from touching feces.

Copycat Crime: A crime inspired by another crime that has been publicized in the news media or fictionally or artistically represented; the offender incorporates aspects of the original offense into a new crime.

Copycat Effect: The influence of media, popular culture, literature, or other cultural artifacts on human behavior. Term usually refers to suicide or criminal behavior in which an individual mimics behavior he or she sees in the media, reads in a book, etc. (also called the *contagion effect*).

Copycat Loop: A type of media loop involving showing and reframing an image of a copycat crime in another context, such as reference to a real-life copycat crime in a television show, film, or computer game.

Correctional Classification: The process by which offenders are matched with the appropriate level of security, supervision, programs, and services in a correctional system.

Correctional Rehabilitation: Programs and interventions in correctional settings that encourage prosocial functioning (e.g., anger management, substance abuse treatment, conflict resolution, victim awareness).

Correctional Supervision: Correctional surveillance methods in institutional and community settings.

Correctional Treatment: Therapeutic interventions in correctional settings that target mental health issues/disorders.

Correlate: To have a relationship to.

Crackers: Criminal hackers, individuals who break into computer systems without authorization, flood Internet sites resulting in denial of service to legitimate users, make a copy-protected program run by digging into the code, deliberately deface Web sites for fraudulent purposes.

Crime: The collective amount of criminal behavior in a society, community, subculture; an event in which the law is broken.

Crime Clock: Method of presenting statistical information on crime in the United States by the FBI showing how many times per second, minute, or hour different types of crime occur in the United States.

Crime Index: The average of all Part I offenses in the FBI's Uniform Crime Reports. The crime index provides a measure of crime often reported in the form of the crime rate (*x* number of offenses per 100,000 people) that can be compared over time and across geographical location.

Crime Prevention Through Environmental Design (CPTED): Term coined by C. Ray Jeffrey referring to a problem-solving approach to crime prevention that involves a comprehensive crime reduction strategy encompassing principles of routine activity theory and environmental and situational crime prevention.

Criminal Behavior: A special category of behavior that has been defined through social-cultural-legal-political-economic processes as outside the bounds of the law. The term is often used to reflect the micro-level dynamics of individual criminality.

Criminal Investigative Analysis: Crime scene patterns, crime scene indicators, victimology, and data collected from interviews with offenders used to determine type (organized/disorganized) of offender who committed the crime. Method developed by the FBI is used by law enforcement officers trained in profiling.

Criminal Personality Theory: Developed by Samuel Yochelson and Stanton Samenow in their work in Saint Elisabeth's Hospital in the 1970s and published in 1977 in their three-volume work *The Criminal Personality*. Based on this theory, a subset of chronic offenders with *criminal personalities* engage in chronic criminal behavior across their life-span as a result of a unique pattern of thinking and use of specific thinking errors.

Criminal Profiling: The inference of offender traits from physical and behavioral evidence involving the application of social science research on criminal behavior to law enforcement investigations.

Criminality: The propensity and motivation to engage in criminal behavior.

Criminogenic Factors: Factors that have been empirically linked to criminal behavior such as delinquent peers, cognitive thinking errors, antisocial personality disorder, psychopathy, social alienation, use/abuse of facilitators (drugs, alcohol, pornography), history of abuse and/or family dysfunction, and social/physical isolation.

Criminological Verstehen: Criminological understanding, that is, understanding crime from the insider perspective. Associated with cultural criminology and the notion that crime is a subcultural product that needs to be understood from the perspective of the person engaging in the criminal behavior within a cultural and subcultural context.

Criminology: The study of crime and criminal behavior. The term *criminology* is often used to refer to the study of crime from a macro-level framework.

Critical Criminology: Critical approach to crime that views crime and its definition as a social construction of those in power used as a mechanism of control. Often used synonymously with Marxist or radical criminology; associated with other critical approaches such as postmodernism, chaos theory, semiotics, edgework, catastrophe theory, critical race theory, peacemaking criminology.

Crowe-Zahm Mixing Principle: Crime prevention through environmental design principle originating in Crowe and Zahm's (2004) article on "Crime Prevention Through Environmental Design" in *Land Management*, which states that crime can be reduced by placing safe activities in unsafe locations and unsafe activities in safe locations.

Cultural Criminology: Branch of criminology that recognizes criminality and criminalization as cultural enterprises that must be studied through a synthesis of divergent perspectives including social, feminist, and cultural theories. From this perspective, criminal behavior (and its control) is constructed, in part, through media, popular culture, and the aesthetics of authority that dictates what is "beautiful," "decent," "clean," and "appropriate." Criminal identities are born and shaped within culture and within criminal subcultures; collective criminal aesthetic and style, symbolism, and meaning are important factors in understanding the criminality.

Cybercrimes: Activities in which computers, telephones, cellular equipment, and other technological devices are used for illicit purposes such as fraud, theft, electronic vandalism, violating intellectual property rights, and breaking and entering into computer systems and networks.

Cyberprostitutes: Individuals who unlawfully promote or participate in sexual activities for profit or attempt to do so by offering services from personal Web sites.

Cyberstalkers: Individuals who gain online access to information about a target for the purpose of intimidation or physical harm. Information such as financial information, personal letters, or blog journal entries is used to find out about an individual for the purpose of eventually harming him or her. Cyberstalking can result in assault, kidnapping, or murder.

Cyberterrorists: Individuals/groups who engage in unlawful attacks or threats of attack against computer networks and the information they contain to intimidate or coerce a government or its people to further a political objective. Activity involves violence or psychological harm through the threat of violent attack against persons or property if specific demands are not met.

Dangerous Offender: Offenders who commit violent crimes, often resulting in victim injury.

Dark Figure of Crime: All of the unknown crimes that do not make it into official crime data, victimization surveys, or research studies; the discrepancy between crime known to police and the true extent of crime.

Decision Errors: Term used in risk prediction to refer to errors in prediction; false positives and false negatives.

Democide: The murder of any person or people by a government, including genocide, politicide, and mass murder.

Dependent Personality Disorder: *DSM-IV-TR* Axis II, Cluster B personality disorder characterized by a pervasive and excessive need to be taken care of that leads to submissive and clinging behavior and fear of separation.

Destructive Hacktivists: Individuals who target Internet sites for political purposes to disrupt but not destroy normal operations. Activity ranges from nuisance activities such as Web sit-ins, virtual blockades, automated e-mail bombs, and URL redirection to computer break-ins, computer viruses and worms, and Web defacement.

Developmental Criminology: Emerged from recent developments in sociology and psychology focusing on critical life events and the interaction between individuals and their social environments in connection with life events, transitions, and turning points. Addresses criminological controversies such as the age-crime curve, career criminality, juvenile delinquency and adult criminality, as well as the pushes and pulls toward and from criminality and the persistence and desistance in crime for different populations at different times and situations across the life course; also referred to as life-course criminology.

Deviance: A sociological concept that refers to acts, beliefs, values, and behaviors that deviate from the norm. Deviance can be viewed from absolutist/objectivist (the idea that some things are universally deviant), social constructionist (what is considered deviance changes across time, place, culture), and statistical (anything that falls at the ends of the normal bell-shaped curve) perspectives.

Diagnostic and Statistical Manual of Mental Disorders (DSM): First published in 1952 by the American Psychiatric Association and now in the fourth edition text revision (*DSM-IV-R*), the *DSM* is a categorical system for classifying mental disorders for the purpose of communication, diagnoses, education, research, and treatment.

Differential Association Theory: Theory of deviance, delinquency, and criminal behavior that suggests individuals' actions reflect who they associate with. People learn criminal behavior through interaction with friends and family members who engage in such behavior.

Differential Association-Reinforcement Theory: Combines differential association with conditioning theories to suggest that people learn to engage in crime through differential association but then criminal behavior is maintained through operant and classical conditioning.

Dissociation: A defensive process that involves splitting or unconscious detachment of (usually painful or anxiety-provoking) emotional experience from conscious awareness.

Dissociative Identity Disorder: Severe *DSM-IV-TR* Axis I clinical disorder characterized by alternation between two or more distinct personality states with impaired recall of important information among these states.

Dissociative State: An altered state noted to occur in 30 to 70% of the normal population, including *depersonalization* (a temporary alteration of the perception or experience of the self in which the usual experience of the self is changed or lost) and *derealization* (a temporary alteration in the perception of one's surroundings in which one loses the sense of reality of the external world). Dissociation in individuals with severe personality disturbance (e.g., psychopaths) is long term and chronic. Dissociative states in normal populations can range from daydreams to pathological states such as psychogenic amnesia or experiences of depersonalization and derealization.

Domestic Espionage: Governmental spying, information-gathering, and domestic surveillance of dissident groups by police and state agents.

Driving Under the Influence (DUI): Pertaining to driving under the influences of any substance (alcohol, illegal drugs, prescription drugs, etc.).

Drug: A substance that has mood-altering, psychotropic, or psychoactive effects.

***DSM-IV-TR* Axis I Disorders:** *DSM* clinical disorders such as schizophrenia, substance-related disorders, mood disorders, anxiety disorders, dissociative disorders, sexual and gender identity disorders, eating disorders, sleep disorders, adjustment disorders, and disorders first diagnosed in infancy, childhood, or adolescence such as learning disorders, conduct disorder, and attention deficit/hyperactivity disorder.

***DSM-IV-TR* Axis II, Cluster A Disorders:** *DSM* personality disorders including paranoid, schizoid, and schizotypal disorders. Individuals with Cluster A disorders appear odd or eccentric.

***DSM-IV-TR* Axis II, Cluster B Disorders:** *DSM* personality disorders that involve acting out behaviors and are more likely than other types of personality disorders to be associated with criminal behavior including antisocial personality disorder, borderline personality disorder, histrionic personality disorder, and narcissistic personality disorder.

***DSM-IV-TR* Axis II, Cluster C Disorders:** *DSM* personality disorders including avoidant, dependant, obsessive-compulsive disorders. Individuals with Cluster C disorders appear fearful or anxious.

Durham Rule: Legal test of insanity established in 1954 in the case *Durham v. United States.* The Durham Rule, also known as the Irresistable Impulse Test, required that for a defendant to be determined "not guilty by reason of insanity," his or her act must be the product of a mental disease or defect that rendered the accused incapable of controlling his or her behavior.

Dynamic Risk Factors: Risk factors that change over time such as age, education level, thinking patterns, attitudes.

Economic Crime: Criminal behavior for the purpose of material gain motivated by economic survival and disadvantageous economic circumstances.

Economic Criminality: Dishonesty, criminal career, and the pursuit of material gain as a motivation for criminal behavior.

Economic (or Industrial) Espionage: Corporate spying of trade secrets.

Ectomorph: One of three body types in Sheldon's body type theory. The ectomorph is characterized by predominance of skin and limbs, and is lean, fragile, and delicate with a small face, fine hair, and sharp nose. The ectomorph is *cerebrotonic*—introverted, sensitive to noise and distractions, socially anxious, expresses physical complaints, and is troubled by allergies and skin problems.

Embezzlement: The unlawful misappropriation or misapplication by an offender to his or her own use of money, property, or some other thing of value entrusted to his or her care, custody, or control.

Empirical Type: Deductively constructed type describing patterns that exist in the real world through multivariate statistical methods.

Endomorph: One of three body types in Sheldon's body type theory. The endomorph is characterized by roundness, short limbs, velvety skin, and tendency to put on fat. In terms of temperament, the endomorph is *viscerotonic*—a comfortable, generally relaxed, extroverted "softie."

Erotomaniacs: The rarest type of stalkers who delusionally believe that the victim loves them.

Erotophonophilia: Sexual arousal from killing.

Espionage: Spying. Aiding the enemy by spying on one's own country and providing secrets to the enemy is a form of treason. Espionage and treason are punishable by death in the United States.

Eugenics: The idea that human hereditary qualities can be improved through interventions such as genetic engineering, selective breeding, and sexual sterilization.

Evolutionary Criminology: Application of theory from evolutionary psychology to criminal behavior. Evolutionary criminologists explain criminal behavior in terms of evolutionary history, arguing that behaviors seen as criminal today were adaptive in ancestral environments. Evolutionary theories of crime are based on the notion that natural selection is the inevitable result of three fundamental features of life.

Evolutionary Psychology: Branch of psychology that uses a Darwinian framework to explain human behavior in terms of natural selection and adaptation processes.

Exhibitionism: *DSM-IV-TR* Axis I paraphilia characterized by sexual arousal from and compulsion to display one's genitals to a nonconsenting person.

Existentialism: Body of philosophical thought that emphasizes uniqueness of individual experience. An outgrowth of phenomenology found in the writings of 19th- and 20th-century European philosophers including Kierkegaard, Nietzsche, Sarte, Camus, and Frankl. Phenomenological perspectives on criminal behavior are rooted in existentialist thought.

Ex Post Facto: Term used to refer to a law that applies retroactively, criminalizing conduct that was legal when originally performed; Latin for "from a thing done afterward."

False Negative: Term used in offender (and other) risk prediction to refer to a decision error. When applied to offender risk prediction, it refers to the prediction outcome whereby the offender is inaccurately predicted to not reoffend and does.

False Positive: Term used in offender (and other) risk prediction to refer to a decision error. When applied to offender risk prediction, it refers to the prediction outcome whereby the offender is inaccurately predicted to reoffend and does not.

Felony-Murder: Homicide committed during the course of another felony crime in which there is intent to commit the felony; the felony-murder doctrine states that the offender can be charged with felony-murder if a homicide occurs during the course of a felony.

Feminist Criminology: Subfield of criminology that studies crime as if women matter, and focusing on the gendered nature of crime and feminist issues in criminological theory. Feminist criminology asks the questions, "Do theories of men's criminality apply to women?" (generalizability problem) and "Why do girls and women commit so much less crime then boys and men?" (gender-ratio problem), questions highlighted in Kathleen Daly and Meda Chesney-Lind's now classic 1988 article, "Feminism and Criminology."

Fence: A professional dealer in stolen property.

Fencing Networks: Systems of relationships and functions that develop between producers and marketers in the theft and disposal of stolen goods.

Fetishism: *DSM-IV-TR* Axis I paraphilia characterized by sexual arousal from inanimate objects such as underwear, shoes, and so on.

Filicide: The murder of a child by a parent.

Firesetter: Individuals who set fires without intent.

Forgery and Counterfeiting: The altering, copying, or imitating of something without authority or right, with the intent to deceive or defraud by passing the copy or thing altered or imitated as original or genuine; or the selling, buying, or possession of an altered, copied, or imitated thing with the intent to deceive or defraud.

Fraud: The intentional perversion of the truth for the purpose of inducing another person or other entity to part with something of value or to surrender a legal right; the predatory transfer of wealth from victim to offender by deception.

Fraud Triangle: Hypothesis developed by Cressey that explains embezzlement and fraudulent acts in terms of three points of a triangle: opportunity, pressure, and rationalization.

Frotteurism: *DSM-IV-TR* paraphilia characterized by sexual arousal from and compulsion for rubbing against a nonconsenting person.

Gateway Model: The view that most people get involved with drugs slowly moving from marijuana or alcohol to more serious drugs in order to experience a better "high."

Gender Identity Disorders: A type of *DSM-IV-TR* Axis I sexual dysfunction characterized by cross-gender identification and persistent discomfort with one's assigned sex.

Gender-Ratio Problem: Because there are so few female offenders in the criminal justice system, resources are more likely to be directed to male offenders and issues associated with male criminality; highlighted in Kathleen Daly and Meda Chesney-Lind's now classic 1988 article, "Feminism and Criminology."

General Theory of Crime: Developed by Gottfredson and Hirschi to explain all crimes in all places at all times as a failure in self-control. Commonly viewed as a sociological theory, but can be considered a partially integrative theory in that it uses both sociological and psychological concepts.

Generalizability Problem: The misapplication of male theories of crime to female offending; highlighted in Kathleen Daly and Meda Chesney-Lind's now classic 1988 article, "Feminism and Criminology."

Genocide: A crime against humanity and a form of state terrorism and mass murder. The term *genocide*, coined from the Greek word *genos* (race) and the Latin root -*cide* (killing), is a crime under international law as defined by the *International Criminal Court*. Some authors distinguish between *genocide* (state mass murder of members of certain racial, ethnic, religious groups) and *politicide* (state mass murder of people for their political views).

Genotype: The genetic constitution of an individual encoded in the DNA contained within chromosomes of cells.

Geographical Profiling: Method of offender profiling involving the use of mathematical model to predict a serial offender's probable location by analyzing data on locations of a series of related crimes and characteristics of the local neighborhoods to produce a map showing the areas in which the offender most likely lives, works, entertains, and travel routes.

Gerontophilia: Sexual interest in elderly persons.

Hacker: Cyberoffender who attacks a system to steal or destroy information. Originally a Yiddish term referring to an inept furniture maker, the term has taken on a range of meaning from the person who benignly enjoys learning about the ins and outs of computer systems to one who maliciously, deceptively, and illegally uses this ability to acquire information.

Hacker Paradigm: Ethical belief among hackers that any and all information that teaches individuals about the way the world works should be free.

Hate Crime: A form of domestic terrorism involving violent crime motivated by anger or ideology targeting a particular group or individual (also called *bias crime*).

Hebophilia: Sexual preference for children who have reached puberty.

Hedonistic Serial Killer: Serial killer motivated by lust and thrill. Killing is an eroticized experience fueled by the linking of sex and violence in the offender's developmental history. One of four types in Holmes and DeBurger serial killer typology.

Heredity: Passing of physical and behavioral traits from parent to offspring through genetics.

Heterogeneous: Comprising different parts or qualities.

High-Rate Offender: Term used to refer to offenders who commit numerous crimes per year when they are not incarcerated or when the opportunity arises.

Histrionic Personality Disorder (HPD): *DSM-IV-TR* Axis II, Cluster B personality disorder characterized by excessive emotionality, attention-seeking, self-centeredness, superficial charm, flirtatiousness, dramatization, sexual provocativeness, seductiveness, use of physical appearance to attract attention, inappropriate and excessive reactions, theatricality, suggestibility, and flights into romantic fantasy.

Homicide: The behavioral outcome of a wide range of motivations and circumstances whereby one or more individuals inflict harm on another that results in death. Homicide is legally defined as murder or non-negligent manslaughter, with a charge of aggravated, first-degree, second-degree, or manslaughter depending on the degree of premeditation, level of intent, and circumstances.

Homogeneous: Comprising the same parts or qualities.

Ideal Type: Type inductively constructed based on a subjective clinical impression.

Ideology: Distinctive belief systems, ideas, and abstract ideals that are perceived as providing the true meaning of life.

Impulse Control Disorder: *DSM-IV-TR* Axis I disorder characterized by recurrent failure to resist impulsive behaviors that may be harmful to themselves or others; includes intermittent explosive disorder, kleptomania, pyromania, pathological gambling, and trichotillomania.

Impulsivity: Reacting on impulse without weighing consequences.

Incest Offender: Individual who engages in sexual activity with his or her own children for selfish pleasure.

Individual-Level Factors: Unique influences and chain of events in an individual's life that can be attributed to the individual's criminal behavior.

Infanticide: The murder of an infant by a parent.

Infibulation: Engaging in self-torture such as piercing genitals with sharp objects (e.g., needles, pins).

Insanity: A legal concept that refers to diminished mental ability at the time of a crime that dismisses criminal responsibility.

Insanity Defense: Legal defense in which a defendant can be determined to be "not guilty by reason of insanity" (NGBRI). The defense is based on the historical belief that crime can be committed only by rational persons and that those who commit a criminal offense who are not aware of what they are doing do not possess criminal intent, and therefore deserve treatment rather than punishment. The insanity defense has changed over time and differs across cultures and jurisdictions. In the United States, there are different versions of insanity defense in the federal and state systems and in variations among individual states including the M'Naughten Rule, the Durham Rule, the American Law Institute Model Penal Code, the Insanity Reform Act of 1984, and the Guilty but Mentally Ill verdict.

Insider Trading: Making decisions about securities trading based on information that is not available to the general public with the intent of making a profit or avoiding a loss.

Interactionist Theories: Interactionist theories explain crime in terms of the interactional dynamics between people. These theories come from a social-psychological perspective focusing, at a more micro level, on the ways in which individuals are defined and come to define themselves as criminal. Examples of interactionist theories include Sutherland and Cressey's differential association theory, Becker's labeling theory, and Hirschi's social bond theory.

Interdisciplinary Criminology: Approach to criminology that rejects the notion that scientific evolution is achieved through the falsification of theories, with the view that criminal behavior is so complex that most theories have something to offer, and explain part of the picture, for at least some types of crimes.

Interdisciplinary Risk Factor Approach: Approach that challenges the either-or view that criminal behavior is the product of free will (classical criminology) or determinism (positivist criminology) with view that it is impossible to empirically verify or falsify free will/rational choice or to demonstrate deterministic causality. Criminal behavior is explained in terms of probability rather than choice or causality, whereby the interaction between risk and protective factors increases or decreases the likelihood of criminal behavior.

Intermittent Explosive Disorder: *DSM-IV-TR* Axis I impulse control disorder characterized by recurrent failure to resist impulsive aggressive destruction of property or assault of other persons far in excess of what might be considered appropriate with respect to any precipitating event.

International Classification of Diseases: Classification of physical diseases and health problems including mental disorders, published by the World Health Organization (WHO). Now in the 10th edition, the first edition was called the *International List of Causes of Death* and was adopted by the International Statistical Institute in 1893. WHO took over the responsibility for the ICD at its creation when the sixth revision was published in 1948.

International Criminal Court: An independent, permanent court that tries persons accused of the most serious crimes of international concern, namely, genocide, crimes against humanity, and war crimes. The ICC is based on a treaty, joined by 104 countries.

Investigative Psychology: Techniques and theories from psychology, psychiatry, and criminology used to develop a profile based on statistical probability. Conducted primarily by academic psychologists and criminologists without investigative training who use typologies and empirical studies to construct profiles. Term used primarily in reference to the work of David Canter and the Investigative Psychology program at the University of Liverpool.

Item Response Theory (IRT): A psychometric model used to measure performance on a test item in relation to other items on a test. IRT enables psychologists to measure individuals on the latent trait defined by the set of items while simultaneously scaling each item on the same dimension.

John: Slang term for individual who solicits prostitutes.

Kleptomania: A *DSM-IV-TR* Axis I impulse control disorder characterized by recurrent failure to resist impulses to steal items not needed for use or monetary value; increasing tension before committing theft; relief, gratification, or pleasure while committing theft; theft not committed out of vengeance or anger or in response to delusion or hallucination; when stealing is not better explained by other disorders such as antisocial personality disorder or conduct disorder.

Klismaphilia: Sexual arousal through receiving or administration of enemas.

Labeling Theory: Individuals who are caught and defined as criminals develop a self-identity consistent with this view. A self-fulfilling prophecy then ensues whereby a person defined as a criminal will self-identify as such and continue to commit criminal behavior. Individuals who are labeled and stigmatized as criminals will develop a criminal identity, style of behaving, and associated auxiliary traits consistent with stigma theory. Labeling theory originated with the work of Howard Becker and Erving Goffman.

Larceny-Theft: Unlawful taking, carrying, leading, or riding away of property from the possession or constructive possession of another.

Learning Theory: Psychological theory contending that behavior is learned through a combination of environmental influences and individual interpretation and response to those influences.

Legalistic Typology: Typology organized around violations of the criminal law. Legalistic typologies are the oldest and most frequently used forms of crime and criminal classification. An example of a simple legalistic typology is the distinction made in the criminal law between "misdemeanors" and "felonies."

Level of Service Inventory–Revised (LSI-R): 54-item instrument developed by Andrews and Bonta that includes a range of risk factors associated with criminal conduct. The content of the LSI-R reflects the recidivism literature, professional opinions of community corrections officers, and the social learning theory of criminal behavior.

Levels Hypothesis: The hypothesis, proposed by Gacono and Meloy in 1988, that defensive process can be inferred from cognitive style in psychopaths.

Liberation Hypothesis: View in early writings on female criminality (by Freda Adler and Rita Simon) that as women become more liberated and have more access to economic success and power, female criminal behavior will increase. Adler and Simon suggested that as women gain more economic power in society, they will engage in more criminal behavior. The view that increased participation in crime by women is a byproduct of the feminist movement.

Life-Course Criminology: Emerged from recent developments in sociology and psychology focusing on critical life events and the interaction between the individual and their social environments in connection with life events, transitions, and turning points. The life-course perspective addresses criminological controversies such as the age-crime curve, career criminality, juvenile delinquency, and adult criminality, as well as the pushes and pulls toward and from criminality and the persistence and desistance in crime for different populations at different times and situations across the life course. Also referred to as developmental criminology.

Life-Course Persistent Offender: An offender whose criminal behavior persists from childhood through adulthood and across the life course.

Linnean Classification: Traditional classification of plants dividing attributes, events, or individuals into classes on the basis of a common principle, such as a variation in form or function. Classes are defined by necessary and sufficient criteria of class membership, and assumed to be homogeneous and mutually exclusive.

Love Obsessional Stalkers: Stalkers who have no existing relationship with the victim and usually target celebrities.

Low-Fear Hypothesis: One of the most consistent findings regarding psychopaths, that they experience low anxiety and low fear reactions to aversive stimuli.

Mala en se Offenses: Crimes considered by society as inherently wrong (e.g., murder, robbery), with consensus with respect to the seriousness of the offenses and the laws against them.

Mala Prohibita Offenses: Crimes that are considered wrong simply because they are prohibited by some legal body, with minimal or no consensus on how serious these offenses are or whether or not laws should be enacted against them or enforced.

The "Man Question": Feminist criminologists (e.g., Naffine in *Feminism and Criminology*) argue that the Man Question—*What is it about men that makes them commit crime and what is it about women that makes them law abiding?*—should be the central preoccupation of criminologists.

Marxist Theory of Crime: Marxist theory contends that the criminal justice system is a tool to repress the working class, but the theory has little to say about crime. Karl Marx himself did not write about criminal behavior. Marxist (and conflict) theorists explain criminal behavior as an inevitable response to the capitalistic system. People engage in crime because either they are brutalized by and are trying to accommodate the capitalistic system or their crimes are conscious or unconscious acts of revolution and resistance.

Masculinity-Predator/Femininity-Prey Dichotomy: The culturally reinforced notion that males are predators/ crime-prone and females are prey/victim-prone.

Mass Murder: When an offender kills four or more victims in one location in one incident.

Massachusetts Treatment Center Child Molester and Rapist Typologies: Empirical typologies of rapists (MTC:R3) and child molesters (MTC:CM) developed at the Massachusetts Treatment Center by Knight and Prentky (1990). The typologies are the most empirically validated rapist and child molester typologies and are widely used in research and sex offender treatment.

Mens Rea: Criminal intent; guilty mind.

Mesomorph: One of three body types in Sheldon's body type theory. The mesomorph is characterized by predominance of muscles and bone, large trunk, heavy chest, and large hands and wrists. The mesomorph is *somotonic*— active, dynamic, assertive, and aggressive and, according to the theory, the most likely of the three types to engage in criminal behavior.

Mission Serial Killer: Serial killer motivated by revenge/ retaliation against a particular group of people. Offender is in touch with reality and acts on a conscious, self-imposed duty to rid the world of a particular group of people. One of four types in Holmes and DeBurger's serial killer typology.

Mixoscopia: Sexual arousal from seeing oneself in sexual scenes or sharing a sexual partner with another person and watching (*also called triolism*).

M'Naughten Rule: First legal test of insanity used in the 1843 case of Daniel M'Naughten. Required evidence that, at the time of the offense, the defendant's actions were committed under a defect of reason, a disease of the mind, resulting in the defendant's inability to know what he or she was doing or that what he or she was doing was wrong. The M'Naughten Rule, sometimes called the *right/wrong test*, is the historical foundation of the insanity defense in Britain and the United States.

Modus Operandi (MO): Method of operation; manner in which offender carries out his or her criminal behavior including all behaviors necessary to commit the crime.

Monkeywrenching: The deliberate intent to slow, halt, or sabotage actions by corporate or other entities perceived as destructive.

Moral Entrepreneurs: Individuals and groups who promote the idea that a particular behavior, issue, group, or type of individual is morally repugnant or dangerous, often with the goal of enacting legislation against the offensive target.

Motor Vehicle Theft: The theft or attempted theft of a motor vehicle.

Multicide: Multiple murder.

Munchausen Syndrome by Proxy: A rare form of child abuse whereby a parent falsifies or induces symptoms in his or her child to obtain attention by seeking medical care.

Narcissistic Personality Disorder: *DSM-IV-TR* Axis II, Cluster B personality disorder characterized by a pervasive pattern of grandiosity (in fantasy or behavior), need for admiration, and lack of empathy.

National Crime Victimization Survey (NCVS): The most comprehensive victimization survey in the United States. Conducted by the National Institute of Justice, Bureau of Justice Statistics, the NCVS, developed in 1972 and redesigned in 1989, obtains annual data from a nationally representative sample of 77,200 households, including approximately 134,000 individuals on the frequency, consequences, and characteristics of criminal victimization in the United States.

National Criminal Justice Reference Service: Central clearinghouse offering justice and substance abuse information with links to resources, reports, and data sources to support research, policy, and program development.

National Incidence-Based Reporting System: Data collection method added to the Uniform Crime Reports in 1987 as a more comprehensive and in-depth source of information about criminal events. The NIBRS views crimes as incidents and collects detailed information about crime and all of its components. Whereas the traditional UCR collects data in aggregate, the NIBRS sorts each incident and arrest into one of 22 different categories that span 46 offenses and 53 data elements collected about the victim, property, and offender.

National Survey of Drug Use and Health (NSDUH): Survey administered annually by the Substance Abuse and Mental Health Services Administration (SAMHSA) that is

Glossary ❖ **539**

the primary source of information about the extent of drug use in the United States.

Naylor Typology of Profit-Driven Crime: Motivational, process-based typology that divides economic crime into three categories: predatory offenses (involuntary transfer of property and illegal redistribution of existing wealth), market-based offenses (consensual market exchange of illegal goods and services and the illegal earning of a new income), and commercial offenses (transfer of legal goods and services and illegal redistribution of legally earned income).

Necrofetishism: Fetish for dead bodies that may involve keeping bodies or body parts in one's home.

Necrophilia: Engaging in sexual acts with dead bodies.

Neurotransmitters: Chemical messengers in the brain that convey "information" in the form of an electrically charged signal across neurons and from brain structure to brain structure. The balance, metabolism, and activity level of neurotransmitters (in part, a function of genetics) regulate emotion, impulse control, mood, hunger, thirst, arousal of the nervous system, and other psychological and behavioral processes. Certain neurotransmitters have been strongly and consistently associated with aggressive and antisocial behavior and appear to play a primary role in the behavioral display of different types of aggression.

Obsessive-Compulsive Personality Disorder: A *DSM-IV-TR* Axis II, Cluster C personality disorder characterized by a pervasive pattern of preoccupation with orderliness, perfectionism, and mental and interpersonal control, at the expense of flexibility, openness, and efficiency.

Occupational Fraud: The use of one's occupation for personal enrichment through the deliberate misapplication of the employing organization's resources or assets.

Offender Reentry: Term used to refer to offenders reentering free society after a period of incarceration; encompasses issues, policies, and practices associated with offender transition from jail or prison to community life.

Operant Conditioning: The increase of behaviors through reinforcements and decrease of behaviors through punishments. Based on the work of B.F. Skinner.

Oppositional Crime: Crimes against the government including nonviolent offenses such as dissent/political protest, sedition, espionage, and treason, and violent offenses such as assassination and domestic and international terrorism.

Organized Crime: A continuing criminal enterprise that rationally works to profit from illicit activities; it is maintained through the use of force, threats, monopoly control, and the corruption of public officials.

Organized Crime Scene/Offender: Organized crime scene reflects offender who commits crime out of a need for power. Motivation is associated with psychopathy. Crime scene characteristics reflect planning and premeditation or attempt to alter scene to avoid detection.

Organized-Disorganized Typology: Typology developed by FBI profilers that makes inferences about an offender based on whether the crime scene is left organized or disorganized. The typology was a primary component of the original FBI profiling method and continues to be a starting point for classifying crime scene evidence, and it is the most widely cited classification of violent, serial offenders.

Paparazzi: Photographers who follow celebrities.

Paranoid Personality Disorder: *DSM-IV-TR* Axis II, Cluster A personality disorder characterized by a pervasive pattern of distrust and suspiciousness of others such that their motives are interpreted as malevolent.

Paraphilias: A group of *DSM-IV-TR* Axis I sexual disorders characterized by sexual fantasies, urges, or behaviors involving nonhuman objects (fetishism, transvestic fetishism), suffering or humiliation (sexual sadism, masochism), children (pedophilia) or other nonconsenting person (voyeurism, frotteurism, exhibitionism). The word paraphilia literally means "abnormal love." In contrast with sexual dysfunctions and gender identity disorder, symptoms of many paraphilias are criminal behaviors.

Part I Offenses: Serious crimes including criminal homicide, aggravated assault, robbery, forcible rape, burglary, larceny-theft, motor vehicle theft, and arson.

Part II Offenses: Less serious offenses such as simple assault, forgery, fraud, embezzlement, prostitution, and gambling.

Partialism: Exclusive sexual focus on particular parts of the body.

Pathological Gambling: *DSM-IV-TR* Axis I impulse-control disorder characterized by persistent and recurrent maladaptive gambling behavior that leads to disruption of major life pursuits.

Patricide: The murder of parents by a child.

Payne Fund Studies: Studies conducted in the 1930s that found that many in a sample of 2,000 respondents were conscious of having directly imitated acts of violence they saw in films. This research spawned decades of controversy and research on the subject of media violence.

PCL-R Factor 1: Items included in the PCL-R associated with personality traits and the aggressive-narcissistic component of psychopathy.

PCL-R Factor 2: Items included in the PCL-R associated with antisocial behavior and the behavioral component of psychopathy.

Pedophilia: *DSM-IV-TR* Axis I paraphilia involving sexual activity with a prepubescent child.

Persistent Offender: Term used to refer to offenders who commit crimes over a long period of time (at least one-third of their lifetimes; also called career criminal, habitual offender, and chronic offender).

Personality Disorder: An enduring pattern of inner experience and behavior that deviates markedly from the expectations of the individual's culture. The enduring pattern must be inflexible and pervasive across a range of circumstances and situations, lead to clinically significant impairment or distress, and be stable, having originated in adolescence or early adulthood.

Personality Profiling: Personality theory and clinical diagnostic categories used to construct a personality profile representing the type of offender most likely to have committed the crime; generally conducted by psychiatrists, psychologists, academic criminologists.

Phenomenology of Offending: The unique meaning of the offense in the moment it is committed.

Phenotype: Observable product of the interaction between the genotype and the environment, such as physiological response and behavior.

Phishing: Method of obtaining personal information from victims through Internet ruses that trick people into giving out Social Security numbers and other information.

Phreaking: An early precursor to hacking that involves telecommunications fraud through the illegal manipulation of PBXs, access codes, access tones, or switches. Many hackers started their careers as phreakers.

Physiological Addiction: Addiction characterized by progressive tolerance, withdrawal symptoms if the individual ceases the behavior, and craving especially during periods of withdrawal.

Pimp: Slang term for individual who promotes prostitution.

Piquerism: Sexual arousal through stabbing, wounding, or cutting.

PMS Defense: A defense sometimes used in which the defense attorney argues that the offender suffered from premenstrual syndrome, which diminished her capacity to control her behavior.

Political Assassination: The murder of public figures for political reasons.

Political Crime: A crime motivated by political *ideology* committed both by and against the government and in organizational, occupational, or individual contexts; an illegal or socially harmful act aimed at preserving or changing the existing political or social order.

Pornography: Obscene material. Word comes from the Greek *porne*, which means prostitute, and *graphein*, which means "to write."

Positivist Criminology: The view that criminal behavior is determined by a range of biological and environmental factors and the causes of crime could be scientifically investigated, measured, and predicted. This view emerged in the early 1800s with the writings of Cesare Lombroso, Adolphe-Jacques Quetelet, and Andre-Michel Guerry.

Potato Chip Principle: Coined by criminologist Marcus Felson, the idea that free will is constrained by deterministic forces with the result that people have control some times but not others and that situational and other factors influence the amount of self-control a person can have in any given situation.

Power Assertive: Applied to rape and sexual homicide offenders, describing an offender who is motivated by power while seeking reassurance from the victim whom he has built up a fantasy about.

Power/Control Serial Killer: Serial killer motivated by power, omnipotence, and entitlement, who gets sexual gratification from domination of the victim. One of four types in Holmes and DeBurger's serial killer typology.

Power Reassurance: Applied to rape and sexual homicide offenders, describing an offender motivated by power who uses increasing aggression to control victim.

Predatory Aggression: Form of aggression that is instrumental and proactive, characterized by planning, purpose, and intent, the absence of autonomic arousal and emotion, and increased self-esteem. In animals, predatory aggression occurs between species, resulting in the destruction of prey to secure food. In humans, predatory aggression occurs within species. Some psychopathological conditions such as psychopathy are particularly suited to predatory aggression.

Prediction of Dangerousness: Term generally used to refer to the prediction of general and violent recidivism and the identification of conditions under which an offender is likely to commit a crime or behave aggressively or violently.

Primary Psychopath: An individual who engages in antisocial behavior as a result of a genetic or biological predisposition, directed by particular psychodynamic forces that occur in infancy. The primary psychopath forms no attachments as a result of early developmental obstruction, and thus is capable of harming others with little or no anxiety. Generally associated with a score of 30 or above on the PCL-R and assessed through identification of personality and behavioral features reflecting affective, interpersonal, antisocial, and lifestyle components of the disorder.

Primitive Defenses: Defense mechanisms used by borderline and psychotic personalities, including splitting, primitive idealization, projective identification, devaluation, omnipotent control, and denial.

Prohibition Era: Era in which alcohol was illegal in the United States, from 1919 to 1933.

Prostitution: The unlawful promotion of or participation in sexual activities for profit, including attempts. Literally means "up front" or "to expose."

Psychological Addiction: Addiction characterized by cognitive preoccupation with the behavior, use of neutralizing techniques (excuses and justifications), negative behavioral or physical consequences resulting from the addictive behavior, and negative emotions.

Psychological Typology: Typologies based on psychological theories organized around personality or some other individual psychological feature (e.g., mental illness, intelligence, cognition, psychodynamic development, motivation). The purposes of psychological typologies are theoretical understanding and correctional management and treatment.

Psychometrics: Branch of psychology that deals with the design, administration, and interpretation of quantitative tests for the measurement of psychological variables.

Psychopathology: The study of mental illness; spectrum of abnormal psychopathological conditions.

Psychopathy: Severe personality disorder characterized by an inability to form human attachment, aggressive narcissism, and antisocial behavior. Generally associated with a score of 30 or above on the PCL-R.

Psychopathy Checklist–Revised (PCL-R): The first standardized, valid, and reliable tool to assess psychopathy, which offers researchers a means to measure psychopathy to ensure all studies are measuring the same clinical entity. Developed by Robert Hare, the first edition was published in 1991 and the second edition in 2003 by Multi-Health Systems.

Psychosis: Clinical mental disorder classified in Axis I of the *DSM-IV-TR*, characterized by delusions, hallucinations, and loss of contact with reality.

Public Order Crime: Criminal behavior that violates the moral sentiment of society without a clearly identifiable victim. Sometimes called "victimless" or "vice" crimes.

Pygmalionism: Sexual involvement with dolls or mannequins.

Pyromania: *DSM-IV-TR* Axis I impulse-control disorder characterized by deliberate and purposeful firesetting, tension and affective arousal before setting a fire, fascination and curiosity about fire and firesetting, pleasure and release of tension after setting a fire, lack of material gain or instrumental motivation for setting the fire, and absence of cognitive impairment.

Racketeer Influenced and Corrupt Organizations Act (RICO): Part of the federal Organized Crime Control Act of 1970 passed by the U.S. Congress for purpose of eradicating organized crime in the United States. The RICO provision enables prosecutors to charge groups engaged in criminal enterprise activity, to obtain forfeiture of assets seized in racketeering activity, and to seek stiffer penalties on conviction.

Radex Model: Model developed by Canter and Alison suggesting that there are general and specific variations between and within crime categories that can be ascertained by identifying offense themes.

Rape: Nonconsensual vaginal, oral, or anal penetration by force, or threat of force.

Recidivism: Return to criminal behavior. Recidivism is defined and measured in different ways across research studies (i.e., rearrest, reconviction, reincarceration).

Response Modulation Hypothesis: Deficit in automatic shift of attention to peripheral stimuli and inability to alter behavior accordingly, resulting in maladaptive response perseveration or inability to pause/interrupt behavior in response to nonsalient stimuli after becoming fixated on a particular goal. Psychopaths are hypothesized to be unable to self-regulate their behavior as a result of this cognitive deficiency, which impairs the ability to shift attention from implementation to evaluation of behavior (Wallace et al., 2000).

Risk Assessment: Actuarial tools or other measures used to evaluate or predict level of risk.

r/K Theory: Evolutionary theory that explains a continuum along which organisms function. Organisms that are r-selected produce large numbers of offspring with little or no parental care. K-selected organisms produce few offspring and devote inordinate energy and time to their care and nurturing, maximizing each offspring's potential for reproduction. r/K theory assumes that altruistic and criminal behavior are at opposite ends of a continuum and that criminality should be found among individuals who exhibit all or most r-selected traits.

Robbery: Taking or attempting to take anything of value from the care, custody, or control of a person or persons by force or threat of force or violence, or by putting the victim in fear. Robbery is both a person and a property crime.

Routine Activity Theory: Based on the work of Marcus Felson and others, routine activity theory states that crime occurs as a result of increased temptations and reduced controls. From this perspective, *setting* and *opportunity* are the most important factors contributing to criminal behavior; crime is a normal everyday activity that occurs when opportunities in the environment support or discourage criminal behavior. Crime can be controlled through strategies that harden targets and alter settings in ways that make crime less opportune and desirable for offenders.

Sadism: Arousal through the intentional infliction of pain and suffering. Term coined by Krafft-Ebing in 1898 based on writings of the Marquis de Sade.

Sadistic Personality Disorder: Personality disorder that appeared in the *DSM-III-R*, characterized by a pervasive pattern of cruel, demeaning, and aggressive behavior, beginning by early adulthood, in which the person takes pleasure in physical cruelty, humiliation, and other means of harming others. The disorder was removed from the *DSM* and was not included in the *DSM-IV* or *DSM-IV-TR* because of concern that it would be used as a mitigating factor in criminal cases.

Sadomasochism: Sexual arousal or excitement resulting from receiving and inflicting pain, suffering, or humiliation. The pain, suffering, or humiliation is real and not imagined and can be physical or psychological in nature.

Schizoid Personality Disorder: *DSM-IV-TR* Axis II, Cluster A personality disorder characterized by a pervasive pattern of detachment from social relationships and a restricted range of expression of emotions in interpersonal settings.

Schizophrenia: *DSM-IV-TR* Axis I clinical disorder characterized by dramatic mood swings or episodes of mania, hypomania, or major depression; a persistent, often chronic and usually serious mental disorder affecting a variety of aspects of behavior, thinking, and emotion. Individuals with schizophrenia who have delusions and hallucinations may be described as psychotic.

Schizotypal Personality Disorder: *DSM-IV-TR* Axis II, Cluster A personality disorder characterized by little capacity for close relationships and eccentricity in behaviors, perceptions, and thinking.

Scoptophilia: The sexualization of looking; predatory staring.

Scriptkiddies: A term used for less sophisticated computer hackers who are usually teenagers out to be challenged and recognized by their peers for their exploits.

Secondary Psychopath: An individual who engages in antisocial behavior as a result of strictly environmental forces (such as membership in a deviant group) that occurs at developmental stages beyond infancy. The secondary psychopath forms human attachments, possibly to deviant subgroups, or possibly not. However, whether or not the secondary psychopath appears to be attached to others, emotional connection to other human beings is present. Generally associated with a score of 20–30 on the PCL-R.

Sedition: The communication of information for the purpose of inciting governmental resistance, defamation, or treason.

Selective Incapacitation: Identification of a select group of offenders who pose the greatest risk to society for incarceration/incapacitation.

Self-Report Surveys: Surveys that attempt to gather information from the offenders' perspective to provide information about criminal incidents from the offenders' perspective and to capture information about crimes that do not come to the attention of the police, that victims are not willing to report, and public order and other offenses that may not have a clearly identifiable victim. Self-report surveys were developed beginning in the 1940s and 1950s out of concern among criminologists that official statistics were reflecting a distorted picture of crime.

Semantic Dementia: Term coined by Hervey Cleckley in his classic 1941 work on psychopathy, *The Mask of Sanity,* refering to the psychopath's attempt to mimic emotion and manipulate meaning through language.

Separatist-Nationalist Terrorists: Well-adjusted, non–mentally disordered people who are highly educated and suffer low social status, projecting this suffering onto an external entity.

Serial Murder: Generally defined as two or more murders committed in two or more separate locations without an emotional cooling-off period between each. However, the definition has been expanded by a number of authors.

Sex Addiction: Preoccupation with and compulsion to engage in sexual behavior to the extent that it has adverse consequences.

Sex Offender Risk Appraisal Guide (SORAG): 14-item scale developed by Quinsey, Harris, Rice, and Cormier for male offenders who have committed sexual offenses. Scored based on review of a comprehensive psychosocial history, including information gathered from third parties and review of records with statistical probability from 0 to 100% that an offender will violently or sexually violently recidivate.

Sexual Deviance: Sexual behavior outside of the norm, including socially deviant as well as criminal sexual behavior.

Sexual Disorders: *DSM-IV-TR* Axis I disorders that involve behaviors that are sexually deviant in the sense that they are associated with some form of individual or interpersonal distress. Sexual disorders include paraphilias, sexual dysfunctions, and gender identity disorders. Some, but not all, of the *DSM* sexual disorders are crimes.

Sexual Homicide: The intentional killing of a person during which there is sexual behavior by the perpetrator.

Sexual Masochism: *DSM-IV-TR* paraphilia characterized by achieving sexual arousal through pain and suffering.

Sexual Predator Laws: A variant of the habitual offender laws involving identifying the worst of the worst habitual offenders who engage in predatory sex offenses and whose criminal behavior is determined to be the product of a mental disease or defect. Current laws, referred to as *sexually violent predator* or SVP laws, are a revival of the old *sexual psychopathy* laws of the early 1900s. Like habitual offender laws, the purpose of sexual predator laws is to protect the public by identifying the subtype of offenders deemed most dangerous. Sexual predator laws take habitual criminal legislation a step further in that they apply after an offender has served his or her sentence and involve civil commitment on completion of a sentence of confinement.

Sexual Psychopath: Legal term used to impose civil commitment of dangerous sex offenders whose behavior is associated with mental illness and pathological tendency to reoffend.

Sexual Sadism: *DSM-IV-TR* paraphilia characterized by sexual arousal through the intentional infliction of pain and suffering.

Sexually Violent Predator (SVP): Legal term used to impose civil commitment of dangerous sex offenders whose behavior is associated with mental illness and pathological tendency to reoffend.

Shakhidka: Term coined by Russian reporters to refer to female Islamist suicide bombers, combining the Arabic word for martyr, *shahid*, and the Russian female suffix, *ka*.

Signature: Offender's behaviors that reflect psychopathology, fantasy, and the unique need of the offender; behaviors that go beyond modus operandi or what's needed to carry out the offense.

Simple Obsessional Stalker: Stalkers who have some prior (usually intimate) relationship with the victim and are the most common types of stalkers.

Situational Crime Prevention: Crime prevention method involving altering situations to crime targets less rewarding while increasing risks, effort, and guilt to reduce temptation to commit crime.

Six Percent Solution: The hypothesis that incarcerating a small number of dangerous offenders will significantly reduce the crime rate and protect public safety based on the landmark 1972 study by Marvin Wolfgang and colleagues, *Delinquency in a Birth Cohort,* which found that 6% of a cohort of 10,000 young men in Philadelphia born in 1945 were responsible for over 50% of total crime.

Social Addiction: Term used to refer to the social basis of addiction. Addicts cannot function without enablers or codependents—people who support, cover up, or otherwise facilitate the addict's addictive behavior.

Social and Behavioral Sciences: Disciplines and subdisciplines involved in the study of criminal behavior, with scholars from a wide range of fields in sociology, psychology, criminology, and criminal justice engaged in the study of crime.

Social Bond Theory: Developed by Travis Hirschi, social bond theory (also referred to as *control theory*) is the most frequently tested and discussed of all theories in criminology. The main proposition in social control theory is that crime occurs when an individual's bond to society is weak or broken. Social bonds consist of four elements: *attachment* to others, *commitment* to conventional goals, *involvement* in conventional community activities, and *belief* in conventional norms and values. Based on this theory, people who are attached, committed, involved, and believe in conventional values are less likely to engage in criminal behavior because they have a stake in the community and have too much to lose.

Social Construction: Constructed through a process of social interaction; the process by which meaning is created through a combination of cultural, social, political, and economic forces in society.

Social Dream: A term coined by Reiber and Vetter in *The Psychopathology of Language and Cognition,* referring to a cultural product distinctive in that it so closely captures an aspect of current impulses and conflicts of society that its content, though quite fantastic, passes without reflection or comment by the general public.

Sociological Typology: Typology based on sociological theory and organized around social and cultural interactions and social context. Sociological typologies classify offenders and offenses based on features such as place of crime, relationship to victim, the activities involved in the crime, and so on. The purposes of sociological typologies are generally theoretical understanding and social policy development.

Sociopathic Personality: Term historically used synonymously with psychopathy, especially in the 1960s and 1970s, when many clinicians and researchers adopted this term to designate a less severe form of psychopathy characterized by social factors rather than psychopathology. Today, the term sociopath is more appropriately reserved for individuals who would be considered "secondary psychopaths" or individuals with antisocial personality disorder who would score between 20 and 30 on the PCL-R.

Sourcebook of Criminal Justice Statistics: Supported by the U.S. Department of Justice, Bureau of Justice Statistics, a collection of data from more than 100 sources on many aspects of crime and criminal justice in the United States.

Specialized Courts: Courts established to address the needs of offenders whose criminal behavior is the product of substance abuse or mental illness. These courts are based on the notion that mental illness and substance abuse play significant roles in the commission of crime for some offenders and that reducing offense behavior for these offenders requires addressing underlying substance abuse or mental illness at the root of offending patterns.

Spree Murder: When an offender murders at two or more separate locations without an emotional cooling-off period between each.

Staging: The intentional manipulation of a crime scene for purpose of throwing off police investigation.

Stalker: An individual who willfully, maliciously, and repeatedly follows, harasses, or pursues someone without the person's consent. Stalkers are likely to have criminal, psychiatric, and drug abuse histories, and show evidence of a range of *DSM* Axis I and Axis II (primarily Cluster B) disorders, though most are not psychotic at the time of their offense.

Stalkerazzi: Photographers who stalk celebrities to get their photos to sell for high prices and are willing to engage in risky behaviors with sometimes fatal consequences.

State Crime: Crime committed by governmental agents for the purpose of maintaining power, including political corruption, illegal domestic surveillance, human rights violations, state corporate crime, and state violence (genocide, torture, deadly force; also called *state organized crime*).

State Violence: An extreme form of political criminality that generally consists of illegal, physically harmful actions committed by a country's coercive organizations (i.e., police, national security agencies, and military) against individuals and groups.

Static Risk Factors: Risk factors that do not change over time, such as biological predisposition, sex, personality, early childhood trauma.

Stolen Property System: Model proposed by White and Chappel that explains economic crime as a multistage process involving acts and actors spanning a broadly defined set of roles and behaviors including six modes: research and planning (determination for the demand for the item, its location, and how it can be acquired), extraction (separation of property from owner), exchange (transfer of item from extractor to marketer), marketing (transportation and storage), redistribution (determination of where, what price, and when item will be resold), and evaluation (analysis of system performance).

Strain Theory: A sociological and structural theory of criminal behavior that says that crime is the product of differential opportunity. Based on the work of Emile Durkheim and extended by Robert Merton, suggests that anomie results when there is lack of access to prescribed goals and lack of availability of legitimate means to obtain those goals. Crime occurs when individuals do not have access to legitimate noncriminal means to obtain the success that everyone strives for.

Stranger Homicide: Homicide in which victim is a stranger to the offender.

Street Ethnography: Qualitative method that involves entering the natural habitat of the subject of study.

Structural Functionalism: The dominant sociological theory of crime from the first half of the 20th century based on the work of Durkheim, Erikson, and others. Structural functionalists see crime and deviance as products of social distancing and *anomie,* a state of normlessness, and see deviance and crime, despite their negative effects, as serving a social function by promoting social solidarity among the law abiding.

Subclinical Psychopath: Noncriminal psychopath. Also referred to as successful, extrasocial, or industrial psychopath. Such an individual would likely score high on Factor 1 but low on Factor 2 of the PCL-R or manifest antisocial behavior in corporate or white-collar deviance or antisocial but noncriminal behavior such as adultery, lying, and manipulative behaviors.

Substance-Induced Disorders: Conditions such as anxiety, delirium, intoxication, sexual dysfunction, and amnesia that occur either from the use of a substance or the withdrawal after discontinuing use.

Substance Use Disorders: Abuse of and dependence on substances taken voluntarily for their effect on the central nervous system or to prevent withdrawal symptoms.

Taxon: A discrete (either/or) group or category.

Techniques of Neutralization: Term coined by Sykes and Matza in 1957 referring to a range of neutralization techniques people use to rationalize their behavior and maintain a positive self-image: condemnation of the condemners, appeal to higher loyalties, denial of injury, denial of victim, and denial of responsibility.

Technology: The application of science to human endeavors.

Technology Transfer: The process by which knowledge and information gets into the hands of those who need it (in criminal justice, mental health, and other systems/organizations).

Terrorism (Domestic): Domestic terrorism is the unlawful use, or threatened use, of violence by a group or individual based and operating entirely within a particular country (e.g., the United States) without foreign direction, committed against persons or property to intimidate or coerce a government, the civilian population, or any segment thereof, in furtherance of political or social objectives.

Terrorism (International): Violent acts or acts dangerous to human life that are intended to intimidate or coerce a civilian population, influence the policy of a government, or affect the government's conduct. These acts transcend national boundaries in the means by which they are accomplished, the persons they appear intended to intimidate, or the locale in which perpetrators operate.

Theoreticism: The tendency of researchers to accept or reject knowledge on the basis of personal values and experiences; the inclination to ignore or disparage knowledge bases and entire disciplines outside of one's own affiliation or framework.

Three Strikes Legislation: Legislation enacted in over half of the United States requiring long-term sentences for repeat offenders. The laws are a revival of the old habitual offender laws of the early to mid-1900s and are said by proponents to reduce crime by deterring and selectively incapacitating the most dangerous and criminally active offenders. Washington State was the first jurisdiction to enact three strikes legislation, in December 1993. California followed in 1994 and by the late 1990s over 26 states and the federal government had also introduced similar laws that differ in the lengths of the long-term sentence (e.g., 25 years, life without parole) and the range of offenses included under the law (e.g., all felonies, select felonies).

Trauma Control Model: Integrative model proposed by Eric Hickey to explain the development of a serial killer that takes into account biological predisposition, early childhood trauma, dissociative processes, fantasy development, facilitators, low self-esteem, and life events.

Treason: An act or acts aimed at overthrowing one's own government.

Tree Spiking: A method of sabotage involving hammering a rod into tree trunks, often used by members of ecoterrorist organizations to discourage logging. If a logging blade hits the rod, the blade can be damaged or the logger can be injured or killed.

Trichotillomania: *DSM-IV-TR* Axis I impulse-control disorder characterized by recurrent impulses to pull out one's own hair. Pulling hair may provide relief or gratification related to tension experienced prior to the act. Unlike the other impulse-control disorders, this disorder does not tend to be associated with criminal behavior.

True Negative: Term used in offender (and other) risk prediction to refer to a correct decision. When applied to offender risk prediction, it refers to the outcome of prediction in which the offender is accurately predicted not to reoffend (i.e., predicted not to reoffend and does not).

True Positive: Term used in offender (and other) risk prediction to refer to a correct decision. When applied to offender risk prediction, it refers to the outcome of prediction in which the offender is accurately predicted to reoffend (i.e., predicted to reoffend and does).

Typology: System of grouping phenomena based on shared characteristics; An abstract category or class (or set of categories or classes) consisting of characteristics organized around a common principle relevant to a particular analysis.

Uniform Crime Reports (UCR):   National crime statistics collected annually by the Federal Bureau of Investigation from police departments around the country. Developed by the International Association for Chiefs of Police (IACP) in 1927 in response to the need for a reliable national crime reporting system.

Urophilia: Sexual interest in drinking or touching urine.

Violence: A behavioral manifestation of aggression that involves overt threat or application of force likely to result in injury.

Violence Inhibition Mechanism (VIM):   A cognitive mechanism that reduces the likelihood of aggressive attack when the aggressor is faced with distress cues.

Violence Risk Appraisal Guide (VRAG):   12-item scale developed by Quinsey, Harris, Rice, and Cormier for male offenders who have committed serious, violent (including sexual) offenses. Scored based on review of a comprehensive psychosocial history, including information gathered from third parties and review of records with statistical probability from 0 to 100% that an offender will violently or sexually violently recidivate.

Visionary Serial Killer: Serial killer motivated by psychosis, with auditory and visual hallucinations telling them to kill and engage in particular acts. One of four types in Holmes and DeBurger's serial killer typology.

Voyeurism: *DSM-IV-TR* paraphilia characterized by sexual arousal from watching nonconsenting persons undress or engage in sexual activity.

Weak Superego Theory: One of the most popular psychodynamic theories of criminal behavior in the psychodynamic literature and the topic of much discourse and discussion in the 1940s, 1950s, and 1960s. Behavioral indicators of a weak superego include reckless disregard for conventional rules, lack of conscience and antisocial cognitions, weak ambition, absence of guilt, early conduct problems, expressions of bravado, authority conflicts, and isolation.

Werther Effect: Term coined by sociologist David Phillips in 1974 to refer to the copycat phenomenon in reference to the 1774 novel *The Sorrows of Young Werther* by Johann Wolfgang von Goethe.

White Hat: Computer hacker who uses hacking skills to engage in prosocial behavior motivated by creativity, self-exploration, and the desire to push the envelope for the betterment of society. White Hats operate from an ethical perspective or "hacker paradigm," believing that any and all information that teaches individuals about the way the world works should be free.

World Trade Organization (WTO): A global international organization of 148 countries established in 1995 to deal with rule of trade between nations.

Zoophilia: Sexual activity with animals (also called bestiality).

References

A third car dragging incident is reported. (2001). *RaceMatters.org:* Retrieved May 10, 2007: http://www .racematters.org/nytarchjb169.htm.

Abbott, J. H. (1981). *In the belly of the beast.* New York: Vintage Books.

Abbott, J. H., & Zack, N. (1987). *My return.* Buffalo, NY: Prometheus Books.

Abel, G. G., Lawry, S. S., Karlstrom, E. M., Osborn, C. A., & Gillespie, C. F. (1994). Screening tests for pedophilia. *Criminal Justice and Behavior, 21,* 115–131.

Abel, G. G., & Rouleau, J. (1990). The nature and extent of sexual assault. In W. L. Marshall, D. R. Laws, & H. E. Barbaree (Eds.), *Handbook of sexual assault: Issues, theories, and treatment of the offender* (pp. 9–21). New York: Plenum.

Abidinsky, H. (1985). *Organized crime.* Chicago: Nelson-Hall.

Abidinsky, H. (2004). *Drugs: An Introduction.* Belmont, CA: Wadsworth.

ACLU of Washington. (July, 2000). Out of control: Seattle's flawed response to protests against the World Trade Organization. Retrieved July 14, 2005: http://www.aclu-wa.org/Issues/police/WTO-Report.html#Executive%20Summary.

Adam, B. A. (April 3 2004). "Woman jailed six years for gang-related stabbing." *The Star Phoenix,* p. A10.

Adler, F. (1975). *Sisters in crime.* New York: McGraw-Hill.

Adler, F. (1995). Who are we?: A self-analysis of criminal justice specialists. *ACJS Today, 14*(1), 1, 3, 21–26.

Adler, P. A., & Adler, P. (Eds.) (2003, 2006). *Constructions of deviance: Social power, context, and interaction.* Belmont, CA: Wadsworth.

Agnew, R. (1994). The techniques of neutralization and violence. *Criminology, 32*(4), 555–580.

Agnew, R. (2005). *Why do criminals offend? A general theory of crime and delinquency.* Los Angeles: Roxbury.

Ahmed, S. (August 3, 2005). Cyberstalking the innocent. Cox News Service.

Aichorn, A. (1935). *Wayward Youth.* London: Putnam.

Ainsworth, M.D.S. (1989). Attachments beyond infancy. *American Psychologist, 44*(4), 709–716.

Akers, R. L., & Sellers, C. (2004). *Criminological theories.* Los Angeles: Roxbury.

Åkerström, M. (1995). *Crooks and squares: Lifestyles of thieves and addicts in comparison to conventional people.* New Brunswick, NJ: Transaction Publishers.

Alalehto, T. (2003). Economic crime: Does personality matter? *International Journal of Offender Therapy and Comparative Criminology, 47*(3), 335–355.

Albanese, J. S. (2000). The causes of organized crime. *Journal of Contemporary Criminal Justice, 14*(4), 409–423.

Albanese, J. S., Parker, M., & Chapman, T (2002). *Organized Crime.* National White Collar Crime Center (http://www.nw3c.org/research/site_files.cfm?mode=p).

Alderson, A. (February 20, 2005). "Confessions of the world's most successful madam." *Sunday Telegraph,* p. 21.

Alison, L., Bennell, C., Mokros, A., & Ormerod, D. (2002). The personality paradox in offender profiling: A theoretical review of the processes involved in deriving background characteristics from crime scene actions. *Psychology, Public Policy, and the Law, 8*(1), 115–135.

Allen, F. A. (2004). Criminal justice, legal values, and the rehabilitative ideal. In G. F. Cole, M. G. Gertz, & A. Bunger (Eds.), *The criminal justice system* (pp. 63–70). Belmont, CA: Wadsworth.

Allen, H. (1987). *Justice unbalanced.* Milton Keynes: Open University Press.

Allen, T. W. (January 10, 2007). Final action on the administrative investigation into the diving mishap and the resulting deaths of USCGC Healy's crewmembers that occurred on 17 August 2006. Memorandum, U.S. Department of Homeland Security U.S. Coast Guard. Retrieved January 14, 2007, at: http://www .uscg.mil/ccs/cit/cim/foia/Healy/HEALY_FAM.pdf.

American Psychiatric Association (APA). (2000). *Diagnostic and statistical manual of mental disorders, Fourth Edition, Text Revision (DSM-IV-TR)*. Washington, DC: American Psychiatric Association.

Anderson, C. A., Berkowitz, L., Donnerstein, E., Huesmann, L. R., Johnson, J. D., Linz, D., et al. (2003). The influence of media violence on youth. *Psychological Science in the Public Interest, 4*(3), 81–110.

Anderson, C. A., & Dill, K. E. (2000). Video games and aggressive thoughts, feelings, and behavior in the laboratory and life. *Journal of Personality and Social Psychology, 78*, 772–790.

Anderson, J. F., Dyson, L., & Brooks, Jr., W. (2002). Preventing hate crime and profiling hate crime offenders. *The Western Journal of Black Studies, 26*(3), 140–148.

Andrews, D. A., & Bonta, J. (1995, 2001). *Level of Service Inventory-Revised*. North Tonowanda, NY: Multi-Health Systems.

Andrews, D. A., & Bonta, J. (2003). *The psychology of criminal conduct* (3rd Ed.). Cincinnatti: Anderson Publishing.

Andrews, D. A., & Bonta, J. (2006). *The psychology of criminal conduct* (4th Ed.). Cincinnati: Anderson Publishing.

Andrews, D. A., & Dowden, C. (2006). Risk principle of case classification in correctional treatment: A meta-analytic investigation. *International Journal of Offender Therapy and Comparative Criminology, 50*(1), 88–100.

Annon, J. S. (1995). Investigative profiling: A behavioral analysis of the crime scene. *American Journal of Forensic Psychology, 13*(4), 67–75.

Appeals court tosses suit blaming movie for killing spree. (June 7, 2002). Associated Press. Retrieved March 24, 2006, at: http://www.fac.org/news.aspx?id=3801.

Arena, M. P., & Arrigo, B. A. (2005). Social psychology, terrorism, and identity: A preliminary re-examination of theory, culture, self, and society. *Behavioral Sciences & The Law, 23*(4), 485–506.

Arnot, C. (March 4, 1998). Crime prevention: Living space. *The Guardian*, p. 6.

Arrigo, B. A. (1998). *Social justice/criminal justice: The maturation of critical theory in crime, law, and deviance*. Belmont, CA: Wadsworth.

Arrigo, B. A., & Purcell, C. (2001). Explaining paraphilias and lust murder: Toward an integrated model. *Journal of Offender Therapy and Comparative Criminology, 45*(1), 6–31.

Arrigo, B. A., & Shipley, S. L. (2005). *Forensic psychology: Issues and controversies in law, law enforcement, and corrections*. San Diego, CA: Elsevier Academic Press.

Arrow, T. (July 9, 2005). Tre Arrow speaks out—part 2. *Free Tre Arrow*. Retrieved July 15, 2005, at: http://www3.telus.net/public/trearrow/.

Atkinson, M. (1999). The movies made me do it. How much are 'Natural Born' Killers affected by film violence? *The Village Voice*. Available at: http://www.villagevoice.com/news/9918,atkinson,5325,1.html.

Auchard, E., & Li, K. (February 19, 2006). MySpace: Murdoch's big hope, parents' nightmare. Reuters. Retrieved March 21, 2006, at: http://www.boston.com/news/education/k_12/articles/2006/02/19/myspace_murdochs_big_hope_parents_nightmare/?p1=email_to_a_friend.

Austin, J., Clark, J., Hardyman, P., & Henry, D. A. (1999). Three strikes laws. *Punishment and Society, 1*, 131–162.

Austin, J., Coleman, D., Peyton, J., & Johnson, K. D. (January 9, 2003). Reliability and validity study of the LSI-R risk assessment instrument. Final Report to the Pennsylvania Board of Probation and Parole. Washington, DC: The Institute on Crime, Justice, and Corrections.

Babiak, P., & Hare, R. D. (2006). *Snakes in suits: When psychopaths go to work*. New York: HarperCollins.

Baby found alive; woman arrested. (December 18, 2004). Retrieved October 10, 2006, at: http://www.cnn.com/2004/US/12/18/fetus.found.alive/.

Bailey, F. Y., & Hale, D. C. (1998). *Popular culture, crime, and justice*. Belmont, CA: Wadsworth.

Barak, G. (1998). *Integrating criminologies*. Needham Heights, MA: Allyn & Bacon.

Barbaree, H. E. (1990). Stimulus control of sexual arousal: Its role in sexual assault. In W. L. Marshall, D. R. Laws, & H. E. Barbaree (Eds.), *Handbook of sexual assault: Issues, theories, and treatment of the offender* (pp. 115–142). New York: Plenum.

Barber, M. (January 13, 2007). Scathing report on fatal dive. *Seattle Post-Intelligencer*, B-1.

Barbour-McMullen, J., Coid, J., & Howard, R. (1988). The psychometric identification of psychopathy in mentally abnormal offenders. *Personality and Individual Differences, 9*, 817–823.

Barefoot v. Estelle (1983). 463 U.S. 880.

Barkan, S. E. (2005). *Criminology: A sociological understanding*. Upper Saddle River, NJ: Pearson/Prentice-Hall.

Bartol, C. R. (2002). *Criminal behavior: A psychosocial approach.* Upper Saddle River, NJ: Pearson/Prentice-Hall.

Bartol, C. R., & Bartol, A. M. (2005). *Introduction to forensic psychology.* Thousand Oaks, CA: Sage.

Beauregard, E., & Proulx, J. (2007). A classification of sexual homicide against men. *International Journal of Offender Therapy and Comparative Criminology, 51*(4), 420–432.

Beck, A. J., & Shipley, B. E. (1989). *Recidivism of prisoners released in 1983.* Washington, DC: National Institute of Justice, Bureau of Justice Statistics.

Beck, J. C. (1998). Legal and ethical duties of the clinician treating a patient who is liable to be impulsively violent. *Behavioral Sciences and the Law, 16,* 375–389.

Becker, H. (2003). Labeling theory. In *Constructions of deviance: Social power, context, and interaction* (pp. 70–74). Belmont, CA: Wadsworth.

Beech, A. R. (1998) A psychometric typology of child molesters. *International Journal of Offender Therapy and Comparative Criminology, 42,* 313–339.

Beech, A. R., & Ward, T. (2004). The integration of etiology and risk in sex offenders: A theoretical model. *Aggression and Violent Behavior, 10,* 31–63.

Beeghley, L. (2003). *Homicide: A sociological perspective.* Lanham, MD: Rowman & Littlefield.

Beetz, A. M. (2004). Bestiality/zoophilia: A scarcely-investigated phenomenon between crime, paraphilia, and love. *Journal of Forensic Psychology Practice, 4*(2), 1–36.

Belfrage, H. (1998). A ten-year follow-up of criminality in Stockholm mental patients: New evidence for a relation between mental disorder and crime. *British Journal of Criminology, 38*(1), 145–155.

Belfrage, H., Fransson, G., & Strand, S. (2004). Management of violent behaviors in the correctional system using qualified risk assessments. *Legal and Criminological Psychology, 9,* 11–22.

Belknap, J. (2004). Meda Chesney-Lind: The mother of feminist criminology. *Women & Criminal Justice, 15,* 1–23.

Bell, R. (2005). The Tylenol terrorist. *The Crime Library.* Retrieved August 31, 2005, at: http://www.crimelibrary.com/terrorists_spies/terrorists/tylenol_murders/index.html?sect=22.

Bellingham Police Department. (October 10, 2002). Level III Sex Offender Notification. Retrieved February 14, 2004, at: http://www.cob.org/police/source/htm/sexovasquez.htm.

Benda, B. B. (2001). Factors that discriminate between recidivists, parole violators, and nonrecidivists in a 3-year follow-up of boot camp graduates. *International Journal of Offender Therapy and Comparative Criminology, 45,* 711–729.

Benda, B. B., Corwyn, R. F., & Toombs, N. J. (2001). Recidivism among adolescent serious offenders: Prediction of entry into the correctional system for adults. *Criminal Justice and Behavior, 28,* 588–613.

Beres, L. S., & Griffith, T. D. (1998). Do three strikes laws make sense? Habitual offender statutes and criminal incapacitation. *Georgetown Law Review, 87,* 103–138.

Best, S., & Nocella, II, A. J. (2004). *Terrorists or freedom fighters?: Reflections on the liberation of animals.* New York: Lantern Books.

Bibes, P. (2001). Transnational organized crime and terrorism. *Journal of Contemporary Criminal Justice, 17*(3), 243–258.

Bickley, J. A., & Beech, A. R. (2002). An empirical investigation of the Ward and Hudson self regulation model of the sexual offense process with child abusers. *Journal of Interpersonal Violence, 17,* 373–393.

Bjorkqvist, K., & Niemela, P. (Eds.) (1992). *Of mice and women: Aspects of female aggression.* San Diego, CA: Academic Press.

Black, D. (1983). Crime as social control. *American Sociological Review, 48,* 73–95.

Black, J. (1991). *The aesthetics of murder: A study in romantic literature and contemporary culture.* Baltimore: Johns Hopkins University Press.

Blackburn, R. (1993). *The psychology of criminal conduct: Theory, research, and practice.* New York: John Wiley & Sons.

Blackburn R. (1998). Psychopathy and personality disorder: Implications of interpersonal theory. In D. J. Cooke et al. (Eds.), *Psychopathy: Theory, research, and implications for society* (pp. 269–301). Netherlands: Kluwer.

Blackburn, R., Logan, C., Donnelly, J., & Renwick, S. (2003). Personality disorders, psychopathy and other mental disorders: Co-morbidity among patients at English and Scottish high-security hospitals. *Journal of Forensic Psychiatry and Psychology, 14*(1), 111–137.

Blair, J. (July 4, 1998). Arrests reveal new ways to steal phone card data. *New York Times,* B1.

Blair, J., Mitchell, D., & Blair, K. (2005). *The psychopath: Emotion and the brain.* Oxford: Blackwell Publishing.

Blair, R. J. R. (2006). Subcortical brain systems in psychopathy: The amygdala and associated structures. In C. J. Patrick (Ed.), *Handbook of psychopathy* (pp. 296–312). New York: Guilford Press.

Blair, R. J. R., Sellars, C., Strickland, I., Clark, F., Williams, A. O., & Smith, M. (1995). Emotion attributions in the psychopath. *Personality and Individual Differences, 19,* 431–437.

Block, A. A., & Griffin, S. P. (2002). Transnational financial crime: Crooked lawyers, tax evasion, and securities fraud. *Journal of Contemporary Criminal Justice, 18*(4), 381–393.

Block, D. (January 5, 2006). Teen faces charges in Arlington blaze: Christmas eve fire damaged row of shops. *The Boston Globe,* 3.

Blume, P. (2004). Mall rapist arrested twice before in Madison area. WMTV NBC15 Madison, Wisconsin. Retrieved July 22, 2004, at: http://www.nbc15.com/Global/story.asp?s=%20%201902520.

Blumstein, A., Cohen, J., Roth, J. A., & Visher, C. A. (eds.). (1986). *Criminal careers and "career criminals."* Washington, DC: National Academy Press.

Boer, D., Hart, S., Kropp, P., & Webster, C. (1997). *Manual for sexual risk-20.* Burnaby, British Columbia: Mental Health, Law & Policy Institute, Simon Frazier University.

Bonta, J., Wallace-Capretta, S. & Rooney, J. (2000). A quasi-experimental evaluation of an intensive rehabilitation supervision program. *Criminal Justice and Behavior, 27,* 312–329.

Boothby, J. L., & Clements, C. B. (2000). A national survey of correctional psychologists. *Criminal Justice and Behavior, 27*(6), 716–732.

Borum, R., & Fulero, S. M. (1999). Empirical research on the insanity defense and attempted reforms: Evidence toward informed policy. *Law and Human Behavior, 23*(3), 375–394.

Bourne, L. E., Dominowski, R. L., Loftus, E. F., & Healy, A. E. (1986). *Cognitive processes.* Englewood Cliffs, NJ: Prentice Hall.

Bowcott, O. (April 30, 2005). Veteran animal rights activist jailed after threat in court. *The Guardian.* Retrieved July 14, 2005, at: http://www.guardian.co.uk/animalrights/story/0,11917,1473780,00.html.

Bowie, S. I., Silverman, D. C., Kalick, S. M., & Edbril, S. D. (1990). Blitz rape and confidence rape: Implications for clinical intervention. *American Journal of Psychotherapy, 44* (2), 180–188.

Bowlby, J. (1969). *Attachment and loss, Volume 1: Attachment.* New York: Basic Books.

Boyle, K. (2001). What's natural about killing? Gender, copycat violence and *Natural Born Killers. Journal of Gender Studies, 10* (3),311–321.

Bralley, J., & Prevost, J. (2001). Reinventing community supervision: Georgia parole's results-driven supervision. *Corrections Today, 63,* 120+.

Brantingham, P. J., & Brantingham, P. L. (1991). *Environmental criminology.* Prospect Heights, IL: Waveland Press.

Brass, M. (July 8, 2005). Canadian native leader convicted of hate crimes. Reuters Canada. Retrieved July 8, 2005, at: http://ca.today.reuters.com/news/newsArticle.aspx?type=topNews&storyID=2005–07–08T205514Z_01_N08394557_RTRIDST_0_NEWS-CRIME-CANADA-HATE-COL.XML.

Brett, A. (2004). "Kindling theory" in arson: How dangerous are firesetters? *Australian Journal of Psychiatry, 38,* 419–425.

Brinkley, C. A., Bernstein, A., & Newman, J. P. (1999a). Coherence in the narratives of psychopathic and nonpsychopathic criminal offenders. *Personality and Individual Differences, 27,* 519–530.

Brinkley, C. A., Newman J. P., Harpur T. J., & Johnson M. M. (1999). Cohesion in texts produced by psychopathic and nonpsychopathic criminal inmates. *Personality and Individual Differences, 26,* 873–885.

Britz, M. T. (2004). *Computer forensics and cybercrime.* Upper Saddle River, NJ: Pearson/Prentice Hall.

Brown, L. S., & Ballou, M. (1992). *Personality and psychopathology: Feminist reappraisals.* New York: The Guilford Press.

Brown, S. E., Esbensen, F., & Geis, G. (2001). *Criminology: Explaining crime and its content.* Cincinnati: Anderson Publishing.

Brownmiller, S. (1975). *Against our will: Men, women, and rape.* New York: Bantam Books.

Buddie, A. M., & Miller, A. G. (2001). Beyond rape myths: A more complex view of perceptions of rape victims. *Sex Roles, 45*(3–4), 139–160.

Burgard, M. (March 4, 2006). A crime-fighting overture neighbors hoping city adopts plan to use classical music to help clean up park. *HartfordInfo.org.* Retrieved August 6, 2007, at: http://www.hartfordinfo.org/issues/documents/Crime/htfd_courant_030406.asp.

Burgess, A. W., Harner, H., Baker, T., Hartman, C., & Lole, C. (2001). Batterers stalking patterns. *Journal of Family Violence, 16* (3), 309–321.

Burgess, R., & Akers, R. L. (1966). A differential association-reinforcement theory of criminal behavior. *Social Problems, 14,* 363–383.

Burk, L. R., & Burkhart, B. R. (2003). Disorganized attachment as a diathesis for sexual deviance developmental experience and the motivation for sexual offending. *Aggression and Violent Behavior, 8,* 487–511.

Burke, S. J., & Barnhart, F. D. (2002). *The collapse of Enron: A bibliography of online legal, government, and legislative resources.* Available at: http://www.llrx.com/features/enron.htm.

Bushman, B. J., & Anderson, C. A. (2001). Is it time to pull the plug on the hostile versus instrumental aggression dichotomy? *Psychological Review, 108*, 273–279.

Caetano, R., & McGrath, C. (2005). Driving under the influence (DUI) among U.S. ethnic groups. *Accident Analysis & Prevention, 37*(2), 217–224.

California Department of Corrections and Rehabilitation. (September 30, 2007). Second and Third Strikers in the Adult Institution Population. Sacramento, CA: California Department of Corrections and Rehabilitation, Offender Information Services Branch, Estimates and Statistical Analysis Section, Data.

Campbell, A. (1994). *Men, women, and aggression.* New York: Basic Books.

Campbell, A., Muncer, S., McManus, I. C., & Woodhouse, D. (1999). Instrumental and expressive representations of aggression: One scale or two? *Aggressive Behavior, 25*, 435–444.

Campbell, K. (October 10, 2002). As sniper hunt grows role of media blurs. *Christian Science Monitor.* Retrieved November 4, 2005, at: http://www.csmonitor.com/2002/1010/p01s03-usju.htm.

Camus, A. (1942, 1988). *The stranger.* New York: Everyman's Library.

Can a video game lead to murder? (March 6, 2005). CBS News. Available at: http://www.cbsnews.com/stories/2005/03/04/60minutes/main678261.shtml.

Cannibal case to go to Germany's highest court. (March 19, 2007). Belfast Telegraph. Retrieved April 16, 2007, at: http://www.belfasttelegraph.co.uk/breaking-news/world/europe/article2372284.ece.

Cannibal could kill again, expert tells German Court. (January 20, 2004). GMax.co.za. Retrieved January 29, 2004, at: http://www.gmax.co.za/look04/01/20-germany.html.

Canter, D. (2000). *Criminal shadows: The inner narratives of evil.* Irving, TX: Authorlink Press.

Canter, D., & Alison, L. (Eds.) (2000). *Profiling property crimes.* Burlington, VT: Ashgate.

Canter, D., Alison, L. J., Alison, E., & Wentink, N. (2004). The organized/disorganized typology of serial murder: Myth or model? *Psychology, Public Policy, and Law, 10*(3), 293–320.

Capowich, G. E. (2003). The conditioning effects of neighborhood ecology on burglary victimization. *Criminal Justice and Behavior, 30*(1), 39–61.

Carnell, B. (August 28, 2004). Security guard receives $25,000 reward for capture of Michael Scarpitti (AKA Tre Arrow). *AnimalRights.net.* Retrieved July 15, 2005, at: http://www.animalrights.net/archives/year/2004/000332.html.

Carpenter, B. (1998). The prostitute and the client: Challenging the dualisms. *Women's Studies International Forum, 21*(4), 387–399.

Carruthers, S. (2001). Past future: The troubled history of Stanley Kubrick's *A Clockwork Orange. National Forum, 81*(2). Available at: http://www.find articles.com/p/articles/mi_qa3651/is_200104/ai_n8930524.

Carter, C. J. (2001). Abducted 5-year-old girl is found dead in what investigators say is a "calling card" from killer. *DodgeGlobe.* Retrieved January 12, 2004, at: http://www.dodgeglobe.com/stories/071802/nat_girl.shtml.

Casella, R. (2001). *At zero tolerance: Punishment, prevention, and school violence.* New York: Peter Lang.

Casey, D. (March 19, 2004). 3 years in jail for beating. *The Ottowa Sun,* p. 16.

Catalano, S. M. (September 2006). *National Crime Victimization Survey, Criminal victimization, 2005.* Washington, DC: U.S. Department of Justice, Bureau of Justice Statistics.

Catan, T., & Peel, M. (March 3, 2003). Bogus websites, stolen corporate identities: How Nigerian fraudsters steal millions from western banks. *Financial Times—London,* 21.

Chaiken, M., & Chaiken, J. (1990). *Redefining the career criminal: Priority prosecution of high-rate dangerous offenders.* Washington, DC: U.S. Department of Justice, National Institute of Justice, Office of Justice Programs.

Chambliss, W. J. (1978, 1988). *On the take: From petty crooks to presidents.* Bloomington: Indiana University Press.

Chandler, R. K., Peters, R. H., Field, G., & Juliano-Bult, D. (2004). Challenges in implementing evidence-based treatment practices for co-occurring disorders in the criminal justice system. *Behavioral Sciences and the Law, 22*, 431–448.

Chapman, J. R. (1980), *Economic realities and the female offender.* Lexington, MA: Lexington Books.

Chesney-Lind, M. (1997). *The female offender: Girls, women, and crime.* Thousand Oaks, CA: Sage.

City of Seattle v. Mighty Movers, Inc. (2004). Supreme Court of the State of Washington. Retrieved February 28, 2005, at: http://www.courts.wa.gov/opinions/?fa=opinions.opindisp&docid=730059MAJ.

Clark, J., Austin, J., & Henry, A. (1997). *"Three strikes and you're out": A review of state legislation*. Washington, DC: U.S. Department of Justice, National Institute of Justice.

Clarke, R. V. (1997). *Situational crime prevention: Successful case studies*. Monsey, NY: Criminal Justice Press.

Clarke, R. V. (2004). Technology, criminology, and crime science. *European Journal on Criminal Policy and Research, 10*(1), 55–63.

Classical music on West Palm corner deters crime. (July 8, 2001). *USA Today*. Retrieved at: http://www.usato day.com/news/nation/2001/07/08/music.htm.

Clear, T. R. (2001). Has academic criminal justice come of age? *Justice Quarterly, 18*(4), 709–726.

Cleckley, H. (1941, 1976, 1988). *The mask of sanity*. Saint Louis, MO: Mosby.

Clements, C. B. (1996). Offender classification: Two decades of progress. *Criminal Justice and Behavior, 23*(1), 121–143.

Clemmer, D. (1958). *The prison community*. New York: Holt Rinehart.

Cleveland, H. H., Koss, M. P., & Lyons, J. (1999). Rape tactics from the survivors perspective: Contextual dependence and within-event independence. *Journal of Interpersonal Violence, 14*(5), 532–547.

Clinard, M. B., & Meier, R. F. (2004). *Sociology of deviant behavior*. Belmont, CA: Wadsworth.

Clinard, M. B., Quinney, R., & Wildeman, J. (1994). *Criminal behavior systems: A typology*. Cincinnati, OH: Anderson Publishing.

Cloward, R., & Ohlin, L. (1960). *Delinquency and Opportunity*. NY: Free Press.

Coid, J. (1993). Current concepts and classifications of psychopathic disorder. In P. Tyrer & G. Stein (Eds.), *Personality disorder reviewed* (pp. 113–164). London: Royal College of Psychiatrists Gaskell Press.

Coleman, L. (2004). *The copycat effect: How the media and popular culture trigger mayhem in tomorrow's headlines*. New York: Paraview Pocket Books.

Colvin, M. (2000). *Crime and coercion: An integrated theory of chronic criminality*. New York: St. Martin's Press.

Cook, P. E., & Hinman, D. L. (1999). Criminal profiling: Science and art. *Journal of Contemporary Criminal Justice, 15*(3), 230–241.

Cooney, M., & Phillips, S. (2002). Typologizing violence: A Blackian perspective. *International Journal of Sociology and Social Policy, 22*(7/8), 75–107.

Copes, H. (2003). Streetlife and the rewards of auto theft. *Deviant Behavior: An Interdisciplinary Journal, 24*, 309–332.

Copes, H., Kerley, K. R., & Carroll, A. (2002). Killed in the act: A descriptive analysis of crime-precipitated homicide. *Homicide Studies, 6*(3), 240–257.

Cops arrest 23 in online shopping scams. (December 8, 2005). Associated Press.

Copson, G. (2004). Goals to Newcastle: Police use of offender profiling. In R. Keppel (Ed.), *Offender profiling* (pp. 145–160). Belmont, CA: Wadsworth.

Cordozo, B. (1930). *What medicine can do for the law*. New York: Harper.

Corley, S., Smith, B. L., & Damphouse, K. R. (2005). The changing face of American terrorism. In L.L. Snowden & B. C. Whitsel (Eds.), *Terrorism: Research, Readings and Realities* (pp. 49–62). Upper Saddle River, NJ1: Prentice Hall.

Cornell, D. G., Warren, J., Hawk, G., Stafford, E., Oram, G., & Pine, D. (1996). Psychopathy in instrumental and reactive violent offenders. *Journal of Consulting and Clinical Psychology, 64*(4), 783–790.

Corum, K. (September 28, 2006). IL Bodies in washer/dryer, coroner distraught. 14 WFIE. Retrieved September 28, 2006, at: http://www.14wfie.com/Global/story.asp? S=5445719&nav=menu54_3.

Court allows states to throw the book. (March 5, 2003). Associated Press. Retrieved May 20, 2006, at: http://www.cbsnews.com/stories/2003/03/05/supreme court/main542863.shtml.

Cowan, G. (2000). Beliefs about the causes of four types of rape. *Sex roles, 42*(9–10), 807–823.

Coyle, J. (April 21, 2007). A well known movie may have played a role in killer's mind. *The Seattle Times*. Retrieved May 9, 2007, at: http://seattletimes .nwsource.com/html/nationworld/2003674650_web virginiatechmovieins21.html.

Cressey, D. R. (1973). *Other people's money*. Montclair, NJ: Patterson Smith.

Crick, N. R., & Nelson, D. A. (2002). Relational and physical victimization within friendships: Nobody told me there'd be friends like these. *Journal of Abnormal Child Psychology, 20*, 599–607.

Croall, H. (2003). Combating financial crime: Regulatory versus crime control approaches. *Journal of Financial Crime, 11*(1), 45–55.

Cromwell, P. F. (Ed.). (1996) *In their own words: Criminals on crime*. Los Angeles: Roxbury.

Cromwell, P., Curtis, J., & Withrow, B. (2004). The dynamics of petty crime: An analysis of shoplifting. In D. A. Dabney (Ed.), *Crime types: A text/reader* (pp. 220–228). Belmont, CA: Wadsworth.

Cromwell, P., & Olson, J. N. (2004). *Breaking and entering: Burglars on burglary.* Belmont, CA: Wadsworth.

Cromwell, P. F., Olson, J. N., & Avary, D. W. (1996). Who buys stolen property? A new look at criminal receiving. In P. F. Cromwell (Ed.), *In their own words: Criminals on crime* (pp. 47–56). Los Angeles: Roxbury.

Crowe, T., & Zahm, D. (2004). Crime prevention through environmental design. *Land Management, 71,* 22–21.

Cullen, D. (April 20, 2004). The depressive and the psychopath: At last we know why the Columbine killers did it. *Slate.* Retrieved October 19, 2005, at: http://slate.msn.com/id/2099203/.

Cullen, D. (April 20, 2007). Psychopath? Depressive? Schizophrenic?: Was Cho Seung-Hui really like the Columbine killers? *Slate.* Retrieved August 17, 2007, at: http://www.slate.com/id/2164757/.

Cullen, F. (1995). Fighting back: Criminal justice as an academic discipline. *ACJS Today, 13*(4), 1–3.

Cullen, F. T., & Agnew, R. (Eds.) (2006). *Criminological theory: Past to present.* Los Angeles: Roxbury.

Cullen, F. T., & Gendreau, P. (2001). From nothing works to what works: Changing professional ideology in the 21st century. *The Prison Journal, 81,* 313–338.

Cunningham, K. J. (2003). Cross-regional trends in female terrorism. *Studies in Conflict and Terrorism, 26,* 171–195.

Cusick, L. (2002). Youth prostitution: A literature review. *Child Abuse Review, 11,* 230–251.

Dabney, D. A. (2004). *Crime types: A text/reader.* Belmont, CA: Wadsworth.

Daéid, N. N. (1997). Differences in offender profiling in the United States of America and the United Kingdom. *Forensic Science International, 90,* 25–31.

Daly, K. (1995). *Gender, crime, and punishment.* New Haven: Yale University Press.

Daly, K., & Chesney-Lind, M. (1988). Feminism and criminology. *Justice Quarterly 5*(4), 101–143.

Danner, M. (November 30, 1984). The place of pornography. *Harper's.* Available at: http://www .markdanner .com/articles/print/121.

Danni, K. A., & Hampe, G. D. (2000). An analysis of predictors of child sex offender types using presentence investigation reports. *International Journal of Offender Therapy and Comparative Criminology, 44*(4), 490–504.

Darke, J. L. (1990). Sexual aggression: Achieving power through humiliation. In W. L. Marshall, D. R. Laws, & H. E. Barbaree (Eds.), *Handbook of sexual assault: Issues, theories, and treatment of the offender* (pp. 55–72). New York: Plenum.

David, P. R. (Ed.). (1974). *The world of the burglar.* Albuquerque: University of New Mexico Press.

Davies, P. A. (2003). Is economic crime a man's game? *Feminist Theory, 4*(3), 283–303.

Davis, J. A. (1999). Criminal personality profiling and crime scene assessment: A contemporary investigative tool to assist law enforcement public safety. *Journal of Contemporary Criminal Justice, 15*(3), 291–301.

Davis, M. (October 10, 2004). Hot cars: FBI breaks major chop shop. *The Car Connection.* Available at: http://www.thecarconnection.com/Shoppers/Drivers_News/Hot_Cars_FBI_Breaks_Major_Chop_Shop.S 241.A7621.html.

Day, K., Gough, B., & McFadden, M. (2003). Women who drink and fight: A discourse analysis of working-class women's talk. *Feminism & Psychology, 13*(2), 141–158.

Deadheads behind bars. (n.d.). Web site: http://www .hr95.0rg/Deadheads.html.

Decker, S., Wright, R., Redfern, A., & Smith, D. (2004). A woman's place is in the home: Females and residential burglary. In D. A. Dabney (Ed.), *Crime types: A text/reader* (pp. 183–192). Belmont, CA: Wadsworth.

Delacoste, F., & Alexander, P. (Eds.). (1988). *Sex work: Writings by women in the sex industry.* London: Virago Press.

DeLisi, M. J. (2005). *Career criminals in society.* Thousand Oaks, CA: Sage.

DeLong, D. F. (February 8, 2001). Hackers said to cost U.S. billions. *NewsFactor Network.* Retrieved February 5, 2006, at: http://www.newsfactor.com/perl/story/7349.html.

DeMatteo, D., & Edens, J. F. (2006). The role and relevance of the Psychopathy Checklist-Revised in court. *Psychology, Public Policy, and Law, 12*(2), 214–241.

Denno, D. W. (2003). Who is Andrea Yates?: A short story about insanity. *Duke Journal of Gender, Law, & Policy, 10*(1), 1–58.

Devine, M. (September 9, 2004). The rise of women warriors. *The Sydney Morning Herald.* Retrieved May 6, 2007, at: http://www.smh.com.au/articles/2004/09/08/1094530691850.html.

Dickey, C. (December 12, 2005). Women of Al Qaeda. *Newsweek, 146*(24), 27–36.

Did American commit treason? (December 11, 2007). *The Dallas Morning News.* Retrieved: December 11, 2007 at: http://multimedia.belointeractive.com/attack/perspective/1222walker.html.

Dietz, P. E. (1983). Sex offenses: behavioral aspects. In S. H. Kadish (Ed.), *Encyclopedia of crime and justice.* New York: Free Press.

Dingley, J. C. (1997). The terrorist—developing a profile. *International Journal of Risk, Security, and Crime Prevention, 2*(1), 25–37.

Dixon, L., & Browne, K. (2003). The heterogeneity of spouse abuse: A review. *Aggression and Violent Behavior, 8,* 107–130.

Documents, neighbors reveal possible murder motive. (June 29, 2005). KIRO TV.com. Retrieved July 8, 2005, at: www.kirotv.com/news/4665129/detail.html.

Dodd, N. J. (2000). The psychology of fraud. In D. Canter & L. Alison (Eds.), *Profiling property crimes* (pp. 211–231). Burlington, VT: Ashgate.

Doley, R. (2003). Pyromania: Fact or fiction? *British Journal of Criminology, 43,* 797–807.

Douglas, J. E., Burgess, A. W., Burgess, A. G., & Ressler, R. K. (1992, 1997). *Crime classification manual.* San Francisco: Josey-Bass Publishers.

Douglas, J. E., & Olshaker, M. (1999). *The anatomy of motive.* New York: Pocket Books.

Douglas, J. E., Ressler, R. K., Burgess, A. W., & Hartman, C. R. (2004). Criminal profiling from crime scene analysis. In R. Keppel (Ed.), *Offender profiling* (pp. 23–34). Belmont, CA: Wadsworth.

Douglas, K. S., Vincent, G. M., & Edens, J. F. (2006). Risk for criminal recidivism: The role of psychopathy. In C. J. Patrick (Ed.), *The handbook of psychopathy* (pp. 533–554). New York: Guilford Press.

Dowden, C., & Andrews, D. A. (2000). Effective correctional treatment and violent reoffending: A meta-analysis. *Canadian Journal of Criminology and Criminal Justice, 42* (4), 449–467.

Dowden, C., & Andrews, D. A. (2004).The importance of staff practice in delivering effective correctional treatment: A meta-analytic review of core correctional practice. *International Journal of Offender Therapy and Comparative Criminology, 48,* 203–214.

Dowden, C., Antonowicz, D., & Andrews, D. A. (2003). The effectiveness of relapse prevention with offenders: A meta-analysis. *International Journal of Offender Therapy and Comparative Criminology, 47,* 516–528.

Dunbar, E. (2003). Symbolic, relational, and ideological signifiers of bias-motivated offenders: Toward a strategy of assessment. *American Journal of Orthopsychiatry, 73*(2), 203–211.

Durkheim, E. (2003). The normal and the pathological. In *Constructions of deviance: Social power, context, and interaction* (pp. 55–59). Belmont, CA: Wadsworth.

Dworkin, A. (1987). *Intercourse.* New York: The Free Press.

Dworkin, A. (1993). I want a twenty-four-hour truce during which there is no rape. In E. Buchwald, P. R. Fletcher, & M. Roth (1993), *Transforming a rape culture* (pp. 13–22). Minneapolis, MN: Milkweed Editions.

Eagan, M. (August 10, 1999). Abortion "choice" for many is one of desperation. *The Boston Herald,* O22.

Eby, D. W., Hopp, M. L., & Streff, F. M. (1996). *A profile of adolescent drivers convicted of felony drunk driving.* Ann Arbor, MI: The University of Michigan Transportation Research Institute.

Edens, J. F. (2001). Misuses of the Hare Psychopathy Checklist-Revised in court. *Journal of Interpersonal Violence, 16*(10), 1082–1093.

Edens, J. F., & Petrila, J. (2006). Legal and ethical issues in the assessment and treatment of psychopathy. In C. J. Patrick (Ed.), *Handbook of psychopathy* (pp. 573–588). New York: Guilford Press.

Egger, S. A. (1999). Psychological profiling: Past, present, and future. *Journal of Contemporary Criminal Justice, 15*(3), 242–261.

Egger, S. A. (2002). *The killers among us.* Upper Saddle River, NJ: Prentice Hall.

Ehrich, P., & Feldman, M. (2003). Genes and cultures: What creates our behavioral phenome? *Current Anthropology, 44*(1), 87–107.

Elliot, D. S., Ageton, S. S., & Canter, R. J. (1979). An integrative theoretical perspective on delinquent behavior. *Journal of Research in Crime and Delinquency, 16*(1), 3–27.

Ellis, L. (1989). Sex differences in criminality: An explanation based on the concept of r/K selection. *Mankind Quarterly, 30*(2) 17–37.

Ellis L. (2001) The biosocial female choice theory of social stratification. *Social Biology. 48*(3-4), 298–320.

Ellis, L. (2005). A theory explaining biological correlates of criminality. *European Journal of Criminology, 2*(3), 287–315.

English, K. (1999). *Sex Predator Risk Assessment Screening Instrument.* Colorado Division of Criminal Justice. Retrieved August 18, 2007, at: http://dcj.state.co.us/ors/pdf/docs/svp1a.PDF.

Epperson, D. L., Kaul, J. D., Huot, S., Goldman, R., & Alexander, W. (2003). Minnesota Sex Offender Screening Tool–Revised (MsSOST-R) technical paper: Development, validation, and recommended risk level cut-off scores. Retrieved August 18, 2007, at: http://www.psychology.iastate.edu/faculty/epperson/TechUpdatePaper12–03.pdf.

Epstein, S. C. (1995). The new mythic monster. In J. Ferrell & C. R. Sanders (Eds.), *Cultural criminology* (pp. 66–70). Boston: Northeastern University Press.

Erickson, K. T. (1966). *Wayward puritans: A study in the sociology of deviance.* Boston: Allyn & Bacon.

Ewing v. California, 538 U.S. 11. (2003). Retrieved March 6, 2003, at: http://supct.law.cornell.edu/supct/pdf/01-6978P.ZO.

Ewing, C. P. (1983). "Dr. Death" and the case for the ethical ban on psychiatric and psychological predictions of dangerousness in capital sentencing proceedings. *American Journal of Law and Medicine, 8*(4), 407–428.

Fagan, P. J., Wise, T. N., Schmidt, C. W., & Berlin, F. S. (2002). Pedophilia. *Journal of the American Medical Association, 288,* 2458–2465.

Faigman, D. L. (1999). *Legal alchemy: The use and misuse of science and law.* New York: W.H. Freeman and Company.

Faith, K. (1993). *Unruly women: The politics of resistance and confinement.* Vancouver, BC: Press Gang Publishers.

Faller, K. S. (2003). *Understanding and assessing child sexual maltreatment.* Thousand Oaks, CA: Sage.

Farley, M., & Kelly, V. (2000). Prostitution: A critical review of the medical and social sciences literature. *Women and Criminal Justice, 11*(4), 29–64.

Farrell, N. (2005). *Grand Theft Auto* player gets the death penalty. *The Inquirer.* Retrieved October 24, 2005, at: http://www.theinquirer.net/?article=25370.

Farrington, D. P. (2003). Developmental and life-course criminology: Key theoretical and empirical issues—The 2002 Sutherland Award Address. *Criminology, 41,* 221–255.

Farrington, D. P. (2006). Family background and psychopathy. In C. J. Patrick (Ed.), *Handbook of psychopathy* (pp. 229–250). New York: Guilford Press.

Farrington, D. P., Petrosino, A., & Welsh, B. C. (2001). Systematic reviews and cost-benefit analyses of correctional interventions. *The Prison Journal, 81,* 339–359.

FBI investigates tape of men vandalizing university research lab. (November 23, 2004). Retrieved July 14, 2005. at: 2004http://www.loca16.com/news/3943452/detail.html.

Federal Bureau of Investigation. (2004). *Hate Crime Statistics 2003.* Washington, DC: U.S. Department of Justice.

Federal Trade Commission. (n.d.). *Investment fraud.* Retrieved December 31, 2004, at: http://www.ftc.gov/reports/Fraud/invest.htm.

Felson, M. (2002). *Crime and everyday life.* Thousand Oaks, CA: Sage.

Felson, M. (2006). *Crime and nature.* Thousand Oaks, CA: Sage.

Felson, R. B. (1996). Mass media effects on violent behavior. *Annual Review of Sociology, 22,* 103–128.

Female Arab terrorism on the rise. (June 21, 2005). *Arutz Sheva—Israel National News.com.* Retrieved July 15, 2005, at http://www.israelnn.com/news.php3?id=84266.

Female terrorists. (2005). Intelligence Bulletin No. 7. *Highway Information Sharing and Analysis Center (ISAC), American Trucking Association (ATA).* Retrieved July 15, 2005, at: https://www.highway isac.org/intel_bulletins/intel_n07.html#Female.

Ferguson, A., Philipson, I., Diamond, I., Quinby, L., Vance, C. S., & Barr Snitow, A. (1984). The feminist sexuality debates. *Signs: Journal of Women in Culture and Society, 10*(1), 106–135.

Fernandez, M. E. (October 14, 1996). "Study helps Liberty Heights plot renovation; Group eyes environmental changes to prevent crime, improve appearance." *The Atlantic Journal and Constitution,* p. 01J.

Ferrell, J. (1995). Culture, crime, and cultural criminology. *Journal of Criminal Justice and Popular Culture, 3*(2), 25–42.

Ferrell, J. (1997). Criminological *verstehen:* Inside the immediacy of crime. *Justice Quarterly 14,* 3–23.

Ferrell, J., & Hamm, M. S. (1998). *Ethnography at the edge: Crime, deviance, and field research.* Belmont, CA: Wadsworth.

Ferrell, J., & Sanders, C. R. (1995). *Cultural criminology.* Boston: Northeastern University Press.

Final action on the administrative investigation into the diving mishap and the resulting deaths of USCGC Healy's crewmembers that occurred on 17 August 2006. (June 10, 2007). Memorandum by Allen, T. W. Washington, DC: U.S. Department of Homeland Security, U.S. Coast Guard. Retrieved January 14, 2007, at: http:// www .uscg.mil/ccs/cit/cim/foia/Healy/HEALY_FAM.pdf.

Finkelhor, D., & Ormrod, R. (2004). *Prostitution of juveniles: Patterns from NIBRS.* Washington, DC: U.S. Department of Justice, Office of Justice Programs, Office of Juvenile and Deliquency Prevention.

Fiore, F. (December 29, 2006). Domestic violence found to fall by half over decade; The statistics mirror a national crime drop, but some are skeptical. *The Los Angeles Times,* A17.

Fischoff, S. (2004). No link between media violence and youth violence has been established. In L. I. Gerdes (Ed.), *Media violence: Opposing viewpoints* (pp. 28–38). San Diego: Greenhaven Press.

Fishbein, D. (2001). *Biobehavioral perspectives in criminology.* Belmont, CA: Wadsworth.

Fisher, B. A. (2004). *Techniques of crime scene investigation.* New York: CRC Press.

Fisher, B. S., Cullen, F. T., & Turner, M. G. (2000). Sexual victimization among college women. U.S. Department of Justice, Office of Justice Programs, Bureau of Justice Statistics.

Fisher, D., & Mair, G. (1998). A review of classification systems for sex offenders. Home Office Research Study No. 78. London: Home Office Research and Statistics Directorate.

Fleming, Z. (2004). The thrill of it all: Youthful offenders and auto theft. In D. A. Dabney, *Crime types: A text/reader* (pp. 229–238). Belmont, CA: Wadsworth.

Flowers, R. B. (2001). *Runaway kids and teenage prostitution: America's lost, abandoned, and sexually exploited children.* Westport, CT: Praeger.

Foden, G. (July 18, 2003). Death and the maidens. *The Guardian.* Retrieved May 6, 2007, at: http://www.guardian.co.uk/women/story/0,3604,1000647,00.html.

Ford, M., & Widiger, T. (1989). Sex bias in the diagnosis of histrionic and antisocial personality disorders. *Journal of Consulting and Clinical Psychology, 52*(2), 301–305.

Foucault, M. (1977, 1995). *Discipline and punish: The birth of the prison.* New York: Vintage.

Fourth girl dies after Amish school shooting. (October 3, 2006). CNN. Retrieved October 3, 2006, at: http://edition.cnn.com/2006/US/10/02/amish.shooting/.

Fowles, D. C., & Dindo, L. (2006). A dual-deficit model of psychopathy. In C. J. Patrick (Ed.), *Handbook of psychopathy* (pp. 14–34). New York: Guilford Press.

Fowles, J. (1999). *The case for television violence.* Thousand Oaks, CA: Sage.

Fox, J. A. (April 18, 2007). A dubious record. *The Boston Globe:* Retrieved May 11, 2007, at: http://www.boston.com/news/globe/editorial_opinion/oped/articles/2007/04/18/a_dubious_record/.

Fox, J. A., & Levin, J. (2001). *The will to kill: Making sense of senseless murder.* Boston: Allyn & Bacon.

Fox, J. A., & Levin, J. (2003). Mass murder: An analysis of extreme violence. *Journal of Applied Psychoanalytic Studies, 5*(1), 47–64.

Fox, J. A., & Levin, J. (2005). *Extreme killings: Understanding serial and mass murder.* Thousand Oaks, CA: Sage.

Fox, J. A., & Zawitz, M. (2002). *Homicide trends in the United States.* Washington, DC: Bureau of Justice Statistics.

Freeman, D. (2001). False prediction of future dangerousness: Error rates and the Psychopathy Checklist–Revised.

Journal of the American Academy of Psychiatry and Law, 29, 89–95.

Frese, B., Moya, M., & Megias, J. L. (2004). Social perception of rape: How rape myth acceptance modulates the influence of situational factors. *Journal of Interpersonal Violence, 19,* 143–161.

Friedrichs, D. O. (2004). *Trusted criminals: White-collar crime in contemporary society.* Belmont, CA: Wadsworth.

Fritzon, K. (2000). The contribution of psychological research to arson investigation. In D. Canter & L. Alison (Eds.), *Profiling property crimes* (pp. 147–184). Aldershot, England: Ashgate.

From Daniel M'Naughten to John Hinkley: A brief history of the insanity defense. (n.d). *Frontline: A crime of insanity.* Available at: http://www.pbs.org/wgbh/pages/frontline/shows/crime/trial/history.html.

Gabor, T. (1994). *Everybody does it!: Crime by the public.* Toronto: University of Toronto Press.

Gacono, C. B. (Ed.). (2000). *The clinical and forensic assessment of psychopathy: A Practitioner's Guide.* Mahwah, NJ: Lawrence Erlbaum Associates.

Gacono, C. B., & Meloy, J. R. (1988). The relationship between conscious cognitive style and unconscious defensive process in the psychopath. *Criminal Justice and Behavior, 15,* 472–483.

Gacono, C. B., & Meloy, J. R. (1994) *The Rorschach assessment of aggressive and psychopathic personalities.* Hillsdale, NJ: Lawrence Erlbaum Associates.

Gacono, C. B., & Meloy, J. R. (2002). Assessing psychopathic personalities. In J. N. Butcher (Ed.), *Clinical personality assessment: Practical approaches* (pp. 361–375). New York: Oxford University Press.

Garland, D. (1990). *Punishment and modern society: A study in social theory.* Chicago: University of Chicago Press.

Garland, D. (Ed.). (2001). *Mass imprisonment: Social causes and consequences.* Thousand Oaks, CA: Sage.

Garland, D. (2002). *The culture of control: Crime and social order in contemporary society.* Chicago: University of Chicago Press.

Garland, D., & Sparks, R. (2000). *Criminology and social theory.* Oxford: Oxford University Press.

Gauthier, D. K., & Bankston, W. B. (2004). "Who kills whom" revisited: A sociological study of variation in the sex ratio of spouse killings. *Homicide Studies, 8*(2), 96–122.

Geberth, V. J. (1996). *Practical homicide investigation: Tactics, procedures, and forensic techniques.* Boca Raton, FL: CRC Press.

Geen, R. G. (1998). Processes and personal variables in affective aggression. In R. G. Geen & E. Donnerstein (Eds.). (1998). *Human aggression: Theories, research, and implications for social policy* (pp. 2–21). San Diego: Academic Press.

Geen, R. G., & Donnerstein, E. (Eds.). (1998). *Human aggression: Theories, research, and implications for social policy.* San Diego: Academic Press.

Gendreau, P. (1996). Offender rehabilitation: What we know and what needs to be done. *Criminal Justice and Behavior, 23*(1), 144–161.

Gendreau, P., Cullen, F. T., & Bonta, J. (1994). Intensive rehabilitation supervision: The next generation in community corrections? *Federal Probation, 58,* 72–78.

Gendreau, P., Goggin, C., & Smith, P. (2002). Is the PCL-R really the "unparalleled" measure of offender risk? A lesson in knowledge cumulation. *Criminal Justice and Behavior, 29*(4), 397–426.

Gendreau, P., Little, T., & Goggin, C. (1996). A meta-analysis of the predictors of adult offender recidivism. What works? *Criminology, 34,* 575–607.

Gendreau, P., & Ross, R. R. (1987). Revivification of rehabilitation: Evidence from the 1980s. *Justice Quarterly, 4*(3), 349–407.

Gerbner, G. (1994). Reclaiming our cultural mythology: Television's global marketing strategy creates a damaging and alienated window on the world. *The Ecology of Justice, 38.* Retrieved February 28, 2004, at: http://www.context.org/ICLIB/IC38/Gerbner.htm.

German cannibal tells of fantasy. (December 3, 2003). BBC News. Retrieved January 29, 2004, at: http://news.bbc.co.uk/2/hi/europe/3286721.stm.

German court sentence cannibal to life in jail. (May 9, 2006). Associate Press. Retrieved August 12, 2007, at: http://www.msnbc.msn.com/id/11909486/.

Gerstenfeld, P. B. (2004). *Hate Crimes: Causes, Controls, and Controversies.* Thousand Oaks, CA: Sage.

GI rape-slay hearing begins in Iraq. (August 6, 2006). CBS News.com. Retrieved September 29, 2006, at: http://www.cbsnews.com/stories/2006/08/06/iraq/main1868218.shtml.

Giles, C. (April 6, 1995). Sentence plea on station rape. *Herald Sun,* 7.

Gilligan, J. (1996). *Violence: Reflections on a national epidemic.* New York: Vintage Books.

Giobbe E. (1993). An analysis of individual, institutional and cultural pimping. *Michigan Journal of Gender and Law, 1,* 33–57.

Girard, L., & Wormith, J. S. (2004). The predictive validity of the Level of Service Inventory-Ontario Revision on general and violent recidivism among various offender groups. *Criminal Justice and Behavior, 31*(2), 150–181.

Girl fatally stabbed before decapitated. (February 19, 2007). *News14 Carolina.* Retrieved February 19, 2007, at: http://www.news14charlotte.com/content/top_stories/default.asp?ArID=134418.

GIs drank whiskey, hit golf balls before alleged Iraqi teen rape-slay, military hearing told. (August 7, 2006). Fox News.com. Retrieved September 29, 2006, at: http://www.foxnews.com/printer_friendly_story/0,3566,207265,00.html.

Glasser, S. B. (April 28, 2005). Global terrorism statistics released. *Washington Post,* p. A07.

Glaze, L. E., & Palla, S. (November, 2005). Probation and parole in the United States, 2004. Bureau of Justice Statistics Bulletin. Washington, DC: U.S. Department of Justice Office of Justice Programs.

Glueck, S., & Glueck, E. (1956). *Physique and delinquency.* New York: Harper & Row.

Godwin, M. (1998). Reliability, validity, and utility of extant serial murder classifications. *The Criminologist, 22*(4), 195–210.

Goffman E. (1963). *Stigma: Notes on them 1: Management of spoiled identity.* Englewood Cliffs, NJ: Prentice Hall.

Gohlke, J. (May 6, 2004). Foster parents indicted in starvation of 4 boys; Camden County case became symbol of failed system. *The Record,* A05.

Going undercover/Criminalizing dissent? (March 5, 2004). *NOW with Bill Moyers.* PBS. Available at: http://www.pbs.org/now/politics/cointelpro.html.

Goldner, E. M., Geller, J., Birmingham, C. L., & Remick, R. A. (2000). Comparison of shoplifting behaviours in patients with eating disorders, psychiatric controls, and undergraduate control subjects. *Canadian Journal of Psychiatry, 45*(5), 471–475.

Goldstein, A. S. (1967). *The insanity defense.* New Haven/London: Yale University Press.

Gottfredson, M. R., & Hirschi, T. (1990). *A general theory of crime.* Palo Alto, CA: Stanford University Press.

Gottfredson, M. R., & Hirschi, T. (2001). The true value of Lambda would appear to be zero. In A. Piquero & P. Mazerolle (Eds.), *Life-Course Criminology* (pp. 67–86). Belmont, CA: Wadsworth

Gottfredson, M. R., Mitchell-Herzfeld, S. D., & Flanagan, T. J. (1982). Another look at the effectiveness of parole supervision. *Journal of Research in Crime and Delinquency, 19,* 277–298.

Gottfredson, M. R., & Tonry, M. (Eds.) (1987). *Prediction and classification: Criminal justice decisionmaking.*

Crime and justice: A review of the research. Chicago: University of Chicago Press.

Greene, J. A. (2003). Smart on crime: Positive trends on state-level sentencing and corrections policy. Washington, DC: Families Against Mandatory Minimums. Retrieved December 28, 2006, at: http://www.soros.org/initiatives/justice/articles_publications/publications/smart_on_crime_20031101/smart_on_crime.pdf.

Greenfeld, L. A. (1997). *Sex offenses and offenders.* Washington, DC: U.S. Department of Justice, Office of Justice Programs, Bureau of Justice Statistics.

Greenfeld, L. A. (1998). *An analysis of national data on the prevalence of alcohol involvement in crime.* Washington, DC: U.S. Department of Justice, Office of Justice Programs, Bureau of Justice Statistics.

Greenstone, J. L., Kosson, D. S., & Gacono, C. B. (2000). Psychopathy and hostage negotiations: Some preliminary thoughts and findings. In C. B. Gacono (Ed.), *The clinical and forensic assessment of psychopathy: A practitioner's guide* (pp. 385–404). Mahwah, NJ: Lawrence Erlbaum Associates.

Greer, C. (December 2, 1998). Mastermind agrees to show authorities how he rigged slots. *Las Vegas Review Journal.*

Griset, P. L., & Mahan, S. (2003). *Terrorism in perspective.* Thousand Oaks, CA: Sage.

Groth, A. N. (1979). *Men who rape: The psychology of the offender.* New York: Plenum.

Grudzinskas, A. J., Clayfield, J. C., Roy-Bujnowski, K., Fisher, W. H., & Richardson, M. H. (2005). Integrating the criminal justice system into mental health service delivery: The Worcester diversion experience. *Behavioral Sciences and the Law, 23,* 277–293.

Habel, U., Kuhn, E., Salloum, J. B., Devos, H., & Schneider, F. (2002). Emotional processing in psychopathic personality. *Aggressive Behavior, 28,* 394–400.

Hagan, F. E. (1997). *Political crime: Ideology and criminality.* Needham Heights, MA: Allyn & Bacon.

Hagan, J., Simpson, J., & Gillis, A. R. (1987). Class in the household: A power-control theory of gender and delinquency. *American Journal of Sociology, 92*(4), 788–816.

Haggard, U., Gumpert, C. H., & Grann, M. (2001). Against all odds: A qualitative follow-up study of high-risk violent offenders who were not reconvicted. *Journal of Interpersonal Violence, 16,* 1048–1065.

Haghighi, B., & Sorensen, J. (1996). America's fear of crime. In T. J. Flanagan & D. R. Longmire (Eds.), *Americans view crime and justice* (pp. 16–30). Thousand Oaks, CA: Sage.

Hainsworth, J. (July 7, 2005). Canada to extradite U.S. firebomb suspect. *The Bakersfield Californian.* Retrieved July 15, 2005, at: http://www.bakersfield.com/24hour/world/story/2540448p-10931727c.html.

Hall, W. (2004). "Girls getting increasingly violent." *CBS News.* Retrieved February 6, 2008: http://www.cbsnews.com/stories/2004/04/29/national/main614781.shtml?source=search_story/.

Hall, J. R., & Benning, S. D. (2006). The "successful psychopath": Adaptive and subclinical manifestations of psychopathy in the general prison population. In C.J. Patrick (Ed.), *Handbook of psychopathy* (pp. 459–478). New York: Guilford Press

Hambright, B. (October 3, 2006). Execution style slayings planned; boys unharmed. *Lancaster Online.* Retrieved October 3, 2006, at: http://local.lancasteronline.com/4/26345.

Hamilton, S., Rothbart, M., & Dawes, R. M. (1986). Sex bias, diagnosis, and *DSM-III. Sex Roles, 5,* 269–274.

Hanlon, T. E., Nurco, D. N., Bateman, R. W., & O'Grady, K. E. (1999). The relative effects of three approaches to the parole supervision of narcotic addicts and cocaine abusers. *The Prison Journal, 79,* 163–181.

Hanson, R. (1997). *Development of a brief actuarial risk scale for sexual offense recidivism.* Department of the Solicitor General of Canada. Public Works and Government Services Canada.

Hanson, R. K. (2005). Twenty years of progress in violence risk assessment. *Journal of Interpersonal Violence, 20*(2), 212–217.

Hanson, R. K., & Thornton, D. (1999). *Static 99: Improving actuarial risk assessments for sex offenders* (User Report: 99–02). Ottawa: Department of the Solicitor General of Canada. Retrieved August 18, 2007, at: http://ww2.ps-sp.gc.ca/publications/corrections/199902_e.pdf.

Harcourt, B. E. (2007). *Against prediction. Profiling, policing, and punishing in an actuarial age.* Chicago: Chicago University Press.

Hare R. D. (1991, 2003). *Manual for the Psychopathy Checklist–Revised.* Toronto: Multi-Health Systems.

Hare R. D. (1993). *Without conscience: The disturbing world of psychopaths among us.* New York: Pocket Books.

Hare, R. D. (1996a). Psychopathy: A clinical construct whose time has come. *Criminal Justice and Behavior, 23*(1), 25–54.

Hare, R. D. (1996b). *The psychopathic mind* [Video recording]. Canadian Broadcasting Corporation. Princeton, NJ: Films for the Humanities & Sciences.

Hare, R. D. (1998). Psychopaths and their nature: Implications for the mental health and criminal justice systems. In T. Millon, E. Simonsen, E. Birket-Smith, & R. D. Davis (Eds.), *Psychopathy: Antisocial, criminal, and violent behavior* (pp. 188–212). New York: Guilford.

Hare, R. D. (2001). Psychopaths and their nature: Some implications for understanding human predatory violence. In A. Raine & J. Sanmartin (Eds.), *Violence and psychopathy* (pp. 5–34). New York: Kluwer/Plenum.

Hare, R. D. (2003). *Hare Psychopathy Checklist–Revise,* (2nd Ed.). Toronto: Multi-Health Systems.

Hare, R. D. (2007). Forty years aren't enough: Recollections, prognostications, and random musings. In H. Herve & J. Yuille (Eds.), *The psychopath: Theory, research, and practice* (pp. 3–28). Mahweh, NJ: Lawrence Erlbaum Associates.

Hare, R. D., & Hart, S. D. (1993) Psychopathy, mental disorder and crime. In: S. Hodgins (Ed.), *Mental disorder and crime* (pp. 104–115). Thousand Oaks, CA: Sage Publications.

Hare, R. D., Hart, S. D., & Harpur, T. (1991). Psychopathy and the *DSM-IV* criteria for antisocial personality disorder. *Journal of Abnormal Psychology, 100,* 391–398.

Hare, R. D., McPherson, L. M., & Forth, A. E. (1988). Male psychopaths and their criminal careers. *Journal of Consulting and Clinical Psychology, 56*(5), 710–714.

Hare, R. D., & Neumann, C. S. (2006). The PCL-R assessment of psychopathy: Development, structural properties, and new directions. In C. J. Patrick (Ed.), *Handbook of psychopathy* (pp. 58–88). New York: Guilford Press.

Hare, R. D., & O'Toole, M. E. (2006). Psychopathy and its application to understanding violent criminals and their behavior. Workshop presentation at the *American Academy of Forensic Sciences,* Seattle, WA, February 20–24, 2006.

Harpur, T. J., Hare, R. D., & Hakstian, R., (1989). Two-factor conceptualization of psychopathy: Construct validity and assessment implications. *Psychological Assessment: A Journal of Consulting and Clinical Psychology, 1*(1), 6–17.

Harrington, A. (1972). *Psychopaths.* New York: Simon & Schuster.

Harris, G. T., Rice, M. E., & Cormier, C. A. (1991). Psychopathy and violent recidivism. *Law and Human Behavior, 15*(6), 625–637.

Harris G. T., Rice, M. E., Quinsey, V. L. (1994). Psychopathy as a taxon: Evidence that psychopaths are a discrete class. *Journal of Consulting and Clinical Psychology, 62*(2), 387–397.

Hart, S. D. (1998). Psychopathy and risk for violence. In D. J. Cooke et al. (Eds.), *Psychopathy: Theory, research, and implications for society* (pp. 355–373). Netherlands: Kluwer.

Hart, S. D., & Hare, R. D. (1989). Discriminant validity of the Psychopathy Checklist in a forensic psychiatric population. *Psychological Assessment, 2,* 338–341.

Hart, T. C., & Rennison, C. (2003, March). *Reporting crime to the police, 1992–2000.* Washington, DC: U.S. Department of Justice.

Harvey, D. (2002). *Obsession: Celebrities and their stalkers.* Dublin, Ireland: Merlin Publishing.

Hazelwood, R., & Burgess, A. (1987). *Practical aspects of rape investigation: A multidisciplinary approach.* New York: Elsevier.

Hazelwood, R., & Warren (1990) The criminal behavior of the serial rapist. Retrieved December 11, 2007: http://www.holysmoke.org/fem/fem0126.htm.

Heartfelt thanks from Letterman. (March 22, 2005). *CBS News.* Retrieved December 27, 2005, at: http://www.cbsnews.com/stories/2005/03/22/entertainment/main682106.shtml.

Heimer, K. (2000). Changes in the gender gap in crime and women's economic marginalization. In G. LaFree (Ed.), *Criminal justice, volume 1, The nature of crime: Continuity and change* (pp. 427–483). Washington, DC: National Institute of Justice.

Heineman, M. (1992). *Losing your shirt: Recovery for compulsive gamblers and their families.* Center City, MN: Hazelden.

Heitzig, N. A. (1996). Traditional theories and methods of deviance. In *Deviance: Rule makers and rule breakers.* St. Paul, MN: West Publishing.

Helfgott, J. B. (1992). The relationship between unconscious defensive process and conscious cognitive style in psychopaths. (Doctoral Dissertation, Penn State University, 1992). Dissertation Abstracts International, 54-03A, 1102–374.

Helfgott, J. (1997a). Ex-offender needs versus criminal opportunity in Seattle, Washington. *Federal Probation, 61,* 12–24.

Helfgott, J. B. (1997b). The unconscious defensive process/conscious cognitive style relationship in psychopaths. *Criminal Justice and Behavior, 24,* 278–293.

Helfgott, J. B. (2004). Primitive defenses in the language of the psychopath: Considerations for forensic practice. *Journal of Forensic Psychology Practice, 4*(3), 1–29.

Helfgott, J. B., Lovell, M. L., & Lawrence, C. F. (2002). Citizens, victims, and offenders restoring justice: Accountability, healing, and hope through storytelling and dialogue. *Crime Victims Report, 6,* 3–4.

Helfgott, J. B., Lovell, M. L., Lawrence, C. F., & Parsonage, W. H. (2000). Development of the citizens, victims, and offenders restoring justice program at the Washington State Reformatory. *Criminal Justice Policy Review, 10,* 363–399.

Helfgott, J. B., Lutze, F., Chang, H., & Goodstein, L. (1990). Institutional responses of inmates with opposing attachments. Paper presentation at the *American Society of Criminology,* November 1990, Baltimore, MD.

Hemphill, J. F., & Hare, R. D. (2004, April). Some misconceptions about the Hare PCL-R and risk assessment: A reply to Gendreau, Goggin, and Smith. *Criminal Justice and Behavior, 31*(2), 203–243.

Hemphill J. F., Templeman R., Wong S., & Hare R. D. (1998). Psychopathy and crime: Recidivism and criminal careers. In D. J. Cooke et al. (Eds.), *Psychopathy: Theory, research, and implications for society* (pp. 375–399). Netherlands: Kluwer.

Hendrix, G. (April 20, 2007). Violent disagreement: What Cho Seung-Hui got wrong about Oldboy. *Slate.* Retrieved May 9, 2007, at: http://www.slate .com/id/2164753/.

Henggeler, S. W. (1996). Treatment of violent juvenile offenders—we have the knowledge: Comment on Gorman-Smith et al. *Journal of Family Psychology, 10,* 137–141.

Henry, S. (1978). *The hidden economy: The context and control of borderline crime.* Port Townsend, WA: Loompanics Unlimited.

Henry, S., & Milovanovic, D. (1996). *Constitutive criminology: Beyond postmodernism.* Thousand Oaks, CA: Sage.

Hiatt, K. D., & Newman, J. P. (2006). Understanding psychopathy: The cognitive side. In C. J. Patrick (Ed.), *Handbook of Psychopathy* (pp. 334–352). New York: Guilford Press.

Hickey, E. W. (2002, 2006). *Serial murderers and their victims.* Belmont, CA: Wadsworth.

Hickey, E. W. (2003). *Encyclopedia of murder and violent crime.* Thousand Oaks, CA: Sage.

Higgins, A. (2002). How al Qaeda put Internet to use: From Britain, Webmaster kept "the brothers" abreast on terror. *Computer Crime Research Center.* Retrieved March 21, 2006, at: http://www.crime-research.org/news/2002/11/Mess1203.htm.

Hill, G. (1992). *Illuminating shadows: The mythic power of film.* Boston: Shambhala Publications.

Hirschi, T. (1969). *Causes of delinquency.* Berkeley, CA: University of California Press.

Hislop, J. (2001). *Female sex offenders: What therapists, Law enforcement and child protective services need to know.* Ravensdale, WA: Issues Press.

Ho, V., Johnson, T., & Castro, H. (November 6, 2003). Gary Ridgway said: "I killed so many women I have a hard time keeping them straight." *Seattle Post-Intelligencer,* A-1, 14.

Hodgins, S. (Ed.) (1993). *Mental disorder and crime.* Newbury Park, CA: Sage.

Hodgins, S. (1997). An overview of research on the prediction of dangerousness. *Nordic Journal of Psychiatry, 51,* 33–38.

Høigård, C., & Finstad, L. (1992). *Backstreets: Prostitution, money, and love.* University Park: Pennsylvania State University Press.

Holland, M. (October 5, 2007). Judge says Linehan jurors won't see movie. *Anchorage Daily News* (adn.com). Retrieved December 8, 2007, at: http://www.adn .com/news/alaska/crime/stripper/story/9356628 p-9269574c.html.

Holland, M. (October 22, 2007). Former stripper convicted in fiance's murder. *Alaska Daily News* (adn.com). Retrieved December 8, 2007, at: http://www.adn.com/news/ alaska/crime/stripper/story/9398965p-9312346c.html.

Hollin, C. R. (Ed.). (2004). To treat or not to treat: An historical perspective. In *The essential handbook of offender assessment and treatment* (pp. 1–13). New York: John Wiley & Sons.

Holmes, R. M. (1989). *Sex crimes.* Thousand Oaks, CA: Sage.

Holmes, R. M., & Deburger, J. (2004). Profiles in terror: Serial murder. In S. T. Holmes & R. M. Holmes (Eds.), *Violence: A contemporary reader* (pp. 211–219). Upper Saddle River: NJ: Prentice Hall.

Holmes, R. M., & Holmes, S. T. (2002). *Profiling violent crimes: An investigative tool.* Thousand Oaks, CA: Sage.

Homant, R. J., & Kennedy, D. B. (1998). Psychological aspects of crime scene profiling: Validity research. *Criminal Justice and Behavior, 25*(3), 319–343.

Horney, J. (2006). An alternative psychology of criminal behavior. *Criminology, 44*(1), 1–16.

Horowitz, M. J. (1977). *Hysterical personality*. New York: Jason Aronson, Inc.

Howells, K., Day, A., Bubner, S., Jauncey, S., Williamson, P., Parker, A., & Heseltine, K. (June, 2002). Anger management and violence prevention: Improving effectiveness. *Trends and Issues in Crime and Justice.* Canberra: Australian Institute of Criminology.

Hucker, S. J., & Baine, J. (1989). Androgenic hormones and sexual assault. In W. L. Marshall, D. R. Laws, & H. E. Barbaree (Eds.), *Handbook of sexual assault: Issues, theories, and treatment of the offender* (pp. 93–102). New York: Plenum.

Huesmann, L. R., Enron, L. D., & Lefkowitz, M. M. (1984). Stability of aggression over time and generations. *Developmental Psychology, 20*(6), 1120–1134.

Hull, D. (April 7, 2003). Police violence shocks protestors, others at Port of Oakland protest. *San Jose Mercury News.* Retrieved July 11, 2005, at: http://www.commondreams.org/headlines03/0407–07.htm.

Humphrey, S. E., & Kahn, A. S. (2000). Fraternities, athletic teams, and rape: Importance of identification with a risky group. *Journal of Interpersonal Violence, 15,* 1313–1322.

Husband "admitted weakest link killing." (January 28, 2002). *BBC News.* Retrieved August 18, 2007, at: http://news.bbc.co.uk/1/hi/england/1787111.stm.

Hyman, R. (2004). Medea of suburbia: Andrea Yates, maternal infanticide, and the insanity defense. *Women's Studies Quarterly, 32*(3/4), 192–210.

Inciardi, J. A., O'Connell, D. J., & Saum, C. A. (2004). The Miami sex for crack market revisited. In D. A. Dabney (Ed.) *Crime types: A text/reader* (pp. 278–292). Belmont, CA: Wadsworth.

Injured husband talks to action news. (May 17, 2006). 6 ABC Action News Philadelphia, PA WPVI-TV/DT. Available at: http://abclocal.go.com/wpvi/story?section=local&id=4183089.

International Association of Chiefs of Police. (1999). What do victims want: Effective strategies to achieve justice for victims of crime. *1999 IACP Summit on Victims of Crime.* Retrieved April 14, 2006, at: http://www.iacp.org/documents/pdfs/Publications/victim%2Epdf.

Inter-University Consortium for Political and Social Research. General Social Survey Series. (n.d.). Available at: http://webapp.icpsr.umich.edu/cocoon/ICPSR-SERIES/00028.xml.

Irwin, J. (1980). *Prisons in turmoil.* Boston: Little Brown.

Jackson, R., & Richards, H. (2007a). Diagnostic and risk profiles among civilly committed sex offenders in Washington State. *International Journal of Offender Therapy and Comparative Criminology, 51*(3), 313–323.

Jackson, R., & Richards, H. (2007b). Psychopathy in women: A valid construct with clear implications. In H. Herve & J. Yuille (Eds.), *The psychopath: Theory, research, and practice* (pp. 389–410). Mahweh, NJ: Lawrence Erlbaum Associates.

Jacobs, J. (1961). *The life and death of great American cities.* New York: Random House.

Jacobs, J. B. (1989). *Drunk driving: An American dilemma.* Chicago: University of Chicago Press.

James, S. H., & Nordby, J. J. (2005). *Forensic science: An introduction to scientific and investigative techniques.* Boca Raton, FLA: CRC Press.

Jarboe, J. F. (2002). The threat of eco-terrorism. *Congressional Testimony before the House Resources Committee, Subcommittee on Forests and Forest Health.* Retrieved June 30, 2005, at: http://www.fbi.gov/congress/congress02/jarboe021202.htm.

Jeffrey, C. R. (1971). *Crime prevention through environmental design.* Beverly Hills: Sage.

Jenkins, P. (1994). *Using murder: The social construction of serial homicide.* New York: Aldine de Gruyter.

Jenkins, P. (1996). *Pedophiles and priests: Anatomy of a contemporary crisis.* Oxford: Oxford University Press.

Jenkins, P. (1998). *Moral panic: Changing concepts of the child molester in modern America.* New Haven, CT: Yale University Press.

Jenkins, P. (1999). *Synthetic panics: The symbolic politics of designer drugs.* New York: New York University Press.

Jenkins, P. (2001). *Beyond tolerance: Child pornography on the Internet.* New York: New York University Press.

Jesilow, P., Pontell, H. M., & Geis, G. (1996). How doctors defraud Medicaid: Doctors tell their stories. In P. Cromwell (Ed.), *In their own words: Criminals on crime* (pp. 74–83). Los Angeles: Roxbury.

Jhally, S. (1999). *Tough guise* [film]. Media Education Foundation.

Jhally, S., Kilbourne, J., & Gerbner, G. (1994). *The killing screens* [Video]. Media Education Foundation.

Johnson, T. (November 5, 1998). Baranyi found guilty. *The Eastside Journal.* Retrieved September 28, 2003, at: http://www.theescapist.com/. ./baranyi1.htm.

Jones, L., & Finkelhor, D. (2001). *The decline in child sexual abuse cases.* Washington, DC: U.S. Department of Justice, Office of Justice programs, Office of Juvenile Justice and Delinquency Prevention.

Jones, O. D. (1999). Sex, culture, and the biology of rape: Toward explanation and prevention. *California Law Review, 87,* 829–941.

Jones, P. (2004). Mothers with monkeywrenches: Feminist imperatives and the ALF. In S. Best & A. J. Nocella II (Eds.), *Terrorists or freedom fighters? Reflections on the liberation of animals* (pp. 137–156). New York: Lantern Press.

Jones, W. T. (1969). *A history of Western philosophy. Kant to Wittgenstein and Sartre,* 2nd Ed. New York: Harcourt, Brace.

Jurors: Yates drowning of her children seemed premeditated. (March 18, 2002). Associated Press. Retrieved July 3, 2006, at: http://www.courttv.com/trials/yates/031802-b_ap.html.

Jury shown Manson video. (December 23, 2004). BBC News. Retrieved May 9, 2007, at: http://news.bbc.co.uk/1/hi/scotland/4121491.stm.

Kamphuis, J. H., & Emmelkamp, P. M. (2005). Twenty years of research into violence and trauma. *Journal of Interpersonal Violence, 20*(2), 167–174.

Kansas v. Hendricks (1997). 117 S. Ct. 2072, 138 L.Ed. 2d 501.

Karlsson, G., & Romelsjö, A. (1997). A longitudinal study of social, psychological and behavioural factors associated with drunken driving and public drunkenness. *Addiction, 4,* 447–57.

Karmen, A. (1994). "Defining deviancy down": How Senator Moynihan's misleading phrase about criminal justice is rapidly being incorporated into popular culture. *Journal of Criminal Justice and Popular Culture, 2*(5), 99–112.

Karpman, B. (1954). *The sexual offender and his offenses.* New York: The Julian Press.

Kassman, L. (September 2, 2004). Women Terrorists Force Changed Thinking by Security Officials. Retrieved May 6, 2007, at: http://www.iwar.org.uk/news-archive/2004/09–02.htm.

Katz, J. (1988). *Seductions of crime: Moral and sensual attractions in doing evil.* New York: Basic Books.

Katz, J. (2006). *Macho paradox: Why some men hurt women and how all men can help.* Napperville, IL: Sourcebooks.

Kaye, K. (2003). Male prostitution in the twentieth century: Pseudohomosexuals, hoodlum homosexuals, and exploited teens. *Journal of Homosexuality, 46* (1/2), 1–77.

Keiser, G. (1992). Applied criminology: Possibilities and limits. *EuroCriminology, 4,* 29–49.

Kelleher, M. D., & Kelleher, C. L. (1998). *Murder most rare: The female serial killer.* Westport, CT: Praeger.

Kelling, G. L., & Coles, C. M. (1996). *Fixing broken windows: Restoring order in American cities.* New York: Martin Kessler Books/Free Press.

Kelly, R. J. (1998). Black rage, murder, racism, and madness: The metamorphosis of Colin Ferguson. In R. J. Kelly & J. Maghen (Eds.), *Hate crime: The global politics of polarization* (pp. 22–36). Carbondale: Southern Illinois University Press.

Kelly, R. J., & Maghan, J. (Eds.) (1998). *Hate crime: The global politics of polarization* (pp. 22–36). Carbondale: Southern Illinois University Press.

Kelly, T., & Bernstein, D. (April, 2006). Psychedelic POWs. *Z Magazine.* Retrieved August 15, 2007, at: http://www.zmag.org/zmag/articles/apri196bernstein.htm.

Kennedy, D. J., & Finckenauer, J. O. (1995). *Organized crime in America.* Belmont, CA: Wadsworth.

Kennedy, M. A., Gorzalka, B. B., & Yuille, J. C. (2004). Men who solicit prostitutes: A demographic profile of participants in the Vancouver Police Department's Prostitution Offender Program. Report prepared for the Vancouver Police Department. Retrieved May 1, 2005, at: http://www.jhslmbc.ca/pdf/Men%20Who%20Solicit-Demo%20Profile-Feb%2004.pdf.

Keppel, R. D., & Birnes, W. (1997). *Signature killers.* New York: Pocket Books.

Keppel, R. D., & Walter, R. (1999). Profiling killers: A revised classification model for understanding sexual murder. *International Journal of Offender Therapy and Comparative Criminology, 43*(4), 417–437.

Kerley, K. R., & Copes, H. (2004).The effects of criminal justice contact on employment stability for white-collar and street-level offenders. *International Journal of Offender Therapy and Comparative Criminology, 48*(1), 65–84.

Kernberg, O. F. (1966). Structural derivatives of object relationships. *International Journal of Psychoanalysis, 47,* 236–253.

Kernberg, O. F. (1967). Borderline personality organization. *Journal of the American Psychoanalytic Association, 15,* 641–685.

Kernberg, O. F. (1976). *Object relations theory and clinical psychoanalysis.* New York: Jason Aronson.

Kernberg, O. F. (1984). *Severe personality disorders: Psychotherapeutic strategies.* New Haven, CT: Yale University Press.

Kernberg, O. F. (1985a). *Borderline conditions and pathological narcissism.* New York: Jason Aronson.

Kernberg, O. F. (1985b). *Internal world and external reality.* New York: Jason Aronson.

Kernberg, O. F. (1992). *Aggression in personality disorders and perversions.* New Haven, CT: Yale University Press.

Kids of woman slain in fetus theft found dead. (September 24, 2006). Associated Press. Retrieved October 10, 2006, at: http://www.msnbc.msn.com/id/14954419/.

Kimmel, M. S., & Mahler, M. (2003). Adolescent masculinity, homophobia, and violence: Random school shootings, 1982–2001. *American Behavioral Scientist, 46*(10), 1439–1458.

Kinder, G. (1982). *Victim: The other side of murder.* New York: Atlantic Monthly Press.

King County Journal. (2003). *Gary Ridgway: The Green River Killer.* Bellevue, WA: The King County Journal.

King County Prosecutor's Summary of Evidence in The State of Washington v. Gary Leon Ridgway.(n.d.). Available at: http://seattletimes.nwsource.com/news/local/links/ridg_summary.pdf.

King 5 News. (August 5, 1996). Interview with Mark Klaas re Richard Allen Davis sentencing.

King, R., & Mauer, M. (2001). *Aging behind bars: "Three-strikes" seven years later.* Washington, DC: The Sentencing Project.

Kinsey, A. C., Pomeroy, W. B., & Martin, C. E. (1948). *Sexual behavior in the human male.* Philadelphia: W.B. Saunders Company.

Kirsta, A. (1994). *Deadlier than the male: Violence and aggression in women.* Hammersmith, London: HarperCollins.

Kiselyak, C. (Producer, Director) (1996). *Natural Born Killers—Director's Cut* [Film]. Warner Brothers Productions.

Kittrie, N. (1971). *The right to be different: Deviance and enforced therapy.* Baltimore: Johns Hopkins University Press.

Klein, D. (1973). The etiology of female crime: A review of the literature. *Crime and Social Justice: Issues in Criminology,* 3–30.

Klein, M. W. (1971). *Street gangs and street workers.* Englewood Cliffs, NJ: Prentice-Hall.

Klein, M. W. (1995). *The American street gang.* New York: Oxford University Press.

Klockars, C. B. (1974). *The professional fence.* New York: The Free Press.

Knight, R. A., & Prentky, R. A. (1987). The developmental antecedents and adult adaptations of rapist subtypes. *Criminal Justice and Behavior, 14,* 403–426.

Knight, R. A., & Prentky, R. A. (1990). Classifying sexual offenders: The development and corroboration of taxonomic models. In W. L. Marshall, D. R. Laws, & H. E. Barbaree (Eds.), *Handbook of sexual assault: Issues, theories, and treatment of the offender* (pp. 23–52). New York: Plenum.

Knowles, G. J. (1999). Gambling, drugs, and sex: New drug trends and addictions in Honolulu, Hawaii, 1998. *Sociological Practice: A Journal of Clinical and Applied Sociology, 1*(1), 45–69.

Kochanik, K. D., & Smith, B. L. (2004). Deaths: Preliminary Data for 2002. *National Vital Statistics Reports, 52*(13). Hyattsville, MD: National Center for Health Statistics.

Kohut, H. (1971). *Analysis of the self.* New York: International Universities Press.

Kosson, D. S., Smith S. S., & Newman J. P. (1990). Evaluating the construct validity of psychopathy in black and white male inmates: three preliminary studies. *Journal of Abnormal Psychology, 99*(3), 250–259.

Kosson, D. S., Gacono, C. B., & Bodholdt, R. H. (2000). Assessing psychopathy: Interpersonal aspects and clinical interviewing. In C. B. Gacono (Ed.) *The clinical and forensic assessment of psychopathy* (pp. 203–229). Mahwah, NJ: Erlbaum.

Kovacich, G. L., & Boni, W. C. (2000). *High-technology crime investigator's handbook: Working in the global information environment.* Boston: Butterworth-Heinemann.

Kovaleski, S. F. (July 21, 1996). The Unabomber: Based his life on novel. *The Guardian Weekly.* Retrieved May 9, 2007, at: http://www.ibiblio.org/eldritch/jc/sa/una.html.

Krafft-Ebing, R. V. (1906). *Psychopathia sexualis.* Chicago: Login Brothers.

Kraska, P. B. (2004). *Theorizing criminal justice.* Long Grove, IL: Waveland Press.

Lachkar, J. (2002). The psychological make-up of a suicide bomber. *The Journal of Psychohistory, 29*(4), 349–367.

Laddin, M. (January, 11, 2004). Family's horror at mother and daughter stabbing. News.scotsman.com. Retrieved January 12, 2004, at: http://www.news.scotsman.com/latest.cfm?id=2397243.

Lafarge, L. (1989). Emptiness as defense in severe regressive states. *Journal of the American Psychoanalytic Association, 37,* 965–995.

Langevin, R (2003). A study of the psychosexual characteristics of sex killers: Can we identify them before it is too late? *International Journal of Offen der Therapy and Comparative Criminology, 47*(4), 266–382.

Lansford, J. E., Kirby, D., Dodge, K. A., Bates, J. E., & Pettit, G. S. (2004). Ethnic differences in the link between physical discipline and later adolescent externalizing behaviors. *Journal of Child Psychology and Psychiatry, 45*(4), 801–812.

Laub, J. H., & Sampson, R. J. (2003). *Shared beginnings, divergent lives: Delinquent boys to age 70.* Cambridge, MA: Harvard University Press.

Laumann, E. O., Gagnon, J. H., Michael, R. T., & Michaels, S. (2003). Survey of sexual behavior of Americans. In P. A. Adler & P. Adler (Eds.), *Constructions of deviance: Social power, context, and interaction* (pp. 106–115). Belmont, CA: Wadsworth.

Laurell, J., & Dåderman, A. M. (2005). Recidivism is related to psychopathy (PCL-R) in a group of men convicted of homicide. *International Journal of Law and Psychiatry, 28,* 255–268.

Laws, D. R., & Marshall, W. L. (1990). A conditioning theory of the etiology and maintenance of deviant sexual preference and behavior. In W. L. Marshall, D. R. Laws, & H. E. Barbaree (Eds.), *Handbook of sexual assault: Issues, theories, and treatment of the offender* (pp. 209–229). New York: Plenum.

Laws, D. R., & O'Donohue, W. (1997a). Fundamental issues in sexual deviance. In D. R. Laws & W. O'Donohue (Eds.), *Sexual Deviance: Theory, assessment, and treatment* (pp. 1–21). New York: The Guilford Press.

Laws, D. R., & O'Donohue, W. (Eds.). (1997b). *Sexual deviance: Theory, assessment, and treatment.* New York: Guilford Press.

Lederhendler, I. I. (2003). Aggression and violence: Perspectives on integrating animal and human research approaches. *Hormones and Behavior, 44,* 156–160.

Lee, N. (2001). *Recidivism: An analysis of adult felons.* Olympia: State of Washington Sentencing Guidelines Commission.

Leigh, C. (2004). *Unrepentant whore: Collected works of Scarlet Harlot.* San Francisco: Last Gasp.

Levin, J., & Fox, J. A. (2001). *Dead lines: Essays in murder and mayhem.* Boston: Allyn & Bacon.

Levitt, S. D. (2004). Understanding why crime fell in the 1990s: Four factors that explain the decline and six that do not. *Journal of Economic Perspectives, 18*(1), 163–190.

Lieb, R. (2000). Social policy and sexual offenders: Contrasting United States' and European policies. *European Journal on Criminal Policy and Research, 8,* 423–440.

Lillienfeld, S., VanValkenburg, C., Larntz, K., & Akiskal, H. (1986). The relationship of histrionic personality disorder to antisocial personality disorder and somatization disorders. *American Journal of Psychiatry, 143*(6), 718–722.

Linder, D. (2002). The trial of John Hinckley. Retrieved July 3, 2006, at: http://www.law.umkc.edu/faculty/projects/ftrials/hinckley/hinckleytrial.html.

Lionel Tate released. (January 27, 2004). CNN.com. Retrieved May 9, 2007, at: http://www.cnn.com/2004/LAW/01/26/wrestling.death/.

Liptak, A. (June 14, 2004). Appealing a death sentence based on future danger. *The New York Times.* Retrieved May 28, 2006, at: http://query.nytimes.com/gst/fullpage.html?sec=health&res=9E03E7DC1030F937A25755C0A9629C8B63.

Lipton, D., Martinson, R., & Wilkes, J. (1975). *The effectiveness of correctional treatment: A survey of treatment evaluation studies.* New York: Praeger.

Litwack T. R., & Schlesinger L. B. (1998). Dangerous risk assessments: Research, legal, and clinical considerations. In A. K. Hess & I. B. Weiner (Eds.), *Handbook of forensic psychology* (pp. 171–217). New York: John Wiley & Sons.

Lloyd, B. T. (2002). A conceptual framework for examining adolescent identity, media influence, and social development. *Review of General Psychology, 6*(1), 73–91.

Lombroso, C. (2003). The criminal man. In F.T. Cullen & R. Agnew (Eds.), *Criminological Theory: Essential Readings* (pp. 23–25). Los Angeles: CA: Roxbury.

London bomb victims identified. (2007). CNN Special Report. Available at: http://www.cnn.com/SPECIALS/2005/london.bombing/victims.html.

London Home Office. (2004). Paying the price: A consultation paper on prostitution. London: Home Office.

Looman, J., Gauthier, C., & Boer, D. (2001). Replication of the Massachusetts Treatment Center Child Molester Typology in a Canadian sample. *Journal of Interpersonal Violence, 16,* 753–767.

Lopez, R. (February 15, 2007). Prison gang linked to 16 Dallas murders. WFAA.com Dallas/Fort Worth.

Retrieved February 19, 2007, at: http://www.wfaa.com/sharedcontent/dws/wfaa/localnews/news8/stories/wfaa070215_mo_prisongang.2bdcdaf.html.

Lovell, M. L., Helfgott, J. B., & Lawrence, C. F. (2002). Narrative accounts from the Citizens, Victims, and Offenders Restoring Justice program at the Washington State Reformatory. *Contemporary Justice Review, 5*, 261–272.

Low, P. W., Jeffries, J. C., & Bonnie, R. J. (1986). *The trial of John W. Hinckley, JR: A case study in the insanity defense.* Mineola, NY: The Foundation Press.

Loza, W., & Green, K. (2003). The Self-Appraisal Questionnaire. *Journal of Interpersonal Violence, 18*(7), 781–797.

Loza, W., & Loza-Fanous, A. (1999). The fallacy of reducing rape and violent recidivism by treating anger. *International Journal of Offender Therapy and Comparative Criminology, 43*, 492–502.

Lueck, T. J., Stowe, S., & Hussey, K. (July 24, 2007). Mother and 2 daughters killed in Connecticut home invasion. *The New York Times,* Section B, p. 1.

Lykken, D. T. (1957). A study of anxiety in the sociopathic personality. *Journal of Abnormal and Social Psychology, 55,* 6–10.

Lykken, D. T. (1995). *The antisocial personalities.* Hillsdale, NJ: Lawrence Erlbaum Associates.

Lynam, D. R., Piquero, A. R., & Moffit, T. E. (2004). Specialization and the propensity to violence. *Journal of Contemporary Criminal Justice, 20*(2), 215–228.

Lyon, D. R., & Ogloff, J. R. P. (2000). Legal and ethical issues in psychopathy assessment. In C. B. Gacono (Ed.), *The clinical and forensic assessment of psychopathy* (pp. 139–173). Mahwah, NJ: Lawrence Erlbaum Associates.

MacKinnon, C. (1983). Feminism, Marxism, method, and the state: Towards a feminist jurisprudence. *Signs, 8*(4), 635–658.

MacLin, O. H., Meissner, C. A., & Zimmerman, L. A. (2005). PC_Eyewitness: A computerized framework for the administration and practical application of research in eyewitness psychology. *Behavior Research Methods, 37*(2), 324–334.

Mailer, N. (1958). *The white negro: Voices of dissent.* New York: Grove Press.

Mailer, N. (1959). *Advertisements for myself.* New York: J.P. Putnam's Sons.

Malcolm, J. G. (April 29, 2003). Statement before the subcommittee of crime, terrorism, and homeland security committee on the judiciary. U.S. House of Representatives. Retrieved March 21, 2006, at: http://www.usdoj.gov/criminal/cybercrime/Malcolmtestimony42903.htm.

Maltz, M. (1976). On defining organized crime: The development of a definition and typology. *Crime and Delinquency, 22*(3), 338–346.

Malvo Trial CNN Transcripts. (December 9, 2003). Malvo Trial. Retrieved November 4, 2005, at: http://transcripts.cnn.com/TRANSCRIPTS/0312/09/ltm.06.html.

Manhunt on as toll set to rise. (July 8, 2005). CNN.com. Retrieved July 8, 2005, at: www.cnn.com—manhunt on as toll set to rise—July 8, 2005.

Manning, P. (1998). Media loops. In F. Bailey & D. Hale (Eds.), *Popular culture, crime, and justice* (pp. 25–39). Belmont, CA: Wadsworth.

Marshall, W. L., Anderson, D., & Fernandez, Y. (1999). *Cognitive behavioral treatment of sexual offenders.* New York: John Wiley & Sons.

Marshall, W. L., Laws D. R., & Barbaree H. E. (Eds.) (1990). *Handbook of sexual assault* (pp. 143–159). New York: Plenum.

Martin, G. (2003). *Understanding terrorism: Challenges, perspectives, & issues.* Thousand Oaks, CA: Sage.

Martin, J. (March 31, 2006). Absence of motive adds an extra layer of grief. *The Seattle Times.* Retrieved April 4, 2006, at: http://seattletimes.nwsource.com/html/localnews/2002901117_nomotive31m.html.

Martin, S. S., & Scarpetti, F. R. (1993). An intensive case management approach for paroled IV drug users. *Journal of Drug Issues, 23,* 43–59.

Martinez, R. (1997). Predictors of violent recidivism: Results from a cohort study. *Journal of Interpersonal Violence, 12,* 216–229.

Martinson, R. (1974). What works?—Questions and answers about prison reform. *The Public Interest, 35,* 22–54.

Martinson, R. (1979). New findings, new views: A note of caution regarding sentencing reform. *Hofstra Law Review, 7,* 243–258.

Marsa, F., O'Reilly, G., Carr, A., Murphy, P., O'Sullivan, M., Cotter, A., & Hevey, D. (2004). Attachment styles and psychological profiles of child sex offenders in Ireland. *Journal of Interpersonal Violence, 19*(2), 228–251.

Marx, G. T. (1988). *Undercover: Police surveillance in America.* Berkeley: University of California Press.

Marx, G. T. (1995). *Electric eye in the sky: Some reflections on the new surveillance and popular culture.* In

J. Ferrell & C. R. Sanders (Eds.), *Cultural criminology* (pp. 106–141). Boston: Northeastern University Press.

Massacre in Madrid: Madrid bombings one year on. (2005). *CNN.com Special Report.* Retrieved July 8, 2005, at: www.cnn.com/SPECIALS/2004/madrid.bombing/.

Masters, W. H., & Johnson, V. E. (1974). *The pleasure bond.* New York: Bantam Books.

Matlin, M. W. (2005). *Cognition.* New York: John Wiley & Sons.

Matthews, R. (2002). *Armed robbery.* Portland, OR: Willan Publishing.

Matthews, R., Matthews, J. K., & Speltz, K.(1989). *Female sexual offenders: An exploratory study.* Orwell, VT: Safer Society Press.

McCabe, D. (2003). The influence of situational ethics on cheating. In P. Adler & P. Adler (Eds.), *Constructions of deviance: Social power, context, and interaction* (pp. 263–271). Belmont, CA: Wadsworth.

McCabe, M. P., & Wauchope, M. (2005). Behavioural characteristics of rapists. *Journal of Sexual Aggression, 11*(3), 235–247.

McCarthy, B. (1995). Not just "for the thrill of it": An instrumentalist elaboration of Katz's explanation of sneaky thrill property crimes. *Criminology, 33*(4), 519–539.

McCord, W., & McCord, J. (1964). *The psychopath: An essay on the criminal mind.* New York: Van Nostrand Reinhold Company.

McCown, W. G., & Chamberlain, L. L. (2000). *Best possible odds: Contemporary treatment strategies for gambling disorders.* New York: John Wiley & Sons.

McDevitt, J., Levin, J., & Bennett, S. (2002). Hate crime offenders: An expanded typology. *Journal of Social Issues, 58*(2), 303–317.

McEllistrem, J. E. (2004). Affective and predatory violence: A bimodal classification of human aggression and violence. *Aggression and Violent Behavior, 10,* 1–30.

McGough, M. (March 31, 2005). Inmate-transfer rules defended. *Pittsburgh Post-Gazette,* A6.

McMillan, E. A. (March 4, 2004). Woman sentenced for role in attack; Michelle Lee Murphy was found guilty of aiding assault of Penn Twp. woman in 2003. *The Evening Sun* (Local News Section).

McMurray, H. L. (1993). High risk parolees in transition from institution to community life. *Journal of Offender Rehabilitation, 19,* 145–161.

Meadows, B. (January 10, 2005). How could she do it? : L. Montgomery accused of killing B. J. Stinnett for the baby in her womb. *People Magazine, 63*(1), 127–128.

Meadows, R. J., & Kuehnel, J. (2005). *Evil minds: Understanding and responding to violent predators.* Upper Saddle River, NJ: Pearson/Prentice-Hall.

Meloy, J. R. (1988). *The psychopathic mind: Origins, dynamics, and treatment.* New York: Jason Aronson.

Meloy, J. R. (1992). *Violent attachments.* Northvale, NJ: Jason Aronson.

Meloy, J. R. (1997). Predatory violence during mass murder. *Journal of Forensic Sciences, 42*(2), 326–329.

Meloy, J. R. (Ed.) (1998). *The psychology of stalking: Clinical and forensic perspectives.* San Diego, CA: Academic Press.

Meloy, J. R. (2000). The nature and dynamics of sexual homicide: An integrative review. *Aggression and Violent Behavior, 5,* 1–22.

Merry, S., & Harsent, L. (2000). Intruders, pilferers, raiders, and invaders: The interpersonal dimension of burglary. In D. Canter & L. Alison (Eds.), *Profiling property crimes* (pp. 33–56). Burlington, VT: Ashgate.

Messerschmidt, J. W. (1993). *Masculinities and crime.* Lanham, MD: Rowman & Littlefield Publishers.

Messing, J. T., & Heeren, J. W. (2004). Another side of multiple murder: Woman killers in the domestic context. *Homicide Studies, 8*(2), 123–158.

Messner, S. F., McHugh, S., & Felson, R. B. (2004). Distinctive characteristics of assaults motivated by bias. *Criminology, 42*(3), 585–618.

Merz-Perez, L., & Heide, K. M. (2004). *Animal cruelty: Pathway to violence against people.* Walnut Creek, CA: AltaMira Press.

Meyers, W. C. (2002). *Juvenile sexual homicide.* San Diego: Academic Press.

Meyers, W. C., Gooch, E., Meloy, J. R. (2005). The role of psychopathy and sexuality in a female serial killer. *Journal of Forensic Sciences, 50*(3), 652–657.

Meyer, C. L., & Oberman, M. (2001). *Mothers who kill their children.* New York: New York University Press.

Miethe, T. D., & McCorkle, R. C. (2001). *Crime profiles: The anatomy of dangerous persons, places, and situations.* (2nd Ed.). Los Angeles: Roxbury Publishing.

Miethe, T. D., McCorkle, R. C., & Listwan, S. J. (2006). *Crime profiles: The anatomy of dangerous persons, places, and situations* (3rd Ed.). Los Angeles: Roxbury Publishing.

Miethe, T. D., & Meier, R. F. (1994). *Crime and its social context. Toward an integrated theory of offenders, victims, and situations.* Albany: State University of New York Press.

Mik, H. M., Ehtesham, S., Baldassarra, L., DeLuca, V., Davidge, K., Bender, D., et al. (2007). Serotonin system genes and childhood-onset aggression. *Psychiatric Genetics, 17*(1), p. 1.

Miller, J. (1998). Up it up: Gender and the accomplishment of street robbery. *Criminology, 36,* 37–67.

Milloy, C. (2003). Six year follow-up of released sex offenders recommended for commitment under Washington's Sexually Violent Predator Law, where no Petition was filed. Olympia: Washington State Institute for Public Policy.

Minoño, A. M., Heron, M., & Smith, B. L. (2004). Deaths: Preliminary data for 2004. National Center for Health Statistics. Retrieved February 14, 2007, at: http://www.cdc.gov/nchs/products/pubs/pubd/hestats/prelimdeaths04/preliminarydeaths04.htm.

Minzenberg, M. J., & Siever, L. J. (2006). Neurochemistry and pharmacology of psychopathy and related disorders. In C. J. Patrick (Ed.), *Handbook of psychopathy* (pp. 251–277). New York: Guilford Press.

Mitchell, K. J., Becker-Blease, K. A., & Finkelhor, D. (2005). Inventory of problematic Internet experiences encountered in clinical practice. *Professional Psychology: Research and Practice, 36*(5), 498–509.

Modestin, J., & Ammann, R. (1995). Mental disorders and criminal behavior. *British Journal of Psychiatry, 166,* 667–675.

Moffit, T. E. (1993). Adolescent-limited and life-course-persistent antisocial behavior: A developmental taxonomy. *Psychological Review, 100*(4), 674–701.

Monahan, J., Steadman, H. J., Silver, E., Appelbaum, P. S., Robbins, P. C., Mulvey, E. P., et al. (2001). *Rethinking risk assessment: The Macarthur study of mental disorder and violence.* Oxford: Oxford University Press.

Montgomery, L. (September 24, 1995). Charged issue: The possibilities of a killer gene, violence therapy. *Seattle Times,* A-3.

Moore, M. (Director) (2002). *Bowling for Columbine.* [film/DVD]. MGM Distribution.

Moore, M. J. (Director) (1999). *Legacy: Murder and media, politics and prison* [video recording]. Princeton, NJ: Films for the Humanities.

Moore, R. F. (November 17, 2006). Jihad's femme fatales: Women terrorists real threat, SEZ NYPD. *New York Daily News.* Retrieved May 6, 2007, at: http://www.nydailynews.com/news/2006/11/17/2006–11-17_jihads_femmes_fatales_women_terrorists_r.html.

Morris, S. (November 3, 2005). Classical deterrent in store for loitering youths. *The Guardian.* Retrieved August 6, 2007, at: http://www.guardian.co.uk/crime/article/0,2763,1607375,00.html.

Morse, E. V., Simon, P. M., Balson, P. M., & Osofsky, H. J. (1992). Sexual behavior patterns of customers of male street prostitutes. *Archives of Sexual Behavior, 21*(4), 347–357.

Mosher, C. J., Miethe, T. D., & Phillips, D. M. (2002). *The mismeasure of crime.* Thousand Oaks, CA: Sage.

Moskowitz, A. (2004). Dissociation and violence: A review of the literature. *Trauma, Violence, & Abuse, 5* (1), 21–46.

Mothers Against Drunk Driving (MADD). (2005). New survey: Teens report pressure to engage in high-risk behaviors on prom and graduation nights, impacting driving safety. Retrieved May 29, 2005, at: http://www.madd.org/news/0,1056,9731,00.html.

Moyer, K. E. (1968). Kinds of aggression and their physiological basis. *Communications in Behavioral Biology, Part A, 2,* 65–87.

Moynihan, D. P. (1993). Defining deviance down. *The American Scholar,* Winter.

Mullens, C. W., & Wright, R. (2003). Gender, social networks, and residential burglary. *Criminology, 41*(3), 813–839.

Murnen, S. K., Wright, C., & Kalunzy, G. (2002). If "boys will be boys" then girls will be victims? A meta-analytic review of the research that relates masculine ideology to sexual aggression. *Sex Roles, 46,* 359–375.

Murphy, J. G. (1972). Moral death: A Kantian essay on psychopathy. *Ethics, 82*(4), 284–298.

Murray, D. (December 1, 2005). Opera is new weapon in fight against crime. ThisisLondon.co.uk. Retrieved August 6, 2007, at: http://www.thisislondon.co.uk/news/article-15898882-details/Opera+is+new+weapon+in+fight+against+crime/article.do;jsessionid=M1ydG3nGkydgH11JR6YTTQ2zn6KLWhTD7LqlvpCP51GDgykQRbPG!890633107!-14073 19224!7001!-1.

Murrin, M. R., & Laws, D. R. (1990). The influence of pornography on sexual crimes. In W. L. Marshall, D. R. Laws, & H. E. Barbaree (Eds.), *Handbook of sexual assault: Issues, theories, and treatment of the offender* (pp. 73–91). New York: Plenum.

Myers, W. C. (2002). *Juvenile sexual homicide.* San Diego, CA: Academic Press.

Nacos. B. L. (2005). The portrayal of female terrorists in the media: Similar framing patterns in the news coverage of women in politics and in terrorism. *Studies in Conflict & Terrorism, 28,* 435–451.

Naffine, N. (1996). *Feminism and criminology.* Philadelphia: Temple University Press.

National Commission on Terrorist Attacks in the United States. (2004). *The 9/11 Commission report: Final report of the National Commission of Terrorist Attacks on the United States.* New York: W.W. Norton & Company.

National Committee to Reopen the Rosenberg Case. (n.d.). Retrieved May 6, 2007, at: http://www.rosenbergtrial.org/comitfrm.html.

National Genome Research Institute. (n.d.). Retrieved December 11, 2007, at: http://www.genome.gov/.

National White Collar Crime Center. (2005). *IC3 2004 Internet Fraud—Crime Report.* Retrieved March 20, 2006: http://www.ic3.gov/media/annualreport/2004_IC3 Report.pdf.

Naylor, R. T. (2003). Towards a general theory of profit-driven crimes. *British Journal of Criminology, 43*(1), 81–101.

NBC News. (July 14, 2006). Violent crime rates on the rise nationwide: FBI statistics show murders in the U.S. jumped 4.8 percent last year. Retrieved January 8, 2007, at: http://www.msnbc.msn.com/id/13863336/.

Neumann, C. S., Kosson, D. S., & Salekin, R. T. (2007). Exploratory and confirmatory factor analysis of the psychopathy construct: Methodological and conceptual issues. In H. Herve & J. C. Yuille (Eds.), *The psychopath: Theory, research, and practice* (pp. 79–104). Mahwah, NJ: Lawrence Erlbaum.

New twist in fetus theft try. (October 14, 2005). CBS News. Retrieved at: http://www.cbsnews.com/stories/2005/10/14/earlyshow/main943428.shtml.

Newkirk, I. (2000). *Free the animals: The amazing story of the animal liberation front.* New York: Lantern Books.

Newman, G. (1998). Popular culture and violence: Decoding the violence of popular movies. In F. Bailey & D. Hale (Eds.) *Popular culture, crime, and justice* (pp. 40–56). Belmont, CA: Wadsworth.

Newman, K. S., Fox, C., Harding, D., Mehta, J., & Roth, W. (2004). *Rampage: The social roots of school shootings.* New York: Basic Books.

Newman, O. (1972). *Defensible space: Crime prevention through urban design.* New York: MacMillian.

News 24.com. (January 26, 2004). I gave him a nice death. Retrieved February 14, 2004, at: http://www.news24.com/News24/World/News/0,,2–10–1462_1474277,00.html.

Ngyuen, K. N., Harrison, W., & Armstrong, K. (September 29, 2006). Gunman's motives remain unclear as new clues surface. ABC News/TheDenverChannel.com.

Retrieved September 29, 2006, at: http://www.thedenverchannel.com/news/9958178/detail.html.

O'Brien, J. (1999). In defense of Oliver Stone, *Natural Born Killers,* and attacks against violent films. Available: http://www.oscarworld.net/ostone/default.asp?PageId=3

O'Donohue, W., Yeater, E. A., & Fanetti, M. (2003). Rape prevention with college males: The roles of rape myth acceptance, victim empathy, and outcome expectancies. *Journal of Interpersonal Violence, 18*(5), 513–531.

Oetting, T. (July 10, 2006). The predator-industrial complex wins again! One Strike Law.org. Retrieved August 25, 2006, at: http://onestrikelaw.blogspot.com/.

Office of National Drug Control Policy. (2000). *Drug related crime.* Rockville, MD: Drug Policy Information Clearinghouse.

O'Hagan, M. (June 3, 2005). WTO no-protest zone upheld; but demonstrators can pursue lawsuits. *The Seattle Times,* B1.

O'Hare, P. (January 1, 2007). City sees 13.5% rise in slayings for 2006. *The Houston Chronicle,* A1.

Oliver, M. B. (2002). Individual differences in media effects. In J. Bryant & D. Zillman (Eds.), *Media effects: Advances in theory and research.* Mahwah, NJ: Lawrence Erlbaum.

Oliver Stone and *Natural Born Killers* timeline. (2005). *Freedom Forum.* Retrieved August 18, 2005, at: http://www.freedomforum.org/templates/document.asp?documentID=3962.

Olsen, J. (1983). *Son: A psychopath and his victims.* New York: MacMillan Press.

Olsen, J. (1991). *Predator.* New York: Delacorte Press.

Olsen, J. (1995). *Charmer: The true story of a lady's man and his victims.* New York: Avon Books.

O'Neil, R. M. (2001). *The first amendment and civil liability.* Bloomington: Indiana University Press.

Orion, D. (1997). *I know you really love me: A psychiatrists journal of erotomania, stalking, and obsessional love.* New York: Macmillan.

O'Sullivan, C. (1993). Fraternities and rape culture. In E. Buchwald, P. R. Fletcher, & M. Roth (Eds.), *Transforming rape culture* (pp. 25–30). Minneapolis: Milkweed Editions.

O'Toole, M. E. (1999). Criminal profiling: The FBI uses criminal investigative analysis to solve crimes. *Corrections Today, 61,* 44–46.

O'Toole, M. E. (2007). Psychopathy as a behavior classification system for violent and serial crime scenes. In H. Herve & J. Yuille (Eds.), *The psychopath: Theory,* research, and practice (pp. 301–325). Mahweh, NJ: Lawrence Erlbaum Associates.

Paletz, D. L., & Schmid, A. P. (1992). *Terrorism and the media.* Thousand Oaks, CA: Sage.

Palmer, C. T., Thornhill, R., & DiBari, D. N. (2002). Biology, sex, and the debate over "chemical castration." In J. F. Hodgson & D. S. Kelly (Eds.), *Sexual violence: Policies, practices, and challenges in the United States and Canada* (pp. 35–49). Westport, CT: Praeger.

Pankratz, H., & Ingold, J. (2003). Columbine killers left paper trail. Violent writings by killers released along with horrific details of massacre. *The Denver Post.* A-1.

Patrick, C. J. (2001). Emotional processes in psychopathy. In A. Raine & J. Sanmartin (Eds.), *Violence and psychopathy* (pp. 57–77). New York: Kluwer/Plenum.

Patrick, C. J. (Ed.) (2006). *Handbook of psychopathy.* New York: Guilford Press.

Patrick, C. J. (2007). Getting to the heart of psychopathy. In H. Herve & J. C. Yuille (Eds.), *The psychopath: Theory, research, and practice* (pp. 207–252). Mahwah, NJ: Lawrence Erlbaum.

Patsuris, P. (2002). The corporate scandal sheet. *Forbes.* Available at: http://www.forbes.com/2002/07/25/accountingtracker.html.

Patten, D. (1997). Rising body count. Salon.com. Retrieved August 25, 2005, at: http://archive.salon.com/sept97/news970916.html.

Paul, R. J., & Townsend, J. B. (1998). Managing workplace gambling—some cautions and recommendations. *Employee Responsibilities and Rights Journal, 11*(3), 171–186.

Pavalko, R. M. (2000). *Risky business: America's fascination with gambling.* Belmont, CA: Wadsworth.

Peaslee, D. (1993). An investigation of incarcerated females: Rorschach indices and psychopathy Checklist scores. Unpublished doctoral dissertation. Fresno: California School of Professional Psychology.

Petersilia, J. (2003). *When prisoners come home: Parole and prisoner reentry.* New York: Oxford University Press.

Petersilia, J., & Turner, S. (1993). Intensive probation and parole. In M. Tonry (Ed.), *Crime and Justice: A review of research* (Vol. 17, pp. 281–335). Chicago: University of Chicago Press.

Peterson-Manz, J. (2002). Copycats: Homicide and the press. *Dissertation Abstracts International.* Unpublished Doctoral Dissertation, Claremont Graduate University.

Phipps, P., Korinek, K., Aos, S., & Lieb, R. (1999). Research findings on adult corrections' programs: A review. *Research Report,* Document No. 99–01–1203. Olympia: Washington State Institute for Public Policy. Available at: http://www.wa.gov/wsipp/crime/pdf/researchfindings.pdf.

Phoenix, J. (2004). An analysis of women's involvement in prostitution. In D.A. Dabney (Ed.), *Crime types: A text/reader* (pp. 292–306). Belmont, CA: Wadsworth.

Pierce, P. (October 15, 2002). Expert links sniper, violent video games. *Tribune Review.* Retrieved January 12, 2004, at: http://www.pittsburghlive.com/x/tribune-review/s_96886.html.

Pinzotto, A. J., & Finkel, N. (1990). Criminal personality profiling: An outcome and process study. *Law and Human Behavior, 14*(3), 215–233.

Piquero, A., & Mazerolle, P. (Eds.). (2001). *Life-course criminology.* Belmont, CA: Wadsworth.

Police say Madison's "Mall Rapist" behind bars. (2004). WMTV NBC15 Madison. Retrieved July 22, 2004, at: http://www.nbc15.com/Global/story.asp?s=%20%201895621.

Police: School shooter asked for girls by name. (September, 29, 2006). CNN.com. Retrieved September 29, 2006, at: http://www.cnn.com/2006/US/09/29/school.shooting/index.html.

Poling, S. (2007). Luke Mitchell: The devil's own? *BBC News.* Retrieved May 9, 2007, at:

Pollock, J. M. (1999). *Criminal women.* Cincinnati: Anderson Publishing.

Pomeroy, G. (Producer) (1991). *Male rape* [video]. Great Britain: Community Programme Unit, BBC Television.

Porter, S., & Porter, S. (2007). Psychopathy and violent crime. In H. Herve & J. C. Yuille (Eds.), *The psychopath: Theory, research, and practice* (pp. 287–300). Mahwah, NJ: Lawrence Erlbaum.

Potter, H. (2006). An argument for Black feminist criminology. *Feminist criminology, 1*(2), 106–124.

Prendergast, M. L., Anglin, M. D., & Wellisch, J. (1995). Treatment for drug abusing offenders under community supervision. *Federal Probation, 59,* 66–74.

Prentky, R. A. (2003). A 15-year retrospective on sexual coercion: Advances and projections. In R. A. Prentky, E. S. Janus, & M. C. Seto (Eds.), *Sexually coercive behavior: Understanding and management* (pp. 13–32). New York: The New York Academy of Sciences.

Prentky, R. A., & Burgess, A. W. (2000). *Forensic management of sexual offenders.* New York: Kluwer/Plenum.

Prentky, R. A., Burgess, A. W., Rokous, F., Lee, A., Hartman, C., Ressler, R., & Douglas, J. (1989). The presumptive role of fantasy in serial sexual homicide. *American Journal of Psychiatry, 146*(7), 887–891.

Prentky, R. A., Janus, E. S., & Seto, M. C. (Eds.) (2003). *Sexually coercive behavior: Understanding and management.* New York: The New York Academy of Sciences.

Presdee, M. (2000). *Cultural criminology and the carnival of crime.* New York: Routledge.

Publisher considers O.J. Simpson book "his confession." (November 15, 2006). *USA Today.* Retrieved January 16, 2007, at: http://www.usatoday.com/life/people/2006–11–15-simpson-reaction_x.htm.

Quayle, E., & Taylor, M. (2003). Model of problematic Internet use in people with a sexual interest in children. *Cyberpsychology & Behavior, 6,* 93–106.

Queen, C. (2000). Toward a taxonomy of tricks: A whore considers the age-old question, "what do clients want?" In M. B. Sycamore (Ed.), *Tricks and treats: Sex workers write about their clients.* New York: Harrington Park Press.

Quinney, R. (1970). *The social reality of crime.* Boston: Little, Brown, & Co.

Quinney, R. (1977). *The problem of crime: A critical introduction to criminology.* New York: Harper & Row.

Quinsey, V. L., Harris, G. T., Rice, M. E., & Cormier, C. A. (1998). *Violent offenders: Appraising and managing risk.* Washington, DC: American Psychological Association.

Racketeering law goes too far. (May 15, 2002). *St Petersburg Times, 14A.*

Radzinowicz, L. (1966). *Ideology and crime.* New York: Columbia University Press.

Rafter, N. (2000). *Shots in the mirror: Crime films and society.* Oxford: Oxford University Press.

Raine, A. (1993). *The psychopathology of crime: Criminal behavior as a clinical disorder.* New York: Academic Press.

Raine, A. (2002). Biosocial studies of antisocial and violent behavior in children and adults: A review. *Journal of Abnormal Child Psychology 30,* 311–326.

Raine, A., & Duncan, J. J. (1990). The genetic and psychophysiological basis of antisocial behaviour: Implications for counseling and therapy. *Journal of Counseling and Development, 68,* 637–644.

Raine, A., Meloy, J. R., Bihrle, S., Stoddard, J., Lacasse, L., & Buchsbaum, M. S. (1988). Reduced prefrontal and increased subcortical brain functioning assessed using positron emission tomography in predatory and affective murderers. *Behavioral Sciences and the Law, 16(3),* 319–332.

Raine, A., & Sanmartin, J. (Eds.) (2001). *Violence and psychopathy.* New York: Kluwer Academic/Plenum.

Raine, A., & Yang, Y. (2006). The neuroanatomical bases of psychopathy: A review of brain imaging findings. In C. J. Patrick (Ed.), *Handbook of psychopathy* (pp. 278–295). New York: Guilford Press.

Rantala, R. R. (2000). Effects of NIBRS on crime statistics. *Special Report.* U.S. Department of Justice, Bureau of Justice Statistics, Office of Justice Programs.

Raphael, J., & Shapiro, D. L. (2004). Violence in indoor and outdoor prostitution venues. *Violence Against Women, 10(2),* 126–139.

Ratliff, E. (October 10, 2005). The zombie hunters: On the trail of cyberextortionists. *The New Yorker,* p. 44.

Rayburn, N., Earleywine, M., & Davidson, G. C. (2003). Base rates of hate crime victimization among college students. *Journal of Interpersonal Violence, 18(10),* 1209–1221.

Recer, P. (February 12, 2001). Gene research may lead to pills that fix behavior. *Vancouver WA Columbian,* A-4.

Reentry Policy Council. *Report of the Reentry Policy Council.* Retrieved June 25, 2006, at: http://rp.webassembler.net/rp/main.aspx?dbID=DB_TheREPORT409.

Regnier, T. (2004). Barefoot in quicksand: The future of "future dangerousness" predictions in death penalty sentencing in the world of Daubert and Kuhmo. *Akron Law Review, 37,* 469–507.

Reiber, R. W., & Green, M. (1989). The psychopathy of everyday life: Antisocial behavior and social distress. In R. W. Rieber (Ed.), *The individual, communication, & society* (pp. 48–89). Cambridge: Cambridge University Press.

Reiber R. W., & Vetter, H. J. (1995). The language of the psychopath. In R. W. Reiber (Ed.), *The psychopathology of language and cognition* (pp. 61–87). New York: Plenum Press.

Reid., A. (December 31, 2006). No pattern to rise in murders, police say. *The Boston Globe,* Reg6.

Reid, T., & Baldwin, T. (October 2, 2006). Gunman kills girls "execution style" at Amish School. *Times Online.* Retrieved February 19, 2007, at: http://www.timesonline.co.uk/tol/news/world/us_and_americas/article657922.ece.

Reid, W. H. (Ed.). (1978). *The psychopath: A comprehensive study of antisocial disorders and behaviour.* New York: Brunner/Mazel.

Reid, W. (1985). The antisocial personality: A review. *Hospital and Community Psychiatry, 36,* 831–837.

Reinarman, C. (2003) Geo-political and cultural constraints on international drug control treaties. *The International Journal of Drug Policy.* April *14*(2), 205–208.

Reisman, J. (1999). Media-initiated killers? *World Net Daily.* Retrieved February 14, 2004, at: http://www.worldnetdaily.com/news/article.asp?ARTICLE_ID=16083.

Reitman, B. L. (1931). *The second oldest profession.* New York: The Vanguard Press.

Rennison, C. M. (2002). *Rape and sexual assault: Reporting to police and medical attention, 1992–2000.* Washington, DC: U.S. Department of Justice, Office of Justice Programs, Bureau of Justice Statistics.

Repeat offender arrested for the 7th time. (February 15, 2006). *The Boston Globe,* B2.

Ressler, R. K., Burgess, A. W., & Douglas, J. E. (1992). *Sexual homicide: Patterns and motives.* New York: Simon & Schuster.

Reuter, P. (1985, 2004). *Disorganized crime: Illegal markets and the mafia.* Cambridge, MA: MIT Press.

Reuter, P. (2004). The political economy of drug smuggling. In M. Vellinga (Ed.), *The political economy of the drug industry* (pp. 127–147). Gainsville: University Press of Florida.

Robinson, M. B. (2004). *Why crime?: An integrated systems theory of antisocial behavior.* Upper Saddle River, NJ: Pearson/Prentice-Hall.

Rondeaux, C. (January 7, 2007). Most types of crime declined last year. *The Washington Post,* T03.

Rosebraugh, C. (2004). *Burning rage of a dying planet: Speaking for the Earth Liberation Front.* New York: Lantern Books.

Ross, J. I. (2003). *The dynamics of political crime.* Thousand Oaks, CA: Sage.

Ross, J. I., & Richards, S. C. (2003). *Convict criminology.* Belmont, CA: Wadsworth.

Rothman, D. (1971). *Discovery of the asylum.* Boston: Little, Brown, & Co.

Rowe, D. C. (2001). *Biology and crime.* New York: Roxbury.

Rozek, D. (January 2, 2007). Homicides up, but violent crime down: City recorded 466 murders last year. *Chicago Sun Times,* p. 08.

Rule, A. (1993). *Small Sacrifices.* New York: Penguin.

Rule, J. (December 6, 2003). Man charged with assault pleads guilty. *Wyoming Tribune-Eagle,* p. A3.

Rummel, R. J. (1996). *The miracle that is freedom: The solution to war, violence, genocide, and poverty.* Moscow, ID: Martin Institute for Peace Studies and Conflict Resolution. Available at: http://www.hawaii.edu/powerkills/NOTE7.HTM.

Ryan, K. M. (2004). Further evidence for a cognitive component of rape. *Aggression and Violent Behavior, 9*(6), 579–604.

Sabo, D., Kupers, T. A., & London, W. (Eds.) (2001). *Prison masculinities.* Philadelphia: Temple University Press.

Salekin R. T., Rogers R., & Sewell K. W. (1996). A review and meta-analysis of the Psychopathy Checklist and Psychopathy Checklist–Revised: Predictive validity of dangerousness. *Clinical Psychology: Science and Practice, 3,* 203–215.

Salfati, C. G. (2000). The nature of expressiveness and instrumentality in homicide and its implications for offender profiling. In P. H. Blackman, V. L. Leggett, B. L. Olson, & J. P. Jarvis (Eds.), *The varieties of homicide and its research: Proceedings of the 1999 meeting of the Homicide Research Working Group* (pp. 99–110). Washington D.C.: Federal Bureau of Investigation.

Salter, D., McMillan, D., Richards, M., Talbot, T., Hodges, J., & Bentovim, A. (2003). Development of sexually abusive behaviour in sexually victimised males: A longitudinal study. *The Lancet, 361*(9356), 471–476.

Sampson, R. J., & Laub, J. H. (1993). *Crime in the making: Pathways and turning points through life.* Cambridge, MA: Harvard University Press.

Santos, M. (July 30, 2007). Will ruffians run from Mozar. *Tacoma News Tribune.* Retrieved August 6, 2007, at: http://www.thenewstribune.com/front/topphoto/story/121533.html.

Santtila, P., Häkkänen, H., Alison, L., & Whyte, C. (2003). Juvenile firesetters: Crime scene actions and offender characteristics. *Legal and Criminological Psychology, 8,* 1–20.

Sargeant, J. (1996). *Born bad: The story of Charles Starkweather and Caril Ann Fugate.* London: Creation Books.

Sarre, R. (1999). Beyond "What Works?" A 25 year jubilee retrospective of Robert Martinson. Paper presented at the *History of Crime, Policing, and Punishment Conference,* Canberra Australia, December 9–10, 1999.

Savage, J. (2004). Does viewing violent media really cause criminal violence? A methodological review. *Aggression and Violent Behavior, 10,* 99–128.

Scarce, M. (1997). *Male on male rape: The hidden toll of stigma and shame.* New York: Insight Books/Plenum.

Schell, B. H., & Dodge, J. L. (2002). *The hacking of America: Who's doing it, why, and how?* Westport, CT: Quorum Books.

Scheidler v. National Organization for Women, 267 F. 3d 687 (2003). Legal Information Institute. Retrieved July 7, 2005, at: http://straylight.law.cornell.edu.

Schenck v. the United States, 249 U.S. 47 (1919). Legal Information Institute. Retrieved July 7, 2005, at: http://straylight.law.cornell.edu.

Schinkle, W. (2004). The will to violence. *Theoretical Criminology, 8*(1), 5–31.

Schmalleger, F. (2004). *Criminology today: An integrative introduction.* Upper Saddle River, NJ: Pearson/Prentice-Hall.

Schrink, J. (2000). Understanding the correctional counselor. In P. Van Voohris, M. Braswell, & D. Lester (Eds.), *Correctional counseling and rehabilitation* (pp. 41–60). Cincinnatti, OH: Anderson.

Schwaner S. L. (1998). Patterns of violent specialization: Predictors of recidivism for a cohort of parolees. *American Journal of Criminal Justice, 23,* 3–17.

Schwaner, S. L., McGaughey, D., & Tewksbury, R. (1998). Situational constraints and absconding behavior: Toward a typology of parole fugitives. *Journal of Offender Rehabilitation, 27,* 37–55.

Scientist jailed for animal-testing sabotage. (September 20, 2006). The Guardian Unlimited. Retrieved September 29, 2006, at: http://www.guardian.co.uk/animalrights/story/0,,1876987,00.html.

Scottish Executive. (2000). Report of the Committee on Serious Violent and Sexual Offenders. Retrieved April 9, 2006, at: http://www.scottishexecutive.gov.uk/maclean/docs/svso.pdf.

Scully, D., & Marolla, J. (1984). Convicted rapists' vocabulary of motives: Excuses and justifications. *Social Problems, 31,* 530–544.

Seattle City Council. (September 14, 2000). Report of the WTO Accountability Committee. Retrieved July 14, 2005, at: http://www.ci.seattle.wa.us/wtocommittee/arcfinal.pdf.

Second RICO suit filed against fur protesters. (August 8, 1999). *Fur Commission USA.* Retrieved July 7, 2005, at: http://www.furcommission.com/news/newsE54.htm.

Secret confessions of BTK. (August 12, 2005). *Dateline NBC.* Retrieved October 24, 2005, at: http://www.msnbc.msn.com/id/8917644/#storyContinued.

Segal, K., & Enos, L., (Directors) (1991). *Investigative reports: Copycat crimes* [Documentary].

Segal, Z. V., & Stermac, L. E. (1990). The role of cognitions in sexual assault. In W. L. Marshall, D. R. Laws, & H. E. Barbaree (Eds.), *Handbook of sexual assault: Issues, theories and treatment of the offender* (pp. 161–174). New York: Plenum.

Seling v. Young (2001). 531 U.S. 250.

Senate Committee on the Judiciary. (1999). Children, media, and violence: A report for parents and policymakers. Retrieved November 1, 2005, at: http://judiciary.senate.gov/oldsite/mediavio.htm.

September 11th 2001 Victims. (2004). 9/11 victims list. Retrieved June 30, 2005, at: http://www.september11victims.com/september11Victims/victims_list.htm.

Serin, R. C., & Amos, N. L. (1995). The role of psychopathy in the assessment of dangerousness. *International Journal of Law and Psychiatry, 18*(2), 231–238.

Serin, R. C., & Brown, S. L. (2000). The clinical use of the Hare Psychopathy Checklist–Revised in contemporary risk assessment. In C. B. Gacono (Ed.), *The clinical and forensic assessment of psychopathy* (pp. 251–268). Mahwah, NJ: Lawrence Erlbaum.

Serin, R., & Kennedy, S. (1997). Treatment readiness and responsivity: Contributing to effective correctional programming. *Research Report R-54.* Ottawa, Canada: Correctional Service of Canada.

Shapiro, D. M. (n.d.). Natural Born Killers. *The Crime Library.* Retrieved March 31, 2006, at: http://www.crimelibrary.com/notorious_murders/celebrity/natural_born_killers/1.html.

Sheehy, K. (January 28, 2003). Copycat choppers—Brothers mimic *Sopranos,* Decapitate mom. *The New York Post,* p. 003.

Shelden, R. G. (2001). *Controlling the dangerous classes: A critical introduction to the history of criminal justice.* Needham Heights, MA: Allyn & Bacon.

Sherman, L. W., Gottfredson, D., Mackenzie, D., Eck, J., Reuter, P., & Bushway, S. (1997). *Preventing crime: What works, what doesn't, what's promising.* Report to the U.S. Congress. Washington, DC: U.S. National Institute of Justice—Office of Justice Programs. Available at: http://cjcentral.com/sherman/sherman.htm.

Shipley, S. L., & Arrigo, B. A. (2004). *The female homicide offender: Serial murder and the case of Aileen Wuornos.* Upper Saddle River, NJ: Prentice Hall.

ShortNews.com. (December 30, 2003). Woman kills pregnant woman and cuts out fetus. Retrieved January 11, 2004, at: http://www.shortnews.com.

ShortNews.com. (January 4, 2004). Man kills wife with telephone cord during sex. Retrieved January 12, 2004, at: http://www.shortnews.com.

Shrum, H. (2004). No longer theory: Correctional practices that work. *Journal of Correctional Education, 55*(3), 225–235.

Siegal, L. J. (2004). *Criminology: Theories, patterns, and typologies.* Belmont, CA: Wadsworth.

Siegal, L. J. (2006). *Criminology.* Belmont, CA: Wadsworth.

Sikes, G. (1996). *8 Ball chicks: A year in the violent world of girl gangsters.* New York: Doubleday.

Silverman, D. C., Kalick, S. M., Bowie, S. I., & Edbril, S. D. (1988). Blitz rape and confidence rape: A typology applied to 1,000 consecutive cases. *The American Journal of Psychiatry, 145,* 11, 1438–1441.

Silverman, I. J. (2001). *Corrections: A comprehensive view.* Belmont, CA: Wadsworth.

Simon, D. R. (1996). *Elite deviance.* Needham Heights, MA: Allyn & Bacon.

Simon, R. (1975). *Women and crime.* Lexington, MA: Lexington Books.

Simourd D. J., & Hodge, R. D. (2000). Criminal psychopathy: A risk-and-need perspective. *Criminal Justice and Behavior, 27,* 256–272.

Simpson, S. S. (1989). Feminist theory, crime, and justice. *Criminology, 27*(4), 605–631.

Sims, S. (July 7, 2006). Dylan's law fails to make ballot. KREM.com. Retrieved August 25, 2006, at: http://www.krem.com/cgi-bin/bi/gold_print.cgi.

Slobogin, C. (2003). The integrationist alternative to the insanity defense: Reflections on the exculpatory scope of mental illness in the wake of the Andrea Yates trial. *American Journal of Criminal Law, 30*(3), 315–341.

Smart, C. (1977). *Women, crime, and criminology: A feminist critique.* Boston, London: Routledge & Kegan Paul.

Smiling cannibal cleared of murder. (January 30, 2004). Thomas Crosbie Media. Retrieved June 29, 2004, at: http://www.breakingnews.ie/2004/01/30/story131930.html.

Smith, K. C. (September 10, 2004). New York cops bust $20 million dollar chop shop. *New York Post.* Available at: http://www.officer.com/article/article.jsp?id=16877&siteSection=1.

Smith, R. J. (1978). *The psychopath in society.* New York: Academic Press.

Smith, S. R., & Meyer, R. G. (1987). *Law, behavior, and mental health policy and practice.* New York: New York University Press.

Snowden, L. L., & Whitsel, B. C. (Eds.) (2005). *Terrorism: Research, readings and realities.* Upper Saddle River, NJ: Prentice Hall.

Snyder, H. (2000). Sexual assault of young children as reported to law enforcement: Victim, incident, and offender characteristics. Washington, DC: Bureau of Justice Statistics, U.S. Department of Justice.

Sorenson, S. L., & Walsh, E. W. (1995). Crime prevention through environmental design & situational prevention in public housing. Technical Assistance Workshop. Washington, DC: U.S. Department of Housing and Urban Development. Retrieved April 10, 2006, at: http://www.housingresearch.org/hrf/HRF_REFLIB.nsf/320d38b6b455f6fb8525699a005e0617/752d93a9c07cb16a8525699a005e5062?OpenDocument.

Soronsen, J. R., & Pilgrim, R. L. (2000). An actuarial risk assessment of violence posed by capital murder defendants. *The Journal of Criminal Law & Criminology, 90,* 1251–1270.

Soule, S. A., & Van Dyke, N. (1999). Black church arson in the United States, 1989–1996. *Ethnic and Racial Studies, 22*(4), 724–742.

Spalt, L. (1980). Hysteria and antisocial personality: A single disorder? *The Journal of Nervous and Mental Disease, 168,* 456–464.

Sparks, C. G., & Sparks, C. W. (2002). Effects of media violence. In J. Bryant & D. Zillman (Eds.), *Media effects: Advances in theory and research* (pp. 269–285). Mahwah, NJ: Lawrence Erlbaum Associates.

Sparks, R. (1992). *Television and the drama of crime: Moral tales and the place of crime in public life.* Philadelphia: Open University Press.

Speer, D. L. (2000). Redefining borders: The challenges of cybercrime. *Crime, Law, and Social Change, 34,* 259–273.

Spiess, M. (2003). *Drug data summary.* Rockville, MD: Office of National Drug Control Policy, Drug Policy Information Clearinghouse.

Spiess, M., & Fallow, D. (2000). *Drug-related crime.* Rockville, MD: Office of National Drug Control Policy, Drug Policy Information Clearinghouse.

Sragow, M. (April 20, 2007). Cho's link to violent movie is discounted. *The Baltimore Sun.com.* Retrieved May 9, 2007, at: http://www.baltimoresun.com/features/lifestyle/bal-to.oldboy20apr20,0,7182839.story?coll=bal-artslife-today.

Stalans, L. J. (2004). Adult sex offenders on community supervision: A review of recent assessment strategies and treatment. *Criminal Justice and Behavior, 31*(5), 564–608.

Stamper, N. (2005). *Breaking rank: A top cop's exposé of the dark side of American policing.* New York: Nation Books.

Stanton, G. H. (1998). The eight stages of genocide. *Genocide Watch.* Retrieved July 10, 2005, at: http://www.genocidewatch.org/eightstages.htm.

State of New York Office of the Attorney General, Bureau of Investor Protection and Securities. (December, 1997). *New York Attorney General Report on microcap stock fraud.* Retrieved December 31, 2004: http://www.oag.state.ny.us/investors/microcap97/report97a.html#overview.

State of Washington v. Ridgway. (2004). [video recording]. Seattle, WA: Chameleon Data; prepared on behalf of King County Prosecutor's Office.

Statistics Canada. (n.d.). *General Social Survey.* Available at: http://www.statcan.ca/english/Dli/Data/Ftp/gss.htm.

Stehlin, I. (April, 1997). A time to heal: Chronotherapy tunes in to a body's rhythms. *FDA Consumer Magazine.* U.S. Food and Drug Administration.

Stermac, L. E., Segal Z. V., & Gillis, R. (1989). Social and cultural factors in sexual assault. In W. L. Marshall, D. R. Laws, & H. E. Barbaree (Eds.), *Handbook of sexual assault* (pp. 143–159). New York: Plenum.

Stern, S. (June 12, 2003). The "Matrix" made me do it. *The Christian Science Monitor.* Available at: http://www .csmonitor.com/2003/0612/p13s02-lire.html.

Steuerwald, B. L., & Kosson, D. S. (2000). Emotional experiences of the psychopath. In C. B. Gacono (Ed.), *The clinical and forensic assessment of psychopathy* (pp. 111–135). Mahwah, NJ: Lawrence Erlbaum.

Stohr, M. K., & Vazquez, S. P. (2000). *Idaho Crime Victimization Survey.* Meridian: Idaho Statistical Analysis Center. Available at: http://www.isp.state.id .us/pgr/PDF/cvs2000.pdf.

Stuart, G. L., Moore, T. M., Gordon, K. C., Ramsey, S. E., & Kahler, C. W. (2006). Psychopathology in women arrested for domestic violence. *Journal of Interpersonal Violence, 21,* 376–389.

Student describes Colorado gunman's takeover of classroom in deadly high school standoff. (September 28, 2006). *Statesboro Herald.* Retrieved September 28, 2006, at: http://www.statesboroherald.net/showstory .php?$recordID=8322.

Substance Abuse and Mental Health Services Administration. (2006). *Results from the 2005 National Survey on Drug Use and Health: National findings* (Office of Applied Studies, NSDUH Series H-30, DHHS Publication No. SMA 06–4194). Rockville, MD.

Sullivan, E. A., & Kosson, D. S. (2006). Ethnic and cultural variations in psychopathy. In C. J. Patrick (Ed.), *Handbook of psychopathy* (pp. 437–458). New York: Guilford Press.

Sullum, J. (1993). Weighty matters—use of drug carrier weight in calculating sentences—Drugs. *Reason.* Retrieved August 15, 2007, at: http://findarticles.com/p/ articles/mi_m1568/is_n5_v25/ai_14536893/pg_1.

Sung, H. (2004). State failure, economic failure, and predatory organized crime: A comparative analysis. *Journal of Research in Crime and Delinquency, 41*(2), 111–129.

Sung Koo Kim gets nearly six years for underwear theft. (November 7, 2005). *KATU.com.* Portland. Retrieved August 12, 2007, at: http://www.katu.com/news/ 3651561.html.

Supreme Court rules RICO law doesn't apply to pro-life protesters. (2003). Retrieved July 7, 2005, at: ten nesseerighttolife.org/news_center/archives/ 03012003–02.htm.

Surette, R. (1990). Estimating the magnitude and mechanisms of copycat crime. In R. Surette (Ed.), *The media and criminal justice policy: Recent research and social effects.* Springfield, IL: C Thomas Publishers.

Surette, R. (1998). *Media, crime, and criminal justice: Images and realities.* Belmont, CA: Wadsworth.

Surette, R. (2002). Self-reported copycat crime among a population of serious and violent juvenile offenders. *Crime & Delinquency, 48*(1), 46–69.

Suris, A., Lind, L., Emmett, G., Borman, P. D., Kashner, M., & Barratt, E. S. (2004). Measures of aggressive behavior: Overview of clinical and research instruments. *Aggression and Violent Behavior, 9,* 165–227.

Sutherland, E. (1950). The sexual psychopath laws. *Journal of Criminal Law and Criminology, 40.*

Sweetingham, L. (July 20, 2006). Expert: Andrea Yates believed she was battling Satan when she drowned her children. *Court TV.* Retrieved May 9, 2007, at: http://www.courttv.com/trials/yates/071906_ctv.html.

Sycamore, M. B. (Ed.) (2000). *Tricks and treats: Sex workers write about their clients.* New York: Harrington Park Press.

Sykes, G. M., & Matza, D. (1957). Techniques of neutralization: A theory of delinquency. *American Sociological Review, 22,* 664–670.

Szaz, T. S. (1974). *The myth of mental illness.* New York: Harper & Row.

Talvi, S. J. A. (November 12, 2003). The truth about the Green River Killer. *AlterNet.org.* Retrieved May 26, 2004, at: http://www.alternet.org/story.html?StoryID=17171.

Taylor, B. (1998). Religion, violence, and radical environmentalism: From Earth First! to the Unabomber to the Earth Liberation Front. *Terrorism and Political Violence, 10*(4), 1–42.

Tedeschi, B. (January 28, 2003). Crime wave washes over cyberspace. *New York Times,* A1.

Templeman, T. L., & Stinnett, R. D. (1991). Patterns of sexual arousal and history in a "normal" sample of young men. In D. West (Ed.), *Sex crimes* (pp. 183–196). Brookfield, VT: Dartmouth Publishing.

Tengström, A., Hodgins, S., Grann, M., Långström, N., & Kullgren, G. (2004). Schizophrenia and criminal offending: The role of psychopathy and substance use disorders. *Criminal Justice and Behavior, 31,* 367–390.

Tennessee Statistical Analysis Center. (1997). *A study of criminal habits: Recidivism and rearrest rates of Tennessee offenders.* Nashville: Tennessee Bureau of Investigation.

The case of the American Taliban. (2001). CNN.com. Retrieved July 8, 2005, at: http://www.cnn.com/CNN/Programs/people/shows/walker/profile.html.

Theoharis, A. (2004). *The FBI and American democracy.* Lawrence: University Press of Kansas.

Therolf, G. (April 27, 2007). Woman held in attack on Sandra Bullock's husband. *Los Angeles Times.com.* Retrieved May 7, 2007, at: http://www.latimes.com/entertainment/news/la-me-bullock27apr27,0,4324527.story?coll=la-home-entertainment.

Thomas, C. W. (April, 2002).The rise and fall of Enron; when a company looks too good to be true it usually is. *Journal of Accountancy.* Available at: http://www.forbes.com/2002/07/25/accountingtracker.html.

Thompson, T. (April 18, 2004). Teen love, teen hate: girl gang takes savage revenge: 17-year-old's horrific fireball death highlights the rise of the feral young females. *The Observer,* p. 10.

Thornberry, T. P. (1987). Toward an interactional theory of delinquency. *Criminology, 25(4),* 865–891.

Thornberry, T. P., & Krohn, M. D. (2000). The self-report method for measuring delinquency and crime. In D. Duffee (Ed.), *Measurement and analysis of crime and justice* (pp. 33–84). Washington, DC: National Institute of Justice.

Thornhill, R., & Palmer, C. T. (2000). *A natural history of rape: Biological bases of sexual coercion.* Cambridge, MA: The MIT Press.

Three defendants indicted, fourth pleads guilty in takedown of major international spam operation. (August 25, 2005). *U.S. Newswire.*

Tietchen, T. F. (1998). Samples and copycats: The cultural implications of the postmodern slasher in contemporary American film. *Journal of Popular Film and Television, 26,* 98–101.

Tiihonen, J., Hakola, P., Nevalainen, & Eronen, M. (1995). Risk of homicidal behavior among persons convicted of homicide. *Forensic Science International, 72,* 43–48.

Tilly, C. (2004). Terror, terrorism, terrorists. *Sociological Theory, 22*(1), 5–13.

Timberg, S. (February 18, 2005). Classical music as crime stopper. SantaFeNewMexico.com. Retrieved August 6, 2007, at: http://www.freenewmexican.com/artsfeatures/10701.html.

Tittle, C. R. (1995). *Control balance: Towards a general theory of deviance.* Boulder, CO: Westview Press.

Tjaden, P., & Thoennes, N. (2000). *Full report of the prevalence, incidence, and consequences of violence against women: Findings from the National Violence Against Women Survey.* Washington, DC: U.S. Department of Justice, Office of Justice Programs, National Institute of Justice.

TLC.com. (2005). Hacker Hall of Fame. Retrieved August 13, 2005, at: http://tlc.discovery.com/convergence/hackers/bio/bio.html.

Toensing, V. (February 12, 2002). Charge Lindh with treason. *National Review Online.* Retrieved July 8, 2005, at: http://www.nationalreview.com/comment/comment-toensing021202.shtml.

Tonry, M. (2004). *Thinking about crime: Sense and sensibility in American penal culture.* New York: Oxford University Press.

Travis, J. (1996). Crime prevention through environmental design and community policing. *Research in Action.* National Institute of Justice, U.S. Department of Justice.

Tremblay, P., Clermont, Y., & Cusson, M. (1994). Jockeys and joyriders: Changing patterns in car theft opportunity structures. *British Journal of Criminology, 34*(3), 307–321.

Tseng, H. C., Duane, J., & Hadipriono, F. (2004). Performance of campus parking garages in preventing crime. *Journal of Performance of Constructed Facilities, 18*(1), 21–28.

Tunnell, K. D. (1992). *Choosing crime: The criminal calculus of property offenders.* Chicago: Nelson-Hall Publishers.

Tunnell, K. D. (1993). *Political crime in contemporary America: A critical approach.* New York: Routledge.

Tunnell, K. D. (1998). Reflections on crime, criminals, and control in newsmagazine television programs. In F. Bailey & D. Hale (Eds.), *Popular culture, crime and justice* (pp. 111–122). Belmont, CA: West/Wadsworth.

Turk, A. T. (1982). *Political criminality: The defiance and defense of authority.* Newbury Park, CA: Sage.

Turner, J. S., & Rubinson, L. (1993). *Contemporary human sexuality.* Englewood Cliffs, NJ: Prentice-Hall.

Turner, S., & Petersilia, J. (1992). Focusing on high risk parolees: An experiment to reduce commitments to the Texas Department of Corrections. *Journal of Research in Crime & Delinquency, 29,* 34–62.

Turner, S., Petersilia, J., & Deschenes, E. P. (1992). Evaluating intensive supervision probation/parole (ISP) for drug offenders. *Crime & Delinquency, 38,* 539–556.

Turvey, B. E. (1999, 2002). *Criminal profiling: An introduction to behavioral evidence analysis.* San Diego, CA: Academic Press.

Tyuse, S. W., & Linhorst, D. M. (2005). Drug courts and mental health courts: Implications for social work. *Health & Social Work, 30*(3), 233–240.

Uniform Crime Reports. (2002). Federal Bureau of Investigation. Available at: http://www.fbi.gov/ucr/02cius.htm.

Uniform Crime Reports. (2003). Federal Bureau of Investigation. Available at: http://www.fbi.gov/ucr/cius_03/pdf/03sec4.pdf.

Uniform Crime Reports. (2005). Federal Bureau of Investigation. Retrieved at: http://www.fbi.gov/ucr/05cius/about/offensedefinitions.html.

U.S.C. § 2384, Title 18, Part 1, Chapter 115 (Seditious Conspiracy). (2005). Legal Information Institute. Available at: http://www.law.cornell.edu/uscode/html/uscode18/usc_sec_18_00002384——000-.html.

U.S. Department of Health and Human Services. (2003). *National Survey on Drug Abuse and Health (NSDUH).* Washington, DC: U.S. Department of Health and Human Services Substance Abuse and Mental Health Services Administration (SAMHSA). Retrieved May 16, 2005, at: http://oas.samhsa.gov/nhsda/2k3nsduh/2k3ResultsW.pdf.

U.S. Department of Health and Human Services. (December 31, 2004). The *National Survey on Drug Abuse and Health (NSDUH) Report: Driving Under the Influence (DUI) among young persons.* Washington, DC: U.S. Department of Health and Human Services, Substance Abuse and Mental Health Services Administration (SAMHSA), Office of Applied Statistics.

U.S. Department of Health and Human Services. (April 1, 2005). *Alcohol use and delinquent behaviors among youth.* Washington, DC: U.S. Department of Health and Human Services, Substance Abuse and Mental Health Services Administration (SAMHSA), Office of Applied Statistics.

U.S. Department of Justice, Bureau of Justice Assistance. (1997, 1999). *Addressing community gang problems: A practical guide.* Monograph. Washington, DC: U.S. Department of Justice, Office of Justice Programs.

U.S. Department of Justice, Bureau of Justice Statistics. (2001).*Hate crimes reported in NIRS,* 1997–99. Washington, DC: U.S. Department of Justice Office of Justice Programs.

U.S. Department of Justice, Bureau of Justice Statistics. (2002).*Compendium of Federal Justice Statistics, 2002.* Washington, DC: U.S. Department of Justice Office of Justice Programs.

U.S. Department of Justice, Bureau of Justice Statistics. (2003). *Criminal victimization, 2002.* Washington, DC: U.S. Department of Justice Office of Justice Programs.

US Department of Justice, FBI. (2000). Crime reporting in the age of technology. *Criminal Justice Information Services Division Newsletter, NIBRS Edition, 4*(1).

U.S. Department of Justice, Federal Bureau of Investigation. (2000/2001). *Terrorism 2000/2001.* Washington, DC: U.S. Department of Justice, Federal Bureau of Investigation. Available at: www.fbi.gov/publications/terror/terror2000_2001.pdf.

U.S. Department of Justice, Federal Bureau of Investigation. (2003). *Hate Crime Statistics 2003.* Washington, DC: U.S. Department of Justice, Federal Bureau of Investigation. Available at: http://www.fbi.gov/ucr/03hc.pdf.

U.S. Department of Justice, Office of Justice Programs. (2000). Arrestee Drug Abuse Monitoring (ADAM) Annual Report. National Institute of Justice, Bureau of Justice Statistics. Available at: http://www.ojp.usdoj.gov/nij/adam/welcome.html.

U.S. Department of Justice, Office of Justice Programs. (2003). Violent crime and property crime fall to lowest levels since 2003. *Bureau of Justice Statistics.* Available at: http://www.ojp.usdoj.gov/newsroom/2003/BJS03126.htm.

U.S. Department of Justice, Office of Justice Programs.(n.d.). *National Crime Victimization Survey.* National Institute of Justice, Bureau of Justice Statistics. Available at: http://www.ojp.usdoj.gov/bjs/cvict.htm#ncvs.

U.S. Department of Justice, Office of Victims of Crime. (n.d.). Victim services in community policing programs: A practitioner's guide. National Organization for Victim's Assistance and the International Association of Chiefs of Police. Retrieved April 14, 2006, at: http://www.iacp.org/research/VictimServCommunity%20PolicingParticipantGuide.pdf.

U.S. Department of Transportation. (2003). *Traffic safety facts: 2003 Data.* Washington, DC: National Center for Statistics & Analysis.

U.S. Securities & Exchange Commission. (2003). SEC charges Martha Stewart, broker Peter Bacanovic with illegal insider trading. Retrieved January 11, 2005, at: http://www.sec.gov/news/press/2003–69.htm.

U.S. Sentencing Commission. (2004). Federal sentencing guidelines. Retrieved May 6, 2005, at: http://www .ussc.gov/2004guid/2g1_1.htm.

Utah animal rights criminals sentenced to jail. (December 17, 1997). *Fur Commission USA.* Retrieved July 14, 2005, at: http://www.furcommission.com/news/ news3.htm.

Vandenburgh, H. (2004). *Deviance: The essentials.* Upper Saddle River, NJ: L Pearson/Prentice-Hall.

Vandiver, D. M., & Kercher, G. (2004). Offender and Victim Characteristics of Registered Female Sexual Offenders in Texas: A proposed typology of female sexual offenders. *Sexual Abuse, 16*(2).

Van Natta, D., & Johnston, D. (July 9, 2005). London bombs seen as crude: Death toll rises to 49. *The New York Times.* Retrieved July 9, 2005, at: http://www .nytimes.com/2005/07/09/international/europe/09i ntel.html?th&emc=th.

Van Voorhis, P., Braswell, M., & Lester, D. (Eds.) (2000). *Correctional counseling and rehabilitation* (4th ed.). Cincinnatti, OH: Anderson.

Van Voorhis, P., Cullen, F. T., & Appelgate, B. (1995). Evaluating interventions with violent offenders: A guide for practitioners and policymakers. *Federal Probation, 59*(2), 17–27.

Vasilenko, V. I. (2004). The concept and typology of terrorism. *Statutes and Decisions, 40*(5), 46–56.

Vellani, K. H., & Nahoun, J. (2001). *Applied crime analysis.* Woburn, MA: Butterworth-Heinemann.

Verona, E., & Vitale, J. (2006). Psychopathy in women: Assessment, manifestations, and etiology. In C. J. Patrick (Ed.). *Handbook of psychopathy* (pp. 415–436). New York: Guilford Press.

Victim of 1989 rape mutilation dies in motorcycle crash. (June 22, 2005). King 5.com. Retrieved April 16, 2007, at: http://www.king5.com/topstories/stories/NW_ 062205WAKhadeEL.3519d0d0.html.

Virginia Tech shooter a self-described "question mark." (April 18, 2007). *CNN.com.* Retrieved May 11, 2007, at: http://www.cnn.com/2007/US/04/18/cho.profile/ index.html.

Vito, G. F., & Wilson, D. G. (1990). Drug testing, treatment, and revocation: A review of program findings. *Federal Probation, 54,* 37–43.

Vold, G. B., Bernard, T. J., & Snipes, J. B. (2002). *Theoretical criminology.* New York: Oxford University Press.

Vogelman, L. (1990). *The sexual face of violence: Rapists on rape.* Johannesburg: Ravan Press.

Walker, S. (1998). *Popular justice: A history of American criminal justice.* New York: Oxford University Press.

Wallace, J. F., Schmitt, W. A., Vitale, J. E., & Neman, J. P. (2000). Experimental investigations of information-processing deficiencies in psychopaths: Implications for diagnosis and treatment. In C.B. Gacono (Ed.), *The clinical and forensic assessment of psychopathy* (pp. 87–109). Mahwah, NJ: Lawrence Erlbaum Associates.

Walsh, A. (2002). *Biosocial criminology.* Cincinnati: Anderson.

Walsh, A., & Ellis, L. (2007). *Criminology: An interdisciplinary Approach.* Thousand Oaks, CA: Sage.

Walsh, D. A., & Gentile, M. (2003). *Sex, murder, and video games* [video recording]. Seraphim Communications. Minneapolis, MN: National Institute on Media and the Family.

Walsh, D. P. (1978). *Shoplifting: Controlling a major crime.* New York: Holmes & Meier Publishers.

Walsh, M., & Chappell, D. (2004). Operational parameters of the stolen property system. In D. A. Dabney (Ed.), *Crime types: A text/reader* (pp. 193–206). Belmont, CA: Wadsworth.

Walsh, M. E. (1977). *The fence: A new look at the world of property theft.* Westport, CT: Greenwood Press.

Walters, G. D. (1990). *The criminal lifestyle: Patterns of serious criminal conduct.* Newbury Park, CA: Sage.

Wang, E. W., & Diamond, P. M. (1999). Empirically identifying factors related to violence risk in corrections. *Behavioral Sciences and the Law, 17,* 377–389.

Ward, T., Hudson, S. M., Johnston, L., & Marshall, W. L. (1997). Cognitive distortions in sex offenders: an integrative review. *Clinical Psychology Review, 17*(5), 479–507.

Warner, R. (1978). The diagnosis of antisocial and hysterical personality disorders. *The Journal of Nervous and Mental Disease, 166,* 839–845.

Washington State Department of Corrections. (2001). *Recidivism Briefing Paper No. 19.* Olympia: Planning and Research Section, Washington State Department of Corrections.

Washington State Institute for Public Policy. (December, 2003). Washington's Offender Accountability Act: An analysis of the Department of Corrections' risk assessment. Olympia: Washington State Institute for Public Policy.

Washington State Institute for Public Policy. (January, 2006). Evidence-based adult correctional programs: What works and what does not. Olympia: Washington State Institute for Public Policy.

Washington State Institute for Public Policy. (February, 2006). Sex offender sentencing in Washington State: Predicting recidivism based on the LSI-R. Olympia: Washington State Institute for Public Policy.

Weatherston, D., & Moran, J. (2003). Terrorism and mental illness. Is there a relationship? *International Journal of Offender Therapy and Comparative Criminology, 47*(6), 698–713.

Webster, C., Douglas, K., Eaves, D., & Hart, S. (1997). *HCR-20 Assessing Risk for Violence: Version II.* Burnaby, British Columbia: Mental Health, Law & Policy Institute, Simon Frazier University.

Weekes, J. R. (1992). Long term offenders: Who are they and where are they? *Forum on Corrections Research, 4,* 3–18.

Weinshenker, N. J., & Siegel, A. (2002). Bimodal classification of aggression: affective defense and predatory attack. *Aggression and Violent Behavior, 7*(3), 237–250.

Wells, J. T. (2005). *Principles of fraud examination.* Hoboken, NJ: John Wiley & Sons.

West, A. (2000). Clinical assessment of homicide offenders: The significance of crime scene in offense and offender analysis. *Homicide Studies, 4*(3), 219–233.

White, J.R. (2002). *Terrorism: An introduction.* Belmont, CA: Wadsworth.

Whitman, T. A., & Akutagawa, D. (2004). Riddles in serial murder: A synthesis. *Aggression and Violent Behavior.*

Wilks, D. (2004). Revisiting Martinson—Has corrections made progress in the past 30 years? *Corrections Today, 66*(6), 108–111.

Williamson, S., Harpur, T. J., & Hare, R. D. (1991). Abnormal processing of affective words by psychopaths. *Psychophysiology, 29,* 260–273.

Willott, S., Griffin, C., & Torrance, M. (2001). Snakes and ladders: Upper middle class male offenders talk about economic crime. *Criminology, 39*(2), 441–466.

Wilson, D., & Byrnes, S. (January 14, 1997). Teen charged with 4 murders—police say he planned to kill for a year. *The Seattle Times,* p. A1.

Wilson, P., Lincoln, R., & Kocsis, R. (1997). Validity, utility and ethics of profiling for serial violent and sexual offenders. *Psychiatry, Psychology, and the Law, 4*(1), 1–12.

Winfree, L. T., & Giever, D. M. (2000). On classifying driving-while intoxicated offenders: The experiences of a citywide DWI drug court. *Journal of Criminal Justice, 28,* 13–21.

Wise, T. N., & Goldberg, R. L. (1995). Escalation of a fetish: Coprophagia in a nonpsychotic adult of normal intelligence. *Journal of Sex and Marital Therapy, 21*(4), 272–275.

Wolf, B. (March 18, 2005). Stalkers, controversy thwart late-night host's yearning for privacy. *ABC News.* Retrieved December 27, 2005, at: http://abcnews.go.com/Entertainment/story?id=593753&page=1.

Wolf, N. (1994). *Fire with fire: The new female power and how to use it.* New York: Ballantine Books.

Wolfgang, M. E., Figlio, R. M., & Sellin, T. (1972). *Delinquency in a birth cohort.* Chicago: University of Chicago Press.

Woman charged with scalping Mohawk-wearing teen. (July 14, 2005). Associated Press. Retrieved February 19, 2007, at: http://www.usatoday.com/news/nation/2005–07–14-scalping-mohawk_x.htm.

Women's Firearm Network. (2000). Fighting back against rapists. Retrieved February 14, 2004, at: http://www.womenshooters.com/wfn/fight.html.

Wong, S., & Hare, R. D. (2005). *Guidelines for a psychopathy treatment program.* Toronto: Multi-Health Systems.

Wooden, W. S., & Blazak, R. (2001). *Renegade kids, suburban outlaws: From youth culture to delinquency.* Belmont, CA: Wadsworth.

Woodworth, M., & Porter, S. (2001). Historical foundations and current applications of criminal profiling in violent crime investigations. *Expert Evidence, 7,* 241–261.

Woodworth, M., & Porter, S. (2002). In cold blood: Characteristics of criminal homicides as a function of psychopathy. *Journal of Abnormal Psychology, 111:* 436–445.

World Health Organization. (1992). *Manual of the International Statistical Classification of Diseases, Injuries, and Causes of Death,* 10th Ed. (ICD-10). Geneva: WHO.

World Trade Organization (WTO). (2003). World Trade Organization. Geneva Switzerland: WTO. Retrieved July 13, 2005, at: http://www.wto.org/english/res_e/doload_e/inbr_e.pdf.

World Trade Organization: Seattle Protests. (1999). Retrieved June 24, 2005, at: http://www.zmedia.org/WTO/index.html.

Wright, R. T., & Decker, S. H. (1996). Choosing the target. In P. Cromwell (Ed.), *In their own words: Criminals on crime* (pp. 34–46). Los Angeles: Roxbury.

Wright, R. T., & Decker, S. H. (1997). *Armed robbers in action: Stickups and street culture.* Boston: Northeastern University Press.

Wulach, J. S. (1988). The criminal personality as a *DSMIII-R* antisocial, narcissistic, borderline, and histrionic personality disorder. *International Journal of Offender Counseling and Comparative Criminology, 33*(3), 185–199.

Yacoubian, G. S., & Kane, R. J. (1998). Identifying a drug use typology of Philadelphia arrestees: A cluster analysis. *Journal of Drug Issues, 28,* 559–574.

Yates, N., Shaw, A., & McGurran, A. (December 18, 2003). Experts brand Huntley "Psycho." *Mirror.co.uk.* Retrieved December 11, 2007, at: http://www .mirror.co.uk/archive/2003/12/18/experts-brand-huntley—psycho—89520-13736221/.

Yochelson, S., & Samenow, S. E. (1977). *The criminal personality. Volumes 1–3.* New York: Jason Aronson.

Young, M. H., Justice, J. V., Erdberg, P. S., & Gacono, C. B. (2000). The incarcerated psychopath in psychiatric treatment. In C. B. Gacono (Ed.), *The clinical and forensic assessment of psychopathy* (pp. 313–331). Mahwah, NJ: Lawrence Erlbaum Associates.

Zamble, E., & Porporino, F. (1990). Coping, imprisonment, and rehabilitation: Some data and their implications. *Criminal Justice and Behavior, 17,* 53–70.

Zedalis, D. D. (2004). Female suicide bombers. Monograph # 1–58487–162–8. Carlisle, PA: Strategic Studies Institute United States Army War College. Retrieved May 6, 2007, at: http://www.strategicstudiesinstitute .army.mil/pdffiles/PUB408.pdf.

Zimring, F. E., Hawkins, G., & Kamin, S. (2001). *Punishment and democracy: 3 Strikes and you're out in California.* New York: Oxford University Press.

Zona, M. A., Palarea, R. E., & Lane, J. C. (1998). Psychiatric diagnosis of the offender-victim typology of stalking. In J. R. Meloy (Ed.), *The psychology of stalking: Clinical and forensic perspectives* (pp. 69–84). San Diego, CA: Academic Press.

Author Index

Subject Index

Abel Assessment for Sexual Interest, 465 (tab)

Abortion, legalization effect on crime rate, 26

Absolute contraband, 265

Abu Ghraib scandal, 356

Accidental criminals, 102

Acquaintance homicide, 172, 527

Acquaintance robbery, 185

Actuarial justice, 494, 495–496

Actuarial risk prediction instruments, 463–465 (tab), 527

Actus reus, 14, 430, 527

Adaptive psychopath, 134

Adaptive traits, 52

Addiction, 304, 527
   nature and dynamics of, 316–317
   substance abuse-related offenses, 304–317

Adolescent-limited offender, 84, 527

Adolescent sex offender, 207

Aesthetic-critical approach, 391–392, 527

Aestheticized hyperreality, 391–392, 527

Affective aggression, 58, 151–153, 151 (fig), 426, 481–482, 527

Affective violence, 176, 186, 187

Aggravated assault, 166

Aggregate-level factors, 11, 12, 13, 527

Aggression, and violence, 6, 149–164
   affective aggression, 58, 151 (fig), 426, 481–482, 527
   biology and, 57–58
   defining, 527

displaced aggression theory, 224
   gender and, 39–40, 59–60, 160–164
   predatory, 151 (fig), 426, 481, 541
   predatory and affective aggression, 150–159, 151 (fig)

Alcohol use
   alcohol-related offenses, 311–314
   reported, 32 (tab)

Alien conspiracy theory, 270

Amateur fence, 268–269

American Civil Liberties Union (ACLU), 527

American Law Institute Model Penal Code, 434 (box), 435, 527

Amygdala, 58, 126, 127, 128, 181, 492, 514n, 527

Anarcho-ideological terrorists, 348, 527

Androgens, 59

Anecdotal evidence of copycat crimes, 379–384 (box)

Anger excitation (AE), 105, 527–528

Anger rapist, 211

Anger retaliatory (AR), 105, 528

Animal Liberation Front (ALF), 337 (box)–340 (box), 341, 518n15

Animal torture, 197, 224

Anomie, 70, 528

Anthropophagy, 197, 528

Antisocial behavior, 6, 528

Antisocial offender, 104–105

Antisocial persistent offender, 439

Antisocial personality disorder (APD), 52, 64, 125, 136, 138, 512n7, 528

Applied criminology, 418–486
   corrections, 477–483
   courts, 430–460
   dangerousness/violence assessment, 460–477
   defining, 419, 528
   police and public safety, 420–430

Armchair theorizing, 110

Arousal hypothesis, 375

Arrestee Drug Abuse Monitoring (ADAM) program, 309, 528

Arson, 517n7
   communicative, 518n16
   crime-concealment, 263
   defining, 528
   hate, 518n17
   profit-motivated, 263
   vandalism, 263

Assassination, 330, 355

Assault, 166–171, 528
   offense themes, 171
   predatory *vs.* affective aggression and, 168–171
   situational context of, 167–168

Associational fence, 266, 267

Attachment theory, 233–234

Attention deficit/hyperactivity disorder, 97, 264, 528

Atypical assassin, 355

Autoeroticism, 197, 528

Autonomic nervous system (ANS), 60–61

Autonomist terrorism, 349

Autotelic violence, 165

Avoidant personality disorder, 97, 528

Regressed type offender,
111, 217
Rehabilitation, 496
Relative contraband, 265
Religious terrorism, 349
Reptilian stare, 127
Response modulation hypothesis,
67, 131–132, 542
Revenge arson, 263
Ridgway, Gary, 103, 155, 156
(box)–159 (box), 175, 205,
221, 236, 385
Riots, 331
Risk assessment, 542
Risk assessment instruments,
462–472, 463 (tab)–465 (tab)
Risk factor approach, 48–49
Robbery, 182–188
as economic crime, 517n6
as predatory crime, 186
defining, 542
offense themes, 187–188
predatory *vs.* affective aggression
and, 186–187
Queens of Armed Robbery,
184 (box)
situational context, 183–186
See also Burglary
Roberts, Charles, 489–490
Role-career model, 102
Rosenberg, Ethyl, 334
Rosenberg, Julius, 334
Routine activity theory, 76
(box)–77 (box), 106–107,
428–429, 512n15, 542
Rushdie, Salman, 521n2

Sadism, 198, 199, 542
sexual, 196, 543
Sadistic personality disorder,
definition of, 542
Sadistic rapist, 211
Sadistic theory, 224
Sadomasochism (S&M), 191,
197–198, 199, 542
SARA model, 77 (box)–78 (box)
Scarpitti, Michael (Tre Arrow),
330, 340
Schizoid personality disorder, 97,
515n1, 542

Schizophrenia, 97, 147, 542
Schizotypal personality disorder,
97, 542
School shooting, 175, 487–489
Columbine, 375, 378, 379, 381,
385, 399, 481, 508
media influence on, 385
Scientific profiling, 149
Scoptophilia, 196, 542
Scriptkiddies, 405, 542
Seattle telephone pole poster ban,
286 (ban)–287 (box)
Secondary psychopath, 542–543
Sedition, 332–333, 543
Seditious libel, 332
Selective incapacitation,
438, 543
Self-Appraisal Questionnaire,
463, 465 (tab)
Self-esteem
elevated, 186
heightened, 154, 159 (box), 426
inflated, 158 (box)
low, 152, 153, 181, 222, 233,
353, 480
Self-fulfilling prophecy, 73
Self-report survey, 22–25, 24 (tab),
164, 543
Semantic dementia,
66, 131, 543
Separatist-nationalist terrorists,
348, 543
Separatist terrorism, 349
Serial arson, 263
Serial killer
female, 226
local, 103
media influence on, 385
mission, 223, 538
mobility typology of, 103
place-specific, 103
power/control, 223, 540
visionary, 223, 546
Serial murder, 173–174, 543
Sex act, 199
Sex addiction, 304, 543
Sex crime, 165, 191–238
cybercrime, 407–408
development of sex offending
behavior, 231–236

developmental factor overview,
232–233
deviant
preferences/urges/fantasies,
233–234
general categories, 207–224
legal definitions of, 198–200
normal sexuality, 193–194
paraphilias, 196–198
sex offender typologies, 206–236
sex offending and gender,
224–231
sexual deviance, 194–195
sexual disorders, 195–198
sexual dysfunctions, 195–196,
197–198
sexual psychopathy/predator
laws, 201–206
triggers for, 234–236
typologies, 206–236
See also Child sexual assault;
Pornography; Prostitution;
Sexual homicide; Sexually
violent predator
Sex Offender Risk Appraisal Guide
(SORAG), 464 (tab), 543
Sex Predator Risk Assessment
Screening Instrument,
465 (tab)
Sex trafficking, 290
Sexual arousal disorders, 196
Sexual assault not classified
elsewhere, 207
Sexual contact, 199
Sexual desire disorders, 196
Sexual deviance, 198, 543
Sexual disorders, 543
Sexual homicide, 219–224
against children, case
examples, 221
cultural factors in, 221–222
defining, 543
female offender, 225–229,
227–228 (box),
230 (box)
offender features, 207, 222–224,
516n8
serial offenders, 221, 222
typologies, 105, 107, 108 (tab),
223, 224

About the Author

Jacqueline (Jackie) Helfgott is an associate professor and chair of the Department of Criminal Justice at Seattle University, where she has taught since 1993. She received her BA from the University of Washington in Psychology/Society and Justice and masters and PhD from the Pennsylvania State University in Administration of Justice with a graduate minor in Psychology. Her work has been published in *Criminal Justice and Behavior, Journal of Forensic Psychology Practice, Journal of Contemporary Criminal Justice, The Journal of Police and Criminal Psychology, Federal Probation, The International Review of Victimology,* and other journals. Her research has focused on two areas—the intersection of psychology, criminology, and criminal justice and institutional and community corrections. Specific research foci and areas of expertise include psychopathy—its role in the criminal justice system and the prediction of violent recidivism and dangerousness; criminal behavior and the use of crime typologies at different stages of the criminal justice process; offender reentry; correctional program evaluation; and restorative justice—balancing victim, offender, and citizen needs, rights, and interests.